# HISTORY OF IDAHO

# History of Idaho

## Volume I

BY

LEONARD J. ARRINGTON

UNIVERSITY OF IDAHO PRESS
MOSCOW

IDAHO STATE HISTORICAL SOCIETY
BOISE

1994

Most of the illustrations used in this history are from the archival collection of the Idaho State Historical Society's Library and Archives in Boise (denoted ISHS) and the Special Collections of the University of Idaho Library in Moscow (denoted UIL). The Clarence Bisbee photos at ISHS are particularly valuable in illustrating the way of life of pioneer settlers in south-central Idaho. Photos from the Archives of The Church of Jesus Christ of Latter-day Saints in Salt Lake City are denoted LDS Church Archives. Those from the Utah State Historical Society Library in Salt Lake City are denoted USHS. Other sources are given in full. Where applicable, the identifying numbers of the photographs are supplied.


Printed in the United States of America

The *History of Idaho* is published by the Idaho State Historical Society and the University of Idaho Press. The research, writing, and publication were funded by an appropriation from the Second Regular Session of the Idaho Centennial Legislature.
Maps by Allan Jokisaari

5 4 3

Library of Congress Cataloging-in-Publication Data

Arrington, Leonard J.
History of Idaho / by Leonard J. Arrington.
p. cm.
Includes bibliographical references and index.
ISBN 0-89301-176-2
1. Idaho—History. I. Title.
F746.A75 1994
979.6—dc20
92-36968
CIP

TO MY PARENTS

N. W. and Edna Corn Arrington
Pioneer Settlers in Twin Falls County
and to
Merle Wells
Superb Idaho State Historian

# CONTENTS

## Volume 1

MAPS

# FOREWORD

IN RESPONSE to widespread public interest in events surrounding Idaho's statehood centennial celebration in 1990, a group of leaders in the Idaho legislature called upon the state's most distinguished senior historian—Leonard Arrington, a native of Twin Falls with over half a century of scholarly experience—to prepare a definitive and complete history of Idaho for its citizens.

Such an undertaking would have been nearly impossible until relatively recently. Nothing approaching an adequate investigation of many fascinating aspects of Idaho's history had provided information essential to a true survey of that history. While many more scholarly accounts of specific topics still need to be written, enough has now been published to enable a competent historian to undertake the assignment given by the legislature.

Leonard Arrington is far more than competent to complete this ambitious project. Trained in both history and economics, and a specialist in western history, he has himself previously investigated a remarkably wide spectrum of Idaho's heritage. His interests encompass—among others—mining, religious, social, and business history. Such broad interests have made possible an equally broadly based interpretation of Idaho's long history before statehood as well as the century we have recently celebrated.

Arrington's own experience encompasses nearly three quarters of Idaho statehood, which gives him an especially valuable perspective. Historians who study their own time take special care to employ proper scholarly methods that they would use in studying any era; but they can also understand and articulate concepts and assumptions that their contemporary citizens take for granted. Later generations of scholars may introduce new varieties of analysis and can use information that becomes available in subsequent years, but they also encounter problems as they try to comprehend the context of bygone eras. In this study, Arrington provides a contemporary understanding of our institutions that will serve future generations as well as present readers.

Many thousands of pages could be filled with a complete account of Idaho's past. Complex issues and situations could be explained in lengthy chapters that could create more confusion than enlightenment. Arrington's study offers a healthy balance between oversimplification and excessive detail. In it, an Idahoan who was raised on an irrigated tract typical of southern Idaho's Snake River Plain and who is a graduate of the state university in northern Idaho does justice to both sections of his native state. His understanding of life throughout the state is a significant contribution to this book's merit.

In the next decades, a substantial—and, happily, growing—number of Idaho historians will continue to explore many important aspects of Idaho's history. Their future work will support later enterprises of this kind, as their past research and writing have supported Arrington's work. Idahoans are fortunate to have this excellent appraisal of their state's achievement to initiate a new era in its rich heritage.

Merle W. Wells
Boise, Idaho
August 1992

# PREFACE AND ACKNOWLEDGMENTS

IN MANY WAYS Idaho is four states. The northern section is part of the Inland Empire centered on Spokane, Washington, only sixteen miles from the Idaho border. Southwestern Idaho, focused on Boise, the state capital, includes an agricultural and industrial area reaching into eastern Oregon. Southeastern Idaho is usually regarded as part of the Mormon culture region centered in Salt Lake City, Utah, one hundred miles south of the Idaho border. South-central Idaho owes no particular allegiance to any of the other three or to any outside cultural center; its residents are independent farmers and business people who help hold the state together and strengthen its unity.

The state's economic and cultural diversity is partly a product of its contrasting geography. The north touches the borders of Canada, and the south includes the northern edge of Utah's temperate Cache Valley. In the southwest corner an arid plain edges the Nevada desert, while in the east the famed Tetons in the high Rockies dominate the landscape. The central west is in the Columbia Plateau region, the southeast in the Basin and Range region. Part of the state harvests crops under ample rainfall; other sections record less than five inches of moisture a year. In altitude the state reaches fingers of the Rockies that include the towering Bitterroot Mountains and Continental Divide along the Montana border and plummets to Lewiston, a little over one hundred miles to the west, only 738 feet above sea level. Parts of the state rest at times under eight feet of snow; others lie bare all winter.

Idaho contrasts its huge semiarid plains with an enormous body of running water. Caves hold cavities of boiling water and massive mountains with towering trees are covered with snow in winter. With its basalt benches, deep canyons, lofty mountain peaks, immense forests, and vast stretches of sagebrush plain, Idaho is the last remaining wilderness state in the "lower 48." The state is dotted with thousands of small irrigated farms; the major metropolitan region includes 205,000 persons, a fifth of the population.

For many years the United States could not make up its mind about this large inland area. It was included in the British Northwest until 1820, when it became part of the Oregon Country. In 1848 it was recognized as a piece of Oregon Territory, and in 1853 the northern half was inserted in newly created Washington Territory. When Oregon became a state in 1859, the entire area and parts of western Wyoming and Montana were absorbed in Washington Territory. But in 1863, when the difficulties of transportation made it impossible to govern the region from Olympia, Idaho was declared a separate territory that included all of present-day Montana and nearly all of present-day Wyoming. Not until 1868 did Idaho Territory emerge with its present state boundaries.

This land of spectacular diversity and brilliant contrasts has occupied a strategic position in the interior Northwest. All direct lines of communication from the northern plains to Pacific

Northwest ports cross Idaho. The Snake River Plain has furnished transportation routes for Pacific-bound travelers in a region filled with mountain barriers. Idaho has fostered cultural interchange between peoples of the Great Basin desert to the south and the forest and plateau inhabitants of the Columbia Basin to the north and west, between British fur traders from the north and the American trappers headquartered in St. Louis whom they confronted. Mormon farmers moving out of Utah into Idaho encountered non-Mormon miners and stockmen who were originally from Texas, Missouri, and Nebraska. Idaho has always had a cultural diversity rivaling the area's geographical differences.

Nevertheless, the peoples of Idaho have adjusted to these divers tugs and pulls, and a resolute citizen loyalty to the state has emerged. Idahoans enjoy their historical uniqueness. Revelations of the theft of the entire territorial treasury, of the abandonment of the territory by all of the executive branch, of the fact that even the name of the state was invented—all of these and the other distinctive stories of Idaho history are taken in stride. Indeed, Idahoans take pride in their singularity—their unique blend of conservatism and progressivism, their freewheeling democracy, and their deep commitment to traditional values. The motto of Idaho is "Esto Perpetua"—may it be forever. As one who was born, reared, and educated in Idaho and knows from experience the attachment native Idahoans have to their state, I have been glad for this opportunity of reviewing its history.

During Idaho's Centennial Year the Idaho Legislature passed a measure approved by Governor Cecil Andrus commissioning me to write a centennial history. Senator Laird Noh of Twin Falls County, sponsor of the bill, has been especially helpful in assisting with the arrangements to complete the history.

As specified by legislators with whom I have talked, I have written this book for the general reader. In this spirit I have restricted reference notes to quotations and the sources of information for which there is some controversy. For the benefit of serious students, I have listed the monographic literature as well as the principal sources relied upon for each chapter. For some chapters I have depended rather heavily on one or two sources, clearly evident in my statement on sources. Because of the need to keep the book to a manageable length, I have had to omit many fascinating aspects of Idaho history. Where there has been little previous research, I am perhaps more silent than I ought to be. I regret that many occurrences important to some readers have been more scantily treated than I would have liked. I have not included everyone's grandfather or grandmother, nor every community, nor every happening to satisfy all.

Fortunately, most of the surviving primary documents relating to Idaho history—the early newspapers, diaries, letters, memoirs, and personal histories—have already been intensively studied. Several informative *Stories of Idaho* have been written for students in Idaho schools; professors and students at the state's colleges and universities have written theses, dissertations, and papers on many aspects of our history; and hundreds of well-researched articles have appeared in *Idaho Yesterdays*, *Pacific Northwest Quarterly*, and other publications. I have made use of all of these, and I have acknowledged those that were particularly helpful in the list of sources for each chapter. This volume owes much to the work of other scholars.

In addition to such early historians as H. H. Bancroft, John Hailey, William J. McConnell, Hiram T. French, Cornelius J. Brosnan (a professor at the University of Idaho when I was a student there), James H. Hawley, Byron Defenbach, and Thomas C. Donaldson, I am indebted to many contemporary historians. Merle Wells, long-time Idaho State Historian and friend, made available copies of materials he has written and suggested outlines and bibliographical material. He has read the entire manuscript, chapter by chapter, and made helpful comments. So have Davis Bitton, my friend of many years and an Idaho-born historian now at the University of Utah, and Heidi Swinton, a Salt Lake City researcher, editor, and friend. Their help has been indispensable. Jack Peterson, formerly director of the Idaho Mining Association and a former student of mine, has helped with some of the chapters. Carlos Schwantes, a brilliant young historian at the University of Idaho, has been generous in furnishing me bibliographical and other materials he has written and has contributed comments on the manuscript. F. Ross Peterson, also a former student, native of Montpelier, and author of Idaho's bicentennial history, shared the many insights that came from his study of Idaho history. His expert help on the last chapter is particularly appreciated. Clark Spence, raised in Glenns Ferry and distinguished professor of western history at the University of Illinois, and Richard W. Etulain, graduate of the Northwest Nazarene College, former professor of history at Idaho State University, and now director of the Center for the American West at the University of New Mexico, have both read the manuscript and made valuable suggestions. Dean Robert Sims, Gwynn (Glenn) Barrett, and Hugh Lovin at Boise State University; Ron Hatzenbuehler at Idaho State University; Larry Coates at Ricks College; Louis Clements in Rexburg; Jeff Simmonds and his staff at Utah State University; and my brother Ken Arrington of Twin Falls have all been helpful, and I thank them. None of them, however, should be held responsible for anything I have written or for my own inadequacies.

The Idaho State Historical Society has handled the administrative chores connected with this project with dispatch. I am grateful to David Crowder, former director, and Ken Swanson, acting director, for their encouragement and help. I am especially indebted to Judith Austin, editor, for her careful and constructive editing. She has saved me from egregious errors. I also thank the University of Idaho Press and its director, Peggy

Pace, for their excellence in design, production, and marketing, and Doug Easton for his indexing. The Society and Press and other readers have given me confidence in referring to Idaho's diverse people in ways that are both politically correct and historically authentic. One will find here tribal names, Indian, Native American, and early American, and also Negro, black, Afro-American, and African American. I hope readers will be patient with my attempts to show respect and yet be historically responsible.

Not everybody may agree, but throughout the book I have regarded as Idahoans persons who were born here, even if they moved away when young; people who were born elsewhere but came to Idaho; people who have lived here for extensive periods even though they may have been born elsewhere and moved away after a sojourn here. It may not be fitting to say "Once an Idahoan always an Idahoan," but I am confident that readers of this history will be interested in their compatriots who have shared life in the Gem State, even for a brief period.

My greatest indebtedness is to my precious wife, Harriet, who volunteered to suspend her own research and writing projects for a year and one-half in order to enter my manually typewritten drafts into her computer, thus providing up-to-date working chapters at each stage of the preparation of the final manuscript. Her cooperation was essential in completing the project ahead of schedule.

Leonard J. Arrington
Twin Falls, Idaho
3 July 1991

CHAPTER ONE

# Idaho's Natural Setting: The Geology and the Beauty

To Ernest Hemingway, Pulitzer Prize-winning author and seasonal resident of Ketchum for twenty-five years, Idaho was "unspoiled." Looking back on a high switchback on the snaky Old Summit road above the River of No Return, Hemingway said softly, "You'd have to come from a test tube and think like a machine not to engrave all of this in your head so that you never lose it."[1]

He thought it had an "indescribably different look about it, a bit of Spain in this hemisphere." In a 1959 letter to a friend he applauded his setting.

> You would love the high open valleys—beautiful streams with trout and some with salmon in the spring. There are duck and geese along all the streams and yesterday we hunted along small streams in the lava rock with water-cress in them. The duck jumping so high and fast. Very nice people live here in the valleys. The farmers and the ranchers.

Hemingway loved the warm sun of summer and the high mountain meadows, the trails through the timber and the sudden clear blue of the lakes. He loved the hills when the snow came. Best of all he loved the fall. No wonder that he wrote a tribute at the death of an Idaho hunting pal that appropriately is carved on his own stone memorial, in a lovely grove of aspen and willow overlooking Trail Creek near Sun Valley:

Best of all he loved the fall
The leaves yellow on the cottonwoods
Leaves floating on the trout streams
And above the hills
The high blue windless skies
. . . now he will be a part of them
Forever.

His was the Idaho of today formed by millions of years of geologic activity. Comparable in size to Great Britain, Idaho has about one million residents spread across the state in moderate-sized communities. It is a harsh but beautiful land that has molded the lives of its people. Steep mountains cut by racing rivers, lava beds and lakes—two thousand of them with names and thousands more without—vast forests and fertile farms in the river valleys are all part of Idaho today.

## GEOLOGIC HISTORY

For millions of years, much of ancient Idaho was part of a seaway that rose and fell with alterations in the earth's atmosphere. Small sponge-like creatures floated over the sandy flats, and worms crawled through the mud near the shores. Shelled creatures began to emerge, and their shells eventually formed the limestone in our landscape.

More than 220 million years ago, the inner heat broke through the earth's surface and the Seven Devils Volcanoes in

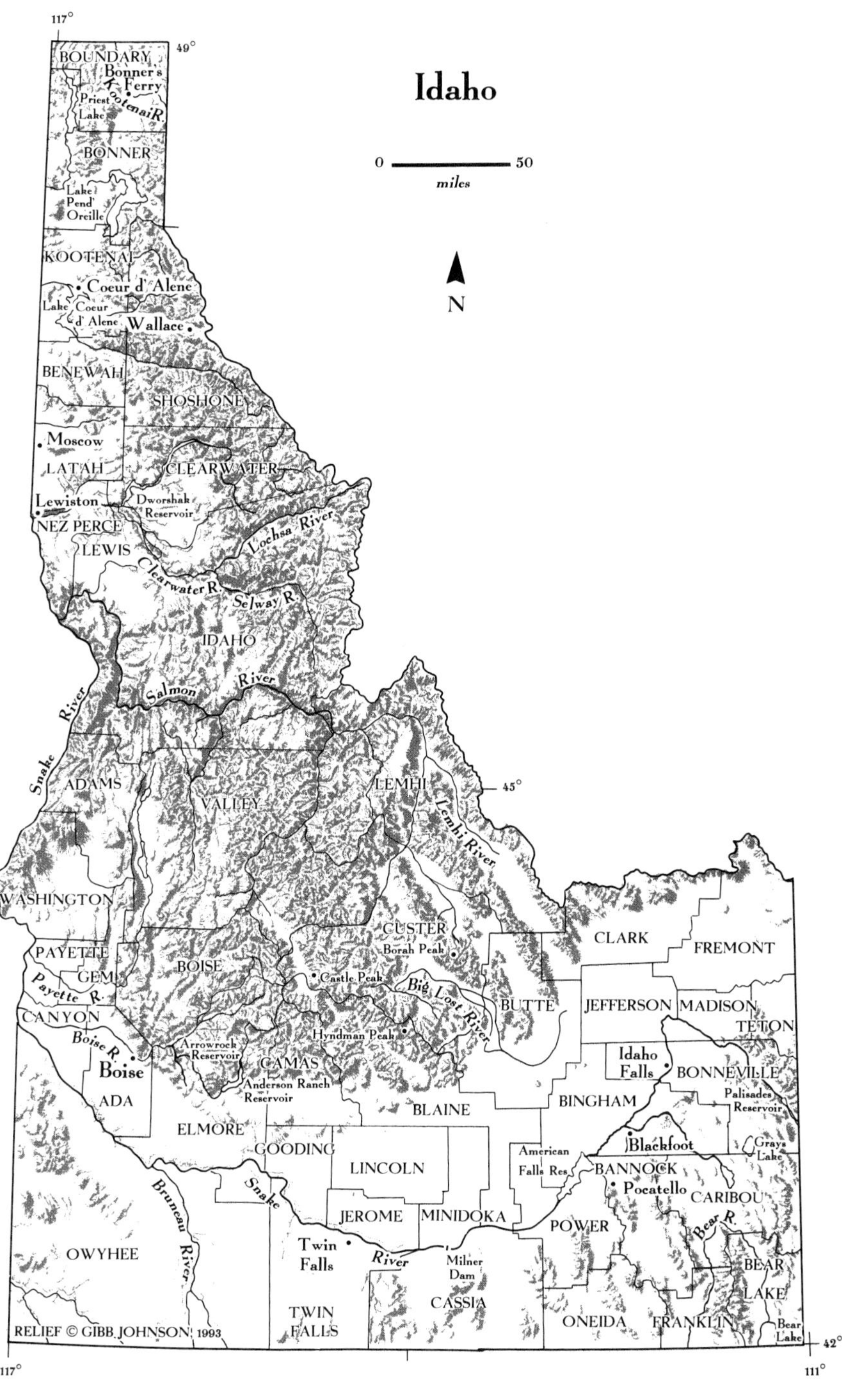
Idaho
0 50
miles
N
117°
49°
45°
42°
111°
BOUNDARY
Bonner's Ferry
Kootenai R.
Priest Lake
BONNER
Lake Pend' Oreille
KOOTENAI
Coeur d' Alene
Lake Coeur d' Alene
Wallace
BENEWAH
SHOSHONE
Moscow
LATAH
CLEARWATER
Lewiston
Dworshak Reservoir
NEZ PERCE
LEWIS
Lochsa River
Clearwater R.
Selway R.
IDAHO
Salmon River
Snake River
ADAMS
VALLEY
LEMHI
Lemhi River
WASHINGTON
CUSTER
Borah Peak
CLARK
FREMONT
PAYETTE
GEM
Payette R.
BOISE
Castle Peak
Big Lost River
BUTTE
JEFFERSON
MADISON
TETON
CANYON
Hyndman Peak
Boise R.
Boise
Arrowrock Reservoir
CAMAS
Anderson Ranch Reservoir
Idaho Falls
BONNEVILLE
ADA
BLAINE
BINGHAM
Palisades Reservoir
ELMORE
Blackfoot
Grays Lake
GOODING
LINCOLN
American Falls Res.
BANNOCK
Pocatello
CARIBOU
Snake
Bruneau River
JEROME
MINIDOKA
POWER
Bear R.
OWYHEE
Twin Falls
River
Milner Dam
BEAR LAKE
CASSIA
TWIN FALLS
ONEIDA
FRANKLIN
Bear Lake
RELIEF © GIBB JOHNSON 1993

western Idaho arose—peaks in a semicircle that reached thousands of feet into the sky. The surrounding seas (not our present seas) swarmed with animals—corals, sponges, sea anemones, armored shellfish, mollusks, lumpy sea urchins, starfish, and trilobites. Low mossy plants offered nutriment, and tall fern-like trees matured with no growth rings, suggesting there were no winters and no droughts. In the forests, over time, innumerable insects came to live. The luscious plants and swarming bugs were tempting fare to evolving amphibians on the ancient shores west of Sun Valley.

Most of the area was above sea level. For perhaps 100 million years, it was a land of hills, low mountains, and wide lowlands. Mountains had risen in the west and cut off much of the rainfall, but forests still grew, streams still eroded the hills, and sand and silt were dumped into the basins. A stark contrast is today's landscape, as more than half the state looms up 5,000 to 10,000 feet.

About 100 million years ago heat began to rise from within the earth's core and throughout most of western Idaho the older rocks melted, becoming the granite that forms the state's mountains and wilderness. Many of Idaho's ore deposits were born at this time. Hot fluids carried gold and silver, lead and zinc, and many other metals that were deposited in cracks to form veins as the fluids cooled.[2] But streams destroyed most of these primitive Rocky Mountains, and soon (by geologic time) only low hills rose above valleys filled with the debris from the mountains. Much of Idaho was gradually flooded by a sea that spread in from the Arctic Ocean and the Gulf of Mexico.

About 75 million years ago the earth's crust was squeezed, accumulated strata folded into colossal wrinkles, the lands rose on a grand scale, and towering new chains of mountains arose. Forests of sequoia and cypress and thickets of cedar and juniper grew. Grasses and lilies evolved, and broadleaved trees became common.

Dinosaurs exercised supremacy. Although no dinosaur fossils have been located in Idaho, they flourished in every environment represented in the region, from desert to swamp. Pterodactyls glided over the lakes, the immense Diplodocus moved half-submerged in the weedy sloughs, and the savage carnivore, Tyrannosaurus, ranged through the valleys terrorizing everything in its path.

About 70 million years ago mammals appeared and the scenery began to be sculptured to its present form. The mountains were still very high, but frost and streams wasted them away and the debris spread again in the valleys. The climate became almost tropical. At first the mammals were miniature: horses were smaller than hunting dogs, camels the size of jackrabbits, and rhinos about as big as sheep. Tree-living animals populated the forests and ate fruits, nuts, insects, and birds' eggs. Beavers and muskrats lived in the wetlands, and bears dominated the cool regions. Flying squirrels glided through the air, and seals, dolphins, and whales swam in the oceans west of Idaho.

This idyllic era was interrupted several times when volcanoes erupted. The earth trembled, and molten lava spread over eastern Idaho and the Yellowstone country. Forests were buried. Then something happened to cool the climate of the whole world. The fig and breadfruit trees that once had flourished in the warm climate disappeared. Grasses took over the plains, while evergreens, poplar, and alder grew on the silts. As the coolness continued, the mammals declined. No longer did the elephant-sized Uintatherium roam Idaho, nor the giant peccary eat the acorns. One sort of mammal prospered, though—the primates, small forest-dwellers, with improved vision and minds.

About a million years ago the climate of Idaho—and the rest of the world—became much cooler. Several times ice gathered in the mountains; glaciers formed, moved sluggishly down the valleys, and then melted away. The glaciers transported and dumped massive boulders and bodies of gravel, sand, and clay that were eroded from the steep mountain valleys. In the wetter times the streams spread gravel down the valleys and far out onto the plains. Lakes formed where lavas dammed streams, and then more lava spilled out and displaced the lakes.[3]

Particularly impressive creatures in Idaho during the ice age were the mammoths and mastodons, huge, hairy elephant-like mammals with rigid molars. Judging by the number of their teeth found in the bottomlands, herds of them grazed in Idaho's wet bottoms, using their trunks to pluck bunches of tall grass and stuff it in their mouths. They were joined by giant bison and sloths.

In northern Idaho, the ice may have been four or five thousand feet thick in the area around Sandpoint. The Sawtooths cradled vast snowfields. Because of heavy rains and snow the streams of Idaho carried enormous amounts of water, and large lakes formed in the closed basins. They spilled out to cause two spectacular floods, the Spokane Floods and the Lake Bonneville Flood, within the past 20,000 years.

The Spokane Floods—there were actually several as the ice advanced and retreated—were caused by an immense glacial dam that blocked Clark Fork Valley, where the mouth of the river opens into Lake Pend Oreille. This ice dam towered several thousand feet above the valley floor. Massive Lake Missoula behind the dam covered about 3,000 square miles in western Montana, with a small projection into present-day northeastern Idaho. The lake did not extend farther into Idaho because Idaho's two-thousand-foot Cabinet Gorge was so close to the Montana boundary. Eventually, as water from thawing glaciers, rain, and melting snow of nearby mountains flowed into the lake, the water began to overflow the glacial block. The glacier, weakened by spilling water, collapsed and the immense body of water rushed pell-mell toward the Columbia Plateau. From there it flowed west and southwest across the Rathdrum Prairie, down the Spokane Valley to the Columbia Gorge, and on to the Pacific Ocean. The volume of water was more than existing river valleys could handle. It ripped apart existing channels and cut into the basalt bedrock. Some of it splashed back up the Snake River in a mighty surge above Lewiston. The powerful current carved canyons and moved land mass, blocking river valleys to create Lake Coeur d'Alene and Priest Lake in Idaho and Liberty Lake in northern Washington. Geologists have found evidence of seven separate cycles of lake formation, ice-dam failure, and flooding.

The other large flood was that from ancient Lake Bonneville, a deep fresh-water lake unrelated to ice dams. During the wet glacial stage, it covered more than 20,000 square miles of land in northern and central Utah, eastern Nevada, and southern Idaho. The lake was deep; today's downtown Salt Lake City was under 1,200 feet of water. Prehistoric residents of Idaho, Utah, and Nevada may have camped on its shores; ancient utensils have been found on the slopes of the high mountain peaks that towered above the lake.

About 14,500 B.C., Lake Bonneville overflowed its banks at Red Rock Pass south of Pocatello. Billions of gallons of water in the top 300 feet of the lake rushed with unbelievable force northward and down Marsh Creek and Portneuf River canyons, tumbled into the Snake River at Pocatello, roared across the Snake River Plain toward Oregon, tore away soil and basalt above the level of Shoshone Falls, and created the deep canyons in the northern part of Magic Valley, extending on westward. Eugene Walker points out: "The rushing waters moved boulders as big as cottages and dropped them helter-skelter where the current slackened. Small boulders were rolled far downstream and became well-rounded, like large melons."[4]

As Lake Bonneville drained, and then dried up to the level of the present-day Great Salt Lake, the flow in the Snake River slowly receded to modern levels, leaving high, abrupt walls of rock on each side of the dwindling river. Among the first to profit from the canyon were cliff swallows that made their nests in rock crevices of the walls and eagles that bred on the surviving pinnacles of rock adjacent to the stream. Prehistoric hunters made homes in caves and rock shelters near the edge of the surviving river, living primarily on Snake River fish—including sturgeon and salmon that came up from the ocean to spawn.

A description of Idaho's natural environment requires a catalogue-like treatment that seems to be unavoidable. It is, however, essential to an understanding of the state and its history.

## IDAHO'S NATURAL ENVIRONMENT

The winds, waters, and volcanoes that Idaho inherited from its ancient past fashioned a diverse terrain of mountains, canyons, rivers, lakes, and sagebrush deserts. Much of Idaho is remote country where mountain ranges are tangled into mazes and where rivers run every way but east. Meriwether Lewis and William Clark in 1805–6 first mapped the region while searching for a Northwest passage—a usable all-water route from the Atlantic to the Pacific. They thought they had found such a passageway, only to be disappointed.

Idaho falls into three distinct natural regions: the north and northeast belong to the Rocky Mountain region, the south and southwest to the Columbia Plateau, and the southeast to the Great Basin. Most of Idaho's mountain ranges are a central part of the Rockies that extend from Alaska to Mexico, and Idaho has more mountain ranges than does any other Rocky Mountain state. In the north are the Bitterroot, Clearwater, Coeur d'Alene, and Palouse. The Bitterroot Range, the longest mountain range in Idaho, forms almost all of the Idaho-Montana border. Its deep canyons and snowy peaks seemed impassable to explorers and trappers until they found the Lolo Pass, used for generations by the Nez Perce. The land is a traditional wilderness area where bighorn sheep, mountain goats, elk, and deer roam. The adjacent Clearwater Mountains are well watered and rarely exceed 8,000 feet, offering plentiful timber and abundant minerals.

The highest mountains in Idaho are found in the Lost River Range of central Idaho. Except for a few passes they have an elevation of more than 10,000 feet and include Idaho's two tallest peaks: Mount Borah (12,622), which was once three miles under water (coral limestone can be found on the top), and Leatherman Peak (12,230). Diamond Peak in the Lemhi Range at 12,197 is not far behind. Mount Hyndman (12,078), Idaho's next tallest named peak, is near Hailey.

Central Idaho's Salmon River Mountains, the most important range after the Bitterroots, contain the large Idaho Primitive Area and the Bighorn Crags, one of the most rugged mountainous areas in the nation. The range also contains Castle Peak (11,830 feet) and the White Cloud peaks. The other large range in Central Idaho is the Sawtooths, just south of the Salmon River Range. To the east of the Salmon River and south of the Bitterroots are the Beaverhead Mountains, forming the southern part of the boundary with Montana. On the western edge of the region lie the Seven Devils, near the Oregon border; the Smoky and Boise ranges lie south of the Sawtooths; the White Knob, south of the Lost River.

The isolated Owyhee Mountains of southwestern Idaho include 11,000 square miles of high desert, lava, and sandstone. In southeastern Idaho are, from north to south, the Henry's Lake, Centennial, Big Hole, Snake River, Caribou, and Blackfoot ranges and, from east to west at the bottom end of the state, the Bear River, Portneuf, Malad, Blue Springs, Deep Creek, and Sublette ranges.

Nearly all of Idaho's extensive mountain land belongs to the federal government and is maintained in its primitive condition. Over 10 million acres of this Forest Service land are still without roads, more than in any other state except Alaska. Because these mountains are rich in forest and mineral resources, they are the subject of endless debate between persons who want their resources used to build the economy and those who want their beauty left undisturbed.

## IDAHO'S MAJOR RIVERS AND LAKES

Because so much of the state is mountainous—one person has counted eighty-one separately named ranges—the state has many rivers, creeks, and lakes. Several major river systems cross the state and two large rivers are contained completely within it. The single most unifying geographical feature is the Snake River, which has its source in the mountains of Yellowstone National Park and meanders west to the Oregon border and then north through Hells Canyon, is joined by the Salmon, and then rolls on to Lewiston, where the Clearwater enters, and heads west to join the Columbia River. The river is more than 1,000 miles long and drains more than 100,000 square miles of country. By the time it empties into the Columbia it carries 40 million acre-feet of water and has dropped more than 7,000 feet in elevation. The five major cities of Idaho are located on the Snake or its tributaries. A dozen or more dams have been constructed along its course to provide irrigation water and hydroelectric power for thousands of farms and homes and most of Idaho's industries. Two-thirds of the population of Idaho live in the fertile Snake River Valley. Because of the fall in elevation the Snake has deep canyon gorges and several important waterfalls, including the spectacular Shoshone Falls, 212 feet high—52 feet higher than Niagara—near the present-day city of Twin Falls. Snake River water that is captured in reservoirs or flows on to the ocean comes, not from rainfall, but from the snow that accumulates on the vast peaks of Idaho's mountains. The fragile environment of the semiarid Snake River Plain is revealed by shifting sand dunes near St. Anthony, Bruneau, and Weiser.

The untamed and imposing Salmon River—"River of No Return"—winds 425 miles through the mountains of central Idaho, its canyon gorge deeper than the Grand Canyon of the Colorado. It flows through the Sawtooth Wilderness Area and finally joins the Snake about fifty miles south of Lewiston. A spawning stream for Pacific salmon, it is one of the longest and most rugged rivers lying wholly within one state.

A second major river system lying entirely within the state is the Clearwater of northern Idaho, which is fed by streams from the Bitterroots. Not as wild as the Salmon, the Clearwater was used as a passageway by explorers and trappers, and later by miners and loggers.

Far to the south is the Bear River, 300 miles long, which originates in Utah's Uinta Mountains, winds back and forth north to Wyoming, back to Utah, back to Wyoming, and then enters Idaho. It moves north (staying south of the tributaries of the Snake) and then back southwest, to where it enters Utah and deposits its water in the Great Salt Lake. Early trappers found beaver along the Bear. The Oregon and California trails entered Idaho with the Bear River and followed it for a considerable distance.

Major rivers in northern Idaho include the Kootenai and Pend Oreille, which flow into the Columbia; the Clark Fork, which flows into Lake Pend Oreille; and the Saint Maries, Saint Joe (St. Joe), and Coeur d'Alene, which flow into Coeur d'Alene Lake. The Spokane River carries the waters of Coeur d'Alene Lake to the Columbia. The Boise, Payette, and Weiser flow into the Snake in southwestern Idaho as it forms the Oregon border, and there are many shorter tributaries of the Snake in southern Idaho.

Idaho has more than 2,000 lakes, most of them in high alpine valleys. The largest in the state is Lake Pend Oreille, in the northern Panhandle, with a surface area of 180 square miles.

Farther north is Priest Lake, early a heavily used trapper area. A few miles south of Pend Oreille are Hayden Lake and Coeur d'Alene Lake, both popular resort areas. Surrounded by forested mountains, all of these lakes are in spectacular settings.

Payette Lake in central Idaho north of Boise is a source of summer recreation. Farther east, in the Sawtooth National Recreation Area, Redfish, Stanley, and Alturas lakes fulfill the same role. In northeastern Idaho, only fifteen miles from Yellowstone, is Henry's Lake, a favorite trapper hangout and trout-fishing lake. Farther south is turquoise Bear Lake, half in Idaho and half in Utah. Some of the state's large lakes are man-made reservoirs: Palisades Lake, near the Wyoming line; American Falls Reservoir on the Snake; and Blackfoot, Anderson Ranch, Arrowrock, Lucky Peak, Cascade, and Dworshak Dam reservoirs, all used for fishing and recreation and in some cases for hydropower generation.

## THE NATURAL WONDERS OF IDAHO

Idaho is an outdoor paradise. It possesses glacial valleys, unusual landforms, mysterious caves, and magnificent scenery. Hells Canyon, through which the Snake River flows on the Oregon border, is the deepest canyon in North America—at one spot it is 7,900 feet from the top to the river below—and one of the narrowest. Historical novels have been set in the canyon, and it is frequently the focus of environmental disputes.

Craters of the Moon, a National Monument for whom some are seeking National Park status, is a lava bed where astronauts trained before going to the moon for the first time. The monument covers 47,210 acres in Central Idaho.

Two sites in south-central Idaho are called City of Rocks. The one at Gooding is made up of shale and sandstone formations that resemble a beautifully colored city; that in Cassia County is the result of erosion of the granite rock, some of the oldest on the continent. Pioneer travelers often thought they were coming to a prehistoric city as they approached one of these landmarks.

Three ice caves demonstrate nature's mysteries. Shoshone Ice Cave is under a lava field; its floor, ceiling, and walls are covered with ice. Crystal Ice Cave, near Paris, has many large rooms that honeycomb the center of the Bear River Range. Crystal Falls Cave, near St. Anthony, has a frozen "river" running along part of its length.

Two of Idaho's rivers are "lost": the Big Lost and Little Lost flow into chasms, caves, and lakes buried in the porous lava fields northeast of Arco and are believed to flow underground through tiny openings in lava beds for about 150 miles until they empty into the Snake River at Thousand Springs, near Hagerman. The flow of this underground river or aquifer is only about one mile a year, so the water now emerging at Thousand Springs disappeared during the period of the fur trade in about 1840. Few springtime sights are as beautiful as the Thousand Springs gushing from the canyon cliff.

Important to Idaho's history was the existence up to the time of agricultural settlement in the 1870s of three vast prairies that produced immense quantities of camas. A blue-flowered lily with a sweet bulb that, when harvested in the fall, was ground into a meal-like flour, camas was a staple in the diet of Native Americans for thousands of years. The rolling plain of Camas Prairie between Grangeville in Idaho County and Winchester in Lewis County encompassed about 200,000 acres from the Snake River on the west to the Clearwater on the north and east. Camas is no longer a critical source of food for most Native Americans, but its name appears throughout the countryside as a reminder of its historic significance. The area now produces grain and peas and livestock fodder. Big Camas Prairie in Camas County near Fairfield (not as large as Camas Prairie in Idaho County) and Camas Meadow on Camas Creek in Clark County were also locations of great amounts of camas. At each of these locations, and elsewhere as well, large bands of natives gathered to dig camas bulbs in what was regarded as communal territory. In full bloom, the camas created a striking blue-flowered landscape.

The Clearwater Plateau of northern Idaho, incorporating the productive Palouse Hills, Nez Perce Prairie, and Camas Prairie, is today among the finest farming (and lumbering) sections of Idaho and the Pacific Northwest.

With its many mountains and its broad areas of sagebrush plain, Idaho has a wide diversity of climate, vegetation, and wildlife. Some mountains get fifty inches of snow each winter; some arid lands in the south get no snow and less than five inches of rainfall a year. Prevailing westerly winds bring moisture and mild weather from the Pacific Ocean to northern Idaho, but there is little moisture left for the Columbia Plateau and Snake River Plain to the south where winters are mild with sparse snowfall and the summers are dry. In the eastern portions of the state the Continental Divide protects the mountain valleys so the weather does not get as cold as on the eastern slopes of the Rockies, but there is heavy snow. Wind blows steadily from west to east along the Snake River Basin. Many mountain valleys, like the popular resort of Sun Valley, enjoy a great deal of sunshine. In some areas of foothills and high plateaus of southern Idaho, grain is grown; at lower elevations farmers plant Idaho's luscious potatoes and many other crops.

## MOST TIMBERED STATE IN THE ROCKIES

Idaho's northern forests are covered with Douglas fir, white pine, and mountain hemlock. Lodgepole pine is one of the most common evergreens and was used by Indians for their lodges—as well as for buildings at Yellowstone Park. Farther up the mountain slopes are Engelmann fir and spruce. Farther down the mountains are mountain mahogany (also called Pacific yew), maples, quaking aspen, ash, willow, birch, cottonwood, and alder. Idaho's western white pine, the state tree, and its cousin, ponderosa pine, are known to tower 200 feet. Mountain undergrowth includes rhododendron, beargrass, and woodbrush. Central Idaho's hills bear bitterbrush, serviceberry, and buckrush as well as syringa, the state flower, and a native variety of mock orange whose stems were used by Indians for bows, arrows, tobacco pipes, and woven cradles. Its leaves were crushed for soap. Semidesert areas in the south have sagebrush and many hardy grasses—fescue, bunch grass, wheatgrass, and bluegrass.

Idaho lies along the flyway of migrating waterfowl, and during spring and fall many birds pass through its skies. Of the 500 species of birds in the state, the mountain bluebird—the state bird—is one of the most colorful. Juncos, nutcrackers, and thrushes also abound in the north and in high altitudes. The sage grouse ("sage hen"), largest grouse in North America, has been plentiful, along with blue grouse, spruce grouse, and sharptail grouse. Ring-necked pheasants have populated the valleys and plains, as have partridges and several varieties of quail. The Canada goose nests in the state, along with mallards, wood duck, baldpate, spoonbill, American pintail, and merganser, canvasback, and ruddy duck.

Because of the lakes, rivers, and reservoirs, many sea and water birds—cormorants, blue herons, white egrets, pelicans, and tundra swans, for which Swan Valley was named—nest here. Island Park and Harriman State Park are the year-round home of the trumpeter swan, of which there are about 400 in Idaho.

Many fishermen regard Idaho as a fisherman's paradise. Bull trout and rainbow trout are common in the higher streams. Sturgeon, the largest freshwater fish in the world, have been common in the Snake River. Now protected by law, this prehistoric fish, if caught, must be returned to the river. Idaho has always had many salmon (some varieties of which are now endangered as are steelhead, varieties of trout and sculpin, whitefish, and cisco).

The largest rodent is the beaver, once numbering in the millions but now below 50,000 animals with a carefully controlled harvest; other furbearing mammals include mink, badgers, martin, fisher, bobcats, lynx, red fox, and desert fox.

Idaho's natural wilderness area holds perhaps the finest big-game population of the United States, with thousands of American elk, moose, white-tailed deer, black-tailed deer, and mule deer. The fast-running pronghorn antelope can be seen along highways; mountain goats are rarely seen but are abundant on the headwaters of the Big Lost and Little Lost rivers and in the Owyhee County desert. Mountain lions plague stockmen and also live on porcupines, raccoons, squirrels, beaver, rabbits, and deer. The Rocky Mountain Bighorn sheep is noted for its heavy curved horns that decorate many "dens" in the state. Idaho always had many grizzly, black, brown, and cinnamon bears. The voice of the coyote can be heard throughout the state as can the howl of the grey wolf. These shrewd animals are responsible for much aboriginal and early American folklore.

Just catching a glimpse of some of the wild animals is a treat for tourists and residents. Ernest Hemingway and his wife encountered a black bear on the road to Yellowstone and stopped to chat with the "beast" standing coyly by the side of the road. Mary reported the event in *How It Was*:

> "How you doin' boy? They treatin' you right?"
>
> Six or seven yards away the bear looked the other direction.
>
> "All that posing for pictures. Gets to be a bore, eh boy?"
>
> The bear looked back at us, his eyes sleepy in the sunshine.
>
> "With no compensation. That's tough. You fellows ought to get together. Charge ten shillings a shot. Or a goat's leg."

The bear ambled off.

"Very uncommunicative bear," said Ernest.

Mary Hemingway called Idaho "Papa's country." Indeed, Idaho residents love the diversity of the land, the unique nature of its features, the habitat it provides for wildlife—those vanishing and those plentiful. All seem to have found a place of their own in a country as diverse as they come—carefully crafted by millions of years of geologic activity.

## CHAPTER ONE: SOURCES

Particularly helpful in writing this chapter were: F. Ross Peterson, *Idaho: A Bicentennial History* (New York: W. W. Norton & Co., 1976), 1–19; Vardis Fisher, *Idaho: A Guide in Word and Picture* (Caldwell: Caxton Printers, 1937), 73–162; Bill Gulick, *Snake River Country* (Caldwell: Caxton Printers, 1971); Robert O. Beatty, *Idaho* (Caldwell: Caxton Printers, 1975); Donald W. Meinig, *The Great Columbia Plain: A Historical Geography, 1805–1910* (Seattle: University of Washington Press, 1968); Don Moser, *The Snake River Country* (New York: Time-Life Books, 1974); and a pair of articles by Herman J. Deutsch, "Geographic Setting for the Recent History of the Inland Empire," *Pacific Northwest Quarterly* 49 (October 1958):150–65; and ibid. 50 (January 1959):14–25. I have also studied *Climates of the States: Idaho* (Washington, D.C.: Government Printing Office, 1960), a publication of the U.S. Weather Bureau.

Other helpful Idaho histories include Byron Defenbach, *Idaho: The Place and Its People*, 3 vols. (Chicago: American Historical Society, 1933) 1:2–40; Cornelius J. Brosnan, *History of the State of Idaho*, rev. ed. (New York: Charles Scribner's Sons, 1948), 10–22; Merrill D. Beal and Merle W. Wells, *History of Idaho*, 3 vols. (New York: Lewis Historical Publishing Co., 1959) 1:1–28; and Earl H. Swanson, Jr., "The Snake River Plain," *Idaho Yesterdays* 18 (Summer 1974):2–11.

For the Geologic History section I have used Clyde P. Ross and J. Donald Forrester, *Outline of the Geology of Idaho* (Moscow: Idaho Bureau of Mines and Geology, 1958); Eugene H. Walker, "The Geologic History of the Snake River Country of Idaho," *Idaho Yesterdays* 7 (Summer 1963):18–31; and Richard E. Ross and David Brauner, "The Northwest as a Prehistoric Region," in William G. Robbins, Robert J. Frank, and Richard E. Ross, eds., *Regionalism and the Pacific Northwest* (Corvallis: Oregon State University Press, 1983), 99–108.

Sources on Ernest Hemingway and Idaho include: Matthew J. Bruccoli, *Conversations with Hemingway* (Jackson: University of Mississippi Press, 1986), 63–64; Mary Walsh Hemingway, *How It Was* (New York: Alfred A. Knopf, 1976), esp. 521–30; and Lloyd Arnold, *High on the Wild with Hemingway* (New York: Grosset & Dunlap, 1968), 160–62.

1.

2.

1. Shoshone Falls, 212 feet high, was a spectacular sight for overland emigrants passing through south-central Idaho. UIL 6–116–1A.
2. Idaho Falls on the Snake River in eastern Idaho was the location of ferries and eventually became the site of a railroad roundhouse. ISHS 69–4.73.

3. 

4. 

3. Craters of the Moon National Monument is a reminder that volcanoes have been active in parts of Idaho in the past few thousand years. UIL 6–69–4.

4. Thousand Springs near Hagerman were created by the emergence of water from Lost River and Little Lost River that disappears in eastern Idaho and flows slowly underground to emerge at this point. PHOTOGRAPH BY MILDRED DOLE DOWNING, UIL 6–27–1B.

5.

5. Balanced Rock, west of Buhl. Two enterprising businessmen arranged for a drop on this rock in the 1930s, and a *Life* photographer took pictures of them eating breakfast on the top. ISHS 73–221.58.

CHAPTER TWO

# Idaho's Earliest Residents: The Big-Game Hunters

ABOUT 15,000 years ago the first humans moved into Idaho. Some of them may have come from the north—from present-day Alberta and British Columbia; some from the west—from present-day Washington and Oregon; some from the east—from present-day Montana and Wyoming; and some from the south—from present-day Nevada and Utah. Archaeologists suppose that the earliest migrants to the New World came from northeastern Asia by way of Beringia, the ancient broad plain between Siberia and Alaska, around 28,000 years ago. That the oceans were several hundred feet below their present level would have simplified the crossing. Beringia would have been a relatively level grassland sixty miles across and a thousand miles wide. Families might have been pursuing browsing animals—mammoths, mastodons, giant ground sloths, musk oxen, moose, bison, elk, and caribou. Over the millennia they would have moved south, through what is now Canada into what is now the United States, and on down into Mexico and

Central and South America. Some archaeologists believe they have found evidence of humans in Central and South America at least 20,000 years ago.

The weather was cold. Glaciers stretched down the mountains and into the valleys of western Canada, but an ice-free corridor ran east of the Rocky Mountains down through the Saskatchewan River Valley. The migrants might also have moved south through the mountain valleys of the Fraser River Valley in British Columbia. The going was not easy; between 20,000 and 18,000 years ago the ice was at its maximum, reaching south of the Great Lakes and covering most of Montana.

A second migration from Asia followed between 20,000 and 12,000 years ago, after the glaciers had melted and created great lakes no longer in existence: Lake Bonneville in Utah, Lake Lahontan in Nevada, and Lake Missoula in Montana. A third migration of Aleuts and Eskimos occurred about 6,000 B.C.[1]

These people had brown skin and may have come before "races," as we know them, developed, but they bore many resemblances to the Mongoloids of Siberia. They were hunters, fishermen, and collectors. Out of select stones, wood, and imperishable bones, they made axes, knives, scrapers, and large lanceolate (shaped like the head of a lance) projectile points, and they chased big-game animals into bogs where they killed them. They conversed, knew how to use fire, roasted meats, and made robes out of the hides of the great-horned bison. They cooperated in hunting, painted pictures and sometimes chiseled designs on the rocks, made beads and other ornaments, participated in religious rites, and buried their dead with respect and ceremony. They probably told ancestral legends and repeated traditional religious stories in the evenings. The camps of these people have been found lining the banks of streams that no longer exist in areas once frequented by native American horses, camels, and other animals long since extinct in North America.

The so-called Pleistocene ice age, which began about a million years ago, continued during this period of migration. There were, in fact, four periods when ice gathered and then melted. In southern Idaho ice covered all the highlands that were more than 7,500 feet high, and the Sawtooths were blanketed with snowfields. As the glaciers ebbed and flowed, plants, animals, and prehistoric peoples moved northward and southward. Groups of these people were in Idaho when the ice tongues in the Sawtooths were building the moraines that hem in Redfish Lake. Some of them in southern Idaho may have witnessed the Bonneville Flood of around 14,000 B.C., and some in northern Idaho may have seen one of the Spokane Floods as late as two thousand years after. Some may have witnessed the eruption of Glacier Peak in the Cascade Range about 12,000 B.C. Others west of the Bitterroot Mountains were present during volcanic eruptions that created the mass of basalt which makes up the Craters of the Moon. Present estimates suggest that volcanic activity began about 15,000 years ago and went through eight or more periods of eruption that produced about forty flows from twenty-five different vents—the most recent as recently as 2,000 years ago. Witnesses surely expressed wonder at the craters of fire and the burning rock.

The earliest known campsite of Idaho's original Big-Game Hunters was discovered by Ruth Gruhn and other Idaho archaeologists in Wilson Butte Cave, near Dietrich. Carbon dating suggests that remains found at the bottom of this cave—bones of Idaho's primitive horse, an extinct Idaho camel, and a sloth—date from 13,000 B.C. One of the instruments found near the bottom of the camp detritus was a spear point that is dated 12,500 B.C. These points, presumably secured to spears to kill ancient beasts, were glassy rock shaped by percussion flaking on both faces of the rock, the tip long and steeply tapered. This "find" is one of the earliest conclusive evidences of ancient human habitation in the United States.

As these people looked out of their caves, they would have

seen shaggy, long-tusked mastodons grazing in herds in the wet bottomland, perhaps not far from a lake. Occasionally their children might have wondered at the rare spectacle of a surviving Emperor Mammoth, fourteen feet high, or a large bison, known as Bison antiquus. They might have awakened to hear the monstrous scream of an angry mastodon and laughed at the attempt of a lumbering twenty-foot sloth to escape a giant saber-toothed tiger. They were surely captivated watching Idaho's small horses racing over the grassy prairie. We have no knowledge that they ever attempted to ride or domesticate any animal. However, archaeologists believe these people used dogs in hunting sheep and other animals.

When the continental ice retreated about 12,000 years ago and the weather warmed, the grassland expanded and bison, deer, and mountain sheep and goats became more prevalent. The result was that many peoples established "home territories" in Idaho. The many archaeological digs in recent years have provided abundant evidence of human occupation in the Snake River Plain, the Lower Salmon River region, the mountain valleys in central and eastern Idaho, and the desert area in southwestern Idaho in the years after the end of the ice age, and more particularly after 10,000 B.C. The finds also suggest interchange between peoples from different areas—between the Snake River Plain and the Great Plains east of the Rockies, between the Snake River Plain and the Great Basin farther south, and between southwestern and northern Idaho and what is now eastern Oregon and Washington.

Archaeologists have distinguished three different periods in the prehistory of Idaho's peoples: Early Big-Game Hunting, 15,000–6,000 B.C.; Archaic, 6,000 B.C. to A.D. 500; and Late Period, A.D. 500 to 1805.[2] The peoples of these three periods might be called the Big-Game Hunters, the Migratory Hunters and Gatherers, and the immediate ancestors of the Kutenai, Nez Perce, Coeur d'Alene, Pend Oreille, Shoshoni, Bannock, and

Northern Paiute who lived here when the first white men arrived in 1805. During each period there were some cultural differences among the peoples along the Snake River Plain, those in the high mountain valleys next to Montana and Wyoming, those in western and northern Idaho, and those to the south of the Snake River Plain. Nevertheless, one can give some general impressions of those in Idaho in each of the three time periods.

The Big-Game Hunters, following migrating game, favored springs and waterholes where mammoths, mastodons, bison, horses, camels, bears, rabbits, and other animals went to drink. They may well have collected seeds, wild vegetable foods, fruit, and camas roots to balance their diet. They were inventive and made exquisite tools and weapons of fine-grained rock (obsidian, flint, quartz) and worked with wood and leather. Archaeologists have found some of their stone knives, scrapers, and projectile points. They did not use the bow and arrow; those were introduced only two thousand years ago.

Big-Game Hunters led a migratory life within a loosely defined homeland, moving about to take advantage of seasonal food resources. An extended family or "tribe" had a home base, but one or two families usually moved about together to forage. They lived in caves, rock shelters, and flimsily built dwellings. They did not engage in agriculture, nor did they have pottery—too fragile and bulky for families constantly on the move. Horns and gourds were used as containers.

Archaeologists tell us that, over the years, the tools and methods of Big-Game Hunters were refined through several stages. Sharing skills with Plains peoples between 12,000 and 9,000 years ago, they made and used Clovis projectile points, mounted and hafted on long lances or spears of remarkable beauty and craftsmanship. A large cache of these was found in the 1960s at the Simon site near Fairfield, Idaho. Clovis points were widely used in attacking the large game that was gradually disappearing. About 9,000 years ago these evolved into Folsom points, even more expertly made—the finest product of the toolmaker's art—and presumably more suited to the smaller animals that remained, particularly bison and mountain sheep. However, archaeologist Susanne Miller and others have found fragments of these points in association with extinct elephant-type remains on the eastern end of the Snake River Plain. Many bison were obtained not by means of spearing but by bison drives, in which rock and brush were piled to create a path drawing animals to a steep slope over which they plunged to their deaths. Such a "jump" has been found near Challis. The fine workmanship of these bison hunters is also indicated in their decorative work on hide and wood, their use of bone and antler for projectile points, and in general their well-developed bone and antler technology.

In a third phase, the Big-Game Hunters used Plano projectile points. Many of these have been found in southern Idaho, a few dating back as far as nine thousand years. Their users had a more diverse culture than did those who preceded them. Apparently, without the herds of camel and horse, and with bison found largely in vast grassland areas, the people foraged and hunted to provide food, clothing, shelter, and medicine.

The Archaic Period peoples (6,000 B.C. to A.D. 500) were also migratory hunters and gatherers. In the early stages of their culture the earth experienced a warming trend called the altithermal. The climate of Idaho became much warmer and drier than it is now, and it remained warm for perhaps two thousand years. As ice disappeared from the mountains, vegetation and animals moved up the slopes and northward, and descendants of the Big-Game Hunters and other groups from farther south followed. Water from the melting glaciers caused the Salmon River to grow in depth, volume, and velocity. Taking advantage of the rivers and lakes, the people caught salmon and steelhead trout with harpoons (the fish migrated up the Columbia and thence up the Snake and its tributaries to spawn).

Whole bands of natives came to depend on this important source of protein for their major food, and they also used river mussels extensively. Many followed a seasonal pattern: fishing in the waters under Shoshone Falls, moving north to the headwaters of the Salmon, and then returning to the Snake River Plain. Those who went farther north moved into the Palouse Country and fished in the Columbia, the Clearwater, and other streams. They interacted with several other Northwest groups.

The people of the Archaic Period also depended heavily on camas bulbs for storage and winter consumption. Attendance at large fish runs and use of blue-flowering camas roots continued until the frontier era, and this lifestyle was noted by early explorers, trappers, and overlanders.

As the climate continued warm and the glaciers had melted, less water flowed in the rivers and there was space for suitable habitats along the canyon floors. Some groups remained in mountain retreats, others adopted a river-based culture. They fished and, at the same time, killed elk, deer, antelope, sheep, and ground squirrels. Temporary winter camps were established along the Salmon. Archaeologists have discovered large, circular pit houses built one to three feet deep, with poles lashed together at the top and with benches, for winter use. The few of those that have been uncovered are the oldest houses in Idaho. Finely woven mats made out of tule or cattail were attached to the poles as "walls." A thick layer of grass was put on the mats around the base of the structure, with dirt on the grass as insulation. The house was heated by a fire in the center of the floor. Some scraps of basketry have also been found in a cave across the border in Oregon, which suggest that these people did fine twine weaving. In this cave were dozens of pairs of partly burned sandals made—well made—of shredded sagebrush bark that, together with some bits of wood, horn, and bone, were carbon-dated to 9,000 years ago.

Each extended family was a self-sufficient unit, although it might occasionally trade with other groups. Women were in charge of butchering meat, cooking, and collecting plant roots, seeds, and berries. Some of them made pots and hopper mortars. Men were responsible for hunting and fashioned knives, awls, scrapers, and chipped stone projectile points used in the search. Although families sometimes settled near each other, joined in buffalo hunts and rabbit drives, and participated in group dances and sacred observances, there were no villages, "nations," or "communities." They did not grow maize or develop any agricultural capability.

Archaic hunters were expert in the use of the atlatl, a wooden throwing-stick or spear-thrower with a handle at one end and a groove at the other that provided extra mechanical advantage by adding length to the hunter's arm. This launch-pad handle increased the throwing distance, the velocity, and the accuracy of the spear. Lanceolate spear points, modifications of the Plano, were side-notched or stemmed-indented. Archaic hunters who lived in northern and western Idaho made long, thin spearpoints that are sometimes referred to as Cascade Points. Archaeologists have found that these peoples had a distinctive burial pattern: burial offerings included bifacially worked blades, large corner-notched and side-notched points, and other tools as well as religious symbols.

The Late Period inhabitants of Idaho, the ancestors of the Indian peoples that Lewis and Clark and other explorers met in 1805 and succeeding years, were still more diverse than earlier peoples. Most of them were descendants of the Archaic peoples, keeping alive the hunting, fishing, and food-gathering practices of their nomadic ancestors. From them grew the Shoshonean culture that was to dominate much of south Idaho's civilization from the fifteenth century until Idaho's permanent white settlement began in 1860.

To the Shoshoni people that descended from Big-Game Hunters was added the gradual in-migration of persons reared in a

Desert culture (archaeologists refer to them as the Northern Fremont peoples). The Desert Culture developed during the Archaic Period among the descendants of peoples who had moved southward during the Great Migration from Siberia and who either stopped in the Great Basin or, having moved into the Southwest, had returned or been driven back into the Great Basin. The nature of the culture was made clear with the examination of Danger Cave in western Nevada in the 1950s by archaeologists from the University of Utah. As described by Jesse Jennings, the effective social unit was small—an extended family of perhaps twenty-five or thirty. The band moved from place to place in search of seasonal plant and animal resources. Its members had little material wealth and gathered with others only for pine-nut harvests and animal drives.

The hallmarks of Desert Culture, wrote Jennings, were the basket and the flat milling stone. Its members were expert in making the most of small seed and berry harvesting and cookery. They were also expert in using plant fibers. Some of their cordage was as fine as today's machine-twisted thread and was used in mats, nets, baskets, and twine. They had characteristic, if somewhat crude and simple, projectile points and also made scrapers, drills, bone tools, and bark sandals. They collected pine nuts, made clothing of rabbit skins, and fashioned rattles out of the dew-claws of deer. They made pottery, and about the time the Late period commenced they began to use bows and arrows. About 1650 A.D. they obtained horses.

As the altithermal continued—perhaps as early as 5,000 B.C., when there was widespread drought—many of these people moved into the Snake River Plain and occupied the caves and territories that had been abandoned by the Big-Game Hunters. Their remains have been found in many locations in southern and western Idaho. Here the migrants found deer in place of the small mammals they had been accustomed to killing. Here, instead of pinenuts, they gathered camas roots; they also joined in fishing for salmon and steelhead. Among their camping sites archaeologists have found ornaments, molded clay objects, and figurines: further indications that they may have had a religious practice of visiting an established sacred site, perhaps to have personal visions and reassurance of a god's protecting care.

In many respects the Shoshonean and Northern Fremont cultures continued up to the nineteenth century. The culture of the Big-Game Hunters developed into the Archaic, and the Archaic into the Northern Shoshoni that explorers, emigrants, missionaries, and settlers encountered on the eastern Snake River in 1850. The Cascade group of the Archaic and late Archaic may be the ancestors of the Nez Perce of the early nineteenth century. The Northern Fremont eventually evolved into the Western Shoshoni and Northern Paiute of the modern era.

We do not know much about the inner motivations of these prehistoric people—their hopes and fears, their dream life, their personal aspirations. We can be reasonably sure that they tried to live with nature, not change it. They respected and tried to find meaning in the movement of the sun, the moon, and the stars, in lightning, thunder, and the wind. We do not know what they made of birth, of death, of the lunar flow of women's blood. We suppose that they laughed and played jokes on each other, and we know that they felt an intimate kinship with fellow creatures. We have also found cairns, tipi rings, and other indications that they had religious dances and ceremonials. They believed in the power of magic and had a strong sense of pride in their own small hunting groups.

The earliest residents of Idaho, over a period of more than 15,000 years, achieved remarkably successful adaptation to the frequent and often extreme natural and human changes in their environment. They provided a sound foundation, culturally and materially, for the Idaho Indians of historic times.

## CHAPTER TWO: SOURCES

Helpful sources on early humans in America include Earl H. Swanson, Warwick Bray, and Ian Farrington, *The Ancient Americas* (New York: Peter Bedrick Books, 1975, 1989); Brian M. Fagan, *The Great Journey: The Peopling of Ancient America* (London: Thames and Hudson, 1987); Richard Shutler, Jr., ed., *Early Man in the New World* (Beverly Hills: Sage Publications, 1983); Jesse D. Jennings, ed., *Ancient North Americans* (San Francisco: W. H. Freeman, 1983); L. S. Cressman, *Prehistory of the Far West: Homes of Vanished Peoples* (Salt Lake City: University of Utah Press, 1977); Jesse D. Jennings and Edward Norbeck, eds., *Prehistoric Man in the New World* (Chicago: University of Chicago Press, 1962); H. M. Wormington, *Ancient Man in North America*, 4th ed. (Denver: Denver Museum of Natural History, 1957); Julian Steward, *Basin-Plateau Aboriginal Socio-Political Groups*, Bureau of American Ethnology Bulletin No. 120 (Washington, D.C.: Smithsonian Institution, 1938); Roger C. Owen, James J. F. Deetz, and Anthony D. Fisher, eds., *The North American Indians: A Sourcebook* (New York: The Macmillan Co., 1967); Jesse D. Jennings, *Prehistory of North America*, 2d ed. (New York: McGraw-Hill Book Co., 1974); C. Vance Haynes, "Elephant Hunting in North America," *Scientific American* 214 (1966):104–12; P. S. Martin, "The Discovery of America," *Science* 179 (1973): 969–74; and George Frison, *Prehistoric Hunters of the High Plains* (New York: Academic Press, 1978).

Sources that deal specifically with early humans in Idaho include Sven Liljeblad, "Indian Peoples of Idaho," in Beal and Wells, *History of Idaho*, 1:33–38; Earl H. Swanson, "Folsom Man in Idaho," *Idaho Yesterdays* 5 (Spring 1961):26–30; Earl H. Swanson, "Prehistoric Environments in Southeastern Idaho," *Idaho Yesterdays* 11 (Winter 1967–68):20–22; Ruth Gruhn, *The Archeology of Wilson Butte Cave, South-Central Idaho*, Occasional Papers of the Idaho State University Museum No. 6 (Pocatello, 1961); *Our Cultural Heritage* (Cottonwood, Idaho: Idaho State Office, U.S. Bureau of Land Management, 1987); Earl H. Swanson, Jr., "The Snake River Plain," *Idaho Yesterdays* 18 (Summer 1974):2–11; B. Robert Butler, *A Guide to*

*Understanding Idaho Archaeology: The Upper Snake and Salmon River Country*, 3d ed. (Pocatello: The Idaho Museum of Natural History, 1978); B. Robert Butler, "Prehistory of the Snake and Salmon River Area," in Warren L. D'Azevedo, ed., *Handbook of North American Indians: Great Basin* (Washington, D.C.: Smithsonian Institution, 1986), 127–34; Mark G. Plew, *An Introduction to the Archaeology of Southern Idaho* (Boise: Boise State University, 1986), a Hemingway Western Studies Center Publication; Earl H. Swanson, Jr., "Idaho Yesteryears," *Idaho Yesterdays* 9 (Spring 1965): 19–24; Earl H. Swanson, Jr., *Birch Creek: Human Ecology in the Cool Desert of the Northern Rocky Mountains 9,000 B.C. to A.D. 1850* (Pocatello: Idaho State University Press, 1972); and Eugene Walker, "The Geologic History of the Snake River Country of Idaho," *Idaho Yesterdays* 7 (Summer 1963): 18–31.

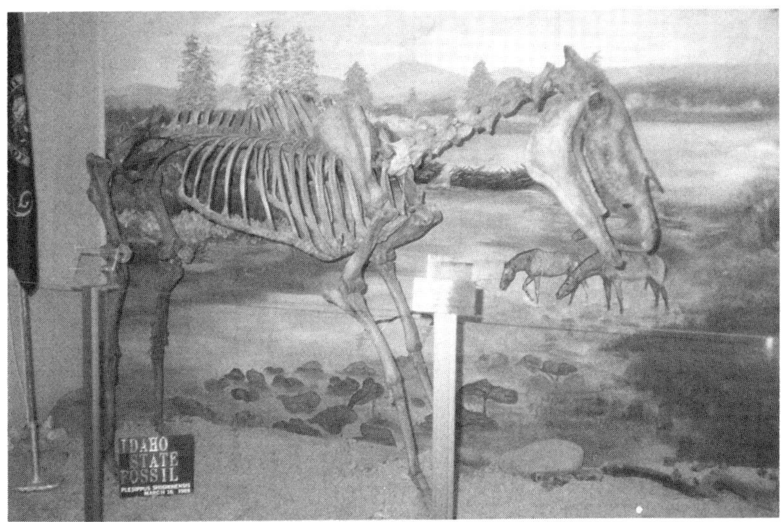


6.

7.

6. In prehistoric times Idaho was the location of elephants, mastodons, sabre-toothed tigers, giant bears, and ancient horses. This fossil skeleton of a prehistoric horse *(equus Idahoensis)*, dated about 1,000,000 B.C., was found in the Hagerman Valley. HAGERMAN VALLEY HISTORICAL SOCIETY.

7. At Wilson Butte Cave, near Eden in south-central Idaho, archaeologists found artifacts used by prehistoric hunters that date back to 14,000 B.C. ISHS 66–1.5.

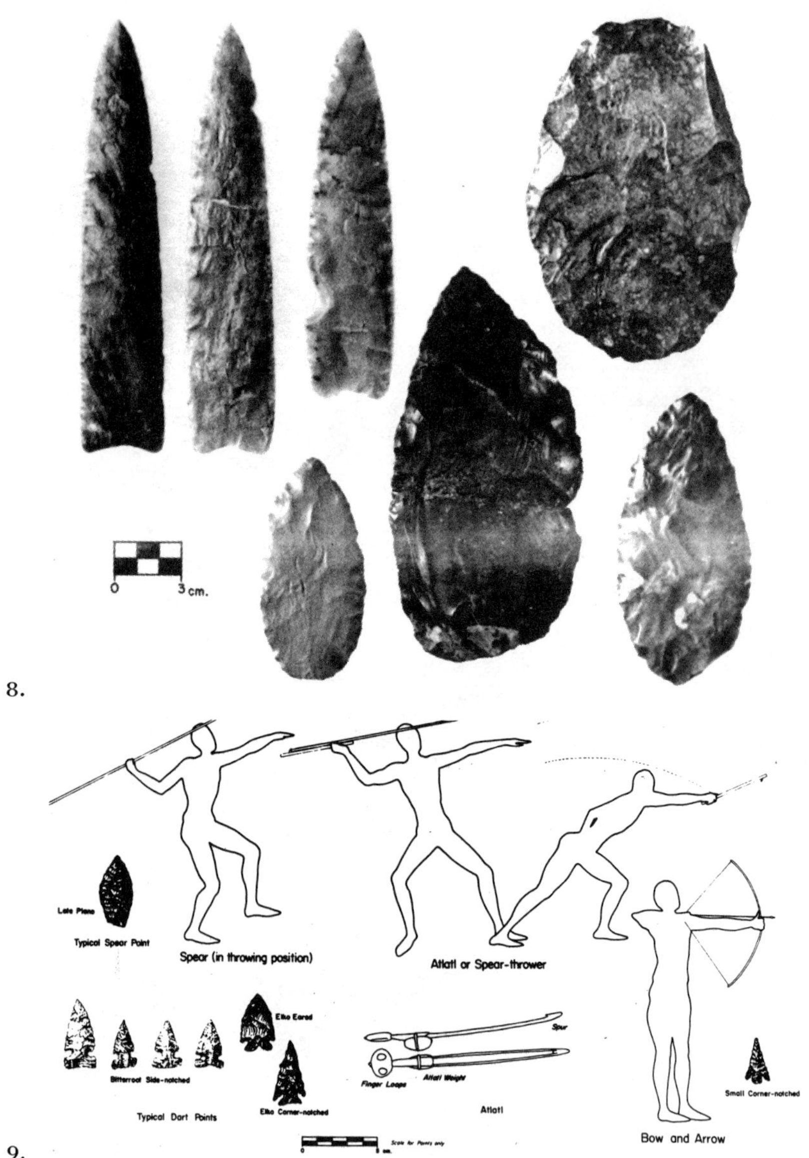


8.

9.

8. Among the artifacts uncovered at the Simon Site Clovis cache near Fairfield were these Clovis spear points that date to 10,000 B.C. UTAH STATE UNIVERSITY SPECIAL COLLECTIONS.

9. Successive forms of prehistoric weaponry in Idaho and nearby states. UTAH STATE UNIVERSITY SPECIAL COLLECTIONS.

## CHAPTER THREE

# Idaho's Native Americans

When the first white men came to Idaho in 1805, the number of Indian aborigines within the modern state varied from 6,000 to 10,000. Because Idaho's boundaries do not conform to the general patterns of Indian residence and migration, it would have been difficult to decide which roving bands or groups to assign to Idaho. Sven Liljeblad has estimated that about 3,000 Shoshoni-Bannock and about 3,000 Nez Perce could be assigned to Idaho. About 700 Coeur d'Alene and about 300 Pend d'Oreille (or Kalispel) might also be counted as Idaho Indians. Another 200 or more Kutenai and perhaps some Northern Paiute were also in Idaho some of the time. Each of these groups lived in and roamed over the country that included parts of Idaho and nearby states.[1]

The Kutenai were the northernmost and smallest of the groups. Most of them now live on the Flathead Reservation in Montana or north of the Canadian border, although one small band still lives near Bonners Ferry. Linguistically unrelated to any of the other Idaho Indians, they lived in a well-watered region with open valleys, small lakes, a mild climate, and abundant fish and game. The Pend d'Oreille were part of the Kalispel group that occupied a vast forested and mountainous area south of the Kutenai and extending into Montana, Washington, and Canada. The territory of the Coeur d'Alene, who were related to the Flatheads of Montana and the Spokanes of Washington, encompassed about four million acres centering on Lake Coeur d'Alene and reaching into Montana and Washington. Now most live near Plummer. The Nez Perce were a populous group inhabiting a large territory between the Bitterroot Range and the Blue Mountains of Oregon. Today, while some of them live on the Colville Reservation in Washington, most live in the lower Clearwater Valley. They were renowned horsemen and had large herds of horses and elaborate horse trappings made of rawhide, horse hair, bone, and antler, which they decorated with dyes, skins, porcupine quills, and beads. While these northern aboriginal people were banded together in groups, they were not supervised by formal "chiefs."

Horses were introduced to America by the Spaniards, and they reached Idaho peoples from New Mexico about the middle of the eighteenth century—forcing the Indians to adapt quickly to a procession of changes. Like their eastern neighbors, Idaho's Native Americans began to alter their lifestyles and patterns of dress and to develop the organization that went with hunting buffalo on horseback. This included living in tipis and traveling from one camp site to another using the travois—a carrier to transport belongings suspended from poles and dragged behind dogs or a horse; "jerking" meat for preservation; wearing ornamented clothing made from skins and fancy feather headdresses; and performing ceremonial dances. Eventually each of the bands came to be organized under a trusted leader to facilitate cooperation in finding food and protecting each other in hostile territory. At first, the political and social structure still in its early stages, the "chiefs" were not autocratic. Individual Indians could move freely from one band to another.[2]

Living conditions among the Kutenai, Pend d'Oreille, Coeur d'Alene, and Nez Perce were quite similar. In the summer they caught salmon, plentiful in most rivers, and dried and stored them for winter. They also caught steelhead, white fish, mountain trout, and sturgeon. They migrated to Montana to conduct communal bison hunts as well as killing bighorn sheep, Rocky Mountain goat, grizzly, black bear, moose, elk, deer, antelope, caribou, and such small game as beaver, squirrel, badger, and rabbits. They hunted grouse, ptarmigan, ducks, and geese. They dug for tuberous roots and bulbs—the blue-flowering camas lily, sego, bitterroot, wild onion, and the kouse or "biscuit root." They mashed and dried huckleberries, chokecherries, serviceberries, blackberries, wild rhubarb, and other fruits.

Permanent dwellings were semisubterranean, mat-covered longhouses. Clothing resembled the styles of the Plains Indians: men wore a long, fringed buckskin shirt with loose sleeves, and leggings, breechcloth, belt, and moccasins. Women wore an undecorated, fringed, long Plains skin frock and knee-length leggings, belts, moccasins, and headbands or caps. In winter both wore robes made from small animal furs. Hats were made from rawhide, fur, and willow withes. Distinguished warriors wore feathers.

These people were quite individualistic and maintained autonomous villages, each with elected headmen. Before the organization under chiefs, local leaders had little authority. In addition to a band leader and a war leader, each band might have a fishing leader, deer-hunting leader, and duck-hunting leader. After they adopted the horse, bands cooperated much more. On their migrations they traded tools, ornaments, and foods with other native groups in Washington, Canada, and Montana.

The social pattern of the Nez Perce is representative of most other North Idaho Indians.[3] Family was a major focus in their life-style, and the opinions of relatives mattered. An expectant mother would receive advice from the older female relatives that ranged from an exercise program to personal hygiene including hot and cold baths and administration of medicinal herbs. An expectant mother was counseled not to observe, touch, or scorn deformed animals or persons for fear the child she was carrying would face a similar fate. Women avoided tying knots or participating in any activities that suggested difficulties encountered in the birthing process.

Typically babies were delivered in specially designated small houses. A Nez Perce woman was attended by a midwife or a shaman and her own mother or another older female member of the family. If problems arose a male shaman with obstetrical skills participated. Usually he would apply healing herbs, physical manipulation, and rituals drawing upon the power of tutelary or guardian spirits. Recognized as an intimate part of the child, the umbilical cord was saved in a special buckskin pouch affixed to the cradleboard. New babies and their mothers were honored with feasts and presents.

Cradleboards were home to the baby until it could walk. The mother strapped the cradleboard on her back or kept it near her all the time. Mothers nursed their infants often for several years and other women relatives assisted in feeding the baby if necessary until it was weaned; then softened vegetables and meats were introduced. A chewy gristle was used to keep the baby satisfied between meals. If a mother died, other family members cared for the baby.

Aboriginal parents and grandparents wished for large families. The children were treated very formally by their parents; the grandparents shared a more relaxed attitude and tended to treat the children as equals, while they also taught the basics of behavior and expectations. A young boy was schooled in fishing and hunting, sweat-bathing, and horse-riding by his grandfather; a young girl was tutored in domestic skills by her grandmother. Children were educated by listening to hours of Indian tales told by grandparents as passed from generation to generation. Aunts, uncles, cousins, and other siblings also were actively engaged in the training of youth. Each morning all the children flocked to the bathing area for the daily regimen of proper exercise and hot and cold baths. There were stern lectures on proper conduct. Infants were rarely disciplined, but older children who misbehaved were often whipped, sometimes in groups. Northern Indian youth spent most of their time with siblings or cousins whom they viewed as brothers and sisters.

At a formal ceremony children were named after important family ancestors with the hope that the youth's development would thus be favorably influenced. Nicknames were common and sometimes names were changed to reflect a great accomplishment, a tutelary-spirit vision, or the refinement of a desirable personal trait.

By the age of three or four boys and girls were expected to contribute to the family's lifestyle. Sometimes strapped to a horse to keep from falling, they would accompany the family in various hunting, fishing, root-digging, and berry-picking duties where they would learn the process with toy bows, digging sticks, and other tools designed just for them. By the age of six, they were expected to make a meaningful contribution to the family's reserves. At special ceremonies the boys were honored for their first kill of game and the girls were recognized for their initial root digging and berry picking.

At this point, the children were individually lectured by one of their significant elders. Attention was again focused on morals, behavior, and attitudes. During adolescence youths actively sought visions from tutelary spirits to learn what their specialty or "power" would be in life. Some pursued a visionary experience many times before receiving a personal endowment or

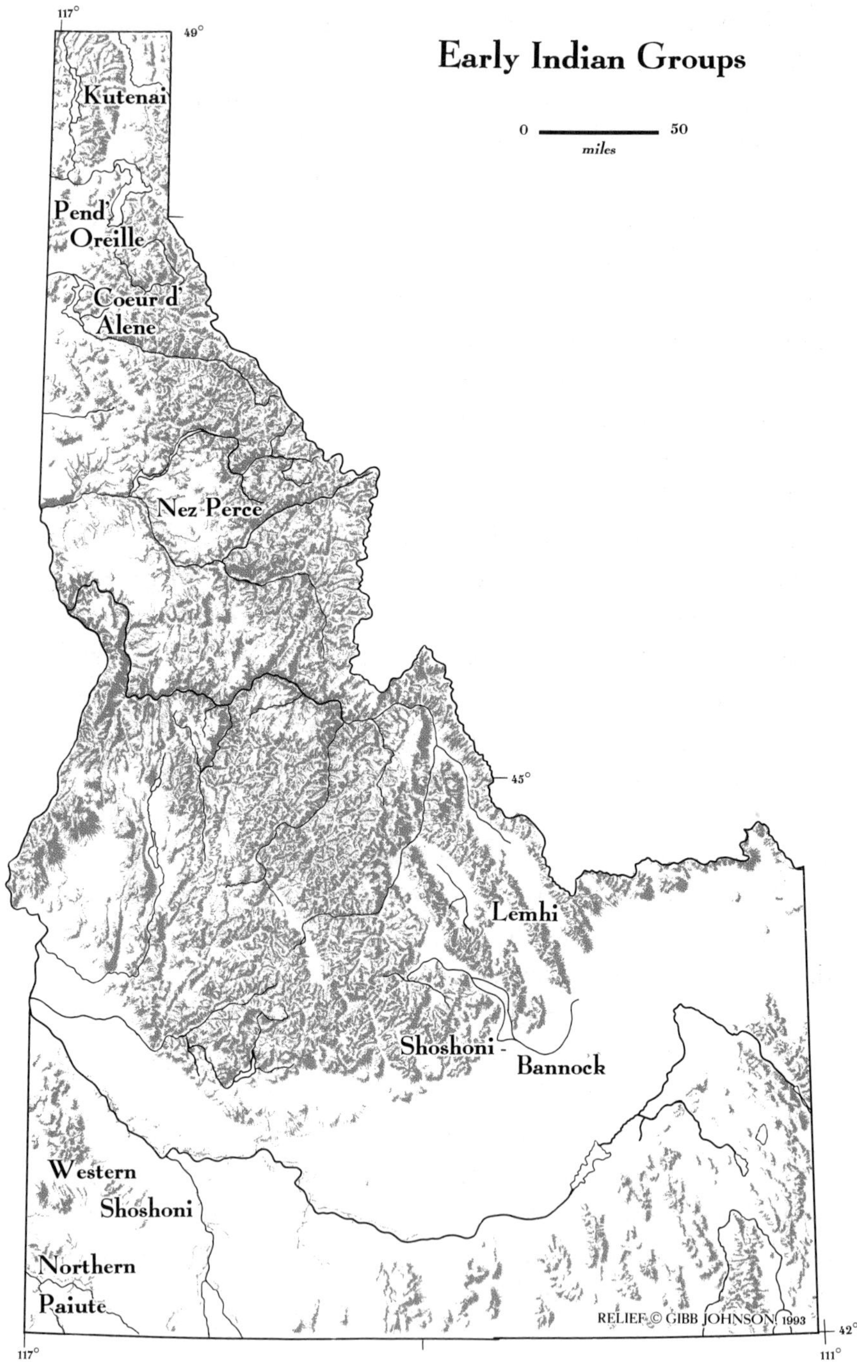
Early Indian Groups
0
50
miles
117°
49°
Kutenai
Pend' Oreille
Coeur d' Alene
Nez Perce
45°
Lemhi
Shoshoni - Bannock
Western Shoshoni
Northern Paiute
RELIEF © GIBB JOHNSON 1993
42°
117°
111°

mission. If successful in receiving a vision, they were almost assured of a successful life as an adult. If no vision was received they could expect a lackluster existence.

Upon reaching puberty a Nez Perce girl faced an elaborate ceremony to mark her transition. At the first indication she would be isolated from the village in a special house and cared for by older female relatives. She was prompted to think good thoughts and engage in worthwhile activity since this period would establish a pattern for the rest of her life. She stayed indoors all day, venturing out only after dark and only for a short time. She had an elaborately carved instrument to scratch her body that was prepared for this event. She ate meals cooked over a special fire. At the end of her isolation, usually about a week, she returned to the community with new status—she was ready for marriage. New clothes, a more mature hairstyle, and gifts from friends accompanied her new role.

Marriage among the Kutenai, Pend d'Oreille, Coeur d'Alene, and Nez Perce was a serious step usually arranged by relatives. The main issue was the social standing of the families involved. Three levels of class structure defined relative wealth and social prestige. The lowest bracket was made up of slaves captured in war or traded for goods, who performed the servile jobs and had no voice in the operation of the family or the village. Children of slaves were treated much better than their parents. The middle class was the largest group and focused on work responsibilities, while the upper class was composed of strong leaders and their families. Their wealth was apparent and often measured in horses. Upper- and middle-class marriages were made usually within their own groups though slave women were sometimes taken as second wives. Slave men married within their class or sometimes into poor middle-class families.

If a young man was interested in a certain girl, his family reviewed his choice in light of her family's social standing. Genealogies were checked to make sure no family lines crossed, as marriage to relatives was not allowed. Marriages within families where one son had already taken a wife were commended since family ties were critically important.

An older female relative of the boy negotiated for the hand of the bride. If the girl's family was responsive to the overture, the relative moved in with them to observe the girl and the two families held occasional feasts. If the two seemed compatible, the couple began living together. If the union was harmonious a ceremony was planned with an elaborate exchange of gifts, first from the family of the groom and about six months later from the family of the bride. Gifts from the groom's relatives would include such items as horses, hunting and fishing tools, and buckskin. The bride's gifts would favor her role with materials like root bags, baskets, beads and beaded bags, and clothing.

With the second exchange of gifts the couple was considered legally married. Very few divorces occurred since the ties between the two families were as important as between the individuals. The couple normally moved in with the parents of the bride although they might later relocate with the family of the groom if conditions seemed better suited to their needs.

Among these bands age meant wisdom and often wealth. The senior males commanded respect and usually held the prominent leadership positions. A leader's death resulted in an official mourning period. A herald crier announced the death to the village and close female relatives immediately began wailing in a high-pitched lamentation. They were joined in their weeping by a larger group of friends and relatives around the corpse until the body was buried the following day. In preparation the body was bathed, dressed in ornate new clothes, and decorated with red face paint, and the hair was combed. Those who prepared the corpse underwent a ritual purification. The grave, usually dug on a high point overlooking the area, was marked with a wooden stake. Wrapped in a robe and surrounded by some of the deceased's precious possessions, the body was carried to the grave by a horse-drawn travois. If the horse was a favorite of the departed, it sometimes was killed and left near the site. The shaman concluded the burial by performing rituals to prevent the ghost of the deceased from bothering the living.

At a feast following the ceremony the family distributed the remaining personal wealth according to the wishes of the deceased. Men received the horses, robes, necklaces, and war and hunting materials, while the women were given cooking implements, beaded bags, and robes.

During the extended period of mourning the spouse's hair was cut, old clothes worn, laughing and public appearances eliminated, and remarriage banned for one year. To assist in eliminating memory of the deceased, the spouse was prohibited use of the name and homes and furnishings, and sweat houses were often abandoned or destroyed. At the end of a year, relatives lifted the mourning period and the surviving spouse received new clothes and a new spouse, usually a kin to the deceased if one was available.

Southern Idaho Indians, most of whom now live at Fort Hall, differed from the northern groups both in language and in way of life. The two major southern groups were the Shoshoni and Northern Paiute. The name "Bannock" has been given to a people of Northern Paiute origin who also live at Fort Hall.[4] Moving north from Nevada and Utah into the Snake River Plain, perhaps in the sixteenth century, and related to the Northern Paiute of Oregon, Nevada, and the eastern portion of California, they were closely associated with the Shoshoni by 1805. In fact, by the time the white men arrived in Idaho the so-called Northern Shoshoni and Bannock were for the most part blended into one, most of them speaking both languages. They shared the same region for their villages, and there was some intermarriage between them.

Prior to the horse era these people congregated in their related families called patrilocal bands, referring to the tradition of the bride moving in with the husband's family. The experienced family heads were the acknowledged leaders. There was little political unity beyond bands, who were often referred to by their primary source of food such as "squirrel eaters," "sagebrush eaters," "mountain sheep eaters," "elk eaters," and "bison eaters." Wandering in search of food, the bands often fell into camps together. As they associated and shared caches of food they also intermarried.

The aboriginal territory of the Shoshoni-Bannock extended across most of southern Idaho into western Wyoming and down into Nevada and Utah. This area was very dry, although the higher areas on the northern and eastern periphery supported vegetation and animal life more abundantly, as did the borders of Snake River tributaries.

The Northern Paiute were part of a large language and cultural grouping that extended south from Oregon and Idaho into south-central Nevada and eastern California and even into northern Mexico. They exploited the same resource areas as the Shoshoni-Bannock, although much of their country was desert, with little water, alkaline soils, and very sparse fauna and flora. They had few mountains to relieve the heat and desiccation of the desert. One small Paiute band, separate from the Bannock, still lives at Duck Valley on the southern boundary of Idaho.

The cultures of the Shoshoni-Bannock and Northern Paiute reflected their differing environments from that of the northern Indians. The Idaho Shoshoni, for example, made more use of the flat grinding stone than did their northern neighbors, who, in turn, were more familiar with the mortar, suitable for pounding meat and bulbs. North Idaho groups excelled in housebuilding; their long gabled structures covered with mats were home to several families. In the south the conical grass hut was the traditional dwelling. Northern Indians excelled in basketmaking. The sophisticated designs on their beautiful soft bags were passed down through generations. The Shoshoni produced more pottery. Shoshoni clothing was skimpy; a robe with woven strips of rabbit skins served as a coat. Southern people had few weapons for warfare, while their best bows were fashioned from the horns of mountain sheep.

The Shoshoni-Bannock fished for salmon below Shoshoni Falls and also found an abundance of roots in this area. Prior to the introduction of the horse these Indians lived on food supplies made up of insects from grasshoppers and crickets to ants and larvae, birds, and occasionally their eggs, seeds, nuts, and small game such as groundhog, jackrabbit, cottontail, porcupine, prairie dog, and badger.

The horse probably reached the Shoshoni-Bannock before it reached the northern Indians. By 1700 these people's lifestyles had been altered dramatically; the new mobility allowed them to hunt bison in southeastern Idaho and, as it reached extinction, to move east into the Great Plains. Hunting expanded to such large game as deer, antelope, bears of several varieties, and mountain sheep. They also dug camas and other roots in distant well-watered regions in south central Idaho as far as Smith Prairie and Camas Prairie on Wood River.

The integration of the horse into Shoshoni-Bannock life refocused much of the daily activity. In the spring, they divided into groups to gather foodstuffs; some sought large game and roots in the mountains while others returned to proven fishing grounds on the Snake River. This cycle continued until midsummer when parties assembled to search for bison in Wyoming and Montana. Also in midsummer intertribal gatherings were held in locations such as Weiser and Lemhi Valley where each group brought items to trade. The women gathered berries, roots, nuts, seeds, and insects from spring to early fall. Birds were most plentiful in summer but were stalked almost year round. Late fall was a time to prepare the foods for the winter, and caches of meat and plants were stored in protected areas where the Indians expected to linger during the winter months. Little hunting or gathering was done during the bitter winter season.

Shoshoni-Bannock used fishing implements that were probably borrowed in design from their northern neighbors. Fish from small streams were scooped up in twined conical baskets. Fish weirs used on the larger Snake River were a community effort in construction and application. Deer hunts on the other hand were much more individualized, although communal nets were used for capturing antelope, rabbits, and some waterfowl. The groups used clubs to kill waterfowl or simply wrung their necks. Snares, decoys, blinds, and spring-pole traps were employed to capture birds and small game. Rodents were prodded out of their holes by a "skewer," a long thin pole that dug into the animal's skin. Sinew backed the bows made from both wood and horn. Obsidian was used for the tips of knives and arrows, and bone was used for salmon spears, awls, and other hand tools. Utensils were carved primarily from horns of bison and mountain sheep. Serving pieces like bowls, pots, and cups were usually fashioned out of soapstone.

The Shoshoni-Bannock collected and carried seeds in conical baskets. Foods prepared in twilled baskets covered in rawhide were transported in baskets of woven sagebrush and bark strengthened by straps of skin or vegetable fibers. Water was stored in a special basket lined with pitch. A loaf similar to bread was prepared from a ground mixture of sunflower seeds, lamb's quarter, and serviceberries. Seeds were pounded into a mash and roasted in willow trays; chokecherries were mashed and spread in the sun to dry. Camas and other tuberous roots were baked in earth ovens and shaped into loafs to dry in the sun. Meat was either broiled or sun-dried.

The Shoshoni-Bannock lived first in conical long-poled dwellings thatched with bundles of grass, bark, and tule before advancing to the conical skin lodge, the "tipi," adopted from the Great Plains Indians. Sunbreaks and windbreaks provided shelters while some lived in caves. Sweat houses and menstrual huts were common, as they were in northern Idaho.

Indians wore few clothes for centuries, but by the time white explorers and settlers arrived the Shoshoni-Bannock were mounted on horseback and dressed in the typical buckskin attire. Men wore the long fringed shirt made from deer, antelope, or big-horn sheep, with fur caps and leggings that often displayed scalps. Women wore dresses from the same hides ornamented with porcupine quills and girdles of polished leather, and often specially woven basket-caps. Men, if facing warfare, shielded themselves with armor of laminated layers of glue, sand, and antelope skin.

The Shoshoni-Bannock were the major political force in southern Idaho. Despite the differences among these Idaho bands, they were unified in halting aggressions from the Plains. Joining with the Shoshoni in western Wyoming, they were able to repel encroachments by the Blackfeet and Crow, and they were also known to link up with the Nez Perce to oppose the Blackfeet.

Traditionally, the Northern Paiute did not ride horses. Indeed, the rare horse that ventured into their territory was killed for food. They lived off the land and exploited their bleak environment more intensively than any other group in Idaho. Since large game like deer, elk, antelope, and mountain sheep were scarce, they focused their efforts on small game animals like cottontail, jackrabbit, mink, gopher, kangaroo rat, mouse, muskrat, woodchuck, squirrel, raccoon, bobcat, badger, and beaver. They caught small minnows, a few trout, and suckers to augment their meager supply of salmon. Fowl such as doves, horned owls, quail, robins, woodpeckers, ruffed grouse, prairie chickens, sage hens, blackbirds, loons, ducks, and geese made up an important part of their diet. Insects used for food ranged from caterpillars and ants to crickets and grasshoppers. Seeds such as wada (a desert plant) and sunflowers were staples, as were tuberous roots like camas and the so-called Indian potato. Currants, chokecherries, huckleberries, and serviceberries added variety to their nutritional fare.

In aboriginal times, the Northern Paiute spent most of their time searching for food. In early May the women started canvassing the countryside for edible roots while the men repaired salmon traps. At the end of the salmon run, the fishermen returned to family units and browsed the countryside for deer, sagehens, and seeds or roots. In midsummer the women gathered crickets, in early fall currants and huckleberries. Men turned to the mountains for deer and elk and joined together for rabbit and antelope campaigns. By November, they, like other Indians, were preparing for winter, depositing stores of food for the cold months to follow.

Deer were hunted with dogs who would herd them into traps by trails or springs. The hunters also used fire, scarecrows, and even deer costumes to lure their game. Antelope and mountain sheep were enticed into corrals of sagebrush-bark rope or stalked by individual hunters. Nets, clubs, and bows and arrows were used to kill rabbits and other small game. Ducks, geese, and mudhens or coots were taken in communal hunts, some with bare hands from cleverly designed blinds. Skewers snared small animals in holes and tunnels. Hook and line, dip nets, weirs, traps, baskets, harpoons, and even hands were employed to catch fish.

Tools to gather and prepare food were often simple, often ingenious. Simple bows of juniper and serviceberry were used. Sometimes the tips of arrows, made of obsidian, bone, or horn, were poisoned. Digging sticks were fashioned from mahogany or serviceberry wood. Grinding seeds, roots, and meat was done with stone pestles and mortars and thin, oval metates. Willow cups, made of coiled and twined sticks, were used with animal stomachs and basketry to serve as water canteens. Horn, bone, and stone scrapers were used in many ways; hammers and choppers were fashioned from bone awls and broken cobbles. Fire was made with the familiar fire drill.

Fish, game, and insects were dried for storage while small

animals were roasted for eating. As with the north Idaho Indians, meat was pulverized and mixed with fat. Spawn eggs were combined with seeds; marrow was scooped out of split long bones. Most foods were stone-boiled or broiled over the fire on forked sticks. To parch seeds, the Indians layered them in baskets hung over hot coals.

The Northern Paiute lived in frame structures of pine, poplar, or willow pole construction sheathed with tule mats, usually either domed or tripodal. In winter they added extra matting for additional protection. As with the Shoshoni-Bannock, their communities often included simple sun shades, sweat houses, and menstrual and birth huts.

Elderly Paiute females hovered over an expectant mother to see that her diet was low in fatty foods; a large baby was too hard to deliver. They prepared mostly roots and warmed water for her to eat and protected her from jolts or sudden cold spells. The babe was delivered in a special house with the assistance of midwives, also the practice of northern Indians. The father ritually bathed the child at birth and would often fast until the child's umbilical cord detached. Unlike the northern tradition, the cord was ceremonially buried to ensure that the child would grow up strong. At the time of the birth, the father took a cold bath and a rigorous run. He was forbidden to smoke, gamble, or sweat bathe for five days, and must not hunt or have any contact with the mother for a month. The new mother returned to the family and home three or four weeks after delivery, freshly bathed and clothed in new attire. The father must dress in fresh clothes in honor of the occasion.

The care of the infant was entirely up to the women. A cradleboard was made for the new child which was essentially its environment for the first year. Only if the child grew up well would the cradleboard be reused for the next infant. At the end of the first year, the child graduated to a robe carried on his mother's back.

Children were named by the mother's parents, usually at the time they were withdrawn from the cradleboard. Boys were usually named for their grandfathers and girls for their grandmothers. As with most Indian groups, the boys' and girls' activities were closely aligned with their roles as adults. The girls gathered roots and seeds and wood; boys learned the habits of small animals and hunted with relatives. Warfare was insignificant in the social system, in sharp contrast to the Shoshoni-Bannock, whose boys were encouraged to pursue honor in battle.

When the child could walk, he or she was cared for by siblings and grandparents who also lived with the family. Shoshoni-Bannock society was permissive with children, who were rarely whipped for fear of breaking their spirit. If a child struck his father, he was considered brave rather than disrespectful. A child's dreams were considered a foreshadowing of his or her eventual contribution to society. As a result, they were questioned carefully after a night's sleep, and some of the children were allowed to follow their dreams to the mountains for special visions.

While girls faced an abrupt transition as they reached adolescence, boys made gradual steps to manhood, beginning with public honor for their first kill and, in the case of Shoshoni-Bannock, advancing to hunting parties, raids into the Great Plains, and eventually an invitation to join a warrior society. Usually this training culminated with marriage at about age twenty.

The Shoshoni-Bannock girl's experience at puberty was similar to that of the northern and central Indians. But, unlike those aboriginal inhabitants, she did not face taboos of touching her body. Still, her time isolated in a special house was believed to have great significance to her adult personality.

Youth activity following puberty was dominated by courtship. There were many formal dances where boys and girls paired off with little adult supervision. A boy played a flute late at night to draw the girl outside her tent for a tryst. Family marriages were also common. When a young man announced his choice for a mate the negotiations were accomplished by an older family member of either sex. If the prestige and wealth of each family were considered mutually acceptable, the prospective groom awarded the father of the bride-to-be a gift of horses. At the marriage ceremony the father reciprocated. Among Shoshoni-Bannock the girl's family could also initiate marriage negotiations.

Marriage among both Shoshoni and Northern Paiute was extended beyond traditional Indian culture to permit polygyny, polyandry, and what Euro-Americans would describe as marriage of first cousins. Primarily, the arrangements were simply a result of few potential partners. Polyandry, the marriage of one woman to several husbands, was practiced by brothers and the children she bore called all the men father. With the arrival of the horse, these marriages declined since the circle of prospects was widened. Polygyny, the practice of multiple wives for one husband, continued despite the introduction of the horse; in fact, it may have increased because of the slave-raiding practices of the Shoshoni-Bannock. Men who were rich in horses often used their wealth to purchase additional wives, reducing the number of women of marriageable age for the young men to select. They were then forced to marry very young girls or women who were slaves. Because the Shoshoni-Bannock, like most other aboriginal Indians, did not live long lives—in part because of their precarious hunting and warrior activities—a dead brother's wife might be added to an existing family unit. The oldest surviving brother might well be married to all his brothers' surviving wives.

Most of the rituals of mourning employed by the northern Indians were also employed by the Shoshoni-Bannock. At burial, the corpse was placed with the head to the west and shamans performed rites to protect the surviving family members from the ghost. Among the Northern Paiutes, where harsh living conditions shortened life expectancy, the mourning family buried the body in a rock shelter, rocky slope, or mountain; they observed mourning periods similar to those of other aboriginals.

Class differences so prominent among the Nez Perce and Shoshoni-Bannock were not an issue to the bands of Northern Paiute. They were few in number and had such meager wealth that class distinction was impractical. Occasionally they were taken as slaves by Nez Perce, Cayuse, and Umatilla and traded throughout the Northwest, or captured by bands of Shoshoni-Bannock.

At the beginning of the nineteenth century white men moved overtly into the Indian territories of Idaho. The Blackfeet, brandishing firearms procured from Canadian trappers, were also systematically terrorizing the Indian camps, stealing horses, and destroying property. The Kutenai, Pend d'Oreille, Coeur d'Alene, Nez Perce, Shoshoni-Bannock, and Northern Paiute frantically traded for guns to protect themselves and occasionally used them against each other. However, years of fairly satisfying relations between Indians and whites were mutually advantageous to the fur traders and natives. Some trappers married Indian women and adopted Indian ways of life. Trading furs to the trappers, the Indians obtained not only guns but knives, tools, traps, fish hooks, kettles, cloth, glass beads, tobacco, and—to later dismay—whiskey. The Hudson's Bay Company, which monopolized the fur industry, eventually eliminated the liquor trafficking.

The Indians of north Idaho were visited by Protestant and Catholic missionaries in the 1830s and 1840s, and thousands of white migrants moved across southern Idaho in the next twenty years on their way to Oregon and California. Except for the Jesuit Coeur d'Alene mission, a post at Fort Hall, and a mountain man or two, no white settlers lived in Idaho for any length of time until 1855. Through the 1860s the aboriginal culture continued to thrive. Living with the advantage of horses and manufactured tools in their primitive environment, the Indians could not have predicted the enormous upheaval ahead for them and their families.

The "Indian summer" then suddenly ended with gold rushes and white settlements. Irrigated farms, white men raising stock, telegraph lines, and railroads intruded on the life natives had known for centuries. Bewildered by the white demand for ownership of land signified by pieces of paper, and pushed from their traditional hunting and fishing grounds, the Indians responded with bows and arrows and gunfire. A tragic sequence of provocations and wars resulted in the inevitable internment of Indians on reservation lands. Governed by vacillating national policies that were administered by insensitive political appointees, the Idaho Indian people suffered the indignities imposed to control "savages."

Little remains of a varied but productive culture that nurtured Indian bands for hundreds, even thousands, of years. When Idaho Indians gave up their lands, they also gave up the only life they knew. They have sought in recent years to respond to the challenge of finding a bridge between the past and the present.[5]

## CHAPTER THREE: SOURCES

The finest sources on Idaho Indians in historic times are Deward E. Walker, Jr., *Indians of Idaho* (Moscow: University Press of Idaho, 1978); Sven Liljeblad, *Indian Peoples of Idaho* (Pocatello: Idaho State College, 1957); Patricia K. Ourada, ed., *Indian Peoples of Idaho* (Boise: Boise State University Press, 1975); Sven Liljeblad, *The Idaho Indians in Transition, 1805–1960* (Pocatello: Idaho State University Museum, 1972); and Deward E. Walker, Jr., *Myths of Idaho Indians* (Moscow: University Press of Idaho, 1980). In addition to these there are chapters in most Idaho histories, including Beal and

Wells, *History of Idaho*, 1:29–59 (written by Sven Liljeblad); Defenbach, *Idaho: The Place and Its People*, 1:41–78; Brosnan, *History of the State of Idaho*, 23–34; James H. Hawley, *History of Idaho: The Gem of the Mountains*, 4 vols. (Chicago: S. J. Clarke Publishing Co., 1920), 1:31–50; Thomas Donaldson, *Idaho of Yesterday* (Caldwell: Caxton Printers, 1941), 276–335; and Floyd R. Barber and Dan W. Martin, *Idaho in the Pacific Northwest* (Caldwell: Caxton Printers, 1956), 111–18.

Several books on Indians in the Northwest and Great Basin treat Idaho Indians. They include Robert H. Ruby and John A. Brown, *Indians of the Pacific Northwest: A History* (Norman: University of Oklahoma Press, 1981); Robert F. and Yolanda Murphy, "Northern Shoshone and Bannock," in Warren L. D'Azevedo, ed., *Handbook of North American Indians: Great Basin*; John R. Swanton, *The Indian Tribes of North America* (Washington, D.C.: Government Printing Office, 1953); Francis Haines, *Indians of the Great Basin and Plateau* (New York: G. P. Putnam's Sons, 1970); and Omer Stewart, *Indians of the Great Basin: A Critical Bibliography* (Bloomington: Indiana University Press, 1982).

Histories of particular Indian nations include: Paul E. Baker, *The Forgotten Kutenai* (Boise: Mountain States Press, 1955); *Century of Survival: A Brief History of the Kootenai Tribe of Idaho* (Bonners Ferry: Kootenai Tribe, 1990); John Fahey, *The Kalispel Indians* (Norman: University of Oklahoma Press, 1986); Francis Haines, *The Nez Perces: Tribesmen of the Columbia Plateau* (Norman: University of Oklahoma Press, 1955); Alvin M. Josephy, Jr., *The Nez Perce Indians and the Opening of the Northwest*, abridged edition (Lincoln: University of Nebraska Press, 1979); Edward Dorn, *The Shoshoneans: The People of the Basin Plateau* (New York: William Morrow Co., 1966); Virginia Cole Trenholm and Maurine Carley, *The Shoshonis: Sentinels of the Rockies* (Norman: University of Oklahoma Press, 1964); Brigham D. Madsen, *The Bannock of Idaho* (Caldwell: Caxton Printers, 1958); Brigham D. Madsen, *The Lemhi: Sacajawea's People* (Caldwell: Caxton Printers, 1979); Brigham D. Madsen, *The Northern Shoshoni* (Caldwell: Caxton Printers, 1980); Hank Corless, *The Weiser Indians: Shoshoni Peacemakers* (Salt Lake City: University of Utah Press, 1990).

Helpful scholarly articles include: Alvin M. Josephy, Jr., "Origins of the Nez Perce People," *Idaho Yesterdays*, 6 (Spring 1962):2–13; Albert W. Thompson, "Coeur d'Alene: The Names Applied to Tribe and Lake," *Idaho Yesterdays* 21 (Winter 1978):11–15; J. C. Yerbury, "Kootenay Linguistics: An Unsolved Mystery," *Idaho Yesterdays* 22 (Spring 1978):11–15; Clifford M. Drury, "Lawyer, Head Chief of the Nez Perce 1848–1875," *Idaho Yesterdays* 22 (Winter 1979):2–12; Omer C. Stewart, "The Shoshoni: Their History and Social Organization," *Idaho Yesterdays* 9 (Fall 1965):2–5, 28; and Haruo Aoki, "What Does Chopunnish Mean?" [origin of the name Nez Perce], *Idaho Yesterdays* 10 (Winter 1966–67):10–11.

Although not specifically focused on Idaho Indians, the life of other Indian women is discussed in Gretchen M. Bataille and Kathleen Mullen Sands, *American Indian Women: Telling Their Lives* (Lincoln: University of Nebraska Press, 1984); and John Upton Terrell and Donna M. Terrell, *Indian Women of the Western Morning: Their Life in Early America* (New York: The Dial Press, 1974).

10. 

11. 

10. Native American camps like this one on the Snake River, near Lewiston, featured tipis in a circle with a large tent in the center. UIL 6–24–7B.

11. This 1904 photo shows five Coeur d'Alene women mounted for a horse race. ISHS 1875–K.

12.

12. Kutenai in Hope, Idaho. ISHS 79–128.37/A.

13.

14.

15.

13. This proud young Nez Perce chief wears a feather headdress indicating his rank; a decorated tomahawk and ermine skins on his arm symbolize prowess. C. J. BROSNAN COLLECTION, UIL 6–24–1AB.

14. Sophie and James Reuben, shown in regalia with their horses, were Nez Perce Indians. ISHS 656.

15. A 1904 scene of a Nez Perce tribal powwow. ISHS 1875–L.

16.

16. Ah-Yah-Toe-Tuhn, a Nez Perce woman, is gathering camas, the root of which she dried and ground into a meal. ISHS 3793.11.

17.

17. W. H. Jackson photographed these three Shoshoni women and baby on a cradleboard in Indian Dick's lodge on October 10, 1878. USHS.

18.

18. Shoshoni Indians, mounted and on foot, about 1878. USHS.

## CHAPTER FOUR

# The First Explorers: Lewis and Clark

IN 1801 newly elected President Thomas Jefferson, always fascinated with western North America, began planning an expedition to explore the West. He employed twenty-six-year-old Meriwether Lewis as a private secretary, intending to prepare him to lead the expedition. Born on his family's plantation in Albemarle County, Virginia, Lewis had enlisted in the state militia at the age of twenty and soon advanced to the rank of captain. Most of his service was on the then western frontier beyond the Alleghenies, where he acquired experience with the wilderness and with aborigines. At Jefferson's urging Lewis was given special scientific and technical training from the faculty of the University of Pennsylvania; he collected equipment and supplies and studied maps of the West.

When the enterprise was secretly approved by Congress in January 1803 and Lewis was designated commander, he invited William Clark to join him as co-leader. Clark, who was also born on a Virginia plantation, was the younger brother of George

Rogers Clark, hero of the American Revolution in the West. Four years older than Lewis, William Clark had been commissioned a lieutenant in the army in 1792, had fought under General Anthony Wayne in the battle of Fallen Timbers, and had been an acquaintance of Lewis in a campaign in 1795–96. He was a mapmaker, had experience fighting Indians, and was a skillful negotiator with them. Clark eagerly accepted the assignment and was henceforth treated as a captain. The two men acted as equals on the journey.

The expedition was charged with exploring the Missouri River to its source in the Rocky Mountains and then proceeding down the nearest westward-flowing stream to the Pacific. The explorers would not only prepare the way for the extension of the American fur trade to the tribes throughout the area, but also advance geographical knowledge of the continent. Reflecting Jefferson's interest in natural science, the party was to gather information about plants, animals, fossils, soils, and geology and to report on the Indian cultures the explorers encountered.

Twenty-eight-year-old Lewis left for the West on July 5, 1803, two months after the United States had gained possession of much of that region by the Louisiana Purchase. He picked up Clark and several recruits at Louisville, Kentucky, and then ascended the Mississippi to Camp Wood River, Illinois. The party remained at the junction with the Missouri River not far from St. Louis throughout the winter of 1803–4, recruiting and training their men, gathering supplies and equipment, and collecting information from traders and boatmen familiar with the Missouri. In addition to Lewis and Clark the permanent exploring party in April 1804 included twenty-seven unmarried soldiers, a half-Indian hunter and interpreter named George Drouilliard (often anglicized to Drewyer), and Clark's black slave, York. In addition, a corporal, five privates, and several French boatmen were to accompany the expedition the first season and then return with its records and scientific specimens.

The "Corps of Discovery" began its journey on May 21, 1804. By October the group had reached the villages of the Mandan and Minnetaree Indians near the mouth of the Knife River in North Dakota. They built a log fort and remained there for the winter. Now numbering thirty-three persons, they resumed their journey on April 7, 1805. They took with them as an interpreter Toussaint Charbonneau, his young Shoshoni wife, Sacagawea, and her baby, Jean Baptiste, born two months earlier.[1]

On June 13, 1805, the expedition reached the Great Falls of the Missouri, where the river tumbled downward almost 100 feet. After a month portaging their goods around the obstacle the explorers headed through wild mountain country to Three Forks, northeast of present Bozeman in southwestern Montana. They named the streams that joined to form the Missouri the Jefferson, Madison (after James Madison, Jefferson's Secretary of State), and Gallatin (after Albert Gallatin, Jefferson's Secretary of the Treasury). Lewis and Clark chose to follow the northernmost of the streams, the Jefferson, which Sacagawea claimed would take them to her Shoshoni people; she had been captured by the Minnetarees at Three Forks and knew the approximate direction and distance to her homeland. Following the Jefferson and its tributaries, the Corps came to what the Shoshoni called Beaver Valley, where a prominent cliff bears a strong resemblance to a beaver. Thirty miles farther they reached the head of the valley, Beaverhead (the site of Dillon, Montana); the stream is also named the Beaverhead.

At this point, on August 9, 1805, Lewis and three companions left the main expedition. Not hindered by boats or baggage, they reached the headwaters of the Missouri near Armstead, just a few feet below Lemhi Pass. On August 12 they stood on the summit of the Continental Divide. It was the first time the eyes of a white man had beheld any part of the state of Idaho—the last of the fifty states to be seen by a Euro-American. It was also an event that the United States could use in claiming the right of discovery to the "lower" part of Oregon Country, which was not part of the Louisiana Purchase. On this historic day, Drouilliard crossed the divide into present-day Idaho. Significantly, the nation's flag was erected on Idaho soil on that first day of its recorded history.[2]

Did Lewis appreciate the drama of this accomplishment? He did. Here are the words in his journal of August 12:

> The road took us to the most distant fountain of the waters of the mighty Missouri in search of which we have spent so many toilsome days and restless nights. Thus far I had accomplished one of those great objects on which my mind has been unalterably fixed for many years. Judge then of the pleasure I felt in allaying my thirst with this pure and ice-cold water which issues from the base of a low mountain or hill of a gentle ascent for one-half a mile. The mountains are high on either hand, [but] leave this gap at the head of this rivulet through which the road passes. Here I halted a few minutes and rested myself. . . . After refreshing ourselves, we proceeded on to the top of the dividing ridge [Continental Divide] from which I discovered immense ranges of high mountains still to the west of us [in Idaho] with their tops partially covered with snow. I now descended the mountain about three-fourths of a mile, which I found much steeper than on the opposite side, to a handsome bold running creek of cold clear water. Here I first tasted the water of the great Columbia river.[3]

The spot where Lewis and his partners crossed the divide is now known as Lemhi Pass and in itself is not impressive. With an elevation of 7,373 feet, Lemhi Pass is a ridge only slightly lower than the ground on either side. To the east is the arid country of Montana; to the west, across the Lemhi River some twenty miles distant, is the northern projection of Idaho's Lemhi Range.

Lewis determined that the western slope of the divide was

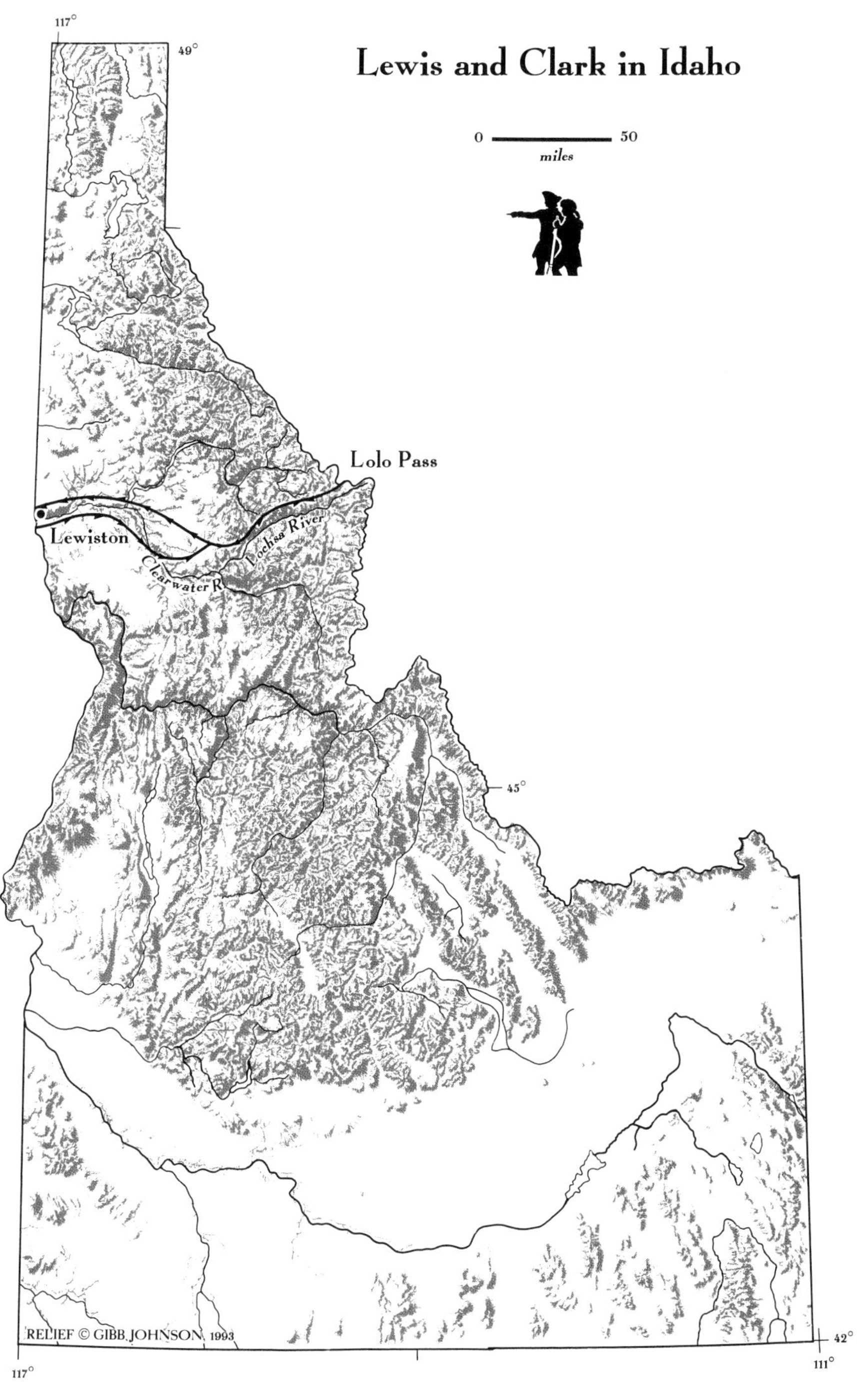

Lewis and Clark in Idaho
0
50
miles
117°
49°
Lolo Pass
Lewiston
Lochsa River
Clearwater R.
45°
RELIEF © GIBB JOHNSON, 1993
42°
117°
111°

very steep. The creek below the men, later named Agency Creek after the Lemhi Indian Agency, was 3,900 feet below the pass. Sure that this creek eventually ran into the Columbia and on to the Pacific Ocean, Lewis and his associates followed the stream for a short distance, then crossed hills and hollows into the ravine formed by Pattee Creek, where they camped on the night of August 12.

The next day the men took the Indian trail west and that afternoon spied an Indian on horseback; frightened, the rider quickly fled. As the whites rounded a hill, they came upon three "Snake" (Shoshoni) women. One started to run; an older woman and girl about twelve, sure that they would be killed, sat on the ground with bowed heads. Captain Lewis tried to reassure the old woman, who called back the one trying to escape. Lewis then painted the cheeks of all three with vermillion rouge, a sign of peace, and gave them gifts of beads and awls and a small mirror. The captain was able to convey to them that he wished them to lead his party to their camp. They walked about two miles, where they met about sixty mounted men. The women informed the warriors of Lewis's peaceful intentions and exhibited the gifts they had received. There were more presents, embraces, and smoking, and the whole party traveled about four miles farther to the Indian camp in "a pretty little meadow" on the bank of the Lemhi River—a tributary of the Salmon—about seventeen miles south of present-day Salmon City. (The river, valley, and pass were later given the name Lemhi by Mormons, who settled the region in 1855.) Lewis noted the Shoshoni custom of removing their moccasins before they would receive or smoke the pipe, indicative, he wrote, "of a sacred obligation of sincerity in their profession of friendship . . . as much as to say that they wish they may always go barefoot if they are not sincere; a pretty heavy penalty if they are to march through the plains of their country."[4]

The "Snakes," as Lewis and Clark referred to them, were

actually Shoshoni. Half-starved, they were in wretched condition. In the days before horses they had held their own against the Blackfeet and Minnetarees, but when the Blackfeet had obtained guns from English traders the Shoshoni had been driven in terror into their mountain retreat where hunting was poor. As their leader, Cameahwait ("He who does not walk"), told Lewis, they had been compelled to hide themselves "in these mountains and live on roots and berries as the bear do."[5] Lewis and his party were the first white men the band of about five hundred had ever seen, and all eyes were fixed upon them every minute. The men were fed cakes of serviceberries and chokecherries, which was all the food the Shoshoni had.

Lewis worked to persuade Cameahwait to accompany him back over the divide with sufficient horses to supply the main party for the return expedition over the pass. The suspicious Shoshoni would agree, then change their minds. Four days later, on August 16, Lewis reached the Beaverhead (Armstead), expecting to find Clark and the twenty-eight men in the main company. However, Clark, weary and ill, was still struggling with his canoes up the winding Beaverhead Creek. Lewis sent out a search party to find him.

The next day, August 17, was a happy reunion. As the still-fatigued, red-haired Clark was walking with Charbonneau in advance of the canoes, Sacagawea, who was ahead of the leader, suddenly rushed forward "to dance and show every mark of the most extravagant joy, turning round to him and pointing to several Indians, sucking her fingers at the same time" to indicate that among these people she had been suckled as a baby.[6] Coming toward them were several Shoshoni who had come with Lewis, and the expedition's half-breed hunter, Drouilliard, this time in Indian costume. Sacagawea recognized her people by their dress and manner of wearing their hair.

As the group drew closer to the Beaverhead camp, a Shoshoni woman made her way through the crowd toward Sacagawea. The two recognized each other as childhood companions who had been taken prisoners three or four years earlier at Three Forks by the Minnetarees. The young Shoshoni woman had later escaped and returned to her homeland while Sacagawea had been passed on to the Hidatsa and then to Charbonneau. As the chronicle says: "They [the two young women] embraced with the most tender affection." There followed a salmon and berry feast, the solemn removal of moccasins, and the passing of the peace pipe.

In the ensuing council meeting, Lewis and Clark sent for Sacagawea so she could interpret. She had only begun the translation when she recognized the "chief," Cameahwait, as her brother (or cousin).[7]

> She instantly jumped up and ran and embraced him, throwing over him her blanket and weeping profusely. The chief was himself moved, though not in the same degree. After some conversation between them she resumed her seat, and attempted to interpret for us, but . . . she was frequently interrupted by her tears. After the council was finished [she] learned that all her family were dead except two brothers, one of whom was absent, and a son of her eldest sister, a small boy, who was immediately adopted by her.[8]

Sacagawea was born of a Shoshoni leader's wife in the Bitterroot Mountains not far from Salmon, Idaho. At about age twelve, during a Shoshoni hunt into Montana for buffalo, she and her friend were captured by a party of Minnetaree Indians. They traded her to the Hidatsa Indians, and she was purchased or won from them on a wager by Toussaint Charbonneau, a French-Canadian living with the Hidatsa. Charbonneau, who was a fur trader with the North West and American Fur companies, took her to wife. When Lewis and Clark met him, Charbonneau had three Indian wives, of whom the youngest was Sacagawea. Her

Hidatsa captors named her Sakagawea, meaning Bird Woman. The babe she carried on her back throughout the journey, her first child, was named Jean Baptiste Charbonneau, but Sacagawea called him Pomp or Pompey, a term of endearment expressing hope that he might become a head person or leader. Captain Clark acknowledged the importance of this sixteen-year-old woman to the expedition in his journals: "The wife of Shabono [Charbonneau] our interpreter we find reconciles all the Indians as to our friendly intentions—a woman with a party of men is a token of peace."[9]

Sacagawea's most significant contribution was establishing friendly relations with the Shoshoni, from whom the party had to secure horses and guides to continue the journey on to the Columbia. The Americans argued that they would provide ample compensation and that the result of their mission would be to open commerce with peoples to the east and west that would be mutually beneficial.[10]

While that request was being negotiated at Beaverhead, Clark and eleven men left on August 18 to accompany the Shoshoni back to Idaho. The party confirmed that the Lemhi flowed into a larger stream, the Salmon. Continuing on, they found the Salmon was not a good route. The mountains on each side were "eternally covered with snow." The river tumbled into steep canyons that could not readily be navigated by boat; perpendicular and jutting rocks hemmed in the river, so that a company could not pass along the shore. Clark sent Lewis a note that the Salmon was not passable; another route should be chosen. After conversations with the Shoshoni, Lewis came to the same conclusion. Both men independently selected the Nez Perce route over the Lolo Trail, 140 miles to the north, which the Shoshoni had advised against.[11]

With Sacagawea's urging, Cameahwait and his band agreed to provide the horses necessary for the northern passage. Lewis and the main party returned to Idaho on August 26 to catch up with Clark and head for the Lolo Trail. The Lemhi Shoshoni headed east on their annual fall hunting trip. Sacagawea tearfully bade her people goodbye and accompanied her husband and the explorers on toward the Pacific.

The expedition, now consisting of the original thirty-three plus six Shoshoni, headed west again. The captains had been able to secure twenty-nine horses. They followed the Lemhi Valley to the Salmon River, moved along the valley to Tower Creek, and worked their way up that bank for four miles to where they reached the valley of the North Fork of the Salmon. Over what one of their party called "the worst road ever traveled," they reached the summit of the Bitterroots on September 4 and left Idaho. They had found the going difficult: "High mountains closed the creek on each side and obliged us to take the steep sides of the mountains—so steep that the horses could scarcely keep from slipping down. Several slipped and injured themselves very much. . . . [we had] but little to eat."[12] They went over Saddle Mountain, west of Lost Trail Pass to the headwaters of the Bitterroot River and then down the Bitterroot Valley into Montana. There they encountered a camp of four hundred Flatheads or Salish with five hundred horses on their way to join the Shoshoni in the buffalo grounds.

The Lewis and Clark expedition continued down the Bitterroot to the mouth of Lolo Creek, about ten miles southwest of present-day Missoula. Heading south and west up Lolo Creek, they crossed the Bitterroot range on the Lolo Trail, reentering Idaho on September 13. They were now about two hundred miles north and a little west of Lemhi Pass, on a trail used by the Nez Perce when they went east to hunt buffalo.

The Corps now experienced the worst privations and greatest hardships of the entire expedition. On September 14 they crossed a very high, steep mountain on a trail "excessively bad and thickly strewn with fallen timber and pine, spruce, fir, hackmatack, and tamarack. Steep and stony, our men and horses much fatigued."[13] The next day was just as bad:

> Proceeded on down the right side of Koos-koos-key River [Clearwater] over steep points, rocky and bushy as usual... ascend[ing] a mountain, winding in every direction to get up the steep ascents.... Several horses slipped and rolled down steep hills, which hurt them very much. The one which carried my desk and small trunk turned over and rolled down a mountain forty yards and lodged against a tree, broke the desk.... From this mountain [top] I could observe high rugged mountains in every direction as far as I could see.[14]

Here was an incident typical of those that delayed them:

> Frazier's horse fell from this road in the evening and rolled with his load near a hundred yards into the creek. We all expected that the horse was killed but to our astonishment when the load was taken off him he arose to his feet and appeared to be but little injured. In twenty minutes he proceeded with his load. This was the most wonderful escape I ever witnessed. The hill down which he rolled was almost perpendicular and [was] broken by large irregular and broken rocks.[15]

Snow fell all day on September 16. They had difficulty finding their way. Delayed in the rugged Bitterroots, short of food, and at the mercy of a confused Indian guide, the expedition split, with Captain Clark taking six men to travel ahead.

After a week, Clark's party entered the open valley of the Clearwater to vistas of the Camas Prairie and Craig Mountain to the southwest. On September 20 they encountered three Indian boys, to whom they gave some small pieces of ribbon, and they soon approached the large Chopunnish (Nez Perce) encampment on Weippe Prairie. The "great chief" was away with a war party, leaving behind the women, who showed signs of fear but presented the expedition with buffalo meat, dried salmon, berries, and bread made of camas roots.

Anxious to establish good relations with the Nez Perce, Clark and a guide went down the creek to the Clearwater, where they found the camp of Twisted Hair, chief of the band. The camp was adjacent to the site of present-day Orofino. Clark gave the Nez Perce leader a presidential medal and smoked with him until after midnight.[16] Then the expedition reunited and journeyed four miles down the river, crossed the Orofino, and established Canoe Camp near the entrance of the North Fork and the site of modern Ahsahka.

The shift in diet from almost no food to the dried salmon and camas flour supplied by the Nez Perce gave the camp dysentery, and they were unable to work or travel. Clark's remedies were strong emetics, the medicine of the day—enough to debilitate those who were perfectly hardy and healthy. Observing this "American shaman" giving powerful medicine, the Indians also crowded around seeking help. Clark gave one Indian some liniment to rub on his knee and thigh for pain; the man recovered and extolled the virtues of the medicines. Near Kooskooske (Lewiston) Clark gave a gentle purgative to a man with a tumor on his thigh, cleaned and dressed the sore, and left him some Castile soap to wash the wound until it got well. "These two cures," wrote Clark, "raised my reputation and gave those natives an exalted opinion of my skill as a physician."[17]

Meanwhile, the men of the expedition settled down near the forks of the Clearwater on September 26 to cut and shape pine trees into dugouts and canoes. Twisted Hair furnished the captains with a white elk-skin map of the country and peoples ahead, showing the junction of the Clearwater and Snake some forty miles below. By October 6 the canoes were completed and the saddles and land equipment cached at Canoe Camp; the company left their horses to the care of the Nez Perces until their return the next spring. The next day they launched their five vessels on the Koos-koos-kie or Clearwater River. To the small stream entering from the north they gave the name of Colter Creek, in honor of John Colter, one of their party.

As the party proceeded down the river the canoes struck

rocks and encountered rapids and eddies that delayed their advance. Their Shoshoni guide and his son left them on October 9 in order to get back to Salmon before snow closed their trail. Reaching the junction of the Clearwater and the Snake, the expedition made camp below the site of Lewiston on the present border between Idaho and Washington. They then left Idaho and continued on to the Columbia. On November 18, 1805, they reached "that ocean, the object of all our labours, the reward of all our anxieties."[18] They built a camp on the south side of the Columbia—Fort Clatsop, above Astoria—and remained the winter.

Lewis and Clark decided the Pacific Ocean was badly named: "It roars like a repeated rolling thunder." They celebrated Christmas by exchanging gifts, firing salutes, shouting, and singing. Their festive dinner consisted of "poor elk, so much spoiled that we eat it through near necessity." They saw a whale, and Sacagawea successfully pleaded "that she had traveled a long way with us to see the great waters, and now that monstrous fish was also to be seen, she thought it very hard she could not be permitted to see either." The winter was dismal; Clark counted only six days of sunshine between January and the last week of March. The men replenished their salt supply by evaporating ocean water; hunted, despite a scarcity of game; and suffered from colds, food poisoning, and Indian thievery. Lewis and Clark gathered and recorded information about the surrounding country and its native inhabitants and planned the expedition's return route.[19]

On March 23, 1806, anxious to be on their way, members of the expedition left Fort Clatsop and followed their original route up the Columbia, then cut across toward the site of Lewiston. On May 5 they returned to the mouth of Colter Creek, now known as the Potlatch, on the site of Arrow Junction. The next day they crossed the Clearwater at a point thirteen miles above modern Potlatch and repossessed the horses they had left with

Twisted Hair the previous fall. The horses had been well cared for. They traveled up to the Nez Perce prairie and proceeded southeasterly to Lawyer's Canyon, four miles above Kamiah, where they rested three days. Then they trekked down the canyon, crossed the Clearwater River, established Camp Chopunnish, and waited a month until the snow should melt sufficiently to make the Lolo Trail passable. Because they had established friendships with the Nez Perce the previous fall, their stay was pleasant. Some of the men ventured down to the Salmon River and the Snake River, partly to see the region but mainly to go fishing.

Clark was now faced by an insistent group of patients. A leading man below Lapwai presented him with "a very elegant gray mare" in return for a phial of eye water and a handkerchief. While Clark did not think of himself as possessing medical skills, he decided to "continue this deception" as a means of earning some provisions to replenish their severely depleted stores. He wrote that he gave them nothing that would injure them (the purgatives?), and in many cases his medical and surgical aid was helpful. On May 6, he wrote: "I was busily employed for several hours this morning in administering eyewater to a crowd of applicants. We once more obtained a plentiful meal, much to the comfort of all the party." Five days later he wrote: "Great numbers of Indians apply to us for medical aid, which we gave them cheerfully . . . scrofula, ulcers, rheumatism, sore eyes, and loss of the use of their limbs were the most common cases among them." Clark and the men also amused themselves "showing them the power of magnetism, the spy glass, compass, watch, air gun, and sundry other articles equally novel and incomprehensible to them."[20] A generation later, these memories still alive, the Nez Perce would ask for missionaries to show them more of the white man's ways.

A group was ready to leave for the East on June 9, when the level of the Clearwater indicated that the melting snows would make crossing the mountains possible. The party moved to Weippe Prairie, hoping they might be able to proceed. Against the advice of the Indians, they left five days later with sixty-six horses. That was a serious mistake; the next fifteen days were a nightmare. Snow twelve to fifteen feet deep made the trail hard to follow, and the air was cold and damp. If a horse slipped crossing the precipices, they would lose it forever. The group returned and waited. They set out again on June 24, this time with three Nez Perce guides. Despite the heavy snow on the mountains, the Indians proved to be "admirable pilots," and they made their way through.[21]

The party reached the Lolo Summit on June 29 and crossed the divide the next day, leaving Idaho and arriving at the hot springs on the Montana slope, where they delightedly bathed in the warm waters.

Lewis and Clark and company experienced many firsts in Idaho. They were the first white men to cross the Lemhi and Lolo passes and the Bitterroot Valley, and the first Euro-Americans to contact the Shoshoni and Nez Perce tribes in their Idaho homelands. They were the first geographers to examine portions of the Lemhi, Lochsa, Clearwater, and Salmon rivers; the first scientists to describe, in something approaching technical language, the grizzly bear, the prairie dog, the pronghorn antelope, the jackrabbit, the black-tailed deer, the mountain goat, and such creatures native to Idaho as the steelhead trout, Clark's nutcracker, and Stellar's jay; the first botanists to collect specimens of the mountain ash, lodgepole pine, and bluebunch wheatgrass. And they were the first non-Indians to feast on camas and huckleberries—both on the same day, September 20, 1805.[22]

They had lived with and established friendly relations with the "Snake" and Nez Perce Indians, an association that was important in the later settlement of Idaho. They had also prepared the way for the St. Louis fur trade to reach up the Missouri toward the Snake country, so important in the next stage of Idaho's development. And they had laid the foundation for the coming of missionaries in the 1830s.[23]

When the expedition reached the mouth of Lolo Creek on July 3, the explorers split. With nine men Lewis went north to Great Falls and then ventured along the Marias River as far as Cut Bank Creek in northern Montana before descending the Missouri. Clark and the rest of the company returned to Three Forks, north of Dillon, and then went down the Yellowstone River. The two groups reunited a few miles below the mouth of the Yellowstone on August 12 and then as a group hurried down the Missouri.

When Lewis and Clark reached the Mandan village near Bismarck, Dakota, Charbonneau and Sacagawea remained with their people. Sacagawea's history from that moment is not certain. The usually accepted view is that she accompanied Charbonneau to St. Louis about 1809, then two years later left her son with Clark and returned upriver with her husband. She fell victim of a "putrid fever" at Fort Manuel late in 1812.[24]

Sacagawea's son Jean Baptiste was educated by William Clark at a Catholic academy in St. Louis. When he was eighteen, he met Prince Paul of Wurttemberg, who was in the west on a scientific expedition, and lived at his castle near Stuttgart for several years. Baptiste later served with the American Fur Company, working with the Robidoux fur brigade in the Utah-Idaho region. He attended the great fur rendezvous of 1833 on the Green River. Several years later he accompanied Sir William Drummond Stewart, a Scottish nobleman, on a pleasure trip to the Rockies via South Pass to the Green River and then north into the Yellowstone country. When the Mexican War began he was guide for Colonel Philip St. George Cooke and his Mormon Battalion on its trek from Santa Fe to San Diego. In California he was alcalde (mayor) for the mission of San Luis

Rey, then went to the gold fields on the American River. In the 1860s he joined the miners' gold rush to Montana but died en route near Jordan Creek, just west of Idaho, probably of Rocky Mountain fever. Charbonneau lived well in two worlds, at home both in educated white circles and on the frontier among his native people.[25]

A second significant personality connected with the expedition was John Colter, one of the nine young men who enlisted for the expedition in 1803. Only a private, he was given dangerous and responsible assignments. When the expedition returned to the Mandan villages in 1806 he was released and joined two fur traders on their way up the Missouri. For four years he was a mountain man in the northern Rockies, during which time he had two narrow escapes from the Blackfoot Indians (including an 1808 encounter in which he ran naked in terror six miles over a thorn-covered plain to find a hiding place under a raft of driftwood). Having been witness to the thermal phenomena of the region, Colter is sometimes given credit for the discovery of Yellowstone National Park.[26]

Minus Sacagawea, Baptiste, and Colter, the party arrived at St. Louis on September 23, 1806, after twenty-eight months' absence. They had long since been given up for lost by nearly everyone except Thomas Jefferson. There was an appropriate celebration.

Lewis was appointed governor of Louisiana Territory and served for two years. In 1809, during a journey to Washington, D.C., he died under mysterious circumstances—probably suicide. Clark was appointed brigadier general of militia and superintendent of Indian affairs for Louisiana Territory, with headquarters in St. Louis. In 1813 he became governor of Missouri Territory, and for several years he was government negotiator for Indian treaties. He died in 1838. Clark's slave, York, returned to Virginia, where he lived to a "ripe, old age."

Lewis and Clark's Corps of Discovery had not found, as Jefferson had half expected, a waterway across the continent, but it had accumulated an enormous wealth of observations, valuable maps, and priceless animal, plant, and mineral specimens, and had left a record of decency and fair play in dealing with Indian peoples. Only one of the Corps had died, of "bilious colic" (ruptured appendix), three months after the expedition began. Dr. Samuel Mitchill, one of the men who had helped Lewis gather information before the expedition was launched, expressed the common feeling that the trip was "a rare performance. It does honour to our national enterprize."[27]

The 8,000-mile journey had opened up the trans-Mississippi West to the American people, and the Corps's experiences offered a fresh approach to American Indians and their way of life.[28] Not only had the explorers taken part in a romantic and stirring event, but they had kept daily journals of their discoveries, impressions, and activities, thus enabling subsequent generations to relive this national epic in words written by men who were both observant and thrilled by the story.[29] As Bernard DeVoto, that devoted student of the expedition, wrote, "It satisfied desire and it created desire: the desire of a westering nation."[30]

## CHAPTER FOUR: SOURCES

Several editions of the fascinating and comprehensive Lewis and Clark journals have been published. The first full publication was Reuben G. Thwaites, ed., *Original Journals of the Lewis and Clark Expedition 1804–1806*, 8 vols. (New York, 1904–5; reprinted in 7 vols., New York: Antiquarian Press, 1959). Important extracts from that original edition were published in Bernard DeVoto, *The Journals of Lewis and Clark* (Boston: Houghton Mifflin Co., 1953). A new edition of the journals in the process of publication is Gary E. Moulton, ed., *The Journals of the Lewis and Clark Expedition*, 7 vols. to date of a projected 11 vols. (Lincoln: University of Nebraska Press, 1983– ). The crossing of Idaho in 1805 is in volume 5.

Other informative sources include: Elliot Coues, *The History of the Expedition Under the Command of Lewis and Clark* (New York: Francis P. Harper, 1893); Bernard DeVoto, *The Course of Empire* (Boston: Houghton Mifflin Co., 1952); Donald Jackson, *Among the Sleeping Giants* (Urbana: University of Illinois Press, 1987); John Logan Allen, *Passage Through the Garden: Lewis and Clark and the Image of the American Northwest* (Urbana: University of Illinois Press, 1975); William H. Goetzmann, *Exploration and Empire: The Explorer and Scientist in the Winning of the American West* (New York: Alfred A. Knopf, 1966); William H. Goetzmann, *New Lands, New Men: America and the Second Great Age of Discovery* (New York: Viking Press, 1986); Donald Jackson, ed., *Letters of the Lewis and Clark Expedition with Related Documents, 1783–1854*, 2nd ed., 2 vols. (Urbana: University of Illinois Press, 1978); David F. Hawke, *Those Tremendous Mountains: The Story of the Lewis and Clark Expedition* (New York: W. W. Norton & Co., 1980); James P. Ronda, *Lewis and Clark Among the Indians* (Lincoln: University of Nebraska Press, 1984); Olin D. Wheeler, *The Trail of Lewis and Clark, 1804–1806*, 2 vols. (Hartford, 1870); John Bakeless, *Lewis and Clark, Partners in Discovery* (New York, 1947); Paul R. Cutright, *Lewis and Clark: Pioneering Naturalists* (Urbana: University of Illinois Press, 1969); John Bakeless, *The Journals of Lewis and Clark* (New York: New American Library, 1964); and a charmingly illustrated book for juveniles by an Idaho teacher: Ronald K. Fisher, *West to the Pacific: The Story of the Lewis and Clark Expedition* (Coeur d'Alene: Alpha Omega, 1989).

A splendid article summarizing these and other publications is Gary E. Moulton, "On Reading Lewis and Clark: The Last Twenty Years," *Montana: The Magazine of Western History* 38 (Summer 1988):28–39.

Western and Pacific Northwest histories that contain substantial accounts of Lewis and Clark include Dorothy O. Johansen and Charles M. Gates, *Empire of the Columbia*, 2d ed. (New York: Harper & Row, 1967), 72–81; Carlos A. Schwantes, *The Pacific Northwest: An Interpretive History* (Lincoln: University of Nebraska Press),

47–53; Ray Allen Billington, *Westward Expansion: A History of the American Frontier*, 2d ed. (New York: The Macmillan Co., 1960), 446–50; LeRoy R. Hafen and Carl Coke Rister, *Western America: The Exploration, Settlement, and Development of the Region beyond the Mississippi*, 2d ed. (Englewood Cliffs, N.J.: Prentice-Hall, 1950), 173–81; Thomas D. Clark, *Frontier America: The Story of the Westward Movement*, 2d ed. (New York: Charles Scribners Sons, 1969), 243–46; George W. Fuller, *A History of the Pacific Northwest* (New York: Alfred A. Knopf, 1931), 61–76; David Lavender, *The Rockies* (New York: Harper & Row, 1968), 40–49.

Histories of Idaho that have chapters or sections on Lewis and Clark include: Beal and Wells, *History of Idaho*, 1:60–77; Defenbach, *Idaho: The Place and Its People*, 1:80–96; Peterson, *Idaho: A Bicentennial History*, 24–32; Brosnan, *History of the State of Idaho*, 39–50. I have been particularly helped by the Beal and Wells chapter. See also Ralph S. Space, *The Lolo Trail* (Lewiston: Printcraft, 1970), and Roy E. Appleman, *Lewis and Clark: Historic Places Associated with Their Transcontinental Exploration* (Washington, D.C.: National Park Service, 1975).

Articles that focus on the experience of the expedition in Idaho include three by John J. Peebles: "Rugged Waters: Trails and Campsites of Lewis and Clark in the Salmon River Country," *Idaho Yesterdays* 8 (Summer 1964):2–17; "On the Lolo Trail: Route and Campsites of Lewis and Clark," *Idaho Yesterdays* 9 (Winter 1965–66): 2–15; and "The Return of Lewis and Clark," *Idaho Yesterdays* 10 (Summer 1966):16–27. The three Peebles articles were combined and published by the Idaho State Historical Society in 1966 under the title *Lewis and Clark in Idaho*.

Also informative are John E. Rees, "The Shoshoni Contribution to Lewis and Clark," *Idaho Yesterdays* 1 (Summer 1958):2–13; and Robert C. Carriker, "Following the Trail of the Captains: The Journals of the Lewis and Clark Expedition at Midpoint," *Idaho Yesterdays* 33 (Summer 1989):25–30.

On Sacagawea, the two principal sources are Harold P. Howard, *Sacajawea* (Norman: University of Oklahoma Press, 1971), and Grace

R. Hebard, *Sacajawea: Guide of the Lewis and Clark Expedition* (Glendale, Calif.: Arthur H. Clark Co., 1933, 1957). An assessment of the legend is provided in C. S. Kingston, "Sacajawea as Guide: The Evaluation of a Legend," *Pacific Northwest Quarterly* 35 (January 1944):3–18.

*(photos on next page)*
19. Meriwether Lewis planned the great expedition to the Pacific and helped realize Thomas Jefferson's dream of a United States reaching from ocean to ocean. Lewis was probably the first white man to set foot on Idaho land. ISHS.
20. The able companion of Lewis, William Clark, helped conduct the great expedition to the Pacific Coast. He was later territorial governor of Missouri. ISHS.
21. A 1931 painting by M. L. Bailey shows the encampment of Lewis and Clark near Tolo Lake where the first United States flag was raised in Idaho in 1805. The Lemhi Mountains and Lemhi Pass are in the background. ISHS 2837.

19. 20.

21.

## CHAPTER FIVE

# Fur Traders and Early Explorers

JUST two years after Lewis and Clark had left Idaho, one of the great geographers of all time, David Thompson, arrived and by 1809 had erected the first house used by white men in Idaho. He would be followed by explorer-trappers with such familiar names as Andrew Henry, Wilson Price Hunt, Donald Mackenzie, William H. Ashley, Jedediah Smith, Francois Payette, B. L. E. Bonneville, Nathaniel Wyeth, and Peter Skene Ogden.

David Thompson was born in England of Welsh parents. Orphaned at an early age, he was trained in mathematics at a charity school for poor children in London. At fourteen he was sent to Canada as an apprentice to the Hudson's Bay Company, a British colonizing and trading company chartered in 1670. The company gradually extended its domain westward until it covered 1.4 million square miles of North America—all the lands draining into Hudson's Bay, more than a third of present Canada. While still in his teens, Thompson began mapping the vast regions west and southwest of his base on Hudson Bay. One of the first whites to deal with the Blackfeet and other Indians living in the borderlands between present-day Montana and Canada, he may have supplied some tribes with their first firearms.

In 1797 Thompson left the Hudson's Bay Company to work for its principal competitor, the North West Company. Organized in 1784 with headquarters in Montreal, the North West Company directed the exploration of much of western North America, including the Columbia River and Snake River country. In this employ Thompson crossed the Rocky Mountains via the Saskatchewan River, scouted the Columbia River from its source to its mouth, and established the first fur posts in Idaho and western Montana.

Thompson, whose ventures in the Pacific Northwest had been thwarted by the warlike Piegan (Blackfeet) Indians, was "released" by them after one group of them had been bested by Meriwether Lewis in 1806; their way of avenging defeat by Americans was to assist a Canadian competitor. Thompson established the first fur trading post on the Columbia, Kootenay (Kootenai) House in modern British Columbia, in July 1807. He spent the winter there and then moved south, instituting a trade with the Kutenai and Pend d'Oreille Indians at Bonners Ferry. He and his associates built a log structure on the eastern shore of Lake Pend d'Oreille near Hope, which, together with tents and a lodge, was called Kullyspell House after the Kalispel Indians. The earliest fort in the Pacific Northwest of the United States and the first white habitation in Idaho, the facility was built only three years after Lewis and Clark had traversed the Lolo Trail on their return east.

Thompson was more than a fur trader. He carefully surveyed and mapped the region. Indeed, he apparently switched from Hudson's Bay to the North West Company because the latter enthusiastically supported his exploratory activities. In Idaho, for example, he skirted along the shore of Lake Pend d'Oreille and came to a place that he noted as "A Point of Sand." It became Sandpoint. He crossed the Priest River and continued to what he called "Pointed Heart's Lake." It became Lake Coeur d'Alene. He drew the first map of northern Idaho. A pious man who always carried his Bible, Thompson was an ardent foe of the liquor traffic; he refused to carry alcohol into areas he visited or supply it to the Indians. However, he was happy to supply the Kutenai with rifles to defend themselves against the Blackfeet because the latter had been an obstacle in his development of the Columbia trade. He thought the Kutenai and Coeur d'Alene were industrious people who "pride themselves in their industry, and their skill in doing anything, and are as neat in their persons as circumstances will allow."[1]

After Thompson left to spend the winter at Saleesh (Salish) House, which he built in western Montana, Kullyspell House was left in charge of Finan McDonald, a native of Inverness, Scotland. Tall, athletic, and red-haired, he had been associated with Thompson in the Columbia venture and remained prominent in the Idaho fur trade until his return to Canada in 1826.

During the winter of 1809–10 Thompson, McDonald, and their associates gathered beaver skins, and in April they took out forty-six packs. (A pack or plew consisted of about eighty beaver skins, each worth from $5 to $10 depending on size and quality. They were pressed and bound by a large leather thong.) The furs went to Bonners Ferry and on to Montreal and London. Thompson was back briefly at Kullyspell House in 1811, but he soon tracked west past Spokane Falls and established a new post, Spokane House. He returned to north Idaho in the spring of 1812, but then left the area to develop other interests in Montreal. In the four years he was in north Idaho he had explored routes still used by transcontinental railways and highways, opened permanent communication with the East, formed friendly relationships with Indians, and established the fur trade as a reputable business.

The second fur outpost pioneered in Idaho was Fort Henry, built beside Henry's Fork or the North Fork of the Snake River. Founder Andrew Henry, a native of Pennsylvania, had moved to Tennessee and then in 1808 to Missouri, where he was a lead miner. In 1809 he became a partner in the Missouri Fur Company organized at St. Louis by Manuel Lisa and others. Their 1809–10 expedition opened up the Three Forks of the Missouri to organized trapping. Impressed with the Lewis and Clark exploration, Lisa had employed John Colter, George Drouilliard, and others before Henry joined him. Henry built a fort at Three Forks, where he was attacked by Blackfeet and grizzly bears. Although Drouilliard and others were killed, Henry managed to send thirty packs of beaver skin down the Missouri to St. Louis.

Henry and his associates crossed a low pass in the Continental Divide into Idaho in 1810 and found what we call Henry's Lake. Impressed with the trapping prospects of the region, he decided to build a post and settled there for the winter. The fort was five miles downstream from St. Anthony on the bench on the west side of Henry's Fork (North Fork) and north of the Teton River. Henry's party struggled through a bitter cold winter. Had they asked the Shoshoni they could have been prepared: the Shoshoni name for the area was "Egin," meaning cold. When the severe winter forced most of the game southward, Henry's party had to subsist mainly on the flesh of their own horses. Nevertheless they were able to secure forty packs of beaver skin in 1810–11. In the spring of 1811 Henry abandoned the site and returned to Missouri. There he occupied himself with other opportunities until 1822, when he returned to the Rockies with William H. Ashley.

Meanwhile, in 1808 John Jacob Astor founded the American Fur Company to free himself from dependence on Canadian and British markets and suppliers and to enable him to trade in furs on the East Coast, in the Pacific Northwest, and in China. His company became the most powerful of the American fur enterprises and made Astor a fortune. A stout and arrogant entrepreneur, Astor built Fort Astoria at the mouth of the Columbia following an expedition from St. Louis. In 1810 he organized the Pacific Fur Company to handle American Fur Company business on the Pacific Coast. After the fort was threatened by a British frigate during the War of 1812, Astor sold the Pacific Fur Company to the North West Company.

Chosen to lead the expedition to the West in 1810 was Wilson Price Hunt, a twenty-eight-year-old businessman from New Jersey who had established a store in St. Louis in 1804. Hunt, the hero of Washington Irving's book *Astoria* (1836) but not an experienced frontiersman, eventually assembled a party of sixty-two men and one woman with two children. An indispensable member of Hunt's party was Pierre Dorion (or Dorian), son of a Frenchman (the first white settler in South Dakota) and an Indian woman, who brought his Iowa Indian wife (Marie Aiowe, or Iowa) and two young boys aged five and three. Dorion knew Indian sign language.

The company sailed up the Missouri in keelboats and spent the winter of 1810–11 with the Arikaras in South Dakota. There they met with John Colter and three mountaineers who had spent the winter at Fort Henry. Hunt's party went overland through Wyoming and entered Jackson Hole in September 1811, camping on the South Fork of the Snake River (which they called Mad River). French Canadian members of the company called the peaks on the west the Trois Tetons (Three Teats), and that name stuck. Crossing Teton Pass, the party arrived in the Teton Basin at modern Victor, Idaho, and occupied vacant cabins at Fort Henry in October.

Assuming they could float down the Snake to the Columbia, they abandoned their horses at Fort Henry (a monumental blunder) and launched fifteen heavily laden canoes fashioned from cottonwood trees in the area. They voyaged down to Idaho Falls, portaged around it, then on to American Falls for another portage. As they continued down the river they lost one man when a canoe hit a large rock in the rapids several miles west of where Milner Dam is located. "Much goods lost," they recorded. Continuing on to a spot in the Snake River's narrow gorge where a pool at the bottom of the high cascade of water churned so fiercely that it reminded them of a witch's brew, they named it Caldron Linn. They beached the remainder of their canoes and scouted the river chasm (from the bluff above) for thirty-five miles. Another attempt was made, another canoe and its goods were lost, and three other canoes were stuck in the rocks. On November 1, calling this stretch of water the Devil's Scuttle Hole, they abandoned their canoes, dug sixteen caches, and filled them with their remaining goods. Divided into three groups, each left to its own resourcefulness, they proceeded afoot to try different routes to the Columbia. One group returned to Fort Henry to get the horses but gave up before they got there and returned without the animals.

Determined to press on to the Columbia, Hunt and nineteen others, including the Dorions, moved ahead suffering from hunger, thirst, and cold. They were able to induce Indians they encountered to give them some salmon and dog meat. They spent one night in Hagerman Valley, another at the site of Glenn's Ferry, and another at Canyon Creek. Mistakenly they left the river to cross the barren sagebrush plain and would have died of thirst if it had not rained. They followed Donald Mackenzie to the Boise River and forded the Payette and Weiser rivers. There were further losses of goods. Guided by friendly Shoshoni, who furnished them horses, Hunt headed westward across Oregon, missing Hells Canyon and the Seven Devils. Crossing the Blue Mountains and the Grande Ronde Valley, the party navigated the Umatilla to the Columbia and finally reached Fort Astoria on February 15, 1812. A group of them returned by essentially the same route to report to Astor. Traveling as they did along the banks of the Snake, they were the first to cover much of what later became the Oregon Trail.

One group of these trappers, under the leadership of John Reed (sometimes Reid), returned to the Payette River Valley in 1813 to trap beaver. Among them were the Dorions. They put up a log house, and at the junction of the Snake and Boise rivers, near the site of Parma, they established another field post. Early in 1814, Reed and his party became victims of the first massacre by a band of Indians in Idaho history. The Indians killed everyone at the log house and everyone at a post farther down the river—a total of nine men, including Reed and Dorion. They took all the guns and ammunition and headed for the post at Parma, where Marie Dorion and her two boys were staying. Warned by a friendly Indian, she hurriedly gathered up buffalo robes and some buffalo meat and, with her boys, set out on the Hunt trail that led about 260 miles to Walla Walla. Knowing she could not go all the way, she traveled nine days to a lonely spot in the Blue Mountains, built a small hut of pine branches and moss, and lined it with horse skin, padded by snow, to keep out the cold. They remained for fifty-three days until spring, living on dried horsemeat. Setting out once more on the trail, the three crossed the Blue Mountains and found friendly Walla Wallas. After a rest, she told her tragic story to trappers.[2]

Another member of the Hunt Party was red-haired Donald Mackenzie, who had moved from the Highlands of Scotland to Montreal in 1800 and worked for the North West Company. In 1809 he transferred to John Jacob Astor's Pacific Fur Company. As a member of Wilson Price Hunt's expedition, he spent the fall of 1811 exploring above a long stretch of the Snake River from Weiser to Lewiston on his way to Astoria. Under the aegis of the North West Company, which he rejoined in 1816 four years after it took control of Astoria, Mackenzie organized the annual Snake Country expeditions that continued until 1832. This activity laid the foundations for the Snake Country fur trade.

A large man (312 pounds), a skillful trader, efficient administrator, and trusted Indian negotiator, Mackenzie took crews consisting of Indians, Owyhees (Hawaiians), and whites who produced fur in quantity far beyond expectations. After 1818, when the United States and England agreed to joint occupancy of the Oregon country and the area was open to the citizens of both countries, he operated out of Fort Nez Perce at the junction of the Snake and the Columbia.

In September 1818 Mackenzie set out with a stock of merchandise, 195 horses, 300 traps, and 55 men for the headwaters and many of the tributaries of the Snake River. They set up winter quarters from Boise River to Bear Lake. Alexander Ross, another Scotsman who had been with both Astor and North West and had helped Mackenzie establish Fort Nez Perce, described this Snake country of southwestern and southeastern Idaho in 1818 as follows:

> Woods and valleys, rocks and plains, rivers and ravines, alternately met us; but altogether it is a delightful country. There animals of every class rove about undisturbed; wherever there was a little plain, the red deer [elk] were seen grazing in herds about the rivers; round every point were clusters of poplar and elder, and where there was a sapling, the ingenious and industrious beaver was at work. Otters sported in the eddies; the wolf and the fox were seen sauntering in quest of prey; now and then a few cypresses or stunted pines were met with on the rocky parts, and in their spreading tops the raccoon sat secure. In the woods, the martin and black fox were numerous; the badger sat quietly looking from his mound; and in the numberless ravines among bushes laden with fruits, the black, the brown, and the grizzly bear were seen. The mountain sheep, and goat white as snow, browsed on the rocks and ridges, and the big-horn species ran among the lofty cliffs. Eagles and vultures of uncommon size flew about the rivers.[3]

It was not a Garden of Eden. Along one stream (Camas Creek) Mackenzie's trappers became ill from eating the tails of beavers that had fed on certain plants. They named the stream Malade, or Malad, a French word for sick. The name stuck for the river and is still frequently used for the stream above its entry into Magic Reservoir.

Three Owyhees in the expedition were lost. The name, which is English, requires an explanation. When Captain James Cook discovered the Sandwich Islands in 1778, he asked the natives what they called themselves. They responded with a sound that he wrote down as "Owyhees" (later usually spelled "Hawaiians"). After stopping at the islands for food and water, English vessels that plied North American West Coast ports often brought Owyhees along as laborers, and each of Mackenzie's three Snake River expeditions included several. When Mackenzie reached southwestern Idaho, he directed three Owyhees to go south of later Fort Boise to trap in the unexplored watersheds of a large unnamed river. The three disappeared and were assumed killed by the Indians.[4] Those associated with the expedition named the river after them, and later the mountains and the county took the same name (and spelling). Other Owyhees were in the contingent in Old Fort Boise in the 1830s and 1840s.

Mackenzie had intended to establish a permanent base in Boise Valley, but he gave up that plan because of the difficulty of supply and Indian hostility. Many horses were stolen, some of his men were killed, and Mackenzie himself had many narrow escapes. But he persisted and tenaciously worked with Indian bands and their leaders. Much of the problem arose from the raids of Indian groups on each other—the Nez Perce on the Sheepeaters, and the Blackfeet on both Nez Perce and Sheepeaters.

Mackenzie's base during the winter of 1819–20 was Little Lost River. He held a grand council of the Snakes (Shoshoni) and secured their assurance of cooperation with his trapping projects, producing a mutually advantageous commerce. He was also able to establish an Indian truce that enabled the Snakes and British traders to maintain good relations throughout the remainder of the fur-trade period.

When Mackenzie's party of seventy trappers arrived at Fort Nez Perce with the season's return in June 1820, they were escorted by a band of four hundred Cayuse Indians from eastern Oregon and Washington. The procession was said to have been more than two miles in length, with 154 horses loaded with beaver.[5]

In 1821, under pressure from the British government, the North West and Hudson's Bay companies merged under the name of the latter, creating a monopoly of the British fur trade in North America. The next year Mackenzie left Idaho and the Northwest to manage Hudson's Bay operations around Winnipeg.

The monopoly was not to be without stiff competition. Americans at St. Louis organized the Rocky Mountain Fur Company in 1822, and the American Fur Company continued its own campaigns. Their encroachment on the British fur trade was substantial.

Finan McDonald led an 1823 Hudson's Bay expedition through the Snake River country. After venturing over to western Montana and then returning to Idaho over Lemhi Pass, McDonald went on to Henry's Fork, the Blackfoot, and the Bear River. On the upper Lemhi, in eastern Idaho, he and his twenty-nine men were forced to fight a battle with a band of seventy-five marauding Piegans (Blackfeet) who ambushed them. By taking advantage of the natural terrain and by astute maneuvers McDonald and his men were able to defeat the attacking hostiles, losing only six men while the Blackfeet suffered sixty-eight casualties. Upon his return to Spokane House, McDonald declared, "I got safe home from the Snake Country . . . and when that Country will see me again the beaver will have a gold skin."[6] Nevertheless, McDonald had broken the power of the Blackfeet in Idaho, opening up a new phase in Idaho's fur trade. St. Louis trappers were now able to penetrate the upper Missouri and Snake country. This victory was particularly significant in the history of Indian wars in Idaho.

Command of the annual Snake brigade was next given to Alexander Ross, who had directed the Hudson's Bay Flathead Post in western Montana in 1821 and led the Snake River expedition of 1824 into southern Idaho. That 1824 brigade, Hudson's Bay's largest expedition up the Snake, consisted of 140 persons—including 25 women and 64 children—and 392 horses. The company was a motley group that included two Americans, seventeen Canadians, five Red River métis (mixed French and Indian), twelve Iroquois, two Abanekees from lower Canada, two natives from Lake Nipissing in Ontario Province, one from Lake Huron, two Cree from Athabaska, one Chinook, two Spokane, two Kutenai, three Flathead, two Kalispel, one Palouse, and one Snake slave. Ross lamented that as many as two-thirds of them were "more expert at the bow and arrow than at the use of the beaver trap." Leader of the Iroquois was "Old Pierre" Tevanitagon, whose name was preserved during the years of the fur trade in Pierre's Hole under the Tetons in Idaho.

Ross and his party finally reached Idaho at Lemhi Pass on April 29, 1824. They were delighted: "Here birds are singing and spring smiles. All traps out for the first time since we left the fort."[7] The brigade trapped the Lemhi and Salmon rivers southward to the Lost and Wood rivers and then moved over to the Boise Valley, where they participated in a peace congress with the Cayuses and Snakes. They covered the Boise, Payette, and Weiser valleys after the conference and then returned to Walla Walla with 5,000 beaver pelts.

The expedition was profitable. But some of Ross's Iroquois trappers were attacked by Indians near Blackfoot and were in grave trouble when stumbled upon by Jedediah Smith and a small party of American trappers. In gratitude, the Iroquois invited the Americans to follow them to Ross's brigade. Fearful that Smith would use the visit to gain further knowledge about the country, Hudson's Bay executives in Vancouver decided that Ross had been too tolerant of a competitor and replaced him with Peter Skene Ogden in 1825. That meeting of British and American fur hunters and the completion of Ross's 1824 venture marked the beginning of a crucial battle for the fur empire in the Oregon Country. The clash between Ross's replacement for Hudson's Bay, Peter Skene Ogden, and America's mountain men for the occupation of the Oregon Country took place largely in Idaho—a disputed borderland in the competition for empire in the Pacific Northwest. Within ten years the British "monopoly" of Oregon fur country was at an end.

Peter Skene Ogden was a major explorer of the fur-trade period. Born in Quebec City, Canada, of American loyalist parents, Ogden grew up in Montreal. He entered the fur trade when he was twenty, worked briefly for John Jacob Astor's American Fur Company in the Great Lakes region, and then joined the North West Company. Sent to the Pacific Northwest in 1818, he was dropped by North West Company in 1821 but picked up by Hudson's Bay Company to run the Spokane House district. When he replaced Ross in the Snake Country fur brigade in the fall of 1824, Ogden was instructed to trap the interior so ruthlessly that there would be nothing left for American trappers and mountain men. His first expedition of 1824–25 took him from the Bitterroot River in western Montana south through eastern Idaho to the Bear River in northern Utah. His second expedition, 1825–26, took him south from the Columbia, east over the Blue Mountains, and down into the Snake River country. He made a magnificent catch of 2,188 beaver and other valuable furs that year, but there was a price to pay on this and nearly every trapping expedition: Ogden lost one of his trusty Frenchmen, "Portneuf," to hostiles along a stream and in a valley that has since borne the victim's name.[8] For three more years, 1827–30, Ogden directed expeditions to the Snake River country, competing with American trappers.

The contest for ascendancy involved two very different sorts of operation. Hudson's Bay Company brigades were regulated as part of a well-managed operation, while the American competitors consisted of many self-reliant frontier individualists who went where they pleased, so long as their resources held out and the Indians did not restrain them.

There were three leading American trappers. One, William Henry Ashley, organized the rendezvous system that fostered the rise of the mountain man, who played such an important role in western history. He had found a way to exploit the fur trade at minimal expense through the organization of fur brigades of free (unattached) trappers, the rendezvous system, and the use of horses instead of boats to penetrate the wilderness. Ashley and/or his men also rediscovered the South Pass and opened the central overland trails to Oregon and California.

Born in Virginia, Ashley moved to Missouri shortly after the Louisiana Purchase. He was associated with Andrew Henry in the manufacture of gunpowder and lead during the war of 1812. A popular officer of the territorial and state militia, he held the title of general by 1822 and was elected Missouri's first lieutenant governor in 1821.

In 1822 Ashley and Andrew Henry advertised for a number of "enterprising young men" to undertake a fur-trading expedition to the upper Missouri. The famous party included young Jedediah Smith, Mike Fink, Jim Bridger, and a dozen others who were significant in the development of the western fur trade. Ashley and Henry succeeded in establishing a post, Fort Henry (later Fort Union), on the Yellowstone River but were resolutely opposed by the Arikara Indians, who wanted to control the river trade in that region. A second expedition the next year was wiped out by the Arikara.

Ashley then sent two parties overland from Fort Kiowa to the Rockies, avoiding the Missouri River route. Trappers were mounted on horseback and went forth in small parties that would be hard to spot. The first group, Andrew Henry's party, traveled across Nebraska and the Dakotas to Fort Henry on the Yellowstone. The second party, led by Jedediah Smith, went west to the Black Hills and into the Wind River region of Wyoming. In 1824, they rediscovered South Pass in western Wyoming (first discovered by returning Astorians), which made it possible to follow a relatively easy route along the Platte and Sweetwater rivers to the Rocky Mountain trapping grounds. No longer would parties have to follow the Missouri into hostile territory. It also meant that wagons might more easily travel a central route.

Both of Ashley's brigades came to Idaho in the fall of 1824. Jedediah Smith's group—six trappers, including William Sublette—reached the Portneuf about the end of September; the other group, under John Weber—Jim Bridger was one of them—did well that fall on the Bear River, north of Franklin. That fall also, Smith and his men discovered a group of Iroquois who had been robbed and left naked on the plains by hostile Bannock. They escorted the Iroquois back to Alexander Ross's Snake brigade on the Salmon and then to their Flathead base in Montana, reaching there the same day that Peter Skene Ogden arrived to save the Snake brigade from St. Louis competition.

Ashley, starting late in the fall of 1824, had to fight storms and snows to take supplies overland by pack trains and wagons to his trappers in the mountains. Arriving in April 1825, he divided his party into small groups to explore and trap. They agreed to rendezvous on the Green River in the summer. The first rendezvous or gathering was held twenty miles north of Henry's Fork on the Green. After a second rendezvous in 1827, Ashley sold out to Jedediah Smith, David E. Jackson, and William L. Sublette and then returned to St. Louis.

The rendezvous attracted hundreds of white trappers and traders who brought furs; negotiated for supplies like salt, flour, tea, and coffee; picked up letters and newspapers, did business, and saw old friends. To these "wilderness fairs" came hundreds of Indians from many bands who brought furs, horses, dried meat, moccasins, and buckskin shirts to trade for kettles, guns, bright cloth, and beads. There was much buying and selling, haggling, bragging, feasting, and card-playing. Trade goods, even with the attendant risks of loss and high costs of transportation, sold at unconscionable prices: tobacco from one to three dollars a pound, blankets from twelve to sixteen dollars each, coats as high as forty dollars, sixpenny calicoes at fifty cents a yard, and beads for a dollar a bunch.[9]

The rendezvous were like medieval fairs. Along with the horseracing, wrestling, shooting matches, gambling, and carousing, some of a different temperament enjoyed the association and excitement but spent their evenings around the campfires reading from the Bible and English and French classics. Some regaled their acquaintances with tall tales, impromptu readings, and the singing of newly composed frontier ballads. There were Indian dances, Scottish reels, and exchanges of medicines.

Some historians have tended to overemphasize the corrosive effects of the wilderness on the mountain men. Picturesque wilderness trailblazers, half-civilized and half-savage, a brave and reckless breed, they have been described as men who, separated from the traditional patterns of civilized life, reverted toward the primitive.[10] The men discussed here do not fit this characterization. They seem to have been "astonishingly similar," to use William Goetzmann's phrase, to their civilized contemporaries. They were "expectant entrepreneurs" who worked tirelessly for the main chance and reveled in the promise of America.[11]

Associated with Ashley on his first and second expeditions,

and one of the partners who bought his interests, was Jedediah S. Smith. Born in Bainbridge, New York, Smith went to St. Louis as a teenager and soon teamed up with Ashley. His stated motives: "I started into the mountains with the determination of becoming a first-rate hunter, of making myself thoroughly acquainted with the character and habits of the Indians, of tracing out the sources of the Columbia River, and following it to its mouth, and of making the whole profitable to me."[12]

A "mild and Christian young man" who did not indulge in profanity, tobacco, or alcoholic liquor or forsake his mild and unassuming manner, Smith always took his religion with him. He was an able leader in Idaho's fur trade although he lived only thirty-two years, and he ranks with Lewis and Clark as one of America's truly great explorers. As Dale Morgan has written:

> During his eight years in the West Jedediah Smith made the effective discovery of South Pass; he was the first man to reach California overland from the American frontier, the first to cross the Sierra Nevada, the first to travel the length and width of the Great Basin, the first to reach Oregon by a journey up the California coast. He saw more of the West than any man of his time, and was familiar with it from the Missouri River to the Pacific, from Mexico to Canada. . . . Jedediah Smith is an authentic American hero. . . .[13]

In his western travels Smith spent many weeks in Lemhi Valley, Teton Valley, Bear Lake Valley, and Cache Valley and in the Boise, Payette, Weiser region. He was one of Idaho's great explorers.

Another notable participant in the fur trade was François Payette, a French Canadian, who arrived at Astoria in 1812 and spent the next thirty-two years in the business. He began with the Pacific Fur Company, transferred to the North West Company when the Astor partners sold out, and finished his career with the Hudson's Bay Company. He was with the Snake expedition of 1818 under Donald Mackenzie, and at that time the Payette River was named for him. He was with Finan McDonald on the Snake Country expedition of 1823 and with the Snake brigade of 1824–25. Peter Skene Ogden had a high opinion of Payette and assigned him to take an advance party of thirteen trappers ahead of the Snake brigade to oppose Jedediah Smith and get a share of the beaver along the Blackfoot River. His party was attacked by Blackfoot Indians, one of his men was lost, and Payette barely escaped by swimming across the river, leaving his horse, traps, and clothes behind. Continuing with the regular group after his escape, Payette and two others, trapping out ahead of the party, came back with 110 beaver pelts. At ten shillings per beaver, the three had £55 for less than a month's actual trapping.[14] He accompanied the next year's expedition as an interpreter.

On one visit to his traps Payette and Baptiste the Iroquois encountered three Snake Indians who had stolen seven horses from fellow Hudson's Bay Company employee Thomas McKay. The two trappers took the horses and demanded payment in addition. Payette began beating the Indians with his whip; in the ensuing scuffle an Indian was killed and the two trappers were severely wounded. Payette soon recovered but lost another horse, gun, and blanket. He was back with the 1827–28 and 1828–29 expeditions as a "free" trapper. On several missions he was given important responsibilities by Ogden, the expedition leader, and he continued to work in eastern Washington, Oregon, and north and central Idaho. Finally he settled at Fort Boise, where he directed affairs until 1844.

One of the many visitors to Old Fort Boise was Thomas Jefferson Farnham, a lawyer in Peoria, Illinois. Inspired by a lecture on the Oregon country by Reverend Jason Lee, Farnham decided to make a trip across the continent. He stopped in Boise on September 13, 1839, and described Monsieur Payette:

> Mr. Payette, the person in charge at Boisais, received us with every mark of kindness; gave our horses to the care of his servants, and introduced us immediately to the chairs, table and edibles of his apartments. He is a French Canadian; has been in the service of the Hudson's Bay Company more than twenty years, and holds the rank of clerk; is a merry, fat old gentleman of fifty, who, although in the wilderness all the best years of his life, has retained that manner of benevolence in trifles, in his mode of address, of seating you and serving you at table, of directing your attention continually to some little matter of interest, of making you speak the French language "parfaitment" whether you are able to do so or not, so strikingly agreeable in that mercurial people. The 14th and 15th were spent very pleasantly with this gentleman. During that time he feasted us with excellent bread, butter made from an American cow, obtained from some of the missionaries; with baked, boiled, fried and broiled salmon—and, at my request, with some of his adventures in the wilderness.[15]

Boiseans can be grateful to French-Canadian Payette for the popularization of the name of their city, meaning "wooded." Many early maps anglicized it to Wood River, but Payette's influence over many years caused the name Boise to prevail.

Partly because of the large number of American trappers in southern Idaho in 1824, 1825, and 1826, Britain agreed with the United States in 1827 to continue the Oregon boundary convention of 1818 for an indefinite period. Idaho and the Oregon country remained open for exploitation by both St. Louis and Hudson's Bay traders on terms of legal equality.

Both British and American trappers continued to ply the Snake and its tributaries in 1827, 1828, and 1829, sometimes with losses of men and equipment to hostile natives—both Snakes and Blackfeet. The double adversity of Indian depredations and competition, plus the exhaustion of the beaver supply, caused a decline in profits; previously, trappers had made good money. Ogden's four expeditions had averaged over $10,000 profit per year; William Sublette earned $36,000 for the fur from the Bear Lake rendezvous—furs that cost him only $9,000 there. By 1830 the six years of sharp competition in the Snake country fur trade had given neither Hudson's Bay nor the St. Louis mountain men a clear-cut victory.

During the early 1830s there were continued forays into Idaho by both British and American trappers. Both continued to have difficulties with Blackfeet and Bannock Indians as well as with each other.

In 1830 John Work took Ogden's place in managing the interests of Hudson's Bay in the Snake River area. Born in Donegal County, Ireland, with the surname of "Wark," Work anglicized his name about the time he joined the Hudson's Bay Company in 1814. He was sent to the Columbia River region in 1823 with a party of men that included Peter Skene Ogden. During the next seven years he was at Spokane House and Fort George (formerly Astoria), traded with the Flathead, explored British Columbia, and helped construct Fort Colville, the successor to Spokane House. (Fort Colville was near Kettle Falls, about seventy-five miles north of Spokane.) His instructions, like those given to Ogden, were to trap out the interior so completely that there would be nothing left for the Americans. His 1830 expedition, consisting of forty men, twenty-nine women, and forty-five children, traveled east from Walla Walla to the Salmon River and then southwest to the Humboldt in Nevada. Detachments trapped the Weiser, Payette, and Boise country but found few beaver remaining. Work went on to southern Idaho's Camas Prairie (where he lost one Snake in his party), up the Lost River to the Salmon, then over to the Blackfoot and Portneuf for the winter. Still not harvesting many beaver, he went on in the spring to the Humboldt.

The 1831 expedition took Work and his party into western Montana and the headwaters of the Missouri. Several of his men were killed in an attack by three hundred Blackfeet, who claimed the territory. Work quickly retreated to the Salmon River to trap and trade with the Snakes. Since too few beaver remained to attract St. Louis trappers, Work took his 1832 brigade south to the Sacramento Valley in California. He was given other responsibilities along the coast and did not return again to Idaho.

In 1834 Hudson's Bay reorganized the Rocky Mountain fur trade by establishing permanent posts to replace the rendezvous system. Fort Hall and Fort Boise (on the Snake) were erected that year. Dissolution of the Rocky Mountain Fur Company at the conclusion of its 1834 rendezvous shifted the St. Louis trade entirely into the hands of the American Fur Company, which lasted only another four years. By 1838 the Hudson's Bay Company became the undisputed leader of the fur empire.

The first leader in the transition to Hudson's Bay control was Benjamin Louis Eulalie de Bonneville. Best remembered as the hero of Washington Irving's *The Adventures of Captain Bonneville* (1837), Captain Bonneville was born near Paris during the middle of the French Revolution. His father was a friend of Lafayette, Condorcet, and Thomas Paine. When Napoleon became emperor of France in 1803, the family migrated to America. Under an appointment arranged by Lafayette, Bonneville attended West Point. After graduation with honors, he served in various army garrisons in New England, then in posts in the West.

In 1830 he decided to lead his own expedition to the West and for that purpose was given a two-year leave of absence from the army (which was later extended). Leaving Fort Osage, Missouri, in 1832 with 110 men and twenty wagons, he went to the Green River country in southwestern Wyoming, where he planned to build Fort Bonneville. When experienced men in the region cautioned that the location was subject to severe winters, Bonneville relocated at the headwaters of the Salmon. His camp was on Carmen Creek, several miles north of where Salmon City now stands. His men trapped along the Snake River, and some of them established a camp near the future site of Fort Hall. He established close relationships with Nez Perce, Flatheads, and Bannocks, who were there hunting buffalo.

The next winter Bonneville set up camp on the Portneuf near present-day Pocatello. He moved between many sites in southeastern Idaho: Bear Lake, Bear River, Pierre's Hole (Teton Valley), and Soda Springs. The latter was his name for the phenomenon; apparently a band of trappers had come upon the spring and in a moment of revelry pronounced it Beer Springs. Here is Washington Irving's account, which describes an experience in the spring of 1834 when Bonneville's men were away from their camp on the Portneuf:

> The most noted curiosity . . . of this singular region, is the *Beer Spring*, of which trappers give wonderful accounts. They are said to turn aside from their route through the country to drink of its waters, with as much eagerness as the Arab seeks some famous well of the desert. . . .
>
> Here the men all halted to have a regale [June 4, 1834]. In a few moments every spring had its jovial knot of hard drinkers, with tin cup in hand, indulging in mock carouse; quaffing, pledging, toasting, bandying jokes, singing drinking songs, and uttering peals of laughter, until it seemed as if their imaginations had given potency to the beverage, and cheated them into a fit of intoxication. Indeed, in the excitement of the moment, they were loud and extravagant in their commendations of "the mountain tap"; elevating it above every beverage produced from hops or malt. It was a singular and fantastic scene; suited to a region where everything is strange and peculiar:—These groups of trappers, and hunters, and Indians, with their wild costumes and wilder countenances; their boisterous gayety, and reckless air; quaffing and making merry round these sparkling fountains; while beside them lay their

> weapons, ready to be snatched up for instant service. Painters are fond of representing banditti at their rude and picturesque carousals; but here were groups, still more rude and picturesque; and it needed but a sudden onset of Blackfeet, and a quick transition from a fantastic revel to a furious melee, to have rendered this picture of a trapper's life complete.[16]

The company traveled over the desert plains north of the Snake River. As the story goes, when they came to Boise River, with its green forested banks, the Frenchmen shouted, "Les bois, les bois, voyez les bois," meaning, "The woods, the woods, see the woods!" But it appears that Boise River—Wooded River—was named by French Canadians in 1811 or 1812, and Ogden was using the French form, Boise, in 1825 or 1827.

Although Bonneville spent three years in the mountains, most of the time in Idaho, he was not able to compete successfully with more knowledgeable trappers. Food was a problem—the region had been hunted out by the Indians; snow and cold weather were obstacles; Blackfeet were always threatening. Historians Beal and Wells suggest that he accomplished little beyond experiencing the adventure later used to embellish Washington Irving's book.[17] Idaho has remembered Bonneville by naming the county in which Idaho Falls is located Bonneville County. The huge prehistoric lake that once covered some of southern Idaho and northern Utah was also named for him.

Another important figure in the fur trade during the middle 1830s was Nathaniel J. Wyeth. Born near Cambridge, Massachusetts, Wyeth spent most of his life in the Boston ice business. After conversations with his fellow townsman Hall Jackson Kelley, a Boston schoolteacher and journalist and booster of the Pacific Northwest, Wyeth arranged to have a ship sail around Cape Horn to the Columbia with a cargo that he hoped to market profitably in the Portland area. Meanwhile in 1832, he led a group of men overland to Oregon, hunting and trapping on the way. He planned, when the ship's cargo was sold, to load the vessel with furs and return to Boston.

The overland trip was not a vacation. Seven men left him at Pierre's Hole.[18] The remaining eighteen continued with Wyeth to Hudson's Bay's Fort Vancouver, on the north bank of the Columbia. Upon their arrival they learned that their ship had been wrecked in the South Pacific, forcing Wyeth to return overland to Boston empty-handed. On his trip east in 1833 he made an agreement with Milton (brother of William) Sublette and others of the Rocky Mountain Fur Company to supply them with goods at the 1834 rendezvous. He also organized the Columbia River Fishing and Trading Company to send salmon and beaver skins to the East by ship around Cape Horn, rather than overland, and he trapped south of the Columbia. When he reached the 1834 rendezvous with $3,000 worth of goods, the Rocky Mountain Fur people refused to buy them. (Another partner apparently had made other arrangements.) Furious, Wyeth told Thomas Fitzpatrick, "I will roll a stone into your garden that you will never be able to get out."[19] Wyeth then built Fort Hall, on the Snake River eleven miles north of present-day Pocatello, hoping to dispose of his goods and conduct his own fur trade. Behind a stockade were cabins and a little garden, and an American flag flew over the fort. The place was named after Henry Hall, a wealthy Bostonian who had backed Wyeth's second trip. Rocky Mountain Fur did retire from the field, but Wyeth had competition from the new Hudson's Bay post at Fort Boise. In the winter of 1836–37 he sold Fort Hall to Hudson's Bay and returned to Boston.

After the rendezvous of 1834, on July 8 and 9, there was a curious get-together of Captain Bonneville, Nathaniel Wyeth, and Thomas McKay at Soda Springs. McKay, who was now in charge of the Hudson's Bay Snake River brigade (he was a stepson of John McLoughlin, chief factor or agent for the Hudson's

Bay Company in Oregon Territory from 1824 to 1845), had with him Sir William Drummond Stuart (or Stewart) of Perthshire, Scotland. Bonneville entertained them royally. Wyeth struck up a friendship with McKay. Surviving correspondence suggests that the two men determined to establish posts to support trapping activities in Idaho—one in eastern Idaho (Fort Hall) and one in the west (Fort Boise). Hudson's Bay's stockholders rejected their expansionary joint enterprise, however. Wyeth may very well from the beginning have had in mind selling Fort Hall to McKay's company once it was well established. At any rate, that was what he did.

One of Wyeth's men was Jason Lee, a Methodist missionary who commenced a ministry at Fort Hall and later went with McKay, driving a herd of cattle across southern Idaho on his way to his permanent location in the Willamette Valley in Oregon. On July 27, at the request of McKay—whose crew was camped nearby during the fort's construction—Lee delivered a Sunday sermon at a cottonwood grove near Fort Hall to a congregation of Indians, trappers, and mountain men. The tall, bearded missionary, dressed in his ministerial garb, gave an exhortation based upon I Corinthians 10:21: "Whether therefore ye eat or drink, or whatsoever ye do, do all to the glory of God." As payment for the sermon, the first in Idaho, McKay presented the missionary with a sack of flour.[20]

Wyeth's description of the dedication ceremony for Fort Hall on August 5, 1834, recalls the excitement he and his men felt on the completion of the historic building:

> We manufactured a magnificent flag from some unbleached sheeting and a little red flannel and a few blue patches, saluted it with damaged powder and wet it in villa[i]nous alcohol, and after all it makes, I do assure you, a very respectable appearance amid the dry and desolate regions of central America. Its Bastions stand a terror to the

> skulking Indian and a beacon of saf[e]ty to the fugitive hunter. It is man[n]ed by 12 men and has constantly loade[d] in the Bastions 100 guns and rifles. These bastions command both the inside and the outside of the Fort.[21]

John K. Townsend, a Philadelphia naturalist and physician who also accompanied Wyeth across the continent, described the revelry that accompanied the christening:

> At sunrise this morning, the "star spangled banner" was raised on the flag-staff at the fort, and a salute fired by the men, who, according to orders, assembled around it. All in camp were allowed the free and uncontrolled use of liquor, and, as usual, the consequence was a scene of rioting, noise, and fighting, during the whole day; some became so drunk that their senses fled them entirely, and they were therefore harmless; but by far the greater number were just sufficiently under the influence of the vile trash, to render them in their conduct disgusting and tiger-like. We had "gouging," biting, fisticuffing, and "stamping" in the most "scientific" perfection; some even fired guns and pistols at each other, but these weapons were mostly harmless in the unsteady hands which employed them. Such scenes I hope never to witness again; they are absolutely sickening, and cause us to look upon our species with abhorrence and loathing.[22]

Although Wyeth was disappointed in the failure of the fort to survive as a supply center for mountaineers and Indians who wished to trade, it became the focus for other activity. The very year of Wyeth's departure, in August 1836, Henry Harmon Spalding and Marcus Whitman were traveling westward with their wives to work with the Nez Perce and Cayuse Indians in north Idaho and eastern Oregon. They stopped at the fort, thus initiating a new role for both Fort Hall and Fort Boise as stations for emigrants on the Oregon Trail. Placed in the charge of

Francis Ermatinger—a Hudson's Bay friend of Wyeth—in 1838, the two forts continued to operate until 1855–56.

Meanwhile, Thomas McKay left his returning company at Glenn's Ferry and went to the Boise region to spend the winter. Two earlier posts on the Boise River had failed, in 1814 and 1819, but McKay confidently built Fort Boise as a means of establishing a supply center close to his Snake River operations. McKay could stock his post with corn, pork, and flour from his Willamette Valley farm, and of course he was backed by the resources of his giant Hudson's Bay Company. His post proved its worth financially as well as practically, and his occupation of the area brought other developments. He planted a vegetable garden at the fort and had onions, peas, and corn on hand when the missionary party of Spalding and Whitman visited in August 1836.[23]

Mountain men continued to trade with Fort Hall—men like Jim Bridger, Osborne Russell, and Andrew Drips. But with the start of the Oregon Trail as the standard route for overlanders bound for the Northwest, the day of the mountain man began to fade. A rendezvous supplied by Andrew Drips on the Green River in 1840 was the last of the sixteen great Rocky Mountain fairs. When Robert Newell, William Craig, and Joe Meek drove a wagon from Fort Hall to Fort Boise, over the Blue Mountains, and then on to the lower Columbia in the fall of 1840, they demonstrated once and for all that the Oregon Trail was a practical wagon route. In the next few years hundreds of wagons followed. At the same time, the fur trade in Idaho had essentially reached its end. Beaver hats represented the past; instead, men began to wear silk hats. Most of Hudson's Bay's competition dropped out, and missionaries and passing overlanders, not fur trappers, dominated the history of Idaho from 1840 to 1860.

Considering the impressive exploratory and exploitative achievements of the Hudson's Bay and North West companies, we are left with a large question: Why did the British lose the Columbia and all its empire south of the 49th parallel? The efforts of American missionaries, settlers, and statesmen are obvious explanations. But William Goetzmann suggests something more. Able men like Thompson, McDonald, Mackenzie, Ross, Ogden, and Work were marvelous explorers and frontiersmen—they deserve respect and gratitude. But they viewed themselves as employees of a gigantic self-governing monopoly that was a product of mercantile England. The Hudson's Bay Company was a commercial enterprise—its goal was the maximization of profit. Only secondarily was it interested in settlement and broad economic development. The British brigade leader was not searching for wagon routes, places for permanent settlement, opportunities for agricultural production or mineral or forest exploration. He was looking for beaver, something that would enhance dividends; when the beaver became scarce, the attraction of the Northwest diminished.

In the spring of 1829, the British governor in North America, George Simpson, questioned Jedediah Smith about the possibility of American migration to the Northwest for reasons of agriculture. Smith replied that he had discovered difficulties likely to deter Americans: the impassable sandy desert and the rugged mountains. The Englishman accepted this appraisal. But in an 1830 letter to John H. Eaton, American Secretary of War, Smith and his two partners, David E. Jackson and William L. Sublette, stated that it was possible for wagons and herds of cattle to go by way of South Pass and on to the Columbia over what was to become the Oregon Trail. They further described the Oregon country (that is, the Willamette Valley) as a fertile farming land. Clearly, they now envisioned the possibility of settlement, of frontier agriculture, mining, and lumbering—the development of a commonwealth, and not just the making of a profit for a great business enterprise.[24]

## CHAPTER FIVE: SOURCES

Most histories of the American West have sections dealing with the early explorations and fur trade. The following were especially helpful: Ray Allen Billington, *The Far Western Frontier, 1830–1860* (New York: Harper & Bros., 1956), 41–68; Dan Elbert Clark, *The West in American History* (New York: Thomas Y. Crowell Co., 1937), 422–41; William H. Goetzmann, *Exploration and Empire: The Explorer and the Scientist in the Winning of the American West* (New York: Alfred A. Knopf, 1966), 105–80; Hafen and Rister, *Western America*, 209–27; John A. Hawgood, *America's Western Frontiers: The Exploration and Settlement of the Trans-Mississippi West* (New York: Alfred A. Knopf, 1967), 93–128; and Robert V. Hine, *The American West: An Interpretive History* (Boston: Little, Brown & Co., 1973), 44–58. Particularly helpful have been the articles in Lamar, ed., *Reader's Encyclopedia of the American West*, most of which were written by Gordon B. Dodds.

Histories of the Northwest that include extensive sections on fur traders and explorers are: Fuller, *History of the Pacific Northwest*, 57–123; Johansen and Gates, *Empire of the Columbia*, 63–149; Schwantes, *The Pacific Northwest*, 47–66; Oscar O. Winther, *The Great Northwest: A History*, 2d ed. (New York: Alfred A. Knopf, 1955), 33–106; and Oscar O. Winther, *The Old Oregon Country: A History of Frontier Trade, Transportation, and Travel* (Lincoln: University of Nebraska Press, 1969 [1950]), 24–105.

Idaho histories that cover the fur trade and exploration in Idaho include: Beal and Wells, *History of Idaho*, 1:78–204; Brosnan, *History of the State of Idaho*, 51–89; Peterson, *Idaho: A Bicentennial History*, 32–47; Defenbach, *Idaho: The Place and Its People*, 1:41–190, 217–36; Hawley, *History of Idaho*, 1:51–75; Merrill D. Beal, *A History of Southeastern Idaho: An Intimate Narrative of Peaceful Conquest by Empire Builders* (Caldwell: Caxton Printer, 1942), 53–84. Among texts for younger students, there are excellent chapters in Jennie Brown Rawlins, *Exploring Idaho's Past* (Salt Lake City: Deseret Book Co., 1963), 35–60; Dwight William Jensen, *Discovering Idaho: A History* (Caldwell: Caxton Printers, 1977), 62–77; Barber and Martin, *Idaho in the Pacific Northwest*, 9–25; Virgil M. Young, *The Story of Idaho*, Centennial Edition (Moscow: University of Idaho Press, 1990), 72–91; Ronald K. Fisher, *Beyond the Rockies: A Narrative History of Idaho*, 2d ed. (Coeur d'Alene: Alpha Omega, 1989), 112–37; and Francis Haines, *The Story of Idaho* (Boise: Syms-York Co., 1942), 29–49.

Books and articles on Fort Hall and Fort Boise include: Jennie Broughton Brown, *Fort Hall: On the Oregon Trail* (Caldwell: Caxton Printers, 1934); Frank C. Robertson, *Fort Hall: Gateway to the Oregon Country* (New York: Hastings House, 1963); Annie Laurie Bird, *Boise, the Peace Valley* (Caldwell: Caxton Printers, 1934); [Merle Wells], "Fort Boise: From Imperial Outpost to Historic Site," *Idaho Yesterdays* 6 (Spring 1962):14–16, 33–39; [Merle Wells], "Fort Hall, 1834–1856," *Idaho Yesterdays* 12 (Summer 1968):18–31; Louis S. Grant, "Fort Hall Under the Hudson's Bay Company, 1837–1856," *Oregon Historical Quarterly* 41 (March 1940):34–39; Francis D. Haines, Jr., "François Payette, Master of Fort Boise," *Pacific Northwest Quarterly* 47 (April 1956):57–61; Richard G. Beidelman, "Nathaniel Wyeth's Fort Hall," *Oregon Historical Quarterly* 58 (September 1957):197–250.

Books on the fur trade and mountain men include: Harrison C. Dale, ed., *The Ashley-Smith Explorations and the Discovery of a Central Route to the Pacific, 1822–1829* (Glendale, Calif.: Arthur H. Clark Co., 1918, 1941); H. M. Chittenden, *The American Fur Trade of the Far West*, 2 vols. (New York: Harper & Bros., 1902), later reissued by the University of Nebraska Press in 2 vols., 1986; E. E. Rich, *The History of the Hudson's Bay Company, 1670–1870*, vol. 2: 1763–1870 (London: The Hudson's Bay Record Society, 1959); John S. Galbraith, *The Hudson's Bay Company as an Imperial Factor, 1821–1869* (Berkeley: University of California Press, 1957); Hafen, ed., *The Mountain Men and the Fur Trade of the Far West*; Paul C. Phillips, *The Fur Trade*, 2 vols. (Norman: University of Oklahoma Press, 1961): Frederick Merk, ed., *Fur Trade and Empire: George Simpson's Journal*, rev. ed. (Cambridge: Harvard University Press, 1968); Warren A. Ferris, *Life in the Rocky Mountains 1830–35* (Salt Lake City: Rocky Mountain Book Shop, 1940); D. E. Livingston-

Little, "The Fur Traders and the Indians," in *An Economic History of North Idaho, 1800–1900* (Los Angeles: Journal of the West, 1965), 5–10; LeRoy R. Hafen, ed., *Trappers of the Far West* (Lincoln: University of Nebraska Press, 1983); Alexander Ross, *The Fur Hunters of the Far West* (London, 1855); and Fred R. Gowans, *Rocky Mountain Rendezvous: A History of the Fur Trade Rendezvous, 1825–1840* (Layton, Utah: Peregrine Smith, 1985).

Books on the trappers active in the fur trade in Idaho include: Charles Norris Cochrans, *David Thompson: The Explorer* (Toronto: The Macmillan Co., 1924, 1928); James K. Smith, *David Thompson: Fur Trader, Explorer, Geographer* (Toronto: Oxford University Press, 1971); Burton Harris, *John Colter: His Years in the Rockies* (New York: Charles Scribner's Sons, 1952); John Edward Sunder, *Bill Sublette, Mountain Man* (Norman: University of Oklahoma Press, 1959); Dale Morgan, *Jedediah Smith and the Opening of the West* (Lincoln: University of Nebraska Press, 1955, 1964); Washington Irving, *Astoria* (1836); Washington Irving, *Adventures of Captain Bonneville* (Paris, 1837); Osborne Russell, *Journal of a Trapper*, Aubrey Haines, ed. (Lincoln: University of Nebraska Press, 1968); J. B. Tyrell, ed., *David Thompson's Narrative of His Explorations in Western America* (Toronto: The Champlain Society, 1916); Francis D. Haines, Jr., ed., *The Snake Country Expedition of 1830–1831: John Work's Field Journal* (Norman: University of Oklahoma Press, 1971.)

Other important articles are: W. C. Eaton, "Nathaniel Wyeth's Oregon Expeditions," *Pacific Historical Review* 4 (June 1935):103–10; A. W. Thompson, "New Light on Donald Mackenzie's Post on the Clearwater, 1812–13," *Idaho Yesterdays* 18 (Fall 1974):24–32; Francis D. Haines, Jr., "François Payette," *Idaho Yesterdays* 8 (Winter 1964–1965):12–21; Frederick Merk, "Snake Country Expedition, 1824–25," *Mississippi Valley Historical Review* 21 (June 1934): 49–62; [Merle Wells], "The Adventures of Alexander Ross in the Snake Country," *Idaho Yesterdays* 14 (Spring 1970):8–15; T. C. Elliott, "David Thompson's Journeys in Idaho," *Washington Historical Quarterly* 11 (April-July 1920):97–114, 167–83; T. C. Elliott, "David Thompson and Beginnings in Idaho," *Oregon Historical Quarterly* 21 (June 1920):49–61; Jacob A. Meyers, "Finan McDonald: Explorer, Fur Trader, and Legislator," *Washington Historical Quarterly* 13 (July 1922):196–208; T. C. Elliott, "Wilson Price Hunt, 1783–1842," *Oregon Historical Quarterly* 32 (June 1931):130–34; T. C. Elliot, "The Earliest Travelers on the Oregon Trail," *Oregon Historical Quarterly* 13 (March 1912):71–84; J. C. Nielsen, "Donald Mackenzie in the Snake Country Fur Trade, 1816–1821," *Pacific Northwest Quarterly* 31 (April 1940):161–79; William T. Atkin, "Snake River Fur Trade, 1816–1824," *Oregon Historical Quarterly* 35 (December 1934):295–312; T. C. Elliott, "Journal of Alexander Ross: Snake Country Expedition, 1824," *Oregon Historical Quarterly* 14 (December 1913):366–88; Robert Carlton Clark, "Hawaiians in Early Oregon," *Oregon Historical Quarterly* 35 (March 1934):22–51; Annie Laurie Bird, "Thomas McKay," *Oregon Historical Quarterly* 40 (March 1939):3–14; Merle W. Wells, "A House for Trading: David Thompson on Pend d'Oreille Lake," *Idaho Yesterdays* 3 (Fall 1959):22–26; Stephen W. Sears, "Trail Blazer of the Far West [Jedediah Smith]," *American Heritage* 14 (June 1963):60–64, 80–83; Louis J. Clements, "Where Was Fort Henry?" *Snake River Echoes* 3 (Spring 1974):51–55.

22.

23.

22. Wilson Price Hunt led the 1811 party that first reported Shoshone Falls and the Boise Valley. UIL 3–58A.

23. This engraving of a summer rendezvous in the 1830s was originally published in Frances Fuller Victor's *The River of the West* (1870). ISHS 76–2.88.

24.

25.

24. Fort Hall, reproduced in this painting by Bethel M. Farley, was a trading post for trappers and emigrants from 1834 to 1856. UIL 5–18–1.

25. Fort Boise, erected in 1834 by the Hudson's Bay Company, served as a post exchange for trappers and emigrants until 1856. UIL 6–92–1.

26. 

27. 

26. Jesus Urquides, a colorful Basque packer, was later celebrated in many Boise parades. JOHNSON & SON, STATESMAN STAFF PHOTOGRAPHERS, UIL 3–746A.

27. Pack strings that supplied miners in Idaho mountains were common in the nineteenth century. U.S. FOREST SERVICE, UIL 6–199–2.

CHAPTER SIX

# The Missionaries

IDAHO'S Indians were fascinated with the "powers" of their white visitors. They had long since accommodated to the horse. But they had no way of explaining the knives, guns, steel traps, beautiful blankets, and glass mirrors that Lewis and Clark, David Thompson, and other sojourners showed them. Whites scribbled on little pieces of paper and seemed to place great store in them. Did these things have something to do with the Book that the whites read and so respected? Did the whites get the power to make these things from the world of spirits? How did they acquire that power? How could Indians get possession of this power? The mighty white God must give the whites powers that were worth acquiring.

The North West Company and later the Hudson's Bay Company had sent several Christian Iroquois, a few of whom had learned to read and write, from the St. Lawrence region into the Columbia and Snake River basins. The Iroquois hunters introduced parts of the Christian religion to the Kutenai, Pend d'Oreille, Coeur d'Alene, Shoshoni, Bannock, and Paiute. Some of the beliefs and practices—for instance, belief in spirits, a future life, and prayers—were not entirely new to the Indians. One could still be an Indian and accept these "new" teachings. But Indians wanted the "big medicine" of the whites and wanted instruction on how to acquire it.

When George Simpson, head of British interests in Canada, went to the Columbia Basin in 1825, Idaho "chiefs" asked him for teachers. Pleased, Simpson drew up plans for a mission school at Spokane. He took two Spokane Indian boys with him to be educated in the company's school at Red River Settlement, the colony the Scottish Earl of Selkirk had established in the valley of the Red River at modern Winnipeg, Manitoba. One of the boys died, but the other, Spokane Garry, returned to his band about 1830. Having learned to read and write, he built a schoolhouse, conducted classes in reading, writing, and religion, and taught farming methods to raise potatoes for food.

The Nez Perce did not wish to be outdone by the Spokanes. How could they get someone to teach them to read, write, and to grow crops? Ever since the visit of Lewis and Clark they had been friendly with Americans and they wanted American—not British—teachers. After their old friend William Clark was assigned as head of U.S. Indian affairs for western Indians, the Nez Perce decided at a conclave in Kamiah in 1831 to send three men to visit with Clark, who was based in St. Louis; a fourth, wanting to see the country, later joined them. The men took the traditional Lolo Trail, and one old man soon turned back. Chief Black Eagle, who led the mission, and the two others went by the Flatheads near Great Falls. Wanting teachers themselves, the Flathead sent three men and a youth with the Nez Perce group.

The party rode down to the Missouri River and boarded an American Fur Company boat loaded with furs. The hot weather and bad drinking water made some sick, and two Flathead and one Nez Perce turned back at Council Bluffs. Black Eagle and one of the Flatheads died of fever (smallpox?) at St. Louis, but the two young Nez Perce who were left, No Horns on His Head and Rabbit Skin Leggins, remained the winter in St. Louis where they visited with Clark. They returned to Fort Union the next spring, but No Horns on his Head later died of fever. Rabbit Skin Leggins reached a Nez Perce group in the buffalo country, only to be killed that fall in a fight with the Blackfeet.

Obviously, the Nez Perce were facing difficulty conveying their initial request for instruction to St. Louis authorities. Their petition for teachers was somehow interpreted as meaning that the tribe wanted to become Christians. William Walker, an Ohio Wyandot chief, son of a white father and part-Indian mother, happened to be visiting William Clark in St. Louis in 1831 at the same time as the Nez Perce. Impressed by their seeking knowledge of the religion and "power" of the white man, he wrote a letter about his experience to a friend in New York, who published it in the Methodist *New York Christian Advocate and Journal.*

The story created a sensation among New England church members. A mission board selected Jason Lee and his nephew Daniel Lee to go to the Nez Perce in 1834. The Lees, staunch Methodists, went west with Nathaniel Wyeth's second expedition, and at Fort Hall the elder Lee, as mentioned earlier, conducted the first church service in Idaho. After he learned of the instability in the region because of the annual Nez Perce defensive battles against the Blackfeet, Jason Lee decided to go on to the Willamette Valley where there were other white men. He became the leader of the first American settlement in the Oregon Country.

In 1835 two Presbyterians were sent west to establish missions: Samuel Parker and Marcus Whitman. They accompanied the American Fur Company caravan, and at the 1835 rendezvous they talked with Snake, Nez Perce, and Flathead and obtained an impression of the tasks that lay ahead. Parker, leader of the two, sent Whitman back to New England for additional funding, while Parker planned to locate sites for missions. The two promised to meet at the 1836 rendezvous. Parker located the sites but did not remain in the Far West. Instead, he ventured on to the Sandwich Islands (Hawaii) and then returned to New York.

Whitman, who was thirty-three in 1835, had received a degree from the medical college at Fairfield, New York, served for four years as a doctor in Canada, and then set up practice in New York. An elder in the Presbyterian church, he knew he would never be assigned as a missionary unless he married; so after his return from his journey with Parker he married Narcissa Prentiss, who also wished to be a missionary and also needed to be married before she could serve in the mission field. The two left for Oregon in February 1836, accompanied by Henry Harmon Spalding, his wife Eliza, and William H. Gray, all under the sponsorship of the American Board of Commissioners for Foreign Missions. Narcissa Whitman and Eliza Spalding were the first white women to cross the Rocky Mountains.

When the Whitmans and Spaldings arrived at the 1836 rendezvous, they were met by a large party of Nez Perce. Eliza Spalding described that meeting in her diary:

> July 4, 1836: Crossed a ridge of land today called the Divide, which separates the waters which flow into the Atlantic from those which flow into the Pacific, and camped for the night on the headwaters of the Colorado. The brave Nez Perces, who have been awaiting our arrival at the rendezvous for several days, on hearing we were near, came out to meet us, and have camped near us tonight. They appear to be gratified to see us actually on the way to their country. Mr. Spalding, Dr. Whitman, and Mr. Gray are to have a talk with the chiefs tonight.

> July 6: We arrived at the rendezvous this evening. Were met by a large party of Nez Perces, men, women, and children. The women were not satisfied short of saluting Mrs. Whitman and myself with a kiss. All appeared happy to see us. If permitted to reach their country and locate among them, may our labors be blessed to their temporal and spiritual good.
>
> July 18: We have commenced our journey for Fort Walla Walla in company with Mr. McLeoud. The Nez Perces seem sadly disappointed because we do not accompany them.[1]

In spite of advice that they were dangerous, Whitman established his mission among the Cayuse Indians, twenty-five miles up the Walla Walla from the Hudson's Bay Company's Fort Nez Perce (Old Fort Walla Walla). The mission at Waiilatpu had plenty of good farmland, water for irrigation, and Indians to help. The Waiilatpu mission ultimately became an important way station for Oregon-bound pioneers.

The Spaldings were assigned to settle among the Nez Perce in Idaho. Henry Spalding, who was thirty-three in 1836, was born out of wedlock in Wheeler, New York, to an uncaring mother and foster father, and was rejected by his sweetheart, Narcissa Prentiss, who later married Marcus Whitman. He studied to be a missionary to the Indians and his wife, Eliza Hart, helped him finance his schooling by taking in boarders. They initially set out for the Osage tribes in Oklahoma but were intercepted by Whitman and persuaded to go to Oregon. Eliza was adept at languages and could talk with the Nez Perce by the time they established their mission. She could spin, weave, sew, and prepare a meal quickly and was a good housekeeper.

For two years the Spaldings established their mission for the Nez Perce on the site of present-day Lapwai (the Valley of Butterflies) on Lapwai Creek about two miles above its mouth and perhaps a dozen miles up the Clearwater from present Lewiston.

In 1838 they moved to the bank of the Clearwater River at the mouth of Lapwai Creek. This location is now part of a national historic park. While Spalding worked to build a cabin, Eliza soon gave birth to a daughter, also named Eliza, the first white child born in Idaho. In addition to family duties Mrs. Spalding taught large classes of eager Nez Perce students of all sizes and ages. Having mastered some of their language on the way to Lapwai, she was able to keep the students busy by writing instructions in her own hand. Hundreds of Nez Perce soon learned to read in their own tongue. In 1839 a Protestant mission in Hawaii sent the Spaldings a small printing press so the lesson sheets could be printed. Several books were printed in Shahaptin, the Nez Perce language, and a small eight-page children's book in the language was the first printing in the Northwest. Other publications included a songbook and parts of the New Testament. These early imprints appeared at a time when fewer than fifty white people resided in all of Idaho.

While Eliza was conducting her school, Henry, wanting to induce the Indians to settle down and live like white people, was teaching the Nez Perce men to farm. He and tribe members planted vegetable gardens, fruit trees, potatoes, corn, and wheat. A water-powered gristmill ground the grain into flour, a sawmill was started to furnish lumber for new buildings, a blacksmith shop helped them make tools. Dr. John McLoughlin, chief factor at Fort Vancouver, assisted in obtaining this equipment, as well as some cattle, pigs, sheep, and chickens. By 1838 their "model farm" was producing 800 bushels of potatoes. In March 1839 Spalding wrote the secretary of the American Board of Commissioners for Foreign Missions:

> We are turning our hoes into horses which are to be sent into the lower Columbia and exchanged for iron which will be made into hoes again for the same purpose and in this way we hope to supply the nation in a few years with the

> means of cultivating their lands. The desire for hoes is far beyond my expectation. I looked for a strong desire to cultivate this spring, but I did not dream of the present enthusiasm. We gave four hoes for a horse, but our stock was gone in two days, and now they would gladly give a horse for a hoe, a horse with us is about $6.00. Yesterday a gun was brought for a hoe. . . . Today we have bought . . . enough old axes and enough [old iron] to make fifty hoes.[2]

That fall Spalding recorded, "The Lord has blessed us with . . . about 2,000 bushels of potatoes, corn, wheat, peas &c plenty."[3]

The summer of 1839 was very dry, and in order to provide water, Spalding dug a ditch and watered the plants in his garden—the first time irrigation was practiced in the region.

Charles Wilkes, who led an exploring expedition to the Northwest by sea, reported after visiting Lapwai that Spalding had "succeeded admirably" in inducing the Indians to give up their roving mode of life and settle down to cultivate the soil.[4] In 1843 Spalding reported that 140 natives had cultivated from one-fourth to four or five acres each and that the Lapwai farmers had thirty-two head of cattle, ten sheep, and forty hogs. Spalding asked for ten or twelve plows to be sent each year.[5]

Not all went easily for the missionaries. Spalding was inflexibly opposed to liquor, gambling, and polygamy; boldly, sometimes tactlessly, he denounced sin, reproved many, and in some instances resorted to the whip. He was denounced by some, ridiculed by others. Eliza Spalding, however, was gentle, patient, and cheerful, and the Indians treated her almost reverently. The Spaldings had three children besides Eliza, all of whom watched the mission lands at Lapwai progress successively as part of Oregon Territory, Washington Territory, and then Idaho Territory. All but one of the children lived to see Idaho become the forty-third state in the nation.[6]

Despite Spalding's positive reports, it is clear that as the years wore on the Nez Perce lost much of their enthusiasm for the schools, their teachers, and the farm. The missionaries had not brought them the expected Big Medicine. There had been no miraculous appearances of guns, food, and other supplies. If they would do His will, they were promised, God would look after them. But their new God had not delivered as the missionaries, in flowery language, had implied He would.

The missionaries, too, were discouraged. Asa B. Smith, who had been sent to join the Spaldings in 1838, had tried and failed to establish a mission at Kamiah, sixty miles southeast of Lapwai. He took the liberty of writing adverse reports about Spalding, an unquestionably hard worker but with limitations and weaknesses. Smith did not hesitate to criticize Spalding, even in front of the Indians. The Indians became half-hearted in keeping up the work they had begun.

The missionaries had additional problems. Some of the mountain men, after the last rendezvous in 1839, chose to settle down with the Nez Perce. They included William Craig, friend of Joe Meek, Jim Bridger, and Kit Carson, who went to Lapwai in 1840, located a farm, and married the daughter of Chief James of Lapwai. Craig expected the Spaldings to pay rent on their mission lands and wanted the Christianized Indians to go back to their villages instead of living at Lapwai.

There was also trouble with the mission board in the East, who thought the mission should support itself by farming and dismissed Spalding in 1840. Whitman, thinking the mission board did not understand the situation, went east in 1842 to get Spalding reappointed and to boost support for both missions. The board relented, and Whitman returned in 1843 with the first large immigration train headed for the Oregon Country.

But Whitman was also in trouble. The Cayuse Indians attributed many deaths to white men's diseases—diseases such as measles and scarlet fever that had reached them because of Dr. Whitman's willingness to help sick travelers. Although the Cayuse disliked travelers who crossed their lands, they were willing to trade fresh horses to those whose teams were tired and worn out. So many Cayuse horses reached Oregon settlements this way that the term "Cayuse horse," or simply "cayuse," became a common term for western range horses.[7]

Dr. Whitman treated both Indians and whites for illness. Usually the whites recovered, but the Indians often died. As we now know, the Indians did not have the resistance that white people had built up over thousands of years. Seeing so many of their band die, the Cayuse came to believe that Dr. Whitman's cures were witchcraft or even that he was administering poison disguised as medicine. Following the severe winter of 1846–47, when many deaths further weakened the Indians, some of the Cayuse killed Marcus and Narcissa Whitman and twelve of the men working at the mission. Several men escaped death, and fifty-three women and children taken prisoner were later rescued by the Hudson's Bay manager at Fort Walla Walla. Settlers in the Willamette Valley raised a volunteer force and tormented the Cayuse until six of them surrendered voluntarily to save the rest of their people from further attacks. The six were taken to Oregon City and hanged after a hasty trial.[8]

After the Whitman massacre, the Spaldings abandoned the Lapwai Mission. Guarded by friendly Nez Perce, they moved to the Willamette Valley, where they engaged in farming. At the time of abandonment the Lapwai mission had forty-four acres under cultivation and 164 horses, cattle, and hogs.[9] For a while Henry was commissioner of schools and Indian agent in Oregon. Eliza Spalding died in 1851.

In 1863 Spalding returned to Lapwai as a teacher. He was forced out by a change of administration in 1867, but in 1871, in accordance with President Ulysses Grant's "peace policy," Spalding resumed his missionary work in Lapwai with a reappointment by the American Board of Commissioners for Foreign Missions. He remained until his death in 1874, when he was seventy-one, and was buried near his wife at Lapwai. Evidence indicates that Spalding had greater success among the

Nez Perces in the early 1870s than in the 1836–47 period.

Spalding's efforts at Lapwai were not in vain. One of his early converts was Tuekakas, who came from the Wallowa River area of Oregon. Spalding baptized him and gave him the Christian name of Joseph; he was one of the two deacons in the Lapwai church. He became known as Old Joseph. In 1840 Old Joseph's wife bore a son, also known as Joseph, who became the Chief Joseph who will be described in Chapter Thirteen—one of Idaho's best-known leaders.

Visitors to Lapwai in subsequent years found the Nez Perce continuing to farm. In 1861, when Captain E. D. Pierce led a party of prospectors onto the Nez Perce Reservation, created in 1855, they became aware of the beef, horses, corn, potatoes, and onions the Nez Perce had to sell. Dr. G. A. Noble reported to the Oregon City *Argus* in 1861: "These Indians have some fine crops here, well-fenced and apparently well-cultivated. I had not seen chicken or egg since June last, but here we saw both chickens and eggs. Chickens three dollars apiece, and eggs four dollars a dozen."[10]

Eliza Spalding Warren, Idaho's first white child, in her *Memoirs of the West*, recalls this picture of the Spalding Mission:

> The Indians were settled in homes; their crops of grain were 20,000 to 30,000 bushels a year; the cows brought by the missionaries had multiplied into numerous herds; the sheep given by the Sandwich Islanders had grown into flocks. In the school which Mrs. Spalding taught there had been 500 pupils. A church of a hundred members had been gathered. The language had been reduced to writing. A patriarchal government had been established. They had adopted a code of laws. The Sabbath was observed.[11]

What Plymouth Rock was to New England, the Spalding Mission was to Idaho.

By 1895 the Nez Perce population was recorded at 2,000 and

was described as having 8,000 acres under cultivation and 10,000 acres fenced. About 350 families were engaged in tilling the soil, and their livestock included 15,000 horses and 7,500 cattle. D. E. Livingston-Little concluded, "Unlike the Indian tribes in other parts of the United States, those of North Idaho had learned how to participate in the region's economic development."[12]

There had been other missionary efforts. Catholic missionaries in Fort Vancouver and the Willamette Valley served the French-Canadians and others in the 1830s. In 1840, Father Pierre Jean de Smet, of Belgium, was sent by the Jesuit Order to the Flathead country of Three Forks, Montana, to locate mission sites. When the Flatheads heard that de Smet was coming they sent 1,600 of their tribe to meet "the black robe" at Pierre's Hole. He was overwhelmed by their interest. This feeling continued as he visited a dozen or more tribes living in the valleys and mountains of Oregon Country. He went back to St. Louis and then to Europe for reinforcements. Returning to the Northwest in 1841, he revisited his Indian hosts and established St. Mary's Mission in the Bitterroot Valley near Stevensville, Montana. This was the first Catholic mission in the Pacific Northwest.

De Smet soon established three other missions, one in Idaho. Even though he settled in St. Louis in 1846, he remained prominent in Northwest Indian affairs until his death in 1873, including serving as an arbitrator in several white-Indian disputes.

In 1842 de Smet commissioned Father Nicolas Point, cofounder of St. Mary's Mission, to expand the work from the Flatheads to the Coeur d'Alenes in North Idaho by establishing the Mission of the Sacred Heart on the north bank of the St. Joe River about one mile from the southern end of Lake Coeur d'Alene. Because the site was subject to spring floods and vicious mosquitoes, the mission was moved in 1846 to a site east of modern Coeur d'Alene on the Coeur d'Alene River.

Father Point, who was born in France, ventured among the Nez Perce in 1845 and remained in the Northwest until 1847. He was a topographical artist and left more than one hundred sketches that have formed illustrative material for Father de Smet's published journal.

When the Flathead mission closed in 1850, Father Antonio Ravalli, born in Italy and skilled in medicine and architecture, went to Sacred Heart. There he designed a larger new church building ninety feet long, forty feet wide, and thirty feet high with a portico supported by six massive wooden pillars. Because the Coeur d'Alenes, who constructed the building, had no nails, they bored holes in the beams and boards and put wooden pegs through the holes to hold the pieces together. For the walls they wove saplings with grass and smeared them with mud. The "Old Mission" building was begun in 1847, finished sufficiently for use in 1854, and finally completed in 1868. Still standing between Kellogg and Coeur d'Alene, the building is the oldest public building in Idaho. In 1853 Governor Isaac I. Stevens of the newly created Washington Territory described the station and its five hundred inhabitants as follows:

> It is indeed extraordinary what the Fathers have done at the Coeur d'Alene Mission. . . . They have a splendid church nearly finished by the labor of the fathers, laymen, and Indians; a large barn, a horse-mill for flour, a small range of buildings for the accommodation of the priests and laymen, a store-room, a milk or dairy-room, a cook room and good arrangements for their pigs and cattle. They are putting up a new range of quarters and the Indians have some twelve comfortable log cabins. . . . They have a large cultivated field of some two hundred acres and a prairie from two to three thousand acres. They own a hundred pigs, eight yokes of oxen, thirty cows and a liberal proportion of horses, mules and young animals.[13]

In 1858 Captain John Mullan, who was building the wagon road that bears his name, was a guest of the Old Mission and called it "St. Bernard in the Coeur d'Alene Mountains." During the winter of 1858–59 it sheltered Father de Smet.[14]

When new boundaries were proposed for the Coeur d'Alene Reservation in 1877, the Sacred Heart Mission was found to lie outside the reservation, so in 1878 a new mission was begun in DeSmet, in Benewah County, where it still functions. (Another group of people wanted to use Father de Smet's name for their town. Since the name was already taken, they decided to use his name spelled backward: Temsed. Someone misspelled the name so the town is known as Tensed.)

In 1877, Father Joseph M. Cataldo was placed in charge of the nine mission stations in the Pacific Northwest, and he served as superior until 1893. A Sicilian by birth, Cataldo had entered the Society of Jesus at the age of fifteen, became a priest at twenty-five, and was assigned to the American West at his own request. During a period of language study at Santa Clara College in California he met Father Gregory Mengarini, who had participated with de Smet in the founding of St. Mary's Mission among the Flathead. From Mengarini he learned the language and customs of the Salish Indians.[15] He was assigned to the Pacific Northwest in 1865 and took station at the Coeur d'Alene Mission of the Sacred Heart. This frail man, called "Dried Salmon" by the Indians, subsequently lived among several other tribes, including the Nez Perce. Cataldo was a peacemaker in the Nez Perce War of 1877. He was also an accomplished linguist, eventually mastering ten Indian languages. He built reservation boarding schools, established Gonzaga College in 1883, and increased the number of missions from nine to fifteen. Cataldo organized Indian-operated, self-supporting farms, some with large herds of livestock, and opened hospitals, mission schools, and orphanages. By 1883 the number of Jesuits in the Rocky Mountain Missions had grown to fifty-three men, of whom twenty-seven were priests. For future personnel needs, Cataldo established a Jesuit novitiate at the Sacred Heart Mission at DeSmet.

One wonders about the success of the Rocky Mountain Mission founded by Father de Smet in 1841, involving as it did such a wide difference in languages. By 1873 the Catholics had baptized and retained as members about 107,000 Indians of different tribes in the Pacific Northwest, compared with 15,000 natives affiliated with Protestant churches.[16]

The Roman Catholics had several advantages over their Protestant counterparts. Catholic priests were unencumbered by families or individual property and could devote themselves completely to the natives and their problems. With Protestants, the challenge of feeding and clothing their families and educating their children must have taken much if not most of their energies. Another reason is that most of the Catholic missionaries were not American-born and thus were not tied to the repressive policies of the American government and military. Nearly all of the "Black Robes" were from Italy, France, Belgium, Holland, and Germany and had been exposed, almost from birth, to a multiplicity of languages. Learning languages was a necessity of life. Moreover, nearly all of them knew French, a second language for many Indians because of the long-term associations with the métis whom the Hudson's Bay Company employed.[17]

A still further reason for Catholic success was theological or doctrinal. About all a potential convert had to do to be baptized was express a belief in Jesus as the Christ. To become a Presbyterian, however, one had to undergo far more rigorous instruction and be able to enunciate far more complex beliefs, absorbing and reciting a full-fledged catechism that must have been difficult, at best.

The very success of the Catholics was a source of Protestant antagonism. The Catholic missionaries who came from Canada by permission of the Hudson's Bay Company were regarded as British reinforcements as well as ecclesiastical competitors. Spalding and his associates believed that the future of Oregon country belonged to their white countrymen; they were advance agents of white civilization. In their view, Catholics were foreigners, their orders came from Rome, and the expansion of their activities was a tragedy. Anti-Catholicism was in many ways an assertion of American nationalism. Spalding was so upset with the Catholic presence that he blamed the priests for the Whitman massacre—a charge that historians have long since dismissed as having no foundation.

Not all early missionary activity occurred in northern Idaho. In 1847, the same year the Whitman Massacre caused the closure of the Lapwai Mission, the Mormons entered the Great Basin. Within a few years Brigham Young, their leader, founded several missions to convert the natives to a more sedentary lifestyle. One of these was within the territory of the Shoshoni-Bannock in central Idaho. That story, because it occurs in a different time period, will be told in Chapter Seven.[18]

Inevitably, there was tension between white culture and Indian culture and between different sects of white Christians. The most enduring achievements of both Catholic and Protestant missionaries were the establishment of permanent settlements, the introduction of agriculture, and the assistance rendered to Indians during their painful transition from nomadic life to the kind of culture imposed by white immigration after 1860.[19]

## CHAPTER SIX: SOURCES

Books on the history of the American West and Northwest that discuss the Idaho missionaries include: Billington, *The Far Western Frontier*, 79–90; Fuller, *History of the Pacific Northwest*, 124–69; Johansen and Gates, *Empire of the Columbia*, 159–77; Winther, *The Great Northwest*, 113–20; and Schwantes, *The Pacific Northwest*, 69–77.

Histories of Idaho that have chapters or sections on the Protestant and Catholic missionaries include Beal and Wells, *History of Idaho*,

1:205–15; Brosnan, *History of the State of Idaho*, 90–114; Defenbach, *Idaho: The Place and Its People*, 1:191–216; and Peterson, *Idaho: A Bicentennial History*, 43–46.

Histories for young people are excellent on this topic: Barber and Martin, *Idaho in the Pacific Northwest*, 28–34; Rawlins, *Exploring Idaho's Past*, 61–80; Young, *The Story of Idaho*, 92–101; Jensen, *Discovering Idaho*, 78–89; Fisher, *Beyond the Rockies*, 141–53; and Haines, *The Story of Idaho*, 50–58.

Books with treatments of topics discussed in the chapter are: Cecil P. Dryden, *Give All to Oregon! Missionary Pioneers to the Far West* (New York: Hastings House, 1968); Clifford M. Drury, ed., *First White Women over the Rockies*, 3 vols. (Glendale, Calif.: Arthur H. Clark Co., 1963–66); R. I. Burns, *The Jesuits and the Indian Wars of the Northwest* (New Haven: Yale University Press, 1966); Clifford Merrill Drury, *The Diaries and Letters of Henry H. Spalding and Asa Bowen Smith Relating to the Nez Perce Mission, 1838–1842* (Glendale, Calif.: Arthur H. Clark Co., 1958); Allen C. and Eleanor Dunlap Morrill, *Out of the Blanket: The Story of Sue and Kate McBeth, Missionaries to the Nez Perce* (Moscow: University Press of Idaho, 1978); Clifford Merrill Drury, *Henry Harmon Spalding* (Caldwell: Caxton Printers, 1936); William N. Bischoff, *The Jesuits in Old Oregon, 1840–1940* (Caldwell: Caxton Printers, 1945); Clifford M. Drury, *Marcus and Narcissa Whitman and the Opening of Old Oregon*, 2 vols. (Glendale, Calif.: Arthur H. Clark Co., 1958, 1973); Narcissa Prentiss Whitman, *My Journal, 1836*, Lawrence Dodd, ed. (Fairfield, Wash.: Ye Galleon Press, 1982); H. M. Chittenden and A. T. Richardson, eds., *Life, Letters, and Travels of Father Pierre Jean De Smet*, S.J., 4 vols. (New York: Harper & Bros., 1905); Robert H. Ruby and John A. Brown, *The Cayuse Indians: Imperial Tribesmen of Old Oregon* (Norman: University of Oklahoma Press, 1972); Cornelius J. Brosnan, *Jason Lee: Prophet of the New Oregon* (New York: The Macmillan Co., 1932); Clyde A. Milner II and Floyd A. O'Neil, eds., *Churchmen and the Western Indians, 1820–1920* (Norman: University of Oklahoma Press, 1985); Nard Jones, *Marcus Whitman, The Great Command: The Story of Marcus and Narcissa Whitman and the Oregon Country Pioneers* (Portland, Ore.: Binfords and Mort,

1959); Pierre J. De Smet, *Oregon Missions and Travels Over the Rocky Mountains in 1845–46* (1847); and Samuel Parker, *Journal of an Exploring Tour Beyond the Rocky Mountains* (repr., Moscow: University of Idaho Press, 1990).

Several helpful articles are published in *Idaho Yesterdays* 31 (Spring-Summer 1987):2–116. The entire issue carries more than a dozen articles by scholars that deal with Catholic, Protestant, and Mormon missionaries among the Indians in north Idaho. These include articles on the Whitmans and Spaldings and Catholic and Mormon missionaries. Also see Erwin N. Thompson, "Joseph M. Cataldo and Saint Joseph's Mission," *Idaho Yesterdays* 18 (Summer 1974):19–29; and Gerald McKevitt, "Jesuit Missionary Linguistics in the Pacific Northwest: A Comparative Study," *Western Historical Quarterly* 21 (August 1990):281–304.

Splendid interpretive work revising some previously held conclusions appears in Julie Roy Jeffrey, "Narcissa Whitman: The Significance of a Missionary's Life," *Montana: The Magazine of Western History* 41 (Spring 1991):3–15, and her *Converting the West: A Biography of Narcissa Whitman* (Norman: University of Oklahoma Press, 1991).

28.

29.

28. The Reverend Henry Harmon Spalding was missionary to the Nez Perce at Lapwai, 1836–47, 1863–74. ISHS 42.

29. This 1901 photo shows the surviving Spalding cabin, built at Lapwai in 1836–37. SARA ANETTE BOWMAN COLLECTION, UIL 5–13–ID.

30. 

 31.

 32.

30. Father Peter de Smet was a Jesuit missionary to the Coeur d'Alene in the 1840s. ISHS 74–195.2.

31. Anthony Ravalli, Jesuit missionary to the Coeur d'Alene from 1850 to 1877, designed the Sacred Heart mission at Cataldo. ISHS 74–195.1.

32. The church of the Coeur d'Alene Mission of the Sacred Heart was built at Cataldo between 1847 and 1868. ISHS 75–5.35.

33.

33. Father Joseph M. Cataldo directed the Sacred Heart Coeur d'Alene Mission, 1877–93. ISHS 75–228.46.

## CHAPTER SEVEN

# Emigrant Trails

IN 1838 the United States dispatched a worldwide naval exploring expedition from Norfolk, Virginia, under the command of Lieutenant Charles Wilkes. In three years and ten months the expedition confirmed that Antarctica was a continent, made excellent charts of islands in the Central and South Pacific, and in April 1841 arrived off the coast of Oregon to strengthen American claims to the Pacific Northwest. In addition to land parties that explored Puget Sound, Grays Harbor, the Willamette and Sacramento river valleys, and Yerba Buena (San Francisco), a group under Lieutenant Robert E. Johnson explored all the way up the Columbia to the mouth of the Snake River, Spokane Falls, Coeur d'Alene Lake, Lapwai, and Fort Walla Walla. The well-publicized expedition confirmed the impressions created by fur traders, Marcus Whitman, Henry Spalding, Pierre Jean de Smet, and other explorers and settlers that the Oregon Country was ripe for agricultural settlements.

The findings of the Wilkes expedition in the Northwest were

soon corroborated by Captain John C. Frémont, who explored the region in 1843. A native of Georgia, educated in Charleston, South Carolina, Frémont was commissioned a second lieutenant in the United States Corps of Topographical Engineers in 1838 when he was twenty-five and accompanied the distinguished French scientist Joseph N. Nicollet on a reconnaissance of the upper Mississippi and Missouri rivers. In Washington, D.C., while engaged in further surveys and in completing maps, Frémont eloped with Jessie Benton, daughter of Senator Thomas Hart Benton of Missouri. In 1842, on an official survey, Frémont followed a path to South Pass and the Wind River Mountains of Wyoming. His report, written with Jessie Frémont's help, stirred the imaginations of Americans and was enormously helpful in pointing the way west.

The 1842 expedition was followed the next year by a reconnaissance that took Frémont to Oregon. The precise and accurate description of the route to Oregon in that report, published immediately by order of Congress, changed the entire picture of the West: no longer an uninhabitable desert, it now appeared as a land of opportunity that invited settlement. Frémont's maps, complete with mileage calculations, descriptions of the terrain, and suggested camping places, provided a prized handbook for thousands of overlanders. His descriptions of the valleys along the Bear River and east of Great Salt Lake were crucial in influencing the Mormons to settle in the Great Salt Lake Valley. Idahoans have remembered him with the naming of Frémont County.

As he crossed South Pass in August 1843, Frémont had first-class equipment and thirty-nine men, including Thomas "Broken Hand" Fitzpatrick and Kit Carson, two of the best scouts and mountain men in Idaho's history. Frémont and his party followed the Bear River into Bear Lake Valley, then up to Soda Springs, which he called Beer Springs. He tested the gurgling carbonated water in the spring; it was eighty degrees Fahrenheit. His party crossed the divide into the Portneuf Valley and proceeded to Fort Hall. They then followed the Bear River, investigated the Great Salt Lake, and returned to Idaho down the valley of "Pannack," now known as Bannock Creek, just west of Pocatello. Coming to the Snake River Plain, Frémont observed to the north the famous Three Buttes. Before him stretched a sagebrush desert.

Upon reaching the Portneuf Frémont described a green valley with scattered timber and the white walls of Fort Hall in the distance.

> Except that there is a greater quantity of wood used in its construction, Fort Hall very much resembles the other trading posts. It is in the low, rich bottom of a valley apparently twenty miles long formed by the confluence of Portneuf River with Lewis Fork of the Columbia [Snake River] which it enters about nine miles below the fort and narrowing gradually to the mouth of Pannack Creek where it has a breadth of only two or three miles.[1]

The Snake River Plain to the west of Fort Hall seemed to him notably barren and hopelessly unproductive:

> There does not occur, for a distance of nearly three hundred miles to the westward, a fertile spot of ground sufficiently large to produce the necessary quantity of grain, or pasturage enough to allow even a temporary repose to the emigrants. On their recent passage, they have been able to obtain, at very high prices and in insufficient quantity only such assistance as could be afforded by a small and remote trading post [Fort Boise]—and that a foreign [British] one. . . . An American military post sufficiently strong to give their road a perfect security against the Indian tribes, who are unsettled in locality and very *uncertain* in their disposition, and which, with the necessary facilities for the repair of their equipage, would be able to afford them relief in stock and grain from the produce of the post would be of

> extraordinary value to the emigration. Such a post (and all others which may be established on the line to Oregon) would naturally form the *nucleus* of a settlement, at which supplies and repose would be obtained by the emigrant, or trading caravans, which may hereafter traverse these elevated, and, in many places, desolate and inhospitable regions.[2]

On September 25 Frémont and party passed through Massacre Rocks and camped on the Rivière aux Cajeaux (Raft River). On the twenty-eighth they crossed Goose Creek and spent the night at Rock Creek a few miles south of the present site of Twin Falls. (They apparently did not see Shoshone Falls.) The next morning they found Thousand Springs. Resuming their journey, on October 1, they camped on the south bank of the Snake at Kanaka Rapids, which Frémont called Fishing Falls. They found several lodges of Indians, unusually jolly and laughing loudly, presumably from the good salmon catch. The next day they were at Upper Salmon Falls, and on October 3 reached Three Island Crossing (downstream from present Glenns Ferry) and crossed to the north side (no ferry there yet) with some difficulty. On October 7, in sight of the Boise—"Wooded"—River, they were delighted to camp under fine old trees. The next two days they traveled fifty miles, camped at the mouth of the Boise, and the next morning arrived at Fort Boise, a simple house on the right bank of the Snake about a mile below the mouth of the river. Here they were hospitably received and fed by François Payette. On the morning of October 11, 1843, they crossed the Snake into Oregon and camped on the "unlucky" river, the Malheur.

Frémont continued on to the Columbia and Fort Vancouver, then down through Oregon to Nevada. Heading west, he made a rash midwinter crossing of the Sierra that is still viewed with wonder. His scattered force regrouped at Sutter's Fort, went to the Sacramento River and Yerba Buena, then moved on to Los

Angeles. Finally, he headed for the Midwest on the Old Spanish Trail. In fourteen months Frémont had completed a virtual circuit of the entire West.

In 1841, two years before Frémont's passage, the first overland migration of pioneers intending to settle permanently in Oregon took place. This company of seventy persons, including Father Pierre de Smet, had Thomas Fitzpatrick and Joseph Meek as guides and John Bidwell and John Bartleson as captains. Fitzpatrick, who as noted above was a guide for the Frémont expedition of 1843–44, was born in Ireland, came to America as a young man, joined Ashley's expedition of 1823, attended the first fur-trading rendezvous of 1825, and was a founder of the Rocky Mountain Fur Company in 1830. He traveled west with Whitman in 1836. Joseph Meek was born in Virginia, fled to Missouri to escape his stepmother, then trapped in the Snake River and Utah regions for many years. As the fur trade declined, he operated out of Fort Hall as a guide.

John Bidwell, a western New Yorker who was educated in Pennsylvania and Ohio, moved to Missouri in 1839, then decided to go on to California in 1840. He formed the Western Emigration Society and by 1841 had promises from five hundred persons to journey from the Missouri River to the West. But Missouri merchants, not anxious to lose customers, furnished sufficient discouragement that Bidwell's party was reduced to sixty-nine. Organizing for the journey, they chose John Bartleson of Jackson County, Missouri, as commander of the company, which included a number of women and children. Fitzpatrick and de Smet guided them to the Platte, Fort Laramie, Independence Rock, and the Sweetwater, to South Pass and Green River Valley, to Soda Springs. At that point the party divided. Thirty-two of the emigrants went to Oregon with Fitzpatrick and de Smet; the remainder, including one woman and her young daughter, joined Bidwell for the trip to California. The Oregon-bound party abandoned their wagons at Fort Hall and continued their journey by pack train. Every experienced person seemed to agree that one could not drive a wagon to Oregon.

In 1842 a larger group of approximately 112 persons and thirty wagons followed the trail under the leadership of Dr. Elijah White, a former missionary heading to his new post as Indian agent for Oregon. Once more, at Fort Laramie, Thomas Fitzpatrick was employed as the guide, and Lansford Hastings was the captain. Born in Ohio, Hastings, who was taking his first trip west with the company in 1842, later wrote one of the early overland guidebooks, *The Emigrants' Guide to Oregon and California*—the guidebook used by the ill-fated Donner Party of 1846. Dr. White's party took with them to Oregon the news that the Presbyterian missions in Idaho and Oregon were to be discontinued, prompting Marcus Whitman to journey east to obtain a reversal.

Dr. Whitman's return to Oregon in 1843 was marked by what is referred to as the Great Migration. Spurred on by favorable publicity about Oregon, by outbreaks of malaria in the Missouri and Mississippi river valleys, by the prospect of an abundance of free land, and no doubt by the patriotic desire to bolster American claims to a rich and resourceful region, about 1,000 men, women, and children gathered at Independence, Missouri, in the early spring of 1843 for the journey. Peter H. Burnett, a Missouri lawyer, was elected captain of the train comprised of about 200 wagons and approximately 5,000 head of cattle.

Since they would not be under United States law for the six months or more on the trail, the large company adopted rules and regulations that would govern them on the journey. The "wake up" bell would be rung at 4 A.M., when they would round up, feed, and water the stock, eat breakfast, "hitch up," and be ready to depart at 7 A.M. There was an hour's stop at noon, and they halted at 6 P.M. There were specified punishments for failure to carry out assigned tasks, sleeping on guard duty, and other derelictions. One group required every couple to carry their Bible; most refused to travel on Sunday. Men (or boys) usually drove the team, although when cholera or other disease or accident took the men, the women did the driving. They averaged from twelve to fifteen miles a day.

Later trains, as protection against possible Indian raids on livestock, drew their wagons into a circle each evening, the tongue of one placed under the body of the next to make a corral. These early emigrants did not have that concern, although in case of a storm or suspected thievery, the stock were gathered inside an enclosure and guards posted to watch the cattle and horses. When the group camped in the evening and circled their wagons, fire was kindled and supper prepared. Jesse Applegate, who was driving a large herd of cattle, describes a typical evening:

> It is not yet 8 o'clock when the first watch is to be set; the evening meal is just over, and the corral [to keep cows out] now free from the intrusion of cattle or horses, groups of children are scattered over it. . . . Before a tent near the river a violin makes lively music, and some youths and maidens have improvised a dance upon the green; in another quarter a flute gives its mellow and melancholy notes to the still night air, which, as they float away over the quiet river, seem a lament for the past rather than a hope for the future. . . . But time passes; the watch is set for the night; the council of old men has been broken up, and each has returned to his own quarter; the flute has whispered its last lament to the deepening night; the violin is silent, and the dancers have dispersed. . . . All is hushed and repose from the fatigues of the day, save the vigilant guard, and the wakeful leader, who still has cares upon his mind that forbid sleep, [until] the last care of the day being removed and the last duty performed, he too seeks the rest that will enable him to go through the same routine tomorrow.[3]

In this and succeeding companies most of the men, the young people, and the women who were not pregnant walked across the plains. Their wagons were loaded with supplies and furnishings, and often a woman had a baby and a small child or two. Most wagons were pulled by oxen, not horses, because oxen had greater endurance and were not as tempting to Indians. Many also took mules—as pack animals and to pull wagons—because they were more sure-footed than horses and had greater stamina.

Although western movies usually feature an Indian attack, John Unruh calculated that during the period 1840 to 1860 a total of 362 overland emigrants were killed by Indians and 426 Indians were killed by emigrants. The fewer than 400 emigrants killed by Indians (a substantial number in Idaho) were less than 4 percent of the estimated 10,000 or more who died on the trail and a miniscule fraction of the 53,062 whites emigrating overland to Oregon and 200,335 traveling overland to California.[4] The overwhelming majority of those who died were victims of accidents or disease. There were drownings, accidental discharges of firearms, and kicks by horses and mules. Children sometimes fell off their perch and were run over by wagons. There were outbreaks of cholera, smallpox, measles, tick fever, and sickness from drinking impure water. There were births of "covered wagon babies" along the way and weddings of couples who had become acquainted on the trail.

The companies followed similar paths but meandered somewhat according to weather conditions and other factors. The Oregon Trail (referred to by Indians as "The Great Medicine Road of the Whites") was a broad avenue of paths, not necessarily one road except in narrow passes. In some places there were many parallel routes miles from each other. Emigrants hated to travel alone and in nearly every case chose to join a group.

Another reason for the bunching of wagons was that they could not leave the Missouri River Valley until the grasses were out to provide feed for their livestock, and they had to be over the Blue and Cascade mountains in Oregon before the snows. Thus the companies left in late April and May and were over the mountains by the end of September.

An emigrant train as large as that of 1843 was bound to have conflicts, particularly between those who traveled without cattle and those who drove herds. At the crossing of the Big Blue River in Kansas a "Light Column" of sixty wagons split off under the leadership of their own captain, William Martin. The wagons in the "Cow Column," led by Jesse Applegate, followed behind. For ninety-eight days the two bands of white-topped wagons rolled westward. At Fort Hall, 1,288 miles from Independence and 786 miles from Fort Vancouver, the two columns were temporarily united. They received the usual advice from the Hudson's Bay people that they should leave their wagons at Fort Hall and go on by pack train. But Whitman had been over the trail four times and counseled them to continue their trek by wagon. There were enough men and boys, he thought, to make a satisfactory road as they went, to remove rocks, fill in holes and depressions, clear away trees, and locate suitable approaches to stream crossings.

The emigrants crossed southern Idaho in August when it was hot, dry, and dusty. The grass was brown, and the animals were tired and thirsty. It was frustrating that the cool waters of the Snake River were at the bottom of impenetrable canyons. The ever-present lava rock of the plains cut into the hooves of the oxen; some were so injured that they had to be left behind. When they reached Three Island Crossing, many found the crossing too deep and were forced to continue on the south side of the Snake to Boise. It was a rugged, dreary desert country. One described it as a "wild, rocky, barren wilderness, of wrecked and ruined nature, a vast field of volcanic desolation."[5] A later emigrant left this description of the country:

> The country all the way down the Snake River is one of the most desolate and dreary wastes in the world. Light,

> soft ground with no soil on top, looking like an ash heap, dust six inches deep and as light as flour. When a man travels all day in it he looks like a miller. You can see nothing but his eyes and they look red... the ground is covered with two of the most detestable shrubs that grow, grease wood and artemesia or wild sage.[6]

No pioneer seems to have given serious consideration to settling down anywhere along the trail in Idaho.

By the time the emigrants reached the Snake River country they had exhausted most of their provisions, the buffalo were behind them, and the wild game had migrated to the cool mountains. There was considerable privation. Moreover, their horses and oxen were worn out, injured, or stolen. When they encountered natives they were eager to do a little trading, and the poorly clothed, destitute Shoshoni, Bannock, and Northern Paiute also were zealous to obtain whatever the whites had to offer. The emigrants bought or traded for horses, fresh and smoked salmon, camas roots, Indian corn, potatoes, tobacco, knives, and herbs. In exchange they offered money, clothing, blankets, needles, thread, mirrors, guns, and ammunition. The diaries, letters, and reminiscences of overlanders are filled with references to swarms of Indians coming to trade and pilfer. One emigrant wrote:

> Whenever we camp near any Indian village we are no sooner stopped than a whole crowd may be seen galloping into our camp, male and female. Some come to swap and others are idle spectators. The squaws do all the swapping except in the pony line. When we will not trade with them they leave with exclamations as no good, NO GOOD.[7]

Although sources suggest that Indians were little or no threat for most of the emigrants, more than one recorded in a diary that the principal problem in Idaho, besides the lack of available water and the dust, was the delight of local Indian bands in stealing horses and oxen and then holding them for ransoms of clothing and blankets. The emigrants were fortunate to find lodges of contented Indians fishing for salmon at Salmon Falls and Thousand Springs, even in off-season.

The appearance of the large 1843 company in Vancouver and the Willamette Valley that fall did not exactly delight Dr. John McLoughlin, chief factor of Hudson's Bay. Although he was polite and helpful, he could see that the Oregon Country was turning into an American, rather than a British, commonwealth. Moreover, passage from the states by wagon was now firmly established, and the way was open for some new bypasses and cutoffs that would shorten the distance and lighten the burden. Ferries were built at river crossings, mills established to provide flour and other "stores," and way-stations constructed. The average number of days required to make the journey decreased from 169 between 1841 and 1848 to 128 during the 1850s.[8]

The annual migration of 1844 was not much larger than that of the previous year because an unusually wet spring forced a late start. But in 1845 an estimated 2,500 migrants traveled to Oregon and in 1846 about 1,200 went to Oregon and 1,500 to California. By the end of 1846, when the southern part of the great Oregon Country officially became part of the United States, approximately 6,300 persons had crossed Idaho headed for Oregon and another 2,900 had cut through part of Idaho to go to California. In 1847 another 4,000 traveled overland to Oregon and 450 to California and in 1848 1,300 journeyed to Oregon and 400 to California.

In 1841, as we have seen, an emigrant party of thirty-two under the leadership of Bartleson and Bidwell left the Oregon Trail at Soda Springs. Heading southwest to the Humboldt River in Nevada, following a route similar to that later known as Hudspeth's Cutoff, they went down the Humboldt and across the Sierra Nevada into California. This was the first group of settlers to take the California Trail. Although no parties took the trail in

1842, some thirty-eight men, women, and children headed that way in 1843 directed by Joseph Reddeford Walker. They took consolation in the fact that from Fort Hall it was 800 miles to Oregon and only 700 to Sutter's Fort, California. They trudged through the sagebrush and greasewood, and at the Raft River they left the Oregon Road to go up the Raft and over the divide to what is known as the City of Rocks, the area where the state lines of Nevada, Idaho, and Utah would meet a half-century later. Then they turned southwest for the Humboldt.

They were followed in 1844 by the Stephens-Murphy party of 53, and another group of 260 in 1845. In 1846, the year of the war with Mexico, 300 wagons on the California Trail carried upwards of 1,500 men, women, and children. With the discovery of gold in California in 1848, thousands took the route beginning in 1849—25,000 in 1849, 44,000 in 1850, and 50,000 in 1852. Some idea of the magnitude of this migration is suggested by the fact that in 1850 soldiers at Fort Laramie counted 9,000 wagons, 7,500 mules, 31,000 oxen, 23,000 horses, and more than 5,000 cows.[9]

The number of overland migrants accelerated rapidly, not only for California but for Oregon as well. In the years 1849 to 1860 an estimated 41,550 persons crossed Idaho to go to Oregon, and approximately 200,000 to take the California Trail.[10] In recognizing its own responsibilities to protect the emigrants, Congress in 1846 provided for a series of emigrant-trail forts to be built by an expedition of mounted riflemen. The Mexican War delayed action on this commitment, but in 1849 Fort Laramie was converted into an army installation, and a temporary Cantonment Loring was started near Fort Hall. The U.S. Army Fort Boise was not established until July 4, 1863, in response to emigrant and mining camp security problems, but it continued to operate until 1912. During the early 1860s Camp Connor functioned at Soda Springs, but it was abandoned in 1866. Travelers continued to use the Oregon Trail; although the Oregon Short Line Railway was completed across southern Idaho in 1884, emigrant wagons continued to cross Idaho for two more decades. The trail was also used for cattle (and sheep) drives from the west to feeding grounds and markets in the upper Plains states and Midwest.

In 1849 a party of about 250 persons—most of them women and children—led by Benoni M. Hudspeth and John J. Myers ventured to shorten the route toward the Humboldt by traveling directly westward from Soda Springs. Myers, an experienced mountain man, had come over the Fort Boise California Trail alternate in 1843; both he and Hudspeth had journeyed to California with Frémont in 1845. Returning to Missouri in 1848, they led this party along a route shown to Frémont's party in 1844 by an old-time Idaho trapper. The shortcut allowed them to bypass Fort Hall but required them to cross four uncharted mountains. They managed to find enough water and ungrazed grasses for the oxen. But when they emerged from the hills east of Raft River and rejoined the regular California Trail, they were surprised to find that they were only eighty miles west of Fort Hall. Although they had saved only twenty-five miles of travel, they were delighted to have spent time at Lava Hot Springs. Because the route was passable and saved two days of travel, it soon drained the California-bound traffic from the Fort Hall road. The older road became almost deserted. Fort Hall was abandoned in 1855 when even the Oregon settlers followed Hudspeth's Cutoff.

The junction of the California Trail and Sublette Cutoff was at the Silent City of Rocks, near Almo, south of Burley and Oakley—a twenty-five-mile-square aggregation of eroded cathedrals, towers, and walls. Because it was a junction of two important trails, thousands of names and dates and messages are recorded on its sheer granite walls, some so high and remote that they must have been written by overland scribes suspended by ropes from the tops of cliffs. The site, with its weird mosques and monoliths, strange pockets and caverns, bathtubs and toad-

Historic Trails
0 50
miles
117°
49°
45°
42°
111°
Mullan Road
Lewis and Clark Trail
Lolo Trail
Spalding Camp
Nez Perce Trail
Ft. Boise
Goodale's Cutoff
Ft. Hall
Oregon
Kelton Trail
Trail
Or. Trail S.
Hudspeth Cutoff
Salt Lk Cutoff
Calif. Trail
RELIEF © GIBB JOHNSON, 1993

stools, Dragon's Head and Old Woman, was visited by more than 80,000 tourists in 1990.

There were other shortcuts to the Oregon and California trails. In 1862 Tim Goodale, a mountain trader well acquainted with the Indian and fur trails north of the Snake River, led a group from Fort Hall directly west to Lost River, then across Camas Prairie, forging an approach to Boise that stayed north of the broad valley of the Snake. The cutoff ran south of Craters of the Moon and the sites of Bellevue and Fairfield and rejoined the Oregon Trail at Ditto Creek, near Mayfield.

In 1859 the government provided funds to enable Frederick W. Lander, an engineer, to locate a new road from South Pass, Wyoming, to Fort Hall that would lead straight west rather than following the original trail down to Fort Bridger and then back up to Fort Hall. Some 13,000 emigrants passed over Lander's Road in 1859, and with further modifications and improvements it became the standard route, obviating the necessity of going south to Fort Bridger. (Jim Bridger, who lost potential business, hated it.) The road saved an estimated 100 miles—at least five days of travel time. The Lander Road went past salt deposits in eastern Idaho later developed by the Oneida Salt Works Company, a concern that sold enormous quantities of salt to mining communities in Idaho and Montana in the 1860s, 1870s, and 1880s. When the transcontinental railroad was completed, traffic over the trail declined. The last wagons crossing it were observed at Fort Piney, Wyoming, between 1910 and 1912.

The Oregon and California trails were the most significant wagon roads through Idaho. Another of historic importance was the Mullan Road, a United States military route that connected Fort Benton, Montana, on the upper reaches of the Missouri (thirty-five miles northeast of Great Falls), with Fort Walla Walla (Wallula), Washington. The road, 624 miles long, was designed to connect the end of navigation on the Missouri with that on the Columbia. Under the direction of army lieutenant

John Mullan, work on the road was started in 1859 and proceeded rapidly. At one time 150 men were at work cutting a 25-foot swath through dense forests for 124 miles and 30 miles of rock, through the Bitterroot and Coeur d'Alene mountains, grading across open country, building hundreds of bridges, and establishing many ferries. The road was completed in August 1860. Almost immediately an army unit traveled its full length, an accomplishment that required fifty-seven days. The road was never important as a military route, but it played a significant role for north Idaho and Montana during the historic gold rush that began in 1861 and was resumed with undiminished vigor in the 1880s.

The road was also used by immigrants and by cattlemen driving many herds from the upper Columbia to the Montana mines. In the years from 1880 to 1910 the Northern Pacific; Chicago, Milwaukee, and St. Paul; and Oregon-Washington Railway and Navigation companies came to traverse Idaho near the line of the Mullan Road. In our day, a broad paved highway winds its way along much of Mullan's original route through scenic Idaho and western Montana.

Years after the completion of the road, Mullan, then a captain, reflected on this supreme achievement of his life:

> Night after night I have laid out in the unbeaten forests, or in the pathless prairies with no bed but a few pine leaves (needles), with no pillow but my saddle, and in my imagination heard the whistle of the engine, the whirr of the machinery, the paddle of the steamboat wheels, as they plowed the waters of the sound. In my enthusiasm, I saw the country thickly populated, thousands pouring over the borders to make homes in this far western land.[11]

For John Mullan, all of those dreams came true.

In 1869, John Hailey, later delegate to Congress, opened a stagecoach line from Kelton to Boise. It ran northwest through the City of Rocks to Rock Creek, where it joined the Oregon Trail to Thousand Springs. There it crossed the Snake at Clark's Ferry and followed an alternate Oregon Trail to Boise. Emigrants took the train to Ogden, Corinne, and Kelton (all in Utah); used the Kelton Road to Boise; and followed the Oregon Trail from there. Until completion of the Oregon Short Line Railway across Idaho in 1883, freight and mail were carried from Salt Lake City and Ogden into Boise over the Kelton Road.

Although Indian difficulties were minor during the years of heavy wagon train migration over the Oregon and California trails, at least three massacres are a part of Idaho history. The first is the Ward massacre, which occurred near the present town of Middleton, twenty-five miles east of Fort Boise, on August 20, 1854. The five-wagon emigration train, the advance portion of a larger company that had previously split into three sections, consisted of twenty people under the leadership of Alexander Ward of Lexington, Missouri. When one of the emigrants spotted an Indian stealing a horse in midday (it was Sunday), he shot the thief. Soon a band of thirty "Winnestah" Snakes launched a furious attack. The day before three white men had been killed in the third segment of the wagon train seventy miles behind when eleven Indians had suddenly opened fire after coming up ostensibly to trade. But the small advance party suffered most. Only two boys of the twenty in the Ward train escaped, one by feigning death after he had been knocked down; the other, unconscious from an arrow wound in his side, was rescued by seven white men who were traveling east. In search of a stray cow, the men came upon the gruesome scene as the Indians were plundering the wagons. They engaged them in battle. One of their number was killed, bringing the death total to nineteen. Two days later eighteen men left Fort Boise in the hope of finding additional survivors. The condition of those they buried was revolting—women raped, scalped, and cut to pieces, and children burned alive. The Indians, who were from east of Fort Boise, took forty-one cattle, five horses, and $3,000 in money. Shortly after the massacre three other whites were shot to death near the fort, and several others were killed on Camas Prairie, seventy-five miles from the post. A federal force of sixty-five men was dispatched to capture the murderers. Three hostile Indians were shot and three others hung at the massacre site; others were imprisoned. Since it was clear that the perpetrators of the massacre were a small band in the region, no general anti-Indian campaign of extermination resulted.[12]

A second massacre occurred in September 1860 on Succor Creek in present Owyhee County, about twenty miles below Shoshone Falls. The Otter-Van Orman emigrant train, consisting of forty-four persons and eight wagons, was ambushed on September 9 by Shoshoni. Four soldiers from Fort Hall helped the group defend themselves from repeated attacks for two days, during which nine of the emigrant train were killed and the covered wagons were set on fire. Then, while the Indians were engaged in plunder, some of the emigrants escaped. The Indians proceeded to kill them as they fled. The soldiers mounted the best horses and rode for help, but two of them were killed before they reached a settlement. Eventually two of the escaping emigrants reached the Umatilla Indian Agency on October 2. Meanwhile the Indians took about one hundred head of stock and all of the emigrants' provisions. The future of the thirty who escaped was bleak. By the time an army detachment, 110 men under Captain F. T. Dent, arrived from Fort Dalles and Walla Walla to rescue the destitute survivors, twenty-three had been killed by Indians, several bodies were mutilated, and four children were abducted (a Van Orman boy was finally retrieved two years later). The remaining eighteen and one soldier had wandered toward the northwest, living on berries and salmon but mainly starving. When the military arrived, there were only twelve still alive, subsisting in part on the flesh of five of their number who had died of wounds and/or starvation. The emaciated survivors, many of them children, were taken by the soldiers to the Willamette Valley.[13]

Major John Owen, who had been instructed to search for the children, insisted that some of the blame for the massacre rested on the whites:

> These Indians [Bannock and Shoshoni] twelve years ago were the avowed friends of the White Man. I have had their young men in my employment as hunters, horse guards, guides, &c &c. I have traversed the length and breadth of their entire country with large bands of stock unmolested. Their present hostile attitude can in a great measure be attributed to the treatment they have received from unprincipled White Men passing through their country. They have been robbed, murdered, their women outraged &c&c and in fact outrages have been committed by White Men that the heart would shudder to record.[14]

On August 9, 1862, about one hundred Shoshoni under Chief Pocatello gathered west of American Falls and attacked eleven wagons. By the time the rest of the wagon train approached, most of the men had been killed. The next morning 40 men went out to recover the stolen stock, but they were driven back by 300 warriors and 3 of the whites were killed. The emigrants waited until their group numbered 700 people, but they were harassed all the way to the Humboldt. This was one of the incidents that led to the Battle of Bear River—a massacre of Indians early the next year in which several hundred Indians were killed, about which more in Chapter Twelve.[15]

Not all purported attacks were by Indians; some were by "white Indians" pretending to be Indians. And there was unthinking killing of Indians by whites for reasons that seem ludicrous, if not downright cruel. A reprehensible example of emigrant brutality was a Texan traveling west from Fort Hall in

1845 who saw an Indian near the trail, rode up to him, struck him, handcuffed him, tied a rope around his neck, and fastened it to the rear of his wagon. The rest of the company was so intimidated by the bully that they did not interfere. This cruelty went on for a week until the Texan thought the Indian's spirit was broken, and he put him to work on various tasks including driving the wagon. One night the Indian slave disappeared, taking with him some of the Texan's personal effects, including his $100 gun. The company members were elated, particularly when the Texan's "wonder dog" was unable to track the vanished Indian.[16]

Finally, there was the counterbalancing factor of numerous instances of Indian assistance to whites—providing information, food, horses, labor, and medicine.

In any case, the massacres did not prevent the migration of thousands across the labyrinths of Idaho mountains, valleys, and plains to Oregon and California in the 1850s and 1860s. Eventually, some of them would find places along the trail to establish farms and ranches. The acres of "dreary sagebrush" would be converted into irrigated wonderlands.

## CHAPTER SEVEN: SOURCES

Virtually all histories of the West have chapters or sections on the Oregon and California trails. Among these are Billington, *Westward Expansion*, 509–33; Clark, *Frontier America*, 486–505; Billington, *Far Western Frontier*, 91–115; Dan Clark, *The West in American History*, 467–87; and Hafen and Rister, *Western America*, 228–45.

Histories of the Pacific Northwest with excellent chapters or sections on the Oregon Trail include: Winther, *The Great Northwest*, 107–26; Winther, *The Old Oregon Country*, 109–34; Schwantes, *The Pacific Northwest*, 78–94; Fuller, *History of the Pacific Northwest*, 180–94; and Sidney Warren, *Farthest Frontier: The Pacific Northwest* (New York: The Macmillan Co., 1949), 45–58.

Histories of Idaho that discuss the Oregon, California, and other trails through the state include: Beal and Wells, *History of Idaho*, 1:216–41; Brosnan, *History of the State of Idaho*, 117–30; Hawley, *History of Idaho*, 1:77–87; and Defenbach, *Idaho: The Place and Its People*, 1:217–36.

For young people, texts that have chapters on the trail include: Rawlins, *Exploring Idaho's Past*, 81–89; Haines, *The Story of Idaho*, 59–64; Jensen, *Discovering Idaho*, 90–104; and Fisher, *Beyond the Rockies*, 155–70.

Monographic sources that treat the Oregon, California, and other trails that went through Idaho include Jay Monaghan, *The Overland Trail* (Indianapolis: Bobbs-Merrill Co., 1947); W. J. Ghent, *The Road to Oregon: A Chronicle of the Great Emigrant Trail* (New York: Tudor, 1934); P. A. Rollins, ed., *The Discovery of the Oregon Trail* (New York: Charles Scribner's Sons, 1935); V. E. Geiger, Ann W. Bryarly, and David M. Potter, eds., *Trail to California* (New Haven: Yale University Press, 1945); David Lavender, *Westward Vision: The Story of the Oregon Trail* (New York: The McGraw-Hill Book Co., 1963); George R. Stewart, *The California Trail: An Epic with Many Heroes* (New York: McGraw-Hill Book Co., 1962); *Route of the Oregon Trail in Idaho* (Boise: Idaho Department of Highways, 1963); John Mack Faragher, *Women and Men on the Overland Trail* (New Haven: Yale University Press, 1979); John D. Unruh, Jr., *The Plains Across: The Overland Emigrants and the Trans-Mississippi West, 1840–1860* (Urbana: University of Illinois Press, 1979); H. J. Warre, *Overland to Oregon in 1845: Impressions of a Journey across North America*, edited by Madeline Major-Fregeau (Ottawa: Public Archives of Canada, 1976); Mike Hanley and Ellis Lucia, *Owyhee Trails: The West's Forgotten Corner* (Caldwell: Caxton Printers, 1988); William E. Hill, *The Oregon Trail: Yesterday and Today* (Caldwell: Caxton Printers, 1989); Bureau of Land Management and Idaho State Historical Society, *Emigrant Trails of Southern Idaho* (Boise: Idaho State Office, Bureau of Land Management, 1989); Jesse Applegate, *A Day with the Cow Column in 1843: Recollections of My Boyhood*, Joseph Schafer, ed. (Chicago: Caxton Club, 1934); George W. Goodhart and A. C. Anderson, *Trails of Early Idaho* (Boise: Privately published, 1940); W. Turrentine Jackson, "The California Trail" and

"The Oregon Trail," in Lamar, ed., *Reader's Encyclopedia of the American West*, 155–56, 884–85; Irene D. Paden, *The Wake of the Prairie Schooner* (New York: The Macmillan Co., 1943); Federal Writers' Project of the Works Progress Administration, *The Oregon Trail: The Missouri River to the Pacific Ocean* (New York: Hastings House, 1939); Wilkes, *Narrative of the United States Exploring Expedition*, esp. vol. 4; and W. Turrentine Jackson, *Wagon Roads West: A Study of Federal Road Surveys and Construction in the Trans Mississippi West, 1846–1869* (Berkeley: University of California Press, 1952).

On John C. Frémont, see Allan Nevins, *John C. Frémont: Pathmarker of the West*, 3d ed. (New York: Longmans, Green & Co., 1955); Donald Jackson and Mary Lee Spence, eds., *The Expeditions of John Charles Frémont*, 3 vols. (Urbana: University of Illinois Press, 1970–84).

Articles that are particularly helpful in gaining an understanding of the trails include: [Merle W. Wells], "Thousand Springs and Salmon Falls," *Idaho Yesterdays* 18 (Fall 1974):14–23; Howard Ross Cramer, "Geology and Hudspeth's Cutoff," *Idaho Yesterdays* 19 (Fall 1975):14–24; Clark C. Spence, "Pioneers with Wagging Tails: Dogs on the Trail to Oregon," *Idaho Yesterdays* 25 (Summer 1981):27–31; Francis Haines, Sr., "Goldilocks on the Oregon Trail," *Idaho Yesterdays* 9 (Winter 1965–66):26–30; Jesse Applegate, "A Day with the Cow Column in 1843," *Oregon Historical Quarterly* 1 (December 1900):371–83; Samuel Flagg Bemis, "Captain John Mullan and the Engineers' Frontier," *Washington Historical Quarterly* 14 (July 1923): 201–205; and T. C. Elliott, "The Mullan Road: Its Local History and Significance," *Washington Historical Quarterly* 14 (July 1923): 206–209.

34.

35.

34. Overlanders who crossed Idaho in the 1840s endured vast plains of sagebrush similar to this one north of Shoshone. COURTESY OF CARLOS A. SCHWANTES.

35. The City of Rocks in south-central Idaho was a major landmark for thousands who took the California Trail in the 1840s and 1850s. USHS.

36.

37.

36. Captain John Mullan was a pioneer road-builder in north Idaho. UIL 3–1691A.

37. Olds Ferry, on the Snake River near modern Weiser, was one of many that furnished transportation across Idaho streams until bridges were built near the end of the nineteenth century. DONATED BY F. CUSHING MOORE, UIL 6–29–1.

CHAPTER EIGHT

# The Salmon River Mission

IN a move similar to the location of the Presbyterians among the Cayuse and Nez Perce, and those missions that the Catholics built for the Coeur d'Alene and Flathead, the Latter-day Saints established a farming settlement to work with Idaho Indians in east-central Idaho called the Salmon River Mission. The mission was located in a narrow, well-timbered river valley on an ancient Indian and trapper trail that connected the Snake River with the upper Missouri and the Bitterroot Valley. Lewis and Clark had followed that tributary of the Salmon River after their history-making crossing of the Continental Divide in 1805, but the names in the area that have come down to us are those that were provided by the Latter-day Saints. They named their post after King Limhi, an ancient Indian leader mentioned in the Latter-day Saint scripture the Book of Mormon. The spelling was soon altered to Lemhi, perhaps because that is the way the Mormon colonizers pronounced it, and today's maps now include Lemhi River, Lemhi Pass, Lemhi County, Lemhi City, and Lemhi Indians. Virtually all of the contemporary sources of the Salmon River Mission refer to Limhi, however, and that spelling will be retained in this chapter.

The first contingent of 16,000 Mormons who had been driven from their homes in Illinois in 1846 had arrived in the valley of the Great Salt Lake in 1847, the year of failure and tragedy for the Whitman and Spalding missions. Two years later the Mormons organized the State of Deseret to encompass a large area that included all of present-day Utah and Nevada, the southeastern corner of Idaho, southcentral Oregon, southern California, northern Arizona, northwestern New Mexico, western Colorado, and central and western Wyoming. By the time Congress considered the Mormon request for statehood, however, the California Gold Rush had led to statehood for California. In the Compromise of 1850 Utah Territory, named for the Ute Indians (Congress did not approve of the name of Deseret), had been created to include Utah, Nevada, and adjoining lands in Wyoming and Colorado. Under the impression that northern Utah and southern Idaho were too cold to grow crops, the Mormons had not gone very far north of the southern tip of Cache Valley until May 1855 when Brigham Young, leader of the Mormons—who now included several thousand immigrants from Great Britain, Scandinavia, and emigrants from the American East, South, and Midwest—called twenty-seven men to found a settlement in the Salmon River country. This was the first Anglo-Saxon agricultural settlement in Idaho, and it continued only until it was abandoned in March 1858.

The Idaho colony was one of six the Mormons founded in 1855. Other outpost settlements were established the same year among Indian groups at Carson Valley, in western Nevada; Little Salt Lake Valley, in southern Utah; Elk Mountain, in eastern Utah; Fort Supply, near Fort Bridger in western Wyoming; and among the Cherokees in Indian (Oklahoma) Territory. Some three hundred missionaries were called to establish these six posts.

The persons "called," that is, asked to go to what was then Oregon Territory, represented a variety of skills and were nearly all from northern Utah—Salt Lake Valley, Davis County, and Weber Valley. Their appointed leader was thirty-seven-year-old Thomas S. Smith of Farmington, Utah. A native of New York, and a Mormon since 1844, Smith became one of the LDS Church's leading colonizers. An indispensable member of the party was George Washington Hill, who had performed previous missions to Indians in the West and who knew the language of the Shoshoni. He would serve as interpreter.

Most of the persons called were young men. Some were married but at the beginning were not expected to take their wives and children. Each was given five or six weeks to prepare for the trip. The instructions to the missionaries were to settle among the "buffalo-hunting Flathead, Bannack, or Shoshone Indians," or anywhere near them that the tribes would permit. The missionaries were told to teach the Indians the principles of civilization; that is, teach them to "settle down," grow crops, build houses, take better care of each other, and live in peace with native nations and with whites. The colonists were to pack provisions to last a year so they would not be a burden on the natives but rather would have enough to share if the Indians needed help. They were expected to live exemplary lives.

The group gathered on the west side of Bear River, west of Ogden, and traveled northward to what later became Brigham City, then along the eastern base of the mountains to Collinston, up the Malad Valley, and on to cross the Bannock Mountains. Passing by the present location of Pocatello, they crossed the Portneuf River and Ross' Fork and then reached the Snake River and Fort Hall. They proceeded on to the Blackfoot River and Eagle Rock (Idaho Falls), then north to Market Lake. After crossing the lava beds they went on to Muddy Lake, then the headwaters of what they called Spring Creek (Birch Creek), and finally to the summit of the Salmon Divide at the headwaters of a fork of the Salmon River.

The Mormon men had to make roads as they went along. They built bridges or forded the rivers and creeks as best they could. Their outfit consisted of thirteen wagons, with two yokes of cattle to each wagon, and a few cows. The company was well-organized, with Smith as president, a captain, a secretary, a captain of the guard, and so on. The party was divided into messes with five or six men to a mess, each with a particular duty to perform. Each morning and evening they held a prayer meeting, each member taking his turn according to the roll call.

After a day's journey down the mountain valley, they met Rock-i-kae, also called Sow-woo-koo, chief of the Bannock. He was more widely known as "Le Grand Coquin" (The Great Rogue), having been given this name by French-Canadian trappers who regarded him as an efficient horse and cattle thief. After the missionaries explained their purpose, he said that they were welcome to any land that they might select for farming.

The missionaries traveled down the Limhi River, cutting through a narrow valley, and on June 15 stopped at a point about twenty miles above where the river empties into the Salmon River—about two miles north of the present town of Tendoy. After thirty days of travel, they were 333 miles from Ogden, as shown by the odometer they kept on the wheels of their wagons—about 370 miles north of Salt Lake City. At this location the valley was about a mile wide, the hills on the east well wooded. The location of Idaho's first white farming community, "Fort Limhi," was but a few miles from Idaho's first campground of white people at the famous Lewis and Clark Seventeen Mile Camp of 1805.

The site they chose, after conversations with mountaineers and travelers at Fort Hall and vicinity, was the summer home of three different tribes—Bannock, Shoshoni, and Nez Perce. For many years, perhaps millennia, nomadic bands had gone to the spawning beds of the ocean-run salmon. A central place like this was appealing to the missionaries because of the opportunities for service to more than one tribe. Apparently the chief of the Bannock-Shoshoni had urged them to camp there, not farther north. Most of the missionaries liked the valley and prepared to make it their home. Four of them returned to Salt Lake City almost immediately and brought their families back with them.

In the vicinity the missionaries found a large gathering of Bannock, Shoshoni, and Nez Perce who were there on their annual fishing trip. In meetings with these groups, George Washington Hill helped them to understand that the missionaries had come to teach them and would like to remain there if they had no objection. The missionaries were kindly received and were told that they might cut the necessary timber for their houses, corrals, and forts. They might kill game or catch fish for their own sustenance, but must not do so for sale or profit.

Having determined the site of the fort, the new residents dug a 300-yard ditch to convey water for irrigation and planted a garden. Although it was late in the season, they planted potatoes, peas, turnips, and corn, hoping to grow something for winter's supply. As it turned out, the planting was done too late; the crops did not mature, and each blade, as it grew out of the ground, was devoured by grasshoppers that descended in devastating swarms.

A strong corral was built for their horses and cattle, and the missionaries erected a mud-walled fort, sixteen rods square, with separate abodes to last them through the winter. They set twelve-foot logs into a three-foot ditch for a palisade. The fort wall was 2 feet wide, 7 feet high, and 165 feet long, with a gate on the east and one on the west. Thirteen cabins were initially constructed inside the fort; later the number of cabins was doubled. They also set up a blacksmith shop, a sawmill, and a well. The lumber for doors, windows, and floors was all sawed by hand. Every night a strong guard was kept over the fort and the cattle so as to prevent a surprise attack. The men never went to the timber to get logs for lumber or fuel unless they were armed with a rifle and revolver. Some of the rifles were among the first manufactured by Jonathan Browning of Ogden, who later invented the Winchester—"the gun that won the West"—the repeater pistol, the Browning Automatic, and the modern antiaircraft gun.

The summer's labor was arduous. The missionaries later testified that they had never worked so hard in their lives as during that summer. In addition to plowing, planting, and building, they also assisted Indians in their fishing. The run of salmon was such that, with willow traps, as many as 300 were caught in a few hours, weighing from twenty to sixty pounds each. These were sliced thin and hung up to dry on willow scaffolds, with a small fire underneath to smoke the fish. They were then placed inside the skins of larger salmon, tied up in bales, and put away for winter use. The Mormons later sent eight wagons of the smoked salmon with one of the parties returning to Utah.

In the fall, when it became clear that their supplies would run short and that they needed seed for next year's planting, they sent eleven men back to Ogden. The men returned on November 19 with their families and with fresh supplies. When winter set in, in November, a large number of Shoshoni camped near them, expecting the whites, as their declared friends, to share their food. The settlers complied, giving them grain and beef. They soon discovered that their food would be exhausted by spring, so a group was again dispatched to Utah for more supplies, to return by spring. Nine men made this trip, leaving on December 4 with six yoke of oxen and three wagons. Nine inches of snow were on the ground, and as they traveled the altitude increased, the snow became deeper, and the weather grew colder. They arrived in Ogden on December 26, more or less frostbitten and "mighty hungry." The group left Ogden on their return to Limhi on March 28, taking with them not only additional supplies but also twenty-two new missionaries.

Meanwhile, the Limhi colonists, in harmony with Mormon land policy, surveyed twenty-two five-acre lots south of the fort and apportioned them among the colonists by a community lottery, some of those present drawing for those who were absent. They attended classes in the Shoshonean languages (Shoshoni, Paiute) during the winter, three evenings each week, and some of them became quite fluent. Three of the men married Indian women. Meetings were held each Sunday, and more than one hundred natives were baptized.

In the spring of 1856 the colonists planted ninety bushels of wheat, barley, oats, and peas, as well as many garden vegetables. But the grasshoppers hatched their eggs by the millions and the offspring devoured all the young crops, leaving the fields barren. The mission suffered during the summer from want of bread. For weeks they lived on fish, butter, and milk. Because of their failed crops, about nine of the missionaries left for Utah on June 30 to get new supplies and seed wheat. Four new missionaries arrived during the summer. In August two men were sent to carry mail to Utah and presumably to bring some back. Late in the fall three men were sent with additional mail to Utah, with the understanding that they would return in the spring.

In May 1857 Brigham Young and a large entourage of church authorities and their families visited Fort Limhi. The company included many of Young's closest associates—115 men, 22 women, 5 boys, and fifty-three wagons and carriages, with an average of three horses or mules each. Among those on the trip was Milo Andrus, founder of a large Idaho clan (not, however, a direct ancestor of Governor Cecil Andrus, a Missouri Synod Lutheran). The purpose of the trip was to encourage the missionaries at Fort Limhi, but it was also a pioneer equivalent of a vacation to "see the country": the only known occasion when Brigham Young and his associates took along their families and friends with the primary purpose of enjoying the scenery.

The party left Salt Lake City on April 24, traveled to Ogden and up the Malad Valley to Fort Hall and Bannock Creek, and on May 1 reached the Snake River, which they crossed in safety. Reaching Fort Limhi on May 8, the group remained five days. They left for Salt Lake City on May 13, arriving on May 27 after thirty-three days on the trail.[1]

In a meeting at the fort, Young told the missionaries that they had settled so far from "home" in Utah that immediate help could not be sent if needed. He thought they should have stopped near the Blackfoot River, just north of Fort Hall. Otherwise, he was pleased with their work. Now that they had settled at Limhi, he would strengthen the mission to give it greater chance of success. The men were exhorted to be patient and kind, to encourage and instruct the Indians, and to do everything possible to create good feelings. Young held conferences with Tio-van-du-ah (Snag), head chief of the Shoshoni, and had a smoke and long friendly talk with him. Snag, who succeeded Cameahwait as leader of the Lemhi Shoshoni, was quite possibly a nephew of Sacagawea. Young gave him presents of blankets and other goods. Arrapeen, head chief of the Utahs, had come with Young's party, and he participated in these conversations.

Young made a major effort to acquire Fort Hall and almost succeeded; but the federal government had other ideas. One other consequence of the visit was the formation of an exploring party to go farther north to investigate possibilities of establishing other settlements. The party explored the Bitterroot Valley and the Deer Lodge and other valleys in what later became Montana, including the locations where now stand Butte, Helena, the Flathead Reservation, the Big Salmon Forest, and other places along the Lewis and Clark Trail. Although nothing resulted at the time from this effort, some of the Salmon River missionaries drove teams to supply foodstuffs to miners in these regions after the discovery of gold in the 1860s.

The settlers continued to have trouble with grasshoppers in 1857, but they succeeded in raising a fair crop of potatoes and other vegetables and 2,500 bushels of wheat. They had demonstrated that grain could be raised on the headwaters of the Salmon River. They built a gristmill and dug additional irrigating ditches and a large canal.

Threshing was done by oxen and flails and separated by a fanning mill. The ground was cleared in a circle about thirty feet in diameter and grain was laid lengthwise along the edge of the circle about six sheaves wide. The center of the ring was left bare. Five or six yoke of oxen were then fastened together, one yoke after another, forming a circle, while the driver occupied the center of the circle, driving them in a continuous round. In this way the grain was thoroughly tramped out. The straw was then pitched away while the chaff and grain were pushed into the center of the ring. The edge was again filled with fresh sheaves and the process repeated again and again until a large stack of chaff and grain was in the center of the ring. With the completion of the threshing, the next step was placing the grain in front of the fanning mill to clean it.

In September, as the threshing was being done, two of the men were sent back to Utah to carry the mail and reassure everyone that the mission had raised good crops and had maintained peace with the Indians.

When the men reached Utah, however, they learned of an occurrence that proved to be catastrophic. A federal army of 2,500 men, "the Utah Expedition," was headed for Utah to discipline the Mormons. Disgruntled Utah officeholders had gone to President James Buchanan in Washington and declared that the Mormons were plotting to set up an independent republic, were insubordinate to federal authority, and were conniving with Indian tribes to subvert federal control. Without notifying Brigham Young, governor of the territory, Buchanan appointed a new governor, Alfred Cumming of Georgia, and sent a major force of the U.S. Army to establish and maintain federal dominion. Since they had not been notified and since the troops had been dispatched with much secrecy, the Mormons concluded that the troops were coming to conquer them, to drive them out of their homes, as had been done in Missouri in the 1830s and in Illinois in 1846. Brigham Young and his associates issued a proclamation—"We are being invaded"—declared martial law, and made preparations to defend their homes.[2]

Despite this danger to their Utah refuge, word of which had come to Brigham Young on July 24, 1857, Mormon leaders followed through with their promise to strengthen the Salmon River Mission by calling, in the fall of 1857, an additional thirty-two men, some of them with wives and children, to join the settlers at Fort Limhi. Most of them were from the Farmington area of Utah. They started north in October, following the route first taken in 1855, and reached Fort Limhi on October 27 after twenty-five days on the trail. The Salmon River colony now consisted of one hundred souls.

One would be surprised if the arrival of these additional settlers did not cause the Shoshoni-Bannock to view the growth of the Mormon colony with some concern. They were likely already provoked by the cutting of timber, the two hundred cattle pastured on the meadows, the shipment of salmon to Utah, and the repeated trades with the Nez Perce—who sometimes fought the Shoshoni-Bannock. Now here was evidence of intended permanent and extended settlement.

With the added personnel at Limhi, the missionaries built a new "Lower Fort," four miles below (north of) Limhi, thereby increasing the acreage and giving more room for new arrivals. Milton D. Hammond, a twenty-six-year-old veteran of a Michigan regiment in the Mexican War of 1846–48, was appointed president of the new little community.

Trouble began at Limhi in the early winter of 1857–58. It was apparently touched off by mountaineers. Many of them had spent time in Missouri, where there had been anti-Mormon feeling since 1831; some had visited the camps of the Utah Expedition and had willingly imbibed the prejudices against the Mormons expressed by the soldiers and officers. But there were other troubles. The missionaries maintained friendships with tribes that were enemies of each other. The Mormon friendship with the Nez Perce, for example, was an offense to the Bannock and Shoshoni, even though the many favors rendered to them were even more substantial than the friendship extended to the Nez Perce.

On December 21, forty lodges of Shoshoni arrived at the fort. The Shoshoni—who, unknown to the missionaries at the time, were returning from a raid on the Nez Perce—were treated kindly and were fed by the mission. A few days later a band of Nez Perce arrived looking for stolen horses. They also were treated kindly and fed, were "put up" in the log houses, and their animals were placed in the fort corral. The Bannock, more enterprising and warlike than the Shoshoni, had planned a raid on the Nez Perce horses and were frustrated and offended that the Mormons had put the horses in their corral.[3] There was a contention between the Nez Perce and Bannock, but the trouble was smoothed over by Thomas Smith, the Limhi president. They smoked a pipe of peace, and the Nez Perce left the next day in good spirits. But that was just a facade, for that night they returned and stole some fifty Shoshoni and Bannock horses—at least, this is what the Shoshoni reported to the missionaries. The Bannock vowed to punish the Mormons, who, they thought, were instruments in the damage done to them by the Nez Perce.

On January 13, 1858, six of the men at the fort were sent out to their herd some miles away. On their arrival, they found one or two cattle gone. They went in pursuit of the Indians and after twenty miles found them in possession of meat from one of the oxen whose carcass had been found eight miles back. The missionaries demanded a horse to pay for the slaughtered cattle. The Indians complied but bided their time.

In February a volunteer officer in the Utah Expedition was in the Bitterroot Valley seeking recruits for an onslaught on the fort to carry off the cattle and sell them to the army. Upon learning this, John Owen, Indian Agent in the Bitterroot Valley, persuaded the mountaineers to abandon participation in the scheme to steal the livestock because of the good that the missionaries were accomplishing with the Indians.

On February 7, a large band of Shoshoni arrived at the fort on their way to fight the Nez Perce. They demanded to be fed and housed and the demand was met. They left the next day. Two days later an Indian stole the horse of President Thomas Smith. A company was sent out; they found the horse eighty miles east of the fort. Sensing difficulties, leaders moved the families in the lower settlement into the fort on February 11. On February 24, a mountaineer rode into the camp and warned the missionaries that the Indians were talking of burning their haystacks and stealing their horses and cattle. They took some precautions, but not enough.

The very next day, February 25, some two hundred Bannock and Shoshoni galloped toward the Limhi cattle herd, grazing two miles from the fort. Seeing their approach, a party of ten men from the fort rode out to protect the herd. The Indians reached the herd first and began to encircle the cattle. George McBride "waved his hat around his head a few times, a veritable challenge, uttered a yell, dashed over the hill and down among the Indians" in a brave attempt to turn the cattle back. The Indians shot him and took his horse. He was later found scalped and stripped of his revolver and clothing. Orson Rose, who happened to be on the side of the herd nearest the fort, dropped into heavy sagebrush when the firing commenced. The Indians riddled the brush with shot but did not hit him. He hid until night and returned safely to the fort. President Smith and Ezra Barnard hastened toward the herd to save it. The Indians fired at them. Smith was wounded but managed to return safely to the fort. Fountain Welch was wounded, as were several others;

James Miller was killed. The Indians drove off the entire herd, consisting of 235 cattle and 31 ponies. Several herders barely escaped, and one of them, who had been missing, was later found dead, scalped, and stripped.

For the next two weeks, the men at the fort spent their time in building bastions, strengthening the fort, digging holes in which to cache their wheat and other provisions, and standing guard. On February 28, three days after the attack, President Smith held a camp meeting at which it was decided to send a dispatch to Brigham Young asking his advice on the proper course to pursue. Two men were chosen to carry the dispatch. With trepidation, they left in the night and with good luck were able to slip past the hostiles.

On March 5, three Shoshoni came to the fort as delegates, they said, of the Shoshoni chiefs. They said they wanted to make peace and were willing to bring back the cattle. They said they had only thirty head, as the Bannock had taken the remainder and all the horses. Three days later they brought back twenty-eight cattle. On March 11, they brought back eight more. The Indians now said that a majority of the stolen cattle had been driven to the army at Soda Springs and exchanged for items that the Indians desired.

Those who have studied the matter carefully believe that the causes of the attack are complex. Apparently the Bannock were the chief perpetrators. There is considerable evidence that they were encouraged by mountaineers who charged that the Mormons were planning to take over their lands and drive off the game. The Bannock were also incensed by the friendly treatment the Mormons had given the Nez Perce. Brigham Madsen concludes that the Bannock were encouraged to engage in their age-old custom of horse-stealing and war because the Nez Perce had stolen their horses, which called for retaliation and replacement; white traders in Beaverhead, having been commissioned by the Army, had advertised they would pay high prices for cattle and horses; and the war of the United States against the Mormons assured the Indians that any hostile action would result only in applause, not punishment.[4]

Meanwhile, the two missionaries sent to Brigham Young arrived in Salt Lake City after some narrow escapes. The president ordered Colonel Thomas Cunningham of the militia, with 100 mounted men and twenty wagons laden with needed provisions, to accompany the missionaries back to Fort Limhi. Another company of fifty, under twenty-five-year-old Captain Horton D. Haight, started from Farmington. An advance contingent of these relief expeditions arrived in the fort on March 21. They took with them Young's instructions to abandon the mission and return to Utah. Ten men immediately were sent to Utah with the mail and various other properties. As they neared the Bannock range, while passing through the narrows on Bannock Creek, they were ambushed by Indians and one of the men was killed and scalped; a horse and mule were also killed.

After a few days of preparation Fort Limhi was abandoned and left in the hands of the Indians. As they left, Thomas Smith gave one thousand bushels of mission wheat to Chief Snag, who had been baptized a Mormon and who, along with his followers, wept at the departure of the Mormons. The missionaries arrived in Ogden on April 11. Two births had occurred on the way, but the passage was safe and without serious incident.

When the men reached their northern Utah communities, they discovered to their dismay that their and their neighbors' homes were empty. Most of the people in northern Utah had packed up and gone south—to central and southern Utah. As the federal army had approached Utah in the summer and fall of 1857, the Utah militia had slowed them and delayed them by a variety of tactics, forcing them to "hole up" at Fort Bridger, then in Utah Territory. President Buchanan had been informed of the falsity of the charges that had been made against the Utah Mormons and had sent out a presidential commission to achieve a peaceful solution to the conflict. But the army, under Albert Sidney Johnston, would certainly head for the Salt Lake Valley when the snows melted in the spring, and Brigham Young was fearful that they would seek to occupy the Mormon metropolis and that some of the more belligerent Saints would give them an excuse to start shooting. In a dramatic gesture to win national sympathy, Brigham Young asked his followers, on March 18, 1858, to abandon their homes and move south. Some 30,000 made the move in the weeks that followed, and they included most of the families of the Salmon River missionaries. Within a day or two, most of the missionaries were on the road to try to find their families. After the federal army marched through the Salt Lake Valley on June 28 and went on to establish Camp Floyd forty miles to the south, northern Utah settlers were instructed to return home.

Thus ended the Salmon River Mission; the Mormons had not been able to maintain a settlement at Limhi. Later, a government reservation was established a little above the Limhi location, which began to appear on maps as Fort Lemhi and the Lemhi Valley Indian reservation. Not surprisingly, there were things that none of the missionaries could forget—the beauty of the country, the productivity of the soil, and the friendliness of most of the Indians.

Several of the men later moved to Idaho Territory to make their homes. Among them were Thomas S. Smith, leader of the mission, who went to Wilford, a beautiful tract lying between Henry's Fork and Teton River, where he served as one of the first settlers and bishop. Another was Horton D. Haight, leader of one of the rescue groups, who later moved to Oakley and served as bishop and as first Cassia Stake President of that Latter-day Saint community. He was a Cassia County Commissioner and president of the Oakley Cooperative Mercantile Institution. Captain Haight's chief lieutenant, Thomas E. Ricks, later returned to the Upper Snake River Valley to found

Rexburg and other Mormon settlements in the region. Even Brigham Young, in his brief journey to the fort in 1857, was impressed with the country. After the end of the Utah War episode, he encouraged families to settle northern Cache Valley, Malad Valley, and points north and west. As a result, the first permanent non-Indian settlement in what is now Idaho was made by Latter-day Saints in Franklin in 1860.

## CHAPTER EIGHT: SOURCES

On the Salmon River Mission I have relied heavily on John V. Bluth, "The Salmon River Mission," *Improvement Era* (Salt Lake City) 3 (September, October 1900):801–815, 900–913; Brigham D. Madsen, *The Bannock of Idaho* (Caldwell: Caxton Printers, 1958), 84–110; and John D. Nash, "The Salmon River Mission of 1855: A Reappraisal," *Idaho Yesterdays* 11 (Spring 1967):22–31. Other important sources include "The Salmon River Mission: The Founding of Fort Lemhi," in Beal, *History of Southeastern Idaho*, 136–52; "The Salmon River Mission," in Milton R. Hunter, *Brigham Young the Colonizer* (Independence, Mo.: Zion's Printing and Publishing, 1945), 334–41; Kate B. Carter, ed., "The Salmon River Mission," in *Our Pioneer Heritage*, 20 vols. (Salt Lake City: Daughters of Utah Pioneers, 1958–78), 7:141–200; "The Salmon River Mission, 1855–1858," in Beal and Wells, *History of Idaho*, 1:242–65; David L. Crowder, *Tendoy: Chief of the Lemhis* (Caldwell: Caxton Printers, 1969), 30–37; Henry L. Talkington, *Heroes and Heroic Deeds of the Pacific Northwest* (Caldwell: Caxton Printers, 1942); W. W. Henderson, ed., "The Salmon River Mission: Organization and Founding," *Utah Historical Quarterly* 5 (January 1932):3–24; William G. Hartley, "Dangerous Mission at Fort Limhi," in *Kindred Saints: The Mormon Immigrant Heritage of Alvin and Kathryne Christenson* (Salt Lake City: Eden Hill, 1982), 71–83; and Charles E. Dibble, "The Mormon Mission to the Shoshoni Indians," *Utah Humanities Review* [now *Western Humanities Review*] 1 (January, April, July 1947):53–73, 166–77, 279–93.

There are many original manuscripts in the LDS Church Library-Archives, Salt Lake City. The most important of these are the "Manuscript History of the Salmon River Mission," the 1855–58 diary of Thomas S. Smith, president of the mission; and the journal of David Moore, clerk of the mission. The library-archives also has the diaries and personal histories of about twenty other participants in the mission.

38.

38. This Fort Lemhi cabin, built in 1856, was one of a cluster of cabins that housed the Latter-day Saint colony at Lemhi, the first white settlement in east-central Idaho. ISHS 166–F.

## CHAPTER NINE

# The Gold Rush of the Early 1860s

EXCEPT for the Mormons at Franklin, the settlement of Idaho and the creation of Idaho Territory were indirect outgrowths of the gold rush to California. Some 300,000 Americans, Mexicans, Chinese, and South Americans had rushed to California after James Marshall's discovery of gold at Sutter's Fort in 1848. As that Eldorado began to play out, gold seekers rushed to the Fraser River in British Columbia in 1858, to the Comstock Lode in western Nevada and Pike's Peak in Colorado in 1859, and then to northern Idaho and Montana in 1860–62.

Elias Davidson Pierce is credited with the discovery that led to Idaho's first gold rush. A native of Ireland who migrated to Virginia in 1839, he was practicing law in Indiana when, at the age of twenty-four, he volunteered to serve in the Mexican War. There he earned the rank of captain. Shortly after his discharge he joined the California gold rush as both prospector and trader. He served in the California legislature in 1852 and later that year he joined a retired Hudson's Bay Company trapper on a trip to the Nez Perce country, where he did some trading. He was attracted by the stories of the presence of gold and looked for an opportunity to return. In 1857 he was back trading in the Nez Perce country, but Indian turmoils signified that the time was not yet ripe for prospecting. In 1858 he joined the throng of prospectors going to the Fraser River in British Columbia, north of Lake Okanagan. He returned to the new town of Walla Walla, in Washington, where he tried farming and cattle raising.

Shortly before, the United States Army had defeated the Coeur d'Alene, so at least a part of eastern Washington and northern Idaho was safe for whites. (At the time what is now Idaho was in Washington Territory, and it remained so until 1863.) Remembering his earlier Nez Perce experience, Pierce smuggled a prospecting outfit into the camp of his Nez Perce friend Wislanaeqa. What he found excited him. The Nez Perce had signed a treaty with the whites in 1855 establishing a large Nez Perce reservation in central Idaho. Pierce tried to interest the tribe in letting him and others open mines on the reservation. The Nez Perce refused; they could not understand the white man's eager search for gold and did not want whites on the reservation. Undeterred, Pierce went to Walla Walla, attracted ten returnees from Fraser River, and in August sneaked by Nez Perce guides to establish a camp on the north fork of the Clearwater.

Traveling on foot toward the Clearwater country, Pierce and his party encountered a Nez Perce camp near what is now Lewiston. He attempted to persuade Chief Timothy, who had been converted to Christianity by the Spaldings, that he should allow whites to pass through the reservation to prospect. The Nez Perce were strongly opposed, but the chief restrained his people from using force to prevent Pierce and his associates from prospecting. There is a legend that Chief Timothy's eighteen-year-old daughter, with the Christian name of Jane, guided them past the modern site of Moscow and then southeast near present-day

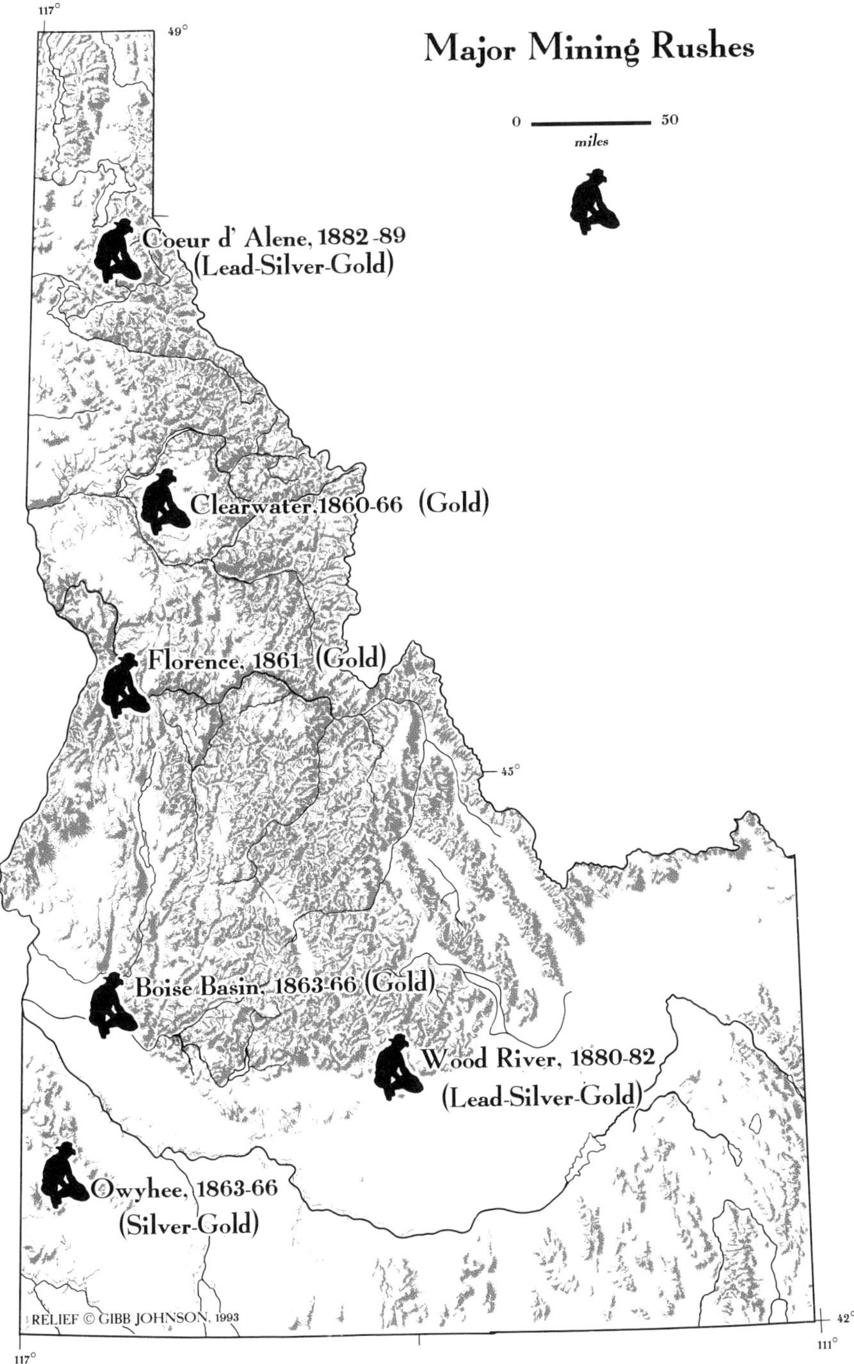
Major Mining Rushes
0 50
miles
117°
49°
Coeur d' Alene, 1882-89
(Lead-Silver-Gold)
Clearwater, 1860-66 (Gold)
Florence, 1861 (Gold)
45°
Boise Basin, 1863-66 (Gold)
Wood River, 1880-82
(Lead-Silver-Gold)
Owyhee, 1863-66
(Silver-Gold)
RELIEF © GIBB JOHNSON, 1993
42°
117°
111°

Kendrick. Recent historians have expressed doubt about the story of Jane (later Jane Silcott) and believe the guide, if there was one, was a young Indian male.[1]

In the Clearwater Valley, about 150 miles from Walla Walla, the group prospected forty miles of rivers and creeks. One afternoon, said to have been September 30, they camped at the mouth of Canal Creek, a tributary of Orofino Creek, itself a tributary of the south branch of the Clearwater River. A member of the party, Wilbur F. Bassett, a carpenter, dug up a shovelful of dirt that contained "flour gold"—also called "oro fino," Spanish for "fine gold." The enterprise was a success.

Pierce returned to Walla Walla with something less than $100 in gold dust. There he organized a party under the leadership of Sergeant John Calhoun Smith to go to Canal Gulch in November. Pierce City was founded on December 3. During the winter the group staked off seventy-one claims; built cabins; sawed lumber for rockers, a long sluice, and sluice boxes; and continued prospecting. They employed proven techniques and equipment used in other gold fields.

Following the California example, the men held an open meeting on January 5, 1861, to organize the Oro Fino Mining District to govern the territory surrounding Oro Fino Creek. They elected officers and drafted rules. The twenty-four rules of this first mining district in Idaho included, for example:

1. All American citizens may locate and hold claims.

2. Each mining claim shall consist of 150 feet from the place of beginning and running up or down the gulch or stream upon which it may be located, and extending from bluff to bluff on said gulch or stream, unless said bluffs be more than 250 feet from each other.

3. [Because claims could not be worked in the winter] No claim shall be considered forfeited from the first of December to the first of June, on Oro Fino Creek, nor on the tributaries thereof, from the first of December until the first of April.

4. All claims shall be considered forfeited within fifteen days from said dates if not worked.

5. All claims shall be worked at least one day in seven, otherwise they are considered forfeited.

12. Any citizen may hold one creek, one hill, and one ravine claim.

14. Any person disabled by sickness shall not forfeit his claim.

15. Claims shall be distinctly marked by notices at each end of the bounds thereof, in the name of the claimant, and no more ground shall be deemed claimed than are included in such notices.

16. Any person, who by proof, shall pull down or destroy any notice on any mining claim, or the laws of this district, shall be fined in any sum that the miner's court of enquiry may direct.

17. No person who may hold a mining claim, shall forfeit said claim by reason of being compelled to leave the district for provisions for himself or company; Provided, he does not absent himelf for a longer period than twenty-five days.

18. Any person or persons who may have grievance to settle, shall do so by arbitration; each party choosing a person to settle the matter, and in case they cannot agree, for the two arbiters to choose a third arbiter, a majority of whom shall settle the difference; and in case they do not settle the matter, then a call for a miners' meeting, who shall assemble and settle such matter as they may deem fit.

24. These laws to be amended hereafter, at the option of the miners, and to take effect from and after their passage.

M. More, Chairman
John W. Park, secretary[2]

"M. More," the chairman who signed the proclamation, may have been J. Marion More, a native of Tennessee, who had gone to California in 1850, joined the Clearwater rush in 1861, represented the miners in the Washington legislature in 1861, and lobbied for the creation of a new territory for the miners.[3] He and his colleagues in the Oro Fino District set up a do-it-yourself kind of jurisprudence that had been widely applied in California, Nevada, and Colorado and would apply until county government was established. (Local laws were recognized by the federal government in 1866 and codified into laws in 1872.) Because the men had made their own rules, they felt free to take the law into their own hands if there was violence or robbery. Little attention was paid to due process.

Early in 1861 Sergeant Smith returned to Walla Walla with $800 worth of gold dust. The dust was shipped to Portland, and within days—just about the time of the booming of cannon at Fort Sumter, South Carolina—hundreds of fortune-seekers were on their way to Pierce City. A new mining camp, Oro Fino, was founded about two miles from Pierce City and about forty miles north of the present Idaho city of the same name.

In this beautiful Clearwater Valley, surrounded on all sides by trees, one thousand persons were reported present by May 1861, including two hundred French, Spanish, Mexicans, and Dutch, and about a dozen families with women and children. The steamer *Colonel Wright* operated on the Snake River, which meant that miners could ship to within fifty or sixty miles of the mines. An enterprising young Nez Perce named Reuben built a ferry across the Snake River at the mouth of the Clearwater, which suggests that at least some of the Nez Perce were not objecting to this "invasion" of their land so long as it did not interfere with their hunting and root lands. There was widespread belief that this was the biggest find since the California gold fields of 1849. Word was that a man could make eight to ten dollars a day.

Although the original miners in Pierce City were mostly from Oregon and Washington, those arriving in the summer of 1861 and succeeding years were mostly from California or returnees from the Fraser River stampede. The men chartered steamers from Victoria and San Francisco and then went up the Columbia to the confluence of the Snake and Clearwater rivers. A leading steamer on the Columbia was the *Idaho*—a name that had originally been proposed in 1859 for Colorado Territory and that was still used at Idaho Springs, a small village beneath Mount Evans west of Denver. Because so many of the miners en route to Clearwater area had sailed on the *Idaho*, persons often referred to them as Idahoans, a name that proved to be prophetic.

Steamship passengers landed at a location on Indian land where, in June 1861, the town of Lewiston was established. Named after Meriwether Lewis (of Lewis and Clark fame), the town for a year or two had so many tent houses that it was nicknamed "rag town." Overnighters could stay at the Luna House, a flimsy structure with canvas roof and walls and an earthen floor, managed by Hill Beachy, of whom more later. In 1862 eggs were $1 per dozen, butter $1 per pound, and whisky $3 to $5 per gallon.

One of those who rushed to the Idaho mines in 1862 was Alonzo Leland, a native of Vermont who had gone to Oregon in 1850. He lost his Idaho mine to claim-jumpers and returned to Lewiston to help John H. Scranton and others establish a newspaper, *The Golden Age*—Idaho's first and its leading newspaper until 1863.

Some contemporaries complained of the lawlessness around Lewiston. Such outlaw activity appeared near most of the gold mines. Among so many men with so little governmental supervision some foul play was inevitable. In the summer of 1862 gangs of highwaymen occasionally held up a miner thought to be carrying dust, so even complete strangers often banded together and traveled in groups to be able to defend themselves if held up. Pat Ford, who conducted a Spanish dancehouse in Oro Fino, was killed by one of these groups, supposedly because he recognized some of them and would betray them.[4]

That same summer Henry Plummer, a professional gambler,

was in north Idaho for a month or two. There were contemporary rumors that he operated one roadhouse between Lewiston and Walla Walla and another between Lewiston and Oro Fino and that he and his "gang" robbed men of valuable property. Historical research has failed to find solid evidence to support these accusations. Later Plummer was hanged by a vigilante group in Montana. (At the time Plummer was hanged the area was still Idaho, but no one today thinks of the vigilantes of Virginia City, *Idaho.*) Men in Lewiston formed their own vigilante group in 1863 and arrested and hanged three men for the robberies of three miners. Other outlaws fled.

By the end of June 1861 about 3,000 men resided in the mines, and more were coming in by the hundreds. Impatient with the failure of Olympia to organize the area politically, the miners held a mass meeting at which Shoshone County—the first county in what is now Idaho—was organized and officers elected. The two-story log courthouse at Pierce City, still standing and one of the oldest public buildings in Idaho, served as Shoshone County's official courthouse until 1884. Application was made for a post office. The community was thriving. Many thousands of dollars in gold dust were being carried out at every opportunity. By the middle of the summer of 1861, according to the contemporary Oregon City *Statesman*, Oro Fino had six restaurants, two hotels, twenty whiskey shops, ten gambling saloons, two bakeries, one watchmaker, thirty stores, one bookstore, one barbershop, four meat markets, three doctors' offices—in all, seventy-five buildings.

There were northerners and southerners, farmers and professors, stoics and profligates, preachers and merchants. There was plenty to quarrel about, even to fight about. It is remarkable that there was so little crime. In the end, wrote W. A. Goulder, who spent four years in the Clearwater region in the early 1860s, they "were fused and blended and moulded into a people that have given us the model political community that we are today proud to call the State of Idaho."[5]

Captain Pierce had always believed that the "show" of gold at Pierce City was an indication of a rich central deposit that would eventually be found in the Clearwater region. Prospectors spread out in every direction. One group of fifty-two left Oro Fino in May 1861 to explore the south fork of the Clearwater. The Nez Perce warned them that the area was closed, and half of the group turned back. Willing to risk war—or perhaps quite sure that the Nez Perce would stop short of that alternative—the other half obstinately continued when Nez Perce backs were turned. In June, with no Indian intervention, they found gold at a place they called Elk City about sixty miles south of Pierce and Oro Fino. Gold was also found at Newsome, a few miles northwest of Elk City.

Another party of twenty-three left Oro Fino in July 1861 and on August 12 found gold on the Salmon River, fifty miles southwest of Elk City and about 110 miles southeast of Lewiston. There were showings in several locations, but the basic settlement was placed at Florence, where the Summit District was organized on September 16. These mines were also within the Nez Perce reservation. The Indians took the strongest measures short of war to prevent a rush, but without success.

From the workings at Pierce City and Oro Fino, Elk City and Newsome, and the Florence area about $3 million worth of gold dust was transported down the Columbia by express companies on Oregon Steam Navigation Company boats. Much more may have been carried out personally by the miners. (The Oregon Steam Navigation Company had been formed in 1860, as if in anticipation of the Idaho miners' rush that began in 1861.)

The winter of 1861–62 was severe and prolonged, not only in the mining areas but throughout the Northwest. The Clearwater, the Snake, and even the Columbia froze over; boat transportation was impossible. Cattle died by the thousands, as did many travelers and settlers. Despite the heavy snowfall, ice-choked streams, and bitter wind, the trails to Oro Fino and to Florence were kept open. Some miners using Norwegian snowshoes (skis) succeeded in beating their way through.[6] The nearby Nez Perce, having been taught principles of compassion and helpfulness by the missionaries, furnished food, medicine, and other supplies.[7] (Judging by their treatment of Lewis and Clark, they might have done so anyway.)

The long winter evenings were devoted to reading old newspapers and available books. Goulder found one person who had a nearly complete set of the novels of the Sir Walter Scott. His cabinmates agreed to buy the books if Goulder would read them aloud evenings. In the process Goulder read aloud all of Scott's stories except *The Fair Maid of Perth*, which he decided was unsuitable for "a wild mining camp." Goulder also says there were games of chess and weekly meetings of the Oro Fino Lyceum and Debating Club.[8]

There was drinking, of course. Saloonkeepers employed men to carry kegs of alcohol, together with what Goulder called vials of chemicals that would convert the alcohol into the "mildly exhilarating fluids of various names and colors, and flavors to suit the whims and tastes of his customers." Wrote Goulder: "With my own eyes I have seen a very superior quality of both Bourbon and Cognac manufactured in five minutes from alcohol, water, and burnt sugar, with a slight admixture of other ingredients, the compound equaling, in its most desired effects, the best imported beverages of the most ancient vintage."[9]

Beginning in 1862, tired of waiting for government service, the miners employed Israel Burr Cowen, a native of Wisconsin who had gone to California in 1849 and remained there twelve years, to carry the mail the eighty miles each way between Pierce City and Lewiston. He used snowshoes during the winter. He also served as probate judge for Shoshone County, was later sheriff, and still later a county commissioner. Cowen performed the mail service on foot, taking ten days each way, carrying a load of between sixty and eighty pounds on his back, in addition to his blankets and provisions. The task was rendered all the more difficult because he was club-footed, his crippled foot making a track at right angles with the other.[10]

Another who carried mail and express between Lewiston and Pierce City in the early sixties was Joaquin Miller (Cincinnatus Heine Miller), who subsequently went to Oregon and also served as a pony express messenger. He later achieved recognition for his poetry, especially in England, where he attained fame as a frontier poet—"The Byron of Oregon." Unfortunately, some of his statements about Idaho in his autobiographical *Memorie and Rime* (1884) are not entirely trustworthy.

As word of the richness of the Salmon River mines spread, several thousand Argonauts moved in. Approximately 10,000 flocked to that basin in June 1862. But not enough mines existed to serve all the newcomers at any of the locations, so many of the new arrivals turned elsewhere for possible opportunities. Among these was James Warren, who on July 22, 1862, organized a settlement just south of the Salmon called Warrens. (Secesh Valley in the Warrens District was named for the many Confederates who worked there.) Another group went south to prospect in Boise Basin.

The Florence area gave the richest promise. Situated near the center of a high basin surrounded by snow-capped mountains, the hundreds of burning campfires gave the appearance of an army camp. Because of the high altitude Florence had severe frost almost every night during the summer of 1862, and on July 3 of that year there was a blinding snowstorm. Nevertheless prospectors continued to come, not only from California and the Pacific Northwest, but also from Missouri, Minnesota, and Colorado, by riverboat, horseback, and stagecoach.

In the summer of 1862 one party heading for the Salmon River mines strayed from its course long enough to prospect on the upper Missouri, then on the westernmost border of Dakota Territory. Their discovery of gold at Grasshopper Creek and the organization of a miners' district at East Bannack in August

1862 resulted in a miners' rush to what is now western Montana. Many of the miners left Florence and headed for East Bannack by the Nez Perce Trail. When prospectors discovered Alder Gulch early in 1863, Virginia City (Montana) became a new mining center. There were more than 11,000 people in Madison County, where Alder Gulch was located, by 1864. An even more important discovery was made that year in Last Chance Gulch, from which Helena emerged. Clearly it was becoming more and more difficult to administer Washington Territory from Olympia and, to the east, Dakota Territory from Yankton.

In the meantime the throng of prospectors spreading over the region discovered gold in the Boise Basin on August 2, 1862. The members of this little party, led by George Grimes and Moses Splawn, had scarcely reached the scene of their discovery before they were reportedly attacked by hostile Indians and Grimes was killed. The group went back to Walla Walla, recruited additional prospectors, and returned to the basin to resume their search. They found paying quantities of dust at several locations, with some claims extraordinarily rich. William Purvine reported from Grimes Creek on October 14 that the new placers were yielding $18 a day. The mad rush was on.

J. Marion More led the party that on October 7 founded Bannack, which became the leading city in the basin. Because the reinforced Grimes-Splawn party claimed all the workable properties in the area of their first discovery, latecomers named it the Hog-Em District (later named Pioneerville) and went on to found other districts at Placerville, Centerville, Buena Vista, and West Bannack (later named Idaho City). More reported that a claim near Placerville had been returning $300 per day and that Lyman Shaffer had found a good quartz lode there. Reports of astonishingly rich claims kept the rush going throughout most of the winter, with a speed-up in the spring of 1863. At Placerville ditches were dug, sluices installed, and miners were hard at work using the water in the spring run-off. By June the

Placerville area had a population of 2,000, eighty-seven frame and log houses, thirteen saloons, five blacksmith shops, seven restaurants, and five meat markets that dispensed two tons of beef daily.[11] By the end of 1863, 16,000 miners lived in Boise Basin, and they had taken out $6 million in gold dust.

Thirty miles in a straight line northeast of the present city of Boise, the basin was a deep, saucer-like, timbered tract of 150 square miles among the mountains. Five hundred miles from Olympia and continuing to increase in numbers, the miners in the basin could hardly be denied having their own territory. More, who continued to represent them in the Washington Legislature, lobbied with the hope of establishing a new territory.

Most of the thousand who joined the 1863 rush to the basin sailed up the Columbia to Umatilla and then took a pack train or saddle train over the Blue Mountains, through the Grande Ronde Valley, and across a long stretch of alkaline desert to the diggings. The first saddle train, which arrived in the Boise Basin in April 1863 with sixteen passengers, was under the management of John Hailey. A native of Tennessee who had moved to Missouri, Hailey went to Oregon in 1853 when he was eighteen and moved on to the Florence mines in 1862. There he decided to become a packer and stage driver in time to serve the rush to Boise Basin in 1863–64. He later became Idaho's delegate to Congress and secretary of the Idaho State Historical Society, and he wrote an informative *History of Idaho* that generations of readers have found fascinating. Stage service to the Boise rushers was also provided by the noted transportation entrepreneur Ben Holladay, who had established the Overland Stage Line from Kansas to Salt Lake City and triweekly service from Salt Lake City to Boise and Walla Walla.

Within a year of its founding, Idaho City (still called West Bannack with the Montana spelling) had 6,167 people, including 360 women and 224 children, and 250 businesses. These included a printing office, eight bakeries, nine restaurants, twenty-five saloons, forty variety stores, fifteen doctors, twenty-five attorneys, seven blacksmith shops, four sawmills, two dentists, three express offices, five auctioneers, three drugstores, four butcher shops, three billiard tables, two bowling alleys, three painters, one photographer, three livery stables, four breweries, one harness shop, one mattress factory, and two jewelers.[12] There were also Protestant and Catholic churches, a school, a hospital, and a theater. Three additional theaters were founded the ensuing winter. Idaho City was now the largest city in the Northwest, even greater than Portland.

The rush was filling the basin. By the end of September 1863, Placerville had 3,254 people; Fort Hogem or Pioneer City, 2,743; and Centerville, 2,638. Boise City, which had just been founded in July, had about one thousand. Many of the newcomers had come from north Idaho. By the fall of 1863 Pierce City was down to 508; Florence, 575; Warrens, 660; Elk City, 472; and Lewiston, 414. Of the 16,000 in the basin, about half were miners and the other half merchants, artisans, and professional people.[13] The *Boise News* was first published September 29, 1863, on a printing press secured from Walla Walla. One of the newspaper carriers was James H. Hawley, later governor of Idaho and author of a four-volume *History of Idaho*. A large number of newcomers were emigrants from Missouri and Arkansas, bent on escaping the guerrilla warfare in their states. They brought "nice" girls, and there were many marriages.

To protect the miners from hostile Indians a military post was established on the Boise River on July 4, 1863, and called Fort Boise. The military had reached Boise on June 30 and selected their fort site on July 4, the day of Lee's battle at Gettysburg and Grant's capture of Vicksburg. The new Fort Boise had no connection with the old Hudson's Bay Company trading post that went under the same name. The location of the new fort, with its tasteful buildings of sandstone and fine parade ground, was the beginning of Boise City—platted July 7 by a small group of local settlers. Boise City thus arose as a trading, not a mining, town, and a year and a half later it was also the state capital. Located in the center of a smooth valley of the Boise River—a valley about fifty miles long by five or six in width—it had an agricultural capacity and was soon producing food for the miners and feed for the livestock. By the fall of 1865 it had about 2,000 inhabitants. An eastern journalist who visited was impressed: "The broad, level, treeless avenues, with their low, white, verandahed warehouses, log-cabins, neat cottages and ever-shifting panorama of wagons and coaches, Indians, miners, farmers, and speculators remind one of a prairie town in Kansas or Iowa."[14]

In tandem with the mining boom came a steady growth of farmers and homesteaders hoping to earn income by filling the demand for food and feed. In 1864 Robert, John, and Alexander McKenzie joined the goldseekers moving eastward along the Oregon Trail to the new Eldorado in Boise Basin. They stopped at a pleasant site on the Boise River just north of Black Canyon, about twenty-five miles downriver from Boise. There they built a cabin where Robert's wife came to live the next year. Some other families settled on the strip of land bordering the river at a community later called Middleton. Many of them were refugees from the Confederate South; others were mostly from the Midwest. Some of these people cleared land and planted crops. The venture proved profitable: peddlers came by every week or two to buy whatever the settlers had to sell and take it to the mines. Ninety percent of the heads of household in Middleton in the 1870 census were farmers or farm workers, many of whom also had ties with nearby mining areas. Nearly all the land between Boise City and the canyon was claimed by such would-be homesteaders. So well developed did the farming become that a gristmill was founded at Middleton in 1869.[15]

The rush to Boise Basin kept up during the winter of 1863–64 and gained momentum during the spring. Production figures for the richer claims were high. On one of them, six men realized $1,000 in one twenty-four-hour day; in another, six men made seventy-two ounces in a twenty-four-hour day, worth a little more than $1,000; in a third seven men recovered thirty-five pounds of gold in nine days, worth perhaps $8,500. While water was available, the work went on twenty-four hours a day, day after day. The water supply began to fail around the end of May, but before that happened, a mine near Idaho City earned $15,000 in one week in May, less $7,000 in expenses, leaving $8,000 in profit for the four partners.[16]

Early in 1863 there were other placer discoveries along the south fork of the Boise River at Rocky Bar, about sixty miles from Idaho City, and in August other discoveries at nearby Atlanta. Both eventually became rich quartz districts.

In May a party of miners under the leadership of Michael Jordan prospected a gold-rich stream, named Jordan Creek, in the Owyhee Mountains about one hundred miles south of Boise Basin. They located a bar called Discovery Bar just above what became Delamar. The men held a miners' meeting, organized a district, established rules, and continued their prospecting up the creek, where they established Happy Camp and appropriated the better ground before the inevitable rush. When word of this discovery reached the basin, some 2,500 men hurried to the new diggings.

The initial Jordan Creek placers that were worked that summer before the water gave out yielded $15 to $18 per day. Gold-bearing gravel was shoveled directly into sluices, and bedrock was only three to six feet below the surface. The work continued through 1864, but by the end of that season most of the placers were finished.

The first camp in the Owyhee District, as laid out in the summer of 1863, was Boonville. The name of the settlement was later changed to Dewey in honor of Colonel W. H. Dewey, a pioneer mining entrepreneur in the district. A little later Ruby City was founded, to be eventually absorbed by Silver City. All were very rich producing areas.

Virtually all of the mining in Idaho from 1860 to 1864 was placer mining, the simplest kind of mining. The earth's core being hot, the molten metal oozed up over time through cracks and crevices. In the millions of years of geologic formation, mountains thrust up, and with erosion these mineral veins cropped out. With further erosion loose fragments or nuggets were mixed with gravel and could be found underneath the surface of existing and extinct streambeds. In some cases the action of the elements broke up the nuggets into infinitesimally fine fragments, so that the gold resembled a kind of flour. It was nevertheless separable with the use of quicksilver (mercury), which clung to the gold and could be separated later by heating.

Prospectors were often young men, some not much more than boys, working with one or more experienced older men, nearly all unmarried. As a group of them, usually four to ten, went to a likely area, they took along food and equipment enough to last several weeks and shovels, picks, axes, and gold pans. They were heavily armed to prevent robbery. They usually walked, leading their pack animals. As they came to a likely-looking gulch, streambed, or hillside ledge, they dug down to bedrock and panned for specks of gold. If, after several tries, they averaged seven cents of gold dust in the pan (gold dust was worth about $15 per fine ounce), they would stake out a claim. After testing the whole area for a mile or two around to see if the field was worth working, they would stake off individual claims and organize a miners' district.

Placer gold was attractive because it could be mined with simple devices—and hard work. The gold was initially located by using a pan, perhaps twelve to eighteen inches in diameter and between three and four inches deep. The sand and gravel to be tested were placed in the pan and submerged in water. The pan was swirled in a circular motion and the heavier material (gold is very heavy) settled on the bottom. Lighter material was poured off, additional water was added, and the same process repeated until the "dust" was recovered. A few verifiable flakes might be worth seven or eight cents per pan—enough to make the work worthwhile.

When the prospectors settled down to more permanent mining, they often used a rocker—a wooden frame about four feet long, a foot or two wide, and two feet high. On top was a hopper with a piece of perforated sheet iron as its bottom. Below the hopper was an apron of canvas or cloth below which were a series of cleats or blocks called riffles that caught the gold and heavier material as the water washed through. Sand and gravel would be shoveled into the hopper and water was poured in as the frame rocked. Some of the gold was caught in the apron. As the water and gold-bearing solution passed over the riffles the heavier gold was caught behind the riffles.[17]

If a running stream could be dammed and diverted to the claim, as at Oro Fino and Florence and to a lesser extent in Boise Basin, miners installed a string of sluice boxes or a flume with riffles across the bottom to catch the gold as it sank while running water carried away the rest of what was shoveled into the sluices. Lumber from the trees on the hillside was whipsawed to make the flumes and sluice boxes. The working of a claim usually required several men—two men to shovel gravel into the sluice boxes; another to fish out the boulders carried down by the stream; a fourth to throw the wasted sand and gravel as far as he could; a fifth to pour quicksilver into the moving mass of water, sand, gravel, and boulders; two others to strip the overburden from the sand and gravel.

Some companies worked both day and night shifts. Obviously, the finding had to be rich to bring a return to all of these partners. In order for each of these seven men to earn $8 per day, their operations would have to yield four ounces of dust. Many reported that the Clearwater claims averaged that much for at least four years.[18] Not only was the process tedious, mining was hard physical labor. The typical picture of a mining district is not one of shooting up saloons and robbing the stage and express companies, but of hundreds of men toiling in the hot sun to earn a worthwhile pouch of dust. The men who laid the foundations for establishing Idaho were hard workers—persistent, patient, and, at times, rewarded.

According to Goulder, all the operations ceased on Saturday evening. Sundays were devoted to paying the workers, repairing equipment, purchasing supplies and provisions, card-playing, and "socializing." In Oro Fino the Wells Fargo express man arrived from Walla Walla on Sunday noon after three days on the trail. He brought papers carrying news of the Civil War, letters from loved ones, and packages with supplies.

The circulating medium of gold-rush society consisted primarily of gold dust. Shortly after the Civil War began, the United States government found it impossible to maintain the gold standard (a fixed quantity of gold backing the currency and gold coins in circulation) and so, beginning in 1861, the government went on a paper basis by issuing United States Notes. These were called greenbacks because of their color. Greenbacks were not well received, especially in the West, where they were called "Lincoln Skins." Until that time, the only paper money consisted of notes issued by state-chartered banks, business corporations, partnerships, and individuals. These notes were printed on all sorts of paper, were of various sizes and designs, and were almost always inadequately secured by gold. Counterfeiting was easy and commonly practiced. Indeed, the nation was flooded with what was called "shin-plaster" money that was largely worthless. Having no need for paper money, the people in Idaho's gold country simply used gold dust or nuggets. There was no gold coin; the government had withdrawn it and private individuals were not yet set up with a mint.

The dust was passed by weight. Small purchases, as for a

glass of whiskey, were made in terms of pinches, a pinch being the amount of gold dust that could be raised out of a miner's pouch between the thumb and forefinger. In fact, a phrase often used in the financial world, "How much can you raise in a pinch," originated in California in 1849, when employers were concerned that their clerks have large hands so they could raise a satisfactory amount in a pinch. A bartender customarily wet his thumb and forefinger before dipping it into the miner's bag of gold dust. The dry dust would be dropped into the saloon's till and the dust that clung to his finger would be rubbed off in his vest pocket as his "tip" on the transaction.

There were problems with this kind of payment because not all gold dust was equally valuable. Some persons added a little sand to the gold dust to increase its bulk and weight; others made imitation gold dust ("bogus") using base metals. Indeed, Bogus Basin, now a popular ski resort, was named for counterfeiters headquartered there who substituted colored lead for gold dust to increase their assets. Even authentic placer gold varied in richness because some silver was always mixed with it. The prevalence of impure gold dust caused some merchants to raise the price of their goods by twenty-five or fifty percent. Saloonkeepers sometimes compensated for adulterated gold dust by providing their scales with heavier weights; honest purchasers were thus short-changed.[19] When persons presented greenbacks for payment, they were depreciated from their face value, sometimes to as low as 35 cents on the dollar. A store would sell an article for $1 in gold or $3 in greenbacks. Most of the greenbacks that reached the region were picked up by merchants and sent east to pay for merchandise or to pay taxes. Nevertheless, even when greenbacks circulated far below par, some merchants preferred them because of experiences with bogus and varying value.

Idaho has always been, historically, a "hard money" state, preferring gold and silver, when possible, to paper. That tradition began with the very founding of the territory during the gold rush. Idahoans have been suspicious of paper money, and since many transactions during the early years were in gold and silver, the use of metal currency became a strong habit.

D. E. Livingston-Little estimates the production in the Nez Perce and Salmon River camps during the years 1860 to 1866 as follows: Elk City, $2.7 million; Pierce, $2.8 million; Warrens, $4.5 million; Newsome, $400,000; and Florence, $9.6 million. Production in north Idaho was estimated as $1,000 in 1860, $2.4 million in 1861, $8.4 million in 1862, $4.5 million in 1863, $4 million in 1864, $2.4 million in 1865, and $2.1 million in 1866.[20] The mines in the Boise Basin, worked for a longer period of time, produced perhaps $66 million in gold.

In subsequent years prospectors would discover numerous deposits of quartz gold and "lodes" and "veins" of gold and silver. A new kind of mineral activity emerged. But in the meantime, Washington Territory had difficulty controlling these thousands of citizens located so far away from Olympia who in fact represented a majority of the citizens of Washington Territory. Puget Sound residents, fearful of losing control, realized that it was necessary to split off the rapidly growing eastern portion.

## CHAPTER NINE: SOURCES

Especially detailed and well-researched are Merle W. Wells, *Gold Camps and Silver Cities*, Bulletin 22 of the Idaho Bureau of Mines and Geology, 2d ed. (Moscow: The Bureau, 1983), which gives the history of mining activity in the Boise Basin and Owyhee County in the 1860s; and Merle W. Wells, *Rush to Idaho*, Bulletin No. 19 of the Idaho Bureau of Mines and Geology (Moscow: The Bureau, 1961), a history of mining in north Idaho in the 1860s.

General histories of Idaho and parts of Idaho that include substantial sections on early mining activities include: Hubert Howe

Bancroft, *History of Washington, Idaho, and Montana, 1845–1889* (San Francisco: The History Company, 1890), 406–41 et passim; John Hailey, *The History of Idaho* (Boise: Syms-York Co., 1910), 19–44, 61–76, 91–99; W. J. McConnell, *Early History of Idaho* (Caldwell: Caxton Printers, 1913), 55–110; Hiram T. French, *History of Idaho*, 3 vols. (Chicago: Lewis Publishing Co., 1914), 1:26–39; Hawley, *History of Idaho*, 1:115–31; Merle Wells and Arthur A. Hart, *Idaho: Gem of the Mountains* (Northridge, Calif.: Windsor Publications, 1985), 35–51; Brosnan, *History of the State of Idaho*, 135–75; Defenbach, *Idaho: The Place and Its People*, 1:257–342; Beal and Wells, *History of Idaho*, 1:281–324; Peterson, *Idaho: A Bicentennial History*, 54–68; and Livingston-Little, *An Economic History of North Idaho*, 23–52.

Local histories that have important chapters on early mining include: M. Alfreda Elsensohn, *Pioneer Days in Idaho County*, 2 vols. (Caldwell: Caxton Printers, 1947–51); Annie Laurie Bird, *Boise, the Peace Valley* (Caldwell: Caxton Printers, 1934); Merle Wells, *Boise: An Illustrated History* (Woodland Hills, Calif.: Windsor Publications, 1982); and Harry B. Averill, John M. Henderson, and William S. Schiach, *An Illustrated History of North Idaho* (n.p.: n.p., 1903).

The books of Idaho history written for young people also include chapters or units on early mining in Idaho.

All of the general histories of the American West and the Pacific Northwest have substantial sections on early mining in Idaho. Histories of mining in the West that include helpful information about mining in early Idaho include: William S. Greever, *The Bonanza West: The Story of the Western Mining Rushes, 1848–1900* (Norman: University of Oklahoma Press, 1963; rpr., Moscow: University of Idaho Press, 1991); T. A. Rickard, *A History of American Mining* (New York: The Macmillan Co., 1932); Clark C. Spence, *British Investment and the American Mining Frontier, 1860–1901* (Ithaca, N.Y.: Cornell University Press, 1958); Muriel S. Wolle, *The Bonanza Trail: Ghost Towns and Mining Camps in the West* (Bloomington: Indiana University Press, 1953); John Fahey, *The Ballyhoo Bonanza: Charles Sweeny and the Idaho Mines* (Seattle: University of Washington Press, 1971); Rodman W. Paul, *Mining Frontiers of the Far West,*

*1848–1880* (New York: Holt, Rinehart and Winston, 1963); Clyde P. Ross, *Mining History of South-Central Idaho* (Moscow: Idaho Bureau of Mines and Geology, 1963); William J. Trimble, *The Mining Advance into the Inland Empire*, Bulletin of the University of Wisconsin, No. 638 (Madison: University of Wisconsin, 1914); Vardis Fisher and Opal Laurel Holmes, *Gold Rushes and Mining Camps of the Early American West* (Caldwell: Caxton Printers, 1968).

A series of nine articles appeared in the issues of *Idaho Yesterdays* from the fall of 1959 to the summer of 1962 reprinting original newspaper accounts of the Clearwater gold rush and the Salmon River rush to Florence. These clarify the Idaho gold discovery just as it was reported in contemporary papers. Other articles, in addition to those mentioned in the notes, include: Merle W. Wells, "History of Mining in Idaho," in *Idaho's Mineral Industry*, Bulletin No. 18 of the Idaho Bureau of Mines and Geology (Moscow: The Bureau, 1961), 9–18; and August C. Bolino, *The Role of Mining in the Economic Development of Idaho Territory*, Information Circular No. 6, Idaho Bureau of Mines and Geology (Moscow: The Bureau, 1960), a reprint from *Oregon Historical Quarterly* 59 (June 1958):116–51.

Several numbers in the Idaho Historical Society Reference Series discuss aspects of the mining history of Idaho. A personal history written with literary flair, which contains significant material on early mining history, is William Armistead Goulder, *Reminiscences: Incidents in the Life of a Pioneer in Oregon and Idaho* (repr., Moscow: University of Idaho Press, 1990), 196–242. An early account of the plunderers and murderers by an unknown author is *The Banditti of the Rocky Mountains and Vigilance Committee in Idaho: An Authentic Record of Startling Adventures in the Gold Mines of Idaho* (Chicago, 1865; repr. Minneapolis: Ross & Haines, 1964).

Theses and dissertations that treat Idaho mining history include: Robert Wayne Smith, "History of Placer and Quartz Gold Mining in the Coeur d'Alene District" (M.A. thesis, University of Idaho, 1932); Ralph Burcham, Jr., "Reminiscences of E. D. Pierce, Discoverer of Gold in Idaho" (Ph.D. dissertation, Washington State College, 1957); Ralph Burcham, Jr., "Elias Davidson Pierce, Discoverer of Gold in Idaho: A Biographical Sketch" (M.A. thesis, University of Idaho,

1951); and Robert L. Romig, "The South Boise Quartz Mines, 1865–1892: A Study in Western Mining Industry and Finance" (M.A. thesis, University of California, Berkeley, 1951).

Also helpful are Otis E. Young, "The Prospectors: Some Considerations on their Craft," in John Alexander Carroll, ed., *Reflections of Western Historians* (Tucson: University of Arizona Press, 1969), 121–33; and Elliott West, *The Saloon on the Rocky Mountain Mining Frontier* (Lincoln: University of Nebraska Press, 1979).

39.

40.

39. Captain E. D. Pierce discovered gold at Pierce City, named after him, in August 1860. ISHS 2749.

40. Many prospectors like this old-timer sought their fortune in gold by panning Idaho streams for nuggets. ISHS 75–209.2.

41.

42.

41. This first photograph of Lewiston, taken in 1863, shows the historical landmarks associated with the establishment of the territorial capital at Lewiston. UIL 5–7–42.

42. Pack trains, like this one on the street of Orofino, were common sights in territorial Idaho. ISHS 1888–G.

# CHAPTER TEN

## The Creation of Idaho Territory

The United States was experiencing its worst moments in 1863. The Civil War battle of Gettysburg occurred in late June and early July and left almost fifty thousand men wounded, killed, or missing. The battles of Chancellorsville, Vicksburg, Chickamauga, and Chattanooga were not quite as deadly, but they were destructive and troubling. In addition, the nation had sought to regulate its banking system in the interests of financing the war by passage of the National Banking Act, general conscription had been ordered, and the Homestead Act of the previous year had been designed to increase the supply of food and fiber by promoting agricultural expansion in the West.

The miners' rush into the Clearwater region (Pierce City, Oro Fino, Elk City), into Salmon River (Florence, Warrens), into Boise Basin (Idaho City, Centerville, Placerville), along with Rocky Bar, Atlanta, and Owyhee, had proceeded apace. By 1863 there were (in addition to the Indians) almost a thousand persons in Clearwater, another five hundred in Florence, perhaps twenty thousand in Boise Basin and Owyhee, and twelve thousand additional in East Bannack and Virginia City. The time was ripe for the creation of a new territory.

From the era of Lewis and Clark's expedition until 1820, Idaho was included in what was known as the Columbia River Country. After 1820 the region was called the Oregon Country, and it included what later became the states of Oregon, Washington, Idaho, western Montana, western Wyoming, and the southern two-thirds of British Columbia. (Most of Montana and Wyoming were in Indian Country—earlier part of Louisiana Territory.) When the British Columbia region was awarded to England in the Treaty of 1846, the northern border of the United States was fixed at the forty-ninth parallel. In 1848 Congress established Oregon Territory; Washington, Idaho, western Montana, and western Wyoming became part of that huge land area. In 1853 Oregon Territory was split when Congress created Washington Territory for the benefit of the 4,000 or fewer scattered settlers north of the Columbia River. Washington Territory thus formed the northern half and Oregon Territory the southern half of the enormous geographic area that had been Oregon Territory for five years. Northern Idaho was in Washington Territory and central and southern Idaho remained in Oregon Territory.

In 1859, when Oregon became a state, the area of it was reduced to its present size. The remainder of Oregon and Washington territories was incorporated as part of the greatly expanded Territory of Washington. That was the situation in 1860 when gold was discovered along the Clearwater River in what is now Idaho. As the population of the region built up in the Clearwater, Salmon, Boise Basin, and Owyhee districts—all regarded as a part of eastern Washington territory, and all separated from the territorial capital by towering mountain ranges and semi-hostile Indians—consideration was given to creating a new territory.

Three proposals to establish the new territory were offered. One proposal would place eastern Washington (east of the Cascades), Idaho, and western Montana (some of which was in a new territory) together with Walla Walla or Lewiston as the capital. Walla Walla and Lewiston favored this proposal, each hoping to be the capital. The second proposal would extend the line separating Oregon and Washington east; all above the line (eastern Washington, northern Idaho, and western Montana) would be Washington Territory, with Walla Walla or Lewiston as the capital, and all south of the line and east of Oregon would be in a new territory to be called Montana Territory. This would include almost all of the Idaho and western Montana gold mining regions and also Wyoming. The capital city would presumably be Idaho City. An actual bill making these provisions was passed by the United States House of Representatives on February 12, 1863, but was never implemented.

The third proposal, the one eventually adopted, provided that the eastern border of Washington Territory should run straight north from the eastern border of Oregon—due north from Lewiston—and Olympia would remain the capital city of Washington. The remainder—all of Idaho, all of Montana, and nearly all of Wyoming—would be placed in a new territory to be called Idaho Territory. Lewiston would be the provisional capital. Eventually, everyone was sure, a new territory or territories would have to be created out of this expansive region to serve the needs of what would become, in due time, Montana and Wyoming.

Puget Sound interests obviously wanted to hold on to as much territory as they could without giving up the capital of Olympia; they left Washington with an area east of the Cascades that had little in common with the coastal area, creating sectional problems that have plagued Washington ever since. On the other hand, the city of Lewiston, as the connecting link with the mining regions in the Clearwater and Salmon Mountains, wanted

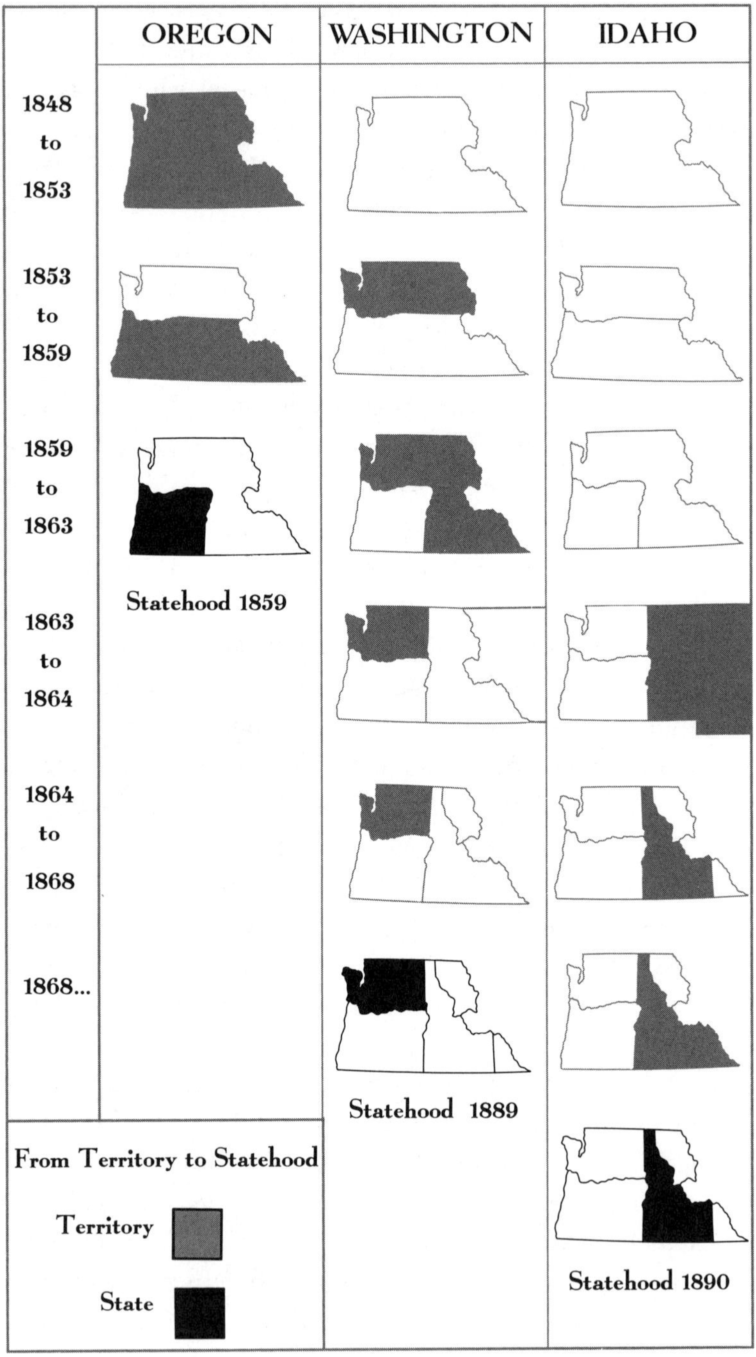

| | OREGON | WASHINGTON | IDAHO |
|---|---|---|---|
| 1848 to 1853 | | | |
| 1853 to 1859 | | | |
| 1859 to 1863 | Statehood 1859 | | |
| 1863 to 1864 | | | |
| 1864 to 1868 | | | |
| 1868... | | Statehood 1889 | Statehood 1890 |

From Territory to Statehood

Territory

State

the boundary to extend as far west as possible. In this way Idaho retained the western boundary of the new territory, and when the state was admitted in 1890 the western border remained intact.

Congress, of course, had expected the inland empire to be settled slowly, over a period of several decades. The gold rush to Idaho changed that perspective. When the Washington elections were held in 1861, the newly organized Shoshone County cast more ballots than any other part of Washington, which forced the Olympia people to acknowledge the need for a new territory lest they lose control of their entire territory. Their plan, the one eventually adopted, was to keep Washington as large as possible and yet get rid of the mining population that was now the controlling majority.

Abraham Lincoln on March 4, 1863, signed the Organic Act creating Idaho Territory, the last great territory in the United States. Covering an area of 325,000 square miles, the territory was larger than Texas but smaller than Alaska. The advantage of territorial government was that Congress supplied most of the essential expenses to run the area. The disadvantage was that those who ran the territory—governors, secretaries, supreme court justices, attorneys, marshals, and other officials—were appointed by the president of the United States and confirmed by the Senate. They often had few roots in Idaho country. Even the territorial legislatures, although elected by the voters in the territory, were paid with federal funds. Along with executive and judicial officials, they received supplementary pay from Idaho's treasury that doubled their salaries, but that was not supposed to be needed. From 1863 on, territorial citizens worked toward the goal of statehood by building stable communities, developing a constitution, and persuading Congress that they were "ready."

By the time Idaho Territory was created, it had four counties: Shoshone, founded in 1861; Nez Perce, 1861; Idaho, 1861; and

Boise, 1863. The territorial legislature consisted of a Council of seven members and a House of Representatives of eleven members. The seven members of the Council were from Boise (two), Madison (Virginia City), Beaverhead, Idaho, Nez Perce, and Shoshone counties. (Boise County included southeastern and south central Idaho.) The eleven members of the House were from Boise (five), Idaho (two), Nez Perce (one), Beaverhead (one), Madison ( one), and Shoshone (one). The voters also elected a territorial delegate to the U.S. House of Representatives, who represented them in deliberations but without voting privileges.

The name given to Idaho Territory is not easily explained. As early as the fall of 1859 the miners in the Pike's Peak region held an election in what they called Jefferson Territory to elect a territorial delegate to Congress to lobby for territorial status. For various reasons the group was represented by three persons. They soon learned that there was opposition to singling out a particular United States president for honor in this way, and a variety of other names was suggested: Lafayette, Columbus, Franklin, San Juan, Yampa, Arapahoe, and Idaho. The last, George M. Willing suggested, meant Gem of the Mountains. Idaho seemed to be the preferred name. As James S. Green, chairman of the U.S. Senate Committee on Territories, declared: "Idaho is a very good name. In the Indian language [he did not say which one] it signifies Gem of the Mountains. Some had proposed the name of Colorado, because the Colorado River is in that region; but Idaho being an Indian name, and its meaning being Gem of the Mountains, as so much mineral is found there, it may be very appropriate."[1]

When promoters of that new territory discovered that Idaho was not an Indian word, the name was changed to Colorado just before passage. On February 28, 1861, President James Buchanan signed the act that created the Territory of Colorado. The name of Idaho was then used in a variety of ways in this developing region. In June of 1860 a steamer was launched on the Columbia bearing the name of *Idaho*. Later that same month the town of Idaho, thirty-five miles west of Denver, received its name; it later became Idaho Springs, Colorado. In October 1861 Nettie Idaho Jackson was born in Blackhawk, Colorado. On December 20, 1861, Idaho County, of Washington Territory, was created as the third county in what is now Idaho (Nez Perce County was the second). Finally, in 1863 the Territory of Idaho was created with the legendary meaning of its name, "Gem of the Mountains," perpetuated.

The first governor of Idaho Territory was William H. Wallace, a lawyer from Steilacoom, Washington. Born in Troy, Ohio, in 1811, Wallace had moved with his family to Indiana when he was six. When his older brother became governor of Indiana in 1837, the younger Wallace moved to Iowa, where he served as speaker of the House and later as a member of the Council. He became a colonel in the Iowa militia and a General Land Office official before moving to the new territory of Washington in 1853. He continued his legislative career, becoming president of the Washington Council in 1855–56. When his friend Abraham Lincoln became president, Wallace was appointed governor of Washington Territory, but before he could take office he was elected delegate to Congress and declined the governorship. Fully aware of the settlements in eastern Washington and of their need for a government closer than Olympia, he used his considerable influence in Washington to secure the passage of the Idaho Act establishing the territory.

Wallace assumed office in Lewiston on July 10, 1863, and organized the government of the new territory that summer. He designated Lewiston as the temporary capital; actually, Lewiston was the only accessible "city" in the territory. Idaho City, though much larger, was a new mining town which could be reached only by saddle and pack animals, and was without a wagon road or a post office. Boise City had not been founded by the time the Organic Act was passed. Lewiston at least had stage and freighting lines connecting with steamboats at Wallula for Portland.

But there was a technical problem, even with Lewiston. In a strictly legal sense Lewiston was not in the territory. In 1855 a treaty between the United States and the Nez Perce Indians had confirmed their reservation, and both Florence and Lewiston were within the reservation. Neither of those places could thus be included within the territorial boundaries of Idaho until the treaty was revised. Treaty negotiations reduced the reservation on June 9, 1863, an action that most of those concerned accepted. Because some dissented, there were now two groups of Nez Perce—those under Chief Timothy and Lawyer, his associate, who had agreed to relinquish Lewiston and the mining lands, and the remainder whose lands were removed from the reservation and who did not consider themselves bound by the treaty. Because of U.S. Senate delays and blunderings in ratifying the new treaty, Lewiston and Florence did not officially become part of Idaho until April 20, 1867. In the meantime, however, the treaty had been signed, the nontreaty Indians did not make a disturbance, and everyone acted as though Lewiston and the mining lands were part of the territory.[2]

Another problem arose. Since Congress had created the territory in the closing hours of the final day of its session, no appropriations had been made for Idaho except those Wallace had been instrumental in securing for the Indians. Wallace came to believe that, because of his congressional and legislative experience as delegate from Washington Territory, he could obtain the needed appropriations more easily than a newcomer, and so he agreed to submit his name as territorial delegate to Congress. Another consideration may have been his loyalty to Abraham Lincoln and the Union and his feeling that his influence might be helpful in keeping the territory loyal during the divisive war. At any rate, he resigned as governor, won Idaho's first election, and left Lewiston for the national capital on December 6.

At the first legislative session in Idaho held a day later, the governor's address was given by William B. Daniels, the territorial secretary. Secretary Daniels, who had lived in Yamhill County, Oregon, served as acting governor until Wallace's replacement, Caleb Lyon, arrived in August 1864. As acting governor during the first legislative session, which lasted from December 7, 1863, to February 4, 1864, Daniels supervised the installation of the first territorial supreme court, consisting of Sidney Edgerton, chief justice, who was assigned to the wild area east of the Rockies; Samuel C. Parks, who was first assigned to the Boise District; and Aleck C. Smith, assigned to the Lewiston District.

The legislature failed to act on a measure to select a permanent capital, but they agreed unanimously that Idaho Territory should be divided. The Virginia City delegates from east of the Continental Divide had to go down the Columbia to Portland, take ship to San Francisco, go east to Salt Lake City, and then head north to Virginia City on their return. That was enough to persuade Congress to create Montana Territory on May 26, 1864. Justice Edgerton was appointed Montana's first governor. In the same act Congress returned most of Wyoming to Dakota Territory. Idaho was left with something close to its final boundaries. With North Idaho effectively separated from the south by the Salmon River Mountains projecting between Washington and Montana, a geographic division between north and south would be a constant challenge to governing the territory, not to mention the eventual state.

In the meantime, the first trial in an Idaho court, in January 1864, was presided over by Justice Parks in Lewiston. Lloyd Magruder, a prominent packer and trader in northern Idaho, purchased a cargo of miners' supplies in Lewiston and loaded his pack train of sixty or seventy mules to go to Virginia City, still in Idaho Territory, about three hundred miles away. Hill Beachy, who kept the principal hotel in Lewiston, was a good friend of Magruder. The night before Magruder was to depart,

Beachy had a dream that his friend would be attacked in the mountains and murdered and robbed. He was telling his wife about the dream the next morning when Magruder arrived to say good-bye. Without saying anything about the dream, Beachy loaned Magruder a fine gun to take on the trip.

Shortly before Magruder reached Virginia City he was overtaken by a party of men who offered to help him into Virginia City in return for grub. They reached the destination and Magruder found a ready sale for his goods. In preparing to return to Lewiston, Magruder had his large train of pack mules and $25,000 to $30,000 in gold dust. Four of the men who had joined the party that rode into Virginia City had ingratiated themselves sufficiently that Magruder gladly employed them for the return trip. The four turned out to be G. C. Lowry, David Renton (alias Howard), and James Roumain (Romain), who were "road agents"—murderous robbers—and William Page, a mountaineer trapper and miner. Also employed were a Mr. Phillips, a Mr. Allen, and two young men from Missouri, names unknown, miners who were returning with $2,000 in gold dust: a total of eight men besides Magruder.

About two-thirds of the way to Lewiston, Lowry, Howard, and Roumain put Page on guard duty, told him to keep his mouth shut under promise of death, and proceeded to murder Magruder, Phillips, Allen, and the two young men. Page later claimed he saw the whole thing. The murderers, wearing moccasins to make it appear that they were Indians, picked out the best mules to ride and drove the rest into the canyon and killed them. The dead men were tied up in their blankets and rolled over a cliff. The camp equipage was burned.

The men, disguised, rode on into Lewiston at night. One had ridden Magruder's fine saddle mule with his elegant saddle. They left their animals with a rancher and took the stage for Walla Walla under fictitious names, then another stage to Wallula, where they boarded a steamer bound for Portland, and then took an ocean steamer for San Francisco.

Hill Beachy was so firmly convinced that the men who had come into Lewiston in the night and left in disguise the next day had murdered Magruder that he swore out a complaint, obtained a warrant for their arrest, got himself appointed deputy sheriff, and got a requisition from Governor Wallace on the governors of Washington Territory, Oregon, and California for the men. Beachy's friends thought he was a little hasty, so he went to examine the mules and saddles the men had left with the rancher. Recognizing them as Magruder's and learning of other evidence that pointed to murder, Beachy and an associate followed the path of the four men to Walla Walla, Wallula, Portland, and San Francisco. Because the next ocean steamer would be two weeks away, Beachy took the stage overland from Portland to San Francisco. When he reached Yreka, the nearest telegraph office, he relayed a description of the men to the chief of police in San Francisco. Captain Lees, the chief, discovered that the men had deposited a large amount of gold dust at the United States Mint for coinage. He arrested them, and threw them in prison. When Beachy arrived, he recognized the men, charged them with murder, and was able to get a full story of what had happened from William Page, who had been with them in San Francisco. Lees, Beachy, and the latter's partner took the men back to Lewiston.

In Lewiston, where the party arrived December 7, 1863, the men in custody were recognized by the citizens, who were quick to get ropes for a hanging. Beachy explained that he had given his word to the governor of California and the San Francisco chief of police that the men would be given a fair trial, and he talked the residents out of the lynching. The trial began January 5, 1864. Found guilty of murder, the three men were hung on March 4. In due time, the gold dust deposited by the murderers in the San Francisco Mint was returned to Magruder's wife and children. The first Idaho legislature, still in session when the verdict was read, appropriated $6,244 to reimburse Beachy for the expenses he had incurred. In the spring, when the snow in the mountains had melted, Beachy and others visited the location of the murder, found the bodies, and verified the story that Page had told at the trial.[3]

While the first legislature had generously agreed on a stipend for Beachy, it failed to agree on a permanent territorial capital. The twelve thousand persons in Virginia City wanted that location. The sixteen thousand persons in Boise Basin wanted Idaho City. And of course all the miners in the Clearwater and Salmon Mountains country wanted Lewiston. Unable to agree—perhaps hoping things would settle down and one location would emerge as the clear choice—the legislature adjourned with no decision.

Caleb Lyon, who was named to replace Governor Wallace, finally arrived in Lewiston in August 1864. Born, as he boasted, in Lyonsdale, in upstate New York, Lyon was educated in Montreal (he was a descendant of the Marquis de Montcalm) and graduated in civil engineering from Norwich University in Vermont when he was only eighteen. He joined the California Gold Rush in 1849, served as a secretary of the 1849 California constitutional convention, and returned to New York, where he served in the legislative assembly and state senate and was elected to Congress. Lyon served as governor of Idaho until June 1866.

When he reached Lewiston, Lyon found the territorial credit in shambles. Congress had not appropriated any money, and yet the territory continued to grow in population and wealth. Oneida County had been created in January 1864 and Ada County in December of the same year. Since the territory had not yet been surveyed and no land patents had been issued, there was no property to be taxed. The necessary revenue to run the government came from license taxes and a tax on "alien" miners at the rate of $4 a month. The latter applied only to Chinese and was intended to discourage them from moving into the mines.

Before the end of 1864 Lyon became embroiled in a battle between Lewiston and the territorial legislature over the location of the capital. Ever since the organization of the territory, the number of miners in Pierce City, Elk City, Florence, and Lewiston had been declining. Of the more than 10,000 who had rushed there in the summer of 1862, scarcely 1,000 remained by the time of the first territorial census in September 1863. The Boise area had more than 16,000 inhabitants, East Bannack and Virginia City close to 12,000. Consequently, in an action fiercely opposed by Lewiston and North Idaho, the second legislature, meeting in Lewiston as the year before, voted on December 7, 1864, to remove the capital to Boise City, which had been founded in July of the previous year. Bitterly resented by north Idahoans, who felt isolated with no control, the action set off urgent agitation for the annexation of the Panhandle to Washington or to Montana. Not until the establishment of better roads and communication after statehood did this turmoil begin to diminish.

Meanwhile, Lyon, in trouble with Lewiston if he signed the bill and in trouble with the legislature if he refused, tried to placate everyone by giving speeches on his experiences in the Holy Land. Boise sought to mollify the northerners by asking Congress to set up a new interior Columbia Territory for Lewiston, Walla Walla, north Idaho, and Missoula. When Montana Territory objected to losing Missoula, the Boise leaders petitioned Congress to form a new Columbia Territory out of northern Idaho and eastern Washington. Congress did not respond to either request. Lewiston tried to delay the move to Boise by getting the local probate judge to declare the legislative session illegal. When the judge and his cohorts sought to serve an injunction on Lyon, he and two Boise legislators devised a plan for Lyon to skip out of the territory on the pretext that he was going duck hunting. On December 29, he hiked six miles to a ferry, where a carriage picked him up across the Snake and took him to Walla Walla. He did not return to the territory until the following November.

Lyon's departure, much resented by irate Lewistonians, left Idaho with no executive department. Three months after Lyon had left, a new territorial secretary, C. DeWitt Smith, arrived. When Smith reached Lewiston, he solicited military support and took the territorial seal and archives away from a vigilant armed guard provided by Lewiston's citizens. He arrived in Boise on April 14, 1865, the very night Abraham Lincoln was assassinated. He did not last long in Boise, however. At the end of a strenuous chess game in Rocky Bar, in August 1865, he suddenly expired from the effects of a "dismal and melancholy disease."[4] Idaho was again left with no government.

At the end of his term as Idaho's Congressional delegate, the territory's first governor, William Wallace, went to his good friend Abraham Lincoln and obtained an appointment to replace Lyon as governor. Wallace's closeness to Lincoln is indicated by the fact that Lincoln had invited him to be with him at Ford's Theater the night that John Wilkes Booth shot and killed the president, and he was a pallbearer at Lincoln's funeral. Lyon's friends managed to sidetrack Wallace's appointment, and, without the support of Lincoln, Wallace was now maneuvered out of the job. Lyon returned to Idaho as governor, and Wallace settled down at his old home at Steilacoom, on the Sound between Olympia and Tacoma, where he stayed until his death in 1879. Wallace was not as famous as his brother David, governor of Indiana, or as his nephew Lew, the Civil War general who authored *Ben Hur*, but he could take some satisfaction in the contributions he had made to Idaho Territory.

Caleb Lyon had given lectures and lived the leisurely life of a gentleman during the months he had been away from Idaho. Upon his return in November 1865, Boiseans felt ill at ease around him. He wore clean linen, took daily baths, wore dress suits, and once appeared at a society function in a swallow-tail coat. William J. McConnell reported that it was even hinted that he wore suspenders![5] Lyon first sought to gain admission for

Idaho Territory as a state so he could run for United States Senator, but that effort failed. He negotiated a treaty with the Shoshoni, but the United States Senate failed to ratify it. He left Boise in April 1866, taking with him some $46,000 in undisbursed Nez Perce Indian funds that he subsequently appropriated for personal purposes. He was an art lover, a scholar, and a poet, but most historians have regarded him as a failure as Idaho's second executive. The historian Hubert Howe Bancroft (or his employed assistant Frances Fuller Victor), writing only twenty years after Lyon's departure, said "he lent his signature to any and every bill of the most disloyal and vulgar-minded legislature that ever disgraced the legislative office, except the one that followed it. . . . His appointments were equally without regard to the welfare of society and the territory." Bancroft quoted a newspaper correspondent who called Lyon "a revolving light on the coast of scampdom."[6]

Was the gargantuan Idaho Territory, including as it did in 1863–64 the mining districts in western Montana, north Idaho, the Boise Basin, and Owyhee, really an effective government? Or was it simply a paper government over a group of recently organized, self-governing mining districts? How well were law and order maintained?

When government is feeble, when lawless elements run rampant and threaten many lives, citizens tend to band together for protection. Citizens' groups were formed in the Lewiston, Idaho City, Payette, Boise, Salmon, and Bannock-Virginia districts. The Lewiston Protective Association, organized in 1862–63, managed to exile some two hundred robbers and gamblers. Beaverhead vigilantes in a mining district in western Montana (then Idaho) executed "Clubfoot Land," "Red," "Spanish Frank," "Dutch John," and "Whiskey Bill." As they "cleansed the Augean Stables," they reportedly hanged twenty-four men in a few weeks during the early months of 1864.[7] A vigilante group was organized in Idaho City in 1865, and at least two persons, including the ex-sheriff of Ada County, David Updyke, were lynched. There was fierce debate among Idahoans. Were vigilantes "a gang of irresponsible outlaws attempting to make their individual hates and interests the governing power"? Or were they "preparing the way for law and order by executing known outlaws and warning others out of the country?"[8]

William J. McConnell, who reported the rise and fall of lawless elements in the Boise Basin, wrote that "the disturbers" were an insignificant minority but they gave the impression that they were really "the whole thing."

> Their ability to impress a community with their numerical strength is usually equal, or superior, to that of the timber, or mountain wolf, one of which can start its calliope and in a few seconds convince the novice that the woods are alive with its kind. The ease and celerity with which the citizens of Boise and Payette valleys rid the country of bad men is proof of the analogy.[9]

Historians Beal and Wells have defended the vigilantes: "In taking this overt course, such citizens [protective societies] do not diminish the power and prestige of law and order. On the contrary, they prepare the way for that higher authority to manifest itself. . . . Their record is praiseworthy. They did what was needed and then dissolved."[10] M. M. McPherson describes the organization of a vigilante committee in Salmon City in 1866. "As soon as this became known," he wrote, "there was an exodus out over the mountains. While there were several men killed at Leesburg, I think it was one of the most peaceful towns in all the mining country."[11]

In Payette Valley, William J. McConnell took the leadership in breaking up a gang led by David Updyke, Ada County's first sheriff. Like Henry Plummer in East Bannack, Updyke led a double life as sheriff and leader of a band of criminals. When a partial disclosure of his deeds came to light, he was forced to resign and later was hung.[12] "Within three months of its organization," McConnell wrote, "the [Vigilance] committee transformed the Payette Valley, with its hitherto unsavory reputation, into a community of peaceful homes, where life and property were as safe as in any of the older states or territories in the Union."[13]

The troublesome feature of territorial government was that the governor and secretary, the men with the money and control, were responsible only to the president of the United States and the Congress, not to the people in the territory. This presented a special problem in Idaho because for every year Idaho was a territory, except four, the president was a Republican, whereas the majority of the people in Idaho and a majority of the legislature were, in almost every year, Democrats. Oddly enough, when the nation had a Democratic president, Idaho voted Republican. Friction was inevitable. Few of the appointed governors got along with the legislature, and few in the legislature were willing to cooperate with the unwanted "carpetbag" governors.

A further complication was caused by the Civil War. While California, Oregon, and Washington Democrats tended to be pro-Union, a large number of southern immigrants in Idaho were Confederate sympathizers, so even the predominant Democratic Party was divided. When Edward D. Holbrook, a California Democrat, was elected delegate to replace William Wallace in 1864, he began a tradition that continued until 1882. In 1886 the election of Fred T. Dubois, a sometime Republican, ended the tradition that the political control of Idaho Territory, at least as far as its elected officials was concerned, was in the hands of Confederate refugees and their Democratic allies from California and Oregon.

Concurrent with these complicated political developments was the growth of a new mining industry in central and southern Idaho. High-yielding quartz mines were discovered in the early 1860s in the Boise Basin, South Boise, Owyhee, Camas Prairie, and elsewhere. Their working attracted miners, mill operators, suppliers, and bankers. If we add to their numbers those coming into the territory to farm and graze cattle, Idaho was accumulating population sufficient to qualify for eventual statehood.

## CHAPTER TEN: SOURCES

All the books on the history of the West and Northwest have sections on the creation of Idaho Territory, as do the books on Idaho history. The relevant pages are as follows: Bancroft, *History of Washington, Idaho, and Montana*, 442–80; Hailey, *The History of Idaho*, 45–48; McConnell, *Early History of Idaho*, 111–253; Donaldson, *Idaho of Yesterday*, 223–75, 368–401; Hawley, *History of Idaho*, 1:133–95; Brosnan, *History of the State of Idaho*, 179–99; Defenbach, *Idaho: The Place and Its People*, 1:367–402; Beal and Wells, *History of Idaho*, 1:325–58, 369–91; Peterson, *Idaho: A Bicentennial History*, 61–68; Goulder, *Reminiscences*, 243–99; and French, *History of Idaho*, 1:53–88. All of the histories of Idaho for young people have units or chapters that tell of the creation of Idaho Territory.

Specialized books on the political history of Idaho and the West that are especially helpful include: Earl S. Pomeroy, *The Territories and the United States, 1861–1890* (Philadelphia: University of Pennsylvania Press, 1947; reissued, Seattle: University of Washington Press, 1969); Ronald H. Limbaugh, *Rocky Mountain Carpetbaggers: Idaho's Territorial Governors, 1863–1890* (Moscow: University of Idaho Press, 1982); and Ronald H. Limbaugh, "Territorial Elites and Political Power Struggles in the Far West, 1865–1890," in David H. Stratton and George A. Frykman, *The Changing Pacific Northwest: Interpreting Its Past* (Pullman: Washington State University Press, 1988), 95–114.

The following periodical articles treat aspects of the creation of Idaho Territory: Herman J. Deutsch, "The Evolution of Territorial and State Boundaries in the Inland Empire of the Pacific Northwest," *Pacific Northwest Quarterly* 51 (July 1960):115–31; Eugene B. Chaffee, "The Political Clash Between North and South Idaho Over the Capital," *Pacific Northwest Quarterly* 29 (July 1938):255–67; C. S. Kingston, "North Idaho Annexation Issue," *Washington Historical Quarterly* 21 (April-October 1930):133–37, 204–17, 281–93; Annie Laurie Bird, "Portrait of a Frontier Politician: William Henson Wallace's Boyhood Background," *Idaho Yesterdays* 1 (Spring 1957):19–23; Ronald H. Limbaugh, "The Case of the Three Musicians," *Idaho Yesterdays* 4 (Winter 1960–61):2–7; W. Turrentine Jackson, "Indian Affairs and Politics in Idaho Territory, 1863–1870," *Pacific Historical Review* 14 (September 1945):311–25; Merle Wells, "S. R. Howlett's War with the Idaho Legislature, 1866–1867," *Idaho Yesterdays* 20 (Spring 1976):20–27; Earl S. Pomeroy, "Running a Territory: They Had Their Troubles," *Idaho Yesterdays* 14 (Fall 1970):10–12; Merle Wells, "The Idaho-Montana Boundary," *Idaho Yesterdays* 12 (Winter 1968–69):6–9; [Merle Wells], "Territorial Governors of Idaho," *Idaho Yesterdays* 7 (Spring 1963):14–23, and "The Idaho Centennial: How Idaho Was Created in 1863," *Idaho Yesterdays* 7 (Spring 1963):44–58; Merle W. Wells, "The Creation of the Territory of Idaho," *Pacific Northwest Quarterly* 40 (April 1949):106–23; Merle W. Wells, "Territorial Government in the Inland Empire: The Movement to Create Columbia Territory, 1864–69," *Pacific Northwest Quarterly* 44 (April 1953):80–87; James L. Thane, Jr., *A Governor's Wife on the Mining Frontier: The Letters of Mary Edgerton from Montana, 1863–1865* (Salt Lake City: University of Utah Library, 1976); Annie Laurie Bird, "Idaho's First Territorial Governor," *Idaho Yesterdays* 10 (Summer 1966):8–15; and Ruth and Mike Dakis, "Guilty or Not Guilty? Vigilantes on Trial," *Idaho Yesterdays* 12 (Winter 1968–69):2–5.

Explanations of the origin of the word Idaho include: Erl H. Ellis, *That Word "Idaho,"* University of Denver Studies in Humanities, No. 2 (Denver: University of Denver Press, 1951); "Footnotes to History," *Idaho Yesterdays* 8 (Spring 1964):33–36. See also *Idaho Yesterdays* 2 (Spring 1958):26–28; John E. Rees, "Idaho—Its Meaning, Origin, and Application," *Quarterly of the Oregon Historical Society* 18 (June 1917):83–92 (repr. Portland: The Ivy Press, 1917); Merle W. Wells, *Origins of the Name Idaho*, Idaho Historical Series, No. 13 (Boise:

Idaho Historical Society, 1964); and Merrill D. Beal, "Epilogue: Idaho, Gem of the Mountains," in Richard W. Etulain and Bert W. Marley, *The Idaho Heritage* (Pocatello: Idaho State University Press, 1974):207–11.

Treatments of the county and state boundaries include: Clyde A. Bridger, "The Counties of Idaho," *Pacific Northwest Quarterly* 31 (April 1940):187–206; Benjamin E. Thomas, "Boundaries and Internal Problems of Idaho," *Geographical Review* 39 (January 1949):99–109; Benjamin E. Thomas, "Demarcation of the Boundaries of Idaho," *Pacific Northwest Quarterly* 40 (January 1949):24–34; Benjamin E. Thomas, "The Historical Geography of Idaho Counties," *Oregon Historical Quarterly* 50 (September 1949):186–208; and D. Brooks Green, "The Idaho-Wyoming Boundary: A Problem in Location," *Idaho Yesterdays* 23 (Spring 1979):10–14.

Helpful theses and dissertations include: M. L. Hulett, "History of the Movement for a Territorial Organization for Idaho, with Special Reference to the Evolution of Idaho's Present Boundary Lines" (M.A. thesis, University of Idaho, 1938); and Fred Woodward Blase, "The Political History of Idaho Territory" (M.A. thesis, University of California, 1926).

43.

44. 

 45.

43. The original courthouse of Shoshone County, the first county in what became Idaho, was built in 1862 in Pierce, a thriving gold-mining community. UIL 5–85–1A.

44. John Hailey, shown here in 1862, was an early Idaho freighter and packer and later delegate to Congress. ISHS 111–A.

45. William H. Wallace, first governor of Idaho Territory, 1863–64, was a close friend of Abraham Lincoln. CHARLES D. MEDERICKS, N.Y., PHOTOGRAPHER, UIL 3–49A.

46.

47.

46. Idaho's territorial capital, established in Lewiston in 1863, was moved shortly after to Boise. UIL 6–21–2.

47. William J. McConnell, later governor, was captain of a group of vigilantes in 1864. First published in his memoir, *Early History of Idaho* (1913). ISHS 74–190.1.

CHAPTER ELEVEN

# Quartz Mines, Stamp Mills, and Chinese Miners

PLACER mining, the simplest and easiest way of obtaining gold, was the first stage in the development of mining in Idaho. But the territory had more lasting riches. By moving upstream as they "panned" for gold, prospectors discovered gold quartz and then followed the surface overburden toward the outcrop or vein from which the gold had come. Quartz mining, in turn, led to large-scale lead-silver-zinc operations that became the major mining thrust of Idaho when railroads and improved technology were introduced. Idaho was a leading mining territory for many years and later a leading mining state. During the early years, 1860 to 1869, twenty thousand or more miners took out about $57 million in minerals, most of it in gold and silver. Approximately half came from placer mines and half from quartz deposits. From 1863 to 1869, the Boise Basin alone yielded 1.4 million ounces in gold.

The mining of gold-bearing quartz was more complicated than placer mining. Lode miners prospected for gold-bearing veins cropping out on an exposed hill and then tunneled underground to reach the minerals. Ore-bearing rock was removed and hauled through access tunnels or shafts to the surface. Once on the surface, the gold-bearing quartz had to be crushed to a powder to free the gold. Next the gold had to be separated from the sand, as in placer mining. Blasting hard rock was slow and expensive, especially before the introduction of dynamite in 1868. Individuals or small groups of men could engage in placer mining, but lode mining required a larger operation—a company or partnership with more capital, labor, and equipment.

Early Idaho quartz miners used two processes of milling the ore. The simplest and most primitive utilized an arrastra, a crude rock-surfaced mill patterned after a type used in northern Mexico in the sixteenth century. Resembling a round bathtub, the arrastra could be assembled locally and operated at low cost. A three- or four-foot hole in the ground with a hard-surface bottom was lined with flat rocks. Two or four large drag stones were placed in it and balanced on one or two long cross poles that projected out from a central pivot. A horse, mule, or ox walked around the edge, dragging the stone over gold-bearing rock dumped into the "tub." Where possible, waterpower was used in place of the horse or mule.

The other device was a steam stamp mill, usually freighted from San Francisco, which pounded rock into powder in a huge mortar. The quartz was first shattered by sledge-hammers into fragments about the size of apples, then shoveled into feeders where heavy iron stamps mounted on vertical stems rose and fell with the turning of a horizontal shaft to which the stems were geared. The stamps, from 300 to 800 pounds in weight, struck sixty times a minute, making a tremendous racket as they beat the rock to a wet powder. The gold in the crushed rock was then caught, as in placer mining, with quicksilver or washed out through sluices and traps. The "soup" was conveyed to a fire retort, the quicksilver was left behind, and the gold was molded into bricks and bars that brought a gleam to all eyes. Frequently quartz could be mined fast enough to keep an arrastra going, but not fast enough to feed a stamp mill, and so the investment in stamp mills was often unproductive.

The placer excitement in Boise Basin in 1862–63 turned to quartz in the fall of 1863. There had been quartz discoveries near Placerville late in 1862, and at Idaho City, Rocky Bar, and Silver City in 1863. Indeed, George C. Robbins, a former mayor of Portland, having employed a large hand mortar pounding 200 pounds of rock daily, left the basin in September 1863 for San Francisco with 400 pounds of ore from a forty-foot shaft. Another arrastra yielded $200 that year. Placer mining continued to dominate for a time, and lode mining did not really begin until the placer season had largely closed in June 1864. But the richness of the quartz discoveries had already led to the ordering of many stamp mills. A ten-stamp Pioneer mill arrived in Placerville on September 15, 1864, a Gambrinus mill arrived on October 16, and other mills were expected to be in operation in 1865. With ore from a 130-foot tunnel, the Pioneer mill turned out $5,000 in its first week and a total of $20,000 by the next spring.[1]

The spring of 1865, however, was something of a disappointment. The rush from Portland to Boise Basin had been deflected to gold fields in Kootenai (or Kootenay) in British Columbia and the Blackfoot Mountains in Montana. Then on May 18, Idaho City burned down—the first fire in a series of four. More than $1 million in property was destroyed. As the town was rebuilt, placer mining continued; but quartz mining could not be resumed until 1867 when the repaired stamp mills were reinstalled. In the two weeks ending April 28, 1867, the Elk Horn produced $9,105; it produced another $8,200 in a run ending June 15 and still another $12,000 in a cleanup of July 9, 1867. In the spring of 1867 William Lent and James Classen reopened the Pioneer operation on Gold Hill. They not only carried out many tests but also employed "the noted and experienced quartz miner" George Hearst, father of the newspaper magnate William Randolph Hearst and a prominent California lode miner. He took to Owyhee a 25-stamp Chickahoming mill, powered by an eighty-horsepower boiler. Twenty-eight men were employed in running a new tunnel and operating the mill. Still, Gold Hill had to wait for future development before it became the major lode mine in Boise Basin.

By 1868 some of the important Basin placers were being worked out and the quartz finds were not rich enough to continue profitable working. New discoveries in White Pine in northeastern Nevada in 1868 and Loon Creek in the Upper Salmon River country in 1869 drew off some of the Basin's miners.[2]

In several instances, Boise Basin miners attacked the problem of deep gravel by hydraulic mining, a technique invented in California in the early 1850s and later used in Nevada. Hydraulicking was a device for bringing water under high pressure and aiming it, through a hose, at the hill believed to be underlain by a gold-laden channel of an ancient river.[3] The water was run through wooden flumes to the top of a hill so that, in falling, the water would build up a great deal of pressure. Conducted through iron pipes, the water when it reached the bottom of the hill was shot through a cannon-like nozzle or "monitor" or "hydraulic giant" to wash away the mountainside. Once washed loose, the soil was run through long sluices that separated and caught the gold behind riffles. This mass-production system could be applied where there were extensive deposits of buried gravels near large streams, with hills that would give the water sufficient fall. In some areas this became an important source of gold. Although the technique required the purchase of patented nozzles, pipes, and other equipment, it enabled water to do the work of men. Beginning in 1867 a big ditch at Centerville delivered sufficient water to operate hydraulic giants, working a great amount of ground for high returns.

Boise Basin continued to be worked both as a placer and as a quartz camp, although on a lesser scale, throughout the early 1870s. But the experience with stamp mills suggested that their introduction had been premature. Nearly all operations were closed down in 1875 and not resumed until 1884 when the completion of the Oregon Short Line Railroad allowed for more efficient shipment of ore.

Far more success was registered in what was called South Boise—mines south and east of Boise Basin, not south of Boise City. Placers had been traced up Feather River to some promising quartz leads on Bear Creek in May 1863. A stampede of 1,500 Boise Basin miners to that location occurred later in the month. They found high-yield placers on Red Warrior Creek and promising ground on Bear Creek near the quartz outcrops. But the placers were not extensive enough to hold all the rushees, and the quartz prospects could not be developed for a season or two. After the excitement had subsided, about 100 miners remained to work the Red Warrior claims; the future of the South Boise mines was in quartz lodes, not in placers.[4]

Discovery of the Idaho ledge on May 7, 1863, started South Boise quartz mining. Four lodes were being explored by the middle of June. One of these was the Elmore, promoted by Henry Thomas Paige Comstock, who gave his name to the famous Comstock lode of Nevada. "Old Pancake," as he was called, believed the Elmore was as rich as the Comstock.

South Boise was, however, inaccessible. There was no regular express serving the area in the spring of 1863, and miners were fearful of the Bannock on the nearby Camas Prairie. A difficult eighty-mile mountain trail connected the Bear Creek area with West Bannack or Idaho City. There was no road over which heavy equipment might be transported to facilitate quartz development, but quartz discoveries continued to be made. Arrastras, which could be constructed from local materials, were built and were operating by late summer of 1863. Seven tons of Elmore ore averaged $347 per ton, four tons from the Golden

Eagle yielded $1,480, and the Spanish company on the Ophir was thought to have done even better. Nevertheless, owners were not yet able to distinguish outcrops of important producers from rich surface seams that at greater depth were valueless.

Swept away by the astonishing prospects and fabulous claims, miners, merchants, promoters, and freighters invested in stamp mills and other heavy machinery but had to await completion of a wagon road from Boise to Rocky Bar. Meanwhile, they continued to use arrastras. Between June and August 1864, the number of South Boise arrastras rose from ten to eighty. The ore milled in these arrastras ranged from $75 to $300 per ton. By the fall of 1864, waterwheels had been installed to propel the arrastras. Larger arrastras, with a circumference of thirty feet, were milling one to one and one-half tons per day. The Wiley Ophir Company in a ten days' run cleared $3,000 from the tubs of two arrastras. Total 1864 South Boise quartz production was $132,000, of which the Confederate Star yielded $51,000 and the Elmore $15,000.

Some engineers mourned that the inefficient arrastras lost all the silver and part of the gold, and Comstock tried to prove this by finding $10 in a single pan of tailings that were deposited one hundred feet below his arrastra. By the end of 1864 owners were anticipating the arrival of expensive and more efficient stamp mills from Chicago and San Francisco. But their success with arrastras was deceiving. Prospecting was limited to surface operations; they had not sunk shafts or driven tunnels sufficiently to explore their veins for stamp-mill purposes. Outcrops of ore, where weathering and fracturing had softened the rock and freed the gold, were worked easily and cheaply; timbering and hoisting were not required. Rich seams, weathered outcrops, and narrow veins were suitable for arrastra milling but could not supply sufficient ore to keep stamp mills running steadily. Arrastras were small and ground slowly enough to thrive on unsorted ore unsuitable for stamp mills.

South Boise promoters devoted 1864 to organizing substantial companies to procure stamp mills. Seven incorporations were filed in Idaho City during the week ending February 27, 1864, their capitalizations ranging from $40,000 to $160,000. The Ada Elmore Corporation, the largest, was capitalized at $800,000, and the Victor Company was organized in San Francisco to develop Red Warrior properties.[5]

Wilson Waddingham went to South Boise in 1864 and secured rich samples of ore. Assured of the value, he sent 1,500 pounds to San Francisco for a test and recovered $800 per ton. The Comstock had assayed $7,112 per ton, the Confederate Star $5,589, and the Elmore $7,434. As a result of these early workings, Waddingham, reasonably confident because the Civil War was winding down, headed for New York to obtain eastern capital. Another South Boise agent in 1864 was S. B. Farnham, who represented the New York and Idaho Gold and Silver Mining Company. Others were Lafayette Cartee and a Mr. Gates, who rushed a five-ton stamp mill to Rocky Bar in August. This first stamp mill in South Boise reached the mines just as Julius Newberg's South Boise wagon road was finished on September 5, 1864.

The road ended the period of the arrastra. Two new stamp mills arrived before the close of the 1864 season; six others were on their way or being built. The Idaho Company's twelve-stamp mill arrived in November, with a freight tariff of $8,400. Rocky Bar now looked forward to rivaling Virginia City. South Boise miners left their arrastras to be destroyed by the elements during the terrible winter of 1864–65. Miners with small arrastras simply tried to sell their mines to the capitalists with stamp mills: Idaho mining law, by act of February 4, 1864, limited quartz-mining claims to two hundred feet along the vein, so mining companies had to secure holdings from many owners in order to keep their mills going.

For a time South Boise prospered. The Idaho Company's

twelve-stamp mill and Cartee and Gates's five-stamp mill ran continuously during the summer of 1865. The former produced $800 to $1,000 each day; the latter, a custom mill, found ready patrons for $25 per ton. Waddingham's company, capitalized at $600,000, was buying mines recklessly regardless of cost, and the Pittsburgh and Idaho Gold and Silver Mining Company likewise paid out sizable sums—acquiring the Idaho mine and mill for $140,000.[6]

A cloud soon appeared on the horizon. Dr. S. B. Farnham, superintendent of the New York and Idaho company, who had erected a magnificent building to house his ten-stamp mill, started operating August 3, 1865. Within two months the work had come to a complete stop. The unpaid teamsters who had hauled freight for the company took Farnham prisoner; the rest of the crew, miners, carpenters, and engineers barricaded the mill, refusing to let anyone in until they received their back wages.[7]

By the fall of 1865 the mines had been worked sufficiently to reveal problems. There was inadequate water to run the steam engines, and miners were plagued by low-quality ore. In the spring of 1866, as the work progressed below the surface zone of gold concentration that resulted from erosion and decomposition of the exposed quartz, company leaders began to realize that they had estimated values on the basis of exaggerated surface indications. They learned that their prized stamp mills were not recovering gold from the sulphurets (gold combined with sulfur). The cost of transportation sometimes exceeded the cost of goods carried to the mines. An enormous amount of hand work was involved and labor was expensive: wages in South Boise were $7 per day, in Owyhee $6 per day, and in the Comstock in Nevada, only $3.50.

But in the spring of 1866 the stamp milling approach seemed to be still succeeding. Wilson Waddingham's Confederate Star cleared $7,200 from a thirteen-day mill run, at an average of

$82 per ton, and his ten-stamp mill produced $60,000 between December 1865 and March 1866. Others reported good production. By the spring of 1866 South Boise had more stamp mills than any other Idaho district. This was the peak of quartz mining excitement, not only in South Boise but throughout the West. Consideration was being given to establishing a branch United States mint in Boise, in the expectation that South Boise would produce $4.5 million in 1866.[8]

There were other problems. The mining stock exchange in New York City was not doing well in 1865–66. Farnham's 1865 disaster, Victor, collapsed in May 1866, and the milling debacle worsened during the ensuing summer. Farnham's New York and Idaho company let its mill go to pay off debts. Even Wilson Waddingham was attacked as a reckless operator for spending too much. Only two of the well-established companies operated during the summer of 1866.

Yet Waddingham's mills continued to run until the fall of 1867. Major James P. Spear's Pittsburgh company started to sink a deep shaft in the Elmore lode in 1866, but incompetent management caused it to be suspended. Twenty years later, in 1886, it reopened with better equipment and superior techniques.

Meanwhile, operations were going on in Owyhee, in a mountain region seventy miles south of Boise City. Those who left Boise to work in the region encountered a dreary plain of sand and alkali, often too barren even for sagebrush. A little steamer plied the Snake River from Bruneau, below Salmon Falls, to a point about one hundred miles downriver.

Owyhee began with placer gold, continued with quartz gold, and ended up as rich silver-mining country. Albert D. Richardson, a national travel writer who visited Owyhee Country in November 1865, declared that the "Owyhee Region . . . [has] the richest and most abundant lodes of gold and silver-bearing rock ever found in the United States."[9] What he said was true. Their richness did surpass anything else yet found in the nation. Unlike the quartz ledges in Boise Basin and South Boise, Owyhee had mines so rich in depth that some operated for a decade or more before they played out. In the earliest days of Silver City, the War Eagle mines had richer ores and a larger initial production than those previously worked, partly because mines at Owyhee were able to take advantage of Comstock recovery methods that were developed just in time for use in Owyhee.

The process used in silver recovery, called the Washoe pan process, was developed by Almarin B. Paul, a California forty-niner who had been a merchant, publisher, miner, and land agent. He went to Washoe (the Comstock) in 1859. Interested in gold-milling techniques, he signed contracts to supply twenty-four stamp mills in Virginia City early in 1860 and furnished the first quartz mill in operation in the district. But Paul knew little about milling silver ores. Most of the world's silver is found in association with such base metals as lead, zinc, and copper and can be separated from them only by smelting, but the silver ores east of the Sierra Nevada were in association principally with gold and could be treated much like California gold ores. This was fortunate, but the owners were also lucky that the Comstock ores were almost as rich in gold as in silver, and they could usefully transfer to Nevada the techniques they were familiar with in California.

What Almarin Paul did was to improve primitive Mexican practices of separating the silver by dumping quicksilver, salt, and copper sulphate into pans and using the sun to provide the heat to stimulate the interaction. Instead Paul used steam. He adopted heavy iron mullers that would grind as well as mix the pulverized rock. The iron filings that wore off the muller and pan by friction provided another essential ingredient. By 1862 Paul and his associates had evolved these mechanical and chemical constituents into the Washoe pan process. Used with elaborate settling devices and traps, it was the final step in the process of separating out the gold and silver. The material mined went through rock breakers, then through the stamp mill, and finally through the Washoe pans.[10]

Mark Twain's humorous remark about the attempt to get the proper combination of chemicals to release the silver was this: "The object with many inventors of 'processes' appeared to be to physic the silver out of the rock, or at least make it so sick that it would be obliged to loose its hold upon its matrix and come out and be caught by the quicksilver lying in wait for it in the bottom of the pans."[11] Mark Twain could make the Washoe pan process interesting, and other colorful and picturesque names came out of Idaho's mining experience.

Mention was made in Chapter Nine of the Michael Jordan party that found placer gold in the Owyhee Mountains in 1863. That July R. H. Wade of the Jordan party found a quartz lode in Whisky Gulch two or three miles farther up the stream from Happy Camp. A few weeks later, a group of prospectors following gold up to veins on War Eagle Mountain discovered the Oro Fino Ledge. Another lode discovery in October occurred on Jordan Creek just below Whisky Gulch on the other side of the mountain from the Oro Fino. This one they called Morning Star. These discoveries were not immediately appreciated by the miners interested in placers, but they began to draw speculators during the winter of 1863–64. E. T. Beatty, of Rocky Bar, visited Owyhee in November and returned with specimens of Morning Star rock that ran $2,800 in gold and $7,000 in silver to the ton. These assays far surpassed those of Comstock.

Boonville, a little up the river from Happy Camp, became the placer center and had thirteen houses by November. Now, with the Morning Star discovery, another mining town above Boonville was built called Ruby City, and another built a mile up the creek named Silver City. Boonville and Ruby City each had a population of around 250 by February 1864. The *Boise News* of February 20, 1864, said that Boonville, located on the creek between high and rugged hills, had narrow, crooked, and muddy streets that "resembled the tracks or courses taken by a lot of angleworms, and might have been laid out by a blind cow."[12] There were perhaps a dozen frame and log buildings. Ruby City, about twenty miles from the Oregon border, consisted of buildings erected quickly on a wooded hillside sloping down to Jordan Creek, near the bottom of a deep canyon. Looming over the city were several mountains that were gashed with gorges, pointed with turrets, and covered with snow in the winter. The king of these peaks was War Eagle, which, Richardson correctly contended, contained "the richest and most wonderful deposit of quartz yet discovered in the United States, even eclipsing the famed Comstock Lode."[13]

Preparations for working the quartz lodes continued during the winter of 1863–64; fifty-six whipsaws supplied lumber to build the towns. By February 1864 the population of Owyhee had risen to about 1,000. J. Marion More, who had led the Oro Fino District in Pierce City and then had founded Idaho City, acquired an interest in both the Oro Fino and Morning Star properties and attracted wide publicity by exhibiting a 1¼-pound rock from which he had recovered nine ounces of gold and silver. He began to extract ore and process it by hand mortaring. New veins of ore were located on War Eagle Mountain, and owners eagerly ordered stamp mills to work the many veins that had been discovered. The Oro Fino shaft had gone down eighty feet, and in that distance the vein had widened from six inches on the surface to thirty inches at depth. D. H. Fogus, representing the company that owned it, started to run a tunnel and to build a mill.[14]

Also owning Owyhee property was the Oregon Steam Navigation Company, holder of the Columbia River steamboat monopoly that had hauled thousands of miners to Idaho after 1860. Among the officers of the company were Simeon G. Reed, who later owned the Bunker Hill and Sullivan Mine in North Idaho and who endowed Portland's Reed College, and John C. Ainsworth, who later sold Oregon Steam Navigation to railroad magnate Henry Villard. Ainsworth's waterpower mill, built on Sinker Creek three miles below the mine it was to serve, went into operation in July 1864 after men had built a road to the newly installed ten-stamp mill. This mill, which cost $70,000, yielded $90,000 in its first forty-five working days. The mill was converted to steam in October. The mill was designed only to recover gold; when the men noticed that the ore was largely silver, they adapted to the Washoe process which was suited to their ores.[15]

By the fall of 1864 A. P. Minear had established a custom mill with ten 450-pound stamps, and More and Fogus were engaged in serious development of the Oro Fino and Morning Star properties. The More and Fogus ten-stamp mill, the best one in the district, began to operate October 3 with ore that was rich enough to compensate for the $100,000 in rock that had to be hoisted by hand from company shafts. On November 27 More arrived in Portland with $60,000 in silver bricks. The owners expected to add twenty-four stamps the next summer. By December 1864 the Morning Star shaft was down 115 feet and the ore was becoming increasingly rich. The mill was converted to the Washoe process in order to complete recovery of silver, and it produced about $1 million in its first year of operation.[16]

One of the weaknesses in the "every man for himself" approach was the failure to consolidate bordering properties on the same vein. Some three hundred ledges had been found on War Eagle Mountain, and several adjacent independent mines were worked at higher cost than would have been incurred had they been combined in a single operation. Since their development would require outside capital, several promoters went to New York to solicit funds and found some investors sufficiently interested that they advanced money to buy stamp mills. Several were rushed in during the summer and fall of 1865. Packing in the machinery for the large mills required several mule trains, described as having "more of the appearance of a cavalcade of mountain howitzers than anything else."[17]

Meanwhile, More and Fogus drilled day and night and kept their mill running during the winter of 1864–65. Both men thought they had enough good ore to keep them busy, and each of their enterprises employed thirty to forty men. The mines on Jordan Creek were closer to Silver City than to Ruby City, so Silver City boomed.

Inevitably there were conflicts over the drift of the veins. On August 5, 1865, a new lode, called the Hays and Ray, was located. Eight 200-foot claims made up the Hays and Ray property; this vein suddenly became the most prominent of the War Eagle lodes. A prospector named Peck secretly found a "pocket" or "chimney" of very rich float-rock (rock eroded from a lode and carried away by water) about 1,000 feet south of the Hays and Ray shaft. He covered up the pocket, said nothing, and learned from the Hays and Ray discoverers that their boundaries included the spot he had located. He tried to purchase the property and left Owyhee when they wanted too much, thinking they would come down by the time he returned. While he was gone, D. C. Bryan and his small company of prospectors found the same spot, called it the Poorman, and began to take out ore of great richness—80 percent gold and silver, mainly silver. Bryan located seven 200-foot claims and recorded them.

Hays and Ray claimed the ground, of course, but the Poorman Company refused to move. Were there two veins, separate and parallel, or was this simply part of the Hays and Ray vein? Hays and Ray gave Peck, now returned, a share for tracing it from their opening. The Poorman people quickly took out what ore they could in the six days that elapsed before Hays and Ray could get an injunction restraining them. In those six days they removed about $500,000 in gold and silver.[18]

Aware that they were almost certainly on the Hays and Ray

vein, the Poorman owners combined with the Oregon Steam Navigation Owyhee interests to get the financial backing they would need to defend their case. A collision occurred on September 24. Armed with shotguns and sixshooters, the Poorman defenders held back the Hays and Ray forces and built a fort, Fort Baker, of logs with portholes and other means of defense. Knowing the law was on their side, Hays and Ray interests did not attack. Instead, they combined with George C. Robbins and the New York and Owyhee Mill Company to get increased financial backing. As it turned out, the Poorman was simply part of the Hays and Ray claim. A compromise was soon reached, however, and the New York and Owyhee organization and the Oregon Steam Navigation Company came out with a share in the consolidation. The Poorman remained closed, however, until July 6, 1866.[19]

Meanwhile, new mills using the efficient Washoe process were placed in operation in the fall of 1865. By the spring of 1866 Owyhee had ten mills with 102 stamps; the district was second only to South Boise, where larger mills had been installed around Rocky Bar. During the year 1865–66 More and Fogus, in 426 days, had taken $1.1 million from the Morning Star alone. Other mills were in profitable operation. By the end of the summer of 1866 eighty-two stamps were going and production was up to $70,000 a week.[20]

By reputation Ruby City and Silver City were both sober, respectable mining communities. The men worked hard and had no time to party half the night. The stamp mills usually observed Sunday closing. J. A. Chittenden, the leading Owyhee assayer, was also Idaho territorial Superintendent of Public Instruction and kept the Silver City school going. Regular church services were held, and a Sunday School was maintained. Silver City sponsored lectures on temperance and Darwinism, had a circulating library, was entertained by dancing schools and a city band, and had access to theatrical productions and lectures that featured Lisle Lester, Carrie Chapman Catt, and Charlotte Crampton. Patrons saw Shakespeare's *Hamlet* and *Richard III*, and *Retribution*, *Cincinnati Tragedy*, and Boucicalt's *Colleen Bawn*. The Silver City Amateur Theatrical Association put on a play to raise money for the town water tanks, held benefits for blind John Oliver, and presented scenes from Shakespeare's *Winter's Tale*.[21]

Whatever the development of community life, less than a month after the Poorman resumed work, More and Fogus, who had been responsible for most of the production in Owyhee, failed financially. Their collapse, which occurred August 24, 1866, was due to their involvement in other mines; they were overextended. By over-expanding and at the same time neglecting to pay their workers and other creditors, they had become insolvent. More, who owed $200,000, announced that he was giving everything he owned to his creditors. He was absolved of any knavery. The creditors, mainly workers, organized the Morning Star and Oro Fino Gold and Silver Mining Company on September 13, 1866, resumed work in April 1867, and for a while engaged in profitable production at a higher output than under More and Fogus. The Poorman, although in actual production less than six months after its discovery, brought in a return of more than $1 million.

There were other problems in Owyhee. Fed up with mismanagements and incompetency, workers in several plants met at the Owyhee County Court House in Silver City on October 1, 1867, to organize a miners' union—the only such union in western mines since the one organized at Comstock in 1863. The surprised mine owners, after a four-day strike, granted the most important demands of the workers: first, that the workers be given contracts instead of being hired informally, and second, that wages be paid in bullion rather than in depreciated greenbacks. The union did not continue as an active force because of the "every man for himself" fever of the boom. But as the camp became more settled, a union was organized again in the spring of 1872 and succeeded in driving out a foreman who had subjected them to "lavish abuse." The Fairview Miners' Union, as it was called, continued as an active organization until the failure of the mines in 1875.[22]

Some cooperation existed among mine owners, at least for a time. Two veins newly uncovered in 1867, both only a short distance from the Oro Fino, were the Ida Elmore, owned by D. H. Fogus and his associates, and the Golden Chariot, owned by the Hill Beachy syndicate. Rather than risk the heavy expenses connected with a protracted litigation, the interests agreed to share the discoveries, even leaving a neutral ground between their two operations so they would not run into each other. Everything proceeded well until late in February 1868, when Golden Chariot violated the neutral ground and broke into the Ida Elmore workings. Both sides armed for conflict. On March 25, the Golden Chariot forces advanced to the Ida Elmore shaft in an offensive marked by heavy firing that threatened to shatter and break up the timbering in the mine. Fogus sent for reinforcements to gain the upper hand on the surface, and several persons responded to his call. The Owyhee War, as it was called, began. The sheriff shut down all the local saloons. Fighting continued underground, where each party claimed its shooting was to protect its property from intruders.

The governor in Boise (sometimes referred to as Bossy Sitty) at the time was David W. Ballard, a native of Indiana who had replaced Caleb Lyon in June 1866. Ballard had crossed the plains on the Oregon Trail when he was thirty and settled in Lebanon, Oregon, where he practiced medicine. A Republican who served during the time that the unpopular Radical Reconstruction of the South was taking place, Ballard was the target of secessionist sympathizers who tried to drive him from office. Indeed, troops were called from Fort Boise to protect the territorial executive officers from attack. Ballard was dismissed from office four times by President Andrew Johnson, but he had not yet been replaced. He went unpaid as a governor for an entire year, supporting himself by fees from his Boise medical practice.

When word reached the governor's office about the Owyhee War, the mild-mannered but determined Ballard dispatched Idaho's renowned deputy marshal and Indian fighter, Orlando Robbins, with a proclamation ordering both sides to desist and settle the dispute by law. In a record six-hour trip Robbins reached Silver City, consulted the sheriff, rounded up the leaders of the two companies, and read them the proclamation. By late that night a new agreement was reached, formal deeds were drawn, and the matter never went to court. An unfortunate anticlimax just five days later was a drunken celebratory brawl during which J. Marion More was killed. More's friends were about to lynch their Golden Chariot opponents when Governor Ballard arrived, addressed the citizens of Silver City, and summoned troops from Fort Boise. Marching to Owyhee with a brass cannon, 95 soldiers occupied Silver City for four days. The Owyhee War was over. Both companies spent virtually all their earnings on the war effort.

Owyhee production went up to more than $200,000 a month after the war. In the summer of 1868 an improvement in technology was introduced—the use of dynamite. Shipments of gold and silver from Silver City totaled more than $3 million by July 1868, and the next year the amount increased by another million. By 1869 three companies had grossed more than a million dollars each: More and Fogus, the Poorman, and the Ida Elmore. Two other large operations, the Ainsworth and the Golden Chariot, had done well over half a million each. Approximately $4.9 million of bullion shipments had been made from Owyhee by the end of 1869.[23]

The easily mined surface bonanzas had kept the stamp mills going, but the lack of investment capital now retarded development of the mines and the construction of more efficient mills. Work on the high-grade War Eagle properties continued until failure of the Bank of California brought about a general mining collapse in 1875. Then in the 1880s, with improved technology and transportation, stepped-up operations on lower-grade ores brought the major Owyhee boom that lasted for about thirty years until the primary producer became depleted around 1912.

Boise Basin, South Boise, and Owyhee were not the only areas in which quartz mining activity in Idaho occurred in the 1860s. There was some initial prospecting and working of quartz at Deadwood, many miles north of Idaho City; in the Volcano district on the Camas Prairie far south of Rocky Bar; in the Little Smoky district east of Rocky Bar; in the Banner District north and east of Pioneerville; in the Atlanta District on the middle fork of the Boise River east of Idaho City; at Warrens, which became a major lode mining district; along the Wood River in the Hailey Gold Belt; at Leesburg just west of Salmon on tributaries of the Salmon River in northeastern Idaho; and at Loon Creek, far to the north of the Stanley Basin and east and north of the Boise Basin operations, to which there was a significant rush in 1869. Unquestionably, Idaho earned its reputation as a mining territory in the 1860s and drew thousands of adventurers to its mountain-fast treasures.

The continued working of the Montana mines also had an impact on eastern Idaho. The rush to the diggings created serious food shortages. The closest supply of food was in the Mormon settlements in Cache Valley, Weber Valley, Davis County, and the Salt Lake Valley. Joseph and Charles Woodmansee drove four hundred miles to Salt Lake City for winter supplies. By way of Bannack Pass, they went down the Snake River Plain, up the Port Neuf River Valley (Port Neuf later modified into one word), down the Malad Valley, and on to Salt Lake City. Others followed them to East Bannack on the return trip. As the 1863 discoveries at Alder Gulch (Virginia City), seventy miles east of Bannack, brought in additional thousands of people, a new wagon road was constructed by way of Monida and Beaver Canyon into the Snake River Plain—a road that went over two hundred miles within what is now Idaho. This road served as the lifeline of food and supplies for the Montana mines, and for the shipping of gold dust to Salt Lake City and on to San Francisco until the Utah and Northern Railway crossed into Montana in 1880.

A regular traffic developed, with dozens of wagons on the road. A ferry established at Eagle Rock (later Idaho Falls) by Harry Richards and William A. Hickman was taken over in 1863 by a Mr. O'Neil, S. M. Hall, and G. F. Simpson and was granted a charter by the Idaho territorial legislature in January 1864. A similar charter was issued to Joseph Meek and John P. Gibson for a ferry on the Blackfoot River. Ben Holladay received a contract for tri-weekly mail deliveries from Salt Lake City to Virginia City by way of Cache Valley, Fort Hall, Eagle Rock, and Beaver Canyon. On January 22, 1864, the legislature incorporated all of this area, from the borders of Owyhee County east to the peaks of the Rocky Mountains, and from the Utah line north to Montana and beyond, as Oneida County.

Perhaps the most fascinating story of this "Idaho gold road," as it was called, was the use of caravans of camels, particularly on the north Idaho supply route between Washington and Montana. In 1855 Jefferson Davis, Secretary of War, sent a committee to the Near East to buy camels to be used in supplying military outposts in the American West. Over a two-year period seventy-seven Arabian camels—dromedaries—were purchased. Davis was informed that they could travel seventy miles a day and carry half a ton of supplies. Three camels could carry on their backs as much as six mules could pull in a wagon and cover the ground nearly twice as fast. The animals were good swimmers and could climb ascents impracticable to the horse. But there were difficulties. Nearly every horse and mule they met bolted in terror at the sight and smell of the beasts. Moreover, unlike the horses and mules to whom riders and drivers were accustomed, camels had a highly effective means of retaliating when they were not treated with care and respect. If a muleteer should abuse a camel, as he might his mule, the camel would turn around and spit in his face a huge, foul-smelling wad of cud. The animal's moaning and groaning, voluminous sneezes, haughty and disdainful expression, and bad odor caused freighters to hate them to the point of obsession.[24]

Camels were used for a few years as pack animals in the mining districts of New Mexico, Colorado, Nevada, Idaho, Montana, and along the Cariboo Trail in British Columbia. The formation of the camel's foot, however, caused it to suffer when it worked constantly in rocky, mountainous country.

The story of an added hazard in the case of one of the Idaho caravans was told by Colonel Hugh McQuaid, a Midwesterner who went to Montana in 1864:

> In 1866, the camels were taken to Montana. They were in [the] charge of an irascible Frenchman, who brought in a large quantity of miners' supplies from the south. Rocky roads ruined their feet, and when they reached the end of the journey it was necessary for the owner to give them a long period of rest in order that their bruised hoofs might heal. They were herded in the neighborhood of Blackfoot [at the base of Blackfoot Mountain just west of Helena, Montana] which was then a lively mining camp.
>
> While there, Tom McNear, late arrival from Iowa, started out in search of game, as fresh meat was scarce. He had heard great stories of moose in the woods, and his hopes were high that he might bring down one of these rather rare animals. He had never seen a moose, of course, nor had he seen a camel for that matter. He had not proceeded far when he saw through the trees and undergrowth the head of one of the camels. The beast was lying down, and only its head was visible. "It's a moose," he thought, and slipped carefully along until he could get a good shot. He let the animal have it between the eyes, and the camel fell dead.
>
> The Frenchman had been dozing under the trees, and his lamentations over the loss of his camel were loud and

> emphatic. McNear thought he had run across a crazy man, and as the other camels came into view, he yelled at the frantic Frenchman: "Keep still, you darned fool, and I'll get the rest of the herd." Not until the Frenchman calmed down did McNear get the idea into his head that he had made a blunder. He finally settled for $300. McNear did not hear the last of his moose hunt for many a day, and it cost him many another dollar for drinks to quiet the joshers. The Frenchman lost no time in taking his humpedback animals out of the country.[25]

As the surface and easily worked quartz operations in Idaho Territory were played out in the late 1860s, many of the disappointing claims were sold to incoming Chinese. The Chinese began to work many of the low-grade and abandoned mines in the Clearwater and Salmon Mountain areas, and more and more of them drifted into Boise Basin, South Boise, and Owyhee. By 1870 there were 4,274 Chinese in Idaho, nearly all of whom listed themselves as miners. In fact, they constituted more than one-third of all the people in the territory and 60 percent of all the miners.

Chinese first began to move into Idaho, principally from California, Nevada, and British Columbia, when the early placer mines began to play out. After considerable opposition, the claim holders at Oro Fino, in September 1864, adopted a resolution to invite the Chinese into the camp. As other mining camps became less productive and laborers left to follow other diggings, they followed Oro Fino's example and invited Chinese labor. Within the next three years Chinese appeared in every mining district of northern Idaho, with as many as two thousand in the region. In the middle sixties the Chinese moved southward into the mining districts of central Idaho, reaching the Owyhee District in the spring of 1865. On June 23, 1866, the Owyhee *Avalanche* reported "Almost every abandoned claim or gulch in which the color of gold can be found has its gang of

Chinamen at work." More than 500 Chinese were said to have been working Jordan Creek.[26]

Chinese were moving into Boise Basin at the same time, buying up the "old, good-for-nothing claims" in the region. By 1869 there were perhaps two thousand Chinese in the Basin, accounting for almost half the population there. By 1870 they held most of the creek and gulch claims of the Basin. That year they also moved into the Warrens District, which had more than a thousand Chinese by 1871. According to a government report, the Chinese "monopolized the gravel workings, going over the mining grounds a second and a third time."[27] Rossiter W. Raymond reported in 1872 that two-thirds of all the claims being worked in Idaho that year were in the hands of the Chinese.[28] The following year he reported that for every paying claim worked by white men in Idaho, there were probably five or six that were returning a profit to the Chinese, and some camps were worked almost exclusively by Chinese.[29]

With their exotic appearance, customs, sing-song chant, and language, the Chinese were very different from Idaho's diverse rabble of miners. In Silver City, where they numbered 700 in 1874, they were generally regarded as reliable and were respected by most of the townspeople. They had a Masonic temple, two joss houses (houses of adoration), four stores, three restaurants, two laundries, five gambling establishments, and many warehouses.[30]

Most of Idaho's Chinese belonged to a company, or tong, that assisted them in finding work, looked after them if arrested, cared for them if ill, and gave them a Chinese burial (transported their bones to China). By and large, they were industrious, patient, and loyal. They reworked the tailings left by quartz reduction mills, repanned gold placers which white men had abandoned, and, in Silver City at least, packed water from mountain springs for deposit in wooden barrels kept at each home and business establishment. As in medieval China, they shouldered a yoke from which two five-gallon cans swung, and delivered one load of ten gallons to each patron daily, with an extra turn on Monday, the community washday. For this service the laborer was rewarded $.50 per week.[31] Some Silver City elite employed Chinese servants at $40 per month; other Chinese contracted to cut wood for residents and business establishments. Still others operated laundries.

If we count the Indians as one brotherhood, the Chinese were the second group to add to the cultural diversity of the territory as well as contribute toward its economic productivity. With their long black braids that swung under wide coolie hats, their baggy blue pantaloons that flopped as they trotted to and from their work, they were distinctive. So were their parades, the darling of which was the great dragon—a writhing, brightly colored monster that, amid a fusillade of firecrackers and the beating of gongs and the clashing of cymbals, twisted and undulated while "his" head turned from side to side hissing and breathing smoke.[32]

Whereas a white worker wanted from five to seven dollars a day, Chinese workmen were willing to earn from one to two dollars a day. They lived frugally, shared a hut in "Chinese row" with eight or ten companions, ate meagerly, and carefully hoarded their money to return to China. Subjected to ridicule and prejudice, often robbed and beaten, they did not fare well in American courts. "He doesn't have a Chinaman's chance" became an American expression. But like Idaho's miners, merchants, and farmers, they doggedly endured.

## CHAPTER ELEVEN: SOURCES

Nearly all the sources listed for Chapter Nine have been used for this chapter as well. That includes the Idaho, Northwest, and Western histories, the listed mining histories, and many of the dissertations and periodical articles.

For this chapter I have relied very heavily on Wells, *Gold Camps and Silver Cities*, and Beal and Wells, *History of Idaho*, 1:359–68. For the South Boise section I have made heavy use of Robert L. Romig, "Stamp Mills in Trouble: Quartz Miners Learned the Hard Way on the South Boise Ledges," *Pacific Northwest Quarterly* 44 (October 1953):166–76. Other sources include: Paul, *Mining Frontiers of the Far West*; H. Leigh Gittins, *Idaho's Gold Road* (Moscow: University Press of Idaho, 1976); Arthur A. Hart, *Basin of Gold: Life in the Boise Basin, 1862–1890* (Boise: Lithocraft, 1986); Rossiter W. Raymond, *Mineral Resources of the States and Territories West of the Rocky Mountains* (Washington, D.C.: Government Printing Office, 1869); Betty Derig, "A History of Silver City, Idaho" (M.A. thesis, Montana State University, 1951); W. W. Staley, *Gold in Idaho* (Moscow, Idaho, 1946); Elliott West, "Five Idaho Mining Towns: A Computer Profile," *Pacific Northwest Quarterly* 73 (July 1982):108–20 (the five towns were Centerville, Idaho City, Pioneer, Placerville, and Silver City); Greever, *Bonanza West*, 257–73; and "Frisky Times in Silver City," in Hanley and Lucia, *Owyhee Trails: The West's Forgotten Corner*, 198–231.

References on camels in the West are found in Lewis B. Lesley, ed., *Uncle Sam's Camels . . .* (El Paso, Texas: Rio Grande Press 1929, 1970); Robert Froman, "The Red Ghost," *American Heritage* 12 (April 1961):34–37, 94–98; William Lewis, "The Camel Pack Trains in the Mining Camps of the West," *Washington Historical Quarterly* 19 (October 1928):271–84; Thomas L. Connelly, "The American Camel Experiment: A Reappraisal," *Southwestern Historical Quarterly* 69 (April 1966):442–62; and an article in the *Deseret Weekly* (Salt Lake City), October 1, 1898, p. 496.

On the Chinese in Idaho in the 1860s and 1870s, I have used: Fern C. Trull, "History of the Chinese in Idaho" (M.A. thesis, University of Oregon, 1946); Betty Derig, "The Chinese of Silver City," *Idaho Yesterdays* 2 (Winter 1958–59):2–5; Randall E. Rohe, "After the Gold Rush: Chinese Mining in the Far West, 1850–1890," *Montana The Magazine of Western History* 32 (Autumn 1982):2–19; Betty Derig, "Celestials in the Diggings," *Idaho Yesterdays* 16 (Fall 1972):2–23; Gunther Barth, *Bitter Strength* (Cambridge: Harvard University Press, 1964); and Li Hua Yu, "The Chinese in Idaho" (Ph.D. dissertation, Bowling Green University, 1991).

48.

48. Chinese immigrants to Idaho in the 1860s surround themselves with carvings, paintings, and furniture from their distant homeland. ISHS 72–28.15.

49.

49. When the early gold mines played out, Chinese miners turned to gardening, peddling, cooking meals, and washing clothes. One-fourth of the population of Idaho in 1870 were Chinese. ISHS 3796.

CHAPTER TWELVE

# Early Latter-day Saint Settlers in Idaho: Mormon Farm Villages

THE major force in the early history of Idaho Territory was mining, and the earliest isolated settlers made their living in part by supplying miners. But another influence became important and remains significant to this date—irrigated agriculture, commenced by Mormons and other farmers who entered the territory in the 1860s.

The first permanent non-Indian settler in what is now Idaho was Colonel William Craig, a Virginian fur trapper who established a home near Spalding's mission at Lapwai in 1846. He was respected by the Nez Perce (his wife was a Nez Perce) and assisted Oregon white leaders in negotiating treaties with the Nez Perce in the 1850s. For this he was given the title of lieutenant colonel. He was the first Indian agent at Lapwai and was buried there in 1869. His son-in-law, Albert H. Robie, in August 1864 in Boise established a large new sawmill that provided doors, molding, and other lumber for Boise's commercial structures and residences. Robie later expanded into central

Oregon, where he operated a large ranch with Alexander Rossi—also his partner in the mill.

A second early settler and close friend of Colonel Craig was "Doctor" Robert Newell, a trapper with the Smith-Jackson-Sublette party of the Rocky Mountain Fur Company, who spent twenty years in Idaho. In 1840 he led the small party that drove the first wagons over the Oregon Trail from Fort Hall along the Snake River Plain to Marcus Whitman's mission at Waiilatpu. Newell joined the rush of gold seekers who went to Pierce City and Oro Fino in 1861–62, served for a period as an Indian agent at Lapwai, helped with treaties with the Nez Perce, and died in 1869 in Lewiston.

After the establishment of the Lapwai Mission in the late 1830s, as we have seen, the first group settlement in what is now Idaho was by Latter-day Saints at Limhi. But the first permanent Latter-day Saint settlers founded Franklin in April 1860. They had already planted and harvested crops by the time of the initial discovery of gold at Pierce City. We have postponed a discussion of this first permanent Idaho settlement because the Franklin settlers thought they were in Utah. (Franklin is only one mile north of the Utah border.) They and their eventual neighbors continued to act on this assumption until an official survey was accepted in 1872.

The Organic Act of Utah Territory (1850) specified the Forty-second Parallel as the northern border of Utah, but no one in the 1850s and 1860s knew its precise location. Until the official survey settled the matter in 1872, the people of Cache Valley paid taxes in Utah, and the Cache County Court created school districts and voting precincts and appropriated money for roads in northern Cache Valley communities. Residents voted in Utah elections and elected a representative who served in the Utah Legislature. The citizens of Oneida County, Idaho, created in 1864, suspected at least as early as 1866 that the Franklin and northern Cache Valley communities might be in their county, but they held no Idaho elections there and did not succeed in collecting taxes. In 1870 federal census enumerators headquartered in Salt Lake City took a census of Franklin, Oxford, and other northern Cache Valley villages, assuming they were in Utah. At the same time, census enumerators from Boise took the census on the assumption that these communities might be part of Idaho.

Although Franklin was Idaho's first permanent settlement, its status was not officially ratified because of the boundary confusion until several years after the town was founded. Not until June 3, 1872, did Cache County, Utah, turn over its assessment records for Idaho towns to Oneida County. The same was true of Bear Lake communities, which were considered part of Richland County, Utah, until Idaho created Bear Lake County in 1875. After the survey was accepted in 1872 Charles C. Rich, founder of the Bear Lake communities, sat in the Legislative Council of Utah, while his son Joseph C. Rich, living nearby, sat in the Idaho Legislature in Boise. The Mormon settlers apparently preferred to have their civil structure follow the familiar Utah pattern. Idaho officials, preoccupied with mining districts in the Clearwater, Salmon Mountain, Boise Basin, and Owyhee regions, may not have cared whether the Mormons were part of "their" territory.

The area was settled partly as a result of the federal military presence in Utah. After the army established Camp Floyd south of Salt Lake City in the summer of 1858, people felt freer to move into areas where Indians were occasionally present. In the spring of 1859, under the guidance of Brigham Young and Peter Maughan (the Cache Valley presiding Mormon bishop), incoming groups planted colonies in Wellsville, Mendon, Logan, and Summit Creek (Smithfield). In the fall they settled Providence. Maughan was ecstatic about Cache Valley, which was about forty miles long and twelve miles wide, and advertised its facilities for irrigation and grazing in June 1859 through the Salt Lake newspaper, the *Deseret News.*[1]

Among those who were influenced by this and other news

about Cache Valley were five men from Weber Valley who went to reconnoiter the region north of existing settlements. Others followed. During the second week of April 1860 several home-seekers went to the confluence of Worm Creek and Cub River (originally called the Muddy), 110 miles from Salt Lake City. One group of thirteen families under the leadership of Thomas S. Smart, a brickmaker from Staffordshire and Normandy who had previously settled in Provo, Utah, arrived April 14; a second group followed on April 15. Still another group arrived on May 1. By the end of 1860 there were approximately sixty-one families, comprising more than one hundred persons. Most of them were young married couples from other Utah settlements—Payson, Provo, Slaterville, Kaysville, and Bountiful. All were Latter-day Saints. Presiding Bishop Maughan appointed three of them, Thomas S. Smart, Samuel R. Parkinson, and James Sanderson, to take charge of affairs until a formal organization, a "ward," was effected. There were Indians in the vicinity and their chief, Kittemere, welcomed the colonists to the land, water, and timber. The Mormons gave him presents of beef and grain.

The families placed their wagon boxes on the ground as temporary dwellings, grouped together as a means of protection from troublesome hostiles, and the undercarriages on the wagons were used to haul logs from the nearby canyon. Meals were cooked on campfires. The men immediately began to lay out a fort-style village, sixty by ninety rods, wherein log cabins were built with doors opening to the inside of the enclosure. The fort was ready for occupancy in August. Corrals for stock were outside the fort with hay ricks beyond the corrals. An important early task was building a pit-sawmill for preparing lumber. Within a year it was replaced by a water-powered sawmill. During the first summer five children were born in the wagon boxes.

On April 19 the settlers met to allot land. There was some discussion of whether unmarried men should be allowed to take part in the drawing, but with only three dissenting votes the group approved their inclusion. Ten-acre lots away from the campsite had been surveyed and numbered, using a rope for measuring distances, and direction determined by sighting on the North Star. The names of the persons were then placed in a hat with a drawing number. Number one had first choice on his lot, number two second choice, and so on. As it turned out, the first two numbers were drawn by single men. They chose their lots close together near the center of the plot. In the summer the men built a bowery as a place to hold church and village meetings. This was an enclosure of brush and boughs that could shelter an audience of 200 persons.

Although it snowed as late as May 12, the men had their land cleared, plowed, and planted to oats, barley, and wheat by the first of June. Next they planted their gardens. Finally, they made ditches to irrigate their land. Except for Spalding's irrigation in the Clearwater Mission in 1838, this was the first irrigation system in Idaho. First, water was conveyed from Spring Creek into the fort for their domestic use. They next dug a ditch from High Creek down to the south field where their crops were planted. Other ditches were made from Oxkiller and South canyons. Landowners worked on the ditches servicing their properties, and the ditches were finished about the middle of July. The next ditch was the city ditch that, enlarged many times, still furnishes water for the city of Franklin.

Most of their food during this first summer came from the Salt Lake Valley, where members of the colony returned from time to time to work on the Church Public Works (temple, theater, roads). For their work they obtained credits to pay for the withdrawals of foodstuffs and supplies from the church's general tithing office.

In early June Brigham Young made a visit to the village; gave it the name Franklin, after Franklin D. Richards, an apostle; and renamed the Muddy the Cub River, because it flowed into the Bear. Young appointed Preston Thomas, a convert from Mississippi and proven pioneer, as bishop. Thomas, who was unpaid, was the principal connection between the central church in Salt Lake City and the settlers in Franklin. He introduced and directed spiritual and temporal programs, collected tithes and contributions, gave counsel, relayed doctrinal pronouncements and policy decisions, solicited volunteers for special missions, and, to use Brigham Young's expression, "notified everyone of his duties." Thomas supervised public works in Franklin; directed the community's common enterprises, including the provision of welfare assistance for the sick, needy, and visiting Indians; settled disputes and conflicts; and conducted Sunday and weekday meetings, funeral services, and marriages.

Thomas also managed the Franklin Tithing Office (the village's general store), which was the central coordinating agency in the village. A similar agency functioned in Mormon villages in Utah and was established in each LDS settlement founded in Idaho in the years that followed. The tithing office was the agency through which tithings of produce, livestock, and other items were received and expended. Above all, it was useful in Franklin in providing flour, beef cattle, grain sorghum, bullets, and other items to visiting Indians. The resulting friendship no doubt helped to prevent contemplated raids on the isolated and vulnerable settlement.[2]

By the fall of 1860, the Franklin settlers had completed their log cabins and dug a well inside the fort. Samuel Parkinson had opened a store, and Alfred Alder and Shem Purnell had started a blacksmith shop. Other early enterprises were a gristmill and creamery. Hannah Comish started a school in her own cabin; she had twenty students. The next spring a one-room combination schoolhouse-meetinghouse, located inside the fort, was completed. Like the log cabin homes, this structure had a sod roof, straw floor, benches made of slab lumber, and a fireplace;

it also had the only window glass in the colony. The building was also Franklin's entertainment center, where readings, lectures, plays, dances, and special dinners were held during the almost four years the settlers lived in the fort.

The first season's harvest consisted of potatoes, onions, and forty-eight bushels of wheat. Although the harvest of 1861 was still small, the settlers felt assured that the land would support them. But with good reason the settlers were apprehensive of Indian depredations. Although Cache Valley was "swarming with Indians," no overwhelming dangers seemed to confront the white settlers—at least at the beginning.[3] Long before the whites came along as fur traders, overland emigrants, and settlers, the Indians had visited this green valley, well watered by many tributaries flowing down from the Bear River Range on the east into the Bear River. There they found an abundance of fish, game, berries, and roots for themselves and their horses.

The Indians of the Cache area were Northern or Northwestern Shoshoni, one of at least five major groups of Shoshoni.[4] The Northwestern bands had camps on Bannock Creek, just south of Fort Hall; near Kelton, Utah, at the northern tip of Great Salt Lake; near the confluence of Bear River with Great Salt Lake; along Logan River above its confluence with Little Bear River; and along Battle Creek, as it flows into the Bear River.

Although Mormons entered into treaty arrangements with various Indian bands and were generous in their gifts to Indians who passed through their villages, Indians became increasingly unhappy with the Mormon tendency to fill up the land with farms and livestock. On the one hand, the Mormons accepted Brigham Young's assertion that it was cheaper to feed Indians than to fight them; on the other hand, they believed they had a right to settle the land, grow crops, and make a living. They became impatient with the constant thievery and aggressive killing. Also, the Mormons suffered when thoughtless emigrant groups killed Indians quite wantonly, and the Indians, insisting on revenge, took it out on the Mormons. One band of Shoshoni established a winter camp near Ogden, Utah, and began to steal cattle and cut fences for firewood. When a Mormon leader, David Moore (who had been at Limhi), protested, Chief Little Soldier replied: "The grass the cows eat and the wood from which the fences are built belong to the Indians."[5]

Although Brigham Young, as Utah's Superintendent of Indian Affairs, and his successors tried valiantly to obtain government support for the Shoshoni, there was little response compared with what the government had done or was doing for other Indian nations. Frequent incidents threatened both whites and natives. In July 1860 an Indian was captured for stealing horses and shot while attempting to escape. The Indians retaliated by shooting John Reed, father of the first child born in Franklin. The settlers had to guard their stock constantly but nevertheless lost many horses and cattle. Raids, kidnappings, and "audacious outrages" provoked the Cache Valley settlers, and pitched battles occurred between local militiamen and angry Indians.

In 1862 President Abraham Lincoln, to insure protection for the overland mail, telegraph, and emigrants (and to keep an eye on the Mormons who, government officials felt, might threaten to secede), called seven hundred California Volunteers to establish Camp Douglas in the hills overlooking Salt Lake City. They were under the command of Colonel Patrick E. Connor, a veteran of the war of 1846 and a California forty-niner. Connor and the Volunteers were disappointed that, instead of being ordered to the front in Virginia, where honor and glory might be won, they had been consigned to a desert area where they might "freeze to death around sage brush fires" while they chased "nondescript bands of Indians away from the mail stations."[6] As historian Brigham Madsen writes: "The stage was set for confrontation between a group of westerners who looked upon all Indians as nuisances at best and the Shoshoni who had abandoned any pretense at peace and were attacking settlers and their herds, and emigrants and miners, with uninhibited determination to stop white encroachment and to secure food and supplies for their families."[7]

During the early winter of 1862–63 a group of miners from the Grasshopper Creek diggings at Bannack, Montana, was attacked by Shoshoni-Bannock, and one of them was killed. A surviving miner asked federal officers for help. Chief Justice John F. Kinney of Utah Territory (a non-Mormon presidential appointee) issued a warrant for the arrest of Chiefs Bear Hunter, Sandpitch, and Sagwitch, along with a request that Colonel Connor support the United States marshal in serving the warrant. Having heard that a large band of Northwestern Shoshoni under the three chiefs was camped in a ravine near the Bear River about twelve miles north of Franklin, the flinty Irishman was glad to oblige and marched his men from their base at Camp Douglas by night so as not to frighten away the Indians. They took fifteen supply wagons and two howitzers. The Indians, as it turned out, had no intention of leaving. Four hundred warriors were prepared to defend their camp. The weather was sub-zero. Connor's troops crossed the ice-choked Bear River on the early morning of January 29, 1863. The colonel did not ask for and was not offered any assistance from the Cache Valley Mormons, who were prepared to flee in the event of an Indian victory.

The ensuing battle, variously called the Battle of Bear River and the Bear River Massacre, resulted in more casualties than did any other Indian disaster in American history. Whereas the notorious Wounded Knee massacre of December 29, 1890, resulted in 146 Oglala Sioux deaths and that at Sand Creek in 130 Cheyenne deaths, the one at Bear River may have cost as many as 368 Indian lives. The battle was important because it brought about a significant change in Indian-white relations.

The Indians fought ferociously, and the battle was deadly. At the beginning the Indians were very confident, and most of the white casualties occurred as the infantry descended from the mountain toward Bear Hunter's redoubt. When Connor's men determined that a frontal assault would probably fail, they began a flanking movement to attack the Indians from either side and from the rear. Near the end of the four-hour battle, when the Indians realized they were not going to win, they began a wholesale attempt to escape. Following Connor's instruction that they take no prisoners, the troops rushed in and began a methodical slaughter. While the Volunteers counted 22 of their own dead, 49 wounded, and 79 disabled by frostbite, the colonel reported 224 Indian deaths (a Mormon observer reported 368) including almost 90 women and children. Some 160 women and children were saved, and a few Indian boys and men escaped via Bear River. The troops destroyed 70 tepees, captured 175 horses, and confiscated 1,000 bushels of grain. Although modern historians now consider the killing of the men, youths, women, and children at the end of the battle as unforgivable, the destruction of this band of Shoshoni was regarded at the time as proper punishment for a group that had terrorized emigrants and citizens of northern Utah and southern Idaho for more than twenty years. Colonel Connor was advanced to the office of brigadier general, and the troops were commended for their "heroic conduct and brilliant victory."[8]

Franklin residents became involved after the battle when they took teams and sleighs and helped remove the wounded soldiers and Indians and the Indian women and children. Many on both sides had frozen feet. Those in need of care were taken to Franklin, and some of the orphaned Indian children were adopted by Cache Valley families. Sagwitch, who Connor had reported was among those killed, was instead seriously wounded. He was nursed back to health and later became a baptized Mormon.

Two sequels affected Idaho history. First, surviving Indians (perhaps 1,500 Northwest Shoshoni were not at the massacre site) sought revenge and booty to replace their losses. The Mormon settlers in Cache Valley suffered heavy losses in cattle and horses, despite their continual handouts of beef, grain, and vegetables. A near disaster occurred at Franklin in September 1863 when a settler shot a drunken Indian who was trying to ride his horse over a white woman. The Shoshoni seized a hostage, demanded that the man who had fired the shot be turned over to them, and resisted all pleas by the Mormon bishop to settle the affair peaceably. The prompt arrival of 300 militiamen from other Cache Valley villages prevented bloodshed and led to a conference with Chief Washakie of the Eastern Shoshoni, who was able to end the affair amicably.

Second, James Duane Doty, the government-appointed superintendent of Indian affairs of Utah Territory, negotiated treaties with the various groups of Shoshoni in July 1863. A treaty was signed with Chief Washakie and the Eastern Shoshoni at Fort Bridger on July 2 and with the chiefs of the Northwestern Shoshoni on July 30 at Box Elder (Brigham City). The signing chiefs solemnly promised an end to plunder and killing, and the government was given permission to construct telegraph lines, overland stage routes, stage stations, and railroads through Indian territory. When the government failed to carry out its promises to provide help to the tribes, the indignant Indians continued to bother local farmers by stealing livestock, grain, and clothing. The Indians were less daring in their raids, however, because Colonel Connor had established a post at Soda Springs. In 1867 the Fort Hall Indian Reservation was established and most of the Cache Valley Indians eventually went there to live.[9]

The Mormons continued their policy of helping the Indians through their Tithing Office. The 1864 "Indian Account" of the Cache Valley Tithing Office shows the following disbursements to Indians:

| Date | Item Disbursed | Value |
|---|---|---|
| Apr. 15 | 104 lbs. flour to Sagwich | $ 6.25 |
| Apr. 19 | 216 lbs. flour to Weber Jack | 12.96 |
| May 2 | 50 lbs. flour to Indian George | 3.00 |
| July 23 | 500 lbs. flour to Indian Bannacks | 30.00 |
| July 5 | 102 lbs. flour to Indian Charles | 6.12 |
| July 31 | 760 lbs. flour to Indian Washakie | 45.60 |
| Aug. 16 | 300 lbs. flour to Indian Madagin | 18.00 |
| Sept. 8 | One beef ox per P. Maughan to Washakie | 70.00 |
| Oct. 7 | One beef ox per T. Tarbet to Washakie | 35.00 |
| Oct. 7 | One beef steer per T. E. Ricks to Washakie | 35.00 |
| Oct. 7 | 116 lbs. beef to Sagwich | 6.95 |
| Nov. 24 | 5 bu. wheat ($10.00); 5 bu. corn ($7.50) to Sagwich | 17.50 |
| Nov. 24 | 10 bu. potatoes ($10.00); 10 bu. carrots ($5.00) to Sagwich | 15.00 |
| Nov. 24 | 1 bu. corn ($1.50); 5 bu. potatoes ($5.00) to Sagwich | 6.50 |
| Nov. 24 | 5 bu carrots to Sagwich | 2.50 |

Source: "Logan General Tithing Office Account Book, 1864–65," 12–13. This record is in the LDS Church Library-Archives, Salt Lake City.

Obviously, Cache Valley contributions toward the welfare of the Indians were not insubstantial. The accounts also contain such notations as "Fixin' gun for Indian George" and "Bullets for Indian Alma."

Whatever the justification for the "battle" or "massacre," the consequence of that encounter and the signing of the Treaty of Box Elder signalled to the settlers in what had become Idaho Territory in July 1863 that there was now less risk in settling new and choice localities. That is precisely what happened. Franklin became "mother" of many settlements in southeastern Idaho.

Reasons for the spread of settlement are not hard to determine. Mormons had a high birth rate, the supply of easily irrigated land was scarce, additional convert-immigrants were coming each summer from England and Scandinavia, and many families were looking for better land to farm. In 1860 Cache Valley had 2,605 people; by 1870 it had 8,299. A. J. Simmonds has estimated that Cache Valley's population had increased about 50 percent between 1861 and 1864, the very years when Indian resistance precluded the establishment of new settlements. As he suggests: "The genocide at Bear River must have seemed a heaven-sent opportunity to break out of the strait jacket into which Shoshoni resistance had placed valley residents."[10]

Brigham Young had asked Colonel James H. Martineau, the Cache County Surveyor, to explore Bear Lake Valley in 1862, and after the Treaty of Box Elder, Young moved quickly. At a meeting held Sunday evening, August 23, 1863, in Logan, "to take into consideration the immediate possession of Bear Lake Valley," Brigham asked for fifty men from Cache Valley to go over to Bear Lake Valley, about a day's horseback ride to the east, to build up a fort before winter. Several hundred Saints would be sent the next year under the direction of Apostle Charles C. Rich to establish settlements north, south, and west of the lake. The president did not want a "single soul" to say anything about the enterprise—"otherwise it will be telegraphed to old Abe Lincoln by some of these officers, and then it will be made a reservation of immediately to prevent us from getting it." "Is the Bear Lake Valley in Utah Territory?" asked one person. "I don't know," responded the president, "neither do I care." He then asked the Cache Valley leaders to make a road to Bear Lake so he could visit the new settlements the next year. "Lay low, watch for 'black ducks,' " he concluded, meaning presumably federal military personnel. "We calculate to be kings of these mountains. Now let us go ahead and occupy them."[11]

Among those assigned to make the journey to Bear Lake were

settlers from Providence, Logan, and Franklin. One of them wrote, on the day of leaving, "Our desire is to build the cities of Zion and by the help of the Lord we hope to accomplish it."[12]

While in Logan, Young picked sites for settlement and negotiated a treaty with Washakie of the Shoshoni and Tagi of the Bannock that allowed Mormon settlement north of Bear Lake. The south end of the lake was a traditional gathering place for the Shoshoni where, among other activities, they engaged in trade with the Utes, which may explain why American fur trappers held two great fur-trade rendezvous there in 1827 and 1828.

General Rich (he had been a Mormon general during the Utah War) led the advance group of settlers across the mountains for Bear Lake Valley on September 18, taking nine wagons. They were eight days in traveling the forty-six miles since it was necessary to cut a road through the timber and construct dugways along steep hillsides until they reached what they later called Paris Creek. (The town was laid out by Surveyor Frederick Perris, but someone misspelled his name when they applied for a post office, and so it became Paris.) The advance company, reinforced by others who arrived in October, built twenty cabins of aspen logs to house the settlers who would remain for the winter. The structures had dirt floors and roofs. Wild hay was cut from the meadows and stored to feed the animals during the winter, which proved to be mild. Between twenty and thirty families spent their first winter at Paris.

The settlers were not without entertainment. Among other things, the drama *William Tell* was presented. Because music was necessary, two men made the winter trip to Franklin to replace some broken violin strings. The men carried back forty pounds of mail to Paris, each with twenty pounds on his back. They were the first in a regular weekly mail service carried by tithing labor, residents donating one day in ten as "public labor."

When the snows melted in the spring 700 additional settlers arrived, and nine more settlements were established: Laketown, Garden City, St. Charles, Ovid, Fish Haven, Bloomington, Bennington, Liberty, and Montpelier. Most of these settlers were from Cache, Davis, and Utah counties. They built homes, erected fences, plowed land, and planted crops.

Brigham Young and other church officials went to Bear Lake Valley in May 1864 to inspect the settlements. As the party left Franklin there were 153 persons, 86 riding in vehicles and the remainder mounted on horses. They had difficulty climbing the mountains separating Franklin from Bear Lake Valley, found themselves struggling through deep mud as they reached the Bear Lake side, and finally arrived at Paris at three o'clock in the morning. At the time Paris consisted of thirty-four log huts with dirt roofs. The Bear Lakers gave the president and company an early breakfast of lake trout fried in butter, after which they understandably took a nap.

The next day the party visited the various settlements in the valley. On Sunday, they held a meeting in front of Apostle Charles C. Rich's cabin in Paris. Young named one settlement, seven miles south of Paris, St. Charles after Apostle Rich. Rich asked Young to name the creek as well. Young replied: "You may call it big water, tall water, large water, big creek, pleasant water, or rich water." With no attempt at poetry or euphony, it was called Paris Creek. Asked about a new-found settlement ten miles northeast of Paris, he said he wished to name it Montpelier, after the capital of his native state of Vermont.

Young was full of advice:

> Make your fences strong and high at once, for to commence a fence with three poles will teach your cows and other stock to be breachy [fence jumpers]. They learn to jump a three-pole fence, you add another pole and they learn to jump that, and thus they are trained to leap fences which would otherwise be sufficient to turn them.[13]

Little children should not be sent out from the settlement to herd cattle or sheep, he admonished, but kept at home or (if old enough) entered in school.

Following the meeting, the pioneers formed St. Charles, dividing the farmland between them by lot, and surveyed the townsite into ten-acre blocks. Twenty-five families built cabins on their village lots in 1864. In 1865 they erected a log meeting-house-schoolhouse and in 1866 added a flour mill. Also in the spring of 1864, north of St. Charles, the town of Liberty was founded where twenty families built cabins, planted crops, and set out an orchard. In the northern end of the valley Montpelier was also established in 1864, and water was brought from Montpelier Creek to irrigate the farms.

For at least two years early frosts damaged a large part of the Bear Lake crops, so many settlers were forced to journey across the mountains to Cache Valley to acquire foodstuffs. Some colonizers ground up their frost-bitten wheat or oats in coffee grinders and sifted out the coarser particles with sieves. In 1865 Francis Pomeroy built a flour mill at the mouth of a nearby canyon, and in 1866 a sawmill was built in Paris Canyon.

The experiences of each of the nine towns founded in 1864 were similar: the colonists laid out townsites, built log cabins, irrigated the land, and tilled the soil. The early years were hard—a plague of grasshoppers damaged the crops in 1867—but the settlers persevered and gradually turned to livestock production.[14]

In 1865 a few settlers violated Rich's instructions about not settling the south end of the lake and began to build fences and make farms. The Shoshoni destroyed their crops and sent the settlers scurrying back to the relative security of St. Charles. This confrontation caused other pullbacks in northern Cache Valley and northern Bear Lake Valley. Not until 1867 were the towns in northern Cache Valley and Bear Lake Valley permanently reoccupied.

In addition to the new colonies in Bear Lake Valley in July 1864, Cache Valley leader Ezra T. Benson, a church apostle, sent an exploring company of seven men under the leadership of Marriner W. Merrill of Richmond to locate sites in northwest Cache. The towns and farm plots were laid out by surveyor Martineau in September.

The first settlers arrived that fall in Stockton and Oxford, in what was called Round Valley, at the far north end of Cache Valley just south of Swan Lake—about twenty miles north of Franklin. Oxford was named, not for the university or city in England, but for a settler's animal that became mired in the little creek. Stockton was named for the herds of Cache Valley cattle that were grazing in Round Valley in 1864. Other settlers arrived in the spring of 1865, most of them settling in Oxford. They built log houses in fort style. When the Indians threatened in the spring of 1866 the settlers removed to the "mother settlement" of Franklin, but in the spring of 1867 they returned to their lots in Oxford. They raised fruit and berries as well as garden-stuffs and grain.

Additional towns established in 1865 by Franklin and other Cache Valley settlers were Rushville, Weston, and Malad. Rushville was on the headwaters of Deep Creek, four miles south of Oxford; its name came from the bushes in the Oxford Slough. The settlement expanded and after an 1869 survey was named Clifton—the name deriving from a high cleft of rock west of the settlement.

Weston, so named because it was on the west side of the valley and was the maiden name of Peter Maughan's wife, Mary Ann Weston Maughan, was settled in April 1865. Lars Frederickson described in his diary the process of settlement, a story quite typical of all the 1863–65 settlements:

> They all dug a hole in the ground and put a roof on (called a dugout); this was the kind of houses they lived in,

> with an open fire place and chimney for heating and cooking. They had no stoves in those days. . . .
>
> They planted some crops mostly wheat this year. Each man had a little strip of land on the creek bottom separated with a ditch. I still remember the names of some of those ditches. There was the Beeswax ditch, the Sheepskin ditch, the Gopher ditch and others.[15]

After planting the crops—later destroyed by crickets—the settlers began the construction of a dam to bring the water onto the farmlands. Frederickson described the dam-building as follows:

> Men started to put in willows, dig sods, and carry them onto the dam. They had to carry all the dirt because they had no other way. They made a rack with two poles and wove it in with small willows so it would hold dirt, load that up, then a man to each end to carry the load over on the dam and unload, then repeat. That was the only kind of wheel scrapers they had. The creek was full of Beavers, so as soon as the Beavers understood that there was going to be a dam built, they would work at night. They would cut willows into three or four foot lengths, sometimes longer, weave these together in the water where the dam was to be, and plaster the whole thing up with mud; the beavers run the night shift, so they were a great help to the first settlers, so in about four weeks they had the water out and getting their grain irrigated and growing fine.[16]

In the summer of 1866, as the crops were growing, the Indians posed a threat, so the settlers left their homes and lands and returned to Richmond. Early in the fall, the men returned to the Weston fields but took refuge again in Richmond after their harvesting was done.

In the spring of 1867 the settlers returned again to Weston, bringing others with them. James Mack completed a gristmill on Weston Creek. Two years later the settlers built log houses to replace the dugouts that had housed them for four years. These log houses had large, open fireplaces and chimneys at one end for cooking and heating. The furniture was, of course, all homemade.

Five miles north of Weston and five miles south of Clifton was Dayton, settled in 1867 by Joseph Chadwick and others of Franklin. The settlement was on the road that led to the Montana mines, and Chadwick opened a store in his home to sell supplies to freighters. By 1882 twenty families were living in Dayton.

When the residents of Franklin moved out of their fort onto their city lots in 1864, they lacked meadowlands for raising hay and pasturing their livestock. Some miles north and west were the Worm Creek bottoms—the flat lands between Worm Creek and the Bear River. This land was covered with wild grasses and had plenty of water. It was tempting to others as well, and herds were driven in from many locations, so the Franklin residents built herd cabins to protect their squatter claims. At first remaining there only in the summers, they later decided to stay. Other settlers joined them. The place was called Worm Creek until 1881, when it was renamed Preston.

At the same time that northern Cache Valley and Bear Lake Valley were being colonized, Mormon families also moved to settle Malad Valley. At this point, one must recognize that Idaho has two Malad River valleys: the tributary of the Snake in central Idaho, with the famed Malad Gorge, and the tributary of the Bear River in southeastern Idaho, with which we are now concerned. Both rivers apparently received their names from French fur trappers who became sick after imbibing the water or after eating the beaver they found in the water.

The Malad Valley in southeastern Idaho was frequented by trappers, mountain men, and explorers in the 1820s and 1830s. Overlanders passed through, particularly those headed for California. John C. Fremont explored the region in 1843, as did

Captain Howard Stansbury in 1849. As we have seen, members of the Salmon River Mission went through Malad Valley on their way to Limhi in 1855. It was along the route of miners and freighters going to and from western Montana in the 1860s.

Mormons used Malad Valley as a herd ground for several years in the early 1850s. In 1855, a colony of fifteen families led by Ezra Barnard located on the east side of the Malad River, built an adobe fort enclosing about an acre of ground in which they dug cellars and erected log houses, and attempted farming. The crops were destroyed by grasshoppers. The little settlement was abandoned in 1858, at the same time as the Salmon River Mission, because of the aggressions of the Shoshoni.

The first man to settle permanently in Malad Valley was A. W. Vanderwood, in 1863. He kept the mail station at Mt. Springs on the east side of the Malad River. The next spring Henry Peck and Judson Stoddard established a livestock ranch opposite the present site of Portage. In the same year Peck and three of his sons settled there to fulfill a contract to cut and sell wheat grass and meadow hay to Ben Holladay's stage line. Peck established his cabin at what he called Deep Creek, the present site of Malad City. He found Chief Pocatello and his band camped there but built his log cabin that fall. About a dozen settlers followed Peck and settled on the present townsite, and the families of Peck and Stoddard went there to live in the spring of 1865. About four hundred horses and many cattle were kept in Peck's large corral.

In the summer of 1865 ten additional families moved to Malad from northern Utah, starting a tradition of settling Welsh converts in the Malad Valley. The names commonly found in Malad Valley throughout its history are mostly Welsh: Williams, Jones, Hughes, Davis, Evans, Waldron, James, Tovey, Thomas, Lewis, Daniels, Parry. As in many Mormon villages, the founders of Malad City patterned their settlement after Salt Lake City, with ten-acre plots, eight lots to the plot.

In 1866 there was an influx of Reorganized Latter Day

Saints—members of a church organized in 1860 with Joseph Smith III, son of the founding prophet of the Church of Jesus Christ of Latter-day Saints, as its leader. The RLDS Church, headquartered at the time in Plano, Illinois, and now in Independence, Missouri, sent missionaries to the Utah church in 1866, and some of those converted went to Malad to settle. Malad thus began as a pluralistic society, with some non-Mormon ranchers, Welsh Latter-day Saints, "Josephite" Latter Day Saints (as the RLDS were called), assorted national groups (Danish, English, Irish, Scottish, German), and some Native Americans (Shoshoni, Bannock, and Northern Paiute).

From Malad City new settlers moved to other areas in the valley. In the spring of 1865 a dozen families moved to Cherry Creek, on Willow Springs, four miles south of Malad. The same year another group went to Woodruff, twelve miles south of Malad but still two and one-half miles north of the present Utah-Idaho line. In 1868 another group settled in Samaria, nine miles southwest of Malad. Most of these also were Welsh Latter-day Saints. St. John, three and one-half miles north of Malad City, was settled in 1869.

As we have seen, the Idaho territorial legislature passed the act creating Oneida County on January 22, 1864. Soda Springs, the post of Colonel Connor, was designated as the county seat. In 1866, when Connor's troops left Soda Springs, the county seat was moved to Malad, where both Mormon farmers and non-Mormon stockmen had settled. In contrast with Franklin and the northern Cache Valley and Bear Lake Valley communities, settlers in the Malad Valley always acknowledged they were in Idaho, not in Utah.

These, of course, were only the first of a steady influx of Mormons into Idaho Territory that eventually spread throughout the Upper Snake River Valley, over to Goose Creek and Cassia Creek, and later into most agricultural regions of southern Idaho. Idaho, as they learned for certain in 1872, was their home, and they sought to make the best of it.

## CHAPTER TWELVE: SOURCES

Basic references for this chapter are: Beal, *History of Southeastern Idaho*; Marie Danielson, *History of the Development of Southeastern Idaho* (Preston, Idaho: Daughters of Utah Pioneers, 1930); Joel E. Ricks and Everett L. Cooley, eds., *The History of a Valley: Cache Valley, Utah-Idaho* (Logan, Utah: Cache Valley Centennial Commission, 1956); Hunter, *Brigham Young the Colonizer*; Leslie L. Sudweeks, "Early Agricultural Settlements in Southern Idaho," *Pacific Northwest Quarterly* 28 (April 1937):137–50; A. J. Simmonds, "Southeast Idaho as a Pioneer Mormon Safety Valve," *Idaho Yesterdays* 23 (Winter 1980):20–30; Lawrence G. Coates, "Mormons and Social Change Among the Shoshoni, 1853–1900," *Idaho Yesterdays* 15 (Winter 1972):2–11; and Leonard J. Arrington, "The Mormon Tithing House: A Frontier Business Institution," *Business History Review* 28 (March 1954):24–58.

The LDS settlement in Franklin is treated in James Ira Young, "The History and Development of Franklin, Idaho, During the Period 1860–1900" (M.A. thesis, Brigham Young University, 1949); Marlow and Zelma Kunz Woodward, *A Brief History of Franklin: First Permanent Settlement in the State of Idaho* (Franklin: Idaho Pioneer Association, 1960); M. D. Beal, "Cache Valley Pioneers: The Founding of Franklin in 1860," *Idaho Yesterdays* 4 (Spring 1960):2–7; and Leonard J. Arrington and Richard Jensen, "Lorenzo Hill Hatch: Pioneer Bishop of Franklin," *Idaho Yesterdays* 17 (Summer 1973):2–8. A basic source is "Manuscript History of Franklin, Idaho," Ms., LDS Library-Archives, Salt Lake City.

On the Bear River Massacre, the principal sources include: Brigham D. Madsen, *The Shoshoni Frontier and the Bear River Massacre* (Salt Lake City: University of Utah Press, 1985); "The Battle of Bear River," in Madsen, *The Bannock of Idaho*, 111–39; Edward J. Barta, "Battle Creek: The Battle of Bear River" (M.A. thesis, Idaho State University, 1962); Newell Hart, *The Bear River Massacre* (Preston, Idaho: Privately published, 1982); Young, "History and Development of Franklin, Idaho," 104–49; Edward W. Tullidge, "The Battle of Bear River," *Tullidge's Quarterly Magazine* 1 (January 1881):190–

98; Trenholm and Carley, *The Shoshonis: Sentinels of the Rockies*; "Slaughter at Bear River," in Harold Schindler, *Orrin Porter Rockwell: Man of God, Son of Thunder* (Salt Lake City: University of Utah Press, 1966), 316–27; Fred B. Rogers, *Soldiers of the Overland, Being Some Account of the Services of General Patrick Edward Connor and His Volunteers in the Old West* (San Francisco: Grabhorn Press, 1938); J. H. Martineau, "The Military History of Cache County," *Tullidge's Quarterly Magazine* 2 (April 1882):122–31; Joel Edward Ricks, *Forms and Methods of Early Mormon Settlement in Utah and the Surrounding Region 1847–1877* (Logan: Utah State University Press, 1964). A splendid short summary that has been enormously helpful is Brigham D. Madsen, "The Northwestern Shoshoni in Cache Valley," in Douglas D. Alder, ed., *Cache Valley: Essays on Her Past and People* (Logan: Utah State University Press, 1976), 28–44.

The settlement of Bear Lake Valley is described in Russell R. Rich, *Land of the Sky-Blue Water: A History of the LDS Settlement of the Bear Lake Valley* (Provo, Utah: Privately published, 1963); Edith P. Haddock, F. Ross Peterson, and Dorothy Matthews, eds., *History of Bear Lake Pioneers* (Salt Lake City: Daughters of the Utah Pioneers of Bear Lake County, 1968); "Settling the Bear Lake Valley" and "Development of the Bear Lake Colony," in John Henry Evans, *Charles Coulson Rich: Pioneer Builder of the West* (New York: The Macmillan Co., 1936), 252–301; "Founding the Bear Lake Colonies" and "Life in the Bear Lake Settlements," in Leonard J. Arrington, *Charles C. Rich: Mormon General and Western Frontiersman* (Provo: Brigham Young University Press, 1974), 247–70.

The principal source on the history of Malad Valley is Glade F. Howell, "Early History of Malad Valley" (M.A. thesis, Brigham Young University, 1960).

50.

51.

50. Cattle ranching was a primary source of income and employment in Idaho Territory in the 1860s and 1870s. ISHS 1277.

51. Early farmers cut their grain by hand and threshed it, as did farmers from ancient times, by having it trod by oxen and the chaff dispersed by the wind. In the early years of the twentieth century, many farmers used a binder like this one, which was later improved so it could bind the stalks into bundles. ISHS 74–75.3.

52. 53.

54.

52. General Charles C. Rich was the founder and religious leader of sixteen communities in southern Idaho in the 1860s and 1870s. ISHS 59–A.

53. Daniel Sylvester Tuttle, Episcopal bishop of Idaho, Utah, and Montana, 1867–86, wrote a reminiscence that details life in early Idaho communities. UIL 3–57C.

54. Statehood for Idaho was facilitated by the large influx of Latter-day Saint settlers in the 1880s. An impression of their number is conveyed by this photo of a Mormon Sunday School in front of their meetinghouse in Burley. LDS CHURCH ARCHIVES PH 2384.

CHAPTER THIRTEEN

# Economic and Political Trials and Indian Conflicts

THE Civil War impacted Idaho in several ways. First, many people came to the territory to escape the war and its consequences in the states where they had lived, particularly Missouri and Arkansas. Second, wartime taxes and financial problems made it difficult for Idaho promoters and developers to raise money to exploit potentially rich mining deposits. Third, the preoccupation of federal personnel with the war effort meant only peripheral interest in remote territories like Idaho. Little attention was given to the government of the territory, to white and Chinese miners, and to Idaho's Native Americans.[1]

As in other wars, there was a heightened demand for many commodities and prices soared. Textiles quadrupled in price; groceries and flour doubled; meat, fuel, and rents increased more than 50 percent. Real wages and salaries lagged far behind; but prices farmers received almost kept pace with the general price increase, rising 86 percent. Because of the mild inflation, gold became more valuable and was seldom used as payment. Banks suspended payment in coin, the government issued $450 million in irredeemable greenbacks (the first government paper money in the nation's history), and the government also distributed short-term Treasury notes that passed almost like money. Paper money thus replaced metallic money as means of circulation. In terms of gold, the greenbacks did not circulate at par; in the summer of 1864, just before war's end, they dropped as low as 39 cents on the dollar.

After the war prices declined, not only because of the drop in demand for many commodities on the part of government and war contractors, but also because of the expansion of agricultural and mineral production that had resulted from the spread of settlement and opening up of new lands and resources west of the Mississippi. Large numbers of farmers, mine owners, and small businessmen had contracted debts during the war to increase production. One would suppose that, in all fairness, the government would now attempt to maintain stability and supply the currency needed for continued industrial and agricultural expansion. Instead, the government was determined to do precisely the opposite: restore prewar "normality" by contracting the paper currency and reducing prices. The government's goal was to resume use of coin as currency and return to the gold standard, a goal finally achieved in 1879 at the cost of substantial injury to farmers, miners, small businessmen, and other pioneer debtors and producers. Those who had borrowed to buy land, livestock, and machinery at 50 cents on the dollar now had to pay their obligations with an 80- or 90-cent dollar. Farm prices declined by 12 percent in 1869, by 30 percent in 1870, and by 35 percent in 1873.

Those who had been hurt by the contraction—and this included nearly all Idahoans—proposed that the government, so anxious to get back to a metal basis, inject more silver into circulation. The ratio of gold to silver had been fixed in 1837 at 16 to 1 (actually 15.98 to 1). This decision overvalued gold slightly, so silver disappeared from the market. Since the silver dollar in 1873 was worth only $1.02 in gold, it was not profitable to coin, and Congress dropped the further minting of the silver dollar. In the eyes of those wanting an expansion—or at least maintenance—of the circulating medium this demonetization of silver was denounced as the "Crime of '73." Idahoans and nearly all westerners attacked this act. Silver, they said, had always stood guard to prevent any considerable rise in gold, and the effect of demonetization was an inordinate rise in gold and further drop in the general price level. The price of silver plunged sharply. By 1876 a silver dollar was worth only 90 cents in gold.

Not only were the financial policies of the nation damaging to the interests of many Idahoans, but the general tenor of federal postwar policy was objectionable, both politically and morally. After the assassination of Abraham Lincoln, a coalition of northerners sought to punish the South and diminish its influence by continuing the hate and abolition idealism that had accompanied the war. The southerners were not compensated for the freeing of their slaves, they were not reimbursed for their holdings of Confederate bonds, they were deprived of voting rights if they had given aid and comfort to the Confederacy (this included virtually all of the South's prominent citizens), they were placed under military rule, and they were punished. (Congress's treatment of the conquered South was far more severe than its treatment of conquered Japanese and Germans after World War II.) This was the intent of Radical Republicans who held control of the national government for seventy years after the Civil War, with the exception of eight years when Democrats achieved a majority in the voting. Those in control, symbolized by South-hating Thaddeus Stevens, sought to establish and maintain northern supremacy. The election of Ulysses S. Grant in 1868 assured the domination of the Radical Republicans and his re-election in 1872 continued the same rule for another four years. Rutherford B. Hayes, elected in a disputed vote in 1876, removed troops from the South in 1877, but Radical Republicans continued to dominate national policies. The setting of national monetary policy was thus largely in the hands of Republican agents of eastern and midwestern industrial and financial interests, to the detriment of Idaho's farmers, miners, and merchants.

A sample of the problems in Idaho Territory occurred at the Fourth Session of the territorial legislature in 1866–67, the first to meet after the death of Lincoln and the end of the Confederacy. On July 2, 1862, Congress had passed a measure imposing an "iron-clad oath" on all federal officials and practicing attorneys, requiring them to denounce the Confederacy as a domestic enemy.[2] That the oath remained in effect after the war was over was interpreted by Idaho's Radical Republicans to mean that the territory's Confederate Democrats were prohibited from serving in the legislature. Since all but five members of the legislature were Confederate sympathizers, the legislators enacted over the veto of David W. Ballard (the Radical Republican governor from 1866 to 1870) a statute specifying that in Idaho at least, the odious test oath applied only to presidential appointees—the governor, secretary, and Supreme Court justices.

That Ballard and the legislature would not get along was clear. The legislature sent an economy bill to the governor suggesting that the governor's salary be cut in half. The governor responded, asking for a "slight amendment" that would cut legislative salaries in half as well. The governor and the legislature agreed that the Supreme Court salaries should be cut in half. (In Idaho, half the pay for the governor and the legislature came from the federal treasury and half from the territory.) The legislature's response to the governor's amendment was that when the governor's advice was required, it would be requested.

Regardless of the act that the legislature had passed over his veto, Ballard insisted that the legislators must sign the required test oath before receiving their pay. When the Radical Republican territorial secretary, Solomon R. Howlett, appealed to Washington, the Secretary of the Treasury instructed Howlett not to pay any legislators who refused to sign the loyalty oath. When Howlett transmitted a copy of the order to the legislators, "[t]he indignation of the Honorable gentlemen was absolutely uncontrollable for some time, and most of them were totally unable to express themselves in terms sufficiently indignant."[3] In actuality, Howlett's predecessor as secretary had absconded with the funds, and there was no Idaho money to pay out anyway.

Some of the legislators expressed their resentment by throwing lamps and chairs out the windows and smashing the furniture. One member threatened to set the town on fire. Others decided upon a concession. They would sign the hated oath and would return their pay if the Washington examiners disallowed the transaction. But Howlett would have none of it. Deciding that a show of force was necessary, he asked for military aid from Fort Boise. Twenty-two soldiers marched up to the legislative hall, loaded their arms, and assumed a belligerent attitude. Meanwhile, legislators hurled epithets and insults at Howlett. Some walked up to him with fists at the ready, while others drew them back. The military intimidation reminded Confederate sympathizers of what the South was experiencing: Reconstruction was being practiced in Idaho as well. Historian John Hailey, who was an observer of these events, reported: "Some of the members [of the legislature] were rather high tempered and fractious, while Secretary S. R. Howlett might be put down as a would-be aristocratic, cranky, old granny. He seemed to think things must go or come his way."[4]

Howlett was finally persuaded by two Supreme Court justices to risk compensating the legislature although that payment was contrary to Treasury instructions. Confederate members, for their part, agreed to his stipulation that they sign the detested oath, which they did on January 14, 1867. Ironically, on that very date, the United States Supreme Court rendered a decision that the test oath was unconstitutional at least when applied to attorneys and teachers. Also on that day, President Andrew Johnson notified the Senate that he had removed Ballard as governor and nominated John M. Murphy of Idaho City to take his place. Murphy was not confirmed by the Senate, however, and Ballard remained as governor for three more years.[5]

Both sides were bitter. Idaho Confederates continued to denounce "the proven villainy, the shameless perjury, the absolute dishonesty, and utter moral rottenness of Secretary Howlett, who had . . . played the knave and pimp continuously . . . [and who was] atrociously corrupt, and totally unworthy of any position under the Government, save as a condemned felon in a Government prison." In another blast, the legislature's press organ continued in the same vein: "Lying and deceit and trouble-brewing come as naturally from the perjured old scoundrel [Secretary Howlett] as poison from an adder or slime from a toad. How long is this old wretch to be permitted outside the penitentiary walls?" Friends of the governor and secretary were equally venomous. The legislators, according to the *Sacramento Daily Union*, were "true and actual representatives of second class hurdy-gurdy houses. . . . The third session was by all good men—irrespective of party—pronounced infamous, but this one is Satanic. With a few harmless acts expected, the present body has made every enactment from a vile motive. . . . The demoniacal Fourth Idaho Legislature has denounced and abused [the governor] . . . in a spirit of constant and fiendish ecstacy."[6]

Something far more damaging than name-calling between Unionists and Confederates occurred in September 1873 when the nation's leading brokerage firm, Jay Cooke & Company, failed. This firm had been principal financier of the Union in the Civil War and in 1873 was engaged in building the Northern Pacific Railroad. Its failure precipitated the most severe panic in the nation's history to that time. Prices of mineral and agricultural products continued to go down, numerous banks closed, and a severe depression ensued that lasted through most of the 1870s. Bank deposits dropped by one-third during the twelve months following the panic. As difficult as it had been for Idahoans to make a living in the late 1860s and early 1870s, it was now even more critical.

Idaho mining had begun its decline as early as 1867. Most of the rich placers had played out. The quartz properties, remote from railroads, lacked access roads for transporting large stamp mills. There were important placer discoveries in Leesburg in 1866, Loon Creek in 1869, and Caribou Mountain in 1870, and some of the richer mines continued to be worked until the failure of the Bank of California in San Francisco in 1875. As a result of the national depression and the slowing of its earlier momentum, Idaho mining production went into a tailspin from which it did not recover until the 1880s.

Idaho's farming communities, at least the largely self-sufficient Latter-day Saint communities in northern Cache Valley, Bear Lake Valley, and Malad Valley, were not affected by the postwar recession and the depression following the Panic of 1873 to the same extent as mining communities, whose products were subject to the whims of government policy and national and international markets. Making a living was nevertheless a struggle. The Mormons' solution, one that was hardly an option to the individualistic mining towns in the Clearwater, Salmon Mountain, Boise Basin, and Owyhee regions, was group cooperation. The central institution was the tithinghouse, which served the community much like a central bank except that there was little coin or currency. By their labor, individuals would accumulate credits that were then used in withdrawing produce that had been brought in by families producing more than they needed. Through this organized barter system the community not only furnished assistance to needy families but also supported persons constructing roads, telegraph lines, and schoolhouse-meetinghouses. By this means also Latter-day Saints supported the establishment of tanneries, woolen mills, tailor shops, carpentry shops, and shingle mills. Each village maintained community herds of cows and sheep, supported a creamery and cheese plant, and patronized craftsmen drafted by the group to do tinwork and make boots, shoes, harness, and furniture. As the village grew, in 1869 in most instances, the bishop established a cooperative store that dovetailed with the tithing-house in retailing goods—particularly those obtained from the church's central wholesaler in Salt Lake City, Zion's Cooperative Mercantile Institution (ZCMI). All of the Idaho Mormon communities had cooperative general stores, the profits of which, if any, were distributed "in kind" among the residents.

After the Panic of 1873, witnessing the failure of many enterprises in Idaho and elsewhere, villages formed United Orders, formally organized community cooperatives under central leadership that controlled the major economic enterprises in the village and ran them as parts of one integrated operation. The organization supplemented but did not supplant the private economic activities of residents. The members elected a general manager, usually the bishop, and persons were assigned to run each of the various shops and industries. For example, community leaders in Bear Lake Valley soon recognized that their future lay in dairying (many Swiss families had settled in Bear Lake Valley), so the community pooled its resources, built up its herd of cattle, acquired additional pastureland, purchased new pasteurizing and cream-separating equipment in the East, and established a flourishing tannery and leather-working shop. Supported by about 125 families (650 persons), the Bear Lake Cooperative continued to expand until the Oregon Short Line Railroad completed a branch line through the valley in 1882. The lowering of transportation costs meant that outside products of superior quality could be acquired more cheaply. In the 1880s, therefore, the cooperative leased out or liquidated its assets. As a result, Bear Lake Valley became more attuned to the rest of the territorial and nationwide economy—as did, for similar reasons, the Mormon cooperatives in northern Cache Valley and Malad Valley.

Nevertheless, the communitarian experience did not die out; there remained a strong group spirit among the Latter-day Saints that continued into the twentieth century. The *History of Idaho Territory* published in 1884 paid tribute to the residents of Paris and other cooperative communities with this observation: "Probably nowhere in the civilized world is cooperation carried on so successfully as it is among this peculiar people." The authors continue:

> This institution has demonstrated that by judicious management, cooperative institutions can be made the means of increasing the wealth of the people; that the citizens of moderate means, and even the poorer classes can, by a combination of their efforts, do their own merchandising and manufacture their own necessities and share the profits among themselves, and thus prevent the growth of monopolies, which become, in many instances, the tyrants of their patrons.[7]

With mining activities declining and Mormon communities operating on an exclusivist basis, merchants, bankers, and freighters in Idaho attached most of the blame for their reverses to continued contraction of the supply of money in circulation nationally. They joined other western interests in insisting that the government do something. In particular, westerners demanded that the government expand the circulating medium by putting silver into circulation. After much urging, with the depression continuing, Congress in 1878 passed the Bland-Allison Silver Purchase Act. The Treasury was required to buy between $2 and $4 million in silver each month to be converted into silver dollars. Although the bill was vetoed by President

Rutherford B. Hayes, Congress voted to override his veto. During the next twelve years, 78 million silver dollars were coined. But the nation was going through such a period of industrial expansion that silver dollars and certificates were absorbed without difficulty and prices of minerals and agricultural products continued to fall. One year after the passage of the Bland-Allison Act the Treasury went back to specie payment.

The impact of the Republican Radicals on Idaho politics is easily demonstrated by reduced appropriations for the territory, particularly during the retrenchment that followed the Panic of 1873, and by the caliber of federal appointees. During the years that the mild-mannered David Ballard was governor, the territory declined in population. The population in 1870, exclusive of Indians, was only 17,804, of whom 4,274 were Chinese. Placer miners, having skimmed the cream of the discoverable gold, left for richer gleanings in other areas or for more comfortable living elsewhere. Ballard, who had won some measure of acceptance from his anti-Radical Idaho constituents, returned to Oregon in 1870 and resumed his medical practice in Lebanon.

Ballard was not replaced until 1871, a year after his term expired. The new appointee, Thomas M. Bowen, served only from July to September 1871. Born near Burlington, Iowa, he was an attorney in Iowa, then in Kansas; served as a general in the Civil War (many of Grant's appointees were generals); and then was a Supreme Court justice in Arkansas. Bowen's objective in accepting the Idaho governorship was to make a fortune in mining. After wandering over the territory, however, he returned to Arkansas, then went to Colorado, where he practiced law, became a judge, and was finally elected to the United States Senate. Certainly qualified by training to be a governor, he had no influence on Idaho because of his short stay.

President Grant was unsuccessful in getting a replacement for Bowen until his sixth appointee, Thomas W. Bennett, accepted and remained for almost four years. Born in Indiana and a graduate of the college that became DePauw University, Bennett practiced law, served in the state senate, became a Civil War general, was elected to another senate term, and served as mayor of Richmond. A "jovially reckless gentleman," according to one observer, Bennett was personally popular with many Idaho residents. Although he tried to get a railroad built in Idaho by inducing the legislature to offer exemptions to railroad corporations, the nationwide depression that followed the Northern Pacific collapse continued to delay Idaho's railroad construction for several years. Bennett also attempted territorial reforms but found Congress to be utterly indifferent. In 1874 he decided to run as Idaho's delegate to Congress. Although he received fewer votes than his opponent, as governor he threw out many ballots on the basis of spelling errors and declared himself elected. He held both offices for a year but finally resigned the governorship in December 1875. He served out most of the term in Congress before his method of counting the vote was rejected and his opponent was seated in his stead. He was then reappointed governor; but when leading Idaho Republicans filed charges of excessive absence from office, theft of public funds, and selling pardons, he decided to return to his home in Indiana.

Bennett was replaced by David P. Thompson, a native of Ohio who had gone in 1853 to Oregon, where he became a surveyor and businessman. He owned or partially owned transportation companies that had contracts with Idaho Territory. When it became evident that he would have to divest himself of these to avoid conflict-of-interest charges, he resigned—after serving only four months as Idaho's governor. For their part, Idahoans rather admired his aggressive business ethic and hated to see him go.

Thompson was replaced in August 1876 by Mason Brayman, who served as governor for four years. Brayman was from

Buffalo, New York, and had been editor of the Buffalo *Bulletin* before he decided to practice law. He became city attorney for Monroe, Michigan; moved to Illinois, where he served as a special commissioner for Governor Thomas Ford in writing the terms for the agreement under which the Mormons left Nauvoo, Illinois, in 1846; served on the planning staff of the Illinois Central Railroad, the nation's first land-grant railroad; and was a general with the Illinois Volunteers in the Civil War. After the war he edited the *Illinois State Journal* in Springfield. Seemingly well qualified, Brayman had never been in the Far West and had no experience in territorial politics. He was a strict legalist who went by the book. Pompous in manner, he was not respected by the Idaho citizenry, who found him just another carpetbag outsider.

Clearly, Idaho's experience with Grant's appointees was not particularly satisfying—nor was it unique. Federal regulations were made all the more burdensome by the limited understanding of administrative and congressional officials in Washington. Most of Idaho's governors refused to serve long: the opportunities for amassing fortunes on the side were not great, particularly during the period from 1866 to 1880, and the pay and "honor" were not tempting.

Not all of the inadequacies of Idaho government can be laid at the door of the carpetbag governors. The governmental structure was so poorly arranged that—as had been true in early Washington Territory—even divorces had to be obtained from the legislature. W. J. McConnell, in his *Early History of Idaho*, gives an example of the manner in which divorces were formally granted in Idaho Territory:

AN ACT

To Dissolve the Bonds of Matrimony now Existing Between Martin Fallon and Mary Fallon, his Wife.

Be it enacted by the Legislative Assembly of the Territory of Idaho, as follows:

Section 1. That the bonds of matrimony heretofore and

now existing, between Martin Fallon and Mary Fallon, his wife, be, and the same are hereby dissolved, and declared void.

Section 2. This act shall take effect and be in force from and after its passage.

Approved February 9, 1881.[8]

There were a number of such acts in Idaho Territory.

The single biggest problem facing the governors was Native Americans' resentment of the intrusion of whites onto their ancestral lands. Until white men came, bands of Shoshoni and Bannock Indians had roamed at will over southern Idaho, regarding the land as theirs, however rarely used. They often levied tribute on traveling emigrants, begging in the daytime and driving away their stock at night. There were a few instances in which entire parties in small trains were murdered. Such violence was more common in southwestern and southeastern Idaho than in the Clearwater country because the Nez Perce were more carefully controlled by their chiefs, some of whom at least were protective of whites. The Boise Basin, on the other hand, was frequented by scattered bands of Shoshoni and Bannock (often called Snakes, Weisers, Malheurs, and Bruneaus) hostile to white invasion.

In March 1863 the thievery and attacks on white invaders had reached the point that miners, freighters, packers, merchants, and saloonkeepers formed a company of eighty men under the leadership of Captain Jefferson J. Standifer to confront the Indians who had killed George Grimes and who had continued to plague the miners. Their guide was "Mountain Jack," a young white who did not know his real name but who had been captured (or found) by Snake Indians when he was a baby and was raised by them, he said, as a slave. The Standifer company killed a number of Indians and captured some of the horses that had been stolen. This campaign, directed entirely at combatants, halted the raids at least temporarily.[9] Another such company was raised in Owyhee in 1864 after a group of Indians killed Michael Jordan, discoverer of the original Owyhee mine, and wounded his partner. The party found the Indian raiders, killed several of them, and then disbanded.[10]

Governor Caleb Lyon attempted to relieve tension with the Bruneau Treaty, signed April 12, 1866. Meeting with 300 Indians across the Bruneau River, he concluded an agreement promising a reservation for them in place of the Boise Valley and assured the natives that whites would stop their aggressive acts if the tribesmen would discontinue theirs. Congress, however, preferred a military solution and did not ratify the treaty. Predictably, a series of encounters followed, usually referred to as the Snake War of 1866–68. Fort Boise was the operating base for army engagements in Oregon and Owyhee until General George Crook took over in December of 1866. An Ohio farm boy who graduated from West Point, Crook had been assigned to the Fourth Infantry on the Pacific Coast and had learned to live off the country, to understand the plight of the Indians, and to mistrust the motives of the volunteer militia. Having served in the Rogue River War, the Yakima War, and (with distinction) the Civil War, he was delighted when he was allowed to return to the Pacific Northwest in charge of southwestern Idaho and eastern Oregon.

During the year and a half after he assumed control, General Crook used Indian allies, undertook night marches, and conducted a devastating winter campaign that kept the hostiles busy. By 1868 he had pacified the region. Crook's subsequent career also has an interest to Idahoans. Assigned in 1871 to Arizona, he forced the first surrender of Geronimo and put pressure on roving bands of Apache. In 1875 he was put in command of the military Department of the Platte, where he led expeditions against the Sioux. He believed that Indian troubles were often the result of tardy and broken faith on the part of the general government. After retirement he gave lectures and wrote pamphlets for Indian-rights organizations. His death in 1890 saved him from witnessing the shame of the Battle of Wounded Knee.[11]

The Nez Perce, influenced as they were by the missionaries in the 1830s and 1840s, were basically friendly toward the whites, even though they had suffered indignities and encroachment by miners in the 1860s. Their land was between the Bitterroot and Blue mountains in north central Idaho, northeastern Oregon, and southeastern Washington, with the Salmon River on the south and the northern Palouse on the north. One group favored their homeland in the Wallowa Valley, east of the Grande Ronde River and west of the Snake at the base of the Blues. White settlers also liked the valley and by force and fraud began to move in; they interpreted Nez Perce patience with their illegal action as a sign of indifference. They fenced in the water and cultivated the valleys. The Nez Perce found it more difficult to find forage for their ponies. White cattlemen began to herd their stock there.

The Yakima were equally alarmed at the swarm of squatters occupying their land in Washington and attempted to form an Indian confederacy to drive out the whites. The Nez Perce refused to join it. General Isaac I. Stevens, governor of Washington Territory and its superintendent of Indian affairs, had assembled all the Indian tribes at Walla Walla in 1855 to arrange for the purchase of Indian lands and sign a treaty. Old Joseph, father of the Joseph noted in Idaho history, and his associate Lawyer, principals of the Nez Perce, were present but did not sign the treaty, which had little effect on their land. After the gold discoveries of the early 1860s, however, whites began to settle the Wallowa Valley and other Nez Perce lands. The government sponsored a treaty session in 1863 to purchase land and reduce the reservation. Old Joseph again refused to sign, although a number of other Indian groups' leaders—including Lawyer—did so. In 1873, President Grant issued an order giving back the ceded land to the Indians. Two years later, under the influence of white lobbyists, Grant revoked the order and made Wallowa a part of the public domain. Just before that action, Old Joseph died and his son, Joseph, became leader. On his deathbed, Old Joseph admonished young Joseph not to give up Wallowa.

In 1877 the Bureau of Indian Affairs in Washington, D.C., ordered the Nez Perce in Wallowa to move to the Lapwai Reservation in Idaho. The Nez Perce replied that they had not signed the treaty and did not consider themselves bound to leave Wallowa. On the third day of the conference at which they were told to move, Too-hul-hul-suit, the religious leader—"tu-at"—defiantly shouted that he would not move to the reservation. He was promptly arrested and placed in the guardhouse by General Oliver O. Howard, commander of the Army's Department of the Columbia. Highly incensed, the Indians contemplated violence but were restrained by young Joseph and his parallel leader, White Bird.

On June 14, 1877, the day set by the government for moving from Wallowa, rebellious Indians—in revenge for personal grievances—went on a rampage and killed several white settlers. Although the Nez Perce were clearly resigned to making the move, however repugnant to their feelings, and although the older Nez Perce were annoyed by the behavior of the young hoodlums, General Howard chose to regard the youthful forays as an indication of major tribal resistance. He sent two cavalry companies to the scene. In doing so he transformed a minor dispute into a full-scale confrontation. Fearful of what Howard's men would do to them, Joseph and White Bird sought to escape his jurisdiction by fleeing to Montana in hope of being welcomed by the Crow. When they were met at the head of White Bird Canyon by Howard's troops, the Nez Perce defeated the troops, inflicting heavy losses.

Howard then took personal charge of the campaign. He was a native of Maine and 1854 graduate of West Point and had fought with distinction in the Civil War, during which he lost his right

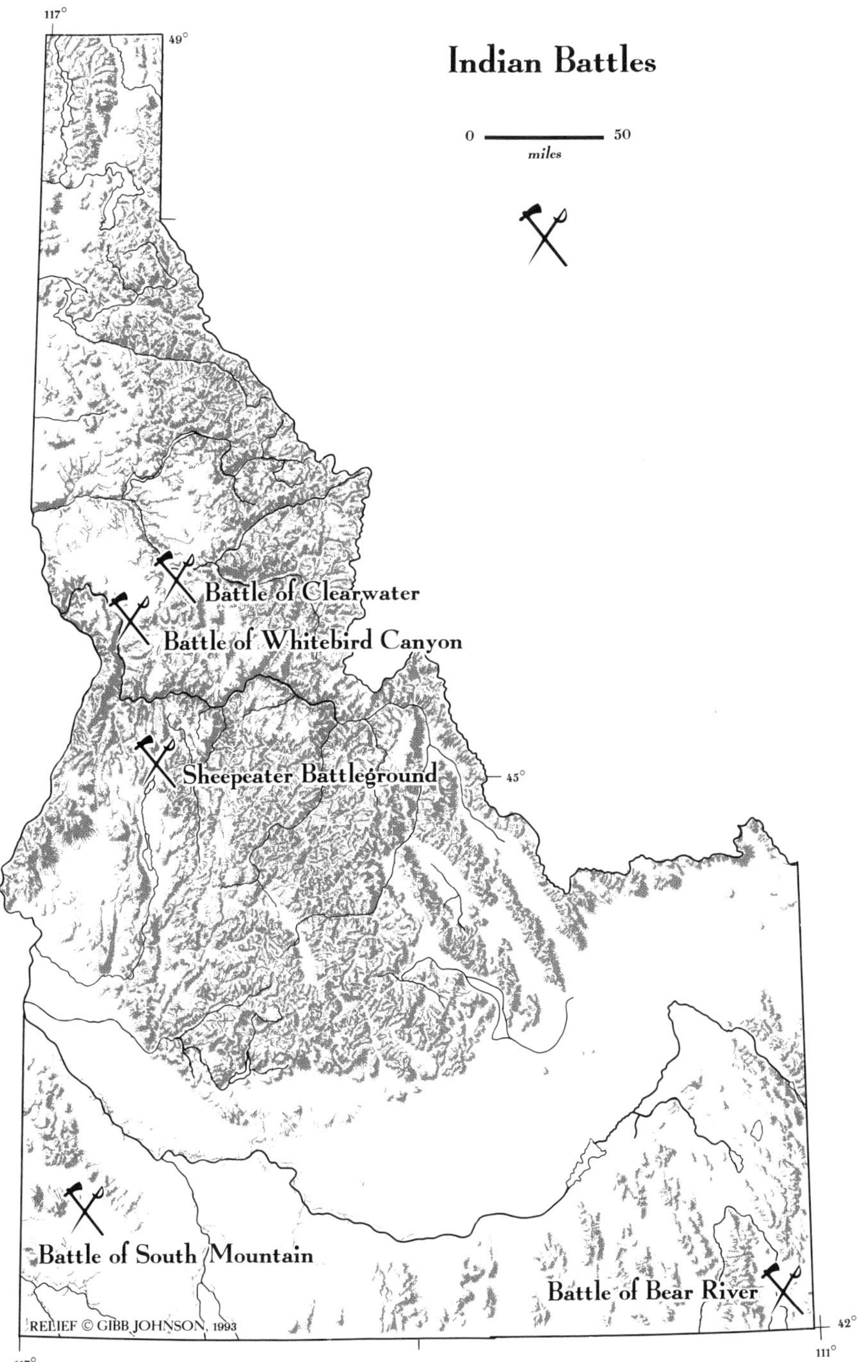
Indian Battles
0
50
miles
Battle of Clearwater
Battle of Whitebird Canyon
Sheepeater Battleground
Battle of South Mountain
Battle of Bear River
RELIEF © GIBB JOHNSON, 1993
117°
49°
45°
42°
111°
117°

arm. Howard had then served as the first director of the Freedmen's Bureau. He helped found and then served as president of Howard University in Washington, D.C., before returning to active duty and was sometimes referred to as the "praying general" and later as the "humanitarian general." Howard assembled a force of about 600 troops and located Joseph's men in a forest region southeast of Kamiah. In a fierce battle the Nez Perce were overwhelmed. They fled across the Clearwater and headed for the Lolo Trail. Although they took along women, children, old men, camp equipage, and livestock, the Nez Perce worked their way quickly over the high mountains, deep canyons, swift currents, and tangled underbrush. On July 18, only eleven days after they began their flight from Idaho, the Nez Perce neared the Montana end of the pass across the Bitterroots. Howard, aware that his troops would never catch the elusive band, wired General W. T. Sherman in Montana to send an intercepting force to capture Joseph.

In Montana, Joseph assured the white settlers in his path that he was fleeing, not on the warpath, and that his group if left alone would not bother the whites. Surprised by a federal force at Big Hole River, Joseph headed for Lemhi Valley, Camas Meadows, and the Henry's Lake country in southeastern Idaho, then eastward into Wyoming through Yellowstone Park. Realizing that the government would not permit him to enjoy the protection of the Crow, he headed north through Montana for Sitting Bull's community in Canada.

On September 17, Colonel Nelson A. Miles, who had earlier accepted the surrender of Crazy Horse, received an order from General Howard to intercept the fleeing Nez Perce. White Bird and 300 of his people had managed to reach Canada; but just thirty miles short of the border, at Bear Paw Mountain, Joseph was captured by Miles on October 4. Joseph's surrender was dramatic. Riding slowly up the hill to where General Howard and Colonel Miles were waiting, he dismounted gracefully and offered his rifle to Howard, who magnanimously motioned him to Miles. Joseph's message in connection with the surrender, as related by one observer, was as follows:

> Tell General Howard I know his heart. What he told me before—I have it in my heart. I am tired of fighting. Our chiefs are killed. Looking-Glass is dead. Too-hul-hul-suit is dead. The old men are all dead. It is the young men now, who say "yes" or "no." He who led on the young men [Joseph's brother, Ollicut] is dead. It is cold, and we have no blankets. The little children are freezing to death. My people—some of them—have run away to the hills, and have no blankets, no food. No one knows where they are—perhaps freezing to death. I want to have time to look for my children, and to see how many of them I can find; maybe I shall find them among the dead. Hear me, my chiefs; my heart is sick and sad. From where the sun now stands, I will fight no more forever![12]

Joseph won the respect of many Americans, including Howard and Miles. Despite Miles's assurance that Joseph and his band would be returned to the reservation at Lapwai, the Secretary of the Interior thought it was risky to return them to a place so close to their former haunt and sent them instead to Fort Leavenworth in Kansas, and then on to Indian Territory (present Oklahoma). After many years of petitioning, Joseph and the surviving members of his band were transferred to the Colville Reservation near Spokane, where Joseph died in 1904.

The Nez Perce War had cost the United States government $930,000 and the lives of 127 soldiers and 50 civilians, with 110 soldiers and 40 civilians wounded. The Nez Perce, who had 191 fighting men and 450 women and children, suffered 151 killed and 80 wounded, mostly warriors.

The year after the war, 1878, there was a skirmish with the Bannock. They had been assigned to the Fort Hall Reservation in 1869, but they continued to roam over southern Idaho. Every summer they went to Camas Prairie. The men hunted while the women dug camas roots, which they ground into meal. They were incensed by the incursions of white cattlemen who grazed their livestock there. Some whites had gone so far as to take swine, which dug up and destroyed the camas, onto the prairie. Inspired by the Nez Perce War, the Bannock followed as their leader young Buffalo Horn, who had been a scout under General Howard in the Nez Perce War and had also had scouting experience under Colonel Miles and General George Armstrong Custer in their Montana wars.

That the Bannock were in a desperate condition, and that much of it was the fault of the government for failing to furnish them promised provisions, is indicated by General Crook—now of the Department of the Platte:

> They have never been half supplied. The agent has sent them off for half a year to enable them to pick up something to live on, but there is nothing for them in that country. The buffalo is all gone, and an Indian can't catch enough jack rabbits to subsist himself and family. . . . What are they to do! Starvation is staring them in the face. . . . There remains but one thing for them to do—fight while they can. . . . Our treatment of the Indian is an outrage.[13]

During the night of May 30, 1878, Colonel Reuben F. Bernard hurried to Camas Prairie from Fort Boise when he heard of the preparations for war and convinced many of the Bannock to return to the reservation. But Buffalo Horn and a group of about 200 dissidents wanted war and started westward across the Snake River, killing settlers, taking provisions, and destroying property. At South Mountain, a mining camp south of Silver City, they were met by a company of volunteer militia. Although the whites failed to win a decisive battle, they killed Buffalo Horn, leaving the Indian militants without a leader. The warriors nevertheless advanced on to Oregon, where they hoped to form an alliance with the Northern Paiute, Umatilla, and

Yakima. General Howard, however, assisted by some companies of volunteers, engaged and succeeded in scattering them.[14]

A third dispute was with the Sheepeater, or Tukuarika, a small band of Shoshoni who, joined by a few families of Bannock and Nez Perce, hid out in the fastnesses of the Salmon River Mountains. Without horses or guns, they lived much as their ancestors had for thousands of years except that, because of the scarcity of mountain sheep and other game, they moved out occasionally and white settlers wrongly blamed them for occasional raids by other Indians on remote white settlements. The Sheepeater were not numerous—perhaps 200 or 300. In 1878 several unwary prospectors and emigrants were killed, their property burned, and their equipage stolen by some group of Indians. In the winter of 1878–79 local Indians were accused of attacking a Chinese camp working on placers at Loon Creek, killing all but one. The Sheepeater afterward denied the attack, and historians now believe they had no connection with it.

In 1878 belligerents in the Nez Perce and Bannock areas escaped to the mountains in the vicinity of the Sheepeater camps and continued to steal horses and cattle. In May 1879, some of these vagabond Indians went to the ranch of Hugh Johnson on the South Fork of the Salmon River, killed Johnson and Peter Dorsey, burned their buildings and haystacks, and drove off the livestock. Under orders issued by General Howard at Vancouver, Colonel Bernard, with sixty men from Fort Boise; Lieutenant Henry Catley, with forty men from Fort Lapwai; and Lieutenant E. S. Farrow, with twenty men and a few Umatilla scouts from the Umatilla Agency, pursued the guilty Indians cautiously in different directions through the Salmon River country. Catley's detachment was surprised by two Sheepeater (yes, only two), one of whom went on to defeat them and capture their pack train and supplies. (Hard to imagine but apparently true.) Lieutenant Farrow's detachment succeeded in flanking the Sheepeater position and, on Loon Creek near its junction with the

Middle Fork of the Salmon, on August 20 got into a battle from which their adversaries retired into rough country. A few weeks later the army contingent, having destroyed most of the Sheep-eater supplies, was able to persuade the entire band of about fifty-one, of whom fifteen were "warriors," to move to Fort Hall. Ironically, the armament of this formidable foe, as Sven Liljeblad wrote, "pursued for three months by the United States cavalry, mounted infantry, and enlisted Umatilla scouts, totaled four carbines, one breech-loading and two muzzle-loading rifles, and one double-barrelled shotgun."[15] After the pathetic group was placed on the Fort Hall Reservation, they merged with other Indians there, and the Sheepeater Indians disappeared. This was the last "Indian War," for such it has been called, in Idaho history.[16]

## CHAPTER THIRTEEN: SOURCES

Most of the general histories of Idaho and several of the histories of the Pacific Northwest cover, in a general way, the political life of Idaho Territory and the conflicts between whites and Indians during the territorial years. Particularly useful are the chapters in Hailey, *History of Idaho*, 201–54, and "Radical Reconstruction in Idaho 1866–1870" and "The Ride of Idaho's Independent Political Tradition, 1872–1876," in Beal and Wells, *History of Idaho*, 1:269–91, 440–93. A carefully researched article is Merle Wells, "Idaho and the Civil War," *Rendezvous: Idaho State University Journal of Arts and Letters* 11 (Fall 1976):9–26.

The political situation in Idaho Territory in the 1870s is covered in Limbaugh, *Rocky Mountain Carpetbaggers*; "Territorial Governors of Idaho," *Idaho Yesterdays* 7 (Spring 1963):14–23; Earl S. Pomeroy, "Running a Territory: They Had Their Troubles," *Idaho Yesterdays* 14 (Fall 1970):10–27; W. Turrentine Jackson, "Indian Affairs and Politics in Idaho Territory, 1863–1870," *Pacific Historical Review* 14 (September 1945):311–25; and Merle W. Wells, "David W. Ballard, Governor of Idaho, 1866–1870," *Oregon Historical Quarterly* 54

(March 1953):3–26. There is also splendid background in Pomeroy, *The Territories and the United States.*

Many books and scholarly articles deal with Idaho's Indians and the conflicts of the 1860s and 1880s. Those particularly useful for this chapter have included:

*General.* Angie Debo, *A History of the Indians of the United States* (Norman: University of Oklahoma Press, 1970); William T. Hagan, *American Indians* (Chicago: University of Chicago Press, 1961); Robert M. Utley, *The Indian Frontier of the American West, 1846–1890* (Albuquerque: University of New Mexico Press, 1984); R. Ross Arnold, *The Indian Wars of Idaho* (Caldwell: Caxton Printers, 1932); "Idaho's Indian Wars," *Idaho Yesterdays* 5 (Summer 1961):22–25; Liljeblad, *The Idaho Indians in Transition*; and Haines, *Indians of the Great Basin and Plateau.*

*Nez Perce.* Books include: "The People of the Plateau," in Alvin M. Josephy, Jr., *Nez Perce Country*, Handbook No. 121 (Washington, D.C.: National Park Service, 1983); Haines, *The Nez Perces: Tribesmen of the Columbia Plateau*; Josephy, *The Nez Perce Indians and the Opening of the Northwest*; Merrill D. Beal, *"I Will Fight No More Forever": Chief Joseph and the Nez Perce War* (Seattle: University of Washington Press, 1963); Lucullus Virgil McWhorter, *Yellow Wolf: His Own Story* (Caldwell: Caxton Printers, 1940, 1986); Alvin Josephy, *The Patriot Chiefs* (New York: Viking Press, 1961); Oliver Otis Howard, *Famous Indian Chiefs I Have Known* (New York: Century Company, 1908); and Mark H. Brown, *The Flight of the Nez Perce* (Lincoln: University of Nebraska Press, 1967).

Articles on the Nez Perce include: Haruo Aoki, "Footnote to History: Chief Joseph's Words," *Idaho Yesterdays* 33 (Fall 1989):16–21; Duncan MacDonald, "The Nez Perces: The History of Their Troubles and the Campaign of 1877," *Idaho Yesterdays* 21 (Spring 1977):2–15, 26–30, (Winter 1978):2–10, 18–26; Merle W. Wells, "The Nez Perce and Their War," *Pacific Northwest Quarterly* 55 (January 1964):35–37; and Robert H. Ruby, "Return of the Nez Perce," *Idaho Yesterdays* 12 (Spring 1968):12–15.

*Shoshoni-Bannock-Paiute.* Madsen, *The Bannock of Idaho*; Trenholm and Carley, *The Shoshonis: Sentinels of the Rockies*; George F.

Brimlow, *The Bannock Indian War of 1878* (Caldwell: Caxton Printers, 1938); Corless, *The Weiser Indians: Shoshoni Peacemakers*; Gae Whitney Canfield, *Sarah Winnemucca of the Northern Paiutes* (Norman: University of Oklahoma Press, 1983); W. C. Brown, *The Sheepeater Campaign* (Caldwell: Caxton Printers, 1926); and John Carrey, ed., *Sheepeater Indian Campaign* (Grangeville: Idaho County Free Press, 1968).

Articles on the Shoshoni-Bannock-Paiute and the Coeur d'Alene include: David L. Crowder, "Nineteenth-Century Indian–White Conflict in Southern Idaho," *Idaho Yesterdays* 23 (Summer 1979):13–18; George M. Shearer, "The Battle of Vinegar Hill," *Idaho Yesterdays* 12 (Spring 1968):16–21; Jack Dozier, "The Coeur d'Alene Indians in the War of 1858," *Idaho Yesterdays* 5 (Fall 1961):22–32; Stewart, "The Shoshoni: Their History and Social Organization"; and Carl Yeckel, "The Sheepeater Campaign," *Idaho Yesterdays* 15 (Summer 1971):2–9.

55.

55. Tendoy, chief of the Shoshoni tribe on the upper Salmon, was friendly to white miners and settlers. UIL 3–1291.

56.

56. Chief Joseph, the highly regarded military and political leader of the Nez Perce, led his nation across Idaho passes in 1877 but failed to reach his intended destination in Canada. ISHS 691.

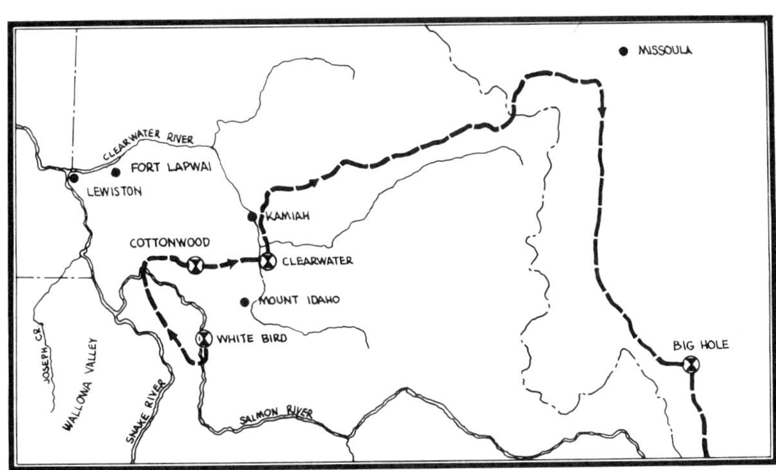


57.

58.

57. This map shows the route of the Nez Perce through Idaho in 1877. ISHS 77–2.67.

58. The Bannock were assigned to the Fort Hall Reservation in 1869, but the government failed to furnish promised provisions. Here is a group at the fort in about 1900. USHS.

59. 

59. Chief Pocatello is shown with a group of his Northwest Shoshoni tribe about 1878. USHS.

CHAPTER FOURTEEN

# Railways and New Settlements

COMPLETION of the transcontinental railroad, with the joining of the rails at Promontory Summit in northern Utah in 1869, meant that Idaho and Montana farmers and miners could now obtain supplies from Ogden, and later Salt Lake City when a connecting branch was completed in January 1870. Construction of the connecting link between Utah and Montana furnished immediate railroad service for Idaho communities, and many families from northern Utah and elsewhere moved to sites along the Utah-to-Montana railroad to farm and engage in other business. The first railroad into Idaho Territory was the Utah Northern, a narrow-gauge line built from Ogden to Franklin in 1873–74. Many Idaho communities owe their existence to the construction of it and other railroads. With the further construction of the Utah Northern—renamed the Utah and Northern—and the arrival of the Oregon Short Line and Northern Pacific railroads in the late 1870s and early 1880s, the population of Idaho almost doubled.

As suggested in Chapter Eleven, the discovery of gold at Grasshopper Creek in western Montana had led to a flood of traffic from northern Utah through eastern Idaho to Montana. Northern Utah settlements—and Franklin and Malad—soon were involved in hauling much-needed supplies to the mining districts. The completion of the transcontinental railroad in 1869 created a new freighting and transportation center on the Central Pacific line at Corinne, at the north end of the Great Salt Lake approximately seventy-five miles north of Salt Lake City. Prior to this connection, freighting was limited to overland or water routes that were less than dependable and influenced by weather conditions. An obstacle in Idaho was the Snake River, finally bridged at Eagle Rock in 1865.

Along the "Gold Road" the most formidable barrier was the Monida (Montana-Idaho) Pass through the Continental Divide, the gateway to Montana. The pass was not usable during winter months of blizzard and freezing weather. Montana could, of course, be supplied from the Midwest by the Missouri River route, but the river was unreliable—usable only during the few months of high water. A few pack trains, some of them camels, moved supplies from Washington Territory via the Mullan Road. But approximately half of Montana's imports during the late 1860s and early 1870s came by ox- and mule-team over the Montana Road in eastern Idaho. From Corinne, the road cut north almost 500 miles to Malad, Marsh Creek, Fort Hall, Eagle Rock, and Pleasant Valley and finally on into Montana.

Many of the freightings used army surplus teams and wagons auctioned off by the government after the U.S. Expedition left Utah to fight, some for the North and some for the South, in the Civil War. Passengers on this route often traveled in stage-coaches operated by Ben Holladay until he sold out to Wells Fargo in 1866. The drivers or "jehus" of the coaches, the bull-whackers with their plodding ox-teams, and the mule-skinners with their heavy freight wagons were occasionally Mormons from

Franklin and other Cache Valley settlements, but more often men from Nevada and the Great Plains states.

The most commonly freighted product was flour, but eggs, butter, and potatoes were carried from Franklin; salt from the Oneida Salt Works on the Lander Emigrant Road eighty-five miles southeast of Eagle Rock; and tobacco, coffee, tea, and mining supplies and equipment from Corinne. On their return from Montana to Utah the freighters took not only mail and passengers, but also gold dust and ores to be refined in Colorado. No reliable figures exist as to the amount of the freight in the 1860s, but in 1872, the earliest year of estimate, 5,000 tons of freight were shipped north from Corinne. Perhaps a thousand or two thousand additional tons were shipped from Ogden, Logan, Franklin, and other northern Utah and southern Idaho points.

The trade was lucrative, particularly in the early years before large freighting outfits dominated. Alexander Toponce recalled that in 1864 he bought a pig in Box Elder (Brigham City) for $36, transported it north to the mines, and sold it for $600. In the same year he bought a train of flour in Ogden, paying $24 per hundredweight, and saw the price in Montana that winter rise to $125 per hundred. On one occasion he loaded up half a dozen six-mule teams with eggs from Franklin and other Cache Valley communities to sell them in Montana for $12 per dozen—a dollar apiece! In 1872, more than $100,000 in butter and eggs and about $250,000 worth of wheat were shipped out of Cache Valley.

## UTAH AND NORTHERN RAILROAD

The transcontinental railroad skirted the north side of the Great Salt Lake, bypassing Salt Lake City. In response, Brigham Young organized the Utah Central Railroad to build a thirty-six-mile line from Ogden to the capital city. Constructed on the cooperative plan by Mormons situated along the line, it was completed on January 10, 1870. The Utah Southern was built in a similar manner to serve Mormon settlements south of Salt Lake City. By 1871 enough freighting business existed to support construction of the railroad north from Ogden to serve the rich agricultural area in Cache Valley and beyond.

William B. Preston, the presiding bishop of Cache Valley, expressed to Brigham Young the local willingness to build the road; the president's son, John W. Young, who had assisted in construction of the Union Pacific, negotiated with Joseph and Benjamin Richardson of New York City to finance the construction north from Ogden to Soda Springs, a distance of about 125 miles. The Richardsons agreed to furnish the rails and equipment if Mormons would build the roadbed and lay the track. On August 23, 1871, seventeen Mormon ecclesiastical and business leaders of northern Utah met in Logan and organized the Utah Northern Railroad Company, with John W. Young as president and superintendent; William B. Preston, vice president and assistant superintendent; and Moses Thatcher, secretary. The directors consisted mostly of bishops of the settlements along the route of the line.

The construction plan called for the bishops to recruit local men to work on the road for stock in the company and some "ready pay" consisting of vouchers redeemable in the local tithing office. There was no government aid. The road was to be narrow gauge, at a cost about one-third that of the standard gauge. The worth of the three-foot road in mountainous terrain had been proven by the narrow-gauge Rio Grande Railway in Colorado.

The road was completed to Logan on January 31, 1873. A month later, on March 3, 1873, Congress passed an act granting the road a right-of-way to build north to Montana "by way of the Bear River Valley, Soda Springs, Snake River Valley to a connection with the Northern Pacific Railroad in Montana."[1] The road was finished to Franklin on May 2, 1874, making the Utah

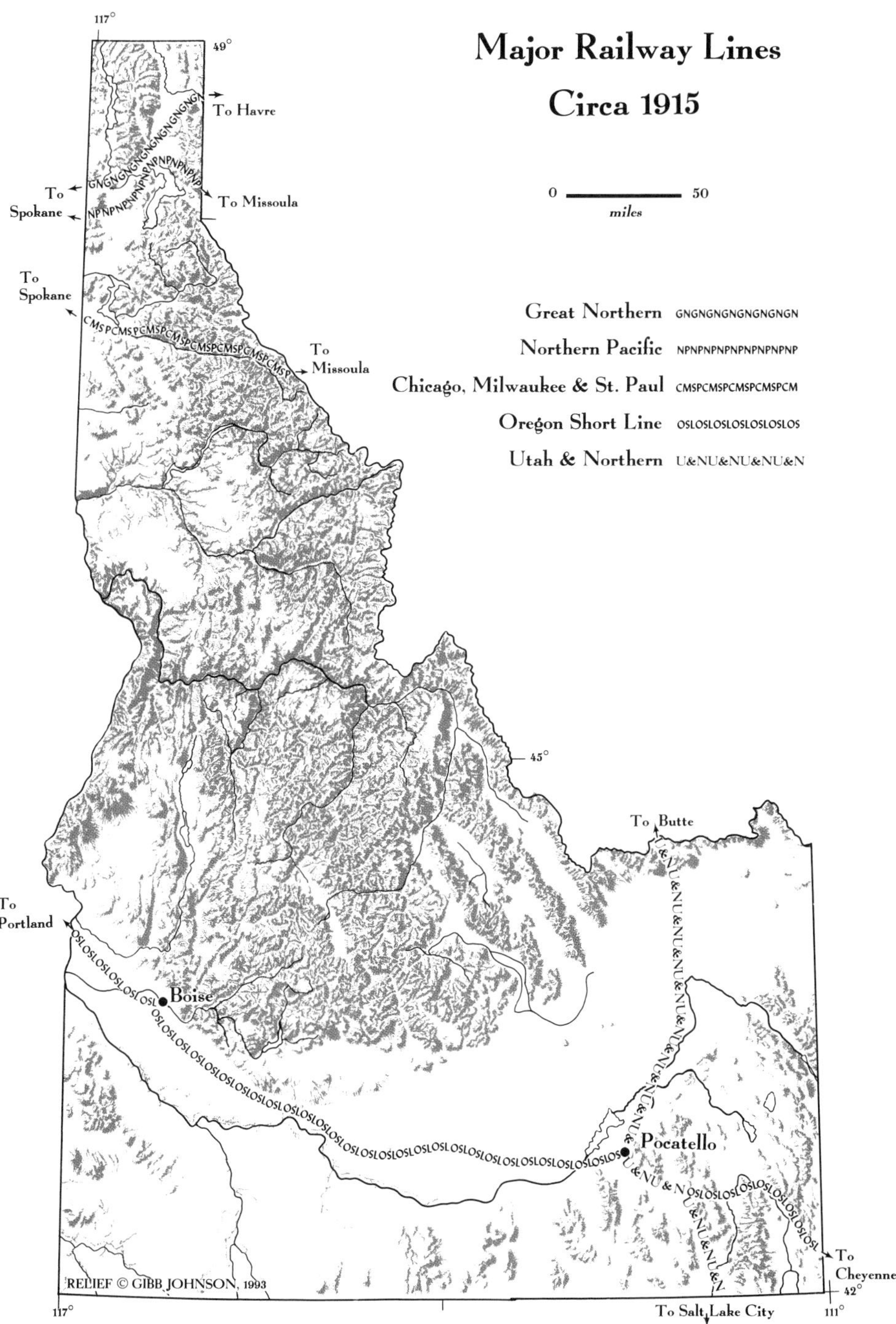
Major Railway Lines
Circa 1915
0
50
miles
Great Northern GNGNGNGNGNGNGNGN
Northern Pacific NPNPNPNPNPNPNPNPNP
Chicago, Milwaukee & St. Paul CMSPCMSPCMSPCMSPCM
Oregon Short Line OSLOSLOSLOSLOSLOSLOS
Utah & Northern U&NU&NU&NU&N
117°
49°
To Havre
To Spokane
To Missoula
To Spokane
To Missoula
45°
To Butte
To Portland
Boise
Pocatello
To Cheyenne
42°
RELIEF © GIBB JOHNSON, 1993
117°
To Salt Lake City
111°

Northern the first railroad to be constructed in Idaho Territory. Fourteen miles of grade were built northeast out of Franklin toward Soda Springs during the summer of 1874. That portion of the track was not completed because of financial problems connected with the Panic of 1873 and because of the realization that the Soda Springs route to Montana was impractical. The road had cost about $1.4 million, of which $700,000 were put up by the Richardsons and the remainder was borne primarily by Mormon farmers along the route working with their teams, wheelbarrows, and scrapers.

As the northernmost point of the line, Franklin now became a principal freighting center for the Montana traffic. Several important freighters, including Diamond R Fast Freight and Express Company, owned by E. G. Maclay of Montana, and the California and Montana Transportation Company, owned by Edward Creighton of Omaha, moved their warehouses and headquarters from Corinne to Franklin. An estimated 600 freighters hauled goods from Franklin to Montana in 1874, with an average of perhaps 80 wagons on the road night and day. The Diamond R alone is said to have had 100 wagons and 600 mules. The freight included hardware, brick, molasses, and clothing. One driver reported having hauled at one time sixty barrels of whiskey. Hauling charges were usually $7 per hundred pounds or $140 per ton. A postal-car system was established to carry the Montana mail to Franklin for forwarding north.

The terminus of the Utah Northern remained at Franklin from 1874 to 1877 because Joseph Richardson failed to furnish additional money after he suffered heavily from the Panic of 1873. Mormon leaders, who were completing the sale of their Utah Central and Utah Southern railroads to Union Pacific, solicited the cooperation of Sidney Dillon, president of Union Pacific, and Jay Gould. Sometimes held up as a "robber baron," Gould grew up in a poor New York family and received little formal education, but he unquestionably had a talent for making money. After he acquired control of the Union Pacific, he worked with

Richardson, Dillon, and Mormon officials to complete the road to Montana. He gave Joseph Richardson $400,000 for his interest in the Utah Northern, paid the Mormon leaders $80,000 (about 10 percent of their investment), reimbursed Mormon laborers at the rate of forty cents on the dollar, and induced church officials to help select the location of the route north and obtain local labor and supplies.

Gould then persuaded the Union Pacific backers to purchase his interests. Under their direction a new corporation, called the Utah and Northern Railroad Company, was formed on October 4, 1877. It represented a coalition between the old Utah Northern and leading stockholders and directors of the Union Pacific. Contracts were let to construct the road from Franklin to Fort Hall and beyond. In December 1877 the Utah Northern was permitted to default on the $1.5 million due on bonds and interest, and the assets were sold at auction for $100,000 to S. H. H. Clark, general superintendent of the Union Pacific. A new operating entity, the Utah and Northern Railway Company, incorporated on April 30, 1878, could now issue new bonds to finance construction to Montana. Congress granted the company the right-of-way to Helena.

As work resumed, the company employed Washington Dunn, a veteran Union Pacific engineer, as general superintendent of construction. Prefabricated houses were set up at the various stations, and the road, "the little bantam rooster," crowed merrily as it moved north.[2] Wells Fargo moved along with the road to freight from successive termini the remainder of the way to Montana. The Mormon laborers, now paid in hard U.P. cash, took along wives as cooks, their sons to work on grading crews, and cows to provide milk. Logging camps and sawmills were set up where needed. Construction stations were located, in succession, at Battle Creek, Dunnville (Banida), Oxford, Oneida (a little west of Arimo), Black Rock (near present Inkom), Pocatello Creek, and Tyhee.

The surveyors ran the road right through the Fort Hall Indian

Reservation. Sidney Dillon went to Washington, D.C., to obtain specific authority to cross the reservation and was advised to obtain the consent of the Indians. Eventually, negotiations were successful: the Indians received a cash settlement and members of the tribe were given free passes and other special benefits.

Construction was completed to Pocatello in August 1878, to Blackfoot in December 1878, to Eagle Rock in April 1879, to Camas in July 1879, to Beaver Canyon (Spencer) in September 1879, to Red Rock at Monida Pass in May 1880, to Dillon (Beaverhead), Montana, in September 1880, to Silver Bow Junction in October 1881, to Butte in December 1881, and to the Northern Pacific connection at Garrison, Montana, in 1884.

The distance from Ogden to Garrison was 466 miles. The Utah and Northern, with its "galloping gooses," was one of the longest narrow-gauge railroads in the world and one of the most profitable of western railroads. Some 206 miles of U&N track were in Idaho, all at the time of construction in Oneida County —a county as large as Maryland and Delaware combined. Eagle Rock replaced Logan as a center of maintenance and repair. The whole road was rebuilt to standard gauge in 1887 and was incorporated into the Oregon Short Line system in 1889.

Most of the workmen along the U&N line were Mormon farmers from Franklin and other Cache Valley settlements. General construction superintendent was Marriner W. Merrill, bishop of the northern Cache Valley ward of Richmond. Thomas E. Ricks and William D. Hendricks were in charge of grading and tracklaying. Ricks in particular became an important figure in eastern Idaho, and after the completion of the U&N road he also played a role in the construction of the Northern Pacific. The cash received by the laborers was of incalculable advantage in building the already established settlements in Cache Valley. But the road's greatest impact on Idaho was in setting the stage for the explosion of Mormon settlement along its Upper Snake River Valley route in the 1880s.

## THE OREGON SHORT LINE RAILROAD

As early as 1844 Asa Whitney had advocated construction of a railway over the Oregon Trail, and in 1865 Governor Caleb Lyon suggested in his annual message to Idaho's legislators that Whitney's railroad ought to be built to connect the Snake River Valley with the Pacific Northwest and with the western-bound transcontinental railroad. In the years that followed Idaho journalists, politicians, and businessmen continued to agitate for such a road that would "unlock the rocks" of the mining regions. Union Pacific engineers did a reconnaissance through Idaho in 1867, but plans did not jell until June 1879, when Sidney Dillon discussed with his directors Henry Villard's proposal to organize a new enterprise "to build a road from Snake River to Oregon which shall secure to the Union Pacific the trade of the Columbia Valley."[3]

Villard was at the time engaged in constructing the road of the Oregon Railway and Navigation Company. This successor to the Oregon Steam Navigation Company was being built on the south bank of the Columbia River from Portland to a junction with the Northern Pacific, then pushing westward across Montana. Born Ferdinand Heinrich Gustav Hilgard in Bavaria, student at the universities of Munich and Wurzburg, Villard migrated to America when he was eighteen and changed his name to avoid military service in his homeland. He learned English well and reported to European newspapers on the Lincoln-Douglas debates, the Colorado gold rush, and the Civil War. In 1874 he became the American representative for a group of investors in the Oregon and California Railroad, was named its president in 1876, and also became president of the Oregon Steamship Company and the Oregon Steam Navigation Company.

Although Dillon's directors declined the purchase of a half-interest in Villard's Oregon Railway and Navigation Company,

Dillon and his friends decided to form their own company, the Oregon Short Line. Government regulations prevented the Union Pacific Railway from building the road for the new line, so holders of Union Pacific stock and their friends subscribed privately for half the bonds and stock on O.S.L. The remainder was held in the U.P. treasury.

One venture vital to the enterprise was the formation of the Idaho and Oregon Land Improvement Company, which, on the basis of O.S.L. plans, purchased lands, laid out townsites, and promoted towns. These activities set the stage for an influx of settlers following the railroad's completion.

Construction of the Oregon Short Line began in 1881. The road would connect with the main U.P. road at Granger, Wyoming, and then angle northwestward toward the Idaho border and on to Montpelier, Soda Springs, Pocatello, Minidoka, Shoshone, King Hill, Mountain Home, Nampa, Riverside, and Weiser. It would then stretch to Huntington, Oregon, to connect with the O.R. & N. The contractors built fifty miles in Wyoming in 1881. By the end of 1882 the track was completed to Shoshone, Idaho, 321 miles from Granger. At that point, work on the main road was suspended while a branch from Shoshone to the Wood River mining district, as far as Ketchum, was built. The main track was extended another 100 miles in 1883, but completion had to await the erection of the 740-feet-long steel bridge across the Snake River just three miles east of Huntington. The road was ready for service on November 17, 1884. Passengers could now board the train in Omaha at eight o'clock Monday evening and reach Portland by eight on Friday morning. Both Pullman and emigrant sleeping cars were furnished, with no extra charge for the latter.[4] The entire track, including the 70-mile Wood River branch, was 542 miles, of which 92 miles were in Wyoming, 434 in Idaho, and 16 in Oregon. In 1889 a consolidation created the Oregon Short Line and Utah Northern Railway Company, and in 1898 both routes were formally merged into the Union Pacific Railroad Company.

The completion of the road stimulated the development of crop agriculture along its route, expansion of the livestock industry, and immigration. One western writer was particularly pleased that, echoing a strangely popular theme, the rails would bring in an independent non-Mormon population that would reduce the influence of the Mormons in Idaho's agricultural development.[5] Actually the Mormons had thrived under the stimulus of the construction. One firm contracted to supply 75,000 ties for the road, while other Mormon workers were employed for the road-grading.

The construction was not simple. The terrain was rocky, water often scarce. Builders encountered rattlesnakes and scorpions, flies and woodticks. Historians have made much of the "hell on wheels" atmosphere—fighting, quarreling, profanity, drunkenness, gambling, prostitution, and crime. Certainly there was some of this, but the speed of construction suggests that the vast majority worked laboriously and effectively. The mighty Snake was spanned four times. Still, the haste of U.P. officials and their desire to conserve costs by not building down to the river bottom is indicated by the beeline road bypassing Boise, going straight from Mountain Home to Nampa. (The twenty-mile branch from Nampa to the capital was completed in 1887 and was referred to by proud Boiseans as "The Stub.") The road created divisional headquarters at Montpelier, Pocatello, and Glenns Ferry, as well as at Granger and Huntington.

The portion of the road connecting Pocatello to American Falls was built by the Utah and Northern Railway, and the steel girders spanning the Snake River at that point were supplied by U&N. Since the entire road from Granger to Huntington was standard gauge, there was a problem in transferring cargo at the junction with the U&N narrow gauge at Pocatello. It was solved by a device called a Ramsey, which raised the car from the standard pair of trucks or wheel carriages and lowered it on the narrow-gauge trucks and vice versa. Hundreds of cars were changed daily, as the procedure required only a few minutes per car.[6]

When the Oregon Short Line was built, it was logical that Pocatello, where the two lines intersected, should replace Eagle Rock as the Gate City. The 2,000-acre townsite of Pocatello, located at the mouth of the Portneuf River, was on the Fort Hall Indian Reservation. Under the influence of Fred T. Dubois and others, the Shoshoni-Bannock agreed to sell the land for $8 an acre. The name of the city came from the noted Shoshoni chief, Pocatello, who died in 1884. With a population of about three thousand residents, mostly railroaders, the village was surveyed and incorporated in 1889. In 1893 the city, now the leading townsite in southeastern Idaho, became the seat of Bannock County.

## THE NORTHERN PACIFIC RAILWAY

The Northern Pacific grew out of a survey made for the War Department in 1853 by Isaac I. Stevens, shortly thereafter appointed governor of Washington. After the Civil War the Northern Pacific was incorporated with the financial assistance of Jay Cooke and Company. Construction began at Thompson Junction, near Duluth, Minnesota, in February 1870. One hundred miles were built that year. In 1871 the westward-moving track reached Fargo, Dakota Territory. The Franco-Prussian War of 1870–71, however, dried up foreign sources of capital, and eastern writers began to refer derisively to the Northern Pacific as "a railroad from no place through nothing to nowhere."[7] In acquiring a controlling interest in other companies, the company overextended itself, and Northern Pacific and Jay Cooke toppled in September 1873, launching the national Panic of 1873.

A subsequent reorganization by General Lewis Cass and others led to a resumption of work. The road reached Bismarck,

Dakota Territory, before the end of 1873. Construction then remained dormant for five years before a reorganization by Frederick Billings in 1878 led to further building. With much cutting, filling, and bridging, the road reached Glendive, on the Yellowstone River in eastern Montana, in December 1880. Inspired by the approach to Butte of the Utah and Northern, Billings concluded an agreement with Henry Villard for the use of the Oregon Railway and Navigation tracks to permit Northern Pacific to construct a road eastward from Wallula, Washington, the site of the old Fort Walla Walla, and at the same time run trains westward to Portland. Villard had previously extended the rail lines of O.R.&N. from Portland to Puget Sound and up the Columbia to Wallula. This layout meant that North Idaho's first railroad would enter the territory from west to east.

Construction proceeded from Wallula northeast across the Palouse through Spokane Falls and Westwood (Rathdrum), reaching Lake Pend Oreille in 1882. Between this lake and the Yellowstone River were 400 miles of alternating mountains and canyons, requiring extensive trestle work. Construction from Sandpoint eastward to Missoula was completed in 1883, and the entire line was in operation just in time for the Coeur d'Alene mining stampede the next year.[8]

Much of Northern Pacific's construction money was supplied by Henry Villard through a secret stock pool of $18 million that secured control of Northern Pacific and facilitated Villard's assuming the presidency of the company. Villard energetically pushed the construction. Boom towns sprang up at the various termini. The railroad bridged the Snake at a temporary town called Ainsworth, not far from the connection of the Snake with the Columbia River, and then headed northeast to Sprague, Cheney, and Spokane. The next stop was Westwood, a town of 200 or 300 people on the westward edge of Idaho that the 189-mile track had reached by the fall of 1881.

To speed construction Villard insisted that 6,000 men be

employed on the western portion of the line as it went through Idaho. The thousands of workmen included Swedes and Norwegians from the Dakotas, Mormon farmers under Hendricks and Ricks from Cache Valley, and itinerants from other states and territories. Unable to get enough Swedes and Mormons, Villard hired 4,000 Chinese, mostly direct from China. Apparently most of them returned to China after the job was completed, for few if any of them remained in North Idaho.

The long road crossed an extremely narrow strip of Idaho, going from Westwood through Cocolalla, Sandpoint, Kootenai, and Hope to reach the territory's eastern boundary at Clark's Fork. George Bird Grinnell, a famous ethnologist and historian of the American West, visited the site of construction in late 1881. Taking the dusty road from Westwood to Dry Lake, near Lake Pend Oreille, Grinnell found an enormous construction camp about ready to lay rails. He wrote:

> It was a veritable canvas city, and its inhabitants white men, Chinamen, horses, mules, and dogs. Everything here is on an enormous scale. The eating tents cover an area equal to that of a large hotel, the sleeping tents are numbered by hundreds; there are great forges, and watering troughs at which twenty-five horses could drink at one time; the bread pan in the cook tent was large enough to serve a full grown man for a bath tub.[9]

From Dry Lake to Lake Pend Oreille, Grinnell wrote, there were several railroad camps, each in a different stage of the construction process. First, the carpenters and bridgebuilders; further along, the road graders; and then the "right of way men," who were cutting their way through the forest, chopping and burning to clear the road of timber for a width of fifty feet. Fifteen miles down the Pend Oreille River (Clark's Fork), west of present Sandpoint, was Siniaqueateen (near Laclede), an ancient crossing place for Coeur d'Alene Indians that had served as a stopping place for traffic headed from the Columbia to British Columbia and Montana during the gold rush of 1864–66. There the Northern Pacific Commissary depot supplied engineer parties laying out the line over the Coeur d'Alene Mountains. Beyond was Clark's Fork, on the eastern border of Idaho, from which the road went southeast to Missoula, and then to Melrose, south of Butte, to the westbound terminus.[10]

The road was completed between St. Paul and Portland in September 1883. Near the end, tracklaying had proceeded at the rate of a mile per day. The joining-of-the-rails celebration was held on September 8 on Gold Creek in Hell Gate Valley near the summit of the Rocky Mountains, scene of the first discovery of gold in Montana. Four palatial trains carried the distinguished guests, who included General U. S. Grant, Secretary of the Interior Henry Teller (formerly U.S. Senator from Colorado), British Minister Sir James Hannon, several governors, and numerous others. More than 5,000 onlookers observed the grand celebration. Among these were a crowd of hitherto unfriendly Indians whose cries of "Grant! Grant! Grant!" (the only name with which they were familiar) were annoying to Henry Villard, who gave the principal address.

## EXPANSION OF SETTLEMENT

Railroad companies were right in expecting the railroads to promote the immigration of families, establishment of settlements, and further development of resources. With substantial federal land grants, railroads offered tempting incentives for location along the line. Each company encouraged settlement in order to develop local traffic.

Not much encouragement was required to induce northern Utah residents, particularly those in Cache Valley, to move into the Upper Snake River Valley. Many of them had worked on construction crews and had seen abundant and fertile land.

Their leaders in Salt Lake City encouraged them to move into the "north country." In a lengthy letter from Mormon President John Taylor to William B. Preston, dated December 26, 1882, the message was:

> Go into the Snake River Country, found settlements, care for the Indians, stand upon an equal footing and cooperate in making improvements. Gain influence among all men [and women], and strengthen the cords of the Stakes of Zion.[11]

In the years between the commencement of construction in 1878 and the final completion of Utah and Northern in 1884, hundreds of Mormons established farms and villages along the 150-mile frontier between Pocatello and Victor.

The settlement process began on February 10, 1879, when John R. Poole of Ogden, who had been on a Mormon U&N grading crew, went deer hunting on lake bottom land north of the present town of Roberts. The land had been occupied since 1867 by John and William Adams and other Virginians who pastured livestock on land watered by the annual overflow from Snake River. Israel Heal ran a large herd on adjacent land, referred to as Heal's Island. Wanting to homestead, Poole asked the permission of Heal, who replied: "I don't believe God intended that a few men should have all this great country to raise horses and cows in." Poole urged friends to visit the "island," and they also were impressed. The first to move was Joseph C. Fisher, grandfather of Idaho novelist Vardis Fisher. Other families followed, and an irrigating ditch was cut. Poole and others informed Apostle Franklin D. Richards of Ogden, who called a meeting to urge settlement by other Latter-day Saints. Heal's Island became Poole's Island, then Cedar Buttes, then Menan—an Indian word meaning "island."

Menan was the parent colony of nine separate communities founded in the 1880s: Egin (Parker), 1879; Louisville (Lewisville), 1882; Bannack (Rexburg), 1882; Lyman, 1883; Salem (Sugar City), 1883; Teton, 1883; Wilford, 1883; Rigby, 1884; and Victor, 1889. These settlements were founded by individual families rather than by group movements. They adopted the cooperative pattern of work characteristic of Franklin, Paris, and other Mormon villages but did not settle fort-style, as was necessary during the period of Indian unrest. Since these homesteaders lived on their 160-acre farms rather than in a village, the communities had a scattered appearance. They were organized into wards or congregations beginning in 1882. Thomas Ricks was chosen the first bishop of Rexburg (named for him), which would become the headquarters ward. By 1884 there were 1,400 Latter-day Saints in the area. Meanwhile, large numbers of Latter-day Saints joined non-Mormon settlers in Pocatello, Blackfoot, and Eagle Rock. This migration suggests both the push of overcrowding in Utah and the attraction of Idaho's fertile volcanic soils.

In time, with the need for getting crops to markets, these new settlements were anxious to obtain railroad service. The Utah and Northern (and the Oregon Short Line that merged with it) was not long in building branch lines. These included a line from Idaho Falls to St. Anthony, built in 1900; Blackfoot to Mackay, 1901; St. Anthony to Yellowstone Park, 1908; Moreland to Aberdeen, 1910; and Yellowstone to Ashton, 1910. Lines were also extended from Montpelier to Paris, Driggs to Victor, and Preston to Cache Junction, Utah.

Settlement also stretched along the route of the Oregon Short Line, occasionally by Mormons but mostly by non-Mormon stockmen, crop farmers, miners, and small-town businessmen from the Great Plains and Midwest. Charles Francis Adams, who became president of Union Pacific in 1884, was particularly interested in building up this "Union Pacific Country." The railroad was not only a means of marketing cattle, gradually replacing the buffalo on the Snake River Valley range, but also a means of stocking the range. In the spring of 1885, a single consignment of cattle comprising 160 cars moved from Wyoming to Idaho.[12]

When the O.S.L. was completed through the upper Portneuf in 1882 and finished the next year to Pocatello, Portneuf Valley north of Soda Springs and east of Pocatello became ready for occupancy. Alexander Toponce, a French-born freighter, had moved a large herd of cattle into the valley in the 1870s to supply his freighting to Montana. Cache Valley Mormons also pastured stock in the area. In 1879 Chester Call, a highly respected bishop in Bountiful, Utah, established a ranch at Chesterfield (named for a city in England). Persuaded that irrigated and dryfarm agriculture was possible, Call began homesteading, and he was joined in 1881 and 1882 by other families from Bountiful. They sold logs for ties and produced grain that was marketed via the railroad. They formed a typical Mormon village, close-knit and with a strong church orientation. Among the early Mormon settlers was William Robertson, father of future Idaho novelist Frank Robertson. Later colonies were established in the vicinity, at Bancroft, Hatch, and Lund.

Another colony near the Montpelier to Pocatello route was Trout Creek (Grace), on the southeast side of Bear River twelve miles southwest of Soda Springs. The town was first settled by Mormon families in 1893.

Several settlements were served by the O.S.L. at the Minidoka station, some fifty-five miles west of Pocatello. Mormon farming settlements in Cassia County included those at Beecherville (Elba), Albion, Sublett, Almo, and Goose Creek (Oakley). Oakley became the principal Latter-day Saint settlement in the region.

Still farther along the line was Shoshone, which provided connection not only with the Wood River area but also with Shoshone Falls. The single most striking natural phenomenon in the Snake River Valley, Shoshone Falls was located about twenty-five miles south of the Shoshone O.S.L. depot. The Snake River there plunged 212 feet over a great basaltic horseshoe rim nearly 1,000 feet wide. Charles S. Walgamott, who worked on the Kelton-to-Walla Walla stage line in the 1870s, posted a squatter's notice on the land below and above the falls, excavated a dugout to "prove up" on his claim, and erected a crudely built "hotel." He then bought a stagecoach and transported tourists from the Shoshone station to the falls. Among those he guided on trips to the Falls were Homer Pound, register of the United States Land Office in Hailey and father of Ezra Pound, poet and leader of America's expatriate literary revolution of the 1920s; Jay Gould; Theodore Roosevelt, not yet president; William Jennings Bryan, later a presidential candidate; Idaho's governor, Mason Brayman; and, in 1898, Edward H. Harriman, who had become president of Union Pacific, and his party of more than one hundred. In the group was seven-year-old Averell Harriman, son of E. H., who later replaced his father as chairman of the board of Union Pacific and became the founding father of the Sun Valley resort.

Another of Walgamott's guests was Edward Roberts, a noted travel writer employed by Union Pacific president Charles Francis Adams to promote the O.S.L. with a series of articles, later published in a book entitled *Shoshone Falls and Other Western Wonders* (New York, 1888). But as far as the development of the Snake River Valley was concerned, Walgamott's most important achievement was inducing I. B. Perrine to establish the latter's Blue Lakes Ranch below the falls. Walgamott also encouraged Perrine in eventually opening the Twin Falls and Northside tracts to irrigation. More about that in Chapter Twenty.

The O.S.L. could do little about developing the agriculture of southwest Idaho, though it tried. Farms had been established in the area as soon as the mines in Boise Basin and Owyhee had created a demand. The 1870 census shows only 414 farms in all of Idaho Territory (not including the Mormon farms in Franklin and Bear Lake, not yet acknowledged to be in Idaho). About 65 percent of those, 269 farms, were in Ada County. Practically all the 76,000 bushels of wheat and 65,000 bushels of potatoes produced in Idaho in 1869 were raised in the Boise Valley. The further development of farming, even with the presence of the nearby railroad, required water. Although easily dug diversion canals were built in the 1860s and '70s, the means of constructing longer, more expensive highline canals had not yet been found. Mormons accomplished this by means of cooperative irrigation companies owned by the farmers, but elsewhere the adoption of legislative devices for the creation of irrigation districts proceeded slowly.

Despite the supposed independence of Idahoans, they asked for federal help. The editor of the Boise *Idaho Daily Statesman* wrote on November 14, 1889, that, following proper surveys,

> The entire Northwest will not only ask, but demand liberal and generous government aid for building reservoirs and opening ditches for irrigating these immense areas of arid government land. It is a pretty state of affairs indeed, if a government which can legally appropriate scores of millions annually for the improvement of harbors and rivers, may not set aside from the surplus a few million for making its own land saleable, and fit for American homes. . . . We are determined to prove that what has been good for the Eastern gander these many years, will be equally good for the Western goose.[13]

If irrigation were expanded, Idahoans contended, more farms could be created, the government could sell more land, and the nation as a whole would benefit. They were on the right track: when the federal government established the U.S. Reclamation Service in 1902, agricultural production in southwestern Idaho rose spectacularly. One of the export industries then developed was fruit. Apples, cherries, peaches, and prunes came to be grown in immense quantities in Caldwell, Payette, Emmett,

Weiser, New Plymouth, Parma, and Council. In the meantime, many mines opened up along the track. The Seven Devils mines above Hells Canyon, for example, hauled tons of ore to the O.S.L. station at Weiser. Weiser was also a gateway for prospectors going to Warren, Roosevelt, and other Salmon Mountain mines.

Branch lines built by the Oregon Short Line or by companies it later absorbed in the years after 1882 include: Nampa to Boise, 1887; Murphy to Emmett, 1902; Weiser to New Meadows, 1902; Blackfoot to Mackay, 1902; Payette to New Plymouth, 1906; Minidoka to Buhl, 1907; New Plymouth to Emmett, 1910; Moreland to Aberdeen, 1910; Twin Falls to Rogerson, 1910; Rupert to Bliss, 1910; Burley to Oakley, 1910; Richfield to Hill City, 1912; and Burley to Declo, 1912.

Henry Villard was forced out of the presidency of Northern Pacific shortly after that line was finished. His successors constructed several branch lines to serve portions of north Idaho and, at the same time, encourage the establishment of new enterprises that would provide traffic. A 112-mile line was built in 1888 from Spokane to Genesee and later from Spokane to Lewiston, thus serving the grain- and pea-growing lands of the Palouse and Camas Prairie areas as well as an increasingly productive timber area. Lewiston, with about 700 people in 1880, was the largest town in north Idaho; Moscow, with about 400, was the second largest. A branch was constructed in 1890 from Pullman, Washington, to Moscow, Troy, Kendrick, and Julietta, following the Potlatch River to the Clearwater. The line was completed to Lewiston in 1898 and to a point adjacent to Camas Prairie in 1899.

In 1886 a thirteen-mile road was built to connect Coeur d'Alene, a city of 200 or 300, with the village of Hauser Junction on Idaho's western border. In 1887, a thirty-mile branch line was extended under the aegis of D. C. Corbin to serve Kingston, Wardner, Osburn, Murray, Wallace, Burke, and

Ryan. (The stretch through the narrow section of Burke Canyon did not have room for both the creek and the railroad, so the rail bed was built directly over Canyon Creek.) Corbin then bought the shipping line that operated from Coeur d'Alene to Cataldo and built a narrow-gauge up the South Fork of the Coeur d'Alene River to the Montana line. The road reached Kellogg in 1887, Wallace in 1888, and Mullan in 1889 and was at the Montana summit in 1891. The entire system was later leased to and eventually purchased by Northern Pacific.

In 1892 North Idaho began to be served by the Great Northern Railway, which stretched from St. Paul to Puget Sound. Under the dynamic leadership of James J. Hill, a Canadian-American, the Great Northern went south of Glacier National Park in Montana, through Bonners Ferry and Sandpoint into Washington, then south to Spokane. The construction continued during the depression of 1893, its payroll thus mitigating the impact of the depression on the region. The railroad was responsible for much of the immigration into the area north of Sandpoint in the 1890s and early years of the twentieth century.

A final transcontinental road was the Chicago, Milwaukee, St. Paul, and Pacific Railroad, which crossed north Idaho in 1909 and is notable as the first railroad to electrify a major segment—a 438-mile section from Harlowtown, Montana, to Avery, Idaho.

The Utah and Northern, Oregon Short Line, and Northern Pacific railroads of the later 1870s and early 1880s, financed as they were by eastern and European capital, brought income to Idaho workers and supplied them with goods and services. The roads facilitated colonization and settlement; stimulated the development of cattle grazing, mining, and other industries that required transportation for their profitability; and encouraged the development of local manufacturing. They brought a larger population that furnished new markets close at hand for the produce of Idaho's farms. By outrunning the course of settlement, the railroads also changed the nature of pioneering. Farmers could now travel with comparative ease to the Snake River Valley and other areas to homestead cheap land, secure provisions and supplies while the land was put under cultivation, and grow specialized products for markets in thriving metropolitan areas on the Pacific Coast and in the Midwest. The railroads were likewise the foundation of Idaho's potato industry; they were also the foundation for the exciting mining developments at Wood River and the Coeur d'Alene region. Within twenty years, stimulated by these railroads, the population of Idaho spiraled from 32,610 in 1880 to 88,548 in 1890 and 161,772 in 1900.

In short, the railroads were catalysts that speeded up the processes of settlement and greatly increased Idaho's income from agriculture, mining, forestry, and commerce. They were mediums of cultural interchange, for they brought visitors from Boston, New York, London, and Berlin who appreciated and publicized Idaho's natural wonders.

## CHAPTER FOURTEEN: SOURCES

Most of the histories of Idaho and of the Pacific Northwest have sections on the topics of this chapter. More specialized studies used in preparing the chapter are given below.

*Utah Northern and Utah and Northern Railroads.* Merrill D. Beal, *Intermountain Railroads: Standard and Narrow Gauge* (Caldwell: Caxton Printers, 1962), 1–140; Robert G. Athearn, *Union Pacific Country* (Chicago: Rand McNally & Company, 1971), 237–63, 279, 299; and Beal and Wells, *History of Idaho*, 1:494–518, the last largely a reprint of Merrill D. Beal, "The Story of the Utah Northern Railroad," *Idaho Yesterdays* 1 (Spring 1957):3–10, and (Summer 1957):16–23. See also [Merle Wells], "Utah Northern Railroad," *Idaho Yesterdays* 22 (Spring 1978):26–28; "The Northern Railroad Right of Way," in Madsen, *The Bannock of Idaho*, 231–48; Leonard J. Arrington, "Mormon Railroads," in *Great Basin Kingdom: An Economic History of the Latter-day Saints, 1830–1900* (Cambridge,

Mass.: Harvard University Press, 1958), 283–89; and Arrington, "Railroad Building and Cooperatives, 1869–1879," in Ricks and Cooley, eds., *The History of a Valley*, 170–86; Robert L. Wrigley, Jr., "Utah and Northern Railway Co.: A Brief History," *Oregon Historical Quarterly* 48 (September 1957):245–53; Robert G. Athearn, "Railroad to a Far-Off Country: The Utah and Northern," *Montana The Magazine of Western History* 18 (October 1968):2–23; Harry Edward Bilger, "A History of Railroads in Idaho" (M.A. thesis, University of Idaho, 1969); and "The Northern Railroads," in Clarence A. Reeder, Jr., "The History of Utah's Railroads, 1869–1883" (Ph.D. dissertation, University of Utah, 1970), 211–56. Recent studies include Maurey Klein, *Union Pacific* (Garden City, N.Y.: Doubleday & Co., 1987); and George W. Hilton, *American Narrow Gauge Railroads* (Stanford, Calif.: Stanford University Press, 1990).

*Oregon Short Line*. Beal, *Intermountain Railroads*, 141–95; Beal and Wells, *History of Idaho*, 1:519–39; Athearn, *Union Pacific Country*, 305–29, 356–57, 373–74, essentially the same as his article "The Oregon Short Line," *Idaho Yesterdays* 13 (Winter 1969–70):2–18; Bilger, "A History of Railroads in Idaho"; Ross R. Controneo, "Snake River Railroad," *Pacific Northwest Quarterly* 56 (July 1965):106–13; Dorothy O. Johansen, "The Oregon Steam Navigation Company: An Example of Capitalism on the Frontier," *Pacific Historical Review* 10 (June 1941):179–88; James H. Kyner and Hawthorn Daniel, *End of Track* (Caldwell: Caxton Printers, 1937; reissued, Lincoln: University of Nebraska Press, 1960); James Blaine Hedges, *Henry Villard and the Railways of the Northwest* (New Haven, Conn.: Yale University Press, 1930).

*Northern Pacific*. Beal and Wells, 1:540–52; "Transportation Development," in Livingston-Little, *An Economic History of North Idaho*, 74–80; George Bird Grinnell, "Building the Northern Pacific," originally published in *Forest and Stream*, February 9, 1882, and republished in *Idaho Yesterdays* 16 (Winter 1972–73):10–13; Bilger, "A History of Railroads in Idaho"; August C. Bolino, "The Big Bend of the Northern Pacific," *Idaho Yesterdays* 3 (Summer 1959):5–10; William Harland Boyd, "The Holladay-Villard Transportation Empire in The Pacific Northwest, 1868–1893," *Pacific*

*Historical Review* 15 (December 1946):379–89; John Fahey, *Inland Empire: D. C. Corbin and Spokane* (Seattle: University of Washington Press, 1965); Eugene V. Smalley, *History of the Northern Pacific Railroad* (New York: G. P. Putnam's Sons, 1883); Oscar O. Winther, *The Transportation Frontier: Trans-Mississippi West, 1865–1890* (New York: Holt, Rinehart and Winston, 1964); and Robert E. Riegel, *The Story of the Western Railroads* (New York: The Macmillan Co., 1926).

Regional settlement is discussed in Beal, *A History of Southeastern Idaho*; Danielson, *History of the Development of Southeastern Idaho*; Ricks and Cooley, eds., *The History of a Valley*; Sudweeks, "Early Agricultural Settlements in Southern Idaho"; Richard Sherlock, "Mormon Migration and Settlement after 1875," *Journal of Mormon History* 2 (1975):53–68; Merrill D. Beal, *The Snake River Fork Country* (Rexburg: The Rexburg Journal, 1935); Davis Bitton, "Peopling the Upper Snake: The Second Wave of Mormon Settlement in Idaho," *Idaho Yesterdays* 23 (Summer 1979):47–52; Dallas E. Livingston-Little, "An Economic History of North Idaho, 1800–1900: Agricultural Developments," *Journal of the West* 3 (April 1964):175–98; David L. Crowder, *Tales of Eastern Idaho* (Idaho Falls: KID Broadcasting Corporation, 1981); Kate B. Carter, comp., *Pioneer Irrigation: Upper Snake River Valley* (Salt Lake City: Daughters of Utah Pioneers, 1955); "Pioneer Irrigation in Southeastern Idaho," in Beal and Wells, *History of Idaho*, 2:119–35; and Janet Thomas, *This Side of the Mountains: Stories of Eastern Idaho* (Idaho Falls: KID Broadcasting Corporation, 1975).

Community studies include: Eugene B. Chaffee, "Boise: The Founding of a City," *Idaho Yesterdays* 7 (Summer 1963):2–7; Bird, *Boise, The Peace Valley*; R. L. Wrigley, Jr., "Early History of Pocatello, Idaho," *Pacific Northwest Quarterly* 34 (October 1943):353–65; Davis Bitton, "The Making of a Community: Blackfoot, Idaho, 1878–1910," *Idaho Yesterdays* 19 (Spring 1975):2–15; Frederickson, *History of Weston, Idaho*; David L. Crowder, *Rexburg, Idaho: The First One Hundred Years, 1883–1983* (Caldwell: Caxton Printers, 1983); Young, "The History and Development of Franklin, Idaho, During the Period 1860–1900"; Arrington and Jensen,

"Lorenzo Hill Hatch: Pioneer Bishop of Franklin"; Mrs. James D. Agnew, "Idaho Pioneer of 1864," *Washington Historical Quarterly* 15 (January 1924):44–48; Paul L. Murphy, "Early Irrigation in the Boise Valley," *Pacific Northwest Quarterly* 44 (October 1953):177–84; Lawrence G. Coates, "Mormons and Social Change Among the Shoshoni, 1853–1900," *Idaho Yesterdays* 15 (Winter 1972):2–11; A. McKay Rich, "The Two Montpeliers," *Idaho Yesterdays* 3 (Winter 1959–60):8–14; Leonard J. Arrington, "The Mormon Settlement of Cassia County, Idaho, 1873–1921," *Idaho Yesterdays* 23 (Summer 1979):36–46.

Additional references include: Betty M. Madsen and Brigham D. Madsen, *North to Montana: Jehus, Bullwhackers, and Muleskinners on the Montana Trail* (Salt Lake City: University of Utah Press, 1980); James Knox Polk Miller, *The Road to Virginia City: The Diary of James Knox Polk Miller*, Andrew F. Rolle, ed. (Norman: University of Oklahoma Press, 1960); Carrie A. Strahorn, *Fifteen Thousand Miles by Stage: A Woman's Unique Experience* (1912; reissued in 2 vols., Lincoln: University of Nebraska Press, 1989); Alexander Toponce, *Reminiscences* (Salt Lake City: Deseret News Publishing Co., 1934); and Peter J. Valora, "A Historical Geography of Agriculture in the Upper Snake River Valley, Idaho" (Ph.D. dissertation, University of Colorado, 1986).

In 1990 the Idaho Humanities Council and the History Committee of the Idaho Centennial Commision funded a project on "Mormon Migration and Idaho" that included papers by Lawrence Coates, Ron Hatzenbuehler, and Peter Boag; copies in possession of the writer.

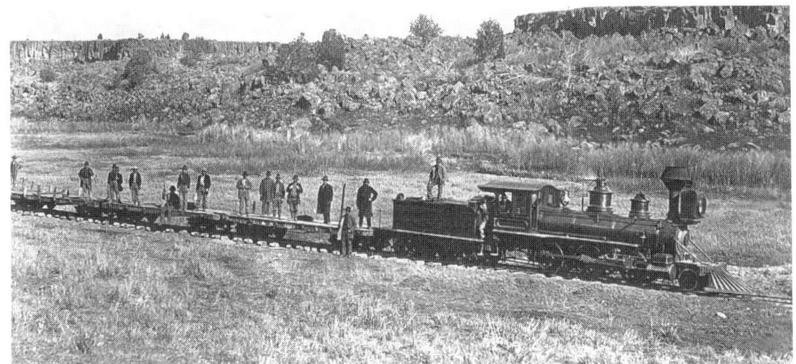

60.

61.

60. Famous Mormon photographer Charles R. Savage took this photo of a Utah and Northern construction train crew working in Portneuf Canyon in 1878. LDS CHURCH ARCHIVES PH 1373.

61. As the Utah and Northern moved north from Franklin to the Montana border, Latter-day Saints settled along its route in southeastern Idaho, especially in the early 1880s. Here are Charles Erastus and Martha Liljenquist with their children and a friend in front of a cabin at Moreland. LDS CHURCH ARCHIVES PH 1228.

62. 

63. 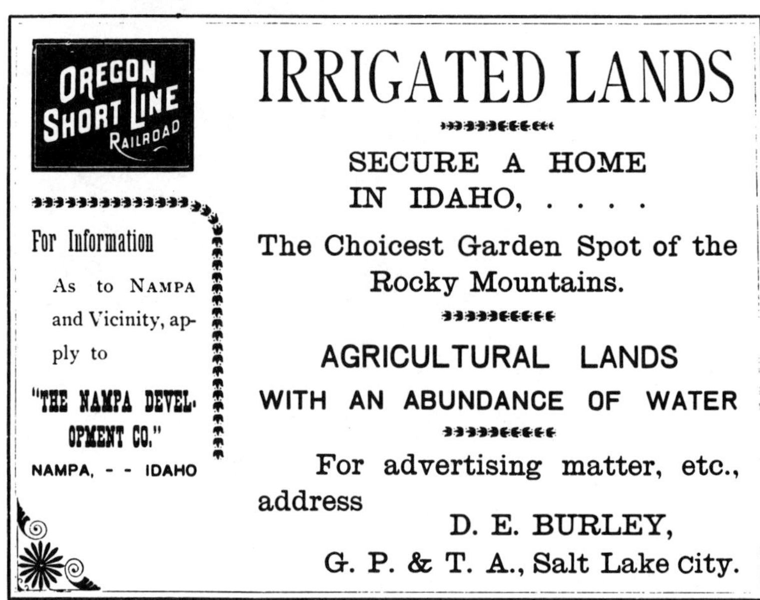


62. This Oregon Short Line Railroad crew worked on the Buhl extension in 1906. ISHS 73–221.178.

63. The completion of the Oregon Short Line Railroad in 1884 initiated a campaign to secure settlers along the route. ISHS 6773.57B.

64.

64. This Northern Pacific construction gang was busy near Green Mountain, west of Lake Pend Oreille, in 1885. ISHS 71–204.0.

65. 

66. 

65. A Northern Pacific train crosses a trestle in Idaho. ISHS 66–15.13.

66. Potatoes were a prime export, as illustrated in these wagons from which sacks were loaded into a train near Twin Falls. PHOTO BY CLARENCE BISBEE. ISHS 73–221.18.

67.

67. This trainload of potatoes was consigned to Wichita, Kansas, by an Idaho Falls shipper. ISHS 64–109.3.

## CHAPTER FIFTEEN

# The Lead-Silver Mining Rush of the 1880s

IDAHO enjoyed another mining boom in the 1880s and 1890s. This was the product of spectacular new discoveries along the Wood and Coeur d'Alene rivers plus the service provided by the Utah and Northern, Oregon Short Line, and Northern Pacific railroads and their branches, and substantial technological innovation and improved scientific understanding. The new mines, and the rejuvenated old mines, became massive industrial enterprises in which millions of dollars were invested by easterners, British, and Europeans. As sophisticated syndicates took charge, workers responded by organizing unions, calling strikes, and eventually engaging in industrial warfare.[1]

Placer mining continued in the 1870s. Pockets of men with burros, picks and shovels, rockers and long toms, sluices and arrastras, trying to make a strike or trying to make earlier strikes pay off, peppered Idaho's mountains. In 1869 Nathan Smith and "Doc" Wilson found gold at Loon Creek (later named Oro Grande), on the Middle Fork of the Salmon River, and a stampede followed. The next year gold was discovered on Caribou Mountain in southeastern Idaho, an area that eventually produced $1.2 million. A major quartz lode was located at Yankee Fork in the Salmon Mountains in 1876, and the principal mine was named the General Custer—who had met his nemesis just two months earlier on the Little Big Horn. In 1878 finds at Vienna and Sawtooth City on the upper Salmon and at the Black Jack at Silver City sustained the momentum. Idaho was achieving a deserved reputation for its wealth in minerals.

The territory was also contributing to American folklore by the imaginative names given to its mines. Governor James Hawley once made up a list of some of the names. There were names of mothers, sisters, daughters, and sweethearts: Esmeralda, Ruby Jackson, Floreta, Henrietta. Others bore the names of admired men, such as Abe Lincoln, General Joseph A. Lane, Light Horse Harry Lee. Still others carried controversial titles: Southern Confederacy, Rattling Jack, Big Cheat. Some names came from phenomena connected with the discovery: Blazing Star, Silver Cloud, Lone Tree, Stormy Hill, Noonday, Twilight. Many of the titles represented a hope that the mine would live up to its name: Home Ticket, Hidden Treasure, Paymaster, Golden Star.[2]

While continuing the search for gold placers and adding considerable lode-mining of gold and silver using the newly developed technology of the time, Idaho mining also came to include lead, zinc, and copper. In doing so, the territory depended more heavily on professionally trained engineers, metallurgists, chemists, and geologists. With the proximity of railroads and the availability of coal from mines in nearby Wyoming and Utah, smelting and refining of base metals became financially feasible. By 1885 the scale of operations exceeded any previous Idaho records.

Advanced technology and expertise led to more hydraulicking and dredging, in which deeply buried and low-paying gravels along the Clearwater, in the Salmon Mountains, in the Boise Basin and Owyhee were worked on a grand scale. But no one could have predicted what was in store on the Wood River and Coeur d'Alene.

## WOOD RIVER MINES

In 1864 Warren Callahan, on his way from Rocky Bar to Montana, discovered galena outcroppings along the Wood River. Returning in 1871–73, he decided silver-lead carbonates were a poor alternative to the free-milling gold he sought. In the summer of 1879, with the Bannock and Sheepeaters no longer a threat and the promised construction of the Oregon Short Line, 3,000 prospectors fanned out from the Rocky Bar, Yankee Fork, Loon Creek, and other locations to comb the gulches and streams in the lower reaches of the Wood River. They found rich veins one to two feet thick, running 40 to 60 percent lead, with silver worth from $80 to $150 per ton. By fall, some 230 miners, including David Ketchum, who built the first cabin in the town originally called Leadville and later Ketchum, located claims. With the coming of spring some prospectors rushed in, coming on foot, on horseback, by wagon, and by stagecoach. Camps were founded at Galena, Ketchum, Deer Creek, Warm Springs Creek, Hailey, and Broadford (at first named Jacobs City). Bellevue had two stores, two restaurants, and four saloons as early as 1880. The principal mine, as it turned out, was the Minnie Moore, located at Broadford across the Wood River from Bellevue. The Minnie Moore produced gold, but its principal wealth was in galena (lead-silver) ore. All told, some 2,000 mines were claimed in 1880. Nearly 200 families and 1,000 single men spent the winter of 1880–81 on Wood River, holed up, as one man wrote, "like a bear."[3]

Like the rushes to Pierce, Florence, Idaho City, and Silver City two decades earlier, the Wood River rush produced acute shortages of supplies. Cats (to keep down mice and rats) sold for $5.00; eggs were $1.50 a dozen; potatoes, $8.00 a hundred; flour, $7.00 a hundred. Sometimes from fifteen to forty deer were killed in a day. No one starved; everyone was counting on the yield of the mines.

In the spring of 1881, hundreds more descended into the region. By the end of April the new town of Hailey (named for John Hailey, who donated the land) had 100 tents and 75 buildings, including five "first class" saloons. Other locations settled in 1881–82 included Muldoon (named for a champion wrestler), which had a peak population of 1,500; Doniphan (named for the Mexican War general), fifteen miles southwest of Hailey, which serviced the Big Camas and Tip Top mines, both of which had stamp mills; Bullion, seven miles west of Hailey, with a population of 700 servicing the Mayflower, Bullion, Jay Gould, May Queen, and Idahoan mines; and Ketchum, with a newspaper, post office, and about 100 businesses. The Philadelphia Mining and Smelting Company near Ketchum had the largest mill in Idaho; it operated until 1893, ran on waterpower from Wood River, and had four tall stacks, electric power, and twenty kilns to feed it with charcoal. By the summer of 1893 there were between 3,500 and 5,000 people on the Wood River, half in towns and the remainder out prospecting.

The branch of the Oregon Short Line reached Hailey in May 1883 and Ketchum by the next year. Wood River was now only fourteen hours from Salt Lake City. The railroad made possible importation of concentrating mills, smelters, tunneling, timbering, shafting, ventilating, and ore hauling. The separation of base metals from gold and silver, as had been developed a few years before in Nevada and Colorado, was now technically possible if the capital were available.

The richness of the finds helped make fortunes. Enos Wall and a partner acquired the Mayflower from its locators for $25,000 and soon sold it to a Chicago group for $375,000. The discoverer of the Minnie Moore sold his quarter interest for $10,000; in 1884 a British combine bought it for $500,000. Ultimately $8.5 million were taken from this mine. Many Wood River mines were sold to companies in Salt Lake City, Denver, San Francisco, Philadelphia, New York, and London. Among the purchasers of mines in Wood River were George Hearst, noted investor in Nevada, Utah, and Dakota mines and smelters and later U.S. Senator from California; and David Eccles, later Utah's first millionaire, who got his big start by establishing a sawmill operation in Gray's Gulch and supplying lumber to nearby Hailey as well as to other camps in the area. He supplied lumber to the Oregon Short Line as it moved through the Snake River Valley and later profited from the completion of the road by establishing the Oregon Lumber Company, an immensely lucrative enterprise.

Since the ore was principally galena, carrying both lead and silver in paying quantities, it had to be smelted. With no smelter in the district, the first products of the mines were taken by freight teams 170 miles to Kelton and then shipped to Salt Lake City or Denver to be processed. When the Oregon Short Line branch was completed, smelters were built at Bellevue; near Hailey at the mouth of Indian Creek; at Ketchum; at Galena; and across the Little Wood River at Muldoon. Each smelter was provided with twenty or more charcoal kilns for fuel.

Prosperity brought amenities not available in many western communities. The telegraph came with the railroad in 1883. By October, Hailey had a telephone system, the first in Idaho; within a month Hailey, Bellevue, Bullion, and Ketchum were all linked by telephone circuit at a cost of $8 a month to the householder. Ketchum's Philadelphia Smelter had electric lights in 1882, thanks to Idaho's initial electric plant. Hailey's town waterworks, opened late the next year, were likewise the first in Idaho. At one time Hailey had three daily newspapers.[4]

The mines drew seasoned miners and novices. Most of the Wood River miners were from California, Nevada, and Boise Basin; in addition to "Old Americans," there were Chinese, blacks, Bohemians, Latin Americans, and a number of Utahans, including some Mormons. The Land Office Receiver was Homer Pound, father of poet Ezra Pound, born in October 1885 in Hailey. Carrie Strahorn, who left a marvelous personal history, described Hailey—which replaced Rocky Bar as the county seat of Alturas County in 1882—as "the most orderly mining town imaginable, and its citizens were largely a class superior to those of frontier settlements."[5] In an article in *Idaho Yesterdays* (Summer 1979) Clark Spence, an Idaho-grown historian, has described the recreational patterns: snow-shoeing (and some skiing) in the surrounding hills, sleighing clubs, bicycle riding, the new (to Idaho) game of baseball, cockfights, and social dancing. Ketchum had a silver cornet band, Bellevue a twelve-piece brass band. Hailey had a quartet and a choral association, and Bullion conducted a dancing school. Ketchum had a debating club and literary society, Bellevue a minstrel group and a liar's club. There were churches, lectures, dramas, and circuses. In 1884 5,000 persons jammed Hailey to watch W. W. Cole's Colossal Shows featuring Samson, a five-ton elephant that broke loose from his trainers and nearly wrecked the town.

One incident marred the harmony in Wood River and presaged problems in the Coeur d'Alenes. In 1884 owners of the Minnie Moore tried to cut wages. Freight rates were unfavorable, and the prices of lead and silver were declining. A neighboring property had shut down two weeks before because of the unfavorable cost-price ratio. The company was unsuccessful in obtaining lower freight rates, and low prices for lead and silver continued. The miners resisted and stopped work on July 20, and the company was forced to resume its customary payments. The company made a second attempt to cut wages, prompting another strike on February 4, 1885. Some strikers were arrested for interfering with company attempts to work the mines with strikebreakers, but public sentiment favored the strikers. When the sheriff provided armed guards to help the mines reopen on February 28, there was resistance. A battle raged for two months. Idaho was without a governor at the time; Governor John Nichol Irwin had come to the territory from Iowa in April 1883, became ill while he was on his first inspection trip, and returned to Iowa to recuperate. He later resigned. The acting governor for the period was Edward L. Curtis, the territorial secretary and son of Edward J. Curtis, a California forty-niner who had come to Idaho in the early 1860s, had become territorial secretary in 1869, and was now an elder statesman of Idaho's Republican Party. Young Curtis and General J. S. Brisbin, of the federal army at Fort Boise, went to Bellevue (and Broadford) to put down the strike by force. Although President Grover Cleveland refused their request for martial law, they provided sufficient military protection for the strikebreakers to continue operating the mines. The strike failed, but angry miners, resentful in their defeat, would later spark the bitter Coeur d'Alene mining wars of the 1890s.[6]

Silver and lead made the Wood River towns, but in the late 1880s both declined in value, silver dropping from $1.50 an ounce in 1880 to $.59 in 1894 and lead from $5 per hundred in 1880 to $3 in 1894. As some of the veins pinched out or were lost, wages were cut and workers drifted on to Coeur d'Alene or elsewhere. By the 1893 depression the Wood River mining region was "deader than a lime fossil."[7] Several of the settlements —Bullion, Galena, Muldoon—had become ghost towns.

## THE COEUR D'ALENE MINES

In the 1850s Captain John Mullan had employed a group of men to build a military road in north Idaho. Some of them were

California forty-niners, and they found placer deposits and "likely looking quartz" along the North Fork of the Coeur d'Alene River, but Mullan, determined to complete the road, persuaded his crew to forget the gold. Charles Wilson prospected the Coeur d'Alenes in the 1860s and found "color." News of the strike spread, and one hundred or more miners followed him back, but he was unable to find the site. Another expedition into the area in 1873–74 was led by John Vollmer, a leading merchant in Lewiston, but that group also failed. In November 1878, however, A. J. Prichard, on his way from New Mexico to Fort Sherman (Coeur d'Alene), found quartz lead on a location he called Evolution. He returned to Evolution from the fort in January 1879, erected a cabin, did some sluicing in Prospect Gulch, and earned sufficient money in 1880 to finance work on his lode claim. He panned along the North Fork of the Coeur d'Alene in 1881, most successfully at a site later called Murray. Apparently Prichard wrote friends about his finds, for in the spring of 1882 several prospectors showed up with a demand that he take them with him. Crossing the North Fork, they were successful in finding gold along Prichard Creek, about three-quarters of a mile below Murray.

The news quickly spread. During the winter of 1882–83 Prichard wrote friends less guardedly, and miners rushed to the area in the spring of 1883. Eagle City emerged. The Northern Pacific Railway passed within thirty miles of the region, and its officials now distributed a circular advertising the "very rich" claims along the creeks running into the Coeur d'Alene: "Nuggets have been found which weigh $50, $100, $166, and $200." They also mentioned the "valuable quartz lode" that Prichard had found. The Coeur d'Alene mines, the circular asserted, "surpass in riches and volume the most fabulous quartz and placers ever discovered, even the famous deposits of Potosi. . . . Although thousands may work them, there will be room for thousands more."[8] Approximately 10,000 people descended on Eagle, Murray, and the North Fork area in 1883, 1884, and 1885. Production ran between $250,000 to $500,000 per year.

Adding to the excitement was the discovery of silver-lead ores in the region. On May 2, 1884, John Canton and Almeda Seymour filed on the Tiger claim on Canyon Creek, a tributary to the South Fork of the Coeur d'Alene, at a place later known as Burke. Three days later Scott McDonald and George P. Carter staked the Poorman claim on the same lode on the other side of the canyon. That same month J. G. Hunter filed on the Gold Hunter silver-lead lode about a mile northeast of Mullan. In July the Morning and Evening lode claims were staked by G. S. Good and C. C. A. Earle two miles north of Mullan and two miles south of Burke. Other locations were identified in August 1884, including the Polaris, across the South Fork canyon two miles south of Evolution, by W. B. Heyburn (later U.S. senator) and others. In September, True and Dennis Blake, brothers, staked the Yankee Lode, destined to become the Sunshine Mine.[9]

The best was still to come. In the summer of 1885, as the placer boom was subsiding, carpenter Noah S. Kellogg found himself unemployed. Kellogg secured a grubstake from O. O. Peck, a Murray contractor, and Dr. J. T. Cooper, a physician. The supplies, obtained at Jim Wardner's store near Murray, consisted of seven pounds of bacon, fifteen pounds of flour, eight pounds of beans, four pounds of dried apples, two pounds of coffee, a dollar's worth of sugar, one pair of shoes, and half a dozen location notices altogether worth about $18.75. Setting out with his burro on August 1, Kellogg prospected in several locations, including Milo Creek. He returned four weeks later, obtained more "stake" from a new set of partners, and returned to Milo Gulch (now Wardner), where he staked out the Bunker Hill and Sullivan claims. The Bunker Hill was named for the Revolutionary War battle; the Sullivan was apparently named for Kellogg's partner, Cornelius Sullivan, although another partner later claimed it was in honor of heavyweight boxing champion John L. Sullivan. Kellogg and his partners were joined at the site by Jim Wardner, who filed on the waters of Milo Creek and 10,000 miners' inches of the South Fork of the Coeur d'Alene. After litigation, Cooper and Peck obtained a judgment awarding them a 25 percent share of the mines.[10]

Wardner took samples to help conclude an agreement with a San Francisco firm to smelt the ore. He also built a wagon road to the head of navigation, and by December 1885 the first shipment of ore was loaded on the steamer *Coeur d'Alene*, transported by water to the city and by wagon from there to Rathdrum, then loaded on Northern Pacific Railway cars for Portland and thence by steamer to San Francisco. Wardner was able to obtain financial help from Governor S. T. Hauser in Montana, D. C. Corbin in Spokane, and others and erected a concentrating mill at Wardner. Obtaining an option for sale in 1887, Wardner sold the mine, mill, and milling contracts to Simeon G. Reed, pioneer Portland industrialist, for $650,000. The mine was destined to become the nation's largest lead-silver mine. Milo was renamed Kellogg.[11]

Meanwhile, D. C. Corbin built a branch-line railroad fifteen miles from Hauser Junction on the Northern Pacific to Coeur d'Alene and a narrow-gauge line from the head of navigation at Cataldo to Wardner Junction. The line was pushed eastward to meet the Northern Pacific standard-gauge line at Lookout Summit on the Montana border. Ores were then shipped to Wickes (Helena), Montana, and later to Denver, Omaha, and Tacoma.[12]

The Tiger and Poorman mines also shipped ore to Helena and Denver, some 440 tons weekly in December 1888. Other lead-silver and gold mines as well were producing and paying dividends. Ten lead-silver mines each had mills of at least 100 tons daily capacity, and the Bunker Hill and Poorman had mills of 150 tons daily capacity. The Bunker Hill and Sullivan became north Idaho's most important economic enterprise of the nineteenth century.[13]

Another mine of great importance was the Hercules, discovered by Harry Day and F. H. Harper in 1889. Henry L. Day, father of Harry, had gone from Maine to California in 1854. He engaged in mining for five years, freighted for another three, and then traveled east to the Comstock Lode in Nevada for four years. Moving back to Truckee and Sacramento, California, he worked in freighting, stagecoaching, and supplying lumber to mines and railroads. In 1886 Henry moved to Wardner, founded a general store which he and Harry operated until 1904, and engaged in dairying and cattle raising. Meanwhile, Henry encouraged Harry to prospect. In 1889, when he was twenty-three, Harry Day and his partner Harper located a rich silver-lead vein near Wallace. They did development work during the next few years; Harper sold his interest and Henry became involved. In 1902 the mine began to pay dividends. During the next twenty-three years the gross output was approximately $75 million, with dividends in excess of $20 million. Harry's assistant, his younger brother Eugene Day, succeeded Harry as general manager in 1912.

There were other mines of this magnitude in the Coeur d'Alenes in the 1890s and early years of the twentieth century. The Bunker Hill and Sullivan Mine, however, was one of the great mines in the history of western civilization, and certain legends have been popularized about its discovery. Most have given credit to Noah Kellogg's jackass. Here is the story told by Jim Wardner:

> Looking across the creek we saw the jack standing upon the side of the hill, and apparently gazing intently across the canyon at some object which attracted his attention. We went up the slope after him, expecting that, as usual, he would give us a hard chase; but he never moved as we approached. His ears were set forward, his eyes were fixed

> upon some object, and he seemed wholly absorbed. Reaching his side, we were astounded to find the jackass standing upon a great outcropping of mineralized vein-matter and looking in apparent amazement at the marvelous ore-shoot across the canyon, which then, as you now see it, was reflecting the sun's rays like a mirror.[14]

T. A. Rickard, a distinguished mining engineer who repeated this tale, was much amused. Argentiferous galena exposed to the atmosphere, he pointed out, becomes a dull sulphate or carbonate, colored dark red by the oxidation of associated iron pyrite. "The talk of a glittering mass of silvery ore sticking out of the mountain-side so brilliantly as to mesmerize the ass, and others not any wiser, is pure moonshine." What did happen, he thought, was that the donkey, in looking for fodder, strayed through the pine forest above the creek toward the outcrop, near which was an open space covered with bunchgrass.[15]

The Coeur d'Alene mining districts, often referred to simply as the Coeur d'Alenes, inaugurated a new era in Idaho mining—a new level of maturity in mine operation and management. Bunker Hill and Sullivan, Tiger, Poorman, and other lead-silver mines employed professionally trained engineers to direct their work, and the Coeur d'Alenes became world leaders in the industry.

Mining engineering in the 1890s and early years of the twentieth century was not as specialized as it has become in recent years, but was already a complex art involving the professions of geologist, surveyor, lawyer, mechanic, chemist, metallurgist, mineralogist, and electrician. The mining engineer located, developed, exposed, measured, and removed ore from the ground; reduced metal from the ore and marketed it; devised intricate machinery; became an expert in mining litigation; and sometimes engaged in corporate promotion and investment.[16] He became a central figure in the production of the silver-lead-zinc ores of the Coeur d'Alenes. He also introduced hydraulicking and gold dredging in Idaho, as he had done in California and Nevada.

Five mining engineers, in particular, participated in the Coeur d'Alenes, where the great Bunker Hill and Sullivan served as a proving ground for western engineers. When Simeon Reed became owner in 1887 he employed Victor Clement, who had been manager of the Empire Mine in Grass Valley, California. Clement was so busy taking charge of the property, directing the exploration and development, making provision for the extracting, processing, and sale of the ore, arranging for underground and surface transportation, supervising the treatment of the ore, managing the accounts and contracts, and overseeing the large labor force, not to mention the inevitable litigation, that he reported to Reed in 1889: "If I find time enough to take my meals I am doing well."[17] Clement tried to keep an eye on the performance of the entire crew, which must have taken some doing. A report on 329 employees of Bunker Hill and Sullivan in the early 1890s showed 84 Americans, 76 Irishmen, 27 Germans, 24 Italians, 23 Swedes, 19 Englishmen, 14 Scots, 12 Finns, 11 Austrians, 8 Norwegians, 7 Frenchmen, 5 Danes, 2 Swiss, and 1 each Spaniard, Portuguese, and Icelander.[18] Engineers often spoke of "ten-day miners" who worked with diligence at one job until they accumulated a stake large enough to take them to another camp.

Clement went to South Africa in 1893 and was succeeded by Frederick W. Bradley, son of a California civil engineer who attended the California School of Mines and had tended several mining properties in Idaho and elsewhere. Bradley had made a reputation in the gold quartz mines of California before his move to the silver ores of Coeur d'Alene. Made president of the company—a position he retained for many years—in 1897, Bradley also remained as manager until 1901, when he appointed Albert Burch. Son of a Methodist minister, Burch went one year to college and then worked on the Chicago, Burlington, and Quincy Railroad as a surveyor. Eventually he became a mine surveyor, a mine operator, and finally manager of the great Bunker Hill and Sullivan. In the early 1890s he was manager of the Bullion Beck and Champion Mine, a silver mine in central Utah. Burch was followed in 1903 by Stanly A. Easton, a University of California graduate, who continued as manager for the next thirty years.

A leading pre-World War I consulting engineer was Gelasio Caetani, an Italian with an English mother. He trained at Columbia, worked for Bunker Hill and Sullivan, and served in an engineering partnership in San Francisco. He left to join the Italian army during World War I (he was the son of the Duke of Sermoneta), became a national hero, returned as Italian ambassador to the United States, and, as Prince Caetani, became an aide of Benito Mussolini and mayor of Rome. Among other things, Caetani designed a concentrating mill built by Bunker Hill and Sullivan in 1909. The feed to the new mill, measured in 1919, assayed 10 percent lead and four ounces of silver per ton; the resulting concentrate was 68 percent lead and twenty-four ounces of silver per ton.[19]

Despite the help of engineers, lawyers, and other professionals, Simeon Reed was so harassed and tormented with suits and personnel problems that he sold the Bunker Hill and Sullivan properties to a group of California and eastern investors headed by the famous mining engineer John Hays Hammond. Ultimately, nearly every Coeur d'Alene silver-lead mine of any stature was bought and developed by corporations. The one insistent holdout was the Hercules Mine.

The year 1892 brought a series of tragic incidents to the Coeur d'Alenes. The miners there had organized in 1886. In 1889 the mine owners had formed a strong Mine Owners Association, of which Fred Bradley of Bunker Hill and Sullivan was the president. Because of low silver and lead prices, a rise in freight rates, and the wish to restore wage levels to the pre-1890 level, mine owners shut down all the major Coeur d'Alene mines on January 16, 1892. The fact that it was winter made it an especially difficult time for the hundreds of miners. The adverse freight-rate increase was rescinded on March 18, but the workers refused to accept a reduction in pay. Mine owners announced that the lockout would continue until June 1. On April 29 a mine in Burke attempted to employ nonunion workers, but the people of the town threw them out. A mine at Wardner decided to employ nonunion workers and sought a federal injunction prohibiting the Wardner union from interfering with the workers. The mine owners recruited a force of fifty-four armed guards in Lewiston, Moscow, and Genesee on May 12. When a trainload of nonunion miners, mostly immigrants, left Missoula on May 14 to work in Burke, the chief guard was promptly arrested by the local court. But other guards concealed their identity, and the mine owners, with the help of their guards, managed to resume operations. By June 1 about 300 nonunion miners were at work; by June 25, about 800. Normally about 4,000 were employed, but at least the mines were able to carry on operations on a reduced scale.

In July 1892 the unemployed union miners decided upon direct action. A large number of armed men congregated at the Gem mine and dynamited a massive but abandoned mill, took the nonunion crew of the adjacent mine captive, and cleared the canyon of nonunion workers. Capturing the mills and concentrators, they threatened to blow them up. The employers, now under duress, agreed to discharge all "scabs." United States troops, called out by President Benjamin Harrison, came from Fort Sherman (at Coeur d'Alene) and from Missoula, and from July 14 to November 18 martial law held sway in the Coeur d'Alenes. Union men suspected of participating in the uprising were confined in a bull-pen—a large outdoor prison. The nonunion workers returned from exile and resumed work. The Mine Owners Association emerged victorious in the "Coeur d'Alene

Mining War of 1892," but, as we shall see, it was only a temporary win.[20]

The Coeur d'Alene discoveries of the early 1880s had transformed the thinly populated agricultural area of north Idaho into a region of nationwide industrial importance. The population of north Idaho grew from 7,000 in 1880 to 25,000 in 1890. Shoshone County, where most of the action took place, rose from 469 to 5,382 in the same decade, and the assessed property valuation rose from $32,000 in 1884 to $1,608,842 in 1890.[21] As mining expanded to large industrial units, the region underwent an uneasy, strife-torn existence. On the one hand, many miners lived in company towns and depended on company benevolence. On the other hand, the companies in Coeur d'Alene, Silver City, Mackay, and the Seven Devils were forging a new industry, producing base metals and rare and strategic metals that became particularly important during and after World War II, establishing payrolls, buying supplies and services, and diversifying Idaho's economy. New skills and technological understanding were developed that would find updated uses elsewhere in Idaho, in the West, and in the nation. Unfortunately, they also contributed to industrial conflict, which, along with other sources of disagreement and friction, would have to be overcome before statehood could be achieved.

## CHAPTER FIFTEEN: SOURCES

Most of the Idaho and Northwest histories contain sections on the Wood River and Coeur d'Alene miners' rushes. Specialized treatments include the following:

*General.* Excellent background is given in "The Latter Days of Mining" in Rodman W. Paul, *The Far West and the Great Plains in Transition, 1859–1900* (New York: Harper & Row, 1988), 252–82. Other general sources include Paul, *Mining Frontiers of the Far West, 1848–1880*, 135–60; Beal and Wells, *History of Idaho*, 1:571–76;

Bolino, *The Role of Mining in the Economic Development of Idaho Territory*; Rickard, *A History of American Mining*, 301–40; Greever, *Bonanza West: The Story of the Western Mining Rushes, 1848–1900*, 272–85; Clark C. Spence, *Mining Engineers and the American West: The Lace-Boot Brigade, 1849–1933* (New Haven, Conn.: Yale University Press, 1970); Lingenfelter, *The Hardrock Miners*, 169–77, 194–218; and Wayne C. Sparling, *Southern Idaho Ghost Towns* (Caldwell: Caxton Printers, 1989).

*Wood River Mines.* I have relied heavily on Clark C. Spence, "The Boom of the Wood River Mines," *Idaho Yesterdays* 23 (Summer 1979):3–12, a splendidly researched article that made good use of contemporary local newspapers and mining periodicals. Other treatments of the Wood River mines include: Bancroft, *History of Washington, Idaho, and Montana*, 529–33; Hawley, *History of Idaho*, 1:491–92.

*Coeur d'Alenes.* Richard G. Magnuson, *Coeur d'Alene Diary: The First Ten Years of Hardrock Mining in North Idaho* (Portland: Metropolitan Press, 1968); D. E. Livingston-Little, "The Bunker Hill and Sullivan: North Idaho's Mining Development from 1885 to 1900," *Idaho Yesterdays* 7 (Spring 1963):34–43, essentially all of which is published in his book, *An Economic History of North Idaho*, esp. 81–122; Eugene V. Smalley, "The Great Coeur d'Alene Stampede of 1884," *Idaho Yesterdays* 11 (Fall 1967):2–10; Richard H. Peterson, "Simeon Gannett Reed and the Bunker Hill and Sullivan: The Frustrations of a Mining Investor," *Idaho Yesterdays* 23 (Fall 1979):2–8; John Fahey, *The Days of the Hercules* (Moscow: University Press of Idaho, 1978); Fahey, *The Ballyhoo Bonanza*; Fahey, *Inland Empire: D. C. Corbin and Spokane*; Wolle, *The Bonanza Trail*, 247–57; and Wendell Brainard, *Golden History Tales from Idaho's Coeur d'Alene Mining District* (Wallace: Crow's Printing, 1990).

Books and articles that discuss the labor unrest, the unions, and the social costs of the Coeur d'Alene and other Idaho mines and industrial disputes include: John Fahey, "Ed Boyce and the Western Federation of Miners," *Idaho Yesterdays* 25 (Fall 1981):18–30; Vernon Jensen, *Heritage of Conflict: Labor Relations in the Nonferrous Metals Industry up to 1930* (Ithaca, N.Y.: Cornell University Press,

1950); May Arkwright Hutton, *The Coeur d'Alenes: A Tale of the Modern Inquisition in Idaho* (Denver: Privately published, 1900); Robert Wayne Smith, *The Coeur d'Alene Mining War of 1892: A Case Study of an Industrial Dispute* (Corvallis: Oregon State College, 1961); Stanley S. Phipps, *From Bull Pen to Bargaining Table: The Tumultous Struggle of the Coeur d'Alenes Miners for the Right to Organize, 1887–1942* (New York: Garland Publishing, 1988); Carlos Schwantes, "The History of Pacific Northwest Labor History," *Idaho Yesterdays* 28 (Winter 1985):23–35; Carlos A. Schwantes, "Patterns of Radicalism on the Wageworkers' Frontier," *Idaho Yesterdays* 30 (Fall 1986):25–30; Richard J. Bonney, "The Pullman Strike of 1894: Pocatello Perspective," *Idaho Yesterdays* 24 (Fall 1980):23–28; Carlos A. Schwantes, "Law and Disorder: The Suppression of Coxey's Army in Idaho," *Idaho Yesterdays* 25 (Summer 1981):10–15; John A. Simpson, "Weldon Heyburn and the Image of the Bloody Shirt," *Idaho Yesterdays* 24 (Winter 1981):20–28; Joseph R. Conlin, "The Haywood Case: An Enduring Riddle," *Pacific Northwest Quarterly* 59 (1968):23–32; W. Earl Greenough, *First 100 Years of the Coeur d'Alene Mining Region, 1846–1946* (Spokane: Hill, 1948); Robert Wayne Smith, "History of Placer and Quartz Gold Mining in the Coeur d'Alene District" (M.A. thesis, University of Idaho, 1932); and Thomas A. Rickard, *The Bunker Hill Enterprise* (San Francisco: The Mining and Scientific Press, 1920).

68.

69.

68. The new Apache Mill in Bullion Gulch near Hailey was built during the Wood River mining rush of the early 1880s. ISHS 63–160.251.

69. Here are the first Bunker Hill and Sullivan bunkhouse and crew at the upper works in 1885. ISHS 79–92.141.

70.

71.

70. Miners' life in the 1880s is depicted in this bunkhouse scene in the Coeur d'Alenes. ISHS 79–92.3.

71. This photo of a group of miners at the entrance of the Mother Lode near Murray was taken about 1885. UIL 8–X993.

72.

72. As mining and milling expanded in the early years of the twentieth century, substantial communities were built. Here is Burke in 1907. UIL 8–X313A.

# CHAPTER SIXTEEN

## Sectional and Factional Contention

IDAHO Territory was Democratic country. In the 1872 elections the candidates for delegate to Congress were John Hailey, Democrat, and Joseph W. Huston, Republican. There were two major issues, both sectional in origin, both related to Idaho's extraordinary—even arbitrary—geography. One was a demand for annexation of north Idaho to Washington; the other was agitation against the Mormons of southeastern Idaho. Both resulted from the boundaries Congress had given to Idaho: the first attempted to correct the unsatisfactory line that had been selected at Olympia's request to separate Washington from Idaho, and the second came from the expansion of settlement from Utah beyond the Forty-Second Parallel, a boundary established arbitrarily in 1819 as a line to separate Spanish claims from those of the United States and continued as the border separating Utah and Idaho.[1]

North Idaho had worked patiently for boundary reform for several years. The annexation of Idaho's panhandle to Washington and establishment of the capital at Walla Walla would, it was argued, satisfy the sectional interests of eastern Washington as well as north Idaho.

As for southeastern Idaho, the Mormons had not fully recognized their presence in Idaho until the official certification of the boundary on February 15, 1872. When Idaho Territory had created Oneida County in January 1864, an anti-Mormon group in Soda Springs and a mixture of Mormons, apostates, Josephites, and non-Mormons in Malad participated in organizing the county, whereas the other border communities had considered themselves part of Utah. The non-Mormon stockraisers did not want Mormon settlements on their public domain grazing land in Gentile Valley (named because of the absence of Mormons) on the bend of the upper Bear River, about thirty miles northeast of Oxford in Cache Valley and twenty miles southwest of Soda Springs. But, despite the efforts of stockmen to drive them out at the point of a pistol, the Mormons' settlement began in 1869.[2]

Huston, a Boise lawyer, supported annexation, but Hailey, a stage-line operator, mirrored the opinion of most southern Idahoans by opposing it. Huston had difficulty obtaining support among the Mormons, who represented a solid vote bloc for Hailey (who, of course, was not a Mormon or even sympathetic). But the Republican Party that nominated Abraham Lincoln in 1860 had declared itself unalterably opposed to "the twin evils of barbarism"—slavery and polygamy—and passed in 1862 the Morrill Act that disincorporated the Mormon Church, declared its property subject to confiscation, and placed heavy fines on its leaders, nearly all of whom had married plural wives. For this reason, and because some Democratic leaders had defended them, the Mormons were Democrats. Ulysses Grant, who led the G.O.P. ticket, was identified with Radical anti-Mormonism as well as with the Radical Reconstruction of the South. Clearly, Huston could not repudiate the actions of

Grant's Radical anti-Mormon appointees in Salt Lake City, so Hailey, a popular figure since the territory was created, was easily elected.

The newly elected, predominantly Democratic Idaho legislature now included Mormons. Bishop Lorenzo Hill Hatch of Franklin was elected from Oneida County and was elected temporary speaker of the House. A Mormon associate of Hatch, Alexander Stalker, also of Franklin, served as chaplain.

Since Republican Party leaders decided that it was useless to appeal for Mormon votes, their tactic after the 1872 election was to discredit the Mormons in such a way that the majority of Idaho voters would vote against Democrats because, it was asserted, they would cater to the Mormons. Thus began a crusade against the Mormons and their influence in Idaho territorial politics. For north Idahoans, boundary readjustment continued to control their elections; but the two issues came to be interconnected. Southern Idahoans asserted that the non-Mormon voters in the north must remain in the territory to keep the Mormons from outvoting the "Gentiles." Likewise north Idahoans must keep down the Mormons because most of the Saints were opposed to annexation.

The two issues figured prominently in every Idaho election until statehood in 1890. Although John Hailey did not run in 1874, his replacement as Democratic candidate was Stephen S. Fenn, the promoter of a new Columbia Territory that would include the north and who also had undivided Mormon support. The Republicans were divided, but Grant's presidential appointee as governor, Thomas W. Bennett, with the support of Idaho Grangers (farmer-members of the secret Patrons of Husbandry) and the anti-Mormons, ran against Fenn. Because he had opposed annexation, Bennett did not do well in north Idaho, and he lost the closely contested election to Fenn. As governor, however, Bennett was in control of the official canvass of the returns. He discarded the votes of three counties because they were submitted on the wrong sheets of paper, and he had 246 of Fenn's Mormon votes from Oneida thrown out illegally because of spelling mistakes. By this strategem he was able to certify his election. He served more than half the term before the Congress declared Fenn elected and seated in late 1874.

In 1876 the Republicans ran John Clark of Lewiston, a north Idahoan opposed to annexation if only because he thought it useless to try. He was, however, sufficiently anti-Mormon to attract many southern Idaho votes. Again, Fenn won primarily because of the solid support of the Mormons. Fenn served four years, or a little less because of the Bennett episode. His replacement in 1878 was George Ainslie, also a Democrat, with similar support and backing. Ainslie also served four years.

The 1882 election signified a sharp turn in the tactics and success of Idaho's Republican Party. Ainslie was replaced by Republican Theodore Frelinghuysen Singiser. A federal appointee from Pennsylvania, Singiser had been Receiver of the General Land Office in Oxford, Idaho, and had then risen to become secretary of the territory. That Singiser was able to establish Republican supremacy for the first time in twenty years—and do so in a traditionally Democratic territory in a Democratic election year nationally—made his victory remarkable. The feat was all the more important because it was a first step in making possible Idaho's admission as a state, which probably could not have happened if Idaho had not been Republican.

The conversion of Idaho voters to Republicanism is explained by three factors. First, the construction of the Utah and Northern and Oregon Short Line railroads across southern Idaho brought in hundreds of settlers from the Republican Midwest. Second, the rapid growth of the Wood River Mining District, together with the smaller rushes to Lemhi and Custer county mines in south-central Idaho, brought additional residents. Third, Singiser was able to forge a political coalition that included anti-Mormons in southeastern Idaho, annexationists of north Idaho, and federal officials (sometimes called the Boise Ring) in Boise. The anti-Mormon movement drew strength from the national offensive against Mormon (i.e., Democratic) political influence. The passage of the Edmunds Anti-Polygamy Act of March 22, 1882, disfranchised polygamists, provided heavy penalties, and stimulated a drive against Mormon leaders throughout Idaho, Utah, and Arizona. The nationwide wave of indignation against the Mormons also swept through Idaho.

Idaho's governor at the time of the 1882 campaign was John B. Neil, a native of Ohio who had been private secretary to Rutherford B. Hayes when the latter was governor of Ohio. Neil, who had served as Receiver of the General Land Office in Salt Lake City and had been part of the Radical Utah anti-Mormon Ring, was appointed Idaho governor in 1880. As President Hayes expected, Neil did his best to inflame the non-Mormon majority of Idahoans against the minority of Latter-day Saints. Neil lasted only until 1883, however, when John N. Irwin replaced him. A resident of Iowa, Irwin lasted only a few months because of ill health; he was replaced early in 1884 by William M. Bunn, an urbane machine politician from Philadelphia, who joined readily in the anti-Mormon crusade now headed by United States Marshal Fred T. Dubois.

Dubois was a native of Springfield, Illinois, where his father had been an intimate friend of Abraham Lincoln for more than thirty years. An 1872 Yale graduate, Dubois came to Idaho in 1880 and became territorial marshal two years later. When the Edmunds Act of 1882 imposed stiff penalties for plural marriage, Dubois found it difficult to obtain convictions in Mormon communities. He became active in county and territorial politics to insure the election of anti-Mormons to local office.

In the 1884 elections popular John Hailey was once more the Democratic candidate for delegate and was elected. Dubois meanwhile concentrated on the territorial election, insuring Radical Republican dominance by securing election of reliably anti-Mormon county officers and legislators. He was charged with having done so fraudulently, but the indictments were never investigated. Anti-Mormons now held the whip hand in both houses of the legislature.

Dubois, not a member of the legislature, worked through Harvey Walker "Kentucky" Smith of Malad, who drafted the harshest anti-Mormon legislation ever enacted. The three acts prevented Mormons from holding county offices, barred them from voting in general elections, and carved a new anti-Mormon county out of the northern four-fifths of Oneida, isolating the Oneida Mormons. The new county was named Bingham. On December 22, 1884, both houses of the legislature passed the act forbidding Mormons from voting and holding county office by means of a test oath. The act declared that members of any organization that "teaches, advises, or encourages the practice of bigamy or polygamy or any other crime" resulting from or arising from the faith or practice of such order was prohibited from voting or holding office. The organization Kentucky Smith had in mind was, of course, the Mormon Church.

Governor Bunn had no difficulty in signing the act creating the new county and requiring the test oath for county officers. But the act that denied voting privileges he considered unconstitutional and unduly strong. Passed by a two-thirds majority of the legislature, the bill arrived on Governor Bunn's desk on February 3, 1885, one day before the session closed. Bargaining for votes for other critical bills, the governor guaranteed three Mormon members of the legislature that he would veto the test oath. After making that guarantee and getting his bills passed, he then proceeded, on the same day, to violate the guarantee by signing the test oath bill and returning it to the legislature commending its members for their "wisdom and broad Americanism in enacting this legislation." For the next eight years, members of Idaho's largest religious denomination were unable to vote, hold office, or even serve on a jury.[3]

In the months that followed, Dubois was out hunting for Mormons to put in jail. He and his associates went one step beyond the legislature in barring Mormons from jury service, whether for polygamy cases or otherwise. Polygamy was a side issue, Dubois admitted; what he and his coterie were aiming at was the elimination of Mormon (Democratic) influence on civil government. Local Mormons leaders, as one might have predicted, went into hiding, as did Mormon county officers. The Mormons developed an underground espionage network so that word of the approach of deputies "got around" and the hunted persons vanished. Some men were, of course, rounded up for trial. They stood no chance of acquittal because the Dubois juries convicted anyone on a polygamy charge regardless of evidence. Idaho's territorial prison overflowed.[4]

An unrelated but contemporaneous crusade was launched against Idaho's Chinese residents, whose lot was in many ways parallel to that of the Indians. The Chinese had taken over most of Idaho's placer mining in the late 1860s and had contributed to the territory's economy when it was on the decline in the 1870s. In the fall of 1885 a hatchet murder occurred in Pierce City, where a large population of Chinese had replaced white miners who had abandoned their mines. Two mercantile firms competed for business in the town, one owned by D. M. Fraser, a long-time resident, and the other by the Chinese firm of Lee Kee Nam and Company. When Fraser's body was found, shot and "terribly chopped to pieces in his own store," suspicions fell on Lee Kee Nam. A white vigilance committee seized Lee, his partner, and three other Chinese—a barber, a gambler, and "a parasite of one of the Chinese prostitutes of the camp." The vigilantes were satisfied that the five were guilty. When the local deputy and his small posse rode out of town with the prisoners to take them to the county seat in Murray, they were intercepted by a lynching party that improvised a gallows and hung the Chinese from a pole lashed to two pine trees. A subsequent investigation by Governor Edward A. Stevenson determined only that the action taken by local citizens seemed appropriate to them and that the Chinese hanged were probably the ones who committed the murder.[5]

Other anti-Chinese agitation and riots had swept the western United States in 1885–86, with ugly incidents in Rock Springs, Wyoming, and Seattle. A standard western slogan was "The Chinese must go." To preclude any further violent action in Idaho, Governor Stevenson issued a proclamation expressing the hope that Congress would deliver Idaho from the presence of Chinese, but it also instructed law officers "to use every precaution to prevent all riotous demonstrations." Although the Boise Anti-Chinese League and similar groups in other towns set May 1, 1886, as the deadline for Chinese to leave the territory, the governor's warning seemed sufficient. There were no armed demonstrations against the Chinese, and most of Idaho's Chinese remained, at least for a while. The Pierce City incident demonstrated that "both racial intolerance and the violation of basic legal rights were sustained . . . by the democratic creed of local self government."[6]

The principal political question confronting Idahoans was whether Congress would vote to correct the injurious, absurd boundary that had handicapped north Idaho and eastern Washington for two decades. North Idahoans were nearly unanimous in preferring union with Washington until the mineral discoveries in the Coeur d'Alenes. Hundreds of miners had flocked to the area from Montana, and they preferred annexation of the region to Montana because they thought Montana was more friendly to miners. Nevertheless, after an 1884 bill providing annexation to Washington passed the U.S. House of Representatives, a flood of petitions from southern Idaho protesting against annexation went to the Senate. In Coeur d'Alene, a petition of Montana miners recommended that north Idaho be divided between Washington and Montana; if that were not possible, its signers would prefer staying in Idaho to joining Washington. An answering petition of Palouse farmers and pro-Washington miners retorted that they would choose Idaho over Montana. Unable to satisfy the competing demands, the Senate committee—dominated by Republicans—delayed action on the annexation bill.

In the next territorial election in 1886, Fred T. Dubois and his Republican associates were successful in defeating John Hailey. Idaho had become a Republican territory, partly because of the support of anti-Mormons who had previously voted Democratic. Idaho's switch from Democratic to Republican and to anti-Mormon control in 1882 was thus confirmed in 1886, and this in turn finally made possible the Idaho admission movement of 1890.

Credit for arousing the "Save Idaho" forces in the Gem State must be given to Senator William M. Stewart of Nevada. Nevada had been made a state at the height of its mining boom in 1864. Now it was losing population and wealth and faced an uncertain future. Stewart's proposal, made in 1886, was that the capital of Nevada should be removed to Winnemucca, a Boise-Winnemucca railway should be constructed, and Idaho should be divided between Washington and Nevada. Southern Idaho was not receptive. Boise, in particular, had no intention of giving up capital city status, with its bevy of well-paid territorial officials. The indignation was sufficient that the territorial Legislative Council, on December 21, 1886, approved a memorial declaring that all sections of Idaho Territory, both north and south, resented any division of the territory. On January 8, 1887, both Idaho houses joined in a legislative admonition against division.

The Nevada legislature, however, heartily approved Senator Stewart's proposal, and he went to Washington in February 1887 to present the proposal to Congress. He was able, as a first step, to induce the Senate Committee on Territories to resurrect the House-approved act to annex north Idaho to Washington.

The next step was the annexation of southern Idaho to Nevada. The Senate committee reported favorably, the bill was passed by the Senate on March 1, the House concurred with the amendments on March 2, and the bill went to President Grover Cleveland. The long-oppressed inhabitants of Lewiston, wrote historian Merle Wells, wept premature tears of joy over their deliverance from the leeches of southern Idaho.[7]

Governor Stevenson, an Idaho pioneer of 1863, long-time member of the legislature, speaker of the House, Boise County Commissioner, and miner and farmer in Payette Valley, could not sit idly by and see the territory dismantled. So on March 3, 1887, he telegraphed President Cleveland asking for a leave of absence allowing him to rush to Washington to explain why the territory ought not to be divided. Cleveland responded that if Stevenson would stay home the bill would not be signed. The next Congress could reconsider the matter. The unsigned bill rested with the president for two days. When Congress adjourned on March 4, Cleveland declared that he did not believe in signing bills after Congress adjourned, and Idaho had a temporary reprieve. Alonzo Leland, leader of the annexation movement, was despondent: "Here endeth another chapter in the wrongs inflicted upon North Idaho at the instance of the Boise ring."[8]

It seemed certain that the annexation bill would pass both houses of the next Congress, but Stevenson and Dubois were not willing to give up. Dubois traveled the territory soliciting support; he also contacted other western senators, some of whom held mining interests in Idaho. He developed a formidable lineup of sentiment against Stewart's proposal. Stevenson journeyed to Washington, D.C., where, as a Democrat, he worked effectively with the Democratic House of Representatives. He carried with him former delegate John Hailey's declaration that nine-tenths of the people of Idaho objected to territorial division. The House Committee on Territories did agree to a Washington-north Idaho admission bill but coupled it with a provision for the acceptance of some Democratic territories (Arizona, for instance)—something they knew the Republican Senate would never approve. When the showdown came on February 29, 1888, the House committee voted unanimously against the bill. Idaho, ungainly as it appeared, was saved from dismemberment.[9]

Not that sectional conflicts disappeared. Before the different geographical interests could be united in a request for statehood, north Idaho had to be placated, the Mormons had to be stifled so as not to endanger Republican control, and other regional interests had to be satisfied.

The concession to north Idaho was an agreement to locate the university there. No one would expect the university to be located in a region about to be annexed to Washington or Montana. Without such an agreement, north Idaho's agitation for removal might continue. In 1887 the legislature had passed a bill to locate the university in Eagle Rock, but Governor Stevenson reluctantly vetoed the measure because of defects in the drafting. By 1889 a political coalition had bolstered the prospect of the north remaining in Idaho so that a northern city could be considered for the university.

In December 1888 Willis Sweet, a thirty-two-year-old Vermont-born attorney and delegate to the Idaho legislature, met in Moscow with Henry Dernham and William Kaufman, merchants, and M. J. Shields, an implement dealer. Sweet had resided in Moscow only seven years, but he had campaigned for Dubois for Congressional delegate and garnered him enough votes in the north to defeat Hailey. Anxious for Moscow to obtain the university, Shields, Dernham, and Kaufman each gave $100 to Sweet to help pay expenses for a "campaign." Also working for Moscow was John Warren Brigham, a thirty-year-old Genesee homesteader and representative of the Latah-Nez Perce legislative district.

In Boise, Sweet dictated Council Bill No. 20, which provided that the University of Idaho be located at Moscow, that the instruction be neither sectarian in religion nor partisan in politics, that the institution be coeducational, that no tuition be charged for any resident of the territory or state, and that $15,000 be appropriated for site purchase, planning costs, and expenses of the Board of Regents. When Brigham introduced the bill on January 10, 1889, there was virtually no opposition. In commending the bill to the House, H. H. Clay, chairman of the Committee on Territorial Affairs, said:

> That the location of the University of Idaho, at the place therein named, is desirable and appropriate, (1) because it is accessible by rail from all points in Idaho that have railway communication with any portion of the country, (2) because it is the center of one of the richest and most populous agricultural sections in the entire Northwest, and is surrounded by a healthy moral atmosphere, and in a community, the wealth of which rests upon a foundation that can not be shaken by the vicissitudes of booms, excitement or speculation. (3) It would be recognized as an olive branch in the interest of peace and good-will extended by one section of the Territory to another, between which there has been long and bitter contention, and in the place of discord and threats of disunion, would unite the sections in the march of progress and improvement for the entire Territory, and a speedy admission into the sovereignty of States. . . . (4) It would be one of the most powerful agents in the field in the great contest now in progress in the Northwest between rival states for desirable immigration.[10]

On January 29, 1889, the "olive branch" bill passed both houses, and on the following day it was signed by Governor Stevenson. When Sweet returned to Moscow, he stopped to see Dernham and Kaufman. One of them walked over to the safe, withdrew Sweet's note for $100, and tore it into pieces.

"You earned the $100," he said.

One other section would, or might, deplore the Idaho admission movement: the Mormon communities in southeastern Idaho. They represented approximately one-fourth of the territory's population. Those working for statehood, or at least all the leaders, were Radical Republican anti-Mormons or anti-Mormon Democrats. The Mormons would have been foolish to want an anti-Mormon territory to become an anti-Mormon state. But they could not effectively oppose Idaho admission if they could not vote. If they should regain the franchise, they would probably vote Democratic, which would disqualify Idaho for admission in 1890 by the Republican Congress—at least according to Fred Dubois' analysis.

Idaho Mormons decided in 1888 that the Latter-day Saints who did not believe in polygamy and who did not practice it (the overwhelming majority of Mormons) ought to subscribe to the test oath and vote if they wished. Richard Z. Johnson, Idaho's Democratic attorney general, concurred. Enough Saints were willing to vote in 1888 to restore Mormon control in Bear Lake County. However, control over registration of voters in most counties was in the hands of radical anti-Mormons who disregarded the opinion of the attorney general. So determined were the anti-Mormons to preserve the test oath as a weapon to exclude Mormons from voting against them that they refused to accept any declaration against polygamy as qualifying Mormons for the franchise.

Some Mormon voters came up with a drastic solution: they would resign their church affiliation, vote, and then be restored to membership later. When Dubois's officials observed these actions, they forced the seceders to declare under penalty of perjury that they would not rejoin the church after voting. In some places, like Preston, seceders were not allowed to vote. Mormon leaders doubted the constitutionality of forbidding people to cease being members of the Mormon Church.

Determined to exclude Mormons from the polls, the Idaho legislature in January 1889 passed a retroactive act under which anyone who had been a Mormon January 1, 1888, would be excluded from voting, holding office, or serving on a jury. Governor Stevenson signed the measure.

Added to the influx of miners and ranchers, enough Mormon farmers had settled in Idaho to enable the territory to qualify for statehood, and they had been rendered politically voiceless so as to remove any possibility that they would be a threat to the Republican Congress. Idaho was now a serious contender for statehood. At this critical moment in her history, we will pause to review the landmarks and lives of Idahoans during the territorial period.

## CHAPTER SIXTEEN: SOURCES

Excellent treatments of the material in this chapter are given in Beal and Wells, *History of Idaho*, 1:440–54, 480–93, 553–70, and 2:58–96. Most of the other histories of Idaho and the Pacific Northwest have briefer treatments.

Specialized book treatments of the topics in this chapter include Limbaugh, *Rocky Mountain Carpetbaggers*; Fred T. Dubois, *The Making of a State*, edited by Louis J. Clements (Rexburg: Eastern Idaho Publishing Company, 1971); Dennis C. Colson, *Idaho's Constitution: The Tie That Binds* (Moscow: University of Idaho Press, 1991); and Merle W. Wells, *Anti-Mormonism in Idaho, 1872–92* (Provo, Utah: Brigham Young University Press, 1978).

Good articles on boundary problems and the annexation movement are Merle W. Wells, "Politics in the Panhandle: Opposition to the Admission of Washington and North Idaho, 1886–1888," *Pacific Northwest Quarterly* 46 (July 1955):79–89; and Wells, "Idaho's Season of Political Distress: An Unusual Path to Statehood," *Montana, The Magazine of Western History* 37 (Autumn 1987):58–67.

Helpful articles on the status of the Mormons include: E. Leo Lyman, "A Mormon Transition in Idaho Politics," *Idaho Yesterdays*

20 (Winter 1977):2–11, 24–29; Michael E. Christensen, "Footnote to History: Charles W. Nibley and the Idaho Test Oath," *Idaho Yesterdays* 22 (Fall 1978):19–20; Merle W. Wells, "Law in the Service of Politics: Anti-Mormonism in Idaho Territory," *Idaho Yesterdays* 25 (Spring 1981):33–43; A. J. Simmonds, "Idaho's Last Colony: Northern Cache Valley under the Test Oath, 1872–1896," *Idaho Yesterdays* 32 (Summer 1988):2–14; Merle W. Wells, "The Idaho Anti-Mormon Test Oath, 1884–1892," *Pacific Historical Review* 24 (August 1955):235–52; Wells, "Unexpected Allies: Fred T. Dubois and the Mormons in 1916," *Idaho Yesterdays* 35 (Fall 1991), 27–33; and Grenville H. Gibbs, "Mormonism in Idaho Politics, 1880–1890," *Utah Historical Quarterly* 21 (October 1953):285–305.

The anti-Chinese crusade is covered in Beal and Wells, *History of Idaho*, 1:577–80; Kenneth Owens, "Pierce City Incident, 1885–1886," *Idaho Yesterdays* 3 (Fall 1959):8–13; and Fern C. Trull, "The History of the Chinese in Idaho from 1864 to 1910" (M.A. thesis, University of Oregon, 1946).

73.

74.

75.

73. Fred T. Dubois, later a United States senator, was leader of the Idaho anti-Mormon crusade of the 1880s. ISHS 83–15.2.

74. Governor of Idaho, 1885–89, was Edward A. Stevenson. ISHS 46–B(2).

75. North Idaho's support of Idaho's application for statehood was strengthened by the agency of Willis Sweet in securing the Moscow location for the state university. Sweet was a regent of the university, 1889–93. UIL 3–9B.

76.

76. The "new" Administration Building of the University of Idaho opened in 1909 and continues to be a focus for campus activity. ISHS 69–4.145D.

CHAPTER SEVENTEEN

# Idaho's Nineteenth-Century Towns and Villages

NINETEENTH-CENTURY Idaho was a territory of small towns and settlements situated in the midst of an array of scattered farms, ranches, mines, and mills. There were river towns, prairie towns, and mountain towns; mining towns, lumber towns, railroad towns, and college towns; ethnic towns, Indian reservations, and Mormon villages. Each had a unique identity, with natural and man-made landmarks that shaped the lives of those who lived and worked there. Each was a "hometown," with a camaraderie of spirit and a solidarity that self-consciously pursued growth and recognition. Had the territory been without these concentrations of population, however small, centrifugal forces might have prevented the achievement of community, of the sense of belonging, that was so important to the territory's consolidation of interests and responsibilities.

People in the localities shared common experiences and developed allegiances; they acquired outlooks and attitudes; and they were subjected to institutions, forces, and personalities that shaped their private and public lives: churches, schools, homes, doctors, lawyers, newspapers, and community festivals. Superimposed on the natural setting, whether in a forest glen, on a mountainside, in an irrigated valley, or at the location of a riverboat landing or ferry, the man-made architecture added to the visual image. Buildings, whether imposing or pretentious, rustic or plain, were not only places of work and worship, learning and leisure, but they also provided reference points for remembered events, people, times, and emotions.[1]

## TOWN AND COUNTRY

The most typical living arrangement in territorial Idaho was a symbiotic town-and-country relationship that was well equipped to meet the needs of early residents. Town dwellers milled the grain; separated cream from the milk; maintained a slaughterhouse to provide the meat; conducted schools; held dances and religious services; erected a watertank and operated a water system; and, while making staples available, offered a market for the farmers' (or housewives') eggs, livestock and poultry, fruits and vegetables. Outlying farmers were part of the town and the town depended on the country for food, feed, "business," and labor.

Most towns began with a store. Silver City in 1864–65 offers an excellent example of an emerging community. The Silver City Meat Market promoted beef, mutton, veal, sausage, and head cheese. The general store of DuRell and Moore listed for sale lard and bacon, dry goods, dress goods, groceries, glass and queensware, liquors, flour, butter, cheese, dried fruits, paints and oils, window glass, hardware, tinware, stoves and irons, mining tools, blasting powder, fuse and steel, quicksilver, and miners' outfits.[2]

Retailer and wholesaler Fred Burnzell, of Ruby City, duplicated his competitors' lists and added "caps, smoking and chewing tobacco, crockery, and carpenters tools." Merchants like J. M. Pearlman also offered horseshoes, nails, butter and cheese, wallpaper, carpets and matting, patent medicines, wheelbarrows, bailing ropes, clocks, large cables, nitric and sulfuric acids, machinery oils, whips, and whiskey.

Some merchants dealt in stoves, tin, copper, and iron sheet ware and offered "repairing done with neatness and dispatch." Drugstores typically listed drugs, medicines, chemicals, perfumery and toilet articles, paints, oils, putty, varnishes, brushes, chewing and smoking tobacco, blank books, stationery, and writing ink. They prided themselves on "Physicians prescriptions accurately compounded."

There were shops for books, stationery, and fancy articles. Photographers advertised "Views taken to order" with the qualification "No Likee, no takee, John," which no doubt played to the abundance of Chinese swarming the gold fields.

Silver City Restaurant offered board at $14 a week and meals for $1 each. They required payment "Invariably in advance." Peaches, apples, and grapes were freighted in from California and melons, cabbages, and turnips sold for 12.5 cents per pound.

Professions provided a wide stretch of services. A town usually had several attorneys, a couple of doctors, a justice of the peace who doubled as a notary public, and a Miners Provision Friend who was essentially a grubstaker.

Ruby City (adjacent to Silver City) at its mining peak saw a great deal of money pass through quickly. The assayer recorded $15,000 worth of bullion in eight days and his revenues for those eight days of work totaled more than $100. Wells Fargo recorded on August 22, 1865, after one month of operation, that it "had shipped two hundred five pounds of bullion valued at $14,371 and gold dust and bars to the amount of $13,373."[3]

Other towns might have different emphases, but there was a great deal of similarity too, as all shared in the goods and services, the fads and fashions of the period. In each town, life was largely shaped by its churches, schools, homes, educated professionals, and newspapers.

CHURCHES. At first, Idaho's frontier was not particularly religious, perhaps because of the predominance of men. Yet there were churches, their members were supportive and devout, and where preachers were not available lay members took charge. Even miners brought their Bibles with them. Churches maintained graveyards, performed marriages, sometimes furnished midwives, and usually conducted a Sunday School that was sometimes the only school. Roman Catholicism was, of course, the predominant faith of the French-Canadian trappers, many Christian Indians, German farming communities, Irish railroad workers, and Hispanics from the Southwest. Many Idaho communities had Catholic schools, hospitals, and fraternal orders.

The principal Protestant denominations were Lutheran, Presbyterian, Methodist, and Baptist, but there were also German Reformed and Dutch Reformed, Disciples of Christ, and Episcopalians. Some church people were leaders in the temperance movement, others opposed dancing and gambling, and visiting preachers held occasional revivals. Nearly every congregation established or supported schools. On weekdays most congregations held prayer meetings, choir practice, and dinners and socials to raise money. Most Idaho towns had only two or three Protestant churches and, with few exceptions, all denominations agreed to work together in their common interest. All church groups agreed on a moral code based on the Ten Commandments and the Sermon on the Mount.[4]

Although Idaho City had a sizable Jewish community during its peak, most of its members soon moved to Boise. Boise had its own Jewish cemetery as early as 1869. Jewish businesses there closed for Jewish holidays, such as the Day of Atonement, but no synagogues were built in Idaho until after statehood.

Typical of the influence that could be exerted by a religiously motivated person was Rebecca Mitchell, a Baptist missionary from Illinois who arrived in Eagle Rock (Idaho Falls) on June 5, 1882. Discovering there was no school, she quickly organized a school for children that she called Providence Mission. She headquartered her educational institution in an abandoned saloon that the mission used for a church as well. Boxes were used for seats and writing desks. Within two years Mitchell had convinced the community to build the first Protestant church between Ogden and Butte. Tuition for the school paid her expenses and allowed her to expand her efforts in organizing a library, the Women's Christian Temperance Union, the Village Improvement Society, and a beautification effort for the city. Eventually, Rebecca Mitchell was named chaplain for the Idaho legislature, the first woman in the United States to be appointed to such a position.[5]

SCHOOLS. Along with churches, town schools were zealous in inculcating proper behavior. Textbooks were uplifting and character-building as well as instructive, whether used in teaching penmanship, history, government, or for that matter arithmetic. Although many of the country schools were one-room, ungraded schools built of logs, with homemade desks, town schools were usually graded with two or three teachers, one for lower grades and one or two for the higher.

As early as January 29, 1864, the legislature created the office of Territorial Superintendent of Instruction. He (always a man in territorial days) helped new localities to establish schools, acquire books and teachers, and set up satisfactory curricula. By 1889, a year before statehood, Idaho had 386 school districts with 12,457 students. The school term averaged 4.4 months. These were public or common schools, but local church congregations also maintained many parochial schools. The first public high school was established by Boise's consolidated school district in 1881.

All of the Mormon stakes (dioceses) in Idaho established

"academies," the equivalent of high schools, in 1887–88. The four included the Bear Lake Stake Academy in Paris, renamed the Fielding Academy in 1901; the Oneida Stake Academy in Preston; the Bannock Stake Academy in Rexburg, renamed the Ricks Academy in 1903; and the Cassia Stake Academy in Oakley. Almost immediately these, although essentially high schools, offered some collegiate classes including normal, commercial, domestic science, and music courses, as well as religious instruction.

HOMES. Because of the predominantly agricultural character of both town and country, parents were usually ever present. Fathers and schoolchildren (except rural children, who took lunches) came home at noon for what was called dinner; in the evening all gathered around the table for supper. Divorces were rare and widows with small children usually remarried. Married women seldom left home to work elsewhere. Girls helped their mothers with housework and sewing; boys split wood for the stove, tended to horses and cows, slopped the hogs, delivered milk, and helped with irrigating and other outdoor tasks. There were frequent visits to and from relatives.

Home was not only a workplace, but also a contributor to community "culture." Some families were able to get pianos, often bringing them in their wagons from the Midwest or the West Coast. Friends from the neighborhood gathered to sing, play, put on skits, and have picnics. Nowhere was there a better demonstration of the universality of art than in the isolated community of Bear Lake Valley, where a few hundred settlers, nearly all farmers, sang in village choirs, played musical instruments for dances and concerts, and identified with Shakespearean characters who were, in turn, humorous, angry, despondent, and eloquent. They listened to their own villagers and artists from Salt Lake City and elsewhere play Mozart, Schubert, and Schumann. Along with producing food, making clothes, and erecting cabins and barns, music and dancing were a vital part of frontier village life.

SALOONS. Nearly every town had a tavern or saloon, and early mining towns had many. Frances Agnew, who arrived in Boise in 1864, wrote: "It seemed to me that over the front entrance of every other building one could read the word saloon. The eating houses and restaurants came next in number and even these usually had a bar near the door."[6] A business census taken in Sawtooth, Idaho, a year after the birth of the camp showed that of forty-one retail stores, twenty were barrooms.[7] The number of saloons was usually an accurate barometer of the prosperity of a camp.

In camps where most of the residents were unattached workingmen the saloon was a haven of companionship, a place of action for the restless and relaxation for the weary. A breeding place for trouble and a magnet for mischief, it was also a place where men could, with inhibitions eased by a bottle or glass, meet and sit and laugh—a gathering ground in a place where men's lives were often solitary and always trying.[8] The colorful names given to the liquor reflected their opinion of a product that was often wretched: "extract of scorpions," "forty-rod" (because it could kill from that distance), "panther sweat," "tonsil paint," "stagger soup," or "milk of the wild cow."[9] Although social conditions and abundance of liquor helped meet genuine psychological needs, the drinking also contributed to public disorder and personal suffering.

A saloonkeeper, to be successful, had to cultivate an attractive public personality—he must be generous, friendly, loyal, and good-humored. James D. Agnew, a thirty-one-year-old Virginian who arrived in Boise in 1863, had tried his hand at mining in Pierce City and Centerville, helped survey the city, and then opened a saloon and a livery stable. His friends later elected him coroner and county sheriff. Thomas Donaldson wrote that Agnew was one of Boise's chief funmakers—a practical joker and storyteller. "Jim Agnew was a good man with whom to sit, drink, and swap lies."[10] He and his customers provided camaraderie, especially important to new arrivals.

Despite the steady presence of saloons and pool halls, "the rank and file of the people," wrote Mrs. Agnew, "had the highest regard for law and order" and worked to make their town and territory a better place to live.[11] They generally accepted the necessity of work and thrift and practiced a basic equalitarianism, and their limited freedoms were usually accompanied by the exercise of responsibility.

Nevertheless, village farm work was often hard, unrelenting, and unrewarding; life in the small towns seemed dull, constricted, with employment opportunities lacking. As a result, many Idaho young people gravitated toward nearby cities—to Boise, Spokane, Portland, or Salt Lake City—where there were jobs that paid well. Some went away to college to become teachers, doctors, lawyers, and engineers.

## TERRITORIAL PROFESSIONALS

**DOCTORS AND MEDICINE.** Although Idahoans boasted of a climate that kept people so healthy that they had to kill a few men to start a cemetery, doctors lived in nearly every town. Herman Ziph, trained in Germany, delivered hundreds of babies in Idaho City and Boise, where he practiced in the 1860s and 1870s. He was the epitome of the devoted country doctor, responding day or night, winter or summer, to mining and lumbering camps, farms, and ranches. Dr. George A. Kenney, a carpenter turned physician, was the agency doctor for the Lemhi Indian Reservation for $50 a month. He cared for a community geographically larger than Connecticut.

Since the family mother or grandmother often treated "ordinary illnesses" and midwives delivered babies, most doctors relied upon other work (mining, farming, newspapers, general store) for support. Some were preachers, others operated drugstores. One problem was collecting from those they helped. When it came, such reimbursement was frequently in the form of fruit, vegetables, meat, or such services as painting or cutting wood. Doctors were usually not among the well-to-do in early settlements. On the other hand, one Idaho governor—Dr. D. W. Ballard—had to rely upon his Boise medical practice for support when he went unpaid during much of his gubernatorial term.

Two kinds of medicine were applied in the early period: heroic medicine, using blood-letting, emetics, and strong purges; and "Thomsonian" or herb medicine, which relied upon nature's power to cure. In either case, the practice was a rugged, frontier medicine—no assistants, no fancy operating rooms or second opinions. Operations were done by candlelight with whiskey to ease the pain. Patients often were too sick to be helped, epidemics ravaged camps, and wounds festered long before the patient reached the doctor. Many pioneer homes had on the shelf, along with the Bible, a home medical adviser such as *Gunn's Domestic Medicine*, written in 1830 by Dr. John C. Gunn of Virginia and Tennessee, or William Buchan's *Domestic Medicine*, which also included a section on the care of livestock.

The most common medical cases were accidents peculiar to travel or work, such as the injuries suffered by miners working in open-faced mining shafts; dietary deficiencies due to lack of fresh fruits and vegetables; diarrhea, cholera, ague (usually malaria), typhoid fever, milk sickness, and tuberculosis.

Midwives played a critical role. Every community had an "Ann, Alice, Mary, Martha, Sarah, or Aunt Lou" who came to assist at times of serious illness and birth. These women not only cared for the mother and child but also fixed meals for the family, cleaned, washed, and sometimes kept the garden.

Many times a doctor cared for his patients in his home or

office. Eventually some of these facilities expanded to more formal hospitals. In 1863 Bannack City (Idaho City) opened a county hospital, the first in the Northwest (there was a military hospital operating in Boise). Patients were charged $34 a week.

LAWYERS. Former governor James H. Hawley, in his *History of Idaho*, wrote that "never before was there assembled in any new section of the United States a more brilliant and learned bar than practiced in Idaho from 1864 to 1875."[12] They were men of remarkably eclectic experience, and many—like physicians—had more than one occupation. The undisputed leader of the Idaho bar during most of the territorial period, Hawley wrote, was Richard Z. Johnson. Born in Akron, Ohio, in 1837, Johnson attended Yale University, practiced law for five years at Winona, Wisconsin, moved to Virginia City, Nevada, and in 1864 settled in Silver City. He practiced there fourteen years and then moved his office to Boise, where he died in 1912. Much of the important litigation in Idaho was handled by Johnson until his retirement. Like many lawyers, he also served in the legislature. He was in the territorial council from 1880 to 1887 and was territorial attorney general prior to statehood. He is said to have had the best library of any lawyer in Idaho Territory.[13] His office is still a landmark on Boise's Sixth Street.

A second well-known lawyer, identified with much serious litigation, was John S. Gray. Born in New York in 1837, he went to California in 1857, to Florence in 1862, and from there to Boise Basin. He was appointed territorial treasurer in 1871 and was a member of the lower house in 1880. Gray was described as "a man who stood four square to every wind that blew and never spoke unless he had something to say."[14]

Francis E. Ensign was born in Painesville, Ohio, in 1829, went to Western Reserve and Oberlin College, and then in 1854 to San Francisco, where he was admitted to the bar four years later. After practicing in Yreka, he moved in 1866 to Silver City and practiced there until 1878, proceeded to Boise, and in 1881 located in Hailey, where he was the town's first attorney. He practiced in Hailey until his death in 1908.

There were other prominent Idaho lawyers. Charles M. Hays, born in Missouri, established himself in Silver City in 1865 and served as sheriff and later as district attorney until 1899. He served in the state senate and was a member of the commission that codified Idaho's laws. William H. Clagett had been a close associate of Samuel L. Clemens (Mark Twain) in Nevada and a delegate to Congress from Montana; he was author of the federal mining law and in 1871 he introduced the bill creating Yellowstone National Park. He moved to Shoshone County, Idaho, a decade later and was president of Idaho's constitutional convention. James W. Poe, a pioneer lawyer of Lewiston, was born in 1838 in Jackson County, Missouri, moved with his parents to Oregon in 1853, and joined the miners' rush to Florence, Oro Fino, and Warrens in the 1860s. After admission to the bar in 1869 he practiced in Warrens and Mount Idaho. In 1876 he was elected district attorney for all of north Idaho, with headquarters in Lewiston. He served in the state senate for many years.[15]

Hawley wrote that it was customary to give Idaho lawyers the honorific title of "judge." The large number of Southerners, he wrote, also insured that there was much "old fashioned oratory" at the bar. Thomas Donaldson, a native of Ohio who served in the U.S. Army during the Civil War and came to Idaho in 1869 as register of the newly opened land office in Boise, gave succinct descriptive evaluations of the lawyers he had observed over the years in Boise, as follows: John R. McBride, ex-chief justice of the territorial supreme court, was "the best general practitioner and ablest lawyer" in the territory; Joseph W. Huston, "a man of genius, a ready lawyer, and an eloquent advocate"; Jeremiah Brumback, "an attorney with the best legal manner"; John C. Henley, "one of the brightest, ablest, and most gentlemanly young men," who died of excessive drink; H. L. Preston, "a splendid speaker who seldom saw the point in his case"; S. S. Fenn, one who, when excited, "got choked in his speech and blurted out his words as if his mouth was full of a substance"; Edward J. Curtis, "Old Ned," one who was "unsurpassed as a conversationalist and yarn-spinner"; Major R. E. Foote, an "ever polite" Southerner; Samuel A. Merritt, "the best man before a jury"; George Ainslie, "too much of a politician to be a strong lawyer"; Albert Heed, "the best natural lawyer in Idaho—he had no culture but had a clear head for judicial principles"; and Henry E. Prickett, "a man of ordinary abilities but with studious habits and impressive manner."[16]

There were also, of course, lawyers in Lewiston, Moscow, Eagle Rock, Blackfoot, and Salmon. A widely known lawyer in Bear Lake County, and representative of many country lawyers, was Joseph C. Rich. Son of Bear Lake's founder, Charles C. Rich, Joseph C., though educated primarily by his mother, taught at the first school in Paris, served as superintendent of schools for the county, was Bear Lake's first surveyor and telegrapher, operated the general store, published the *Bear Lake Democrat*, and later opened the Hot Springs Resort on the shore of the lake. In the 1860s he studied law briefly under Hosea Stout, city and district attorney for Salt Lake City, and he did most of the early legal work for Bear Lake and Oneida counties. Elected to the territorial legislature in 1878 and 1880, he served as district attorney, was elected state senator in 1896, and was president pro tem of the Senate. He was a delegate to the Democratic National Convention that nominated William Jennings Bryan. Near the end of his life he was elected judge of the Fifth Judicial District that comprised the six southeastern counties of Oneida, Bannock, Bingham, Fremont, Lemhi, and Bear Lake. Rich described the practice of law in the 1860s and 1870s before the younger generation arrived with their LLBs from the University of Michigan:

> In those days, we didn't squander on "Demurrer," "Appeals," "Injunctions," "Motions for Nonsuits." No. If a fellow didn't ante up about the square thing, we would take him before Bishop Horne, or Brother Bingham, and fetch him up standing ecclesiastically. We never had the record burdened with long expensive continuances. The fee bill was not regulated as now. The lawyer's poll tax worked out by an ordinary poor devil was considered about an equivalent for the same time consumed by the party of the first part. I am the only lawyer in the county who gave reliable information without taking the last cow that made you a candidate for the poorhouse.[17]

Thomas Donaldson also chronicles—more or less accurately—some colorful episodes in territorial Idaho's legal history. In 1870 the election for sheriff of Ada County was a close contest. Vying for the office were Lute Lindsay, a livery-stable proprietor and a Missouri Democrat, and William Bryon, his Republican opponent. On the third day after the election the returns showed that Lindsay had been elected by a majority of one. Donaldson, who had been offered an appointment as governor but declined, wrote that it suddenly occurred to him that the election judges might not be aware that Congress had passed earlier in the year the universal suffrage bill extending voting rights to blacks. He knew that three of Boise's four blacks had voted and suspected that the judges had not counted their ballots. Donaldson, a Yankee Republican, thought he could see victory for Bryon. He induced attorney Henry E. Prickett to get a fellow Mason who was an election judge to open the ballot box to make certain that the number of ballots counted was, indeed, three votes short in comparison with those registered on the tally sheet. Suit was instituted by Prickett in the district court. The trial lasted several days. The three blacks, John West, John Seavy, and "Old Bill," testified that they had voted for Bryon. The election judges admitted that they had indeed thrust the three ballots under the table. Because no Negro had voted in Idaho before, they discounted their votes as simply a Republican trick. The district judge, after counting the three black ballots, confirmed the election of William Bryon as sheriff of Ada County by two votes.[18]

Another notable trial, also held in 1870, concerned a suit for damages. A driver for the Northwestern Stage Company invited Emma Cox, an unmarried woman of twenty-four, to take a free ride with him from one stage station to another. She was sitting on the box chatting with the driver when the stage was upset. Thrown from her seat, Miss Cox rolled down the slope and hurt her hip. She was taken to Boise for medical attention and submitted a bill to the stagecoach company for payment. When it refused to pay, Miss Cox employed John R. McBride, "the best trial attorney in the territory," to file suit. One of the medical experts who testified for the stagecoach company was asked if he had received a diploma from a reputable medical school. He answered, "Well no! I'm not a diplomatic doctor." The jury, composed of eleven single men and one married man, apparently agreed. Their sympathy was clearly with the young woman. Although most observers thought a free passenger riding contrary to company orders deserved no compensation, the jury rendered a verdict for Miss Cox of $14,000, half of which went to her attorney.

Donaldson learned later how the jury had settled upon the $14,000 judgment. After deciding that the "diplomatic" doctor had dashed the stage company's defense, the jurors agreed to give Miss Cox sufficient to pay medical experts, lawyers, and a large hotel bill due one of the jurors. In the first informal ballot, one juror voted an award of $500; another $1,000, still another $5,000. After other ballots failed to reach a consensus, the foreman suggested that each juror stipulate a sum. They would add up the twelve ballots and then divide by twelve. This sounded reasonable; they all agreed. When they reviewed the ballots, one was for $5,000, another $60,000, still another $80,000, one other, $100,000, and so on. They averaged $14,000 in the end, the figure they submitted to the judge. The juror who explained the action to Donaldson wished he had voted a million dollars in damages. "A husband needs all the money his wife might get from a stage company or any other source," he explained.[19]

NEWSPAPERS. From as early as the 1860s, larger towns were serviced by newspapers. Their coverage included the usual reports on hangings, shootings, political scuffles, and Indian raids. But the paper especially reflected the political views of the editor, usually one of the most educated and articulate persons in town. Frequently newspapers bitterly attacked their opposition. The Boise *Statesman* and *The Idaho World* of Idaho City feuded constantly. Editors were known to refer to each other as "low reptile" or "dirty liar" or worse. Other early publications included Silver City's *Owyhee Avalanche* and *Owyhee Semi-Weekly Tidal Wave*, Eagle City's *Coeur d'Alene Nugget*, Lewiston's *Teller* and *Nez Perce News*, the Grangeville *Idaho Free Press*, the *Coeur d'Alene Record*, and the *Kellogg Evening News*. A one-year subscription to *The Owyhee Avalanche* cost $10 for a four-page weekly. One inch of advertising copy cost $5 for the first insertion and $2 for additional submissions.[20]

Three pioneer newspapers in Idaho were edited, at least for a period, by women: the *Bellevue Herald*, a weekly published in Bellevue in 1895, with a Mrs. Graham as editor; the *Idaho Recorder*, a weekly published in Salmon, 1888–1906, edited by Ada Chase Merritt; and *The Ladies' Mite*, a church weekly published in Idaho City in 1864 with Isabelle Butler and a Mrs. Rees as editors. Little is known about the *Bellevue Herald* and *The Ladies' Mite*, but the story of the *Idaho Recorder* deserves mention.[21]

In 1883 Henry Clay Merritt and Ada Chase Merritt moved

their family from Nevada to Salmon, where Henry was employed as superintendent of the Kentuck Mine near Shoup, downriver from Salmon. A year later he was knocked off one of the flatboats that carried supplies to the mine and was drowned. Left with two children to support, Ada taught school. In 1886 J. E. Booth founded *The Idaho Recorder* as the official journal of Lemhi County, but he put it up for sale two years later. The paper was purchased by Ada Merritt and O. W. Mintzer, who had been the printer. Later the same year Mrs. Merritt bought Mintzer's interest, and she ran the paper until 1906.

Page three of the paper carried a column of "Local Intelligence" that contained short, sprightly notes about activities in the county. One could find out that haying was in full swing, that the circus was coming to Dillon on Friday, and that Henry Monroe had come in from Pine Creek to meet his friend from Missouri. On the same page were "Territorial News," "Mining Notes," "Voyagers on the Salmon," "News of our Neighbors over the Range," and "Telegraphic Brevities." Most of the four-page paper was filled with original material.

Merritt was a Democrat, and she did not hesitate to call the majority Republican Party to task. On one occasion she accused the Republicans of creating unbelievable new offices to provide jobs for members of their party: state rabbit chaser, irrigation agitator, cricket crucifier, artificial rainmaker, herder of the state militia, alfalfa inspector, prune examiner, hop howler, inspector of petrified forests, and opal lapidarist. By 1894 Merritt was supporting the Populists, and from 1895 to 1902 the paper carried the subtitle "Free and Unlimited Coinage of Silver at a Ratio of 16 to 1."

The newspaper carried advertisements for many of Salmon's businesses: the Lemhi Drug Company, the City Livery Stable, Hong Kee & Company, the Elk Horn Meat Market, and the town's doctors and dentists. Events like the Grand Calico Ball, with music by the Eolian Orchestra, were advertised, as were patent medicines like Royal Life Tablets, which promised "The Old Made Young, The Weak Made Strong, The Sick Made Well."

Along with editing the paper, Merritt—like many weekly newspaper publishers—ran a job-printing shop and a store that sold stationery, periodicals, novels, and writing materials. After selling the paper in 1906 she moved to Caldwell, then to Salt Lake City, and finally to Santa Monica, California. While in Salmon, she was a member of the Methodist Episcopal church choir, vice president of the Salmon City Chautauqua Literary and Scientific Circle, occasional reciter for the Washington Reading Club, secretary of the Woman's Relief Corps (an auxiliary of the Grand Army of the Republic), and conductress of the local Order of the Eastern Star. She ran for county treasurer in 1900 and won, was the sole woman delegate to the state's silver convention in 1893, and was an active member of the Idaho State Press Association, of which she was elected vice president in 1905.

## ARCHITECTURAL DEVELOPMENT

All of the institutional and professional activity described above took place within a small-town setting; there were no "cities" (places with more than 2,500 inhabitants) in territorial Idaho. The development of the physical structures of these early towns has been described by architectural historian Jennifer Eastman Attebery.[22]

The first homes in Idaho were pit houses built by aboriginal settlers several thousand years ago. With pole and grass roofs they seemed almost a part of the natural landscape. Nearby were small dome-shaped structures ("sweathouses") made of saplings blanketed with mats, skins, dirt, bark, and brush that functioned as centers of personal renewal and high resolve. The first white settlements, missions, or forts were whole compounds, and the enclaves created a sense of security for the residents. Their builders used adobe, local woods, grasses, and stone for their construction. Fur-trade forts, like the North West Company's Kullyspell House on Lake Pend Oreille in 1809, were suggestive of French-Canadian construction with horizontal beams fitting into grooves of a timber frame. The original Fort Boise and Fort Hall were rectangular facilities with buildings opening onto a center court. Blockhouses constructed primarily of cottonwood and adobe anchored the corners of the compound. The Spaldings lived briefly at their Lapwai mission in tipis made of hides before constructing a house complete with chimneys, window glass, and machine-cut nails. Their entire project at Lapwai eventually included a student dormitory, a blacksmith shop, two school buildings, a meetinghouse, two printshops, a spinning and weaving workshop, a poultry house, a multipurpose building that was also a summer kitchen, a shop, storeroom, granary, wood house, and blockhouse.

The Jesuits first brought real architectural design to the Northwest. Father Antonio Ravalli had studied art, mechanics, and other subjects in Italy before journeying to the Oregon Country. Putting his expertise to work, Father Ravalli directed the construction at Cataldo, east of Coeur d'Alene Lake, of the Sacred Heart Mission. Essentially completed in 1853, it is a resplendent baroque structure with a wooden false front forming a curved pediment embellished with urns and classic columns. Sacred Heart is recognized as a National Historic Landmark.

Service towns, like Middleton, and farm towns, like Paris, were similar in design. Each included a main street for commerce with shops, professional offices, and assorted businesses. Central to the town were its church, school, homes, and street plotting. There were usually saloons, livery stables, and pool halls, but they were not viewed as a credit to the community. Residential neighborhoods stretched around the edges of town and often included acreage for pastures and orchards.

Mormon farm communities, unique in layout and design, were developed according to a concentrated north-south or east-west grid plan with wide streets, homes placed conspicuously on corners, and designated farmland encircling the community. Thus Mormon towns had a rural feeling because of the open pastures, barns, and spacing between houses. Lining the streets were irrigation ditches, often deeper and wider than those found in typical small towns, and trees—usually poplars. Sheep and cattle grazed in the same pastures. There were "inside-out" granaries, clapboard buildings with the vertical studding on the outside to provide a smooth interior, and "Mormon" hay derricks, made of pine poles from nearby mountains, used for stacking hay. "Mormon fences" assembled with various poles, posts, slabs, or finished pickets placed evenly for support, all unpainted, circled pastures and gardens. Bleached by the sun, these fences created a sharp contrast to the earth, grasses, and manure in the corral. In the center of town was a public square with an LDS meetinghouse, Women's Relief Society hall, and schoolhouse. Residents had a duty to build and maintain these structures as a part of their "labor tithing." As the community grew, this central zone became the setting for the general store, post office, bank, and other businesses.

The coming of the railroad in the 1880s and 1890s solidified fledgling communities and established towns at important junctions. Railroads provided access to out-of-state factories able to supply millwork, wrought iron, cast iron, pressed galvanized sheet iron, and steel used for more sophisticated construction. Commercial sections, government facilities, and residential neighborhoods started to embrace an expanded variety of popular styles: Italianate, Romanesque Revival, Moorish, Gothic Revival, Queen Anne, French Chateau, and Colonial Revival.

At first most buildings were simply rectangular boxes ornamented with a gable front and Greek or Gothic revival adornments for special interest. On churches, schools, and town halls, a bell tower might sit at the peak of the front wall. An outside staircase might be added to fraternal lodges to give private access to the second-story lodge while a business enterprise operated on the main floor. Examples of these buildings include the Salmon Odd Fellows Hall built in 1874, the Idaho City Odd Fellows Hall built in 1875, the Idaho City Masonic Hall built in 1865, the Silver City Masonic Hall built in 1869, and the Boise Good Templars' Hall built in 1870.

Many towns were dominated by a single structure that spoke of size, elegance, and grandeur. Paris, in southern Idaho, was dwarfed by an imposing Romanesque tabernacle referred to as the Notre Dame of Paris—Idaho. The cathedral-like structure, built between 1884 and 1889 by skilled Swiss and English stonemasons and carpenters, was stunning in pink, red, and gray sandstone hauled from a canyon eighteen miles away. In winter sled loads of the rock were pulled across a frozen Bear Lake. Shingles and other lumber came from nearby forests. For whatever reason, there were other European influences throughout the community. There are more Mansard roofs in Paris than in any other Idaho town. The gingerbread houses, comfortable porticos, and white picket fences with old-fashioned English stiles were expressions of a generation seeking status and refinement in the western wilderness.[23]

A similar Victorian village, Oakley, was planted in the middle of a road in a bare valley. Elaborately detailed homes of brick, stone, wood, and intricately cut wooden designs were built to last. The Oakley image dispels the theory that early farm life was nothing but drudgery, for ornate castles like the Judge Howell house and neighboring mansions were built with pride and a vision of the future. Juliaetta's "Castle" dominates the Potlatch Creek area. Erected by a successful wheat grower, this fancy structure was created with intricate tin ceilings, classical moldings, and garlands. In Murray, once the setting of flourishing Coeur d'Alene placer-gold activity, the two-story survivors stand tall and narrow-shouldered, their gable ends facing the long main street.[24]

Churches were major components of Idaho's architectural heritage. The railroad town of Rathdrum, on the edge of the prairies north of Coeur d'Alene, featured Gothic revival churches of both wood and brick, along with a Romanesque bank, turn-of-the century commercial blocks, and neat residences of several architectural periods. In Idaho City, St. Joseph's church emphasized gable returns and pediment window heads reflecting the Greek influence, but the steepled roof was purely Gothic. Good examples of Greek and Gothic churches to house Protestant and Catholic gatherings were St. Michael's Episcopal (now Christ Chapel), built in Boise in 1866; St. Joseph's in Idaho City, built in 1867; the Kamiah Presbyterian Church, built in 1874; and St. Joseph's Catholic Mission church near Lapwai, Idaho, built in 1874. The elaborate brick First Methodist Church in Boise, finished in 1874, reached beyond the boxy traditions of the surrounding community churches and employed angular Gothic windows and an English Gothic corner tower—ideas that could have been copied from available pattern books like Holly's *Country Seats*.[25] A typical example of the Mormon church style was the Second Ward building in Rexburg, which blended a "rusticated stone building with a pedimented gable, Romanesque and Gothic arched openings, and a semicircular window."[26]

Early government structures also expressed architectural character. The assay office at Boise—Idaho's only other architectural National Historic Landmark—was designed in 1872 by Alfred B. Mullett, U.S. Treasury Department architect, shortly before he left the government's employ for private practice. Mullett relied on a classical Italianate design that included stone quoining, denticulated eaves, and a bracketed cupola sitting at the crest of the pyramidal roof of the two stories. Inside, the first floor was used for official offices, while the second level housed living quarters. Undoubtedly, the assay office was an inspiration for other Italianate buildings, both homes and commercial properties, that were completed in Boise in the 1870s.

The territorial capital, built in 1886, was designed in the eclectic Romanesque style by Detroit architect Elijah E. Myers, whose credits included numerous state capitals and county courthouses around the nation.

Prominent early commercial buildings in Idaho City include the Boise County Courthouse, originally built as the Kingsley store in 1873; the post office and Boise Basin Museum, first built as the Pinney's bookstore in 1867; the Boise Market, later converted to the Idaho World Building; the Claresy Saloon, later the Miners Exchange block; and the three units of the Boise Basin Mercantile Company, completed in 1865–68.

In Idaho as in most nineteenth-century American communities there were many lodges belonging to fraternal and social organizations. Agricultural areas had grange halls, and laborers in the mills and shops built union halls. Scattered throughout the territory were buildings erected and maintained by Eagles (twenty-two aeries by 1890), Moose (fifteen lodges), Knights of Columbus (twelve Councils), Masons and Eastern Star, Shriners, Foresters, and Miners. Also stemming from the nineteenth century are twenty-four Idaho Elks Lodges, from Sandpoint in the north, to Caldwell in the southwest, to Preston in the southeast, and to Salmon in east central Idaho. Particularly important in the life of the territory were the Masons. In 1863 a Masonic lodge was organized in Idaho City (then called Bannack City) and a hall built. Destroyed during the disastrous fire of 1865, the facility was replaced almost immediately by a Masonic-built community hall, where citizens held not only lodge events but Sunday school, balls, weddings, and other social affairs. A substantial proportion of territorial leaders were Masons. The Independent Order of Odd Fellows was also instituted at Idaho City and soon spread to Silver City and to Boise in

1868. In at least one instance the town sprang up around the I.O.O.F. hall: in 1893, three Odd Fellows decided to establish a lodge in what is now Meridian. A hall for Odd Fellows and Rebekahs was erected in a large alfalfa field; then the surrounding ground was surveyed and the town of Meridian laid out.

## SYMBOLS OF IDENTITY

Settled by people wishing to be free to follow their own fortunes, territorial Idaho was nevertheless able to realize a community of common values and purposes. The dispersed settlements, the repeated movements of people into and out of the territory, the varieties of ethnic groups and culture patterns may have inhibited the attainment of community identity, but there was seldom lack of social enjoyment. Strong gravitational pulls may have drawn Idahoans toward Spokane, Boise, and Salt Lake City, but the very factors that might have promoted social disorganization caused Idaho's settlers to work toward the achievement of common purpose and attachment to their territory. They had a commitment to economic progress, but they also had shared understandings and obligations, affective ties, common enjoyments. As historian Robert Hine wrote: "The need for community bred community."[27]

The symbols of community identity were witnessed in a variety of social enjoyments. Dances, musicals, theatrical performances, picnics, ball games, rodeos, and local fairs added zest to life. In some of the larger communities, like Boise, there were costume parties and splendid masquerades. The *Idaho World* of December 17, 1864, captured the mood of the New Year's plans: "Dancing is the prevailing amusement in this camp, and balls, assemblies, and parties are generously offering sources of enjoyment to all who love that oft-described light fantastic toe."[28] School buildings were often used as dance pavilions. Some had "four-set" rooms specially designed to accommodate four sets of dancers. Popular, too, were the polkas, mazurkas, Monkey Musk, Virginia Reels, and waltzes.

The Idaho theater, more entertainment than "culture," sprang up among bored miners looking for diversion. Theater groups were known to perform in tents as well as community halls and schools. Nearly every town built an "opera house" (a theater) as fast as it could. Paris presented a production of *William Tell* as early as February 23, 1864; there were similar productions in other small towns and villages. Typical drama-club presentations included *The Charcoal Burner*, *The Hidden Hand*, *Above the Clouds*, *Ten Nights in a Bar Room*, *Gun Maker of Moscow*, *The Husband of the Hour*, and *Robber of the Rhine*.

Also popular in Idaho were circuses and rodeo events that allowed participants from the local ranches and neighboring communities to show their skills. There were fairs in most of the counties, horse races, and Pioneer Day celebrations in Mormon communities. The Fourth of July was celebrated by parades, dances, and horse races. A celebration in Whitney in 1889 may have been more seriously structured than most: "A patriotic meeting consisted of two prayers, sixteen readings, dialogues, and recitations, sixteen speeches, eleven musical numbers, and a step dance."[29]

Idaho's momentum as a territory was strengthened by the blend of aggressive individuality and common endeavor that was promoted by Main Street enterprisers, fraternal groups, professional people, religious and political leaders, and the Native Americans, white farmers, and stockmen who fed them all. Idahoans in the generation before statehood shared much. Above all, they were learning to think of themselves as Idahoans. With the coming of statehood in 1890 that sense of identity would be intensified.

## CHAPTER SEVENTEEN: SOURCES

General studies of American communities include Lewis Atherton, *Main Street on the Middle Border* (Bloomington: Indiana University Press, 1954); Merle Curti, *The Making of an American Community: A Case Study of Democracy in a Frontier County* (Stanford: Stanford University Press, 1959); Page Smith, *As a City Upon a Hill: The Town in American History* (New York: Alfred A. Knopf, 1966); Robert V. Hine, *Community on the American Frontier: Separate But Not Alone* (Norman: University of Oklahoma Press, 1980); "The Search for Community," in Hine, *The American West: An Interpretive History*, 252–67; John D. Hicks, "The Significance of the Small Town in American History," in Carroll, ed., *Reflections of Western Historians*, 155–66; T. Scott Miyakawa, *Protestants and Pioneers: Individualism and Conformity on the American Frontier* (Chicago: University of Chicago Press, 1964); and Charles Howard Shinn, *Mining Camps: A Study in American Frontier Government* (New York: Harper & Row, 1884, 1965); helpful also are various articles in Lamar, ed., *The Reader's Encyclopedia of the American West.*

Idaho histories with a chapter or more on Idaho community life include Beal and Wells, *History of Idaho*, 2:40–71; Hawley, *History of Idaho*, 1:315–32, 363–82, 585–854; Vardis Fisher, *The Idaho Encyclopedia* (Caldwell: Caxton Printers, 1938), esp. 153–61, 210–432; French, *History of Idaho*, 1:109–291, 510–14; Wells, *Boise: An Illustrated History*; Cort Conley, *Idaho for the Curious: A Guide* (Cambridge, Idaho: Backeddy Books, 1982); Defenbach, *Idaho: The Place and Its People*, 1:467–549; Leonard J. Arrington, Feramorz Y. Fox, and Dean L. May, *Building the City of God: Community and Cooperation Among the Mormons* (Salt Lake City: Deseret Book Company, 1976); Beal, *History of Southeastern Idaho.*

Especially helpful for the pages on architecture is Jennifer Eastman Attebery, *Building Idaho: An Architectural History* (Moscow: University of Idaho Press, 1991).

Articles in *Idaho Yesterdays* and elsewhere on specific topics are mentioned in the footnote references. A very nice introduction is in Arthur Hart, "Community Identity in Small Town Idaho," *Idaho*

*Heritage*, no. 6 (December 1976), 34–36. There are many histories of specific Idaho communities—too many to list here. Lists are given in Richard W. Etulain and Merwin Swanson, *Idaho History: A Bibliography* (Pocatello: Idaho State University Press, 1974), 9–15; *Idaho Local History: A Bibliography with a Checklist of Library Holdings* (Moscow: University Press of Idaho, 1976); and Merle W. Wells, *Idaho: A Students' Guide to Localized History* (New York: Teachers College Press, 1965).

77.

78.

77. The Idaho Hotel on Jordan Street in Silver City was one of the first public hotels and restaurants in Idaho. DAN WARREN, PHOTOGRAPHER, UIL 5–82–1B.

78. This A.R. Trimble Saloon in Lewiston is typical of the popular pioneer resorts. "Hank" Trimble's barroom goes back to the 1860s. "Ab" Anderson is behind the bar and cowboy "Bill" Anderson stands in front. UIL 5–7–4B.

79. 

80. 

79. Blacksmith shops like this one of J. P. Fitzgerald in Grangeville were common in Idaho villages in the nineteenth century. Donated by Verna McGrane, UIL 5–117–5A.

80. Every village had a livery stable; this was in Orofino. ISHS 2812.

81.

82.

81. After the log-cabin era, many pioneer homes in southern Idaho were made of adobe. Here is Charles C. Rich in his Paris home about 1880, with his wife Mary Ann Phelps and their four sons and two daughters. LDS CHURCH ARCHIVES PH 1323.

82. The Bannock Stake Academy band at Rexburg (1895) had not only fine instruments, but fancy uniforms as well. LDS CHURCH ARCHIVES PH 1023.

83.

84.

83. The Romanesque LDS tabernacle in Paris was built between 1884 and 1889 by skilled Swiss and English stonemasons and carpenters. Stunning in pink, red, and gray sandstone hauled from a nearby canyon, the tabernacle is shown here in 1930 when the community was celebrating Pioneer Day. LDS CHURCH ARCHIVES.

84. This schoolhouse was built in the 1880s to serve the mining communities of Custer and Bonanza. ISHS 73–215.1.

85.

86.

85. Communities sponsored festivities like this Children's Fair at the Maroa Country School, three miles west of Filer. ISHS 73–221.629.

86. The Canyon County Fair, Caldwell, in October 1902, was like most rural turn-of-the-century celebrations. ISHS 78–92.5.

87. 

88. 

87. Beginning in the 1880s, the circus came every summer to most Idaho towns. This was the parade down Main Street in Twin Falls in 1910. ISHS 73–221.794.

88. Many Idaho farmers were members of the National Grange and engaged in many group activities like this Grange Day at Hagerman Valley about 1900. ISHS 69–4.69E.

89.

90.

89. Loading sacked potatoes in "Spud Alley," Idaho Falls, in 1912, was rigorous work. ISHS 64–109.2.

90. Despite the earlier failure of gold mines, the community of Pierce was prospering at the turn of the century. ISHS 64–13.3.

## CHAPTER EIGHTEEN

# Statehood

THE rapid growth in agriculture and mining that followed the advance of railroads through Idaho boosted population sufficiently to warrant serious consideration for statehood. The prospect that north Idaho would consent to statehood in lieu of annexation by Washington or Montana became more likely after the election of 1888 and after the specter of Mormon domination of the territory had been quashed by the adoption of the Test Oath and related anti-Mormon measures. Idaho was now sufficiently Republican to induce the Republican Congress to include it with other territories in a statehood bill.

No new states had been admitted into the Union since Colorado in 1876. When the Republicans captured the White House and both houses of Congress in 1888, the way was cleared for an omnibus bill to admit a number of territories that had lobbied for statehood. Democrats, who had previously delayed approval, now hoped to get credit for supporting statehood by joining Republicans to admit Washington, Montana, and the two Dakotas.

Although not mentioned in the bill, Idaho and Wyoming proceeded without formal congressional approval to hold constitutional conventions and draft constitutions. They were admitted in 1890, a year after the omnibus states.

In advance of a constitutional convention the Idaho legislature adopted a petition to Congress asking for admission. The territorial House of Representatives passed an act calling a convention, but the Council, because of an internal squabble, failed to act on the measure. Nevertheless, arrangements for the convention went ahead. The lame-duck Democrat-controlled U.S. House Committee on Territories voted to approve statehood for Idaho, Wyoming, and Arizona on February 5, 1889, and the Republican Senate committee approved the Idaho bill on February 17. But Congress adjourned without final passage.

At this point Republican congressional leaders assured Idaho Delegate Fred T. Dubois that Idaho should proceed with the constitutional convention without waiting for a congressional enabling act or for formal approval of the Idaho legislature. On this advice Governor Stevenson, on April 2, 1889, called an Idaho constitutional convention to assemble in Boise on July 4. Governor George L. Shoup (who was appointed by Republican President Benjamin Harrison to replace Stevenson) confirmed the proclamation on May 11, 1889. A joint Republican-Democratic committee meeting would be held in each county to elect delegates. In practical terms the absence of a territorial enabling act meant that there would be no funds to cover the expense of the delegates. Each party was allotted half of each county's representation, so all the local and territorial political leaders were there. The seventy men of both parties who gathered in Boise elected William H. Clagett, of Shoshone County, permanent chairman.

The unique element in the Idaho constitution, insisted upon by the Radical anti-Mormon Republicans who were in the majority, was a clause giving the legislature unrestricted power to disfranchise anyone. This was a means of preventing Mormons from using any tactic that would return their franchise. The Test Oath was incorporated in the constitution without change. Except for this extreme anti-Mormon measure, the constitution was typical of many. Boise was confirmed as the state capital; the university was permanently located in Moscow; and a traveling supreme court was established to diminish geographic obstacles to litigation. Aliens (for example, Chinese) were denied the privilege of working for the state or any municipality, and the constitution disqualified from voting all bigamists, polygamists, Chinese or persons of Mongolian descent, and Indians not taxed or who had not severed their tribal relations. The constitution provided for the election of seven state executive officers every two years, gave the governor an item veto over all appropriations, set a ceiling on state salaries (a measure that would later have to be deleted), and established precautionary controls over corporate enterprises, especially railroads. Despite a plea from Abigail Scott Duniway, an Oregonian with an Idaho ranch and a leading suffragist, the constitution did not grant women the vote.

On August 6 the convention issued its document, admonishing voters to approve it. Announced opposition was slim. The Mormons who might oppose the anti-Mormon clause could not vote; no north Idaho paper opposed admission. In the referendum, held November 5, 1889, the people voted 12,126 to 6,282 for the constitution—a large anti-statehood vote. Moscow and the Coeur d'Alene district voted overwhelmingly in favor; only Lewiston, among the larger cities, still favored joining Washington.

In the Fifty-first Congress, which convened in December 1889, Delegate Dubois was made a member of the House Committee on Territories so he could more effectively forward the bill. Governor Shoup led a Republican delegation of lobbyists, and former Governor Stevenson and former Chief Justice Hugh

W. Weir headed the Democrats. There were spirited debates. Although the U.S. Supreme Court upheld the anti-Mormon Test Oath on February 3, 1890, the Democrats argued against that infringement of religious freedom as a part of the constitution. When the House voted, on April 2, 1890, sixty-seven Democrats abstained. The resulting vote was 129 to 1 in favor. The Senate also debated the bill, and primarily the anti-Mormon clause, vigorously and then passed it on July 1. That night there were bonfires and rejoicing in Idaho.

Hundreds of telegrams asked Delegate Dubois to have the president sign the bill on the Fourth of July. On July 3, Dubois went with the congressional clerk to the White House. He met President Benjamin Harrison and Secretary of State James G. Blaine and explained Idaho's desire to be the Fourth of July State. The president's reply, according to Dubois, was that he would be glad to sign the bill the next day but wanted Dubois to understand that the star of a new state goes on the flag the Fourth of July following the date of admission. If he waited until the Fourth to sign the bill, the star of Idaho would not be on the flag for another year. If he signed the bill immediately, the forty-third star would be on the flag the next day. Dubois hesitated for a moment.

> "Mr. President," I replied, "This is rather a momentous position. I am the sole representative of our people. They have wired me what they desire. I am quite sure, however, that they do not know about the star any more than I did. The responsibility is all mine and I ask you to sign the bill now. I want the star of Idaho on the flag tomorrow." "I think you have chosen well," the President remarked, and Secretary Blaine agreed with him. The President then picked up a new, golden penholder, adjusted a brand new pen, signed the bill, and presented the pen and penholder to me saying, "You may wish to keep this as a souvenir. There is no honor which can come to any young man

> greater than that of bringing your state into the Union." Years afterwards I presented this pen and holder to my friend John Hailey, who was at the head of the Historical Society of Idaho, and it is now among the Idaho relics in the State House at Boise. . . . Wyoming was admitted just one week later, on July 10th.[1]

For the first time a band of full-fledged states stretched from the Atlantic to the Pacific.

The next step in Idaho was the election of officers. The Republicans held a state nominating convention in Boise on August 20 and the Democrats on August 26. In the ensuing election, held October 1, 1890, the following, all Republicans, were elected: governor, George L. Shoup; lieutenant governor, Norman B. Willey; secretary of state, A. J. Pinkham; auditor, Silas W. Moody; treasurer, Frank R. Coffin; attorney general, George H. Roberts; superintendent of public instruction, Joseph E. Harroun. Willis Sweet, also a Republican, was elected to the U.S. House of Representatives.

The First State Legislature convened at Boise on December 8, 1890, and continued in session until March 14, 1891. A principal responsibility was the election of two United States Senators (until 1916 Senators were elected by the legislature, not by the voting public). In an odd turn of circumstances Idaho elected three senators on December 18, 1890, and startled everyone by electing a fourth on February 11, 1891. To quote the Helena *Journal*, "Idaho evidently goes on the principle that electing United [States] Senators is like courting a widow—it can't be overdone."[2]

The plenitude of senators lay partly in the fact that north Idaho had been promised one of the two elected senators by both the Republican and Democratic conventions of 1890. After two votes no candidate had received a majority. Dubois, who expected to be one of the senators, wired the chairman of the U.S.

Senate Judiciary Committee asking whether the legislators could elect three senators—one for a full term beginning on March 4, 1891, one whose term would expire on that date, and a third to serve for two or four years, depending on the lot he would draw. The reply sanctioned three under those terms. As power-broker of the election, but not a delegate, Dubois then suggested the election of Governor George L. Shoup, W. H. Clagett, and himself as senators. Dubois would take the full term beginning in March 1891; Clagett and Shoup would draw lots to see which would serve for only sixty days. Clagett refused to go along with the scheme because the election of three senators would make it impossible for the sixty-day senator to be re-elected. Besides, if Clagett lost the draw, north Idaho would be without its promised senator. Dubois then turned to William J. McConnell, a Moscow merchant, who agreed to run in Clagett's place. When the three elected men appeared in Washington to draw lots, McConnell drew the sixty-day term.

North Idahoans believed there was treachery and called the recent election illegal; there were grounds for doing so. After much agitation and behind-the-scenes lobbying, the Idaho Legislature approved a resolution declaring the previous election for U.S. Senators illegal and invalid. In a new election on February 11 Clagett received a majority of the votes and was declared elected. Clagett then prepared a lengthy memorial to Congress stating his claim that Dubois' election had been invalid.

All four men were in Washington when the U.S. Senate adjourned on March 4, 1891. McConnell had just finished his brief term; Senator Shoup would be continuing his four-year-term, and Clagett and Dubois were contesting for McConnell's now vacant seat. The following January, after debate in the Senate, Dubois prevailed. Adam Aulbach, the publisher of the *Wallace Press*, editorialized: "If the Easterners don't think we have anything else, we can point with pride at our four Federal senators. We have got material for some more, too, and it is to be regretted that the Legislature cannot keep on balloting, for every ballot that has been taken has improved the breed."[3] Indeed, the senator's seat was a prized position.

Governor Shoup, who had served as Idaho's last territorial governor from May 1, 1889, to July 3, 1890, really wanted to be senator. Originally from Kittanning, Pennsylvania, Shoup became a stockman in Galesburg, Illinois, before joining the gold rush to Pike's Peak in 1859. He was a merchant in Denver, a member of the Colorado Volunteers during the Civil War, a colonel in the Plains Indian cavalry, and a member of the Colorado constitutional convention. He established a store in Virginia City, Montana, in 1866, opened another store in Leesburg, Idaho, later the same year, and in 1867 settled permanently in Salmon. He maintained a large cattle herd in addition to his store. In politics he made significant contributions at many levels. He was one of the original Lemhi County commissioners in 1869 and county superintendent of schools beginning in 1872, and he was elected to the legislature in 1874 and 1878. He served on the Republican National Committee from 1880 to 1884, and again in 1888. He personally prepared an Idaho exhibit at the New Orleans exposition of 1884–85.

When Shoup was elected senator on December 18, 1890, he relinquished his governorship to Lieutenant Governor Willey. In the meantime, Shoup managed the transition from territory to statehood with great skill. He was also effective in the Senate, where he served until 1900. When the time came to nominate an Idahoan for Statuary Hall in the national capitol, Shoup was chosen and his statue installed in 1910. His statue was joined in 1948 by that of Senator William E. Borah.

The new state of Idaho had sixteen counties. They were, in the order of founding:

| *County* | *Date of Founding* |
|---|---|
| Shoshone | 1861 |
| Nez Perce | 1861 |
| Idaho | 1861 |
| Boise | 1863 |
| Owyhee | 1863 |
| Oneida | 1864 |
| Ada | 1864 |
| Lemhi | 1869 |
| Bear Lake | 1875 |
| Cassia | 1879 |
| Washington | 1879 |
| Custer | 1881 |
| Kootenai | 1881 |
| Bingham | 1885 |
| Latah | 1888 |
| Elmore | 1889 |

The first four of these were created when Idaho was part of Washington Territory. The others were organized as new settlements spread a significant distance from the existing county seat.

The creation of Latah County was so unusual that it deserves comment. In the 1870s pioneers began to settle the upland plateau known as the Palouse country. All the open prairie land north of the Clearwater River, in Nez Perce County, was settled and the towns of Genesee and Moscow were founded. Moscow soon rivaled Lewiston, the county seat, in population and business enterprise.[4] The Moscow people wanted a division of Nez Perce County, and a bill was eventually passed by the legislature submitting the question of county division to the voters. County division was defeated, but the citizens of Moscow were undaunted. They carried the fight to the U.S. Congress, which passed a law on May 14, 1888, to create the new county of

Latah. This was apparently the only time that a new county has been created by an act of Congress.[5] Congress not only set the boundaries and located the county seat at Moscow but also designated the county commissioners and authorized them to sell bonds to erect a courthouse and jail.

One of the first official acts of Idaho was to establish a state seal. Designed by Emma Edwards Green, it was adopted by the first legislature on March 14, 1891. Mrs. Green's explanation for the state seal design was as follows:

> The question of Woman Suffrage was being agitated somewhat, and as leading men and politicians agreed that Idaho would eventually give women the right to vote, and as mining was the chief industry, and the mining man the largest financial factor of the state at that time, I made the figure of the man the most prominent in the design, while that of the woman, signifying justice, as noted by the scales; liberty, as denoted by the liberty cap on the end of the spear, and equality with man as denoted by her position at his side, also signifies freedom. The pick and shovel held by the miner, and the ledge of rock beside which he stands, as well as the pieces of ore scattered about his feet, all indicate the chief occupation of the State. The stamp mill in the distance . . . is also typical of the mining interest of Idaho. The shield between the man and woman is emblematic of the protection they unite in giving the state. The large fir or pine tree in the foreground in the shield refers to Idaho's immense timber interests. The husbandman plowing on the left side of the shield, together with the sheaf of grain beneath the shield, are emblematic of Idaho's agricultural resources, while the cornucopias, or horns of plenty, refer to the horticultural. Idaho has a game law, which protects the elk and moose. The elk's head, therefore, rises above the shield. The state flower, the wild Syringa or mock orange, grows at the woman's feet, while the ripened wheat grows as high as her

> shoulder. The star signifies a new light in the galaxy of states. . . . The river depicted in the shield is our mighty Snake or Shoshone River, a stream of great majesty. . . . As Idaho was a virgin state, I robed my goddess in white and made the liberty cap on the end of the spear the same color. . . . The "Light of the Mountains" is typified by the rosy glow which precedes the sunrise.[6]

Five events following shortly after the granting of statehood had a permanent impact on the forty-third state. The first was the opening of the University of Idaho at Moscow on October 3, 1892. As the state land-grant college, the university established an agricultural experiment station, College of Engineering, state normal school, and school of home economics. The next year, 1893, the state founded two additional state normal schools—one at Lewiston, the other at Albion.

The second event was the invitation to Idaho to prepare an exhibit for the Columbian Exposition in Chicago in 1893. The legislature appropriated $50,000 (private contributions boosted the total to $100,000), commissioners were appointed from each county, and George Manning of Post Falls and John A. Stearns of Nampa were appointed national commissioners. The three members of the national Board of Lady Managers were Mrs. Joseph C. Straughan, Boise; Mrs. A. E. M. Farnum, Post Falls; and Mrs. Louise L. Barton, Moscow. The Idaho Building reflected frontier design and material—a large, rustic log cabin—and was intended to represent the varieties of timber, stone, marble, and brick in the state. All the logs and other materials were shipped from Idaho. The mining exhibit was particularly outstanding, with samples of the silver, gold, lead, zinc, and other metals; precious stones, marbles, salts, and all the paraphernalia used in mining were prominently displayed. Agriculture was represented by fruits, vegetables (including potatoes and sugar beets), grains, wool, and animals. The women exhibited their needlework, from embroidered portières (draperies), tablecloths, and bedspreads to hose, lace, and fans. There were also drawings, paintings, wood carvings, and jewelry.

The Columbian Committee also confirmed the syringa as Idaho's state flower. The flower has four white petals and a yellow center and flourishes in the mountainous regions of Idaho. In 1931 the legislature officially recognized the syringa, giving it the statutory distinction that it had held by common consent since 1890.

The third significant event after statehood was the elimination in 1895 of the anti-Mormon Test Oath for voting and holding public office. The 20,000 or more Mormons in Idaho had not attempted to vote in the state's first election, but the crusade against the old polygamous families had continued.[7] John Codman, a nationally known reporter and summer resident of Soda Springs during some of the 1880s, complained of "the frequent and painful scene which justly arouses indignation" in which old men were dragged to prison "for no other cause than an occasional visit, in open daylight, or taking of a meal sometimes in the house of a plural wife."[8]

On September 26, 1890, Wilford Woodruff, president of the Church of Jesus Christ of Latter-day Saints, issued a manifesto that signaled a cessation of the performance of plural marriages, at least in the United States. The manifesto was accepted by the high leadership of the church, then by an assembled body (general conference) of members in Salt Lake City. Idaho anti-Mormons, who had used polygamy as the basis for the voting restriction, now had to admit that the Test Oath was based not so much on polygamy as on the Mormon tendency to vote as a bloc.

The 1890 manifesto was later accepted as sincere and genuine by Presidents Benjamin Harrison and Grover Cleveland, who agreed that Mormons with plural wives might continue to live together though no new plural marriages were sanctioned, and the Saints must discontinue bloc voting and the church must stop all attempts to control political officers. In Idaho enforcement of the Test Oath would be continued until everyone could be sure that bloc voting would no longer be practiced. Under the influence of Dubois, the Idaho election act of February 25, 1891, retained the proviso that anyone who had been a member of the Mormon Church on January 1, 1888, still could not vote. For the moment Idaho anti-Mormons could continue to assume there would be no Mormon influence in Idaho politics.

Meanwhile, Mormon Church officials sought to eliminate church political influence. On June 10, 1891, the Mormon People's Party was dissolved, and the church undertook to achieve a more or less equal division of the Saints between the two national parties. Although nearly all Mormons had been Democrats since the Republicans had strongly repudiated them in 1856 (and again at each national convention thereafter), most Idaho Democrats had turned against the Mormons in 1884. Some Latter-day Saints could no longer tolerate the Democratic Party and were prepared to become Republicans. A few LDS leaders were friendly with James G. Blaine and other nationally prominent Republicans, and the economy of the Mormons favored the high tariffs proposed by William McKinley. Church authorities decided that to realize a 50–50 split of their members, church apostles who wished to become Republicans would declare so publicly; those who preferred to remain Democrats would keep silent. There was thus a gradual build-up of Republican loyalty. Mormon officers applied to President Harrison for amnesty on December 19, 1891.

On February 15, 1892, under the leadership of a new Boise attorney, William E. Borah—later son-in-law of William J. McConnell, the Republican candidate for governor—the Republican State Committee dropped criticism of the Saints and welcomed them into the party. The Democratic State Committee followed on March 5 with a statement that they were willing to let the Saints vote. A Republican state Supreme Court, however, on October 18, held that the Mormons were still ineligible to vote under existing law. They would have to wait two more years.

Actions were taken to mitigate "the Mormon problem." Late in 1892 Senator Dubois endorsed amnesty for polygamists liable for prosecution before November 1, 1890. In December the Idaho Legislature considered proposals to repeal the Test Oath. One such proposal was passed February 23, 1893, and duly signed by Governor McConnell. Later that year, on October 23, Congress restored confiscated property in Utah to the Mormon Church. On July 16, 1894, an act to grant Utah statehood promised an end to the Mormon disabilities growing out of the national anti-Mormon movement.

In Idaho's 1894 elections, competition by both parties for the Mormon vote was intense. Temporary chairman of the Democratic State Convention was Bear Lake Mormon Joseph C. Rich. At the Republican rally in Paris on November 1 Dubois and William Budge, a leading Mormon in Bear Lake Valley, joined in an appeal to the Mormons to vote Republican. In fact, the Mormons divided almost evenly in the 1894 election.

Following the 1894 election, Republicans, Democrats, and Populists united to repeal the anti-Mormon Test Oath of 1885. By act of February 1, 1895, this vestige of anti-Mormon election practice finally was removed. Because the Mormons no longer voted unanimously as a bloc, non-Mormons were not tempted to vote unanimously against them. The Idaho anti-Mormon movement was over.

Or, at least, that was the expectation. But there was one more surge. Dubois's retirement from anti-Mormon activity lasted only a decade. In 1896 he emerged as a leader of the Silver Republicans, a position from which he made another transition in 1900 to take over Idaho's Democratic Party. Losing to William E. Borah's Idaho Progressive Republican Party in 1902, Dubois found a new cause in leading the national campaign to prevent the seating of Reed Smoot, a Mormon apostle who had been elected U.S. Senator from Utah. In 1904 Dubois successfully insisted on an anti-Mormon plank in the national Democratic platform. But his anti-Mormon crusade ran into trouble because this time the Mormons could vote. Senator Borah ridiculed Dubois's anti-Mormon declarations:

> Mr. Dubois dares not come before you this year and discuss his position on the inter-oceanic canal question, or the tariff question, or any of the questions in which you all are so vitally interested. Instead, he comes before you with a story about some Mormon bishop who back in 1869 married a third wife, and using that as a basis tries to make you ladies believe that you are in an imminent danger of becoming the third wife of some Mormon if you do not vote the Democratic ticket this fall.[9]

He followed with further charges against Dubois:

> When I said that Mormonism was not a political issue, I did not mean that Senator Dubois could not discuss it. He will discuss it, for the very reason that it is not a political question nor a political issue, as he does not propose to discuss the political issues that are involved in this campaign. . . .
>
> Suppose that in his excitement, when the frenzy of moral ecstasy was upon him that he would have declared for the ten commandments, would there have been any political discussion? . . . Suppose somebody should have told him that there was such a thing in the Bible as a Sermon on the Mount, and that he would have declared in favor of that, would it have raised a political controversy? The reason why it cannot be a political question, ladies and gentlemen, is the simple fact that you cannot find a political organization in this state that is in favor of polygamy.[10]

In 1906, Borah replaced Dubois as one of Idaho's senators. Although he had lined up a Senate committee majority against

Reed Smoot on June 1, 1906, Dubois lost that battle as well and Smoot went on to serve thirty years in the U.S. Senate. Efforts to get the courts to prevent Idaho Mormons from voting on constitutional grounds failed on March 24, 1908. Idaho's constitution still contained the anti-Mormon Test Oath (finally removed in 1982), but the Supreme Court held that as long as the Saints refrained from plural marriage there was no legal impediment to their voting, holding public office, and serving on juries. More binding was the provision that guarantees "perfect toleration of religious sentiment."

The fourth significant event after statehood was the adoption of woman suffrage in 1896. When women were granted the vote in Wyoming Territory in 1869 and in Utah the next February, an alert legislator from Malad, Dr. Joseph William Morgan, introduced a similar bill in the Idaho legislature. Morgan had emigrated with his family from Great Britain to the Salt Lake Valley, then to the Mormon community of Malad. Representing Oneida County, which contained most of the Mormon residents in the territory, the thirty-two-year-old physician introduced the bill on December 29, 1870. On the third reading the vote was a tie, 11 to 11, which meant defeat. The legislators tried to make a joke out of it by placing Morgan in charge of food and drink for Ladies' Day at the legislature. If the Idaho House had passed the bill, which it came so close to doing (council leaders said they would have approved it, and acting governor E. J. Curtis said he would have signed it), Idaho would have been the third territory to grant women the franchise.[11]

In the years that followed there was little suffragist agitation. Suffrage lecturers did not come into the territory until after the railroads were completed in the 1880s and 1890s. The principal objection to the proposition when it was mentioned was that enfranchising women would give the Mormons more political power. In 1870 Idaho had nine men for every woman, but the Mormon communities had approximately as many women as men. The suffrage question was not a partisan issue, however; there were supporters and opponents in both parties.

The principal advocate appears to have been the *Idaho Statesman*, a Boise-based paper affiliated with the Republican Party. Both founder-editor Milton Kelly and his wife were strong advocates; Mrs. Kelly was sometimes referred to as the "pioneer suffragist of Idaho." William Balderston, who edited the *Statesman* in the 1890s, was an officer of the Equal Suffrage Association of Idaho. A number of Idahoans subscribed to *The New Northwest*, a weekly newspaper published by Abigail Scott Duniway of Portland in behalf of woman suffrage. Duniway occasionally visited Idaho to give lectures and solicit subscribers. In July 1876 she spoke in Idaho City, Placerville, Silver City, and twice in Boise. Another lecture series was given in Lewiston in 1879, and others were presented in a score of Idaho cities in 1881, 1885, and 1886.

Duniway was invited to speak to the Idaho House of Representatives on January 11, 1887. Her talk was persuasive to some, but in a subsequent vote on the bill the proposal lost by 10 to 14. Duniway was attracted to Idaho. She and two of her five sons filed on federal land and started a livestock ranch in Idaho's Lost River country (in Custer County). She lived there during part of 1887, pausing en route to lecture in Hailey and Ketchum, and she was at the ranch part of each summer thereafter; but, active in the suffrage campaign, she spent most of the year in Portland.

Duniway believed that the chief problem in obtaining suffrage was the energetic lobbying of the Women's Christian Temperance Union, which moved into Idaho in 1883. The Union was interested in suffrage as a springboard to achieving its goal of Prohibition. Recognizing that the liquor interests and miners of Idaho would never support suffrage if it meant the probability of Prohibition, Duniway found herself arguing against the W.C.T.U.

When word came to Duniway that Idaho's constitutional convention, meeting in Boise in the summer of 1889, had been petitioned by the W.C.T.U. to include in the constitution a clause prohibiting the sale of liquor and one enfranchising women, she knew both would fail when associated together. She rushed to the convention to convince the delegates that temperance and suffrage were not inexorably tied. Her efforts failed to persuade, and neither clause for Prohibition or for suffrage was included in the constitution.[12]

After statehood came, various groups of women committed their efforts to suffrage. The Idaho Women's Christian Temperance Union, led by Henrietta Skelton and Rebecca Brown Mitchell, continued its suffrage work despite Duniway's and others' objections. Mormon women, having experienced suffrage in Utah Territory from 1870 and having had Congress deprive them of the vote in 1887 as a part of the same anti-Mormon campaign conducted by Dubois, worked steadfastly for suffrage. Emmeline B. Wells, editor of the *Woman's Exponent* in Salt Lake City, a friend of Susan B. Anthony and other national suffrage leaders and a staunch advocate of women's rights, visited Idaho frequently. Her daughter Melvina (Mrs. W. W.) Woods lived in Wallace, where her husband, a major in the Civil War, was a lawyer and judge. On the way to and from Wallace, Wells—who was an officer of the Women's Relief Society of the LDS Church—stopped to give suffrage lectures to various Mormon and other groups. Emily S. Richards, also a Relief Society officer and national suffrage leader, was another Utahan who went to Idaho to spread the message of equal suffrage. Both women distributed suffrage literature and left money to support local campaigns.

In 1893 the first woman suffrage organization in Idaho was formed by Elizabeth Ingram, a schoolteacher in Hagerman, and her friends and neighbors. In 1894 the Idaho Populist Party announced its support of an amendment in favor of women suffrage; so did the Republican and Democratic parties. Following the 1895 convention of the National American Woman Suffrage Association in Atlanta, Georgia, Abigail Duniway and William Balderston launched a campaign for suffrage. Within a few months, the NAWSA sent Emma Smith DeVoe of Illinois to Idaho to manage the campaign. Melvina "Mell" Woods was assigned to assist her. DeVoe and Woods traveled to twenty-two settlements in the state, from Hope and Rathdrum in the north to Paris and Montpelier in the south and Eagle Rock in the east, organizing suffrage clubs as they traveled. Approximately thirty clubs were established on these tours. In November delegates from these clubs in eight counties met in Boise to form the Idaho Equal Suffrage Association as an auxiliary of the NAWSA.

In the spring of 1896 Laura M. Johns, of Salina, Kansas, a national organizer of the NAWSA, went to Idaho to direct the campaign. She would guide the operation in southwest Idaho from Boise; Blanche (Mrs. Marcus J.) Whitman of Montpelier was assigned to rally the predominantly Mormon communities in the Southeast; Helen Young of Wallace (one of Idaho's few women lawyers and possibly also a Mormon), would take charge of north Idaho. Their arguments included the following: the experience with female voting in Wyoming, Utah, and Colorado (which granted female suffrage in 1893) had been "altogether good and nothing evil"; "our Republic believed in no taxation without representation; white, native-born women should be at least politically equal with native-born Chinese and Indian men; the ballot is a badge of equality in all classes."[13]

The association's secretary, Eunice Pond Athey, wrote to prominent Idaho businessmen and political leaders requesting statements and endorsements. William E. Borah, the rising young statesman, was invited to speak to the 1896 equal suffrage convention held in Boise the first three days of July. National leader Carrie Chapman Catt attended, as did Emily Richards from Utah. Emphasis was put on the moral righteousness of the amendment. When the election was held, committees of women were stationed near the polling places with yellow suffrage banners and circulars beseeching men to "Remember the Amendment." There was little organized opposition. The amendment carried by 12,126 in favor and 6,282 against. Every county except Custer reported a majority in favor. The southeastern Mormon-dominated counties (Bannock, Bear Lake, Bingham, Cassia, Fremont, and Oneida) showed 77 percent favorable; other counties, where there were large numbers of single men, showed an average of slightly over 60 percent in favor.

Even with the successful vote the struggle was not over. The state board of canvassers ruled that the amendment was defeated because it had not received a majority of all votes cast in the election, just a majority of those voting on the amendment. An appeal was carried to the Idaho Supreme Court by two lawyers who donated their services, Borah (who had spoken out in favor of the amendment) and James H. Hawley (who as a legislator had voted for Dr. Morgan's bill in 1871). On December 11, 1896, the judges ruled unanimously in favor of the amendment. Thus Idaho became the fourth state to extend full voting privileges to women. Borah and Hawley would be greatly appreciated by equal-suffrage women in their subsequent careers, Borah as senator and Hawley as governor.

The convention of the National Woman's Suffrage Association held in 1897 at Des Moines, Iowa, celebrated Idaho's victory. Reasons listed for the success of woman suffrage in Idaho included:

> First, the fact that within the state a large colony of people reside who were formerly residents of Utah at the time the women were voting there and who were then converted to the measure; second, the educational and organizational work of the national committee; third, the labors of the various branches of the Idaho Association; fourth, the political endorsement by all political parties.[14]

The delegate from Idaho, Mell Woods, was applauded as she and her mother were called to the platform for a "mother and daughter enfranchised" fanfare.[15] Woods continued to attend the national suffrage conventions for several years thereafter.

Women were soon elected to and made a visible impact in public offices. In 1897, only a few months after the adoption of suffrage, Rebecca Mitchell of Eagle Rock was elected as the first woman legislative chaplain. The next year, Permeal J. French was elected state superintendent of public instruction, and for the next thirty-five years women occupied that office. The same year, Idaho elected three women to the legislature: Clara Campbell, Republican of Boise; Hattie Noble, Democrat of Idaho City; and Mary A. Wright, Populist of Rathdrum. Four women were elected county treasurers, fifteen were chosen county superintendents of schools, and three were made deputy sheriffs. Within two decades from the time woman suffrage was adopted, the legislature passed, at the urging of women legislators and lobbyists, acts that prohibited child labor, gave married women the same right to control and dispose of their property as married men, required saloons to close on Sunday, established a state library commission, increased support for libraries, provided a domestic science department at the University, established an industrial reform school, and made gambling illegal.[16]

Idaho had met an obligation to half its citizens. But there was one other obligation, one to the nation, that was soon to come. The fulfillment of this obligation was the fifth important event that occurred soon after statehood. When the United States declared war against Spain on April 25, 1898, President William McKinley called for 125,000 volunteers. Governor Frank Steuenenberg (elected in 1896 to replace Governor McConnell) confidently offered an Idaho regiment, and in less than three weeks the First Idaho Regiment of infantry Volunteers was organized and mustered into the federal service at Camp Stevenson in Boise. Company A was from Canyon County; Company B, Lewiston area; Company C, Grangeville; Company D, Latah; Company E, Fremont and Bonneville; Company F, Shoshone

County; Company G, Pocatello; and Company H, Boise. The commander of the regiment was Lieutenant Colonel John W. Jones, formerly of the Confederate army and more recently publisher of the *Idaho News* in Blackfoot. Private businesses, caught up in the jingoistic atmosphere of the times, encouraged enlistment. The Bunker Hill and Sullivan Mining Company, for example, offered each employee who enlisted $100, with a promise of employment upon his return. A group from Salmon, organized as Shoup's Rangers, intended to seek service with the Rough Riders of Theodore Roosevelt, but they did not reach Tampa Bay in time to get aboard the ships bound for Cuba.

The 672 members of Idaho's regiment assembled in Boise on May 2 and participated in a mammoth parade on May 19. The entire community turned out, and schoolchildren covered the streets with spring flowers. The next day the soldiers paraded in Portland. Arriving in San Francisco on May 22, the men were treated more like conquering heroes than "poor, ragged, dust-begrimed privates."[17]

The troops were on board ship on June 26, 1898, and arrived at Parañaque, near Manila, on August 6. Their first assignment was to guard army supplies from the natives during the battle for Manila. They did outpost and patrol duty throughout the fall and winter of 1898–99. On February 4, 1899, Emilio Aguinaldo's Filipino army made a desperate effort to liberate their nation in what was called the Philippino Insurrection. Idaho troops were called into service in the Battle of Santa Ana. The Americans were outnumbered two to one, but the 1,500 Idaho and Washington troops rashly charged the 10,000 well-fortified and well-armed Filipinos. Major Daniel W. Figgins (Idaho's adjutant general), who was in charge, was asked if he could not stop his men. "No, I cannot," he replied. To this General Charles King, brigadier general of volunteers in the war, responded: "Then I will give them a command they will obey." Raising his voice, he yelled, "Go it, you damned Idaho savages, go it." As he lowered his sword and settled back in his saddle, he commented: "There goes the American soldier, and all hell can't stop him."[18]

By noon the Idaho and Washington volunteers had captured Santa Ana. They fought again at Caloocan on February 10–11 and at Guadalupe on February 16–18, and participated in the fighting at Santa Cruz during the Laguna Bay campaign in April. Thirty-four men, including Major Edward McConville of Lewiston, were killed in action or died in army service during the war. The men were ordered home on July 29; when they reached San Francisco, Governor Steunenberg and about 100 other citizens of the state were there to greet them.

The State of Idaho had started auspiciously. The university and two state and four private teachers colleges were in operation, the state had gained favorable publicity at the Chicago Columbian Exposition, anti-Mormonism had been shelved at least temporarily, woman suffrage had been adopted, and the state's citizens had achieved recognition in the Spanish-American and Philippine military engagements. The principal roadblock for the citizens was confrontation with a debilitating economic depression.

## CHAPTER EIGHTEEN: SOURCES

I have relied rather heavily on Beal and Wells, *History of Idaho*, 1:597–611, 2:2–118. Other Idaho histories have sections and chapters dealing with this period. Histories of the West and Pacific Northwest likewise mention Idaho statehood. Particularly good is Schwantes, *The Pacific Northwest*, 207–17.

Specialized sources and studies on the granting of statehood include: I. W. Hart, *Proceedings and Debates of the Constitutional Convention of Idaho, 1889* (Caldwell: Caxton Printers, 1912); Colson, *Idaho's Constitution*; Ronald H. Limbaugh, *Rocky Mountain Carpetbaggers: Idaho's Territorial Governors, 1863–1890*; Dennis L. Thompson, "Religion and the Idaho Constitution," *Pacific Northwest*

*Quarterly* 58 (October 1967):169–78; Merle Wells, "Idaho's Season of Political Distress: An Unusual Path to Statehood"; Leo W. Graff, Jr., *The Senatorial Career of Fred T. Dubois of Idaho, 1890–1907* (New York: Garland Publishing, 1988); David L. Crowder, "Pioneer Sketch: George Laird Shoup," *Idaho Yesterdays* 33 (Winter 1990): 18–22; Margaret Lauterbach, "A Plentitude of Senators," *Idaho Yesterdays* 21 (Fall 1977):2–8; Merle W. Wells, "The Idaho Admission Movement, 1888–1890," *Oregon Historical Quarterly* 56 (March 1955):27–46; and Clyde A. Bridger, "The Counties of Idaho," *Pacific Northwest Quarterly* 31 (April 1940):187–206.

Idaho's participation in the Chicago Columbian Exposition of 1893 is discussed in Don Hibbard, "Chicago 1893: Idaho at the World's Columbian Exposition," *Idaho Yesterdays* 24 (Summer 1980):24–29; and James M. Wells, *Idaho at the World's Columbian Exposition* (Boise: Statesman Printing, 1892).

The decline of the Idaho anti-Mormon movement in the 1890s is analyzed in Wells, *Anti-Mormonism in Idaho, 1872–92.*

The adoption of woman suffrage is treated in the Minute Book of the Idaho Equal Suffrage Association, Idaho State Historical Society, Boise; T. A. Larson, "Idaho's Role in America's Woman Suffrage Crusade," *Idaho Yesterdays* 18 (Spring 1974):2–15; T. A. Larson, "Woman's Rights in Idaho," *Idaho Yesterdays* 16 (Spring 1972): 2–19; "The Suffrage Idea in Idaho," in Beverly Beeton, *Women Vote in the West: The Woman Suffrage Movement, 1869–1896* (New York: Garland Publishing, 1986), 116–35; William Balderston and Eunice Pond Athey, "The Idaho Woman Suffrage Campaign," in Susan B. Anthony and Ida Husted Harper, eds., *The History of Woman Suffrage*, 4 vols. (Rochester, 1902), 4:589–97; Abigail Scott Duniway, *Path Breaking: An Autobiographical History of the Equal Suffrage Movement in Pacific Coast States*, 2d ed. (1914; repr., New York: Kraus Reprint Co., 1971); Ruth Barnes Moynihan, *Rebel for Rights: Abigail Scott Duniway* (New Haven, Conn.: Yale University Press, 1983); and Helen Krebs Smith, *The Presumptuous Dreamers* (Lake Oswego, Oregon: Smith, Smith and Smith Publishing Company, 1974).

91.

92.

93.

94.

91. President of the Idaho constitutional convention of 1889 was William H. Clagett, a pioneer of Shoshone County. ISHS 1102.

92. First elected governor of Idaho was George L. Shoup, who served 1890–91 until his election as United States senator. Shoup's statue is in Statuary Hall in the national Capitol. ISHS 1332.

93. William J. McConnell served as governor of Idaho, 1893–97. An early pioneer, he authored a book on the *Early History of Idaho* and was father-in-law of Senator William E. Borah. ERICKSON, MOSCOW, PHOTOGRAPHER, UIL 3–148B.

94. Designer of the seal of the State of Idaho was Emma Edwards Green. ISHS 71–72.1.

95.

95. Members of the Idaho Legislature posed for an official photo on the steps of the old Territorial Capitol in Boise in 1895. LDS CHURCH ARCHIVES PH 578.

96. 

96. Although begun in 1905, the state Capitol, modeled after the national Capitol, was not completed until 1920 at a cost of $2 million. UIL 6–22–4.

97.

97. Idaho proudly furnished troops to fight in the Spanish-American War. Here Idaho soldiers hang a Spaniard in effigy on May 3, 1898. GILBERT, PHOTOGRAPHER, UIL 6–5–5.

98. 

99. 

98. University of Idaho cadets march down Main Street in Moscow in May 1898 prior to their departure for the Philippines. UIL 6–5–3B.
99. Idaho women pack a box of supplies to send to their "boys" in the Philippines in 1898. UIL 6–5–11.

100.

100. A leading promoter of woman suffrage in Idaho was Abigail Scott Duniway. ISHS 461.

101. 

101. A group of both whites and Native Americans participated in a flag ceremony at Orofino on July 4, 1899. ISHS 2779.

## CHAPTER NINETEEN

# Depression, Silver Politics, and Violence

WHATEVER the social, cultural, and political reforms Idaho had adopted after 1890, the economic picture was bleak. First, there was a mild economic decline from July 1890 to May 1891 produced by the failure of the great English banking house of Baring Brothers of London. This started a drain on the United States gold reserve that became increasingly critical. That was followed by a financial panic in 1893 that shattered the mining prosperity of the 1880s and ushered in the worst depression the nation had experienced to that time.

The panic started in March 1893 when the Philadelphia and Reading Railroad Company and National Cordage Company went bankrupt, and the New York Stock Exchange agonized over the greatest selling spree in its history. In April the United States gold reserve fell below the $100 million mark, considered a safe minimum. Foreign investors were selling securities for gold, and gold was leaving the United States at an unprecedented rate. The market collapsed, banks called in their loans, and credit was not available. One great railroad after another went into receivership—the Erie, Reading, Northern Pacific, Union Pacific, and Santa Fe. Mills, factories, and mines shut down nearly everywhere. By the end of 1893 some six hundred banks, more than fifty railroads, and about 15,000 businesses had gone into bankruptcy.

The depression hit Idaho immediately. The banks in Wardner and Wallace closed in mid-April; three Spokane banks closed on June 6 and another two in July. The Boise clothing firm of T. C. Early failed in April; the Small and Colby Lumber Company in Kingston went broke in May; and P. H. Michael's cigar factory in Boise went up in smoke in August. The most noteworthy failure was the McConnell-Maguire Company of Moscow—the largest mercantile in Idaho—whose founder and principal stockholder was William J. McConnell, governor of Idaho from 1892 to 1896. Mining areas were also severely affected. Bunker Hill and Sullivan, Idaho's foremost silver-lead producer, curtailed operations on March 1; Custer County mines discontinued operations. Hundreds of unemployed men walked the streets. The *Idaho Daily Statesman* reduced its pages by half, and the *Pocatello Herald* simply quit publishing.

The impact of the depression on agriculture is suggested by the prices paid Idaho's farmers. Wheat, which had sold for $.82 a bushel in 1892, was down to $.36 in the fall of 1893. Corn was $.21. Apples sold for $.02 a pound, cabbage for $.02, potatoes for hardly more than $1.00 for a hundred-pound sack. Eggs were $.10 a dozen.

## SILVER POLITICS

Surrounded as he was by conservative financiers and business moguls, President Grover Cleveland had a simple solution: repeal the Sherman Silver Purchase Act of 1890 and maintain the gold standard. This approach clashed with the firm belief of

Idaho's silver miners and Populists that the real culprit was the "Crime of '73" that demonetized silver and reduced the circulating medium. Idaho's silver mines also suffered from the demonetization of silver in Europe and India. Westerners supported free and unlimited coinage of silver at a ratio of sixteen ounces to one of gold. They saw free coinage of silver as one hope of relief from currency contraction and declining prices and credit.

When Cleveland called a special session of Congress to repeal the Sherman Act, Idahoans were outraged. Silver rallies were held in Ketchum, Hailey, Moscow, Boise, Silver City, and Pocatello, each of which passed resolutions similar to those a large crowd of angry dissidents adopted at Ketchum on July 10, 1892:

> WHEREAS, The gold bugs and money monopolists of the world have conspired to demonetize the chief element of American currency, and thereby contracting the money of the nation to an amount entirely insufficient and inadequate for the needs of trade and commerce, and sacrificing the products of American labor and American industry for the enhancement of gold and the enrichment of money lenders, and
>
> WHEREAS, In his limited vision, and deluded by the interest sharks and money brokers of England and America, the President of the United States has issued a proclamation convening Congress in extraordinary session on the 7th of August for the purpose of absolutely demonetizing silver by the repeal of the Sherman Act, and
>
> WHEREAS, We believe the free and unlimited coinage of silver, at a ratio of 16 to 1, would relieve the financial distress now prevailing throughout the country, and restore prosperity to our people; therefore be it
>
> Resolved, That we, the people of Ketchum and the Upper Wood River Mining District, in mass meeting assembled, are unalterably opposed to the repeal of the legislation commonly known as the "Sherman Act" of 1890,

> except, that such legislation which repeals said act shall provide for the continued coinage and use of silver upon terms more favorable to the advocates of free coinage of silver than the measure proposed to be repealed, and our members in Congress are requested to adhere to the policy herein outlined.[1]

The repeal of the Sherman Act had little beneficial impact on the nation. The drain on the gold reserve continued, and so did the mounting depression. The editor of the *Idaho World* (Idaho City) wrote that Cleveland was a "thick-skulled, big-necked, beefy Mogul, who is not satisfied with present deplorable conditions which already bring the people to the verge of starvation, but seeks to make these conditions infinitely worse."[2]

Cleveland's action split the Democratic Party; liberals prepared to take control of the party in the 1896 convention. By January 1894 the gold reserve was down to $62 million. Alarmed, the President conducted a $50-million bond sale, followed by a second in November. In February 1895 the president relied upon a syndicate headed by New York banker J. Pierpont Morgan to buy $65 million in bonds, half subscribed by overseas investors who would pay in gold. Westerners, in particular, were indignant at this "sellout" to eastern financial interests. In any case, the depression deepened. Railroad construction fell off, factory workers lost their jobs, wages were cut, and farmers' markets declined. In 1894 approximately 20 percent of the nation's workers were unemployed. Almost no city provided work relief, and the federal government had no programs to provide help.

Jacob S. Coxey, a well-to-do businessman in Ohio, proposed a plan of federal work relief on public roads to be financed by an issue of $500 million in legal-tender Treasury Notes (like the greenbacks Lincoln had issued during the Civil War). When Congress refused to pass it, Coxey declared: "We will send a petition to Washington with boots on."[3] "Coxey's Army," as it was called—about 300 destitute men and a few sympathizers—marched peacefully from Ohio to Washington and paraded in protest on May Day 1894. Some twenty other "industrial armies" started for Washington in 1894 from Boston, Seattle, San Francisco, Los Angeles, and elsewhere, and more than 1,200 men eventually arrived.

Five of the largest of these "industrial armies" originated in the Pacific Northwest, which had been devastated by the depression. Beginning the second week of May they moved eastward across Washington, Oregon, and Idaho. The Portland army, led by stonemason S. L. Scheffler, followed the Union Pacific route across the southern part of the state through Weiser, Payette, Caldwell, Nampa, Pocatello, and Montpelier. Three Washington armies followed Northern Pacific and branch lines through northern Idaho to Helena. Unemployed and blaming their predicament on bankers and wealthy businessmen, they often hitched rides on passing trains. As they "landed" in various communities, residents, feeling compassion and wishing them well in their hope of "waking up" Congress, often provided food, clothing, money, and "three rousing cheers." This was true in Bonners Ferry, Wallace, Weiser, and indeed most Idaho towns. People were not convinced that it was a crime to steal rides or even a train. "Stealing trains," wrote the editor of the Spokane *Chronicle*, "is almost as popular as stealing railroads was a few years ago."[4] The Southern Pacific granted charity rates for their travel. The Union Pacific and Northern Pacific, however, forced into bankruptcy by the exigencies of the depression, refused to provide special rates and consistently appealed to judges to enjoin industrials from stealing rides on their trains.

When the advance guard of Scheffler's army moved from Oregon into Idaho, the Union Pacific threw them off its cars with a judge's injunction. They would be arrested if they tried to reboard. They were stranded in Caldwell, whose townspeople were angered that the railroad had brought the men into town and refused to take them out. After two days of complaint, Union Pacific agreed to haul them out, and they headed for Pocatello. Citizens there had collected 400 pounds of meat and 400 loaves of bread; but when city officials learned that 250 men were coming, they urged Union Pacific to take them through without stopping. Townspeople sent the provisions on to McCammon, where Sheffler's Coxeyites picked them up before they left for Montpelier. Union Pacific officials decided the time had come for a showdown, so they ordered their crews in Montpelier to sidetrack all trains carrying Coxeyites. The protesters were stranded again. The next day, May 13, about fifty of the men, some of whom were unemployed engineers and firemen, decided that if the railroad would not haul them they would haul themselves. They stole an engine and steamed out of Montpelier into Wyoming near Cokeville, about thirty miles away. They left the engine and camped in the sagebrush.[5]

The next morning the industrials who were still stranded in Montpelier decided to follow the example of the advance guard, but as they clambered aboard an engine they saw a special train carrying U.S. Marshal Joseph Pinkham, the U.P. division superintendent, and thirty deputies. The officials told the Coxeyites that anyone stealing a train would be shot. On the same day the mayor and other citizens of Montpelier held a town meeting and demanded that the marshal and U.P. superintendent allow the Coxeyites to move on. The marshal said his hands were tied, and he solicited community help in arresting the men and setting them up for trial in Boise. A saloonkeeper jumped to his feet and announced that he would never help arrest men whose only crime was that they were broke.

When several deputies resigned rather than make the arrests, the marshal and superintendent decided to avoid a "general killing" by allowing the men to go on. The Coxeyites took an engine and five empty boxcars and steamed off to join their comrades in Wyoming. The U.S. marshal and his deputies in Wyoming surprised the advance group near Cokeville and the main group at Green River. Reinforced by 275 soldiers rushed from Fort Russell, near Cheyenne, they confined 150 men and took them in sealed coaches to Fort Boise. They picked up a few who had been taken into custody in Pocatello and arrived in Boise on May 19 with 158 prisoners. There was no room in jail, except for organizer Scheffler and two or three others, so they put the prisoners in a roundhouse and empty boxcars. The men immediately sent a protest to Governor William J. McConnell, who visited the prisoners and complained that they were crowded like wild cattle into a pen without sleeping and sanitary accommodations. He insisted they be furnished with beds and blankets. Union Pacific wanted the whole group jailed; others wanted them slapped on the wrist and released on promise they would steal no more rides. After a trial of several days, Judge James H. Beatty called the movement a conspiracy, found every defendant guilty of contempt of court, and sentenced every one to prison. He suggested that the marshal consider releasing Coxeyites in groups of five to ten and having the Union Pacific transport them back to Portland.

Judge Beatty ordered the marshal and his deputies to construct and operate a special prison in the sagebrush wilderness where the Union Pacific crossed the Snake River from Idaho into Oregon. On June 12 the men, now totaling 184 (others had been caught and imprisoned), were taken to "Camp Pinkham." Deputies armed with rifles and sixshooters herded the men into ten waiting boxcars, the doors were nailed shut, and the special train of twenty cars carried the industrials, two infantry companies, Pinkham and his thirty deputies, and lumber for housing to the camp. The men were released in small groups until September 1, when the last man was freed. Union Pacific transported all of them to Portland.

Such harsh treatment was not unusual. In mid-August, after

other industrials had camped along the Potomac River opposite Washington for several weeks, the governor of Virginia dispatched state militia to destroy their shantytown and drive the men into the District of Columbia. There officials furnished them free transportation to the Midwest.

The wholesale imprisonment of western Coxeyites during June in Idaho ended the crusade, but an impression had been made on the nation's conscience. The poor working class had lost out to big business. The nation was willing to offer federal protection for railroads, but not federal assistance to the needy. This attitude would not change until the New Deal programs of the 1930s. Government authorities and businessmen of the time were fearful of riot, revolution, and violence. Management resorted to preventive violence, employed secret police, and secured injunctions from friendly courts. In some cases federal troops were used to crush striking workers. The administration's primary remedy for the widespread suffering and disorder, it seemed, was to maintain the gold standard.

Idaho's politics were especially affected by three results of the depression: the organization of the Populist Party, the split of the Republicans into Silver Republicans and Republicans, and the silverites' and inflationists' take-over of the Democratic Party.

Populism was a major third-party movement of the 1890s. Farmers, interested in regulating railroads and other public utilities, had formed the National Grange and other alliances and leagues. Laborers had formed the Knights of Labor (of which north Idaho unions were a part) to protect their interests. Idealists had formed Single-Tax Clubs and Bellamy Nationalist Clubs. All of these joined together in Kansas in 1890 to form the People's Party, and Populism was a natural derivative. The organization moved into other Great Plains states and the Northwest and was a viable political force. The National People's Party called for government ownership of the nation's railroads and telegraph and telephone systems; safe and sound national currency that would counter the deflationary trend; a graduated income tax; the return to the public domain of unsold land granted to railroads; a subtreasury system that would permit farmers to obtain government loans on stored crops; recognition of the right of laborers to organize; maximum eight-hour days for labor; and the direct election of United States Senators.

Idaho Populists, who first met in 1892, stood firm until 1904. In addition to national causes, Idahoans were angry at excessive steamship rates on the Columbia River system and the high prices Northern Pacific Railroad demanded for tracts from its land grant. Laborers complained about substandard wages, company-owned boarding houses, inadequate medical attention, and refusal to recognize unions. Moreover, free and unlimited coinage of silver was a universal objective—a rallying cry alike of Idaho's Democrats and Republicans. In the 1892 election the Populists won ten seats in the state legislature. The "Cleveland Depression" and the mistreatment of Coxey's army strengthened their appeal, but when the legislature met in 1894 the Populists were unable to push through any of their reforms. They did manage to delay the election of a Republican to the U.S. Senate until the fifty-second ballot.

When the earnest and gifted orator William Jennings Bryan ran for president in 1896, Idaho's Populists fused with the Democrats, as they did nationally, to support him and to nominate a state slate of offices divided equally between the two parties. Bryan, although losing a close election nationally, carried Idaho four to one, and the entire state Populist-Democrat ticket was swept into office. In the following legislative session the Populists accomplished almost nothing except that, after a great struggle, they secured the election of a political nonentity, Henry Heitfeld, to the United States Senate. In 1898 the Populists lost to the combined Democrat-Free Silver Republicans, who swept all offices at the state level and in all counties except

Shoshone, site of the Coeur d'Alene mining troubles of 1892 and the Populists' main source of strength. When the labor conflict of 1899 climaxed (as will be described later), the local union was destroyed and the Populists weakened. When the party failed to win in 1900, 1902, and 1904, it dissolved. As with the Coxeyites, the principal contribution of the Populists was to demonstrate that many Americans believed the federal government had some responsibility for the public welfare, something that would not happen until the 1930s.[6]

Not until 1897 did the economy improve significantly. Farm prices rose as the wheat crop in India failed. New gold discoveries in the Klondike and new methods of processing precious metals produced more gold and prices climbed. And the war with Spain over Cuba and the Philippines stimulated business and enhanced patriotism.

## THE PROGRESSIVE MOVEMENT

With the opening of the twentieth century many Americans became increasingly alarmed at the changes that had come with industrialization. Small businessmen, country bankers, farmers, clergymen, and newspaper editors spoke out against the political and economic controls exercised by privileged persons of wealth. Reformers demanded elimination of the industrial exploitation of women and children, removal of political bossism in the cities, improvement of conditions in the mines, and reduction in the power of railroads and industrial corporations. Their goal was to make local, state, and national government more democratic—more responsive to the needs of ordinary, unprotected, hard-working citizens. Among the measures advocated were abolition of child labor, limiting the number of hours women could work in factories, establishing minimum wages for women, formation of nonpartisan leagues to overthrow corrupt municipal political machines, adoption of the secret ballot, direct election of senators, direct primary, regulation of the rates and services of public utilities and railroads, and improvement of education. Progressives formed political-action groups aimed at wresting control from Republican and Democratic leaders who resisted changes in the status quo.

The progressive movement in Idaho was delayed because of the preoccupation of political leaders, particularly Fred Dubois, with anti-Mormonism. As Merle Wells has pointed out, progressive achievement in Idaho began with the end of the anti-Mormon revival of 1902–08.[7] In the latter year, for the first time, the local option on Prohibition and the direct primary replaced anti-Mormonism as the leading political issue. Both were enacted in 1908. Senator William E. Borah, who had replaced Dubois as U.S. Senator, helped persuade the U.S. Senate to agree to the direct election of senators and to approve an amendment enacting a graduated federal income tax. Borah also successfully promoted a bill to hasten construction of reclamation projects in the West, and Idaho was one of the first states to benefit from reclamation expenditures. The Idaho legislature chosen through the direct-primary method in 1910 established a state board of education, a state public utilities commission, a new state highway commission, and a Blue Sky law to protect investors in securities, and approved a commission form of city government.

In 1911 progressives formed the National Progressive Republican League in an attempt to secure the renomination of Theodore Roosevelt as president. When this failed, they united in a third (Progressive) party and in 1912 nominated Roosevelt. Predictably, with Republicans split—some voting for the official Republican nominee, William Howard Taft, and some for Roosevelt—the election was won by Democrat Woodrow Wilson. Among the measures supported by Wilson were the Federal Reserve Act, which reformed the currency system; the Clayton Antitrust Act and Federal Trade Commission Act, which extended government regulation of business; and the Keating-Owen Act, which restricted child labor. Constitutional amendments enacting the income tax and direct election of senators amendments were ratified. Under Senator Borah's sponsorship, the Department of Labor was created, and the Smith-Lever Act provided extensive aid for agricultural research.

With America's entry into World War I, however, the energy of progressives was diverted and the movement lost momentum until its reappearance during the 1930s. Its principal legacy was establishing the principle of government regulation of business.

## COEUR D'ALENE LABOR DISPUTE

As a part of the bitterness that grew out of the 1892 Coeur d'Alene labor dispute, the collapse of markets for minerals that caused mining companies to cut wages, and the excitement connected with the organization of Populist groups in the Northwest, the Western Federation of Miners was organized in Butte, Montana, in 1893. The aggressive president who was elected in 1896 and served to 1902 was Edward Boyce of Idaho. He was followed by Charles A. Moyer, president, and William D. Haywood (also an Idaho miner), secretary. The union participated in strikes in Cripple Creek and Leadville, Colorado, in 1894, and in the Coeur d'Alene area in 1899. But the miners' unions were still not recognized by mine management, which hired both union and nonunion laborers.

The Bunker Hill and Sullivan Mining Company, the greatest mineral producer in that section and employer of the largest number of men, was a principal focus of the miners. On April 24, 1899, all of the union men in the region marched in a body to the company offices in Wardner and demanded that all men working underground be paid $3.50 per day and that none but union men be employed. Not intimidated, the superintendent responded that the present scale of wages, varying from $3.00 to $3.50 per day, would be paid. The company would not recognize the union, he said, and any of the company's employees who were not satisfied with their work were free to take their pay and go elsewhere.

The next day similar demands were made of the Empire State Company and the Idaho Mining and Development Company. These companies closed down their operations. Union leaders decided the time had come to force the companies to comply with their demands, and meetings were held at which union members concurred in taking action against Bunker Hill and Sullivan. On April 29, several hundred miners captured a Northern Pacific passenger train connecting Burke with the other mining camps below. They ran the train down the canyon toward Wallace, stopped at Frisco, and stole 3,000 pounds of dynamite. The train then proceeded to Wallace, where many men belonging to the Mullan miners' union who had marched down the South Fork of the Coeur d'Alene were taken on. Many belonging to the Gem union also joined the crowd.

The train was directed on to Kellogg. The miners marched in a line, with almost military precision, to the Bunker Hill office and destroyed it with dynamite. They also demolished the nearby concentrating mill. (Among those placing the dynamite was Harry Orchard, of whom more later.) The unionists then marched back to Kellogg, boarded the captured train, and ran it back to Burke. Most of the participants wore masks so they would not be recognized.

Although the rioters had cut the telegraph wires to prevent communication with Boise, the news soon reached Governor Frank Steunenberg. A native of Keokuk, Iowa, Steunenberg was educated at Iowa State College of Agriculture in Ames, published a newspaper in Knoxville, Iowa, and in 1887 took over the *Caldwell Tribune*. He had served in the Idaho House of Representatives. At the head of a fusion ticket of Democrats, Silver

Republicans, and Populists in 1896, he was chosen governor, and he was reelected in 1898. His terms were colored by strife between sheepmen and cattlemen and by the labor troubles in the Coeur d'Alene district.

When Steunenberg learned of the troubles in the Coeur d'Alenes, he telegraphed President William McKinley (successor to Cleveland), asking for federal troops. On May 1, Captain Batchellor of Company M, First United States Infantry, arrived at Wardner with seventy-five soldiers. About 100 citizens of Coeur d'Alene were also sworn in as special officers to help maintain order. Disorder was rampant: on the way to the swearing-in ceremony three employees of Bunker Hill and Sullivan were captured by the miners, released, and ordered to run. As they fled, the miners fired, killing one of the men and wounding another. On May 3, Governor Steunenberg proclaimed martial law. By that time 600 federal troops were in the region, and more than 1,000 dissidents were arrested. Among those placed in custody were the sheriff and two county commissioners of Shoshone County, charged with having had previous knowledge of the intended outbreak and refusing to take action to prevent it.

The prisoners were kept under guard for a few days until a stockade, the "bull pen," was erected below Wardner to hold the men. The county coroner, in holding an inquest over the body of the Bunker Hill employee who was killed, questioned many miners and others over a period of several weeks. Governor Steunenberg likewise spent several days in the region investigating. He and other state officials, concluding that the state needed additional counsel to conduct the legal aspects of the proceedings, retained William Borah, James H. Hawley, and J. H. Forney, a prominent Moscow attorney.

Trial began on May 29 in the District Court of Shoshone County against parties charged with rioting, murder, and, in the case of the sheriff, dereliction of duty. The Western Federation of Miners employed lawyers from San Francisco, Spokane, and Wallace to conduct the defense. On July 8, Paul Corcoran, secretary of the Burke union, was singled out for punishment. After a hard forensic battle, he was found guilty on July 27 of murder in the second degree and sentenced to life imprisonment. Corcoran served in the state penitentiary in Boise only until the fall of 1901, when he received a full pardon from the Board of Pardons based on the fact that he had been found guilty primarily because he was just one party to a conspiracy formed for an illegal purpose.

Martial law remained in force in the Coeur d'Alenes for a year and a half, and a large number of men were confined in the "bull pen." Some of those men escaped and were never found. An era of good feeling followed, however, and no further efforts were made to prosecute. Most prisoners were released by the fall of 1899. But the troublemakers vowed vengeance against the governor who had set martial law in order, and Steunenberg received many letters threatening his life.[8]

A half dozen years later, on the night of December 30, 1905, when ex-governor Steunenberg opened the gate to the walk leading into his home in Caldwell, a bomb exploded; he was carried dying into his home. There was a speedy investigation, rewards were offered, and soon suspicion centered on Harry Orchard. Orchard (an alias for Albert E. Horsley), who was pretending to be a sheepman, apparently wanted to be caught—at least he was careless in leaving incriminating evidence in his hotel room and in his trunk at the railroad depot. There was an attempt to connect the Western Federation of Miners with the murder, so Moyer and Haywood employed an attorney. The state employed James McParland, head of the Denver office of the Pinkerton Detective Agency, to handle its investigation. McParland won a "confession" from Orchard, who also implicated Moyer and Haywood and George A. Pettibone, a Denver businessman and former union activist. They were arrested and transported to

Idaho in February. In his "confession" Orchard had accused an "inner circle" of the W.F.M. of having hired him to commit the Steunenberg murder and other murders and dynamitings. The case made headlines. The defense attorneys brought in Clarence Darrow, a nationally recognized defender. In the habeas corpus proceedings protesting Haywood's and Moyer's arrests the court ruled for the state; an appeal was made to the U.S. Supreme Court, which later ruled nothing remiss in the "kidnappings."

Many in the W.F.M. and other unions were not convinced of the "confession" of Harry Orchard. But the prevailing opinion held that the "inner circle" was responsible and that, with help and prompting, Orchard had done the deed out of personal revenge for having lost a one-sixteenth interest in the Hercules Mine as the result of the 1899 Coeur d'Alene labor dispute. There seemed to be some substantiation of many parts of his "confession," but few believed it all.

The trial against Haywood and the W.F.M. was watched all over the nation, by business, labor, and government. In his summing up, Borah attempted to demonstrate a network of intrigue, but the jury could find no proof of conspiracy. After an all-night deliberation the jury returned a verdict of not guilty; Haywood was released, and the case against Moyer was later dropped. Orchard, who had admitted his guilt, spent the rest of his life in the Boise penitentiary.[9] Although the W.F.M. was not thoroughly discredited, there were no recognized unions for years around the Coeur d'Alenes. (W.F.M. locals continued to function quietly but had no company agreements.) Borah's handling of the prosecution had brought him national fame, and he later won election six times to the United States Senate. Significantly, as a senator Borah upheld the cause of organized labor and consistently opposed business monopoly, although as an attorney he had worked for several large corporations.

The Haywood trial was sensational, and the labor troubles of

Idaho gained national attention, but the state was experiencing a period of resource development equally sensational. Several major reclamation projects greatly enhanced the state's production of crops; cattle and sheep raising became big business; and an important commercial lumber industry was established. The state was henceforth less dependent on mining.

## CHAPTER NINETEEN: SOURCES

There are treatments of the depression, silver politics, Populism, and Coxey's Army in several Idaho histories, but the most extensive is in Beal and Wells, *History of Idaho*, 2:72–199. Books and articles on these topics include John D. Hicks, *The Populist Revolt* (Lincoln: University of Nebraska Press, 1961); Clark C. Spence, *The Sinews of American Capitalism: An Economic History* (New York: Hill and Wang, 1964); Robert Higgs, *The Transformation of the American Economy, 1865–1914: An Essay in Interpretation* (New York: John Wiley & Sons, 1971); Charles Hoffman, "The Depression of the Nineties," *Journal of Economic History* 16 (June 1956):137–64; Claudius O. Johnson, "The Story of Silver Politics in Idaho, 1892–1902," *Pacific Northwest Quarterly* 33 (July 1942):283–96; William Joseph Gaboury, "The Stubborn Defense: Idaho's Losing Fight for Free Silver," *Idaho Yesterdays* 5 (Winter 1961–62):2–10; Thomas C. Riddle, "Populism in the Palouse: Old Ideals and New Realities," *Pacific Northwest Quarterly* 65 (July 1974):97–109; William J. Gaboury, *Dissension in the Rockies: A History of Idaho Populism* (New York: Garland Publishing, 1988); and Robert W. Larson, *Populism in the Mountain West* (Albuquerque: University of New Mexico Press, 1986).

An excellent treatment of Coxey's Army in Idaho is given in Carlos A. Schwantes, "Law and Disorder: The Suppression of Coxey's Army in Idaho," *Idaho Yesterdays* 25 (Summer 1981):10–15, and his follow-up book, *Coxey's Army: An American Odyssey* (Lincoln: University of Nebraska Press, 1985). See also Donald L. McMurry, *Coxey's Army: A Study of the Industrial Army Movement of 1894* (Seattle: University of Washington Press, 1968).

Good insights into the Progressive era are given in Robert Wiebe, *The Search for Order, 1877–1920* (New York: Hill & Wang, 1967); Higgs, *The Transformation of the American Economy*; Samuel P. Hays, *The Response to Industrialism: 1885–1914* (Chicago: University of Chicago Press, 1957); Arthur S. Link, *American Epoch: A History of the United States Since the 1890's*, 2d ed. (New York: Alfred A. Knopf, 1966), 68–91; and Richard Hofstadter, *The Progressive Movement, 1900–1915* (Englewood Cliffs, N.J.: Prentice-Hall, 1963). The Progressive movement in Idaho is well described in Beal and Wells, *History of Idaho*, 2:221–29; and Peterson, *Idaho: A Bicentennial History*, 161–64.

The labor unrest of the early years of statehood is best discussed in Jensen, *Heritage of Conflict*. Other treatments include: Fahey, "Ed Boyce and the Western Federation of Miners"; Phipps, *From Bull Pen to Bargaining Table*; Carlos A. Schwantes, "Patterns of Radicalism on the Wageworkers' Frontier"; Joseph R. Conlin, "The Haywood Case: An Enduring Riddle," *Pacific Northwest Quarterly* 59 (January 1968):23–32; Fahey, *The Days of the Hercules*; Livingston-Little, "The Bunker Hill and Sullivan: North Idaho's Mining Development from 1885 to 1900"; and James W. Montgomery, *Liberated Woman: A Life of May Arkwright Hutton* (Fairfield, Wash.: Ye Galleon Press, 1974, 1985), which includes a reprint of Hutton's *The Coeur d'Alenes; or, A Tale of the Modern Inquisition in Idaho* (1900).

102.

102. Frank Steunenberg, governor of Idaho, 1896–1900, was assassinated in 1904 in reprisal for calling out the National Guard at the time of a miners' strike in north Idaho. ISHS 66–16.1.

103. 

104. 

103. This panoramic view of the Bunker Hill and Sullivan Mill at Kellogg was taken in 1917. UIL 8–X412.

104. Striking miners drilled with wooden guns in the "bull pen" in Kellogg, 1899. UIL 8–X312.

105.

106.

105. Several hundred National Guardsmen were camped in Wallace in 1899. UIL 8–X486.

106. Ore-dressing mills, like this one at Coeur d'Alene, were essential to the mining business. ISHS 81–136.1.

CHAPTER TWENTY

# The Amazing Growth of Idaho's Agriculture and Forest Industries, 1890–1914

IN the two decades after statehood, Idaho's dramatic economic growth occurred in agriculture and forestry. Population increased from 88,548 in 1890 to 161,772 in 1900 and to 325,594 in 1910—almost a doubling each decade. An estimated 40,000 people came into the state from 1890 to 1900, and more than 100,000 from 1900 to 1910. That approximately 80 percent of the population was rural as late as 1910 suggests the continuing preeminence of agriculture.[1] Moreover, agricultural expansion took place all over the state. The Palouse country in north Idaho became one of the most productive wheat-growing regions in the nation; southwestern Idaho matured as a fruit- and sugar beet-growing region; south-central Idaho became a showcase of rich new irrigation spreads; and southeastern Idaho emerged as a leading producer of potatoes, sugar beets, and peas. In every part of the state hundred of herds of sheep and cattle could be found grazing.

The growth of the timber industry was equally notable. With

one of the largest forest acreages in the country, Idaho was, by World War I, a principal producer of timber. Forestry developed to be recognized as one of Idaho's three most important industries—following agriculture and mining.

Critical to the maturing of agriculture and timber industries was the development of water systems. In a state with a wealth of water and yet much land far distant from the sources, finding ways to irrigate and transfer water was vital. Both private enterprise and governments worked to solve the need for water, eventually producing the sophisticated network still in place today.

## CROP AGRICULTURE

During the placer boom of the 1860s numerous farms were established by whites and Indians around Lewiston to supply food to the thousands of men and women in the mining camps. The passage of the Homestead Act in 1862 encouraged men to claim land in the Palouse Hills just north of Lewiston, and by 1870 there were 1,588 persons in Nez Perce County. When farm prices recovered from the Panic of 1873, and the prospect emerged of the Northern Pacific getting crops to a distant market at reasonable cost, additional homesteads and preemptions were claimed. By 1877 45,000 Nez Perce County acres were producing more than one million bushels of grain. In that year Congress passed the Desert Land Act, which permitted the head of a family to "prove up" on 640 acres instead of the customary 160, and the population of Nez Perce County jumped to 3,965 by 1880. With the opening up of Camas Prairie, which had belonged to the Nez Perce, Idaho County increased from 849 inhabitants in 1870 to 2,031 in 1880. Latah County, formed out of Nez Perce County in 1888, had 9,173 people in 1890. During 1891 and 1892 Latah County produced more than a million bushels of wheat annually in addition to livestock, fruits, and vegetables. By the early 1890s north Idaho had 55,000 residents, of whom approximately 40,000 were engaged in agriculture.

The lower Snake River Valley, lying between King Hill and Weiser, experienced an agricultural boom during the mining development in Boise Basin and Owyhee in the 1860s. Because the waters of the Snake were comparatively inaccessible, farming acreages were served from the lower Bruneau, Boise, Payette, Owyhee, and Weiser rivers. Since the lower elevation afforded an additional month of growing weather, the lower Snake River Valley yielded, with irrigation, the greatest diversity of crops in the state.

In the early 1860s ranchers had been quick to claim the grassy lateral valleys; it was an easy step to irrigate along the creek and river bottoms. By the summer of 1864 all the river bottom land in Boise Valley was under irrigation. Pioneer farmers used sloughs and other natural depressions as links in their canals. Floods and washouts were common, but breaks were repaired with sagebrush and rocks. Farmers felt that prospecting for farms paid as well as prospecting for ledges. Gradually they expanded onto bench lands. But upstream diversion dams and canals required capital, so companies were organized. The key to the boost in agriculture was a dependable water system.

The Idaho legislature passed an act in 1881 entitling a person to file notice on a stream at the point of intended diversion and then record his claim, as miners did, at the county courthouse. Initial attempts were more costly than anticipated. In 1882 John H. Burns of New York organized the Idaho Mining and Irrigation Company and filed claims for 150,000 inches of Boise River water to be carried to both the east and west sides of the river valley. Not able to cover all costs of his intended project, Burns sold the rights to the west-side project to J. M. Stewart and James A. McGee of Philadelphia, who organized the Phyllis Canal. Their resources exhausted, they turned back the property to the Burns Company in 1888. A contract was let to complete the New York (east-side) and Phyllis (west-side) projects. By 1891 the Phyllis Canal extended thirty-five miles and had passed Nampa. Nevertheless, the Idaho Mining and Irrigation Company failed that year. The Phyllis and New York canals, taken over by the construction company, were promptly disposed of to farmers in the area.

In the eastern end of Boise Valley, the Farmers' Cooperative Ditch started a canal in 1875 and sold it in 1887 to Howard Sebree, who completed construction to irrigate 22,000 acres. The project was sold in 1896 to the Irrigation and Colonization Company of Salt Lake City. Several Methodist ministers tapped the Boise River on the opposite side of the Farmers' Cooperative Ditch with the Riverside Canal. Ownership soon passed to Boise businessmen and the operation was called the Boise Land and Water Company, which brought 12,000 acres under irrigation. The Indian Valley Irrigation Company was organized in 1883 to irrigate an extensive area called Dixie Country. Another group completed a canal twenty miles long in Payette Valley. Similar projects were developed in the Bruneau, Owyhee, and Weiser valleys. By 1900, 76 canals, totaling 568 miles of main and lateral ditches, served almost a quarter of the total valley of 400,000 acres. Without these projects the whole area of the lower Snake would have remained desert, providing only scanty feed for cattle and passing bands of sheep.

In southeastern Idaho the earliest projects were cooperatively developed by farmers at relatively low cost. The Cub River and Worm Creek Canal, near Franklin, extended fifteen miles, watered 15,000 acres, and cost only $30,000. The Upper Snake River Valley, settled by ranchers in the 1870s and by farmers starting in 1879, had an abundance of water and many manageable tributaries. The first filing upon Snake River water was entered by the Eagle Rock and Willow Creek Canal Company on June 11, 1880. The 160 second-feet of water from a point below Heise Hot Springs was intended to irrigate land in the Menan district. As the number of settlers multiplied, canal-building became a mania. By 1885, 28 canals had been dug in southeastern Idaho, and by 1906 there were 264 canals—virtually all of them farmer-built, locally owned cooperative canal systems.

A strong organizer of these projects was Thomas E. Ricks.[2] Born in southwestern Kentucky, near the Tennessee border, Ricks came from a farming family of eight children. An accident in 1844, when Thomas E. was sixteen, left him partially disabled the rest of his life. Nevertheless, he crossed the Great Plains in 1848; on the trip he was shot three different times by Indians and left to die. Surviving, he helped to colonize Centerville, Farmington, and Cache Valley, Utah, and Las Vegas, Nevada, and served as sheriff, assessor, and tax collector in Logan, Utah. His introduction to Idaho came from serving in the Salmon River Mission at Lemhi. From his work as a contractor building the grade for the Utah and Northern Railway from Franklin to Butte during the late 1870s, he went on to supervise grading for the Northern Pacific Railway in Montana, northern Idaho, and eastern Washington in the early 1880s.

After spending five years in the Upper Snake River Valley, Ricks was asked by Mormon authorities to direct these burgeoning settlements. He was the first Mormon bishop of the region, the first stake president, and also Idaho's official delegate to the National Irrigation Congress in the 1890s. His major achievement was the massive drive to construct the Great Feeder Dam on the South Fork of the Snake River in 1894–95. The dam was built during the winter by men and teams from a score of small cooperative farmer companies who hauled rock and cottonwood timber from nearby canyons. By 1895 the Great Feeder system was diverting 110,000 inches of water to be used for agricultural purposes. Built and owned by small farmers, it was a testimony both to the favorable topography and to the previous experience with irrigated agriculture of men like Ricks.

The enterprise was completed in June 1895. A thousand

people came to see the project and exult in the accomplishment: it was the largest single irrigation project in the world. Conducting the ceremony was Richard F. Jardine, son of a Scottish Mormon immigrant and founder-bishop of Lewisville, several miles to the south of Menan. The Idaho Canal and Improvement Company, another consolidation of farmer-owned and -managed ditches that included more than three hundred miles of canals and laterals in Fremont and Bingham counties, soon followed.

The first dam on the main channel of the Snake River was a joint undertaking by the Idaho Canal Company and the Great Western Canal Company (a consolidation of local farmer cooperatives). In the spring of 1900 logs, lumber, and rocks were stockpiled 5 feet high and 944 feet across on a site about twelve miles north of Idaho Falls. Built in five months, this dam was replaced by a concrete structure in 1912.

Farther down Snake River the Watson Slough, Corbett Slough, Neilson-Hansen, Fox-Whitten, Center Branch, Reservation Canal, Parsons, Snake River Valley, and Blackfoot Irrigation ditches were all built by farmers. Another pioneer-type irrigation system still farther down the river was in the Oakley area on Goose Creek, where Mormon settlers had dug ditches as early as 1879. The original pioneer tract consisted of about 1,000 acres. As years passed and new settlers arrived, that system was enlarged and the area of cultivation greatly expanded.

## THE CAREY ACT

Because previous land laws had failed to facilitate the settlement of arid agricultural land, Congress in 1894 passed the Carey Act. The government would cede up to one million acres to any western state willing to undertake the reclamation of lands under the grant. The land could then be sold in parcels as small as forty acres. The state and private investors had ten years to complete a project after beginning construction. The construction company sold water rights to the farmer and the state sold the land for 50 cents an acre. Idaho took advantage of these provisions and, in fact, in one of its projects became a national showcase for the success of the Carey Act.

Several men caught the vision for the successful development of south-central Idaho. There were Frank Riblett and John Hansen, Cassia surveyors and farmers, who ran lines for possible reclamation sites; Paul Bickel, chief engineer of the Twin Falls project; John E. Hayes, his young assistant; Stanley Milner, a Salt Lake City banker who financed the initial surveys; and Frank Buhl and Peter Kimberly, iron and steel manufacturers of Sharon, Pennsylvania, who raised $3.5 million. But the single personality dominating the project was Ira B. Perrine.

A native of Indiana, Perrine had come to Idaho in 1883 when he was twenty-two. Working in the Wood River mines near Hailey, he recognized a need to provide food for miners. After many months he rode across the desert to Idaho Falls, bought forty dairy cows, and drove them back to the mines to furnish milk, butter, and meat to the miners. During the fall of 1884, in need of winter pasture, Perrine moved his herd south to the Snake River Canyon and located a few miles below Shoshone Falls in a deep alcove within the canyon walls. There he found abundant grass watered by two clear emerald lakes fed by underground springs—the Blue Lakes, as they came to be known. He planted trees and grew wheat, fruits, vegetables, and berries, which he marketed in mining camps and in villages of Cassia County. After succeeding with irrigation at Blue Lakes, he was ready in 1900 to water 500,000 acres by taking water out of the Snake at a point known as The Cedars, the site of Milner Dam. Appreciative of the work of the surveyors and engineers, he began raising the money to fashion an agricultural empire.

Perrine got $30,000 from Stanley Milner and incorporated the Twin Falls Land and Water Company in 1900, secured money from a Chicago bonding house, filed notice for the diversion of water on both the north and south sides of the Snake, contracted with Idaho to develop 270,000 acres under the Carey Act, and began to sell land at 25 cents an acre and water rights at $25 per acre. Milner Dam was completed by 1905 and water diverted into a canal 10 feet deep, 80 feet wide at the bottom, and 120 feet at the top. Water thus became immediately available to 60,000 acres of Magic Valley farmland. By 1905, Twin Falls had its first bank, doctor, attorney, dentist, barber, school, newspaper, restaurant, and roominghouse. In addition, new towns in the valley sprang up: Hansen, Kimberly, Filer, Buhl. The project included 244,000 acres watered by gravity flow of the Snake for 1,295 farms. One writer described it as "one of the miracles of modern American life"—one reason that people came to call it Magic Valley.[3]

Ultimately, Perrine was able to obtain financial support from Pennsylvanians Williams S. and James S. Kuhn to complete the 185,000-acre North Side Project, eventually encompassing Jerome, Hazelton, Eden, and Wendell as well. The Kuhns were Pittsburgh commercial and investment bankers, coal and traction-car enterprisers and principal stockholders in the American Water Works and Guarantee Company of Pittsburgh. In the financial panic of 1913, however, their industrial and financial empire crumbled, and the Twin Falls North Side Land and Water Company almost collapsed.

Sympathetic to the plight of North Side settlers, the U.S. Reclamation Service (later the Bureau of Reclamation) provided water from the Jackson Lake, Wyoming, storage beginning in 1914–15 in return for a cash settlement to pay for additional dam construction. Beginning in 1916 the project was able yearly to tap 315,000 acre-feet of water from Jackson Lake. The cultivated area increased from 65,000 acres in 1915 to 120,000 acres in 1919, and the tract population rose to about 15,000 people. Unfortunately, this tract, which also obtained water from Milner Dam, then developed significant problems. Because of the porous soil the contemplated storage reservoir would not fill. Perrine and his associates were forced to ask the Reclamation Service to increase the holding capacity of Jackson Lake. These private investors, normally suspicious of government, were delighted when the federal water came to supply their thirsty late-season crops. The North Side project, enlarged over the years to 185,000 acres, was slower in finding success than the South Side but nevertheless reflects Perrine's leadership in building the Magic Valley empire.

The Kuhn interests were also induced to participate in Carey Act projects on Salmon Falls Creek southwest of Twin Falls and near Oakley, almost south of Milner Dam. Oversold, the Salmon Falls tract was never able to deliver water to all the promised acres. But the dam was erected, some 12,000 acres of land were provided with water, and the project is still supplying acreage. The Oakley Dam on Goose Creek, said to have been the largest earth-filled dam in the world, was begun in 1911. When Kuhn Brothers went broke in 1913, the settlers themselves completed the 21,000-acre project.

Although none was as spectacular as Magic Valley, several other Carey Act projects were established in Idaho. Idaho's State Board of Land Commissioners, with the responsibility of contracting with private entrepreneurs and supervising irrigation systems under the Carey Act, authorized twenty-five projects. The first of these was the Aberdeen-Springfield Canal. In 1894 William Reece, John Parsons, Charles Corbridge, and others determined to provide water to a tract west of the Moreland-Thomas district. The farmers filed on 1,250 second-feet of Snake River water at a point three miles downstream from the Firth bridge. The canal reached the Aberdeen tract in 1895.

A second project was a 6,000-acre tract at Marysville, east of Ashton in Fremont County. Designed to convey water from Fall River, thirteen miles to the east, this project was authorized in 1898 but had legal and financial problems. James H. Wilson and others had settled the acres in 1889 and had brought water to the land. Some of these early settlers who had built diversion works opposed the development. When a legal injunction was lifted, construction problems delayed completion. The dam had to be built three times, and the price of the water contracts doubled. The canal, finally completed in 1914, was named Brady Canal after a leading investor in the enterprise, James H. Brady, Idaho's governor from 1908 to 1910.[4]

A third project, accepted in 1899, was the American Falls Canal and Power Company, designed to reclaim about 60,000 acres in Power and Bingham counties. The project was completed in 1910; but with no reservoir to store water for the dry season, the company was unable to provide sufficient water for the entire tract. (The American Falls Reservoir was completed in 1927.)

According to historian Hugh T. Lovin, who has made a careful study of the records of the twenty-five projects authorized by the Idaho Land Board between 1905 and 1914, twenty-three remained functional, placing 850,000 acres under cultivation. The Carey Act had attracted $100 million from out of state and was deemed responsible for a population increase of 50,000 people.[5]

## FEDERAL RECLAMATION IN IDAHO

With the build-up of settlement in Idaho and other arid and semiarid states, national leaders became persuaded that only the federal government could solve the problem of water rights on interstate streams. Moreover, federal construction of storage reservoirs would offset the tendency toward land monopoly that characterized some state operations. A national program was inaugurated in 1902 with the passage of the Newlands Act. The act, which opened reclamation projects to Homestead Act entries, provided that the construction of dams and canals would be supported by the income derived from the sale of arable western land. Frederick H. Newell, of the hydrographic branch of the Geological Survey, was the commissioner in charge, and he employed an extremely capable force of civil engineers to plan and supervise the construction of high-level dams. Among the first of these federal projects were two in Idaho: Minidoka and Boise.

The Minidoka Project used a complex system of storage on distant Jackson Lake, Wyoming, a diversion dam on the Snake River, and both gravity and pumped distribution to enable homesteaders to settle lands in Minidoka County. The earth-fill dam, 85 feet high and almost a mile long across the Snake River, provided water to 120,000 acres on both sides of the Snake near the Minidoka rapids, about thirty-five miles upstream from Milner Dam. Fifteen miles from Rupert, the dam was started in 1904 and completed in 1906 at a cost of $6.5 million. It impounded a volume of 107,000 acre-feet in Lake Walcott, providing water for 116,000 newly cultivated acres. The canal and distributing system, completed in 1907, diverted water on both the north and south sides of the river, irrigating Heyburn, Paul, Acequia, and Rupert. The canal dug on the north side of the Snake, carrying the first water provided by the U.S. Reclamation Service, was suited for gravity flow; the system on the south side that serviced Burley had a series of pumping stations to move the water. At the same time, the Reclamation Service had under construction a timber-crib storage dam on Jackson Lake, Wyoming, 300 miles upstream to provide water to the Twin Falls North Side and Minidoka projects. Population in the area served by Minidoka alone increased 14,500.

In addition to supplying much needed water, the Minidoka Project pioneered the production and distribution of power. The Minidoka Dam created a fifty-foot head for hydroelectric generation, and a 7,000-kilowatt power plant began operating in 1909 to pump irrigation water. A large share of the plant's capacity powered three lifting stations that raised canal water to 50,000 acres of the project's South-Side Unit. Because the reservoir had a relatively constant year-round head, a substantial surplus of energy was available even in summer months when the pumping plants were in full operation. Along the transmission lines groups of farmers and small towns organized cooperative utility companies, built their own distribution systems, contracted with the Reclamation Service for power, and sold it to themselves. Within a decade, household and farm use of electricity was common throughout the project, and reclamation power was helping to process sugarbeets, mill flour, and manufacture cattle feed. By 1920 more than 1,100 farm families were obtaining electricity from twenty mutual power companies that maintained 190 miles of distribution lines. Long before many other rural areas in the state, 6,000 household electrical appliances were operating on the project, including 2,000 electric irons, 1,000 washing machines, 310 vacuum cleaners, and 246 ranges. In 1914 Rupert attracted national attention by building one of the world's first large electrically heated buildings. The town also constructed an all-electric, three-story brick high school for 600 students, the first in the West.

The Boise Project (earlier called the Payette-Boise Project) added water storage and improved privately built canals to supplement the water supply to developed farms in the Boise Valley. Planning for the project began before the Reclamation Act was passed, and the early work concentrated on an off-stream storage reservoir, Lake Lowell in Canyon County, and a canal network. By the summer of 1910 funding was available to construct a dam on the Boise River that would store water for irrigation in the late summer months when the river supply was insufficient. Arrowrock Dam, named for an outcrop of rock that jutted over the river near the dam, was twenty-two miles upstream from Boise. A diversion dam was built in 1912 to channel the river around the Arrowrock construction area. A specially built

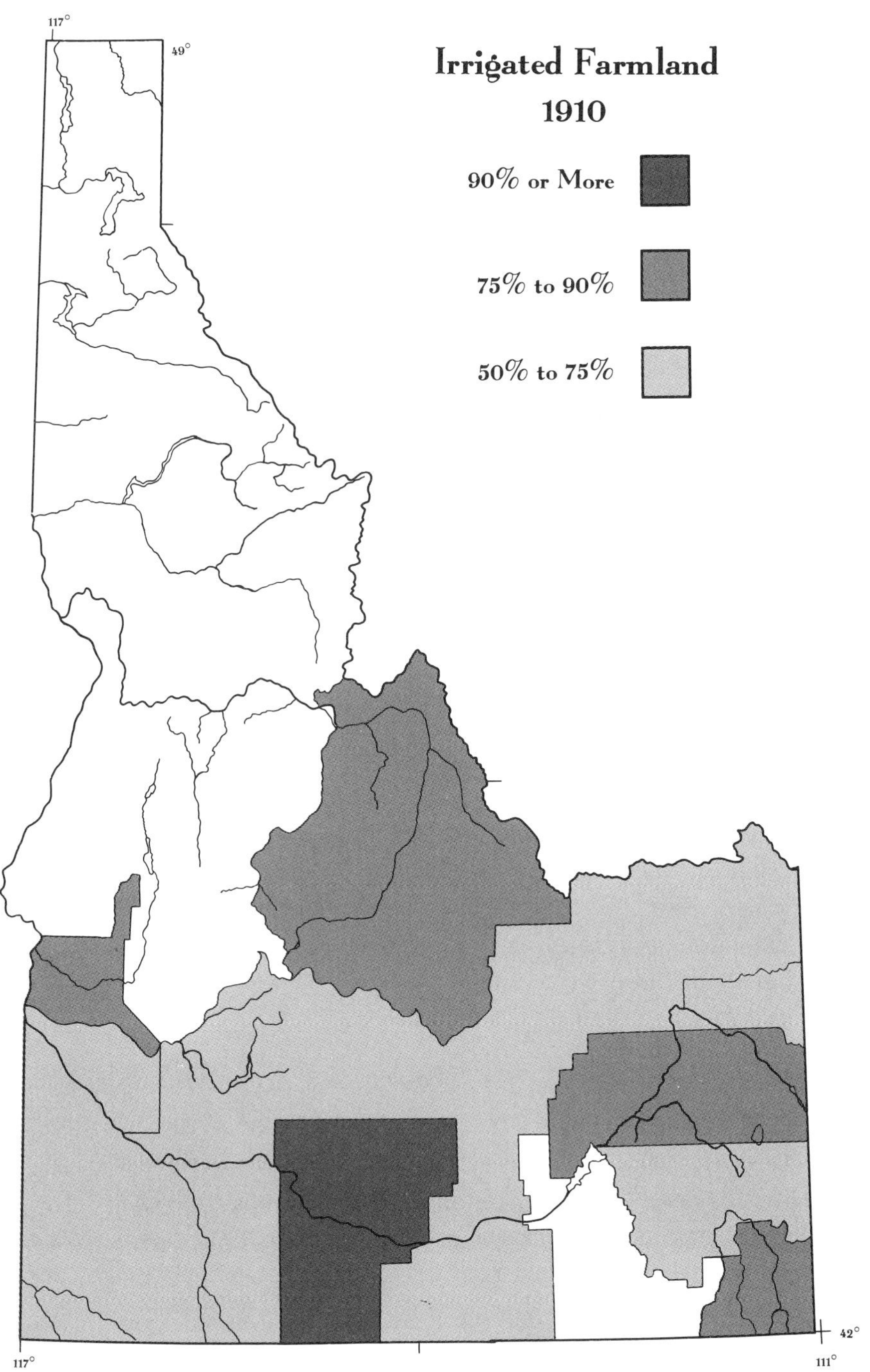
117°
49°
Irrigated Farmland
1910
90% or More
75% to 90%
50% to 75%
42°
117°
111°

1,500-kilowatt power plant ran concrete mixers and other machinery; a sawmill and a sand cement plant were built at the site to supply lumber and cement. A telephone system—some fifty-four miles of lines—was connected with the U.S. Reclamation Service office in Boise; a seventeen-mile standard-gauge railroad connected Arrowrock with Barberton, a timber mill site just northeast of Boise, and with connections to the Oregon Short Line Railway. Some 1,500 men were employed to build the dam, which was begun in 1911 and finished in 1915, two years ahead of schedule.

The $12-million Arrowrock project was built entirely by engineers, mechanics, laborers, and teamsters on the federal payroll. In this way the Reclamation Service received the needed experience for building the American Falls Dam of the 1920s and the gigantic projects of the 1930s and 1940s—Hoover, Grand Coulee, Shasta, and later Glen Canyon. Arrowrock Dam, the highest in the world until 1932, was 348 feet tall (raised to 353 feet in 1937). It was dedicated on October 4 and 5, 1915, and its importance was accurately expressed in Boise's *Evening Capital News* on October 4, 1915:

> Few outside the semi-arid sections of the west realize what this means, this conversion of a vast tract of blistering waste into fruitful gardens, orchards and farms—this transformation of a weary stretch of sagebrush desert into an abode of thrifty and contented citizens with their homes, their villages and their schools.

The reservoir, eighteen miles long, could store 276,000 acre-feet of water. Since the summer of 1915 was one of the driest on record, the availability of water was "a godsend to thousands of settlers."[6] Serving the area around Boise, Nampa, and Caldwell, the Boise Project provided water for about 170,000 acres of irrigable land.

In 1917, about the time the United States entered World War

I, the federal Reclamation Service took control of two small Carey Act projects, called the King Hill Project, between Boise and Twin Falls. This project served about 15,000 acres of land.

The Carey Act and Reclamation Act, of which Idaho took full advantage, were the principal factors in causing the population of Idaho to jump by 164,000 between 1900 and 1910. By the end of that decade all of Idaho's present urban centers had come into existence. In addition, the Carey and Reclamation act projects, along with various farmers' mutual companies, fostered the development of three industries that were significant to Idaho's agriculture: potatoes, peas, and sugarbeets.

DRY FARMING. Much rich farmland in Idaho has inadequate rainfall and yet cannot be irrigated—bench land, undulating terrains, and land distant from streams. Where the soil retains moisture, and where at least ten inches of rainfall falls from April to September, the land might still be farmed by proper soil culture. One must plow in the fall, plow deep, cultivate after every rain, fallow the land every other year, and grow drought-resistant crops, mainly wheat. The Mormons experimented with this dry-farming technique in the 1880s and 1890s and the science was further developed by Dr. John A. Widtsoe at Utah State Agricultural College in the 1890s. Dry-farming was practiced among Mormons and other farmers throughout the region—in Oneida, Caribou, Power, Bingham, Bonneville, Jefferson, Madison, Fremont, and Teton counties.[7]

In 1911 the University of Idaho established a branch agricultural experiment station in Aberdeen. The Aberdeen Valley Land Development Company and its canal system were nearing completion, and dry farms were located nearby, so university scientists could experiment in both irrigated and dry-farm agriculture. Potatoes were the most important crop in terms of the number of research projects conducted.[8]

## FARMING AND ORCHARD PROJECTS

FRUIT. Idaho became a serious contender in fruit production beginning about 1890 when 2,600 acres of fruit were harvested in southwestern and northern Idaho. By 1897 more than 30,000 acres of fruit—mostly apples, prunes, pears, peaches, and cherries—were in production. Latah County led with 5,900 acres; Ada came second with 5,500; Canyon third at 5,300. In 1900, fruit was grown on 36,000 acres; by 1902, 43,000 acres; in 1905, 50,000 acres; in 1915 about 65,000 acres, of which 45,000 acres were in apples, 15,000 in prunes, and 5,000 in peaches, pears, and cherries.[9]

POTATOES. The first potatoes in Idaho were grown by Henry Harmon Spalding at Lapwai in 1837. His 1838 crop was estimated at 800 bushels. In 1860 the Franklin settlers planted potatoes. Ten years later a freighter hauled a load of potatoes from Farmington, Utah, to the Snake River region north of Fort Hall, and these furnished seed for the first potatoes planted in that area. By 1882, 2,000 acres were planted to potatoes in Idaho. The mass of new settlers from Utah introduced the Burbank potato from California, and by 1904 Idaho harvested 17,000 acres. Eleven years later acreage had increased to 33,000. Idaho potatoes yielded well and were large, white, mealy, and delicious. Thousands of carloads of "spuds" were shipped from the state to eastern markets over the Oregon Short Line in the late 1880s and 1890s.

Nearly all potatoes were the russet Burbank. Born in Lancaster, Massachusetts, Luther Burbank became a plant breeder in north central Massachusetts and in the 1870s developed the characteristic Burbank potato. When he moved to Santa Rosa, California, in 1875, he took with him ten of the smooth-skinned, long white tubers and introduced them to growers there.[10]

But the Idaho potato was more than an ordinary Burbank. The russet Burbank of Idaho had a slightly rough, reticulated skin and was commonly called the Netted Gem. The russet, originated by Lon D. Sweet, a plant breeder in Denver, was developed from a chance sport or mutation out of the Burbank. Although not more attractive, the potato was resistant to tuber diseases and "blight"—potato scab and other diseases—a quality that enhanced its value with growers. The russet mutation involves only the outer layers of the tuber.

Potato scientists have speculated that it was not the russet Burbank that made Idaho famous, but rather Idaho that made the russet Burbank famous. Idaho's growing conditions and growers simply produce a superior variety. Potatoes grow well in high altitudes where the growing season is warm and sunny in the day and cool at night, where the soil contains a high level of moisture (regulated by growers with irrigation), and where the soil is light like the volcanic ash in Idaho's potato-growing areas. Moreover, there is a skill in growing a smooth elongated russeted tuber that pleases both the eye and palate; growers without experience often grow russets that are knobby and misshapen. As the only potato-growing area that produced ideally shaped and flavored russet Burbanks, Idaho earned the reputation for being the source of the world's finest bakers. Noted reporter John Gunther once asked an Idaho patriot why the potatoes are so big. His answer: "We fertilize 'em with cornmeal, and irrigate with milk."[11]

SUGAR BEETS AND BEET SUGAR MANUFACTURING. Just as the Idaho soil and climate were well suited to the production of superior potatoes, they were equally effective in the production of sugar beets. An important sector of the French agricultural economy since the days of Napoleon, the industry was introduced in the United States in the 1880s and 1890s with the erection of factories in Wisconsin, California, Nebraska, and Utah. Sugar beets are a labor-intensive product requiring a garden-like culture, particularly suited to the irrigated villages of northern Utah because of the abundance of labor for thinning and harvesting and the strong desire of the oft-persecuted Mormons to achieve self-sufficiency. With the Mormon Church acting as entrepreneur, Utah sugar farmers developed a skilled personnel and successful operating technique. Factories were erected at Lehi, Ogden, Garland, Logan, and Lewiston in northern Utah, and at La Grande, Oregon.

Many Mormons who settled southeastern Idaho were anxious to generate a cash crop. Improved beet seed was imported from Europe. Agricultural implements were designed and refined for preparation of the ground, planting of seed, cultivating the growing plant, digging the beets at harvest-time, and transporting the product to the factory. At the plant, satisfactory equipment was perfected for receiving beets and washing, transporting, and conveying the material to be processed from station to station. The industry was well suited to irrigated agriculture because the water could be supplied in late summer when rainfall was minimal.

The Carey and Newlands acts opened up sun-drenched areas suited to beet culture. The U.S. Department of Agriculture favored the industry, believing that factories would benefit farming communities economically, socially, and even culturally. Indeed, a factory would assure more employment, higher wages, a better market for products, and a more stable farm income. The following is from a U.S.D.A. circular:

> Each sugar factory requires from 200 to 400 laborers. These must all be supplied with produce from the gardens, fields, dairies, poultry yards, orchards, feed yards, etc. A similar demand affects the business of the merchant, the banker, and local businessmen in all other lines. It has been estimated that several towns have been increased in

> two or three years to the extent of one-third or one-half their population, entirely on account of the additional business and opportunities caused by the location of a sugar factory.
>
> The sugar-beet lands of Utah were very much enhanced in value, so that the experience of this country up to the present time seems to be that the location of a beet-sugar factory in a district causes a healthy rise in rents and values of lands. . . . On Saturday afternoons and evenings the people appear on the streets well dressed, looking happy and contented, showing in every way the effects of prosperous conditions. . . .
>
> So prosperous has Lehi become that in 1896 there was not a single delinquent taxpayer.[12]

The Department of Agriculture was also impressed with the beet because the sugar was sold to humans, the tops and pulp and molasses were fed to animals, and the roots remained in the soil to enrich and condition it. Beets were an ideal crop for rotation with grains, vegetables, and other crops. The industry also lent itself to diversification and stock feeding, improved the land, and provided the farmer on irrigation projects with the cash to meet his payments and to buy new equipment.[13]

By 1902, the success of the Lehi and other factories was so marked that Mormon authorities determined to build additional factories in other settlements. Financial backing for this expansion was provided in 1902 by Henry Havemeyer and fellow stockholders in the American Sugar Refining Company of New York City, which owned or controlled 98 percent of the nation's sugar-refining capacity—nearly all in cane sugar.

As the beet-sugar industry became increasingly competitive, ASR began to purchase a controlling interest in independent beet companies. The Mormon Church quite willingly sold a 50 percent interest in its Utah Sugar Company because Havemeyer, as president of ASR, insisted on keeping the same local management, with full local autonomy, and indicated his willingness to participate on a fifty-fifty basis in the construction of additional factories. With the money from this sale, Utah Sugar formed the Idaho Sugar Company, followed shortly by the Fremont County Sugar Company and the Western Idaho Sugar Company, and the acquisition of the Snake River Valley Sugar Company. With Havemeyer's participation, these companies built plants at Idaho Falls (1903), Sugar City (1904), Blackfoot (1904), Nampa (1906), Shelley (1917), and Rigby (1919). The companies and their plants merged with the Utah Sugar Company in 1907 to form the Utah-Idaho Sugar Company. Until its discontinuance in the 1970s, Utah-Idaho was one of the major beet sugar producers in the nation. Most of those involved in the early stages of the industry in Idaho were Mormons.

An example of local management of these factories was Mark Austin. Born in Bedfordshire, England, he emigrated with his parents to Utah in 1868, when he was six. As a young man he had experience working in the factory at Lehi, Utah, then was employed by the Great Western Sugar Company in Loveland, Colorado, and finally was manager of Utah-Idaho factories in Idaho Falls and Sugar City. He was LDS bishop in Sugar City and later Fremont Stake president.

The Idaho factories, costing about $750,000 each, were among the largest in the nation. Approximately 200 persons were employed by each factory during the processing season. The Idaho Falls factory, to give one example, originally had a capacity of 600 tons per day. During its first year it processed 37,000 tons of beets to produce 72,000 100-pound bags of sugar. Within three years the factory processed double this figure. The capacity was raised to 900 tons until 1922, when it jumped to 1,200 tons per day. Still later the daily slicing capacity was increased to 4,000 tons. The plant produced 1.5 million bags of sugar annually in the 1960s. Utah-Idaho expended in excess of $100 million in the district for beets, labor, and materials. When it was built, the Sugar City plant surpassed the Idaho Falls plant. Indeed, it was the largest beet sugar factory in the nation. As early as 1906, for example, it produced more than 200,000 bags of sugar. The Sugar City factory maintained an auxiliary cutting plant on the Egin Bench at Parker, Idaho, some six miles distant. A pipeline carried beet juice from the cutting plant to the refinery.

With the improvement of country roads and transportation and a declining local labor supply, processing beets was more economical at large, efficient, centralized plants. For that reason the Sugar City factory was closed in 1943 and sugarbeets produced in the Sugar City district were then processed in the Idaho Falls factory. During the thirty-seven years of its operation, the Sugar City factory had processed 2.1 million tons of sugarbeets and extracted 8.1 million 100-pound bags of sugar. U&I and its predecessors expended an estimated $25 million in the district for beets, labor, and supplies.

For similar reasons the Blackfoot factory closed in 1949, and the district's beets were also processed thereafter in the Idaho Falls factory. The Rigby and Shelley factories closed in 1939 and 1942 as a result of insect infestation.

Company agent at Nampa was Edward Henry Dewey, born in Ruby City, Idaho, in 1869, the son of Colonel William Henry Dewey, one of the founders of Silver City. The younger Dewey purchased the townsite of Nampa from Alexander Duffus; built the Dewey Palace Hotel, a western showplace; and led the incorporation of the Boise, Nampa, and Owyhee Railroad, which eventually built a line to serve Silver City through Murphy. As a young man, E. H. Dewey served as superintendent of the Black Jack and other mines in Owyhee and supervised the erection of three large quartz mills. He moved to Nampa in 1898, started banks, a power company, and an irrigation company, and served in the state senate. The Nampa factory, however, was not successful. Beets were invaded by the white fly, an insect carrying a virus that caused beet leaves to curl up and turn yellow; both the tops and roots shriveled and ceased to grow. As the "blight," as the disease was called, reduced the production of beets, the harvest was not sufficient to justify operation. The infestation continued for several years, and the company closed the Nampa plant in 1911 and in 1916 moved the machinery to Spanish Fork, Utah.

U&I's only remaining plant in Idaho in the 1970s was the large Idaho Falls factory. As U.S. government policy became increasingly less favorable to the sugarbeet industry, profits evaporated; in 1979 the company closed all of its remaining factories, including the one in Idaho Falls.

Beet sugar factories were also built in Idaho by David Eccles, a Mormon entrepreneur whose fortune was triggered by supplying timber during the Wood River excitement of the 1880s. He had followed the Oregon Short Line and established the immensely successful Oregon Lumber Company at Baker. Eccles founded the Amalgamated Sugar Company, made an arrangement with Henry Havemeyer and the American Sugar Refining Company similar to that of U&I Sugar, and built plants at Burley (1912), Twin Falls (1916), and Paul (1917). Later refineries built or acquired by Amalgamated included one in 1922 at Whitney (near Preston); one in 1938 at Nyssa, Oregon, that served many southwestern Idaho farmers; and one in 1942 at Nampa. The factories in Burley and Whitney were closed in recent years, but those in Twin Falls, Paul, Nampa, and Nyssa are still in operation at this writing.

## SHEEP AND CATTLE

The high price of meat turned many disappointed miners to stockraising and farming. There were abundant grazing resources in Idaho, some of which were opportunely used by Captain Richard Grant of Fort Hall. During the mining rushes of the

1860s herds were driven to Idaho from Nebraska, Texas, California, and Oregon. Longhorns, Durhams, and shorthorns dotted the Lost, Lemhi, and Portneuf river valleys, Cassia and Goose creeks, the Bruneau country, the Beaverhead and Snake River valleys. Mexican vaqueros, American cowboys, and Mormon farm boys were common sights in the summer mountain areas. Inevitably, there were also cattle- and horse-rustlers.[14]

The cost of raising cattle in the early territorial years was slight. Eastern Idaho was almost one big cattle ranch in the 1870s and early 1880s. Cattle grazed on the public range, looked after themselves, and were rounded up and trailed to market. By the thousands they were driven from eastern Oregon and southern Idaho to stockyards at Cheyenne and then shipped to Omaha, Kansas City, and Chicago. Idaho cattlemen did well until the hard winters of the 1880s.

When the Oregon Short Line was completed, sheep were introduced to the open range along with cattle. With an abundance of little-used pastureland, Idaho was attractive to sheepmen. In 1893 the Idaho Wool Growers Association was organized, with Frank R. Gooding (later U.S. senator) as president. Flocks varied from 2,000 to 3,000 head. With his sheepdog as inseparable companion, the herder moved the sheep from one grazing area to another to prevent denuding. Early spring lambs were shipped to market in late summer and early fall. Mountain Home, Ketchum, Idaho Falls, Soda Springs, and St. Anthony were important lamb-shipping centers.

As in other states and territories, cattlemen and settlers regarded sheepmen as intruders. Although some ranchers ran both sheep and cattle, most cattlemen were convinced that sheep cropped the grass too close, fouled the range, and slipped through fences to damage crops. (Sheepmen also complained about cattle, whose feet cut deep pathways in the range.) Cattlemen induced the legislature to pass an act making it illegal to trail sheep where cattle had been grazing, but territorial law could not apply to public land. Ineffective enforcement led cattlemen (and settlers) to resort to extralegal action. Warnings were posted; sheep camps were attacked; springs and sheep were poisoned; and destructive fires were started. In 1892 one sheepman was forced to remove his sheep from Lemhi Valley.

A few herders were murdered. In February 1896 two sheepherders were found dead in their camp in Shoshone Basin; they were presumed shot by an agent of cattlemen. The prime suspect was Jackson Lee "Diamond Field Jack" Davis. The widely publicized trial in Albion, Cassia County, in 1897 featured William Borah for the prosecution and James Hawley for the defense. Davis, found guilty, was given the death sentence. In October, shortly before Davis was to be hanged, two leading ranchers admitted killing the herders and pled self-defense. In 1901 the State Board of Pardons established quite conclusively that Diamond Field Jack had not murdered the sheepherders but only commuted his sentence to life imprisonment. In 1902 Davis was granted an unconditional pardon by Governor Frank W. Hunt, who succeeded Governor Steunenberg. Although many cattlemen adopted a more tolerant attitude toward sheepmen thereafter, raids continued on sheep camps and flocks were scattered for several years.

At the suggestion of President Theodore Roosevelt, who had personally witnessed overgrazing and undisguised range warfare, the United States government adopted an orderly grazing policy for all federal lands in 1905. Grazing permits were required, fees were paid, and grazing lands were controlled as to the number of stock and the length of the season. The program was later strengthened by the Taylor Grazing Act of 1934.

## TIMBER

Idaho's lumber industry, which ranked second only to agriculture in economic importance, reaches back to early days when Lewis and Clark felled large trees near Orofino to make canoes, when the Reverend Mr. Spalding operated a sawmill on the Clearwater in 1840, and when timber was cut for miners' cabins, mines, and business establishments during the gold rush of the early 1860s. Initial methods were crude but effective. Men used a pit saw or whipsaw to split a timber lengthwise. A log was rolled over a pit or onto a scaffold. One man stood under the log and pulled the saw downwards while the other stood on the log and guided the saw. Trees were cut and logs were trimmed with a broadax. As demand for lumber increased, sawmills were introduced—at first powered by water, later by steam. A sawmill was erected in Franklin in 1860, a larger one in the Boise Basin in 1863, and several dozen dotted important mining and agricultural settlements by the 1870s and 1880s. In 1899 the Bureau of the Census reported eighty-seven sawmills in Idaho producing more than 65 million board feet of lumber per year.

The railroads were important customers of sawmill operators, and the completion of the Oregon Short Line and Northern Pacific railroads and their branches around the turn of the century made possible a more thorough exploitation of Idaho's rich timber resources.

The most important figure in Idaho's fledgling forest industry was Frederick Weyerhaeuser of St. Paul, Minnesota. Immigrating from Germany as a youth in 1852, Weyerhaeuser started in the lumber business in Rock Island, Illinois, in 1856 in partnership with his brother-in-law, F. C. A. Denkmann. Their business prospered and they expanded into larger operations in Minnesota and Wisconsin. Through these enterprises Weyerhaeuser and his four sons became associated with prominent lumber families—the Lairds and Nortons of Winona, Minnesota; the Mussers of Muscatine and the Youngs, Lambs, and Joyces of Clinton, Iowa; the Ingrams, Carsons, and Moons in Eau Claire; the Humbirds of Mason; and the Rutledges of Chippewa Falls—all in Wisconsin.

The Great Lakes region, which had been the center of lumber

production in the United States after the Civil War, was largely cut over by 1900; the forests of Michigan, Minnesota, and Wisconsin were being rapidly depleted; and leading lumbermen began to close operations on the upper Mississippi and Chippewa rivers. With the Northern Pacific Railway offering timberlands for sale in Washington, Oregon, and Idaho (lands were granted by the government to help finance the railroad), many timber operators quite naturally shifted to the Pacific Northwest. Frederick Weyerhaeuser had seen the graphic display of Idaho's splendid timber resources at the Columbian Exposition in Chicago in 1893. Now he was determined to acquire such properties for himself and his midwestern lumber associates. Between 1899 and 1908 these families put their money into seven Idaho ventures, five of them north and two of them south of the Salmon River canyon, which represented the bulk of Idaho's lumber production before World War I.

Weyerhaeuser's representative was Charles O. Brown, a native of Maine with lengthy experience in Michigan. Brown had moved to the Clearwater in north Idaho, where his son Nat and son-in-law Theodore Fohl joined him. After exploring the timberland, they assured Weyerhaeuser and John A. Humbird that the forests were worth purchasing. In the summer of 1900 Weyerhaeuser and Humbird purchased Northern Pacific Railway scrip entitling them to 40,000 acres on the Clearwater River. They instructed Brown to choose lands and file claims. Brown was aware that a competitor, W. E. McCord, a wealthy lumberman of Chippewa Falls, Wisconsin, had employed a man named Bussell to do the same. The first to make the selections, fix the legal boundary lines, file descriptions at the General Land Office in Lewiston, and offer payment would get the timberland.

As it happened, the crews of Brown and Bussell finished their surveys on the same September afternoon. Bussell started for the railhead at Orofino. The youthful Nat Brown followed him on horseback. By midnight Brown had covered about twenty-five miles. Reaching a rancher's house, he smelled fresh steaming coffee and guessed that Bussell was inside renewing himself. Brown quietly entered the stable, exchanged his jaded horse for a fresh mount, and galloped on. Suspecting that McCord had a fast locomotive ready at Orofino to speed Bussell on to Lewiston, Brown decided he would try a bluff. He arrived in Orofino, stabled his horse, and asked the hotel owner: "Is my engine ready?" The hotelman responded: "Yes, and I have a letter authorizing you to use it." Brown boarded the train, arrived in Lewiston around 7 a.m., found the holder of the scrip, and copied out the boundary descriptions from notes he had brought with him. He then rushed over to the land office and the deed was done. McCord, who had waited for Bussell in Lewiston, "seemed greatly surprised and agitated."[15]

These promising lands became the nucleus of holdings of the Clearwater Timber Company, organized on December 13, 1900, with an authorized capital of $500,000. With Humbird as president and Weyerhaeuser as vice-president, the company owned one of the finest bodies of Western white pine in the nation, acquired at a cost of a little more than $6 per acre. The company continued to acquire additional land and by 1927 owned about 220,000 acres with about 2 billion board feet of white pine and an equal amount of other species.

At the same time Weyerhaeuser and associates expanded to the Pend Oreille-Kootenai district farther north, where the Northern Pacific crosses the state on its way from Spokane to Missoula. Weyerhaeuser and Edward Rutledge got off the train at Sandpoint; inspected the pine, red fir, larch, and cedar of the Priest River Valley; purchased land from the Northern Pacific; and also bought the Sandpoint Lumber Company, which owned a single-band mill and some appurtenant timberland. On December 6, 1900, Weyerhaeuser, Humbird, and Rutledge organized the Humbird Lumber Company, capitalized at $500,000.

The Sandpoint mill was converted to a two-band operation, another sawmill was set up five miles away at Kootenai, and ample log-storage facilities were provided along the shore of Lake Pend Oreille. By 1931 the company had produced more than 2 billion board feet of lumber.

A few months after the organization of the Clearwater and Humbird companies, Edward Rutledge persuaded the Weyerhaeuser associates to acquire approximately 26,000 acres of Northern Pacific white-pine lands and 30,000 acres of state lands as the nucleus for the Edward Rutledge Timber Company, organized in October 1902 with an authorized capital of $200,000. The timber was in the watersheds of the St. Joe and St. Maries rivers. For a variety of reasons the company was never able to pay any dividends, and in 1930 the properties were taken over by Potlatch Forests, Inc.

A fourth corporation, also organized in 1902 and with an equally unfavorable earnings record, was the Bonners Ferry Lumber Company, which had a mill site, 13,000 acres of timberland, and rights to the waters of the Kootenai River. Unquestionably, the setting of operations was beautiful. One fall a contributor to the company newspaper became lyrical: "The folds of the forest carpet form deep valleys over which the mountains tower in quiet dignity, outlined in sharp, rugged grandeur against the sky."[16] The operation turned out to be not so grand. There were fires, floods, and problems with the railroad. Earnings never exceeded expenses. Production rose to about 13 million board feet in 1904, reached more than 50 million in 1913, and then tapered off until coming to a stop in 1926.

The most ambitious venture of the Weyerhauser group was the Potlatch Lumber Company. In 1901 and 1902 William Deary purchased state timber and other lands in the Palouse-Clearwater drainage areas in the name of the Northland Pine Company. These acquisitions were sold, along with others acquired by Henry Turrish for the Wisconsin Log and Lumber

Company, to Potlatch in March 1903. The Potlatch Lumber Company was organized with a capital of $3 million, later raised to $8 million. Frederick Weyerhaeuser's son Charles was elected president, Henry Turrish vice president, and William Deary general manager. The company soon absorbed several local concerns, including the Palouse River Lumber Company.

Although consideration was given to locating the mill at Moscow, Deary bought a site north of Moscow from independent timber owners and ranchers. In 1906 Deary built a gigantic belt-driven mill at Potlatch, establishing there one of the outstanding company towns in the West. In 1907 he constructed (in the name of the Washington, Idaho, and Montana Railway Company) forty-five miles of common-carrier logging railroad from Palouse, Washington, to Bovill, Idaho, where it connected with the Chicago, Milwaukee, and St. Paul Railroad. Three years later a second mill, this one electrically driven, was built at Elk River, east of Potlatch. The timber was the highest quality. One famous tree, "The King of the White Pines," was 207 feet high, measured 6 feet 9 inches across the butt, and yielded 29,000 feet of lumber when processed in the mill.

Although it sawed an average of 131 million board feet of lumber annually throughout the period from 1908 to 1927, the company was a marginal enterprise, losing money most of those years. Logging and transportation costs were high, regional markets for ponderosa, fir, and larch spotty, and the regional market uncertain. Frederick Weyerhaeuser once declared that the name Potlatch, which signified an Indian feast accompanied by lavish gifts, was appropriate, for the giving of money to the company by lenders and stockholders never ended and little came back.[17]

The first of the companies in southern Idaho, the Barber Lumber Company, also a Weyerhaeuser affiliate, was organized in July 1902. It included 25,000 acres of timberland on Grimes and More's creeks, tributaries to the Boise, purchased from

Frank Steunenberg. The firm was capitalized for $150,000. The second was the Payette Lumber and Manufacturing Company, organized in January 1902, which took over stumpage and timberlands in the Payette Basin originally purchased by William Deary for Northland Pine and Henry Turrish for Wisconsin Log and Lumber. These holdings included 33,000 acres of stumpage purchased from the state for $184,000 in 1902. The firm was capitalized for $500,000.

Barber Lumber struggled. There were problems with log drives; some of the timberlands were more suited to grazing than to logging; and legal hassles plagued the company. One suit (which involved Borah) charged conspiracy to defraud the government in acquiring timberlands. Barber Lumber Company was finally cleared of the charge, but its earnings remained far below expectations.

Meanwhile, Payette Lumber and Manufacturing Company continued to acquire valuable timber: by the end of 1913 the company owned 154,000 acres. On December 24, 1913, the company merged with Barber to form the Boise Payette Lumber Company, with a paid-in capital of $7 million. Total timberlands of the combined firm were 200,000 acres. C. A. Barton, the new manager, built the company's own rail line, the Intermountain Railway, to transport logs from Centerville to Arrowrock Dam Junction and on to a large new mill in Emmett, using rails constructed by the U.S. Reclamation Service to build Arrowrock Dam. The firm had satisfactory earnings until the depression of the 1930s.

The men who worked for Idaho's lumber companies were mostly young, rugged, and tough. Some were Scandinavian immigrants, some were unemployed miners, some were French-Canadians (Canuckers). They took pride in their work, understood the risks, and tolerated the crude dwellings and rough life. The company tried to employ skilled cooks, even though the staples often consisted of pancakes, sourdough, salt pork, baked beans, and strong coffee. Employees worked long hours. They were not unionized until the Industrial Workers of the World (IWW) came to the Northwest shortly after its organization in Chicago in 1905. One of the IWW's organizers was William D. Haywood. Members of the "one big union" were often called Wobblies, a term that is said to have originated as a Chinese distortion of IWW—"I wobbly wobbly." The IWW's Lumber Workers Union did much to alleviate harsh conditions in the logging camps.

Until technology improved, most of the companies built mills alongside railways, used two-man saws, drew logs to streams or to railroad loading points by horses, and transported logs by streams or rail or both. Labor policies were determined by the market, not by collective bargaining. Companies tended to cut tracts swiftly and exit quickly off the land, encouraged by local property taxes, which remained the same year after year whether or not the timber was cut.

Moreover, threats of costly fires were real. The north Idaho and Montana fire of 1910 was unparalleled in the history of the United States. With 744 blazes, Idaho suffered 1.7 million scorched acres—one sixth of its northern forest lands. Many mines were also destroyed, and several communities, including the town of Wallace, were devastated. Smoke from the fire drifted across the continent as far east as Boston and on to Europe. Partly to control fires, and partly out of the desire to stabilize the industry, the operators formed the West Coast Lumbermen's Association in 1911. (The United States Forest Service, which has provided efficient fire control in recent years, did not fight fires effectively until the 1930s.)

Although these companies often earned irregular profits or none at all, their owners and officers adjusted to changing conditions in the market, the forces of nature, and the work force. By rational planning for full utilization of timber, they contributed materially to the economic development of Idaho. They provided employment for hundreds, stimulated the growth of cities and towns, produced lumber for city residents and farmers, paid taxes to local governments and the state, and set the stage for long-term policies that are still benefiting Idaho.

## CHAPTER TWENTY: SOURCES

Sources on Idaho agricultural settlements before World War I include Hugh Lovin, "Sage, Jacks, and Snake Plain Pioneers," *Idaho Yesterdays* 22 (Winter 1979):13–24; W. Darrell Gertsch, "Water Use, Energy, and Economic Development in the Snake River Basin," *Idaho Yesterdays* 23 (Summer 1979):58–72; Hugh Lovin, "Footnote to History: The Reservoir . . . Would Not Hold Water," *Idaho Yesterdays* 24 (Spring 1980):12–19; Charles Coate, "Federal-Local Relationships on the Boise and Minidoka Projects, 1904–1926," *Idaho Yesterdays* 25 (Summer 1981):2–9; Hugh T. Lovin, "Free Enterprise and Large-Scale Reclamation on the Twin Falls-North Side Tract, 1907–1930," *Idaho Yesterdays* 29 (Spring 1985):2–14; Barbara E. Perry, "Arrowrock Dam Is Built," *Idaho Yesterdays* 29 (Spring 1985):15–23; Leonard J. Arrington, "Irrigation in the Snake River Valley: An Historical Overview," *Idaho Yesterdays* 30 (Spring-Summer 1986):3–11; Hugh Lovin, "How Not to Run a Carey Act Project: The Twin Falls-Salmon Falls Creek Tract, 1904–1922," *Idaho Yesterdays* 30 (Fall 1986):9–15, 18–24; Livingston-Little, *An Economic History of North Idaho*, 53–64; Carter, ed., *Pioneer Irrigation: Upper Snake River Valley*; Murphy, "Early Irrigation in the Boise Valley"; H. J. Kingsbury, *Bucking the Tide* (Seattle: Ganis and Harris, 1949); Beal, *A History of Southeastern Idaho*; Lovin, "The Carey Act in Idaho, 1895–1925," *Pacific Northwest Quarterly* 78 (October 1987):122–33; Mikel H. Williams, *The History of the Development and Current Status of Carey Act Projects in Idaho* (Boise: Idaho Department of Reclamation, 1970); Bruce L. Schmalz, "Headgates and Headaches," *Idaho Yesterdays* 9 (Winter 1965–66):22–25; J. Meredith Neil, "A Forgotten Alternative: Reclamation by the States," *Idaho Yesterdays* 9 (Winter 1965–66):18–21; Bureau of Reclamation, U.S. Department of Agriculture, *Boise Federal Reclamation Project*, Conservation Bulletin No. 26 (Washington, D.C.: Government Printing Office, 1942); F. Ross Peterson and W. Darrell Gertsch, "The Creation of Idaho's Lifeblood: The Politics of Irrigation," *Rendezvous: Idaho State University Journal of Arts and Letters* 11 (Fall 1976):53–61; William Darrell Gertsch, "The Upper Snake River Project: A Historical Study of Reclamation and Regional Development, 1890–1930" (Ph.D. dissertation, University of Washington, 1974); Patricia Lyn Scott, "Idaho and the Carey Act, 1894–1930" (M.A. thesis, University of Utah, 1983); Neil H. Carlton, "A History of the Development of the Boise Irrigation Project" (M.A. thesis, Brigham Young University, 1969); William E. Smythe, *The Conquest of Arid America*, rev. ed. (1905; repr., Seattle: University of Washington Press, 1969); Hugh T. Lovin, "A 'New West' Reclamation Tragedy: The Twin Falls-Oakley Project in Idaho, 1908–1931," *Arizona and the West* 20 (Spring 1978):5–24; Michael C. Robinson, *Water for the West: The Bureau of Reclamation, 1902–1977* (Chicago: Public Works Historical Society, 1979); and Alfred E. Golzé, *Reclamation in the United States* (Caldwell: Caxton Printers, 1961).

A broadly focused recent article that summarizes much research is Hugh Lovin, "Water, Arid Land, and Visions of Advancement on the Snake River Plain," *Idaho Yesterdays* 35 (Spring 1991):3–18.

Idaho's early sugar beet industry is described in Kenneth J. Williams, "Sugar-Beet Growing in Ada and Canyon Counties, Idaho," *Pacific Northwest Quarterly* 42 (July 1951):203–10; Leonard J. Arrington, "Launching Idaho's Sugar Beet Industry," *Idaho Yesterdays* 9 (Fall 1965):16–27; Leonard J. Arrington, *Beet Sugar in the West: A History of the Utah-Idaho Sugar Company, 1891–1966* (Seattle: University of Washington Press, 1966); and J. R. Bachman, *Story of the Amalgamated Sugar Company, 1897–1961* (Caldwell: Caxton Printers, 1962).

Sources on the beginnings of Idaho's important cattle-grazing and sheep-growing industry include: Alexander Campbell McGregor, *Counting Sheep: From Open Range to Agribusiness on the Columbia Plateau* (Seattle: University of Washington Press, 1982); Edward N. Wentworth, *America's Sheep Trails* (Ames: Iowa State College Press,

1948); Marion Clawson, *The Western Range Livestock Industry* (New York: McGraw Hill Co., 1950); Fite, *The Farmer's Frontier, 1865–1900*; J. Orin Oliphant, *On the Cattle Ranges of the Oregon Country* (Seattle: University of Washington Press, 1968); and Charles S. Walgamott, *Six Decades Back* (1936; repr., Moscow: University of Idaho Press, 1990).

Sources on the beginnings of Idaho's lumber industry include Beal and Wells, *History of Idaho*, 2:192–99; Hawley, *History of Idaho*, 1:503–16; Ralph Hidy, "Lumbermen in Idaho: A Study in Adaptation to Environment," *Idaho Yesterdays* 6 (Winter 1962):2–17; Ralph W. Hidy, Frank Ernest Hill, and Allen Nevins, *Timber and Men: The Weyerhaeuser Story* (New York: The Macmillan Co., 1963); Keith C. Petersen, *Company Town: Potlatch, Idaho, and the Potlatch Lumber Company* (Pullman and Moscow: Washington State University Press and Latah County Historical Society, 1987); Fred W. Kohlmeyer, *Timber Roots: The Laird, Norton Story, 1855–1905* (Winona, Minnesota: Winona County Historical Society, 1972); S. Blair Hutchison, "A Century of Lumbering in Northern Idaho," *The Timberman* 39 (August, September, and October 1938); Robert Ficken, "Weyerhaeuser and the Pacific Northwest Timber Industry, 1899–1903," *Pacific Northwest Quarterly* 70 (October 1979):146–65; John Fahey, "Big Lumber in the Inland Empire: The Early Years, 1900–1930," *Pacific Northwest Quarterly* 76 (July 1985):95–103; John Fahey, *The Inland Empire: Unfolding Years, 1879–1929* (Seattle: University of Washington Press, 1986), esp. 188–213; and Meinig, *The Great Columbia Plain*.

107.

108.

107. James H. Hawley, governor from 1911 to 1913, wrote a monumental three-volume *History of Idaho* (1920) that gives a detailed description of Idaho's development to 1920. ISHS 64–138.18.

108. The land drawing at Twin Falls in 1905 attracted a large crowd. ISHS 78–32.2.

109.

110.

109. This steam thresher was on the Camas Prairie in Idaho County about 1905. ISHS 1274–B.

110. Harvesting grain in the Palouse, a heavy wheat-producing area, was a community affair. ISHS 60–52.806.

111.

112.

111. This Amalgamated beet sugar factory south of Twin Falls was built in 1916. ISHS 73–221–619B.

112. Sugar beets were a popular commercial crop in most irrigated valleys. ISHS 65–41.6.

113.

114.

113. Basque sheepherder, his wagon, and a dog were a familiar sight in Idaho's grazing country. ISHS 78–37.100/M.

114. Sheep shearing on the Brown-Crocker Ranch northeast of Filer required the efforts of several talented men. ISHS 73–221.646.

115.

116.

115. Summer sheep ranges, like Corral Creek and Trail Creek, provided the best grazing in warm months. ISHS 75–76.12/B.

116. The whipsaw was most commonly used for cutting logs until sawmills were established. ISHS 2746.

117.

118.

117. An example of the many sawmills erected near villages was Erickson's Mill at Reubens, about 1902. DONATED BY GEORGE WELLS, OROFINO, UIL 5–92–1.

118. Forest fires were often devastating before the 1930s, when U.S. Forest Service crews began to provide effective fire-fighting protection. C. J. BROSNAN COLLECTION, UIL 6–169–1.

 119.

119. Workers for the Milwaukee Lumber Company carry burned timber from the 1910 fire. ISHS 72–139.6.

120. 

120. Idaho rivers were jammed with logs during the cutting season. ISHS 70–70.29.

# NOTES

## CHAPTER 1

1. This and the following quotations are from Bruccoli, *Conversations with Hemingway*, 63–64.

2. Walker, "The Geologic History of the Snake River Country of Idaho," 24–25.

3. Ibid., 30.

4. Ibid.

## CHAPTER 2

1. There are differences of opinion among archaeologists about several of the matters discussed in this chapter. I have read the sources listed at the end of the chapter and have made the best judgment possible on the basis of the sometimes conflicting interpretations of the evidence. I am particularly grateful to Thomas Green, former Idaho State Archaeologist, for reading this chapter and suggesting changes. However, he should not be held responsible for any of my conclusions.

2. This classification is used in Butler, "Prehistory of the Snake and Salmon River Area," 127–34.

## CHAPTER 3

1. "Idaho's Indian Population in 1800," Idaho Historical Society Reference Series No. 29, December 1964.

2. [Sven Liljeblad], "The Indians of Idaho," typewritten circular distributed by the Idaho State Historical Society.

3. I have relied very heavily on Walker, *Indians of Idaho*, 132–57. Chapter Three is largely written from this informative book.

4. Contemporary early references to Bannock Indians are vague and unclear. Early trapper-explorer Alexander Ross, while confused about Bannocks and Sheepeaters (or Mountain Shoshoni), usually referred to Banattee or Bannattee, but in his 1855 publication he once varied that with Bannack. Peter Skene Ogden's Banague (June 3, 5, 1828) is relevant, as is John Work's Banack (April 8, 19, 1831). Frémont wrote of the Pannack, and this term was also used by Howard Stansbury. In his chapter for Beal and Wells, *History of Idaho* (1:38), Sven Liljeblad, Idaho's linguistic analyst, concluded that the Paiute newcomers who associated with the Shoshoni called themselves "panakwate," a word that early white visitors changed to "Panak" or "Bannack." By 1862, however, Frémont's identification was ignored and Idaho's Indians were commonly referred to as Bannock, even though in Montana Bannack was the preferred spelling (and was adopted by the first miners in the Boise Basin who called their district West Bannack). Since the Indians who occasionally wandered into Montana were from Idaho, it seems logical to use the common Idaho spelling. Brigham Madsen entitled his book *The Bannock of Idaho*, as did Robert F. and Yolanda Murphy in their essay, "Northern Shoshone and Bannock," in D'Azevedo, *Handbook of North American Indians: Great Basin*, 284–307.

5. The last four paragraphs are almost a paraphrase of Sven Liljeblad, "The Indians of Idaho," Idaho Historical Series, Number 3, 1960.

## CHAPTER 4

1. Brief biographies of Lewis and Clark and a summary of the Lewis and Clark Expedition by John L. Loos appear in Howard R. Lamar, ed., *The Reader's Encyclopedia of the American West* (New York: Thomas Y. Crowell Co., 1977), 221–22, 663–65.

2. Brosnan, *History of the State of Idaho*, 42. Rees says the flag carrier was McNeal, another member of the party. Rees, "The Shoshoni Contribution," 6.

3. Thwaites, ed., *Original Journals of Lewis and Clark Expedition*, 2:335; Moulton, ed., *The Journals of the Lewis and Clark Expedition*, 5:74. The rules of spelling had not yet been agreed upon at the time the captains wrote, and their orthography is both erratic and imaginative. Clark spelled "Sioux" six different ways. The same with capitalization and grammar, which are reproduced faithfully in the published journals. Partly for this reason, the published journals are slow going. I hope professional purists will excuse me for regularizing the spelling, capitalization, and punctuation in this chapter. However, I have changed not a word.

4. Thwaites, *Original Journals*, 2:339–43; Moulton, *The Journals*, 5:79.

5. Moulton, *The Journals*, 5:91.

6. Thwaites, *Original Journal*, 2:362–63.

7. In Shoshoni, what we call brother and cousin is a single word that means both, so we cannot be sure whether Cameahwait was her brother or her cousin.

8. Ibid., 2:362–63.

9. Quoted in Kenneth N. Owens, "Sacagawea," in Lamar, ed., *The Reader's Encyclopedia of the American West*, 1055. Although most biographies of this young Indian woman use the spelling "Sacajawea," the journals of Lewis and Clark suggest that the hard "g" is nearer what they tried to report although they had an incorrect spelling. This is the preferred spelling of the U.S. Geographic Names Board.

10. So much attention has been given to "Sacajawea" that one can be led to believe, as Bernard DeVoto observed, that "Lewis, Clark and their command were privileged to assist in the Sacajawea

Expedition," DeVoto, *The Course of Empire*, 478. The journals of the captains clearly indicate that Sacagawea was a good traveler and helpful in Shoshoni country, but Lewis and Clark were their own guides, sometimes aided by native scouts.

11. Thwaites, *Original Journals*, 2:380, 3:26.

12. Ibid., 3:51; Moulton, *The Journals*, 5:185–86.

13. Thwaites, *Original Journals*, 3:68; Moulton, *The Journals*, 5:205.

14. Thwaites, *Original Journals*, 3:68; Moulton, *The Journals*, 5:206–7.

15. Thwaites, *Original Journals*, 3:74; Moulton, *The Journals*, 5:215.

16. Thwaites, *Original Journals*, 3:82; Moulton, *The Journals*, 5:226–27. The journals mention a son of Twisted Hair who later became the famaous Chief Lawyer, whom we shall refer to in Chapter Thirteen.

17. Thwaites, *Original Journals*, 4:360–61, 365.

18. Quoted in Billington, *Westward Expansion*, 448.

19. The quotations are given in Johansen and Gates, *Empire of the Columbia*, 78.

20. Thwaites, *Original Journals*, 3:365, 5:21.

21. Ibid., 5:120, 139, 143, 166.

22. Robert Carriker, "Following the Trail of the Captains," 29.

23. Compare Beal and Wells, *History of Idaho*, 1:77.

24. Owens, "Sacagawea," in Lamar, ed., *The Reader's Encyclopedia*, 1055.

25. Howard R. Lamar, "Jean Baptiste Charbonneau," in Lamar, ed., *The Reader's Encyclopedia of the American West*, 190–91; and Ann W. Hafen, "Jean Baptiste Charbonneau," in Leroy R. Hafen, ed., *The Mountain Men and the Fur Trade of the Far West*, 10 vols. (Glendale, Calif.: Arthur H. Clark Co., 1965–70), 1:205–24.

26. Burton Harris, *John Colter: His Years in the Rockies* (New York: Charles Scribner's Sons, 1952).

27. Lavender, *The Rockies*, 48.

28. John L. Loos, "Lewis and Clark Expedition," in Lamar, ed., *The Reader's Encyclopedia*, 664–65.

29. See Gary E. Moulton, "On Reading Lewis and Clark," 28.

30. DeVoto, *The Journals of Lewis and Clark*, iii.

## CHAPTER 5

1. Tyrell, ed., *David Thompson's Narrative of His Explorations in Western America*, 414–15.

2. Byron Defenbach, *Red Heroines of the Northwest* (Caldwell: Caxton Printers, 1929); J. N. Barry, "Madame Dorion of the Astorians," *Oregon Historical Quarterly* 30 (1929):272 ff.

3. Alexander Ross, *The Fur Hunters of the Far West*, 2 vols. (London, 1855), 1:202–3, as quoted in Beal and Wells, *History of Idaho*, 1:114.

4. Beal and Wells, *History of Idaho*, 1:122, states that the massacre occurred during Mackenzie's second expedition, 1819–20.

5. Ibid., 1:122–23.

6. Ross, *Fur Hunters*, 2:54–59, quoted in Beal and Wells, *History of Idaho*, 1:130.

7. Ross, *Fur Hunters*, 2:66–67.

8. Defenbach, *Idaho: The Place and Its People*, 1:140–41.

9. Rufus Sage, *Scenes in the Rocky Mountains* (Philadelphia, 1846), 29.

10. Billington, *The Far Western Frontier*, 44–55.

11. William H. Goetzmann, "The Mountain Man as Jacksonian Man," *American Quarterly* 15 (Fall 1963):402–15.

12. Quoted in Sears, "Trail Blazer of the Far West," 60.

13. Morgan, *Jedediah Smith and the Opening of the West*, 7.

14. Francis Haines, Jr., "Francois Payette," 15.

15. Farnham, *Travels in the Far Northwest, 1839–46* (Cleveland: Arthur H. Clark Co., 1906), 120–23.

16. Washington Irving, *Adventures of Captain Bonneville* (Paris, 1837), 55–57, quoted in Beal and Wells, *History of Idaho*, 1:180–81.

17. Beal and Wells, *History of Idaho*, 1:179.

18. Pierre's Hole was the scene of the annual rendezvous of mountain men and suppliers of 1832—"The Great Rocky Mountain Fair."

The valley was permanently settled in 1882 and now bears the name Teton Valley.

19. Francis Fuller Victor, *The River of the West* (Hartford, 1871), 164.

20. Biedleman, "Nathaniel Wyeth's Fort Hall," 211–12.

21. F. G. Young, ed., *The Correspondence and Journals of Captain Nathaniel J. Wyeth, 1831–1836* (Eugene, Ore., 1899), 146–47.

22. John K. Townsend, *Narrative of a Journey Across the Rocky Mountains to the Columbia River* (Philadelphia, 1839), 107, quoted in Beal and Wells, *History of Idaho*, 1:187.

23. Many scholars have posited a vigorous competition between Fort Hall and Fort Boise, and hypothesized that McKay was encouraged to drive Wyeth out. But a careful study of the letters and documents exchanged between Wyeth and his backers in Boston suggests that McKay and Wyeth planned their ventures together and did not see each other as opponents. See Bradford Cole, "The Letter Book of Henry Hall: An Edited Version with an Introduction" (Master's thesis, Utah State University, 1986).

24. Goetzmann, *Exploration and Empire*, 101–4. See also Morgan, *Jedediah Smith*, 187–88, 343–47.

## CHAPTER 6

1. Mrs. Spalding's diary is quoted in Haines, *The Story of Idaho*, 53.

2. Drury, *Spalding and Smith*, 252–53.

3. Ibid., 248.

4. Charles Wilkes, *Narrative of the U.S.A. Exploring Expedition* (Philadelphia, 1844), 460, as quoted in D. E. Livingston-Little, *An Economic History of North Idaho, 1800–1900* (Los Angeles: Journal of the West, 1965), 17.

5. Ibid., 18.

6. Barber and Martin, *Idaho in the Pacific Northwest*, 31.

7. Francis Haines, "Cayuse Indians" in Lamar, ed., *The Reader's Encyclopedia of the American West*, 186.

8. *Ibid.*

9. Drury, *Spalding and Smith*, 336.

10. Oregon City *Argus*, April 5, 1861.

11. Quoted in Barber and Martin, *Idaho in the Pacific Northwest*, 32.

12. Livingston-Little, *Economic History of North Idaho*, 21.

13. Quoted in Cyprian Bradley and Edward J. Kelly, *History of the Diocese of Boise, 1863–1952* (Boise: n.p., 1953), 1:78.

14. Brosnan, *History of the State of Idaho*, 102.

15. See Robert C. Carriker, "Direct Successor to De Smet: Joseph M. Cataldo, S.J., and Stabilization of the Jesuit Indian Missions of the Pacific Northwest, 1877–1893," *Idaho Yesterdays* 31 (Spring-Summer 1987):8–12.

16. Gerald McKevitt, "Jesuit Missionary Linguistics," 284.

17. Ibid., 286, 293–302.

18. See Lawrence G. Coates, "The Spalding-Whitman and Lemhi Missions: A Comparison," *Idaho Yesterdays* 31 (Spring-Summer 1987):38–46.

19. A Nez Perce reaction to the white missionaries is given in Allen P. Slickpoo, Sr., "The Nez Perce Attitude Toward the Missionary Experience," *Idaho Yesterdays* 31 (Spring-Summer 1987):35–37.

## CHAPTER 7

1. *Fremont's Expedition Report*, as quoted in Defenbach, *Idaho: The Place and Its People*, 1:226.

2. Spence and Spence, eds., *The Expeditions of John C. Fremont*, 1:520–21.

3. Applegate, *A Day with the Cow Column*, 62–63.

4. Unruh, *The Plains Across*, 119–20, 185, 408.

5. Quoted in U.S. Bureau of Land Management, *Emigrant Trails of Southern Idaho* (Boise: Idaho State Office, U.S. Bureau of Land Management, 1989), 68.

6. E. S. McComas, as quoted in Fisher, *Beyond the Rockies*, 172.

7. Quoted in Unruh, *The Plains Across*, 165.

8. Schwantes, *The Pacific Northwest*, 90.

9. Fisher, *Beyond the Rockies*, 160.

10. These estimates are based on Unruh, *The Plains Across*, 119–20.

11. Quoted in Winther, *The Great Northwest*, 234.

12. Brigham D. Madsen, *The Bannock of Idaho* (Caldwell, Idaho: Caxton Printers, 1958), 77–79; Unruh, *The Plains Across*, 189–90, 215–16.

13. Madsen, *The Bannock of Idaho*, 124–25; Unruh, *The Plains Across*, 190–92.

14. Quoted in Madsen, *The Bannock of Idaho*, 124–25. I have regularized the punctuation and capitalization.

15. Ibid., 129–31.

16. Unruh, *The Plains Across*, 186–87.

## CHAPTER 8

1. See Brigham Young's remarks in the Great Salt Lake City Bowery, May 31, 1857, in *Journal of Discourses*, 26 vols. (Liverpool, 1855–86), 4:326.

2. The best volume on the Utah War is Norman Furniss, *The Mormon Conflict 1850–1859* (New Haven: Yale University Press, 1960).

3. The Horse, a prominent earlier Bannock leader, and his Bannock band wiped out John Reed's Boise post in 1814 (see Chapter 5) and also raided Etienne Provost's crew near Great Salt Lake in 1824.

4. Madsen, *The Bannock of Idaho*, 107–8; Nash, "The Salmon River Mission," 31; Beal and Wells, *History of Idaho*, 1:261.

## CHAPTER 9

1. Pierce prepared a long detailed account of this trip mentioned in the sources. He refers to no such guidance by Jane. In fact, his party had a hard time finding their way. The legend of Jane may have been an attempt to create another Sacagawea. See Burcham, "Reminiscences of E. D. Pierce, Discoverer of Gold in Idaho."

2. The mining laws of the Oro Fino district, as adopted on January 5, 1861, are given in *Idaho Yesterdays* 3 (Winter 1959–60):18.

3. There is a possibility that J. Marion More, present at Pierce in 1861, was not the M. More who was chairman of the meeting. A

Moore family in recent times believe it was their grandfather, who was often confused with J. Marion More. At any rate, J. Marion was in Pierce and went also to Idaho City, of which he was one of the founders.

4. Goulder, *Reminiscences*, 230–32. McConnell, *Early History of Idaho*, devotes many pages to the outlaws and their methods: 60–78, 100–110. See also Goulder, *Reminiscences*, 221–23.

5. Goulder, *Reminiscences*, 206.

6. Livingston-Little, *An Economic History of North Idaho*, 35–36.

7. Donald N. Wells, "Farmers Forgotten: Nez Perce Suppliers of the North Idaho Gold Rush Days," *Idaho Yesterdays* 2 (Summer 1958):28–32.

8. Goulder, *Reminiscences*, 221–23.

9. Ibid., 240–41.

10. Ibid., 253.

11. Merle W. Wells, *Gold Camps and Silver Cities*, 8.

12. Ibid.

13. Ibid., 9.

14. Albert D. Richardson, *Beyond the Mississippi*... (Hartford, Conn., 1867), 500.

15. Dean L. May and Jenny Cornell, "Middleton's Agriminers: The Beginnings of an Agricultural Town," *Idaho Yesterdays* 28 (Winter 1985):2–11.

16. Wells, *Gold Camps and Silver Cities*, 10–11.

17. *Our Cultural Heritage* (Cottonwood, Ida.: Idaho State Office, U.S. Bureau of Land Management, 1987), 20–22.

18. Goulder, *Reminiscences*, 210–14.

19. Mike Dakis, "Bogus Gold," *Idaho Yesterdays* 5 (Summer 1961):2–7; Ira B. Cross, "Californians and Hard Money," *California Folklore Quarterly* 4 (July 1945):169–77.

20. Livingston-Little, *An Economic History of North Idaho*, 43.

## CHAPTER 10

1. Ellis, *That Word "Idaho,"* 8.

2. A full discussion is in Beal and Wells, *History of Idaho*, 1:335–37.

3. The full story of the episode is given in Hailey, *History of Idaho*, 66–76.

4. Beal and Wells, *History of Idaho*, 1:355.

5. McConnell, *Early History of Idaho*, 288.

6. Bancroft, *History of Washington, Idaho, and Montana*, 467.

7. Dakis and Dakis, "Guilty," 2. See also *Boise News* (Idaho City), March 19, 1864.

8. Dakis and Dakis, "Guilty," 3, 5.

9. McConnell, *Early History of Idaho*, 254.

10. Beal and Wells, *History of Idaho*, 1:322, 324.

11. M. M. McPherson, "Reminiscences," manuscript in Idaho State University Museum, 34, as quoted in Beal and Wells, *History of Idaho*, 323–24.

12. McConnell, *Early History of Idaho*, 234, 250. McConnell spells the name Opdyke. See also Beal and Wells, *History of Idaho*, 1:324, 371. There is now some doubt about the early sensationalistic appraisals of Plummer. See Ruth Dakis Mather and F. E. Boswell, *Hanging the Sheriff: A Biography of Henry Plummer* (Salt Lake City: University of Utah Press, 1987).

13. McConnell, *Early History of Idaho*, 233.

## CHAPTER 11

1. Wells, *Gold Camps and Silver Cities* 12.

2. Ibid., 13.

3. See Paul, *Mining Frontiers*, 29–30.

4. Romig, "Stamp Mills in Trouble," 166–69.

5. Ibid., 169.

6. Ibid., 172.

7. Ibid.

8. Ibid., 174.

9. Richardson, *Beyond the Mississippi*, 501.

10. A more extensive description appears in Paul, *Mining Frontiers*, 64–67.

11. William Wright [Dan De Quille, pseud.], *History of the Big Bonanza: An Authentic Account of the Discovery, History, and Working*

*of the World Renowned Comstock Silver Lode of Nevada* (Hartford, Conn., 1876), 139.

12. Quoted in Wells, *Gold Camps and Silver Cities*, 28.
13. Richardson, *Beyond the Mississippi*, 505.
14. Wells, *Gold Camps and Silver Cities*, 28–29.
15. Ibid., 29.
16. Ibid., 31.
17. Quoted in ibid., 33–34.
18. Ibid., 34–35.
19. Ibid., 35–36.
20. Ibid., 37.
21. Fred Gilliard, "Early Theater in the Owyhees," *Idaho Yesterdays* 17 (Summer 1973):9–15.
22. See especially Richard E. Lingenfelter, *The Hardrock Miners: A History of the Mining Labor Movement in the American West, 1863–1893* (Berkeley: University of California Press, 1974), 79–81.
23. Wells, *Gold Camps and Silver Cities*, 41–43.
24. Robert Froman, "The Red Ghost," *American Heritage* 12 (April 1961):95.
25. *Deseret Weekly News* (Salt Lake City), October 1, 1898, p. 496.
26. Rohe, "After the Gold Rush," 11.
27. H. C. Burchard, *Report of the Director of the Mint* (Washington, D.C., 1882), 194.
28. Rossiter W. Raymond, *Statistics of Mines and Mining in the States and Territories West of the Rocky Mountains*, House Exec. Doc. 210, 42d Cong., 3d Sess. (Washington, D.C.: Government Printing Office, 1873), 198.
29. Ibid., 1874, 143.
30. Derig, "Chinese of Silver City," 2.
31. Ibid., 3.
32. Derig, "Celestials," 19.

## CHAPTER 12

1. "Letter Peter Maughan to Editor *Deseret News*, June 15, 1859," *Deseret News*, July 2, 1859.

2. See Leonard J. Arrington, "How the Saints Fed the Indians," *Improvement Era* 57 (November 1954):800–802, 814.

3. Ricks, ed., *The History of a Valley*, 48.

4. The major Fort Hall group traveled with Bannock associates (all Bannock were Northern Paiute, but not all Northern Paiute were Bannock). Their "homeland" was traversed by thousands of overlanders, and these Shoshoni-Bannock sometimes succumbed to the temptation to attack small and isolated white emigrant trains. The mounted Mountain or Lemhi Shoshoni, Sacagawea's people, ranged along the tributaries of the Salmon River into the Beaverhead country of western Montana. The unmounted Mountain Shoshoni or Sheepeaters were distributed across central Idaho and northwestern Wyoming. The Boise Shoshoni constituted a major mounted band larger than the Fort Hall Shoshoni and Northern Paiute peoples. Often referred to in early Idaho accounts as Snakes, they sometimes preyed upon emigrant parties along the Oregon Trail. Several Northwestern Shoshoni bands occupied the valleys of northern Utah. In addition, there were the Eastern Shoshoni under Chief Washakie, who occupied the Wind River Mountain area of Wyoming; the Gosiute and Western Shoshoni, who occupied the difficult desert area southwest of the Great Salt Lake and northern Nevada and sometimes took advantage of emigrants traversing the Nevada-California Trail; the Southern Shoshoni, who lived around Death Valley in southern California and Nevada and had their own dialect; and the large group of Plains-roaming Shoshoni (whom the Spaniards called Comanche), who introduced their compatriots to the horse. Confusingly, French and English explorers often referred to this last group as Snakes. See the linguistic and ethnological analysis of Sven Liljeblad, as given in Madsen, *The Shoshoni Frontier and the Bear River Massacre*, 4–12.

5. Cited in Madsen, "The Northwestern Shoshoni in Cache Valley," 29–30.

6. Ibid., 33.

7. Ibid.

8. Tullidge, "The Battle of Bear River," 197–98.

9. I have followed very closely Brigham Madsen's brilliant summary in "The Northwestern Shoshoni in Cache Valley," 28–44.

10. Simmonds, "Southeast Idaho as a Pioneer Mormon Safety Valve," 24.

11. Council Meeting, August 23, 1863, Minutes, Brigham Young Collection, 1855–77, LDS Church Library-Archives, 176–80.

12. Thomas Sleight, Journal, typescript, Utah State University Library, 50.

13. Record of President Young's Bear Lake Tour May 16 to May 26, 1864, MS, LDS Church Library-Archives; and Solomon F. Kimball, "President Brigham Young's First Trip to Bear Lake Valley," *Improvement Era* 10 (February 1907):296–303.

14. Sudweeks, "Early Agricultural Settlements in Southern Idaho," 144–45.

15. Lars Frederickson, *History of Weston, Idaho*, edited by A. J. Simmonds (Logan: Utah State University Press, 1972), 10–11.

16. Ibid., 11.

## CHAPTER 13

1. See Wells, "Idaho and the Civil War."

2. The oath is reproduced in McConnell, *Early History of Idaho*, 292–93.

3. Quoted in Beal and Wells, *History of Idaho*, 1:378. See also Hailey, *History of Idaho*, 110–15, 130–35.

4. Hailey, *History of Idaho*, 134–35. A pro-Union account of the Fourth Legislature is given in McConnell, *Early History of Idaho*, 344–49.

5. *Ibid.*, 378–83.

6. Quoted in Beal and Wells, *History of Idaho*, 381–82.

7. [H. N. Elliott, ed.], *History of Idaho Territory* (San Francisco, 1884; repr., Fairfield, Washington: Ye Galleon Press, 1973), 222. See also Dean L. May, "Mormon Cooperatives in Paris, Idaho, 1869–1896," *Idaho Yesterdays* 19 (Summer 1975):20–30.

8. McConnell, *Early History of Idaho*, 370–71.

9. Accounts of two members of Standifer's company are given in Hailey, *History of Idaho*, 50–60.

10. The account of this party is related in ibid., 86–87.

11. *General George Crook: His Autobiography*, Martin F. Schmitt, ed. (Norman: University of Oklahoma Press, 1960).

12. I realize that there are some problems with this text. Joseph spoke in Nez Perce; those who kept notes wrote in English. There are differing accounts, one presumably the text of a message and a shorter one being the substance of his remarks at the moment of surrender. Whatever the exact text, and whatever the contribution of C. E. S. Wood, Joseph was eloquent, and the reported message reminds one of General Robert E. Lee at his Civil War surrender. See Aoki, "Footnote to History: Chief Joseph's Words."

13. *New York Times*, June 23, 1878, as quoted in Canfield, *Sarah Winnemucca*, 135–36.

14. The Bannock War is described in Madsen, *The Bannock of Idaho*, 202–30; Brimlow, *The Bannock Indian War of 1878*; Canfield, *Sarah Winnemucca*, 123–49; and Corless, *The Weiser Indians*, 87–113.

15. Liljeblad, *The Idaho Indians in Transition*, 39.

16. The most recent summary of the Sheepeater campaign is in Corless, *The Weiser Indians*, 115–36.

## CHAPTER 14

1. Arrington, *Great Basin Kingdom*, 286.

2. Madsen, *North to Montana*, 221.

3. Sidney Dillon letter quoted in Athearn, "The Oregon Short Line," 2.

4. Athearn, "The Oregon Short Line," 9.

5. Linus P. Brockett, *Our Western Empire . . .* (Philadelphia, 1882), 795–96.

6. Beal and Wells, *History of Idaho*, 1:512–13.

7. Ibid., 1:541.

8. Livingston-Little, *Economic History of North Idaho*, 75.

9. George Bird Grinnell, "Building the Northern Pacific," 11.

10. Ibid., 11–13.

11. Merrill Beal, *Snake River Fork Country*, 22–23. This is Beal's summary of the letter.

12. Athearn, "The Oregon Short Line," 11.

13. Quoted in Gilbert C. Fite, *The Farmers' Frontier, 1865–1900* (New York: Holt, Rinehart and Winston, 1966), 188.

## CHAPTER 15

1. Paul, *The Far West and the Great Plains Transition*, 252–82.
2. Hawley, *History of Idaho*, 1:486–87.
3. *Idaho Tri-Weekly Statesman*, December 14, 1880, as quoted in Spence, "Boom in the Wood River Mines," *Idaho Yesterdays* 23 (Summer 1979): 4.
4. Ibid., 8; Beal and Wells, *History of Idaho*, 1:572.
5. Strahorn, *Fifteen Thousand Miles by Stage*, 2:49.
6. Beal and Wells, *History of Idaho*, 1:574.
7. Spence, "Boom of the Wood River Mines," 9–12.
8. Quoted in Livingston-Little, *Economic History of North Idaho*, 84–85.
9. Ibid., 85.
10. Ibid., 85–86; Rickard, *History of American Mining*, 320.
11. Livingston-Little, *Economic History of North Idaho*, 86–88.
12. Ibid., 87.
13. Ibid., 90–93.
14. Rickard, *History of American Mining*, 321–22. A similar story, ostensibly told by Kellogg, is given in *The Autobiography of John Hays Hammond*, 2 vols. (New York: Farrar Rinehart, 1935), 1:187–88.
15. Rickard, *History of American Mining*, 322.
16. Spence, *Mining Engineers and the American West*, 1–2.
17. Ibid., 155.
18. Ibid., 170–71.
19. Ibid., 10–11; Rickard, *History of American Mining*, 337.
20. Beal and Wells, *History of Idaho*, 2:75–78.
21. Livingston-Little, *Economic History of North Idaho*, 82.

## CHAPTER 16

1. Beal and Wells, *History of Idaho*, 1:440.
2. Ibid., 440–42.

3. Limbaugh, *Rocky Mountain Carpetbaggers*, 165.

4. Beal and Wells, *History of Idaho*, 1:568–70.

5. *Idaho World* (Idaho City), as quoted in Owens, "Pierce City Incident," 9 and passim.

6. Ibid., 12–13.

7. Beal and Wells, *History of Idaho*, 1:594.

8. Ibid.

9. Ibid., 1:596.

10. Rafe Gibbs, *Beacon for Mountain and Plain: Story of the University of Idaho* (Moscow: University of Idaho, 1962), 16–17.

## CHAPTER 17

1. Arthur Hart, "Community Identity," 34.

2. Victoria Croft, "Saturday Specials on Jordan Creek," *Idaho Yesterdays* 5 (Winter 1961–62):17. The following paragraphs are based on this source.

3. Ibid., 18.

4. Hicks, "The Significance of the Small Town," 159.

5. Leonard J. Arrington, "The Promise of Eagle Rock: Idaho Falls, Idaho, 1863–1980," *Rendezvous: Idaho State University Journal of Arts and Letters* 18 (Spring 1983):2–17.

6. Agnew, "Idaho Pioneer of 1864," 45.

7. West, *The Saloon on the Rocky Mountain Frontier*, xiv.

8. Ibid., 148–49.

9. Ibid., 12, 95.

10. Ibid., 61; Donaldson, *Idaho of Yesterday*, 113–20.

11. Agnew, "Idaho Pioneer of 1864," 44.

12. Hawley, *History of Idaho*, 1:594.

13. Ibid.

14. Ibid., 1:594–95.

15. Ibid., 1:596–97.

16. Donaldson, *Idaho of Yesterday*, 203.

17. Quoted in Ezra J. Poulsen, *Joseph C. Rich, Versatile Pioneer on the Mormon Frontier* (Salt Lake City: Granite Publishing Co., 1958), 301–2.

18. Donaldson, *Idaho of Yesterday*, 211–13.

19. Ibid., 214–20.

20. Mark Wyman, "Frontier Journalism," *Idaho Yesterdays* 17 (Spring 1973):30–36. See also Oliver Knight, "The Owyhee Avalanche: The Frontier Newspaper as a Catalyst in Social Change," *Pacific Northwest Quarterly*, 58 (1967):74–81.

21. These paragraphs are based on Sherilyn Cox Bennion, "Ada Chase Merritt and the Recorder: A Pioneer Idaho Editor and Her Newspaper," *Idaho Yesterdays* 25 (Winter 1982):22–30. See also Bennion's *Equal to the Occasion: Women Editors of the Nineteenth-Century West* (Reno and Las Vegas: University of Nevada Press, 1990).

22. This section borrows heavily from Attebery, *Building Idaho*, passim.

23. Ezra J. Poulsen, "Parisian Life . . . Western Style," *Idaho Yesterdays* 8 (Spring 1964):2–9.

24. Based on Arthur Hart, "Community Identity in Small Town Idaho," 34–35.

25. Attebery, *Building Idaho*, 41–42.

26. Ibid., 71.

27. Hine, *The American West: An Interpretive History*, 254. See also Thomas Bender, *Community and Social Change in America* (New Brunswick, N.J.: Rutgers University Press, 1978); Don Harrison Doyle, *The Social Order of Frontier Community: Jacksonville, Illinois, 1825–1870* (Urbana: University of Illinois Press, 1978); and Dean L. May and Jenny Cornell, "Middleton's Agriminers: The Beginnings of an Agricultural Town," *Idaho Yesterdays* 28 (Winter 1985):2–11.

28. Beal and Wells, *History of Idaho*, 2:45.

29. William Henry Gibbs, Personal Journal, 1886–1904, manuscript, LDS Church Archives, Salt Lake City, Utah, 49.

## CHAPTER 18

1. Dubois, *The Making of a State*, 180.

2. Quoted in Lauterbach, "A Plentitude of Senators."

3. *Wallace Press*, February 21, 1891, quoted in Lauterbach, "A Plenitude of Senators," 8.

4. In 1890 neither Lewiston nor Moscow was as large as Mont-

pelier, Idaho's only town besides Boise with a population of more than 1,000.

5. A copy of the act is given in McConnell, *Early History of Idaho*, 318–24.

6. Emma Edwards Green, "Description of the Idaho State Seal," Idaho Historical Society Reference Series No. 61.

7. William Budge, leading Mormon in Bear Lake Valley, estimated 25,000 persons of Mormon antecedents in Idaho, which would have been about 28 percent of Idaho's 1890 population. A church membership compilation of that year listed 15,167 active Mormons in Idaho's four southeastern counties. Of course there were others scattered throughout the state. The 20,000 figure seems reasonable.

8. Codman in the *National Democrat*, September 17, 1890, as published in *Deseret Weekly* 41 (July 5, 1890):37–38.

9. *Sandpoint News*, October 21, 1904.

10. *Lewiston Tribune*, October 25–26, 1904.

11. Hawley, *History of Idaho*, 1:237.

12. Duniway's address, given July 16, 1889, is published in her autobiography, *Path Breaking*, 130–43, and in *Idaho Yesterdays* 34 (Summer 1990):21–27.

13. Minute Book, Equal Suffrage Association, 21; also Beeton, *Women Vote in the West*, 127.

14. Cited in Beeton, *Women Vote in the West*, 132.

15. Ibid. See also Emmeline B. Wells, Diary, January 19, 1897, Brigham Young University Library.

16. Larson, "Woman's Rights in Idaho," 19; Rebecca Brown Mitchell, "Glimpses From My Life," *Snake River Echoes* 3 (1974): 63–65.

17. Quoted in Beal and Wells, *History of Idaho*, 2:98.

18. Quoted in ibid., 2:103–4, and Hawley, *History of Idaho*, 1:572.

## CHAPTER 19

1. *Ketchum Keystone*, July 15, 1893, as quoted in Gaboury, "The Stubborn Defense," 5.

2. *Idaho World*, September 19, 1893, as quoted in Gaboury, "The Stubborn Defense." 7.

3. Schwantes, "Law and Disorder," 11.

4. Ibid., 12.

5. In this and the following paragraphs I am relying heavily on Schwantes, "Law and Disorder," 10–15, 18–26.

6. Gaboury, *Dissension in the Rockies*, passim.

7. Beal and Wells, *History of Idaho*, 2:221.

8. I have closely followed the recitation given in Hawley, *History of Idaho*, 1:244–56. An excellent treatment is Jensen, *Heritage of Conflict*, 72–87.

9. See "The Idaho Trials," in Jensen, *Heritage of Conflict*, 197–218.

## CHAPTER 20

1. The U.S. Census definition at the time classified as urban people living in towns of 2,500 or more inhabitants. Thus rural included not only those living in country towns and on scattered farms, but also those in small mining camps.

2. See Wanda Ricks Wyler, *Thomas E. Ricks: Colonizer and Founder* (Provo, Utah: M. C. Printing, 1989).

3. Louise Morgan Sill, "The Largest Irrigated Tract in the World," *Harper's Weekly* 52 (October 17, 1908):11; Kingsbury, *Bucking the Tide*, 45–115.

4. Carter, ed., *Pioneer Irrigation*, 262–65.

5. Lovin, "The Carey Act in Idaho," 127, 132–33.

6. Quoted in Perry, "Arrowrock Dam is Built," 16.

7. John A. Widtsoe, *Dry Farming: A System of Agriculture for Countries Under a Low Rainfall* (New York: The Macmillan Co., 1910).

8. James W. Davis and Nikki Balch Stilwell, *Aristocrat in Burlap: A History of the Potato in Idaho* (Idaho Falls: Idaho Potato Commission, 1975), especially 1–43.

9. George Yost and Dick d'Easum, *Idaho: The Fruitful Land* (Boise: Syms-York, 1980), 1–8.

10. Luther Burbank, *Harvest of the Years*, 1927.

11. John Gunther, *Inside U.S.A.* (New York: Harper & Brothers, 1947), 114.

12. Charles F. Saylor, *Methods and Benefits of Growing Sugar Beets*, U.S. Department of Agriculture Circular 11 (Washington, D.C.: Government Printing Office, 1904), 24; Charles F. Saylor in U.S. Department of Agriculture, *Special Report on the Beet-Sugar Industry in the United States* (Washington: Government Printing Office, 1898), 169, 184.

13. See Leonard J. Arrington, "Science, Government, and Enterprise in Economic Development: The Western Beet Sugar Industry," *Agricultural History* 41 (January 1967):6–13.

14. Beal and Wells, *History of Idaho*, 1:422–39.

15. The story of the race is told in Hidy, et al., *Timber and Men*, 250–51.

16. Quoted in ibid., 254.

17. Ibid., 258.

# INDEX

## Volume 2

BY

LEONARD J. ARRINGTON

UNIVERSITY OF IDAHO PRESS
MOSCOW

IDAHO STATE HISTORICAL SOCIETY
BOISE

1994

TO MY PARENTS

N. W. and Edna Corn Arrington
Pioneer Settlers in Twin Falls County
and to
Merle Wells
Superb Idaho State Historian

# CONTENTS

## Volume 2

## CHAPTER TWENTY-ONE

# World War I

WHEN the Great War began in Europe in 1914 Idaho had been a state only twenty-four years. Men and women were still living who had come into the Clearwater, Boise Basin, and Owyhee mining regions in the 1860s; who had worked on the Utah and Northern, Oregon Short Line, and Northern Pacific railroads in the 1870s and 1880s. Men still alive had known Chief Joseph, both on the battlefield and in his retirement. Women still talked of the first vote they cast after suffrage and they were proud and respectful of Permeal J. French, superintendent of public instruction. Six of Idaho's governors were still alive, one of whom, James H. Brady, was serving as United States Senator. Idaho's brilliant and respected Senator William E. Borah had been reelected to his second term in 1912. Blacks on Idaho farms and in cities had been born as slaves in Mississippi, Alabama, and North Carolina, and on the edge of Idaho's capital city groups of Indians still pitched their tents. Idaho was becoming famous for her potatoes and for her

White Satin sugar, as she had been famous for her thunderous Shoshone Falls in the days before Magic Valley had risen like a mirage in the desert.

A few automobiles had appeared in Boise, Pocatello, and Twin Falls. Local opera houses were still scheduling "players" from back east. Schoolteachers had diplomas from Lewiston, Albion, Moscow, the College of Idaho, and Ricks. People enjoyed county fairs and church socials, spelling bees and sleigh rides, Fourth of July and Thanksgiving, rabbit hunts and salmon fishing.

In addition to Senator Borah, Idaho was best known early in the century as the home of Walter Johnson, the "Weiser Wonder," arguably the greatest baseball player of all time. Born in western Kansas in 1887, Johnson drifted to the West in 1905 and tried out for some Pacific Coast baseball teams but failed to make the grade. In 1906 Weiser boosters organized a local baseball team and, through a mutual contact in Portland, offered Johnson a contract. He played a few games in the spring of 1906. Five hundred persons watched Johnson strike out thirteen in a 1-to-0 win against Emmett on June 20. Emmett players, supposed to be the "champs," were so crestfallen that they demanded a rematch, which was held on July 4. Once again Weiser was victorious; Emmett players lamented, "too much Johnson." Weiser won against Nampa, Boise, and Mountain Home but lost to Caldwell. Nineteen-year-old Johnson had pitched eighty-five innings without a score against him and struck out 166 men.

Word soon spread, and the very next year, in 1907, the Washington Senators signed him on. The "Weiser Wonder" again performed his magic. In his second season with the Senators he accomplished the impossible: he shut out the New York Yankees three games in a row. In all, Johnson pitched for the Senators twenty-one years, during which he set a world record for strikeouts (3,508) and shutouts (113) and pitched fifty-six consecutive scoreless innings.[1] In 1913 he won thirty-six games while losing only seven. His 416 victories, next to Cy Young the highest achieved by any pitcher in this century, were all the more remarkable for having been gained on behalf of a perennial second-division team. Johnson's principal weapon was his fastball, which, with the possible exception of Bob Feller, is generally considered the fastest of all time and earned him the nickname "Big Train."

While Idahoans were enjoying small-town baseball, dreadful events were transpiring in Europe. On July 28, 1914, Austria declared war on Serbia, and within a few days Germany, Russia, France, and Great Britain were also at war. Idaho was a long way from the battlefront; but when the Germans overran Belgium, Idahoans conducted a statewide drive to purchase flour for the Belgian Relief Fund.

In the fall of 1914 Idahoans were preoccupied with the political campaign. Republican John M. Haines, a Boise realtor since 1890 and former mayor of Boise, had been elected governor in 1912 and had served well in that office. To most observers his reelection seemed secure—that is, until two weeks before the voting, when the Boise *Statesman* revealed that State Treasurer O. V. Allen, also a Republican, had submitted his resignation. An audit of the treasurer's books showed a defalcation. Charged with embezzlement, Allen pled guilty on October 22 to taking $93,112 and was sentenced to five to ten years in the state penitentiary. When he first took office, Haines had promptly cleared out obvious corruption. Now, although the state treasurer was a constitutional officer in no way responsible to the governor, many voters apparently felt that Haines should have been aware of what was going on. Politically damaged, Haines was defeated by his Democratic opponent. The newly elected governor was Moses Alexander, also a Boise resident, who operated a retail chain of men's wearing apparel. He now became the nation's first elected Jewish governor.

Moses Alexander was born in Bavaria in 1853, the youngest of eight children. In 1867, at the age of fourteen, he immigrated to the United States and settled in Chillicothe, Missouri, where he worked as a salesman in his cousin's store. He became fluent in English, studied history and government, and avidly read the St. Louis *Republic*, a Democratic newspaper. In 1875 he met Hedwig Kaestner, who had emigrated with her family from Saxony in eastern Germany when she was twelve. It pleased Alexander that she decided to convert to Judaism; she was given the new name of Helena. The couple were married in St. Joseph, Missouri, in 1876, and subsequently became the parents of four children. Alexander was elected to the Chillicothe City Council, then mayor of the city for two terms. In 1891 he left Chillicothe bound for Alaska. En route, he stopped in Boise, liked what he saw, bought a former saloon on the corner of Main and Ninth streets, and opened a men's clothing store. He later expanded with stores in Emmett, Weiser, Caldwell, Nampa, Twin Falls, Burley, and Blackfoot.

In 1895 Alexander joined with other Jews to organize a Reform Jewish congregation, Beth Israel, and a synagogue was built in 1896. The next year, he agreed to run for mayor of Boise on a nonpartisan ticket and was elected. He served a second term. In 1908 he ran for governor but was narrowly defeated by James H. Brady. He declined nomination in 1910 but was selected again in 1914. Campaigning strongly for economy in state government and for Prohibition, he was elected.

Alexander's popularity with voters can be partly explained by his sense of humor. "Not far from Caldwell . . . he came upon a cluster of farmers," wrote one reporter. Wanting to address them on "the issues of the day," he noticed a low shed nearby and offered to speak from the top of it. "But they store manure in it," commented one of his fellow-travelers. Alexander mounted the shed, looked out over his impromptu audience, and observed: "This is the first time in my life I've ever spoken from a Republican platform!"[2]

Alexander's first action as governor was against the liquor traffic. Idaho had embraced local option on Prohibition in 1909, but Alexander pressed for statutory Prohibition and also for an amendment to the state constitution that would eliminate the saloon. The Senate passed the resolution unanimously and the House by a three-fourths majority. Alexander signed the bill, and it became effective on January 1, 1916. In the November 1916 election, with Prohibition already in effect by legislation, the citizens approved the amendment to make it a constitutional provision. They also reelected Alexander by a narrow majority. In fact, the Democratic state ticket was swept into office; for the first time since the days of Populism and free silver the Democrats controlled the legislature. A major piece of legislation approved and signed by the governor was an act, directed against Bill Haywood's Industrial Workers of the World, making advocacy of armed revolution a criminal offense. This criminal syndicalism statute was enforced without hesitation, particularly in northern Idaho.

Early in 1916 Francisco "Pancho" Villa and his Mexican troops raided across the border into New Mexico. America was incensed at this violation, and General John J. Pershing was assigned to pursue Villa. Governor Alexander sent a telegram to President Woodrow Wilson offering enlisted men and officers equipped and trained. Wilson signed the National Defense Act authorizing use of state militias to guard against invasion, and in June 1916 the Secretary of War requested that Governor Alexander send a regiment to the Mexican border. He mobilized the Idaho National Guard, Second Regiment, some 1,800 men. Among the volunteers was his son Nathan. They arrived at Nogales, Arizona, on July 12 and served there until December 8. Army instructions were that they should be mustered out at Fort Douglas, Utah, but Governor Alexander was outraged. He fired off telegrams to the Army and to Idaho's congressional delegation, and the orders were revised to permit the Idaho regiment to be discharged out of Boise Barracks.

Early in 1917 the war in Europe that had seemed so remote for two and one-half years suddenly threatened to involve the United States. The Germans began to wage unrestricted submarine warfare; they sank five American ships in the month of March. Responding to a presidential request, Congress on April 6, 1917, declared war on the Central Powers. Governor Alexander echoed support that the President "acted rightly and it was the only thing for him to do to protect the integrity of the flag."[3] The recently demobilized Second Regiment was reassembled and prepared for service as the Second Idaho National Guard. Drafted into United States service on August 5, 1917, the Second Idaho consisted of twelve full infantry companies, a machine-gun company, a supply company, and a headquarters company. The men, who came from all counties and most communities in the state, were trained at Camp Lewis, Washington, shipped to Camp Greene at Charlotte, North Carolina, and there were merged with other units, much to the regret of the officers and men. The first battalion became part of the 146th Field Artillery, which fought in several major engagements during the final year of the war. The second battalion was assigned to guard duty on railroad bridges and tunnels in the Northwest until October 1917, when its members joined the 116th Engineers. The third battalion was incorporated in the 146th Machine Gun Battalion. The machine-gun company was assigned to the 147th; and the field hospital unit was divided among four companies. All these organizations were attached to the 41st Division. From Camp Greene the men were moved to ports of embarkation and boarded British and American transports for France.

The large contingent of the 41st Division arrived at Le Havre, Saint Nazaire, Brest, and Bordeaux, France, in November and December 1917. Another contingent left in June 1918 and arrived at the front in time to assist in wiping out the Saint Mihiel salient near Metz. They also saw service in the Meuse-Argonne drive and the Ypres-Lys offensive. Other major engagements in which Idaho men fought were Cantigny, Chateau-Thierry, and the battles along the Marne, Aisne, Vesle, and Oure rivers. Cantigny, the first offensive in which American troops took part, was a key engagement that gave the Allies confidence in the fighting ability of American soldiers. At Chateau Thierry, the turning point of the war, American soldiers and marines halted the German advance to Paris. The First American Army, in taking the Saint Mihiel salient, prepared the way for the Meuse-Argonne drive through the Argonne Forest that proved to be one of the great battles in American history. These and other offensives resulted in the Armistice of November 11, 1918.[4]

On May 16, 1918, 2,786 young men who had reached the age of twenty-one registered under the Selective Service regulations, and the Selective Service Act of August 21, 1918, boosted the number of Idaho military registrants to 105,337. By July 22, 1918, some 12,590 Idahoans were in Army service, of whom 5,060 were volunteers. The total number of Idaho men and women in United States forces was 19,279, including Army, Navy, Marine Corps, Aviation Corps, and nurses. More than half, 10,028, went overseas. A total of 782 Idaho men lost their lives, and many others suffered from battle wounds and disease. On March 1, 1918, Idaho suffered its first casualty when Captain Stewart W. Hoover, of Blackfoot, was killed in action. Another Idahoan, Thomas C. Neibaur of Sugar City, received the Congressional Medal of Honor for extraordinary heroism. Although seriously wounded, he successfully arrested the counterattack of a German unit, killed four who attacked him at short range, and took eleven prisoners. Twenty-three Idaho men received the Distinguished Service Cross for exceptional bravery in battle.[5]

Since Allied countries could not produce what they needed to carry out the war effort, Idaho farmers and ranchers were urged to step up their production. There was every incentive to do so, because for a few years farmers received unprecedented prices.

Wheat prices rose from $.72 a bushel in 1913 to $1.98 in 1918. The price of oats and hay doubled. Still, the labor shortage was a constraint, so Idaho state officials went so far as to invade saloons and poolrooms where those men who spurned jobs were arrested. Governor Alexander even issued a proclamation closing pool halls during the day so that "pool hall loafers" would have no alternative but to work. Businessmen volunteers in Boise, Twin Falls, and Idaho Falls also helped the farmers. Highway building was postponed so that more men would be available to plant crops. District judges were asked to postpone civil cases where a jury was needed until after the planting (or harvesting) season. Schools were expected to give spring and fall "vacations" to enable young people to thin sugar beet plants and pick potatoes. The governor issued a proclamation in February 1918 calling for 900 skilled workmen to go to the West Coast to work as shipbuilders. Much to the governor's satisfaction, the quota soon was filled.

On May 7, 1917, Governor Alexander appointed a State Council of Defense to coordinate all of Idaho's activity in behalf of the war. A local council was organized in each county to work with the state council in promoting patriotism and waging war on disloyalty, ferreting out deserters, draft slackers, and potential subversives. Because the Second Idaho was called into national service, the state was left without troops for internal defense in case of emergency. Alexander therefore authorized the creation of a battalion of Home Guards. Companies were organized at Boise, American Falls, Pocatello, Sandpoint, and Moscow.[6]

Members of the Industrial Workers of the World had gone to work in lumber camps in north Idaho. Accusations mounted that the IWW was financed by German agents and was intent on shutting down the industry. Keeping in mind the legislature's passage of sabotage laws and the timber interests' repeated requests for intervention, the Council of Defense asked the governor to declare martial law and jail officers of the IWW. When

Alexander went to north Idaho and personally talked with lumber-mill managers, lumberjacks, and IWW organizers, he found that the disturbances were "considerably overdrawn." Nevertheless, local police units imprisoned some IWW members, prompting the union to threaten a general strike until they were released. The governor then asked for federal troops and called up a company of the National Guard. The strike, if indeed one was planned, was averted.

IWW organizing activity continued, however, and in March 1918 the labor group threatened to storm the St. Maries jail to free one of their members charged with criminal syndicalism. Alexander called the IWW "an organization based on sedition, cowardice and treason." The Sandpoint Home Guard was ordered to St. Maries and possible violence was prevented.[7] This crisis was the only time any unit of the Home Guard was called into active service.

A part of the war effort required economizing on wheat, meat, and sugar, with "wheatless Mondays" and "meatless Tuesdays." Herbert Hoover, head of the War Food Administration, asked for "Hoover menus" of rye bread, no meat, and honey in place of sugar. Women were taught how to make sugarless, eggless, milkless, butterless cakes; many of them started home gardens and organized canning clubs. At Pocatello, a regular stop on the transcontinental railroad, local women maintained a Red Cross canteen unit that served soldiers on their way to the West Coast, in both the months preceding and the month after the Armistice. During December 1918, for example, the Pocatello canteen served 500 gallons of coffee, 30,000 sandwiches, and 30,000 doughnuts.[8]

Public demonstrations of patriotism and support were common. Draftees were sent off with parades, dances, and farewell gifts. Women were organized to knit socks, vests, jackets, scarfs, and wristlets; they prepared bandages for hospitals; some of them entered the labor force to replace men, even doing heavy work in railroad shops. To cite the example of one Idaho community, by the beginning of November 1917 Pocatello women had contributed 223 bedshirts, 280 pairs of pajamas, 68 shoulder wraps, 100 bathrobes, 241 surgical gowns, 80 pairs of bedsocks, 84 hot-water-bag covers, 144 ice-bag covers, 60 operating caps, 80 operating helmets, and 2 large boxes of surgical dressings.[9]

Educators were also involved. A student Army Training Corps at the University of Idaho compensated for dwindling enrollment. An angry band of educators in Lincoln County attempted to punish a colleague for "traitorous" behavior (expressing pacifist sentiments) by throwing him into the icy waters of the Wood River. Councils of Defense in Kootenai, Idaho, Minidoka, Twin Falls, and Lincoln counties eventually forced the closure of parochial schools maintained by German Methodists, Lutherans, and Mennonites.[10]

In addition, massive drives were mounted to sell government Liberty Bonds and to gather donations to the Red Cross, Y.M.C.A., Salvation Army, United War Work, and other forms of relief. Former Governor James Hawley, in his *History of Idaho*, summarized Idaho's contributions to war finances as follows (figures rounded out):

| | |
|---|---:|
| Liberty bonds purchased | $44,400,000 |
| War Savings Stamps | 5,900,000 |
| Red Cross Donations | 700,000 |
| United War Drive | 450,000 |
| All other relief work | 1,300,000 |
| Total | $52,750,000 |

A total of $120 was collected for every man, woman, and child in the state—a creditable accomplishment.[11]

Support for the war effort sometimes verged on paranoia. Guards were stationed at Arrowrock Dam, railroad bridges, grain elevators, and power plants, although no evidence exists of any attempted German sabotage. North Idaho mine and smelter operators asked the War Department for bayonets to prevent disruptions. When that request was denied, they asked that the state supply guards.

In 1917 Idaho had about 4,000 German-born citizens and another 1,000 of Austro-Hungarian birth, as well as 18,000 native-born Idahoans of German ancestry and another 3,000 of Austrian origin. The more zealous local citizens scrutinized the 16,000 "German" inhabitants carefully. Dunkard congregations at Cavendish and Teakean were pacifists. Germans also comprised most of the pacifist Mennonite congregations at Aberdeen, Kimama, and Adelaide. They declared their loyalty to America but did not believe in war.

Not surprisingly, anti-German emotions surfaced. In one case a person telephoned county offices in Blackfoot to say that residents of the small "German" settlement at Taber, eighteen miles northwest of Blackfoot, openly opposed the war and had raised the German flag over the schoolhouse. Outraged Bingham County citizens gathered at Blackfoot, and a group of them, estimated at from 40 to 100, fully armed, commandeered a train and went to Taber. No German flag floated aloft; the stunned local citizens watched while the mob raised the Stars and Stripes over Taber and then departed.[12]

Self-appointed vigilantes visited various punishments upon citizens suspected of being disloyal:

> The Pocatello owner of a facsimile gold-plated iron cross was jailed. Snoopers discovered a photograph of Wilhelm II in a hotel room in Troy; thereupon, a "shouting crowd" compelled the owner of the photograph to destroy it and publicly to "kiss the Stars and Stripes." At Rexburg, rowdies masked their identities behind Ku Klux Klan costumes before hunting for "pro-Germans." The mob captured and chained one accused individual to an electric light pole on

which a sign was posted: "I was put here as a warning, also as an example of a Pro-German, a Kaiser lover."[13]

Local vigilance committees and patriot leagues, as they did throughout the nation, kept an eye on aliens, strangers, and suspicious persons, with little concern for civil rights and enlightenment. German books were burned, meetings of groups that permitted talks in German were forbidden, and the teaching of German in high schools was dropped in favor of French or no foreign language. Although he was a German immigrant, the governor did not discourage these moves. Indeed, he declared himself to be "against the German language, German Kultur, and German propaganda."[14] He was also unsympathetic to Idaho's many German immigrants who, because of their accent, were harassed by neighbors. He simply responded that they must prove their loyalty. Perhaps because he was Jewish, no one ever questioned his resolute American patriotism.

The 1918 election went on as usual. Senator Borah was reelected (with the private support of Woodrow Wilson); John F. Nugent, a Democrat who was appointed by Governor Alexander to fill the vacancy in the other senatorial slot when Republican James H. Brady died, was elected. Alexander chose not to run again, and Republican D. W. Davis was victorious in the governor's race. Idaho now had two Congressmen, and both Republican representatives were reelected—Addison T. Smith and Burton L. French.

Thanks partially to the American victory at Saint Mihiel in September 1918 and the substantial American contributions in the Meuse-Argonne offensive that began September 16 and continued into November, Bulgaria, Austria, and Turkey surrendered, and the Germans signed an Armistice on November 11, 1918. Idahoans celebrated with bells, whistles, sirens, drums, horns, and steam calliopes. Thousands marched in parades and listened to victory talks by Governor Alexander and city mayors.

The Kaiser was burned in effigy. Bands played "There'll be a Hot Time in the Old Town Tonight." As health officials warned, however, a deadly price was paid for this exuberance.

In the spring of 1918 a relentless epidemic called Spanish influenza spread through Europe, Asia, Africa, and North and South America in what became the most serious pandemic since the Black Death of the fourteenth century. In a period of twelve months approximately 25 million persons died of influenza-pneumonia, including 500,000 Americans. The disease struck down and killed more American soldiers than did enemy firepower. The disease had touched America in the spring of 1918, but a more virulent wave of infection was brought to army camps throughout the nation as soldiers returned from France in the fall. Far deadlier than earlier strains, this influenza struck quickly and produced a high fever. Many of the cases developed into severe bronchial pneumonia, producing an alarming number of deaths not only among the very young and very old, but also among persons between the ages of twenty and forty.

The epidemic reached Idaho in early October 1918. The front pages of the state's newspapers were covered with reports of the victorious advance of American, British, French, and Italian troops. On the back pages were small dispatches from eastern cities telling of deaths from "The Spanish Flu." A few infections were reported in Boise, Caldwell, and Meridian. In compliance with the recommendation of the U.S. Surgeon General, Idaho's State Board of Health issued a statewide order, effective October 10, 1918, prohibiting all public assemblies "as a precaution." This order included the closure of theaters, churches, town assembly halls, and dance halls. All gatherings of a public nature were canceled, including election-year campaign rallies, Liberty Loan meetings, and dances. Schools were closed. Several communities adopted a quarantine under which no passenger was permitted to leave the train as it passed through the town, nor was any automobile allowed to stop there. Society matrons, members of civic clubs, schoolteachers, church groups, and other volunteers responded to calls for nursing help. Neighborhood women entered homes where everyone in the family was down and drew water, cooked meals, answered the telephone, and scrubbed floors. Some of the volunteer cooks, nurses, and "helpers" contracted the disease and lost their lives in the service of others.

With the announcement of the Armistice, the caution of the previous month was thrown aside. Celebrators gave little thought to the inevitability of contagion, and the result was predictable. Thousands were infected with the disease, hospitals were jammed, and business slowed to a standstill. Local and state boards of health promptly tightened regulations: all influenza cases had to be quarantined, public meetings deferred, and public telephones fumigated. Hotels and eating places were required to disinfect dishes and silver. Barbers were directed to disinfect razors, brushes, and towels. All buildings with influenza patients inside were placarded with a large quarantine sign, "INFLUENZA." Spitting on the sidewalks or floors, even loafing on street corners, were prohibited. Anyone venturing outside had to wear cotton gauze masks to prevent the spread of germs by coughs and sneezes.

Minidoka County placed guards at all roads into the county; anyone trying to enter was forcibly restrained. Challis placed guards on the highway in the mountain divide between the town and Mackay to keep people from bringing in the disease. Among those stopped were the county commissioners, the district judge, and many hunters. Gooding County did the same, as did Bonneville. Most towns continued their quarantines into March 1919, when the epidemic began to subside. The effect of the epidemic on Native Americans was especially baneful. Idaho's Indian population of 4,208 developed 634 cases of influenza and suffered 72 deaths.

Although no reliable statistics recorded the total number of deaths in Idaho, reports from neighboring states (Montana, Utah, Washington, and Oregon) suggest that the impact of the influenza epidemic on Idaho was severe. Rich and poor, farmers and factory workers, lumbermen and miners—many were stricken. Doctors, nurses, and hospitals were taxed as never before. Every hamlet was affected, every neighborhood lost children, parents, and grandparents. To this day medical historians are not certain why the epidemic of 1918–19 took place, why it was so deadly, why it ended, or where it went. But the Idahoans of those years remember it well.[15]

Idahoans proved their patriotism during World War I. The rate of war service was high and the support of citizens was evident in the hearty send-offs to draftees, street demonstrations, band concerts, fireworks, and farewell suppers. Idaho soldiers exhibited courage, resourcefulness, and alertness. Thousands of craftsmen not drafted migrated to Washington, Oregon, and California to work in shipyards and war plants. Laborers who remained supplied the Allied war effort with food and feed, minerals, and timber products in unprecedented amounts. Women found employment in railroad and machine shops, mills, and grain elevators. Housewives organized to furnish aid to soldiers, European refugees, and families of soldiers killed or wounded in action. Idaho's schoolchildren helped with the weeding and harvesting of farm crops, while their teachers served as substitute nurses during the influenza epidemic. Almost everyone bought war bonds or thrift and war savings stamps. Idahoans were fully involved in the great crusade to save the world for democracy. The decade that followed the Armistice, however, brought disillusionment and misfortune to many.

## CHAPTER TWENTY-ONE: SOURCES

The national setting for the World War I period is described in Frederic L. Paxson, *America at War, 1917–1918* (Boston: Houghton

Mifflin Co., 1939); W. E. Leuchtenburg, *The Perils of Prosperity, 1914–1932* (Chicago: University of Chicago Press, 1958), 1–83; George Soule, *Prosperity Decade: From War to Depression, 1917–1929* (New York: Rinehart and Company, 1947), 7–80; Arthur S. Link, *American Epoch: A History of the United States Since the 1890s*, 2d ed. (New York: Alfred A. Knopf, 1966), esp. 171–246; A. B. Genung, "Agriculture in the World War Period," in United States Department of Agriculture, *Year Book of Agriculture, 1940* (Washington, D.C.: Government Printing Office, 1941), 277–95; and Jonathan R. T. Hughes, *American Economic History*, 2d ed. (Glenview, Ill.: Scott, Foresman and Company, 1987), 413–27.

Regional histories that cover the World War I period include Johansen and Gates, *Empire of the Columbia*, 476–91; Schwantes, *The Pacific Northwest*, 279–84, 288–89; Michael P. Malone and Richard W. Etulain, *The American West: A Twentieth-Century History* (Lincoln: University of Nebraska Press, 1989), 17–19, 26, 72–79, 159–60; Gerald D. Nash, *The American West in the Twentieth Century: A Short History of An Urban Oasis* (Englewood Cliffs, New Jersey: Prentice-Hall, 1973), 65–76; and Earl Pomeroy, *The Pacific Slope: A History of California, Oregon, Washington, Idaho, Utah, and Nevada* (New York: Alfred A. Knopf, 1965), 216–17. A good chapter on a neighboring state is T. A. Larson, *History of Wyoming* (Lincoln: University of Nebraska Press, 1965), 386–410.

On Idaho history the best source is the chapter in Beal and Wells, *History of Idaho*, 2:229–37. Other sources include Brosnan, *History of the State of Idaho*, 346–48, 360–67; Defenbach, *Idaho: The Place and Its People*, 1:554–57; Hawley, *History of Idaho*, 1:576–83; Barber and Martin, *Idaho in the Pacific Northwest*, 167–211; and the following articles: Hugh T. Lovin, "The Red Scare in Idaho, 1916–1918," *Idaho Yesterdays* 17 (Fall 1973):2–13; Jo-Ann Ruckman, "Knit, Knit, and Then Knit: The Women of Pocatello and the War Effort of 1917–1918," *Idaho Yesterdays* 26 (Spring 1982):26–36; Leonard J. Arrington, "The Influenza Epidemic of 1918–1919 in Southern Idaho," *Idaho Yesterdays* 32 (Fall 1988):19–29; and Hugh T. Lovin, "World War Vigilantes in Idaho, 1917–1918," *Idaho Yesterdays* 18 (Fall 1974):2–11.

Governor Moses Alexander is treated in David L. Crowder, "Moses Alexander: Idaho's Jewish Governor, 1914–1918" (Ph.D. dissertation, University of Utah, 1972); and David L. Crowder, "Moses Alexander," in Robert C. Sims, ed., *Idaho's Governors: Historical Essays on Their Administrations* (Boise: Boise State University, 1978), 92–102.

121.

122.

121. Governor of Idaho from 1914 to 1918 was Moses Alexander, the nation's first elected Jewish head of a state. ISHS 72–74.238.

122. Armistice Day Parade in Troy, November 11, 1918, included a veteran of the Civil War, Mr. Weaver, who is holding the U.S. flag. UIL 5–77–5A.

## CHAPTER TWENTY-TWO

# The Faltering Twenties

AMERICA'S transition from war to peace was not smooth; the war had borne bitter fruit. With little recognition of the consequences to the domestic economy, the government began to terminate war orders as soon as the Armistice was signed. Federal regulations that had been adopted to buttress the war effort were rescinded, and millions of American troops were discharged. Early in 1919 the pent-up demand for consumers' goods caused prices to soar. Wages failed to advance with the cost of living, and a wave of strikes occurred. In an attempt to curtail inflation, the Federal Reserve Board in late 1919 tightened credit, and prices dropped in 1920. Industrial prices declined modestly; farm prices plummeted. The value of agricultural land nosedived, and rural banks began to fail. Likewise, the markets for Idaho minerals and lumber dried up almost completely. Like its western neighbors, Idaho experienced a depression that continued throughout the 1920s.

Other changes made traditional Idahoans apprehensive and

protective. Although there were many positive developments, they were outweighed by the negative economic momentum. A general strike began in Seattle on February 6, 1919, and lasted for several days. On September 9 of the same year about 1,000 members of the Boston police force went on strike. Because of looting, Governor Calvin Coolidge called out the entire State Guard, the strike was broken, and there was general agreement that no one has a right to strike against the public safety. On November 11, 1919, one year after the original armistice, a group of American Legionnaires and other war veterans in Centralia, Washington, beat up a group of Wobblies and killed at least one of them. Three Legionnaires died. Americans had observed the triumph of the Bolsheviks in Russia and were apprehensive that radicals, aliens, and foreigners were plotting a revolution in the United States.

One solution was the enactment of "syndicalism" laws that made membership in any organization committed to the destruction of the American form of government a crime. Among other states, Idaho adopted such a law in 1919. Idahoans were, in particular, fearful of the I.W.W. Prompted by the demands of the big lumber companies in the north, state authorities imprisoned thirty-one men under this act and effectively destroyed the influence of the I.W.W. in Idaho. By the next year, officers had arrested ninety-eight of them, all in the panhandle counties. Another eight were arrested in southern counties, primarily in Pocatello. Juries, however, convicted only 9 of the 106.

Rumors of radical conspiracy to subvert the government were widespread; people pointed accusing fingers at those persons who spoke German and Russian, Socialists, Wobblies, and even the Non-Partisan League.

Established in North Dakota in 1915, the NPL sought to remedy farmers' grievances by political means. The group began an organizational drive in Idaho in 1917, took over the Democratic Party in 1918, nominated a Republican millionaire from Bonner

County (H. F. Samuels) for governor, and campaigned vigorously for a variety of causes, including the direct primary, a state bank guaranty law, good roads, nationalization or regulation of public utilities, and a moratorium on farm mortgage foreclosures. Some of their candidates were elected, but only to minor offices. By 1919 12,000 Idahoans were on the rolls of the Non-Partisan League. Sympathetic with them, Senator Borah supported their calls for economic and social justice, but many regarded members as "foes of democracy." They were attacked at times—Legionnaires broke up some of their meetings in 1919 and 1920—but the League continued to grow. The movement may have strengthened its opponents by driving conservative Democrats into the Republican Party, which triumphed in the polls in 1920.

The NPL joined forces with other groups in 1922 to form the Progressive Party, and their candidate for governor polled the second highest number of votes—ahead of Moses Alexander, running again as the Democratic candidate—but lost to the Republican candidate, C. C. Moore. Progressives took control of county governments in Jerome, Minidoka, and Canyon counties, but the 1923 legislature defeated nearly all of their reform proposals. It was not a time for reform. People distrusted "radicals," whether native-born or foreign-born—whether seeking justice for farmers or for laborers. The courts, highly conservative, upheld legislative and administrative bodies when they adopted security measures against "radicals." Courts willingly granted sweeping injunctions against strikes. Governors called upon state militias and federal troops to protect strikebreakers and halt union activity. Although the group failed to achieve identified political objectives and eventually collapsed in 1924, it forced some Idahoans to become more tolerant of different ideologies and programs. The League also enjoyed widespread support in 1919–22 in North and South Dakota, Iowa, Colorado, Montana, Washington, and Oregon and was the major force behind the Farmer-Labor Party that controlled Minnesota politics for half a century. Partly as a result of NPL influence, the federal government adopted programs designed to help the farmer in the late 1920s and early 1930s.

Idaho's governor from 1919 to 1923 was David W. Davis. Born in Wales, Davis grew up in Iowa, where his father was a coal miner. For a while Davis managed the Farmers' Cooperative Association store and worked as a cashier in the bank at Rippey, Iowa, before he moved to Dayton, Washington. Relocating at American Falls in 1907, he established a bank, became a booster for the city and state, and was elected governor in 1918. He instituted a massive reorganization of state government by combining forty-six offices and agencies into nine departments. His cabinet consisted of a commissioner in charge of each department. During his term, construction of the state capitol building was finished and a state highway program was begun. But the depression reduced tax payments and frugality was required.

Governor Davis, along with many other Idahoans, was still caught up with the hatreds and cautions that accompanied the war. Firmly of the "old school," he called for compulsory education of foreign immigrants, insisting that they be trained to read, write, and speak English. He ordered a crackdown on the I.W.W. in Idaho, persuaded the legislature to authorize an Idaho Constabulary as a state police force, and insisted that children be required to attend public schools. This last proposal would have eliminated parochial schools, and a bill to require it failed to pass.

Other aspects of the national temper affected Idaho in the early 1920s. One was Prohibition. As early as 1892 a Prohibition Party had been organized in Idaho, primarily through the stimulus of churches, the Young People's Society of Christian Endeavor, and the Independent Order of Good Templars. Gains were made in municipal liquor control: most saloons were forced to close on Sunday, some were shut down completely, and women were prohibited from entering saloons. Some towns became "dry" by force of law. Saloons, it was thought, brutalized the poor, fostered dirty politics, and lined the pockets of the rich.[1] The granting of woman suffrage probably reinforced the growing public morality. In 1909 Idaho passed a local-option law, and many local elections pitted a "saloon" ticket against a "church" slate.

In 1915, in a campaign actively supported by the Women's Christian Temperance Union, Prohibition Party, Anti-Saloon League, Citizens' Leagues, Young Men's Christian Association, Sunday School societies, Salvation Army, Mormon wards and stakes, Methodist Epworth League, Baptist Young People's Union, and the Christian Endeavor societies of the Christian, Congregational, and Presbyterian churches, Idaho amended the state constitution to make Prohibition a part of the organic law of the state. An amendment to the national constitution was ratified by the thirty-sixth state (Utah) on January 29, 1919, and took effect one year later. Congress passed the Volstead Act over President Wilson's veto so that the nation had the power to enforce the Eighteenth (Prohibition) Amendment. As distillers and liquor distributors went out of business, bootleggers—some genuinely criminal elements and some strictly local entrepreneurs—began to operate. The nation learned during the twenties that a much-wanted reform would not work unless it enjoyed widespread popular support and was backed by a determined enforcement effort. The general impression was that as the twenties proceeded, the amendment brought about "disrespect for all laws." The law stayed on the books until 1933, when it was repealed by the Twenty-first Amendment.

A second national movement that blessedly affected only a small minority of Idahoans was the Ku Klux Klan, an organization that fanned intolerance of blacks, Roman Catholics, and Jews. The goal, according to Imperial Wizard of the Klan Hiram

Wesley Evans, was "to recreate a native, white, Protestant America."[2] The Klan had first been organized in the South after the Civil War to restore order and return prewar leaders to their former seats of power. Disbanded in 1869, the organization was reborn in the early 1920s and by 1924 had five million members. It was a force with influence in Arkansas, Texas, California, Colorado, and Oregon and indeed in many other states during the 1920s. By the Depression of the 1930s the Klan had fewer than 100,000 members. Those that remained with the Klan in the 1930s directed their attention to Communism and organized labor, with the traditional parades, cross-burnings, secret initiations, and floggings.

The Klan moved across the border from California to Oregon in 1921; by the spring of 1922 there were 14,000 members in the Beaver State, and the Klan was strong enough to ruin the careers of many otherwise acceptable political aspirants. Successful in Oregon, the KKK flowed over into Washington and Idaho, but it was never a major force in either state. Idaho's two Kleagles (Klan officials) were located in Lewiston and Boise. They organized Klaverns (local branches) in those cities and in Caldwell, Nampa, Twin Falls, Burley, and Pocatello. One historian described the Klan's Idaho activities as follows:

> Located mainly in the farming country along the Snake River [ignoring the panhandle and Mormon southeastern Idaho], the Klan was a social club where the members from time to time sat down to worry about the foreigners and Catholics in the lumber and mining camps to the north, and the Pope in Rome. In one little town, the solitary Jewish family was included in all of the Klavern's social activities to show that the Klan was a strictly nondiscriminatory movement aimed only at outsiders.[3]

As a boy in 1925, the writer witnessed a burned cross on the lawn of a Roman Catholic neighbor named Kelly. In general

KKK members received most of their thrills from their fraternalism. The Klan seems to have made virtually no headway among the Mormons, in either Utah or Idaho. Most Idahoans were not taken up with the Klan, seeing it as neither inspiring nor constructive, and several Idaho communities adopted anti-mask ordinances. There was a similar general reaction to the "skinheads" and Nazi types that existed in pockets in northern Idaho in the 1980s.

If Idaho was exploring wayward paths in the 1920s, it was also adopting new ways of life that would bring abiding pleasure: the automobile, movies, electricity, telephone, radio, clothes washers, refrigerators, and vacuum cleaners. Not least important was the installation of cafeterias to take the place of the outlawed saloons. Cafeterias, created in Los Angeles, were friendlier and more informal than the typical restaurant. The most exciting to Boiseans and the many visitors to the Capital City was the establishment of an automatic restaurant, the Mechanafe, in which food was conveyed by a running belt to the customer; one merely made selections and began to eat, at the counter or in a private booth. A teenager's dream! (Gertrude McDevitt, who operated the business until wartime rationing ruined it, went on to serve as state historian.)

The most pervading influence on the style of life in Idaho was the automobile. Of course, the first automobiles, regarded as "rich men's toys," were expensive and virtually inoperable in bad weather. But after Henry Ford's assembly-line production of his Model T, prices dropped to an affordable level, and in the 1920s the automobile and the truck replaced the pushcart, the buggy, the wagon, and the riding horse. Once satisfactory roads were built one could build a house on the edge of the city and avoid high-rises, apartments, and tenements. The automobile also enabled those on farms and in small towns and villages to take advantage of cultural offerings in nearby cities—libraries, movies, musical performances, and Chautauquas.

The automobile led to the development of larger stores in larger communities. Among those who set the pace were M. B. Skaggs and his four brothers of American Falls, who consolidated their operation with a California group to form Safeway grocery stores. The enlarged Safeway chain, along with Skaggs drugstores, gained national prominence.[4]

Another invention that narrowed the gap between country and city dwellers was the radio. Idaho's first radio transmitter was built by Harry Redeker, a teacher at Boise High School, and his students in 1920. They helped other people build radio stations elsewhere in the state. Their station evolved into KIDO, which was nationally licensed in 1922.

The most amazing product of Idaho schools in the 1920s was Philo Farnsworth. Utah-born Farnsworth, whose family moved to southeastern Idaho in 1918, began to tinker with an electric farm generator at Ucon (a few miles east of Rigby), built an electric motor that operated his mother's washing machine, and won a contest with an invention for an ignition switch for a car. In 1920 he went to Rigby High School, where he was fortunate to have a stimulating chemistry and physics teacher, Justin Tolman, who took extra time after class to respond to his many questions. Tolman also encouraged Philo to sign up for a correspondence course from the National Radio Institute in Washington, D.C.

On the afternoon of February 21, 1922, Tolman came into the classroom to find Farnsworth (called Phil by his school buddies) covering the blackboard with strange drawings. "What is that?" Tolman asked. "It's an electrical system for projecting an image," responded Farnsworth. "It's just a diagram of how my new invention will work," he said. Then the precocious boy went through the whole diagram, explaining how, by means of a "cathode-ray tube" (later known as a "dissector tube"), one could transmit light impulses into electrical impulses and scan an image by means of fast-flying protons in order to display pictures electrically. At the time, radio was in its infancy; there was not yet a licensed broadcasting system in Idaho and only one in the Mountain West.

Farnsworth later moved to Utah, then Los Angeles, then San Francisco, all the while working on his invention. He was supported by San Francisco bankers. Once, when working in his home laboratory, he was surprised by police who thought he must be making liquor and raided his premises. On September 7, 1927, now aged twenty-one, he projected his first image on a screen. The image was a dollar sign, which he hoped would persuade the bankers to continue their investment. In 1930 a hearing on his invention was conducted by the U.S. Patent Office. It demanded proof of his 1922 "discovery." Farnsworth found Tolman, who walked into the hearing with his student's high-school science notebook. The lawyers asked Tolman if he could remember the youngster sketching his system on the blackboard in February 1922. Tolman went to the blackboard, sketched out from memory the system Farnsworth had described in 1922, and exhibited his notebook for proof. Farnsworth was granted the patent on August 26, 1930. In recent years much has been made of his youthful accomplishment. His image appeared on a twenty-two-cent postage stamp in 1983, and his statue was placed in the National Statuary Hall of Fame for Utah in Washington, D.C. in 1990. Appropriately, the drive to place his statue there was initiated by a group of grade-school students who were present at the ceremony in the nation's Capitol.

To shift for a moment out of the 1920s, William Shiflett, a professor at Idaho State University, built Idaho's first television station. Shiflett and his students made their own cameras, television sets, and other equipment, and in November 1940 they televised a football game to a few television sets in buildings on the ISU campus. The first commercial station in Idaho was KIDO-TV (now KTUB) in Boise, in 1953.

The other medium that exerted a lasting influence on the

people of Idaho was the motion picture. At first silent, and after 1928 "talkies" with sound, the films contributed to the enlargement of people's expectations. Unquestionably popular—forty million cinema tickets were sold weekly in 1922—the movies often featured carefree persons engaged in exciting adventures surrounded by frivolous luxuries.[5] Among the notable shows seen in most Idaho villages and towns in the late 1910s and 1920s were *The Birth of a Nation* with Lillian Gish, *The Thief of Bagdad* with Douglas Fairbanks, *The Gold Rush* with Charlie Chaplin, *The General* with Buster Keaton, *The Jazz Singer* with Al Jolson, and *All Quiet on the Western Front* with Lew Ayres.

Another noteworthy event in Idaho in the 1920s was the construction of the American Falls Reservoir. In many respects this was the most important Snake River project in the twentieth century because it furnished ample late-season water for dozens of small cooperative companies on the Upper Snake River, the thousands of farmers under the Twin Falls and North Side canal company ditches, and the Minidoka settlers. Its success required the cooperation of federal, state, and local governments, private interests, and both corporate and individual proprietorships. It is said to have been the brainchild of Ira Perrine.

Several considerations were involved in the success of the project. Farmers had learned that the annual supply of mountain runoff is not constant but goes through periodic cycles. The year 1919 was one of the driest in Idaho's history. (Other dry ones have occurred in 1931, 1934, 1977, and 1992.) On July 1, the Twin Falls Canal Company reported that it would be able to furnish only 30 percent of the normal supply of water. There were altercations along the river. Desperate farmers in the upper valleys of the Snake sometimes made illegal use of water at night, broke the locks on headgates, and in some cases organized vigilante committees. Farmers on the north side of the Snake in Magic Valley, unable to provide water for their livestock and poultry, were forced to haul in water for washing, cooking, and drinking. Such was the sympathy with their plight that the South Side farmers, who had a prior right, voluntarily gave up water to make possible a run for the people north of the Snake. In doing so, Magic Valley farmers suffered a $25 million crop loss. Obviously, additional storage facilities had to be built to provide water for future drought conditions.

To arrive at the accord was not simple. Agreement had to be forged among some thirty water districts and forty irrigation companies along a 300-mile stretch of the river. Organizations such as the Idaho Irrigation Congress and the Western States Reclamation Association, both established in 1919, had to be developed to promote the project. Eastern and southern congressmen, from states not directly impacted, had to be persuaded that the project was necessary and economical. Idaho's national political figure, Senator Borah, had to be enlisted in the cause. The entire town of American Falls had to be purchased, since its existing location would be submerged by the projected reservoir. And the federal government had to acquire 70,000 acres of land, over half of which belonged to the Bannock-Shoshoni tribe on the Fort Hall Indian Reservation.

An editorial in the *Pocatello Tribune* for July 12, 1919, exemplifies the arguments used to persuade reluctant eastern and southern congressmen to support the project:

> Some of the erudite brethren of the South and East should consider that sagebrush will not always be the decorative portion of Western scenery. The East has forgotten its bush days, and the South its tanglewood and skunkbush. Both have rain, but neither understands irrigation nor conservation of water. They know that it will float a steam-boat and is reasonably fair for baptismal purposes, but they don't comprehend canning it for crops.

Despite all odds—the collapse of farm prices after World War I, the obstinacy of Secretary of the Interior Albert B. Fall, the opposition of important absentee landowners and certain business interests—the Department of the Interior signified its approval in November 1924; a contract to construct the large dam was let and in July 1925 its cornerstone was laid. For two years an average of 400 men worked around-the-clock shifts. The gates of the dam were lowered into place in October 1926, and the reservoir was filled to its maximum capacity of 1.7 million acre-feet on July 1, 1927. The event was critical for thousands of Idaho farmers. With the backwater of the reservoir extending up the Snake twenty-five miles, the project provided directly for the reclamation of 115,000 additional acres of public land to the north of the Minidoka Project—what is known as the Gooding division—and supplied supplemental water for over 1 million acres above and below the facility.

When the cornerstone was laid, the community of American Falls presented a historical pageant—in tableau the story of western progress in eight episodes beginning with Lewis and Clark and continuing through fur trading, pony express (which did not in fact operate in Idaho), covered wagon, Fort Bridger treaty, Indian school, Mormon migration, and "the present"—i.e., 1925. The conclusion was one of Idaho's momentous days—equal to the discovery of gold on the Clearwater in 1860, the settlement of Franklin later the same year, and the completion of the Oregon Short Line and Northern Pacific in 1884.

Clearly, the 1920s had both achievements and disasters. In business, agriculture, entertainment, and household comfort, improvements were outstanding. The other side, however, was agricultural depression, exerting an influence that was predominant, even devastating.

The demand for agricultural products during World War I had prompted a land boom—the cultivation of acres that would not be profitable when demand and prices declined. Some of the expansion was financed by small-town bankers, often with little regard for the inflated prices upon which the demand for credit was based. Between 1914 and 1920 more than 1,700 new banks were opened in eleven agricultural states, and frequently two or three banks were located in communities where only one bank could hope to survive.

The severe agricultural depression of 1921 left many rural bankers with little more than "frozen assets"—that is, assets that could not be converted into cash without heavy loss. Local bankers had assisted young men in securing equipment and stock at the high prices of 1918–20; aided farmers in purchasing cattle, sheep, and hogs for feeding in early 1920; and extended credit to inexperienced one-crop "farmers" cultivating marginal land. In so doing, small-town bankers in Idaho and other agricultural states were helping farmers to produce huge surpluses at the very time the value of farm exports was falling from more than $4 billion in 1919 to less than $2 billion in 1922.

The increase in European production of farm crops after the war and the curtailment of United States loans abroad caused the loss of important overseas markets. American grains and meats were crowded from the market by similar, less expensive items from Canada, Australia, and New Zealand. Washington withdrew wartime price supports just when prices began to fall, and by the start of the crisis in 1921, no government program existed to cushion the shock.

When economic disaster threatens, the first recourse of most enterprisers is the local bank. But independent banks have, in a sense, "all their eggs in one basket" and are least able to help when they are most needed. Their resources and their ability to provide financial assistance are largely tied to the welfare of the region they serve. When the enterprises of the region are desperate, the banks have difficulty giving assistance because the same factors burying the enterprises are also curtailing the lending power of the bank. Thus it was in 1921: farmers who had flourished during the war were now submarginal, and extending credit to keep alive their war-demand-induced operations was merely postponing the collapse of their ventures.

An example was the extension of emergency credit to country

banks in the fall of 1921 by the War Finance Corporation. Created in April 1918 to fund war industries, WFC, under the direction of Eugene Meyer, established thirty district offices throughout the nation and made limited advances to banks for loans to farmers. By December 1921, WFC was authorizing loans at the rate of $2 million a day. Most went to large institutions, but WFC did make a $300,000 loan to Idaho livestock loan companies and banks in December 1921 and later approved an additional $450,000. Although the Idaho committee of WFC correctly claimed that the limited WFC sums made available to farmers and ranchers may have saved some banks whose farm loans were delinquent because of the depression, it covered only a small fraction of the deficit. Farmers desperate for the money, it seemed, found it difficult to qualify for the loans.

WFC requirements made it almost impossible to make money available to dirt farmers. The expenses for getting a $500 loan, according to one banker, came to about $157.[6] Farmers who could furnish adequate unencumbered security qualified for credit at 6 percent interest with an additional 6 percent for local banks. Still, collateral had to be approved by WFC. This demand for "gilt-edge security" angered local bankers, who were required to attach their signatures to the small loans made to local farmers and stockmen. Although a government agency designed to serve a useful purpose, WFC was "bad if not colder-blooded than the private concerns," according to one Idaho banker. "I have had to endorse paper for our little bank to the amount of half what I am worth . . . the more I have to do with BUREAUCRATIC government the less use I have for it."[7] Many farmer-borrowers who took WFC money through rural banks paid 10 percent, with commissions of 15 percent added.[8] Nor did the loans stop the decline in farm prices.

In protest against WFC policies, farmers held a series of mass meetings throughout the state and drafted resolutions against the high expense, red tape, and impractical system WFC had for "helping" the farmer. One banker received a letter from a farmer that read:

> I got your letter about what I owe you. Now be patient. I ain't forgot you. Please wait. . . . If this was judgment [day] and you were no more prepared to meet your Maker than I am to meet your account, you sure would have to go to Hell. Trusting you will do this, I remain, sincerely yours. . . .[9]

The agricultural depression worsened, and prices fell dramatically below expectations. By 1922 the value of Idaho farmland had dropped to one-third of the pre-depression price. Potatoes worth $1.51 per bushel in 1919 brought $.31 in 1922. Potato land valued at $154 per acre at war's end in 1918 plummeted to $57 by 1922. The farm rate for sheep in Idaho was $12.20 per hundred pounds in January 1919 and $5.30 per hundred in January 1922. Hay, which brought $22 per ton in 1919, dropped below $10 in 1922. The average national farm price for beef cattle in January 1919 was $9.65; just three years later in Idaho the price was down to $4.50. Sugarbeets that sold to the Utah-Idaho Sugar Company for $12.03 a ton shortly before the depression sold for less than $6.00 in the 1921 harvest. Wheat brought the farmer $2.05 per bushel in 1919, $.72 in 1921, and $.90 in 1922.[10]

As Idaho's farmers and ranchers were unable to meet their obligations to local banks, these institutions began to fail. Twenty-seven Idaho banks, seven of which were nationally chartered, closed in the early 1920s. Nearly all of these served rural areas exclusively. Idaho had 224 banks in 1920, 86 national institutions and 138 state; by 1925 there were only 56 national banks and 103 state banks, or 65 fewer banks than in 1920.[11]

The heavy declines in the farm prices for potatoes, livestock, hay, wheat, and sugar beets—Idaho's major products—meant that granting farmers credit might help them to "hang on" but that was all. Without a change in prices they would sooner or later go under. Farmers attempting to convert from horse to mechanical power found the prices of tractors and machinery inching up. Hay growers receiving low prices found little sympathy from woolgrowers who could afford $8 per ton and no more to avoid loss. Hugh Sproat, president of the Idaho Wool Growers Association, calculated that interest, loss, depreciation, feed, labor, and taxes on an operation involving 10,000 ewes would total $49,000, while wool and lambs would bring in only $35,000, or a net loss of $14,000. By wintering without lambing and buying only enough feed for emergencies, the net loss could be cut to $3,500, but no further.[12]

Farmers and their political leaders failed to obtain legislation favorable to their plight. An early effort attempted to eliminate foreign competition for American farm products by imposing prohibitive customs duties. An Emergency Tariff Act passed in May 1921 was followed by the Fordney-McCumber Act of 1922, which raised rates on 200 agricultural products including huckleberries and reindeer meat. The seeming advantage of the tariff, however, was nullified by increased rates on industrial goods. Using the pretext that higher tariffs raised the cost of their raw materials, eastern and midwestern manufacturers simply raised prices on consumer goods and farm equipment. Again, the farmer was working at a loss.

Farm representatives then embraced the concept of parity: farmers ought to receive price increases commensurate with those of the necessities they had to buy. Using the period before World War I as a base, farm prices should rise as much as the general price index. This was a justifiable goal, but how could it be achieved? One way was by cooperative marketing—a device to eliminate the middleman. But markets were contracting, not expanding, so not much was realized.

In the face of these mounting difficulties, Senator Charles L. McNary of Oregon and Representative Gilbert N. Haugen of Iowa proposed a bill to make the protective tariff effective by subsidizing exporters to sell agricultural surpluses at world prices, even if below the protected prices paid farmers for commodities in America. The exporters would be paid by farm producers who, it was hoped, would benefit by selling at higher prices. Congress twice passed the measure, and Idaho farmers were much encouraged that the official to oversee it would be Idaho-born Secretary of Agriculture William M. Jardine. One of seven children born to English and Scottish settlers in Cherry Creek (near Malad), Jardine had gone to Utah State Agricultural College in Logan and was both a football hero and an honor graduate in agriculture. After a teaching assistantship at Utah State he went on to Kansas State University, where he earned the Ph.D. and became a professor, then dean, and finally a member of President Calvin Coolidge's cabinet. (He was Idaho's first cabinet appointee—appropriately in agriculture.) Despite farmer lobbying, Coolidge twice vetoed the McNary-Haugen bill on the grounds that it would fix prices and lead to overproduction. Borah favored paying the cost of farm support out of the treasury, but that was not achieved until the 1930s. A Federal Farm Board was created in 1929 with power to purchase and store surplus crops to maintain prices, but it began operating just as the Great Depression of the 1930s began and quickly exhausted its funds.

Lumber prices also dropped from 1921 to 1924, and the industry suffered much unemployment. Mining suffered too as the prices of most minerals sagged until 1923. Then there was some recovery, but most producers were mechanizing and needed fewer workers. Depending on agriculture, mining, and forestry as its principal industries, Idaho's overall economy was sluggish throughout the 1920s. Individual businesses failed to flourish, and many families struggled in near poverty. For the first time since the end of the gold rush Idaho suffered a massive loss of population: some 50,600 people over the age of ten migrated out of the state, primarily to California. But however poor the state of the economy was in the twenties, it was merely a prelude to a worse one in the 1930s.

## CHAPTER TWENTY-TWO: SOURCES

Several general histories of the West and Pacific Northwest have chapters on the 1920s that include a discussion of Idaho's experience. Particularly helpful are Schwantes, *The Pacific Northwest*, 288–302; Malone and Etulain, *The American West*, 78–86; and Nash, *The American West in the Twentieth Century*, 74–118. National histories include Frederick Lewis Allen, *Only Yesterday: An Informal History of the 1920s* (New York: Harper & Bros., 1931); George E. Mowry, *The Urban Nation, 1920–1960* (New York: Hill and Wang, 1965); Leuchtenburg, *The Perils of Prosperity, 1914–32*; and Soule, *Prosperity Decade: From War to Depression, 1917–1929.*

Idaho histories with a treatment of the 1920s include: Brosnan, *History of the State of Idaho*, 366–73; Defenbach, *Idaho: The Place and Its People*, 1:557–62; Beal and Wells, *History of Idaho*, 2:238–50; Wells and Hart, *Idaho: Gem of the Mountains*, 123–36.

The plight of the farmer and small-town banks and businessmen is discussed in Gwynn Barrett and Leonard J. Arrington, "The 1921 Depression: Its Impact on Idaho," *Idaho Yesterdays* 15 (Summer 1971): 10–15; James H. Shideler, *Farm Crisis, 1919–1923* (Berkeley: University of California Press, 1957); and Hugh T. Lovin, "The Farmer Revolt in Idaho, 1914–1922," *Idaho Yesterdays* 20 (Fall 1976):2–15.

The politics of the 1920s is discussed in LeRoy Ashby, *The Spearless Leader: Senator Borah and the Progressive Movement in the 1920s* (Urbana: University of Illinois Press, 1972); Robert L. Morlan, *Political Prairie Fire: The Non-Partisan League, 1915–1922* (Minneapolis: University of Minnesota Press, 1955); Hugh Lovin, "The Non-Partisan League and Progressive Renascence in Idaho, 1919–1924," *Idaho Yesterdays* 32 (Fall 1988):2–15; and Hugh T. Lovin, "Idaho and the 'Reds,' 1919–1926," *Pacific Northwest Quarterly* 69 (July 1978):107–15.

Philo Farnsworth's story is told by his wife in E. G. "Pem" Farnsworth, *Distant Vision: Romance and Discovery on an Invisible Frontier* (Salt Lake City: Pemberly Kent Publishers, 1990); Leonard J. Arrington, "Philo T. Farnsworth: Inventor of Television," in *Acceptance and Dedication of the Statue of Philo T. Farnsworth* (Washington, D.C.: Government Printing Office, 1991), 33–48; and George Everson, *The Story of Television: The Life of Philo T. Farnsworth* (New York: W. W. Norton & Company, 1949).

Other aspects of the 1920s are treated in Irvin E. Rockwell, *The Saga of the American Falls Dam* (New York: The Hobson Book Press, 1947); Larry R. Gerlach, *Blazing Crosses in Zion: The Ku Klux Klan in Utah* (Logan: Utah State University Press, 1982); David M. Chalmers, *Hooded Americanism: The History of the Ku Klux Klan* (New York: Franklin Watts, 1981); John M. Mecklin, *The Ku Klux Klan: A Study of the American Mind* (New York: Russell and Russell, 1963); Wyn Craig Wade, *The Fiery Cross: The Ku Klux Klan in America* (New York: Simon and Schuster, 1987); Edison K. Putman, "The Prohibition Movement in Idaho, 1863–1934" (Ph.D. dissertation, University of Idaho, 1979); Edison K. Putman, "Travail at the Turn of the Century: Efforts at Liquor Control in Idaho," *Idaho Yesterdays* 33 (Spring 1989):13–19, 22–24; and Larry Quinn, "The End of Prohibition in Idaho," *Idaho Yesterdays* 17 (Winter 1974):6–13.

123. 

124. 

123. The automobile became common on Idaho roads in the 1920s. This one was headed along a country road near Richfield. C. J. BROSNAN COLLECTION, UIL 6–102–5.

124. With the passage of the Prohibition Amendment in 1918, bootleggers tried to evade the law. This Bisbee photo, taken November 11, 1922, shows the Women's Christian Temperance Union in Twin Falls destroying illegal drink. ISHS 73–221.793.

125.

125. The most popular sports personality in the nation during the 1920s was Walter Johnson, the Weiser Wonder, "The Big Train," one of the great pitchers of all time. ISHS 80–127.1.

126. 

126. Idaho's first appointee to a presidential cabinet was William M. Jardine of Cherry Creek (near Malad), who served as Secretary of Agriculture for Calvin Coolidge, 1925–29. Here he is shown with his mother and sister in front of his parents' Cherry Creek home in 1926 during his period of service. UTAH STATE UNIVERSITY SPECIAL COLLECTIONS.

CHAPTER TWENTY-THREE

# The Great Depression and the New Deal

THE industrial East of the United States underwent the semblance of a boom in the later 1920s. Prices were strong, employment rose, stocks rebounded, and an air of confidence prevailed. During these years of national "prosperity," Idaho's agriculture, mining, and lumbering had risen ever so slightly out of the trough of 1921. The postwar reversal had been massive and the gains modest; by 1929 there was only a partial recovery. Then came the stock market crash of October 1929 that launched the worst economic disaster in the nation's history. The personal incomes of all Americans declined from $83 billion in 1929 to $46 billion in 1933, and the level of total income floundered below the $80-billion mark until 1941, twelve years after the depression began. As many as 13 million people were unemployed in 1933—a fourth of the nation's work force.[1]

Idaho, which had barely weathered depression conditions in the 1920s, was among the states most adversely affected by the nationwide depression. Judging by the percentage decline in income from 1929 to 1932, the states most disastrously affected were, in order of severity, North and South Dakota, Oklahoma, Mississippi, Montana, and Idaho. Although there has been a tendency to regard the depression as primarily an industrial phenomenon, the states that suffered most, in percentage decline in income and absolute level of income, were predominantly agricultural—states that had not recovered from the 1921 crisis before they were hit again by the devastating exigencies of the 1930s. Foreign markets dropped off sharply; domestic markets also declined; an additional calamity was drought. For example, Idaho's farm income dropped 57 percent from 1929 to 1932. Idaho's economy also depended heavily on lead and silver mines, nearly all of which closed during the 1930s, and on the lumber industry, which was largely inactive because people were not building homes.

The evidence of the decline in Idaho's income between 1929 and 1932 is glaring. The price of wheat dropped to $.26 per bushel, and cattle brought less than $20.00 per head in 1932—the lowest average price since the 1890s. Sheep similarly sold for $2.25 per head in 1932—the lowest in the century. Prunes were down from $22.00 per ton in 1929 to $6.50 a ton at the bottom of the depression. Sugar beets sank to $4.00 per ton in 1932, while wool declined from $.36 per pound in 1929 to $.09 per pound three years later.

Production of lumber from Idaho's famous white pine plunged from 438 million board feet in 1929 to 169 million board feet in 1933. The total value of mineral products declined from $32 million in 1929 to less than $10 million in 1933—again, the lowest in the twentieth century. The price of silver fell from $1.39 an ounce in 1919 to $.24 an ounce in 1933—the lowest price for silver in Idaho's history.

The early years of the depression spurred differing behavior in silver and gold. Production of silver fell drastically; gold, on the other hand, gained in value. Inasmuch as the United States was on the gold standard until 1934, the decline in general price levels after 1929 caused gold prices to escalate. This change induced a surge in the production of gold from 21,000 ounces in 1929 to 62,000 ounces in 1933. The combination of the rise in price and rise in production prompted the value of Idaho's gold "crop" to spurt from $429,000 in 1929 to $1,641,000 in 1933. As a contemporary observer pointed out, the Depression of the 1930s induced a rejuvenated gold industry comparable to the boom period of the 1860s. Indeed, it is unfortunate that the New Deal did not try to boost dismal circumstances by taking the gold out of Fort Knox, burying it in various centers of unemployment, letting the unemployed dig it up, and putting it back in circulation for the benefit of trade.[2]

The total cash income of Idaho farmers dropped from $116 million in 1929 to $41 million in 1932. Similarly, wages and salaries fell from $139 million in 1929 to $81 million in 1932. Total income payments of all kinds in Idaho slid downward from $235 million in 1929 to $123 million in 1932, a drop in per capita income from $529 to $268. Manufacturing employment was cut back from 15,644 men and women in 1929 to 7,682 in 1933, and Idaho's manufacturing payroll declined from $22.5 million to $7.1 million during the same period.

Unfortunately, when a calamity as clearcut as a depression occurs, people become fearful that they will "lose everything"—their property and savings as well as their jobs. Banks were pivotal institutions in that regard. Banks received and held the money deposits of businesses and families, made loans to individuals and companies, cashed checks, acted as fiscal agents for local governments, and in general served as community bookkeepers. Since banks provided the local circulating medium that seemed to have "dried up" during the Thirties, they were sometimes, mistakenly of course, held responsible for the depression. One would laugh at a sick person who became angry and broke his thermometer because it registered a high fever.

But citizens of many communities in the 1930s became so hysterical that, without intending to do so, they resorted to action that made the prophecies of financial calamity self-fulfilling.

Before 1933 there was no federal deposit insurance. If a bank failed, the depositor was helpless. Banks were peculiarly vulnerable to the citizenry; when people lost confidence in a bank, they rushed in, demanded their deposits in cash, and left the institution in ruin. This phenomenon occurred hundreds of times in the United States in the 1930s. Some 4,500 banks faced runs that forced them to shut their doors, and in Idaho 38 of 106 banks closed their doors between 1929 and the bank holiday of 1933. Two were in Boise, and one of these was headquarters of a chain-banking arrangement that affected ten banks in Idaho and Oregon. The story of the closure and the subsequent run on other banks is instructive.[3]

In the summer of 1932 Boise had three banks: Boise City National at 8th and Idaho streets; First National Bank of Idaho, at 10th and Idaho; and First Security Bank of Idaho, at 9th and Idaho. The First Security Bank of Idaho was owned by the First Security Corporation, the nation's first registered bank holding company, which by 1929 owned twenty banks in Idaho and Utah with resources of $40 million. Its constituent First Security Bank of Idaho operated banks in Idaho Falls, Blackfoot, Montpelier, Pocatello, Preston, Gooding, Jerome, Shoshone, Hailey, Ashton, Mountain Home, Nampa, and Boise. Managing Boise's First Security was J. Lynn Driscoll, a native of Nebraska who, after his graduation from the University of Nebraska, began his banking career in Idaho as a messenger boy in the Overland National of Boise when it opened in 1915. He moved up rapidly and became a livestock loan specialist "all over hell's half-acre."

Boise City National, the second bank in Boise, had been founded by Henry Wadsworth and Alfred Eoff as early as 1886 and had long been one of Idaho's important banks. In 1932 the bank was headed by C. H. Coffin and Charles A. McLean.

First National Bank of Idaho, the oldest bank in Boise, had been chartered as a national bank in 1867. Founded by B. M. DuRell and Christopher W. Moore, it was Idaho's largest. By 1932 the Moore interests had purchased banks at Ontario and Vale in Oregon, and at Emmett, Meridian, Nampa, Caldwell, Weiser, Buhl, and Rupert in Idaho. Crawford Moore, son of Christopher and president of First National in 1932, was an "old-style" banker; he considered federal regulations something of a nuisance.

In July 1932 Lynn Driscoll, anticipating trouble at Boise banks, had gone to Chicago to observe "runs" on several banks. The last week in July Driscoll received a telephone call informing him that the Boise City National, now paying out in old-style, large-sized bills, was on the verge of closing its doors. Driscoll returned home on the first available train; four days later, on August 1, Boise City National shut down.

The closure of Boise City National set in motion the domino effect. The public anticipated that the two remaining Boise banks might also be forced out of business. This apprehension almost sealed their closure because of what economists refer to as the Law of Self-Justified Expectations: if people expect a bank to go broke, customers will quickly withdraw deposits, and the bank *will* go broke for lack of immediately available cash. First National and First Security both began to suffer a few withdrawals.

On Saturday morning, August 27, Crawford Moore called Driscoll to report in confidence that First National was in trouble and that he was recommending to his board of directors, meeting that afternoon, that the bank and its affiliates not reopen Monday morning.

With Moore's permission, Driscoll immediately called E. G. Bennett, vice president of First Security Corporation in Salt Lake City and a member of the advisory committee of the Reconstruction Finance Corporation. Driscoll arranged for Moore to go to Salt Lake City in an attempt to arrange by telephone for financial help from the RFC. First proposed by President Herbert Hoover in his annual message to Congress on December 8, 1931, the RFC bill was passed by Congress and signed by Hoover in January 1932. Although this new federal agency was generally considered to have been created to render assistance to large banks and industrial corporations, it might also serve smaller banks such as Moore's First National. When it became clear that RFC was willing to see what could be done but would not categorically guarantee all of First National's deposits, Moore decided not to open his banks that Wednesday. The RFC conference was not a complete failure, however, for it initiated negotiations that led to the reopening of Moore's banks two months later.

Driscoll was conferring with Governor C. Ben Ross (Democrat, 1931–37) early Wednesday morning, August 31, when Ross advised him that Moore would not open his banks that day. Rushing back to his office, Driscoll called the First Security banks at Nampa and Mountain Home, and the others scattered across southern Idaho, to warn of the run that was certain to develop within the hour. To Driscoll's dismay, Boise radio got hold of the news and broadcast the closure. Within thirty minutes customers lined up a block long, extending down both 9th and Idaho streets in Boise.

Anticipating a run on his bank, Driscoll had taken significant precautions before the opening of First Security of Boise that morning. For more than a year he had been sending promissory notes of important firms and business leaders, as they obtained loans from First Security, to the Federal Reserve Bank in Salt Lake City. This tactic gave him advance approval on notes that First Security might wish to use as security for borrowing in a future contingency. This arrangement, referred to as "rediscounting," was an important function of the Federal Reserve and made it possible for banks to borrow at low rates of interest on the security of prime business notes. Knowing that he might, in the event of the closing of First National, require a large supply of cash to cover withdrawals, Driscoll also had called the Salt Lake Federal Reserve the preceding Saturday, requesting the shipment to Boise of $500,000 in currency and another $50,000 each for the First Security banks at Nampa and Mountain Home. At the same time, recognizing that the heaviest demand for cash would be in Boise, Driscoll had arranged with the RFC in Salt Lake City for First Security to borrow $1 million. Then, on Tuesday, August 30, reasonably certain that First National would close, Driscoll again asked the Federal Reserve for another shipment to Boise of $500,000 in currency.

As First Security of Boise opened on that fateful Wednesday morning, Driscoll and other executives stood at their regular posts and announced that all deposits would be paid. Tellers were instructed to pay all comers, "but don't break your necks"—meaning pay out slowly and in small bills. Driscoll stood on the counter and announced: "We have wired for a great additional supply of currency to add to the emergency supply on hand, and we can stand a run of any duration. We will pay off every depositor if necessary." Traditionally the bank had closed on this day because of the Western Idaho Fair. It suddenly occurred to Driscoll that he dare not close at noon for the fair, as previously advertised, because customers might associate a closure with financial weakness rather than with support for the festivities. Driscoll promised that the bank would remain open as long as there were customers wishing to make deposits or withdrawals. Employees were told to be prepared to continue on the job until midnight if necessary.

Driscoll also wanted to communicate to all passersby that the bank was remaining open and had an adequate supply of currency. Under his direction Harry Hopffgarten, a Boise sign painter, hurriedly painted this message in red and black paint on a three-by-ten-foot sign with a white background:

For the Benefit of Our Patrons This Bank Will be
OPEN UNTIL LATE TONIGHT
If You Want Your Money Come and Get It!
J. L. Driscoll, President, First Security Bank

The sign was suspended over the entrance to the bank from the second-story window even before the paint was dry. This firm declaration brought a cheer from the crowd outside. Some persons dropped out of line; by 3 p.m. the run had dwindled, although the bank remained open another six hours.

A number of incidents during this first-day run on First Security demonstrated the fundamental irrationality of people stricken with panic at the possibility of losing their lifetime savings. One customer, when he had finally advanced to the teller, declared in a most positive tone: "If you've got my money, I guess I really don't want it. But if you haven't got it, then by heaven, I want it now and in full!"

That day the Boise *Capital News* published a large editorial titled "Steady Boise." During the height of the run, representatives of nineteen of the leading businesses of Boise met in Mayor James P. Pope's office and issued a statement of faith in the local economy. From this meeting came the volunteered service of Idaho's leonine Senator William Borah and Boise's largest merchants. Borah, who was in Boise campaigning for his colleague John Thomas, made his way through the mob into the bank and came to Driscoll's desk. Borah suggested that he would be glad to mount the counter and make a speech to reassure the people that the situation did not merit panic and alarm. "For the first time in your life your offer to make a speech is turned down," replied Driscoll. The mere speech of the senator, thought Driscoll, might create additional alarm. The banker favored handling the crisis in a confident, matter-of-fact way.

The merchants realized that their business problems would be compounded if the last of the three Boise banks failed. To help the cause some businessmen brought deposits to First Security. Among those who exhibited strong support was C. C. Anderson, Idaho's largest merchant, who was a director of First National. Anderson made several appearances in the First Security lobby with checks and currency that he had ostensibly received from customers in payment for dry goods, and with much flourish he deposited the funds, thus bolstering the bank's reserves. This visible manifestation of confidence relaxed the tension on the faces of all present.

Even the Boise postmaster, Harry Yost, entered into the spirit of the day. When Driscoll noted that many of his customers were taking their cash from the bank and depositing it in Postal Savings, he asked Yost to return the money through the back door of the bank and redeposit it to the postmaster's account. Yost did him one better by bringing the money back every half-hour, thus furnishing an additional supply of currency for First Security's use.

Driscoll confidently waited for the half-million dollars in currency he had ordered from the Fed in Salt Lake City. Sure enough, on Wednesday morning as scheduled, two guards walked into the bank to report their arrival. Driscoll asked: "Where's the money?" They replied: "It's supposed to be here." The truth was, as Driscoll discovered, that the money was still at the Railway Express Office in Salt Lake City. No one had thought to put it on the train! Driscoll would surely be excused for uttering some of Idaho's colorful profanity as he telephoned Salt Lake City requesting the Fed to charter a plane to bring the currency immediately to Boise. That flight seemed particularly long to the impatient Driscoll. "No plane," Driscoll afterward recalled, "ever flew slower than that one." Late Wednesday afternoon when the crisp, compact cargo actually did arrive, the worst of the run was over. By nine o'clock that evening First Security's lobby was empty, and officials gratefully closed for the night. Thanks to the sign, the advance arrangements for currency, the atmosphere of confidence, and the good sense of some of Boise's civic and business leaders, First Security had weathered the first day of panic.

It was hard to predict what kind of run might occur on Thursday. Many people would have heard of the failure of First National and of the long lines at First Security. Would they all show up to make withdrawals Thursday morning? First Security opened earlier than usual on Thursday to avoid, if possible, the development of a line. Among the first people to face the tellers were some who had withdrawn deposits the previous day, now redepositing packages of money that they had never bothered to open. Although there were a few large withdrawals, the belated currency shipment from Federal Reserve was not needed. After a few days it was shipped back to Salt Lake City unopened.

From one point of view, the First Security Bank in Boise now enjoyed an enviable position; it was the only bank in Idaho's largest city open for business. But Driscoll decided that the community would best be served when his competitor, Crawford Moore's First National, reopened. Meanwhile he announced that First Security would utilize the facilities of the Boise City National Bank to handle state, county, and school district business and city payroll checks and to receive deposits on accounts already established.

Driscoll told the RFC representative who had arrived at the First National in Boise that $150,000 were needed immediately for the necessary operating expenses of both the First National's and the Boise City National's stockmen, whose herds were scattered far and wide on the range and whose employees had no money with which to buy groceries. Driscoll asked that the RFC take the unusual step of advancing $150,000 without requiring security, and he would then distribute money to the stockmen for absolute necessities. Mortgages, he explained, would be worthless if the established ranches failed. RFC representatives were somewhat taken back by Driscoll's audacity: "We'll see what we can do." The next morning the money was wired to Boise through the RFC, deposited in an account in the First Security Bank in Boise, and distributed to stockmen to meet their most pressing needs. Herders could now be paid, and flocks that might have been lost without adequate supervision were saved. Funds were dispensed by means of sight drafts, or "chippy checkbooks" as they were called, which required an explanation of the expenditure on every draft. Although restrictions of this nature irritated the hitherto independent stockmen, they willingly admitted that they had never seen a checkbook that looked so good. Eventually, when the stockmen were refinanced through a formally organized subsidiary of RFC, every penny of this advance was returned to RFC.

In addition to arrangements for the specific benefit of livestock enterprises, RFC also extended credit to banks, such as First National, which had to be reorganized in order to reopen. Total RFC loans to Idaho banks during the first six years of its existence (1932 to 1938) amounted to approximately $3 million over what RFC's Regional Agricultural Credit Corporation (Spokane) loaned. The First National in Boise was the recipient of nearly half this amount.

Finally, the national bank examiner and Comptroller of the Currency having completed their investigation, the First National Bank in Boise reopened on Monday, October 31, 1932, exactly two months after closing its doors. A corps of fifty-seven solicitors headed by reorganization committee chairman Harry Morrison raised $300,000 through the sale of capital stock, and this, together with the RFC loan, took $1,775,000 of the "frozen" assets out of First National. The threat to Boise's (and Idaho's) financial future was removed.

Shortly after Franklin Roosevelt became president in 1933, he selected E. G. Bennett to head the newly created Federal Deposit Insurance Corporation. The FDIC initiated federal insurance on deposits in all the nation's banks. From that time there was no reason for the public to be concerned about the safety of their deposits. No one would have to fear that the 1932 Boise experience would ever be repeated.

The two leading banking systems of Idaho had survived, but thousands of farmers were losing their farms through foreclosure. Having borrowed money when prices were more favorable, they now had to pay off their loans when prices of farm products were hopelessly below costs. Familiar with the unfairness of the situation all through the 1920s, now substantially magnified, they reacted quite understandably. During the winter of 1932–33 a neighbor of the writer was foreclosed by his creditor and a sheriff's sale ordered for a Monday. All the farmers in the neighborhood gathered together on Sunday evening and agreed upon a plan to help their friend. They would attend the sale and refuse to bid against each other. The next day, as the auctioneer went through his accustomed chant, a splendid team of horses sold for $1.50; a grain binder, $2.00; a hay mower, $1.00. Prices of other animals and equipment ran from a low of $.50 to a high of $3.00. The farmers duly paid the sums they had bid, received the items purchased, and promptly turned them back to the farmer who had been foreclosed.

There were many such conspiracies. In Gem, Boise, Idaho, Valley, Adams, and Lemhi counties, arsonists systematically ignited fires in the forests in order to obtain employment as fire fighters. The situation became so serious that Governor Ross declared those counties to be in a state of insurrection, placed them under martial law, and ordered the National Guard to close off the forests to public access.[4]

As if things were not bad enough already, the year 1934 brought a disastrous drought. The Governor's Emergency Drought Relief Committee, on the basis of reports from forty-five water districts representing 80 percent of the irrigated land of Idaho, estimated that the general average water supply was only 56 percent of normal. Crop losses were estimated at $22.4 million. About 30,000 people required relief.[5]

The reports from six weather observation stations in southern Idaho showed that from October 1933 to April 1934 precipitation was less than 65 percent of the long-term normal for that period. Already farmers had absorbed a heavy crop loss of potatoes, beets, beans, peas, and hay. The year 1934 was already the driest year in southern Idaho since the stations had started keeping records in 1909.

The report estimated that approximately 75,000 Idaho citizens would need aid on account of the drought, and that $2 million in emergency relief funds were required to remove beaver dams obstructing the flow of streams; to pump water from lakes, marshes, sloughs, ponds, and streams into irrigation ditches and canals; to straighten creek and river channels; to pump from wells; to clean canals and ditches; and to provide direct relief.

In a telegram to the Universal News Service in Chicago on July 26, 1934, Governor Ross declared:

> In Idaho the drought is serious, the worst in the history of the white man in this territory. Rivers and creeks are drying up which in previous years furnished irrigation. Thousands of springs that have been used for watering livestock in the mountains have become dry, and water must be furnished from other sections. While people in the affected areas will not be required to evacuate, feed must be shipped in to save the livestock. . . . With assistance of the Federal Government we will be able to sustain our people in their homes without evacuation.

The files of the Ross Administration in the State Archives contain many applications for drought relief.

The problems of the Idaho drought multiplied as the drought in the Great Plains region prompted thousands of families to move into the Far West. Idaho received many thousands of these migrants—from Nebraska, Kansas, Oklahoma, Arkansas, Missouri, and Texas. Although Idaho's economy was incomparably more distressed in the 1930s than in the 1920s, the net emigration of the 1920s was converted by *Grapes of Wrath* migrants into a net in-migration in the depressed thirties. The newcomers, who went principally into the Snake River Valley in southern Idaho and the cut-over area in northern Idaho, escalated a mounting relief load. Clearly, conditions in Idaho, as in other states, required a sustained program of relief and recovery.

When Franklin Roosevelt was nominated for president in 1932 he promised a "New Deal" for the American people. When he took office in March 1933 he promised to "do something" about the depression—to "put people to work." During the first "Hundred Days" (March 9 to June 16) he declared a Bank Holiday to prevent runs on banks, forbade the export and hoarding of gold, raised the price of gold, established federal deposit insurance for national banks, signed an act placing securities under federal supervision, granted $500 million to the states for emergency relief, inaugurated a plan of industrial self-government to be administered by the National Recovery Administration, and adopted the Agricultural Adjustment Act in an attempt to restore farm prices to parity—to levels equivalent to those existing before World War I. There were clearly some experimentation, some "playing by ear," and some inconsistencies, but at least there was action and a general consensus that the federal government was justified in taking measures to solve the problems of unemployment and low income. During the years 1933–34 the goal was to achieve recovery by agricultural and business regulation, price stabilization, and public works. From 1935 to 1941 relief and recovery measures were continued, but the government also enacted social and economic legislation to benefit working people—minimum-wage and maximum-hour legislation, social security, and massive work relief.

The federal anti-depression program in Idaho included unemployment relief, agricultural loans and benefits, programs for youth, social welfare assistance, works programs, and lending programs. While all of these measures were extensive in their coverage, it is surprising how meager the expenditures of the various New Deal agencies proved to be. The nation was not yet accustomed to distributing large amounts for economic resuscitation. Although Idaho ranked eighth among the forty-eight states in per capita federal expenditures during the period 1933 to 1939, the total disbursements in Idaho of all New Deal agencies during those seven years were only $399 per capita, or an average of $57 per person per year. Economists are now satisfied that one primary reason the nation failed to recover from the Depression of the 1930s until World War II was the small reach of the recovery effort. In all the years of the New Deal, the total financial assistance from federal government recovery programs was approximately $24 billion. That is a stout sum, but in the first year of World War II the federal government spent more than twice that figure.

Whatever the amount spent, there is no doubt that the recovery program made a vital contribution to Idaho's debilitated economy. Six significant programs deserve a brief summary.[6]

## UNEMPLOYMENT RELIEF

**FEDERAL EMERGENCY RELIEF ADMINISTRATION.** The most pressing need was direct relief. Local charitable organizations and municipalities were unable to provide adequate assistance to miners and seasonal agricultural laborers who relocated in Idaho's cities. The Reconstruction Finance Corporation was empowered to lend to states and local governments suffering such pressures. The FERA, which became law on May 12, 1933, made grants to local and state public agencies on a matching basis, one dollar of federal money for every three dollars spent by the state on relief programs. The newly created Idaho Emergency Relief Administration provided approximately $16 million in relief for 20,000 destitute Idaho families during the years 1933–35. Where feasible, the money was earned by work; a variety of projects enabled recipients to render useful service. Relief benefits per family in Idaho averaged from $15 to $30 per month. (At the time a common wage for agricultural and other unskilled workers was $1 per day; the average income of Idahoans was about $27 per month.)

CIVIL WORKS ADMINISTRATION. The CWA was established on November 9, 1933, to employ 4 million persons during the winter of 1933–34. It expended $5.4 million in Idaho, providing jobs without reference to need. About half of those hired were previously on relief; the others were unemployed persons receiving no assistance. Average weekly earnings were about $15. While about one-third of the projects were building roads, streets, and bridges, others included repair of schools and hospitals, improvement of parks and fairgrounds, and constructing airports, sanitary facilities, waterworks, and means of flood control. A Women's Work Program provided employment in sewing clothes, making bedding, canning food, nursing, and teaching.

## YOUTH PROGRAMS

CIVILIAN CONSERVATION CORPS. Aware of the heavy impact of unemployment on young people, their lack of opportunity to develop skills and perform useful labor, President Franklin Roosevelt established the Civilian Conservation Corps (CCC) by executive order on April 5, 1933. The goal was to conserve young men physically and psychologically, but also to conserve the nation's natural resources. Approximately 4,500 barracks camps were organized during the nine-year program, usually in forests and national parks, each with about 200 young men. A total of 2.5 million young men eighteen to twenty-five, whose families were eligible for relief, were enrolled; they were paid $1.00 per day, plus maintenance and medical care. Of the $30 received each month, $25 were sent to the enrollee's family. In general, the camps were supervised by military officers, but many of the instructors were drawn from local teachers and well-trained civil-service personnel who conducted educational programs along with work projects.

Because of its bounteous forests, Idaho ranked second among all the states in CCC expenditures. Most of the young men assigned to camps in Idaho were from the industrial East—New York, New England, New Jersey, Pennsylvania, the upper South, and the Midwest. But approximately 2,500 Idahoans were enrolled each year—just over 20,000 in the history of the CCC. About one-third of the enrollees, camp officers, and supervisory workers were from Idaho. A total of 163 camps were established in Idaho and operated for an average of three years each. Among them were 109 Forest Service camps, 20 on state forest, 9 on private forest lands, 8 under the Soil Conservation Service, and 16 under the Grazing Service. Most were south of the Salmon River. At its peak in 1935, CCC had eighty-two camps in Idaho. The projects were substantial: CCC enrollees in Idaho completed pest and disease control (blister rust) on 700,000 acres of forest, devoted 300,000 man-days to fighting forest fires, cleared 3,600 miles of truck trails, constructed 187 lookout towers and houses, built 1,500 miles of telephone lines, planted 10 million trees, controlled rodents on 2.5 million acres, and regenerated 42,000 acres of rangeland. The Idaho CCC also constructed thousands of public facilities, such as picnic tables, benches, fireplaces, and shelters.

One example of the permanent benefit of the CCC is its work in Heyburn State Park, where a camp was established in 1934. Fire circles, boat-landing slips, swimming rafts, bathhouses, seats along the shore of Lake Chatcolet, picnic grounds and tables, parking areas, community kitchens, toilet facilities, two caretakers' houses, a lodge, campsites with fireplaces, roads, and water systems turned the unimproved park into a showpiece for the state.[7] A total of $57 million was spent on the CCC in Idaho.

INDIAN CIVILIAN CONSERVATION CORPS.[8] A separate CCC program was established under the Indian Service for young Indian men living on reservations. Unlike those in regular camps, Indian enrollees could live in their own houses while working in family camps or in camps for single men. Indian families frequently moved their tents close to work projects. A permanent camp was set up for twenty-five or more men who would work on a project for two or three months and then move on to another. The family camps, sometimes supervised by employed Indian women, were visited by teams who instructed the women in sewing, cooking, and child care. At first, Indian enrollees worked twenty days a month at $1.50 a day, earning $30.00 a month; if the individual lived at home he also received $.60 a day for subsistence and thus received $42.00 a month. Later, the work week was changed to eight hours a day, five days a week, for which the enrollee earned $45.00 instead of $30.00. The work programs were designed primarily by Indian leaders on the reservations in the interest of improving their land, water, and forests. The enrollees constructed telephone lines, fire breaks, truck trails, vehicle bridges, horse trails, reservoirs, springs and wells, and range fences, and worked on erosion control and grasshopper and rodent eradication—all on the reservations. The young men were also required to spend ten hours per week in educational and vocational training: arts and crafts, farm and home carpentry, range and livestock management, health, masonry, and poultry raising.

All told, 1,038 Idaho Indians were employed by the Indian CCC from 1933 to 1942. The spendings of the Indian Service for the Idaho Indian CCC program up to 1938 amounted to $615,862.

NATIONAL YOUTH ADMINISTRATION. The NYA was established by executive order in June 1935 and continued into the war period. The program consolidated various types of assistance to youth provided by the Federal Emergency Relief

Administration. A total of nearly 2 million youths from 16 to 24 were employed on NYA work programs during the depression years; 5,000 of these were in Idaho. Students whose families were unable to pay their school expenses or were certified for WPA employment were eligible. In contrast to the CCC, the NYA was focused on education funding. The NYA granted money to schools and colleges that then provided students with enough work to cover their necessary expenses. The writer, who was supported under this program during his four years at the University of Idaho (1935–39), worked on the college farm, in a chemical laboratory, in the library, and for the Department of Economics, receiving $15.05 per month for forty-three hours of work—$.35 per hour. The magnitude of the program in Idaho is suggested by its outreach in May 1939, when 2,264 participants included 1,532 high school students earning an average wage of $4.34 per month (high school students had little school expense) and 725 college students earning an average monthly wage of $26.29. Idaho received $473,772 to administer the program and ranked fourth among all states in per-capita expenditures.

## AGRICULTURAL PROGRAMS

AGRICULTURAL ADJUSTMENT ACT. Because of Idaho's heavy dependence on agriculture, the New Deal's most important assistance was a program designed to restore farm purchasing power. The 1933 Agricultural Adjustment Act authorized paying growers to decrease their plantings of surplus crops and had them devote the acreage to pasture, summer fallow, and other soil-building practices. In return for benefit payments of $2.5 million, Idaho growers during the 1934 crop year shifted approximately 150,000 acres from wheat and corn to soil-building or soil-conserving uses. During the three years of the program (1933–36) 28,134 AAA crop adjustment contracts were accepted by Idaho farmers, about half by wheat farmers.

The remainder were for corn-hog and sugar beet contracts.[9]

When the United States Supreme Court ruled the AAA production control program invalid on January 6, 1936, Congress lost no time in approving the Soil Conservation and Domestic Allotment Act as a replacement. Sponsored by Idaho's New Deal Senator James Pope, this revised program continued restrictions in agricultural output by paying farmers not to reduce production but to adopt land uses and farm practices that would conserve soil and enhance its fertility. About 20,000 Idaho farmers were organized into county associations to participate in the revised program. Approximately 53 percent of Idaho's cropland—that is, about 2 million acres—was covered by these contracts. A total of 170,000 acres was diverted from soil-depleting crops; about 380,000 acres were involved in soil-building practices. Idaho farmers received $1.9 million in conservation payments under the 1937 program.

In 1937 the greatest harvest in the history of the United States threatened to break farm prices with the weight of the surpluses. When it became clear that, in addition to soil conservation, measures were necessary to stabilize the supplies and prices of farm products, Congress approved the Agricultural Adjustment Act of 1938—the so-called Second Triple A—which set up acreage goals to encourage plantings harmonious with domestic demand, foreign markets, and adequate carryovers. Above all, it provided loans on crops stored in an "ever normal granary" to assure sufficient supplies for consumers and favorable markets for farmers. When two-thirds of the producers voted favorably, marketing quotas were established on wheat and other crops. Crop insurance provided parity payments to producers of staples when prices fell below specified levels. Under these programs Idaho farmers received $2.3 million in 1938.

FARM CREDIT ADMINISTRATION. Because much of its farming was commercial, Idaho was in particular need of credit to help farmers with their financial burdens. The commercial banks of Idaho, like those of the nation generally, were designed primarily for small business operations; they specialized in short-term loans. When they sought to offer agricultural aid by extending credit for longer time periods, they were saddled with "frozen assets"—assets that could not quickly be converted into cash. Institutions under supervision of the newly organized Farm Credit Administration loaned $12.5 million to individual Idaho farmers in 1938–39 and extended credit to a number of Idaho farm cooperatives. The largest volume of financing came from the five Idaho production credit associations, which loaned more than $54 million for short periods to 2,500 farmers and stockmen from 1933 to 1939. Long-term mortgage loans made on 11,000 farms in Idaho by the Federal Land Bank of Spokane aggregated more than $35 million by the end of 1939—about 40 percent of the total farm mortgage debt in the state.

Another farm credit institution lending to Idaho agriculture was the Spokane Bank for Cooperatives, which made loans to fruit and vegetable cooperatives, farm-supply associations, and cooperative grain elevators. As of December 31, 1939, the Spokane bank was financing eighteen Idaho cooperatives with loans aggregating more than $600,000.

FARM SECURITY ADMINISTRATION. Because the above-mentioned agricultural programs benefited primarily commercial farmers, the Farm Security Administration was created in 1935 to help low-income families become self-supporting instead of dependent on relief. During its first four years the FSA assisted almost 9,000 struggling Idaho families. The work of the FSA included a rehabilitation loan program, under which $5 million were loaned to 5,000 Idaho farm families for feed, seed, fertilizer, and equipment; small subsistence grants, averaging about $85 each, for the purchase of food, fuel, and other urgent necessities; the establishment of homesteads in Boundary County and "scattered farms" in Ada and sixteen other counties to provide better homes, improved schools, and enhanced farming opportunities; a tenant purchase program enabling fifteen Idahoans to obtain loans of $140,000 to acquire farms of their own; and the establishment of four migratory labor camps to furnish accommodations for 448 seasonal agricultural families.

RURAL ELECTRIFICATION ADMINISTRATION. The REA was created in 1935 to lend the entire cost of constructing electric distribution systems in isolated rural areas. The plan was successful. By the end of 1939 REA had loaned $2.2 million to six farm electric cooperatives that built 1,800 miles of new rural lines to serve 5,000 farmers. Whereas fewer than 30 percent of Idaho farms received highline power at the end of 1934, electrical service was available to 54 percent of the farms in 1939. Idaho rural schools were among the first to draw power from the new lines. Rural electrification facilitated the use of power equipment in dairying and increased the use of washing machines, electric irons, radios, refrigerators, chicken brooders, and tank heaters.

All told, from 1933 to 1939 New Deal appropriations for Idaho agriculture, not counting agricultural education expenditures, were $120 million, of which $32 million were outright grants and $88 million were loans.

## SOCIAL WELFARE PROGRAMS

Under the old-age and survivors insurance program of the Social Security Act of 1936, single cash payments were made to covered workers reaching age sixty-five and to heirs of workers who died. These payments equalled 3½ percent of a worker's wages covered by the system. By July 31, 1939, a total of 1,200 payments amounting to $48,000 had been made to Idaho workers at age sixty-five or to their heirs.

A second section of the Social Security Act financed state unemployment compensation programs. With this encouragement, Idaho passed an unemployment compensation law on August 6, 1936, that covered an estimated 110,000 workers. Although benefits to unemployed workers did not become payable under the Idaho law until September 1938, eleven months later unemployment benefit payments in the state totaled $2.3 million. The average weekly benefit payment in the state was $10 for total unemployment and $9 for those partially unemployed. In administering the law the federal government expended, from 1936 to 1939, some $480,000 in Idaho. In addition, the United States Employment Service in Idaho received some 36,000 applications for jobs during the New Deal era and placed 29,000 people, 70 percent of them with private concerns.

A third section of the Social Security Act allowed public assistance for the needy aged, blind, and dependent children. These programs called for matching funds, with the federal government advancing 50 percent. By August 1939, 8,400 needy aged, 300 blind, and 6,400 dependent children in 2,700 Idaho families were receiving an average of $22 per month from federal and state funds. From 1936 to 1939, federal grants to Idaho for these programs were old-age assistance, $3.8 million; aid to the blind, $130,000; and aid to dependent children, $830,000. Idaho also received $280,000 for maternal and child welfare services, $240,000 for establishing and maintaining adequate public health services, and an undisclosed sum to help some 193 Idaho citizens in the process of rehabilitation.

## WORKS PROGRAMS

Although the most pressing need in Idaho and other states was the provision of a federal system of relief, Congress and the

Roosevelt Administration sought to establish programs that would stimulate business and provide remunerative employment. Some of these merely stepped up the rate of spending of existing bureaus and agencies.

PUBLIC ROADS ADMINISTRATION. The least revolutionary of these programs was road building, in which the federal assistance was granted to provide employment and also to build up an integrated system of state highways and secondary roads. Federal funds were made available for the elimination of railroad grade-crossing hazards, the reconditioning of feeder or secondary roads, and the improvement of main trunk highways. From 1933 through 1939 work was done on 1,650 miles of roads in Idaho with the aid of federal funds. Total federal expenditures in Idaho from 1934 to 1939 were $15 million for highways and $2 million for grade crossings.

PUBLIC WORKS ADMINISTRATION. To stimulate industry and put men back to work, the PWA made available to state and local sponsoring bodies federal funds to aid in construction costs. In general, projects were financed by 45 percent grants from PWA funds. In some instances, in addition to the outright grant, the PWA arranged to lend the applicant the remainder of the cost. PWA payrolls had to meet the prevailing wage scale in the community where the project was located. The PWA also operated a federal program, consisting of construction and repair work on federal property in each state. PWA allotments for federal and non-federal projects in Idaho up to July 1, 1939, included $8.2 million for streets and highways, $1.3 million for sewers and waterworks, $500,000 for administrative buildings, $2.7 million for school buildings, $3.9 million for flood control and reclamation, and $3.5 million for improvements on federal lands.

To improve recreational facilities as a means to stimulate Idaho's lure for tourists, the PWA made an allotment of $5.6

million to the Forest Service for the construction of major and minor forest highways, roads, and physical improvements in Idaho's national forests. The PWA also allotted to the Bureau of Reclamation $5.2 million for various water projects, including canals and structures for irrigation and distribution systems. The most important of these was the Owyhee Reclamation Project in Oregon and Idaho, to which $5.2 million were allotted for the construction of canals and canal structures for the irrigation distribution system of which the PWA contributed $2.2 million. The PWA also provided for the construction of storage reservoirs on tributaries of the Upper Snake River near Ashton.

Principal nonfederal programs were the construction of seventy-eight educational buildings with an estimated cost of $6 million. A grant of $225,000 financed a new junior high school building and additions to Boise High School and a Boise elementary school; a Pocatello High School expansion received $400,000. Drainage work near Bonners Ferry was funded to rebuild dikes, drainage ditches, and a pumping plant.

The peak of site activity on federal and nonfederal programs combined was reached in June 1934, when an average of 10,000 men were at work.

WORK PROJECTS ADMINISTRATION. Some 95 percent of the projects on which funds were expended by the WPA, a work-relief program, were planned and sponsored by the areas in which they took place. In practically all cases the locality contributed to the cost of the project, and in most cases it provided site planning as well. The community's contribution paid the majority of the cost of materials, supplies, and equipment, whereas federal funds were expended primarily for wages. Those employed on these projects were all certified as in need of work. Of every federal dollar spent, 86 cents went directly into wages for workers.

Among the major accomplishments of the WPA in Idaho were the construction of 125 public buildings and the modernization and improvement of 90 others, including 43 schools. In addition, 1,484 miles of highways, roads, and streets in the state were extended or improved. The WPA also constructed and/or repaired more than 1,800 culverts and 400 bridges. Municipal water-supply systems benefited by the addition of ninety-five miles of water mains, aqueducts, and distribution lines, and laterals were added to storm and sanitary sewer systems. The expansion of recreational facilities was accomplished by the construction of twelve new athletic fields and playgrounds and the improvement of eleven others. WPA sewing rooms produced more than 430,000 garments and other articles for distribution to needy families. Some 72,000 quarts of milk and 12 million pounds of other foodstuffs were distributed to persons in need, and 1.2 million lunches were served to school children. Other work included the refurbishing of 287,000 public-school and library books and the cataloging of 70,000 volumes.

In another effort, Idaho's writers employed by the Federal Writers Project produced, under the direction of Vardis Fisher, a splendid state guide—the first in the United States—and two other published compilations and studies. The Federal Music Project of Idaho presented several hundred free concerts. Other Idahoans were employed in art, theater, and education projects and historical records surveys.[10]

On June 28, 1939, 8,574 persons were employed in Idaho on projects operated by the WPA. Earnings of these persons for June amounted to $441,000, for an average of a little over $50 per month per person employed. Total federal expenditures from the beginning of the program to June 30, 1939, amounted to $23 million.

## LENDING PROGRAMS

Through 1939 the Reconstruction Finance Corporation, inaugurated in the fall of 1932, made loans to at least 132 borrowers in Idaho. These included loans to banks and trust companies, mortgage loan companies, and industrial and commercial businesses, as well as catastrophe loans.

During the seven years after the organization of the Federal Home Loan Bank System in 1933, the number of affiliated Idaho institutions grew to eight and they reported total resources of more than $7 million. These were all federal savings and loan associations chartered and supervised by the national government under Act of Congress passed in 1933. Up to August 31, 1939, these member institutions had received $2.6 million in advances from their district Federal Home Loan Bank in Portland. Member institutions of the Home Loan Bank System were operating in almost every large-sized community, making their services available to most of the non-farm population of the state. Federally chartered savings and loan associations were located in Boise, Coeur d'Alene, Idaho Falls, Lewiston, Nampa, Pocatello, and Twin Falls.

The Home Owners' Loan Corporation refinanced 4,700 home loans totaling $8.2 million from 1933 to 1936. About 92 percent of these almost hopeless homeowners refinanced by HOLC saved their homes.

The Federal Housing Administration was established in 1934 to stimulate residential construction, promote improved housing standards, create a sound system of home financing, and insure loans made by banks, building and loan associations, and other private lending institutions for new construction, repairs, alterations, and improvements. It also made possible the modernization of farm properties and of small-business plants and equipment. The net volume of FHA business in Idaho through June 30, 1939, totaled $10.3 million.

## IMPACT OF THE NEW DEAL ON IDAHO

Although no complete summary of all federal expenditures in Idaho for the period from March 1933 to September 1939 has been made, the compilation by the Statistical Section of the

Office of Government Reports in the fall of 1939 shows that federal economic agencies expended more than $209 million in grants, an additional $112 million in loans, and an additional $10 million in insured private loans, for a grand total of about $331 million of federal assistance to Idaho. During the same period federal taxes collected in Idaho probably did not exceed $12 million.

As the result of the injection of federal funds, Idaho's economy did improve. The following summary is suggestive:

Individual income and corporate taxes in Idaho rose from $403,000 in 1933 to $2,012,000 in 1939.

Bank deposits rose from $41 million in 1933 to $90 million in 1939.

Total income payments in Idaho rose from $134 million in 1933 to $234 million in 1939; income per capita rose from $287 in 1933 to $452 in 1939.

Employment in manufacturing rose from 7,700 in 1933 to 9,900, and manufacturing payrolls rose from $7.1 million in 1933 to $13.3 million.

Farm marketings rose from $52 million in 1933 to $80 million in 1939.

Silver production rose from $2 million in 1933 to $15 million in 1939.

It would be misleading, however, to conclude that the 1930s were a period of unalloyed economic stagnation or that all the recovery was a result of the New Deal programs. Significant technical growth occurred nationally in steel, petroleum, chemicals, aircraft, and automobiles. One of the most dramatic advancements in Idaho was made by the Morrison-Knudsen Construction Company of Boise. Harry Morrison, an Illinois farm boy, and Morris Hans Knudsen, a Danish immigrant, became acquainted while working on the Boise Project of the U.S. Reclamation Service in 1905. In 1912 the two men formed their own construction firm. In 1927 they joined with the Utah Construction Company and contracted for the construction of the Bureau of Reclamation dam at Guernsey, Wyoming, and then built

Deadwood Dam, high in the mountains near Lowman. M-K was likewise one of six companies that built Boulder (renamed Hoover) Dam in 1931–35, Parker Dam in 1935–38, and numerous other dams, irrigation works, tunnels and canals, streets, highways, and buildings financed by the PWA. Between 1933 and 1940 M-K and associates completed twenty major dams and hydroelectric works, in addition to other projects. After the government began its preparedness campaign in 1939, the company received many military construction contracts. Although the 1930s are usually remembered as years of sluggishness, to some energetic entrepreneurs they were also years of opportunity and growth.[11]

A second example of a growth enterprise was Sun Valley Lodge, opened in 1936 and giving Idaho status as a winter and summer sports destination. Established by W. Averell Harriman, chairman of the board of Union Pacific Railroad and later governor of New York, this famous sports playground, nestled in a valley near Ketchum, is 6,500 feet above sea level. Once a 3,000-acre sheep ranch, it became one of America's premier resort communities, with swimming pools, ice rinks, ski lifts (including the first chairlift ever built, modeled after a device to load carcasses on freighters), golf course, artistic lodges, and shopping centers. Sun Valley is one of America's favorite convention centers and vacation spots.

Finally, the depression years saw the burgeoning in Moscow of "Psychiana," the world's largest mail-order religion. Frank Bruce Robinson, a native of England, had migrated to Canada as a young man; moved to the United States, where he enlisted in the army; and eventually settled in Moscow, where he was employed as a druggist. In his search for religious truth, he claimed to talk with God and organized a psychological religion that enrolled thousands of interested persons in a correspondence course. Eventually, he became Latah County's largest private employer, wrote twenty books outlining his beliefs, and employed 40 to 100 persons full-time for the assembling and mailing of some 50,000 pieces of mail per day. He perpetuated the myth of the American Dream even at the peak of economic stagnation. It was possible to find the God Power, he asserted, if one followed the steps outlined in his lessons. As his biographer concluded, "He preached the possibility of material success and happiness despite the Depression."[12]

Like other Americans, Idahoans slowly gained in wealth and well-being from 1933 to 1939. By the outbreak of World War II, they were in a reasonably good position to participate effectively in the struggle for national survival during that effort.

## CHAPTER TWENTY-THREE: SOURCES

The depressed thirties form separate sections or chapters in most of the recent histories of the West and Pacific Northwest. Those that are particularly helpful include: Malone and Etulain, *The American West*, 87–107; Nash, *The American West in the Twentieth Century*, 139–91; Schwantes, *The Pacific Northwest*, 302–13; Howard R. Lamar, "Comparing Depressions," in Gerald D. Nash and Richard W. Etulain, eds., *The Twentieth Century West: Historical Interpretations* (Albuquerque: University of New Mexico Press, 1989), 175–206; Lawrence Henry Chamberlain, "Idaho: State of Sectional Schisms," in Thomas C. Donnelly, ed., *Rocky Mountain Politics* (Albuquerque: University of New Mexico Press, 1940), 150–88; and Leonard J. Arrington and Don C. Reading, "Federal Expenditures in Northern Tier States, 1933–1939," in William L. Lang, ed., *The Centennial West: Essays on the Northern Tier States* (Seattle: University of Washington Press, 1991), 227–43.

Idaho histories and biographies with a treatment of the 1930s include: Beal and Wells, *History of Idaho*, 2:251–68; Peterson, *Idaho: A Bicentennial History*, 139–58; Michael P. Malone, *C. Ben Ross and the New Deal in Idaho* (Seattle: University of Washington Press, 1970); "The New Deal," in Claudius O. Johnson, *Borah of Idaho* (New York: Longmans, Green and Co., 1936), 468–89; and Aldrich, *The History of Banking in Idaho.*

There is an extensive literature on the Great Depression and its impact on America and the world. Among the most helpful in the preparation of this chapter were Broadus Mitchell, *Depression Decade: From New Era through New Deal, 1919–1941* (New York: Rinehart and Company, 1947); Dixon Wecter, *The Age of the Great Depression, 1929–1941* (New York: The Macmillan Co., 1948); David A. Shannon, *The Great Depression* (Englewood Cliffs, N.J.: Prentice-Hall, 1960); Caroline Bird, *The Invisible Scar* (New York: David McKay Co., 1966); Lester V. Chandler, *America's Greatest Depression, 1929–1941* (New York: Harper & Row, 1970); John A. Garraty, *The Great Depression* (San Diego: Harcourt Brace Jovanovich, 1986); Charles P. Kindleberger, *The World in Depression, 1929–1939*, revised and enlarged edition (Berkeley: University of California Press, 1973, 1986); Michael A. Bernstein, *The Great Depression: Delayed Recovery and Economic Change in America, 1929–1939* (New York: Cambridge University Press, 1987).

Many worthwhile books also describe the New Deal. Helpful in connection with Idaho include Ernest K. Lindley (an Idaho journalist), *The Roosevelt Revolution: First Phase* (New York: Viking Press, 1933); Basil Rauch, *The History of the New Deal, 1933–1938* (New York: Capricorn, 1944, 1963); Arthur M. Schlesinger, Jr., *The Age of Roosevelt: The Coming of the New Deal* (Boston: Houghton Mifflin Co., 1958, 1965); Paul K. Conkin, *The New Deal* (New York: Thomas Y. Crowell Co., 1967); James R. Patterson, *The New Deal and the States: Federalism in Transition* (Princeton, N.J.: Princeton University Press, 1969); Richard Lowitt, *The New Deal and the West* (Bloomington: Indiana University Press, 1984); Anthony J. Badger, *The New Deal: The Depression Years, 1933–40* (New York: Noonday Press, 1989).

Journal articles on the impact of the Great Depression and New Deal programs on Idaho and the West include: Donald Tanasoca (Elmo Richardson, ed.), "CCC: Six Months in Garden Valley," *Idaho Yesterdays* 11 (Summer 1967):16–24; Leonard J. Arrington, "Idaho and the Great Depression," *Idaho Yesterdays* 13 (Summer 1969):2–8; Leonard J. Arrington, "The New Deal in the West: A Preliminary Statistical Inquiry," *Pacific Historical Review* 38 (August 1969):311–16; Leonard J. Arrington, "Western Agriculture and the New Deal," *Agricultural History* 44 (October 1970):337–53; Leonard J. Arrington,

"The Sagebrush Resurrection: New Deal Expenditures in the Western States, 1933–1939," *Pacific Historical Review* 52 (February 1983): 1–16; Don C. Reading, "New Deal Activity and the States, 1933 to 1939," *Journal of Economic History* 33 (December 1973):792–807; Don C. Reading, "A Statistical Analysis of New Deal Economic Programs in the Forty-eight States, 1933–1939" (Ph.D. dissertation, Utah State University, 1972); James T. Patterson, "The New Deal and the States," *American Historical Review* 73 (October 1967):70–84; Leonard Arrington and Gwynn Barrett, "Stopping a Run on a Bank: First Security Bank of Idaho and the Great Depression of the 1930s," *Idaho Yesterdays* 14 (Winter 1970–71):2–11; James S. Olson, "The Boise Bank Panic of 1932," *Idaho Yesterdays* 18 (Winter 1975): 25–28; Merwin R. Swanson, "Pocatello's Business Community and the New Deal," *Idaho Yesterdays* 21 (Fall 1977):9–15; Glenn Barrett, "Reclamation's New Deal for Heavy Construction: M-K in the Great Depression," *Idaho Yesterdays* 22 (Fall 1978):21–27; Merwin R. Swanson, "The New Deal in Pocatello," *Idaho Yesterdays* 23 (Summer 1979):53–57; Judith Austin, "The CCC in Idaho," *Idaho Yesterdays* 27 (Fall 1983):13–18; Merwin R. Swanson, "The Civil Works Administration in Idaho," *Idaho Yesterdays* 32 (Winter 1989):2–10; Elmo R. Richardson, "Western Politics and New Deal Policies," *Pacific Northwest Quarterly* 54 (January 1963):9–18; Davis McEntire and Marion Clawson, "Migration and Resettlement in the Pacific Northwest, 1930–1940," *Social Science* 16 (April 1941): 102–15; James R. Patterson, "The New Deal in the West," *Pacific Historical Review* 38 (August 1969):317–27; Jonathan Dembo, "The Pacific Northwest Lumber Industry during the Great Depression," *Journal of the West* 24 (October 1985):51–62; and Ronald W. Taber, "Vardis Fisher and the 'Idaho Guide': Preserving the Culture for the New Deal," *Pacific Northwest Quarterly* 59 (1968):68–76.

127.

128.

127. A popular federal agency during the 1930s was the Civilian Conservation Corps (CCC), in which young men were employed to improve the nation's forests. This photo shows Camp F-142 (Kalispell Bay) on the Priest River in 1934. PRIEST LAKE MUSEUM ASSOC. COLLECTION, UIL 17–7.14.

128. This photo shows one company and officers at CCC Camp F–16, at Prichard, 1933. UIL 8–B140.4.

129. 

129. A Works Progress Administration (WPA) unit near Wallace built a channel for this unruly stream in 1939. DONATED BY MRS. HARRY MARSH, UIL 6–59–7.

130.

130. The LDS Church inaugurated a self-help program in 1936 in which LDS stakes operated farms and other enterprises to furnish food for families in need. This is the Hog Project of the 11th Quorum of Seventies in Bear Lake Stake, Paris. LDS CHURCH ARCHIVES PH 1086.

CHAPTER TWENTY-FOUR

# The Impact of World War II

On September 1, 1939, Germany invaded Poland, launching World War II. Britain and France declared war on Germany, and the United States declared its neutrality. As the German military marched to repeated success, Congress authorized trade with friendly belligerents on a cash-and-carry basis. Germany invaded Norway, Belgium, the Netherlands, and Luxembourg. The United States agreed to send outdated and surplus war supplies, including aircraft, to Great Britain.

Having begun a limited rearmament program in 1939, the United States stepped up the effort and appropriated $4.3 billion for defense, including the planned production of 50,000 airplanes per year. As the war raged in Europe, the United States methodically put in place a system of defensive preparation. Germany defeated France in June 1940; the United States appropriated $4 billion to produce a two-ocean navy of two hundred ships. As the Battle of Britain began, the United States passed the Selective Service Act requiring the first compulsory military training in peacetime. Germany invaded Rumania, Italy invaded Greece, and the United States established the Office of Production Management for Defense (later the OPM). President Franklin Roosevelt asked for further aid to the anti-Axis nations (England, France); Germany invaded Yugoslavia. The United States established the Office of Price Administration (OPA) to ward off inflation and supervise rationing. Germany invaded the Soviet Union.

Meanwhile the Japanese government, allied with Germany and Italy, occupied French Indo-China and moved on throughout Asia. On December 7, 1941, Japanese carrier-based planes attacked the United States naval base at Pearl Harbor; Imperial forces also attacked Guam, the Philippines, Wake Island, Midway Island, Hong Kong, and the Malay Peninsula. At Pearl Harbor the Japanese pilots sank or disabled nineteen ships, including eight battleships and three destroyers, and 140 planes. About 2,300 people were killed and 1,200 wounded. Congress declared war on Japan and quickly followed with a declaration of war on Germany and Italy.

Idahoans had become involved in the war when the nation began preparedness in the fall of 1939. Morrison-Knudsen had been assigned by the Defense Department to construct airfields, roads, and maintenance buildings in the Pacific. When the Japanese occupied Wake Island, Guam, and Midway, they took as prisoners more than a thousand M-K employees, mostly from Idaho, and these men remained prisoners until 1945. Some died during their incarceration.

As a part of its defense preparations, the U.S. Navy acquired land near Buttonhook and Scenic bays on the southern end of Lake Pend Oreille, consolidated its holdings through condemnation, and constructed Farragut Naval Base. By the close of the war this vast training center covered an area of more than 4,000 acres and included 800 buildings. Beginning April 10, 1942, some 22,000 men worked on the construction, laboring ten-hour days, thirteen out of every fourteen days. Some $64 million were funneled into the project, and Farragut (named for Admiral David Glasgow Farragut, who achieved Civil War victories aboard the U.S.S. *Hartford*) became the largest city in Idaho. Naval personnel arrived in August 1942, six "boot camps" named after naval heroes were opened, and sailors began training in September. Five thousand men were stationed at each camp, where they lived in twenty-two two-story barracks, were fed in a central mess hall, and were served by dispensaries, recreation facilities, and store buildings. At one time there were as many as 55,000 people at Farragut. "Liberty" trains ran from the base to Spokane three times a day. The naval hospital, the best in Idaho at the time, consisted of 100 buildings connected by covered passageways, with beds for 2,500 patients and their families. Within fifteen months approximately 300,000 sailors passed basic training. The base was decommissioned in 1946 and became a college and technical institute between 1946 and 1949. Secret naval research has continued at nearby Bayview. In 1965 the base was designated Farragut State Park. After an International Boy Scout Jamboree was held there in 1967, the Seventh National Jamboree was held at Farragut in 1969, attracting 42,000 boys, and another National Jamboree was held in 1973, drawing 30,000 Scouts.[1]

Determined to have an ordnance plant away from the West Coast, the Navy built a large facility at Pocatello in the early summer of 1942. Guns up to eighteen inches in size were accommodated in the relining plant. Single lathes 115 feet long and overhead bridge cranes of 150-ton capacity made it possible to handle the massive naval guns. These monsters were lowered lengthwise into an eight-story pit, the bottom of which dropped so far below water level that Navy divers were used in its construction.[2] One of the buildings, only one story yet 135 feet high, covered 200,000 square feet and was designed to maintain the inside temperature with a fluctuation of only two degrees. Repaired and relined guns were tested at a station near Arco. This proving ground was transferred into the National Reactor Testing Station for the Atomic Energy Commission after the war. The ordnance plant was later converted into a factory where the Bucyrus-Erie Company made machines for strip-mining.[3]

In 1940 the United States Army Air Corps established Gowen Field near Boise as a major base for B-24 bombers. The base was named in 1941 for Lieutenant Paul Gowen, a native of Caldwell who died in 1938 in an air crash while on duty in Panama. Gowen Field became the final training center for units headed for Europe and the Pacific. Pilots, bombardiers, navigators, gunners, and other crew members learned to work as a team in flying bomber missions. Large air bases were also established at Mountain Home to train bomber crews and at Pocatello to prepare fighter pilots. The base at Mountain Home is still in operation. The Pocatello base was a closely guarded area near the twenty-six-mile reservoir above American Falls Dam.

In addition to the military facilities, Sun Valley Resort was closed to the public in 1942 and used by the Navy as a convalescent hospital for sailors and Marines with malaria, fatigue, or rheumatic fever. Idaho's colleges and universities were also centers for Army and Navy training.

Idaho furnished approximately 39,000 young men and 818 young women to the Army and Air Corps and 21,115 persons to the Navy, Marine Corps, and Coast Guard. Including Seabees (construction battalions), nurses, and other volunteers and inductees, Idaho had approximately 60,000 young men and women in the military service during the war, of whom 1,784 died, 8 were declared missing, and 31 were held in foreign prison camps. Many were decorated, including Junior Van Noy and Leonard Brostrom of Preston and Lloyd McCarter of St. Maries, each of whom was presented the nation's highest military award, the Congressional Medal of Honor—Van Noy and Brostrom posthumously.[4]

On the civilian front Idaho ranked near the top of the forty-eight states in providing food, lumber, and metals. Idaho supplied beef, mutton, pork, turkey, chicken, eggs, and huge quantities of potatoes, beans, peas, onions, sweet corn, and carrots; apples, prunes, peaches, and cherries; milk, cheese, and butter. Idaho lumber was used to build military bases, ships, airplanes, boxes, and crates. During 1942 mills at Potlatch, Coeur d'Alene, and Lewiston produced 427 million board feet of lumber, principally Idaho white pine and yellow (ponderosa) pine, for the war effort. Idaho lead was used in making bullets and batteries, zinc was used in making brass cartridge cases, and mercury exploded the percussion caps. Idaho antimony contributed metal ingredients in every tire. Idaho silver helped make silver alloy bearings, and Idaho tungsten from Valley and Lemhi counties was used in making the hard-cutting tools in war plants.[5] A single mine, setting aside gold ore for a month, extracted enough tungsten to toughen 75 million pounds of steel. Because tungsten from mines in China (the previous source) had to fly the deadly Himalaya hump to reach Allied mills, the value of Idaho's tungsten was measured not in gold but in blood.[6]

A private entrepreneur who rendered yeoman service was J. R. Simplot. A native of Iowa, Simplot grew up in Declo, Idaho, and at nineteen, in 1928, began as a produce merchant in Burley. At the start of the war in 1941 he was the state's largest shipper of potatoes and onions. Seeing a future in dehydrated foods, he constructed a small onion dehydrator at Caldwell in 1941. After Pearl Harbor he expanded the operation and became the largest supplier of dehydrated potatoes to the Armed Forces. His dehydration method reduced one hundred pounds of potatoes to a neat fifteen-pound carton that could readily be sent overseas. Between 1942 and 1945 Simplot produced more than 33 million pounds of dried potatoes annually for the government and won the Army-Navy "E" for excellence. In 1944 he began construction of a gigantic phosphate fertilizer plant at Pocatello. These were the beginnings of a large industrial and commercial empire that included food distribution and production, lumbering, mining, fertilizer manufacture, microchips, livestock, and real estate development. More of this in Chapters Twenty-six and Twenty-nine.

Much civilian trade and business activity had to be suspended during the war years because of the shortage of materials, gasoline, and skilled labor. For example, the $26-million Anderson Ranch Dam to furnish supplemental water for Boise Valley farms was to have been finished in 1946 but was not completed for another four years.

Many Idahoans worked in shipyards in the Portland-Vancouver area, in airplane assembly plants in Seattle, in aluminum reduction plants near Vancouver, and on the Bonneville and Grand Coulee dams. Add to this the large number serving in the Armed Forces and one understands the chronic shortage of agricultural labor, which typically paid less than jobs in war industries. As a result, Idaho farmers recruited help from Mexico through the bracero program, from prisoner-of-war camps, from the Japanese-American relocation center at Hunt, from the conscientious-objector camp at Downey, from the Navajo Indian reservation in southern Utah, Arizona, and New Mexico, and from groups previously unsalaried, principally women. Those women who remained at home also contributed to the war effort by raising victory gardens, helping to salvage critical war materials, selling war bonds, and coping with rationing regulations.

Idaho was selected for two major and at least sixteen minor German and Italian prisoner-of-war camps. A large base camp was located at Farragut, where 850 German prisoners of war were stationed to work as gardeners and maintenance men. The second base camp was at Rupert, where the prisoners worked in sugar beet and potato fields and fruit orchards. Branch camps were located at Rexburg, Sugar City, Rigby, Idaho Falls, Shelley, Blackfoot, Thomas, Fort Hall, Pocatello Army Air Force Base, Preston, Franklin, Filer, Marsing, Payette, Upper Deer

Flat, and Wilder. The branch camps were hurriedly constructed so the prisoners could live near a farm or orchard where labor was required. The prisoners, always under guard, lived in tents surrounded by a hog-wire fence. Guards left early in the morning to take the prisoners to work in the fields. One German prisoner of war thinning beets at the Preston camp remarked, "Hitler said we would march across North America, but I didn't think we would do it on our hands and knees."[7] According to Geneva Convention rules, their food was to be equal in quantity and quality to that given U.S. troops in the field. Hospital and medical treatment was provided at the base hospitals at Farragut and Pocatello and at Bushnell General Hospital in Brigham City, Utah. The prisoners had organized sports activities—soccer for the Germans and soccer and boccie (an Italian version of bowling) for Italians. They sometimes had motion pictures, musical instruments, crafts, libraries, and camp newspapers. Courses in American history and English language were popular. Those who worked on farms received 80 cents a day, but farmers were required to pay the minimum wage of $2.20 per day; the difference funded housing and food expenses. After Italy capitulated on September 8, 1943, Italian prisoners were given special privileges if they signed the Italian Service Unit parole agreement, which many did. In essence this made them "partners" in the Allied war effort. The conduct of the camps, in general, was a humane and successful endeavor.[8]

Situated at Downey, in the heart of Marsh Creek Valley forty miles south of Pocatello, a depression-era Civilian Conservation Corps camp became the wartime home of some 126 conscientious objectors—most of them men who belonged to one of the "peace churches" (Mennonite, Amish, Quaker, Jehovah's Witnesses) that do not believe in war. The majority were from Indiana, Iowa, Kansas, and Illinois. Under the direction of the Soil Conservation Service, they worked at erosion control, rehabilitating irrigation systems, constructing and digging irrigation drainage ditches, putting in water pipelines, rock-ribbing the Portneuf Mountain slopes, constructing the McCammon Diversion Dam, and doing emergency farm and forest work—thinning and topping sugar beets, picking potatoes, fighting range and forest fires, building fences, and cutting timber. As in POW camps, these men lived in barracks dormitories and had an infirmary, chapel, bathhouse, craft and recreation center, library, classroom, garages, and workshops. A few of the men were married and were able to spend evenings with wives living in Downey, which was within walking distance. Spike (temporary) camps for one or two dozen men were established near farming areas needing their labor, such as those at Fort Hall, Bancroft, Grace, and Tyhee.

A controversial war measure was the relocation of approximately ten thousand Japanese-Americans from the Portland and Seattle areas to an erstwhile "desert" location at Hunt near Rupert in south-central Idaho. These persons formed, for the period September 1942 to October 1945, the eighth largest city in Idaho—a city that no longer exists.

In recent years the United States government has officially apologized and made redress for this unjustified wholesale evacuation, explicable only in terms of the hysteria that followed the attack by the Japanese on Pearl Harbor. All West Coast military installations, airfields, and electrical plants were treated with extensive camouflage netting and blackout regulations. Such precautionary measures were also extended to cities and civilians. At the time, about 127,000 persons of Japanese descent lived in the United States, some 112,000 on the Pacific Coast. In the weeks after the attack on Hawaii the Japanese had launched successful assaults against the Philippines, Thailand, and Singapore. The American public grew increasingly suspicious of persons of Japanese ancestry in the United States. Some even suggested that they represented a racially undesirable element in American life and could not be assimilated. Rumors circulated of sabotage and fifth-column activity in Hawaii, none of them true. Reports of enemy submarine activity off the coast of California added to the mounting sense of panic. Fearful of an invasion of the continent, and conscious of the dangers of resident sabotage, citizens on the West Coast demanded strong precautionary measures.

At the height of the popular suspicion, distrust, and fear, on February 19, 1942, President Franklin Roosevelt signed the unprecedented Executive Order 9066, under which the Army was given blanket power to deal with "the enemy." General John L. DeWitt, commanding general of the Western Defense Command in San Francisco, issued Public Proclamation No. 1 designating the entire western half of California, Oregon, and Washington as a "military area" and announced that all persons of Japanese ancestry would be removed as a matter of military necessity. One of the unfortunate results of the expulsion order was the inadequate protection of evacuee property rights.

The families affected owned about 150,000 acres of lush farming land, some 20,000 automobiles, several thousand businesses, and homes, art works, bank accounts, and other forms of property built up at great sacrifice over a period of many years. Evacuees were expected to dispose of this property quickly and individually. Each person was permitted to take with him or her only what could be carried in hand. Inevitably, they were victimized by the unscrupulous, who bought their homes and farms for a fraction of their true value. Total income and property losses of all Japanese-Americans attributed to the evacuation is estimated at $350 million.

In March 1942 the military constructed assembly centers at racetracks, fairgrounds, and livestock exhibition halls near the principal West Coast settlements. From these, internees were moved in the summer and fall of 1942 to ten newly constructed barracks cities, known as relocation centers, located in eastern California, Arizona, Wyoming, Colorado, Utah, Arkansas, and

Idaho. The Minidoka Relocation Center, on federal land in the Minidoka (Gooding) Reclamation Project at Hunt, was one. (Hunt was named for Wilson Price Hunt, the Astorian explorer and businessman who had passed through Idaho in 1811.) These camps were administered by the War Relocation Authority (WRA), directed by Dillon S. Myer of the Agricultural Conservation and Adjustment Administration. Most of the central and field staff of the WRA came from the Department of Agriculture.

The Minidoka Center was located on 68,000 acres of arid sagebrush and sandy land between the Sawtooth Range on the north and the Snake River immediately to the south, near the towns of Twin Falls, Rupert, and Jerome. The construction contract was awarded to Morrison-Knudsen, and a crew of 3,000 men hastily built row after row of low, black barracks of frame and tarpaper in the summer of 1942. The community, sprawled over an area three and one-half miles long and one mile wide, was divided into areas for evacuee residents, administrative personnel, and military police. The evacuee area consisted of thirty-five residential blocks, each housing and servicing 250 to 300 persons. Within each block there were fifteen single-story barracks buildings, a central mess or dining hall, a recreation hall, a combination washroom-toilet-laundry building, outdoor clotheslines, and an office for the block manager. Each barrack was divided into six single rooms, ranging in size from 16 by 20 feet to 20 by 25 feet. Each room was "home for the duration" for a family with several children or for four or five unrelated individuals. During the early weeks, when the housing was still uncompleted, the rooms often held two families or up to eight bachelor men or women. To many Japanese, the most objectionable aspect of the entire arrangement was the denial of individual and family privacy.

From army stores the WRA furnished pot-bellied stoves, cots, sacks or mattress covers, and blankets, but there was seldom enough bedding. The evacuees were expected to make their own partitions, chairs, benches, tables, shelves, closets, storage chests, and other furniture, which they did by "borrowing" some of the poorly guarded lumber left over from the construction. There were no washing, bathing, or toilet facilities in the barracks; a central building in each block had to be used for these purposes. Each block had only four bathtubs for all the women, and the same number of showers for the men; and even these were lacking for several weeks. All meals were taken in the central dining hall. In the center of the compound were a community auditorium, gymnasium, canteens, schools, libraries, churches, post office, and fire station. There were athletic fields and a community garden plot.

The administrative area consisted of several blocks of office buildings, barracks apartments, dormitories, and a recreation center. Approximately 200 Caucasians, some of them from nearby towns, supervised and staffed the various administrative divisions. In one corner, behind a barbed-wire fence, were the barracks and headquarters of the military police, about a hundred of whom arrived ahead of the first detachment of evacuees. During most of the center's history there were from three to five officers and from 85 to 150 enlisted men. Guardhouses were built at each entrance to the city, and the military police checked the papers and credentials of every person going and coming. Although most such camps (e.g. Topaz, Utah) were surrounded by tall, strong barbed-wire fences, with watchtower guard houses equipped with searchlights every quarter of a mile and manned by armed patrols, observers say the Minidoka Center was far less fortified.

All told, there were about five hundred wooden buildings, all uniformly somber except the white-painted hospital and administrative structures. At the beginning the Minidoka Center was only two-thirds completed, with drafty buildings, crowded barracks, and open trenches. When the houses had neither ceilings nor inside walls, the residents complained of the blowing dust; they slept and worked with faces covered by towels. (It should be noted that many emergency housing facilities built at military camps nationwide for servicemen and their families were of similar construction.)

Construction of the Minidoka camp in the summer of 1942 ended the depression in south-central Idaho. M-K had hired carpenters and masons and helpers in Magic Valley for $72 per week, when wages ranged from $10 to $15 per week for clerks in stores and $20 to $25 per week for carpenters and masons (most of whom were unemployed anyway). Except during the harvest and the sugar factory "campaign," work was scarce; local poolhalls were lined with idle men of all ages, and scores of "loafers" leaned on buildings in the center of town facing the sidewalk. By contrast, those who worked at the "Jap Camp," as it was called, earned unbelievable wages. One of the writer's friends, later a distinguished professor at Northwestern University, was only fourteen, but he was tall and husky and no one asked his age, so he was hired to work in the lumberyard, later on the "cement gang." He learned that some carpenters were paid $300 a week. It was a crash project; speed was the object. Workers often wore respirators to keep from breathing the dust and getting "dust pneumonia."

The M-K payroll was like fireworks in Magic Valley—bringing immediate prosperity. Bars and restaurants suddenly overflowed. People bought newer cars and made improvements in their homes. World War II spending had rescued Magic Valley from the depression. Most of the builders, coming from farms rather than cities, lived in houses and shacks without running water, and they used outhouses. As they constructed the camp's communal kitchens, laundries, and bathhouses they were envious: the incoming "Japs" were being given such "luxuries" as indoor toilets at public expense. It would never have occurred to the workers what a God-forsaken place this would seem to people from Portland and Seattle forcibly exiled into the Idaho desert.

Most of the evacuees sent to Minidoka were residents of western Washington and Oregon—about 7,000 from Washington and 3,000 from Oregon. Since the sewage system had not been installed, the inhabitants were first forced to use outdoor latrines. Knowing this would be their home for an indefinite period, they sought to alter the grim, bleak appearance by beautifying the center with vines, ferns, and flowers. They planted grass and a few large trees donated by residents of Twin Falls and Jerome and brought in cattail reeds, willows, and cactus to put on "their" land.

The administration was limited to a food budget of 45 cents per person per day. Although the individual amount of food was meager, the totals were enormous. In November 1942, the entire Minidoka camp consumed daily: 4,000 pounds of rice, 900 gallons of milk, 3,500 pounds of meat, 4,400 loaves of bread, and 1,126 dozen eggs.[9]

About a year after their incarceration, the residents adopted a system of self-government. A charter was approved, a seven-man Community Advisory Council was elected, and special committees were appointed to deal with food, health, housing, education, employment, and public relations. The center had two elementary schools with 776 pupils and a faculty of ten; five nursery schools for children under six; Hunt High School with 1,200 students; and an adult educational program designed to "Americanize" the Japanese with training in the English language and American history and government. An industrial-arts program taught adults skills in farm machinery, welding, motor mechanics, poultry and dairy husbandry, truck farming, electricity, and carpentry. There were four libraries—one in each of the schools and a public library.

A resident-controlled community cooperative, established in December 1942, set up a shoe repair, a watch repair, two mail-order agencies, four general stores, one clothing and dry goods store, one beauty parlor, two barber shops, one flower shop, a weekly newspaper (the *Minidoka Irrigator*), a motion-picture department, and a dry-cleaning shop.[10] A Community Activities Division sponsored music performances, socials, entertainments, children's activities, arts and crafts, and athletics. A Catholic Church, six Protestant denominations combined into one Federated Christian Church, and three Buddhist denominations provided religious services.

Soon after the center's inception, the administration launched a drive to recruit a labor force for work outside the center. Workers on neighboring farms and orchards were paid $16 a month and professionally trained persons $19 a month. Evacuees worked in potato fields, harvested sugar beets, and picked fruit. Although the residents, mostly from urban centers, were not accustomed to physically strenuous work (and picking potatoes and thinning and topping sugar beets could be very exhausting), they became conditioned and farmers regarded them as efficient and cooperative laborers.

The evacuees learned farming skills quickly. They cleared, irrigated, and placed under cultivation 250 acres in the spring of 1943 and produced more than 1,000 tons of grains and vegetables, including enough potatoes to last the colony for a year. The 1944 crop was nearly twice as large, coming from 800 acres under cultivation. The community also operated a hog ranch and a poultry unit. The poultry farm had 8,600 chickens by the end of 1943, with 3,500 laying hens producing three cases of eggs per day. The hog ranch contained 400 hogs by the end of 1943, furnishing dining halls with 25 animals per week. In 1944 the poultry farm produced 39,000 pounds of chicken meat and 63,000 eggs; the hog farm produced 307,000 pounds of pork. All in all, the farm furnished the center with about one-sixth of its food requirements. An attempt to set up a canning plant failed because necessary machinery and equipment were lacking.

In January 1943 the U.S. War Department announced the formation of a special Japanese combat unit. Of the 300 Minidoka volunteers, 211 were classified as acceptable, more than from any other relocation center. A year later, in January 1944, the War Department announced a program of drafting eligible Nisei (children of immigrants born in America) into the army. By the end of 1944 more than 800 Minidoka residents were serving in the armed forces. Many of these were killed in action in Italy.

The central administration had encouraged relocation out of the compound for students and others. By the summer of 1944 more than 2,000 were doing agricultural and other manual labor outside camp or had permanently relocated to work or to attend a college or university. Not allowed to return to the West Coast, many of the parolees went to the Midwest.

In the middle of December 1944 the WRA announced that all relocation centers would be closed within a year; moreover, the ban on returning to the West Coast was removed. Since many of the men had joined the army, gone to university, or found outside employment, those remaining at the camp were mostly elderly people and children. They were not eager to move, either to the West Coast or elsewhere. But the administration gradually suspended the operation of its various services: the agricultural division was eliminated, schools were closed in May and June, and there was a steady exodus of relocatees. By July 1945 fewer than 5,000 still lived in camp, by September about 3,000, and on October 23, 1945, the center was closed.

Most of the center inhabitants did not return to Oregon or Washington but dispersed all over the nation. With the war over both in Europe and with Japan, Americans hailed the fighting heroism of the Japanese-American combat team, and the relocated internees now found themselves accepted as loyal Americans.

Many "Japanese" today are grateful for the evacuation experience. By uprooting them from the West Coast, it paved the way for their residence and acceptance in the interior. Many lawyers, doctors, business executives, and university professors now attribute their rise out of "second-class citizenship" at least in part to the forced relocation out of the Little Tokyos on the West Coast. Bitter and bewildering as it was, the evacuation is now sometimes referred to as a "blessing in disguise."

World War II exerted a mixed influence on Idahoans. On the one hand, about 25,000 Idahoans left the state to work in the shipyards, aircraft assembly plants, and other industries on the West Coast. Bright young men and women from the state served in the armed forces in North Africa and Italy; in England, France, Germany; in Guadalcanal, New Guinea, Okinawa, and Japan; and at American bases in Texas, Georgia, Maryland, Michigan, and California. Some of them paid the ultimate price. Civilians on the home front could not travel as they would like to have done, buy all the food they were accustomed to eating, or obtain new consumer durables, parts, and materials for building. Even civilians faced social dislocation, privation, and death.

On the other hand, Idaho experienced unprecedented prosperity. Wages were high, new military bases and industrial plants provided employment and added to the state's income, and people worked together as never before to achieve a common purpose—the defeat of the Axis. Many rural villages suffered as people moved to cities. Not everyone appreciated contributions of the Hispanics, Japanese-Americans, and prisoners of war to Idaho's agriculture, but the greater ethnic diversity added to the state's cultural heritage. Whatever one's individual experience, all were determined that the nightmarish aftermath Idaho's citizens had undergone following World War I would not be repeated.

## CHAPTER TWENTY-FOUR: SOURCES

National histories that provide good background include Francis Walton, *Miracle of World War II: How American Industry Made Victory Possible* (New York: The Macmillan Co., 1956); Eliot Janeway,

*The Struggle for Survival: A Chronicle of Economic Mobilization in World War II* (New Haven, Conn.: Yale University Press, 1951); Hughes, *American Economic History*, 472–85; Harold Underwood Faulkner, *American Economic History*, 8th ed. (New York: Harper & Brothers, 1960), 696–711; and Donald M. Nelson, *Arsenal of Democracy: The Story of American War Production* (New York: Harcourt, Brace and Company, 1946).

Histories of the West and of the Pacific Northwest that give the regional experience include Malone and Etulain, *The American West*, 107–19; Nash, *The American West in the Twentieth Century*, 195–216; Gerald D. Nash, *The American West Transformed: The Impact of the Second World War* (Bloomington: Indiana University Press, 1985), passim; Johansen and Gates, *Empire of the Columbia*, 528–31; Pomeroy, *The Pacific Slope*, 297–301; Schwantes, *The Pacific Northwest*, 326–40; Carlos A. Schwantes, ed., *The Pacific Northwest in World War II* (Manhattan, Kansas: Sunflower University Press, 1986).

Histories of Idaho that have sections on the World War II period include Wells, *Boise: An Illustrated History*, 103–7; Brosnan, *History of the State of Idaho*, 373C–373T; Beal and Wells, *History of Idaho*, 2:269–74; Jensen, *Discovering Idaho: A History*, 224–31; and Barber and Martin, *Idaho in the Pacific Northwest*, 212–17.

A considerable literature now exists on the Japanese-American Relocation movement. Of particular relevance to the Minidoka Camp are Roger Daniels, *Concentration Camps USA: Japanese Americans and World War II* (New York: Holt, Rinehart and Winston, 1972); United States Department of Interior, *WRA: Impounded People—Japanese Americans in the Relocation Centers* (Washington, D.C.: Government Printing Office, 1946); John Tateishi, *And Justice for All: An Oral History of the Japanese American Detention Camps* (New York: Random House, 1984), esp. 38–50, 62–93; 213–21, 239–41; *Personal Justice Denied: Report of the Commission on Wartime Relocation and Internment of Civilians* (Washington, D.C.: Government Printing Office, 1982); Robert C. Sims, "The Japanese Experience in Idaho," *Idaho Yesterdays* 22 (Spring 1978):2–10; Robert C. Sims, "Japanese Americans in Idaho," in Roger Daniels, Sandra C. Taylor, and Harry H. L. Kitano, eds., *Japanese Americans: From Relocation to Redress* (Salt Lake City: University of Utah Press, 1986), 103–11; Robert C.

Sims, "A Fearless, Patriotic, 'Clean-Cut Stand': Idaho's Governor Clark and Japanese-American Relocation in World War II," *Pacific Northwest Quarterly* 70 (April 1979):75–81; Donald E. Hausler, "History of the Japanese-American Relocation Center at Hunt, Minidoka County, Idaho" (M.A. thesis, Utah State University, 1964); Leonard J. Arrington, *The Price of Prejudice: The Japanese-American Relocation Center in Utah During World War II* (Logan: Utah State University Press, 1962); Monica Sone, *Nisei Daughter* (Boston: Little, Brown and Company, 1953); Jonathan Hughes, "A Personal Preface: The Jap Camp" and "A Disastrous Blunder," 1984, typescripts generously furnished to the author by Dr. Hughes; Arthur Kleinkopf, "Relocation Center Diary," typescript in the Twin Falls Public Library (Kleinkopf was superintendent of education at the War Relocation Center at Hunt); James Sakoda, "Minidoka: An Analysis of Changing Patterns of Social Interaction" (Ph.D. dissertation, University of California, 1955); and the *Minidoka Irrigator* (camp newspaper) and other materials in the University of California Library, Berkeley. Especially useful in that collection is Harry L. Stafford's Project Director's Narrative.

Other helpful articles include: D. Worth Clark, "Idaho Made the Desert Bloom," *National Geographic Magazine* 85 (June 1944): 641–80; John C. Olinger, "They Called It Camp Downey," *Idaho Yesterdays* 31 (Winter 1988):15–23; Patricia K. Ourada, "Reluctant Servants: Conscientious Objectors in Idaho During World War II," *Idaho Yesterdays* 31 (Winter 1988):2–14; Ralph A. Busco and Douglas D. Alder, "German and Italian Prisoners of War in Utah and Idaho," *Utah Historical Quarterly* 39 (Winter 1971):55–72; and Erasmo Gamboa, *Mexican Labor and World War II: Braceros in the Pacific Northwest, 1942–1947* (Austin: University of Texas Press, 1990).

131.

131. About 8,000 Japanese-Americans from the Seattle area were interned during World War II at Camp Minidoka near Paul. ISHS 73–184.1.

## CHAPTER TWENTY-FIVE

# Political Independence in War and Peace

SINCE the achievement of statehood, and even before, Idaho's political leaders and their constituents have demonstrated a strong spirit of independence. The voting patterns of Idaho citizens have demonstrated, time after time, that Idahoans have maintained ambivalent attitudes toward political parties; they have not identified closely with major political parties; they have shown a high frequency of ticket-splitting and have sometimes given an important role to third parties.

The independent political tradition of Idaho is a major theme in the authoritative three-volume *History of Idaho* by Merrill Beal and Merle Wells.[1] It was also a theme of two recent books discussing Idaho's political history.[2] Focusing on the twenty-seven-year territorial period, Robert Blank, in *Individualism in Idaho*, concluded that the miners, farmers, and cattlemen who settled Idaho began a tradition of conservatism that included home rule, animosity toward "carpetbag" federal officials, and maintenance of pioneer values.[3]

With respect to the federal government, the Idaho tradition has continued to be both independent and dependent. From the beginning, although there has been a resistance to outside authority and control, federal assistance has been not only accepted but demanded. In the words of historian Duane Smith:

> The miner relied upon his government for aid and succor. He cried for mail service, lenient federal policies toward mining and land, military protection, and territorial government. Aroused protests greeted any dereliction of responsibility or failure to meet expectations. Up to a point Uncle Sam was welcome, but the miner and townsman did not want the government to interfere too much. Quite definitely Federal regulation or close supervision was not desired. This ambiguous attraction and repulsion typify the Western attitude toward government.[4]

Because of the lack of strict party affiliation Idaho has been a borderline state politically, and many contests are close. Republican C. A. Bottolfsen and Democrat Chase Clark alternated in the governorship in the late 1930s and early 1940s by winning successive races by only a few hundred votes. Charles C. Gossett, who succeeded Bottolfsen and served briefly in 1945 before he appointed himself senator to replace John Thomas, carried an important county by a majority of one vote. Glen Taylor, who had earlier been bested by Gossett, beat him when he came up for re-election the next year.

John Gunther, who discussed Idaho politics in 1947 in his book *Inside U.S.A.*, summarized the state's major political forces. First, he pointed to the great mining companies, like Bunker Hill and Sullivan at Kellogg and the Sunshine Mining Company near Osburn (west of Wallace) with the world's biggest silver mine; the major lumber companies such as Clearwater Timber Company and other Weyerhaeuser interests; and the Idaho Power Company. Second, Gunther listed the Mormon Church, repeating a local truism: "Eighty percent of the Idaho vote is agricultural and 40 percent of that is Mormon."[5] Third were the Basques, whom Gunther credited with being as "liberal" as the Mormons were conservative and who swung the balance in the 1944 vote that elected Glen Taylor in place of D. Worth Clark. Fourth were the dust-bowl migrants from Oklahoma, Missouri, Kansas, and the Dakotas who represented a dissident vote. Fifth, said Gunther, was the education lobby, and sixth the *Idaho Statesman*, controlled at the time by Margaret Cobb Ailshie.[6]

The decades before, during, and after World War II are evidence of Idaho's independent political heritage.[7] Perhaps the single best illustration occurred in 1936, when Republican fortunes were at their lowest ebb. That year Senator Borah's term was up. Despite his five terms in the Senate, many observers, including one prominent Idaho newspaper, thought he would be defeated. Republicans had faced disaster in 1932 and 1934. Franklin Roosevelt, elected by a wide margin in 1932, was certain to be reelected in 1936 and would likely bring in a Democratic senator on his coattails. The Democrats, who had never run a strong candidate against Borah, now had a popular three-term governor, C. Ben Ross. "Cowboy Ben," a flamboyant campaigner, clearly appealed to the ordinary voter who, it was thought, might be tired of Borah's learned discourses on the Constitution, American history, and America's role in world affairs. But as he had done throughout his political life, Borah reached his rural and small-town coalition of cowboys, ranchers, miners, lumberjacks, merchants, teachers, farmers, and housewives chiefly by making them think. Not that he didn't sometimes inject humor to make them chuckle. His carefully organized, logically argued discourses, as this writer can testify, were never demagogic or partisan, ever thought-provoking, inspiring, and sometimes thrilling. The election figures demonstrated once again the independence of Idaho's voters. In the presidential vote Idaho gave Roosevelt 125,683 votes and

Landon 66,232; in the senatorial race Borah received 128,723 votes and Ross 74,444. Some 60,000 voters had crossed over to the Republican column to support Borah for the Senate. Approximately one-half the voters divided their ballot between the parties in that election—one of the most remarkable instances of "ticket-scratching" on record.[8]

Borah and Ross were both exemplars of Idahoans' political independence. A native of Illinois who became an attorney in Kansas, Borah settled in Boise in 1890, the year Idaho was made a state. He was twenty-five. Active politically, within two years he was named chairman of Idaho's Republican Party. Under his influence Republicans abandoned their traditional anti-Mormonism and focused on national issues. Although he organized a progressive Republican election victory in 1902, a conservative Republican combine preferred Weldon B. Heyburn, of Wallace, who served in the Senate from 1903 until his death in 1912.

In 1906 Borah again led the Republicans to an Idaho victory. Following a highly successful criminal and corporate law practice, and having achieved a national reputation as an attorney for the state in its unsuccessful prosecution of William D. Haywood, Borah was elected senator to succeed Fred Dubois. Borah held the senatorial post for the next thirty-three years. He was a persuasive orator and exerted considerable influence in the Senate. He sponsored two progressive constitutional amendments—direct election of United States senators and the federal income tax—as well as the creation of the Children's Bureau and the United States Department of Labor. Although he was a solid supporter of President Theodore Roosevelt, he chose to remain neutral in the "mugwump" presidential election of 1912. During World War I Borah continued to solidify his independent posture, firmly supporting civil liberties at a time when freedom of speech was not popular. He strongly recommended taxing corporations' excess profits and upheld the Wilson administration in conducting the war against obstructionist tactics of the Republicans.

After the Armistice, Borah led the fight against ratification of the Treaty of Versailles, believing it to be inequitable and imperialist and a likely provocation for war in the future. He regarded the proposed League of Nations as simply a device to maintain an unjust peace and disparaged the World Court as an instrument of the League. For this position he was widely regarded as an isolationist. But unlike other isolationists, he felt that the United States should pursue an active, independent international policy for revision of the Paris treaties in order to promote world peace. Borah was largely responsible for the Washington Disarmament Conference of 1921.

In 1924 Borah was a candidate for his fourth term in the Senate. An independent in his senatorial speeches, votes, and actions and nationally regarded as a powerful champion of the rights and liberties of the people, Borah had the official nominations of both the Republican and Progressive parties and the quiet support of thousands of Democrats. In the election Borah received 99,846 votes and his Democratic opponent 25,199, a four-to-one score.

Borah chaired the Senate Foreign Relations Committee from 1924 to 1933. He fought foreign entanglements while at the same time promoting voluntary cooperation and anticipating much of the Good Neighbor Policy. He championed the unpopular cause of recognition of the Soviet Union and helped to promote a better relationship between the United States and Mexico. He was a potent voice in the 1928 multilateral Kellogg-Briand Pact that outlawed war as an instrument of national policy.

The senator was equally active in domestic affairs. During the New Deal, he supported banking reforms, including a monetary adjustment for gold and silver. He staunchly approved social security legislation but criticized other important New Deal measures, including the National Industrial Recovery Act, which violated his antimonopoly principles. He emerged as a leading Republican presidential contender early in 1936 but fortunately was spared that nomination. Instead, Idaho returned him to the Senate for a sixth term that year by a staggering vote that exceeded Franklin D. Roosevelt's total in the state. During his final Senate term, believing the independence of the judiciary at stake, Borah worked to defeat Roosevelt's proposal to enlarge or "pack" the United States Supreme Court. He also continued to support measures to keep the United States out of European wars, which he had warned against so often. He witnessed Hitler's advance into Czechoslovakia and Poland in 1938 and 1939, but he died before France fell in 1940.[9]

Even though Senator Borah addressed himself to national issues, he was able, through his seniority and exceptional prestige, to serve Idaho as well as the nation. He was a leader in the passage of the three-year (easier requirements) Homestead bill, his influence was important in the construction of the Arrowrock Dam and other reclamation projects, and he promoted such farm legislation as the Perishable Agricultural Commodities Act. Above all, he was proof that Idahoans did not care much about party affiliation.

The man Borah defeated in 1936 was another exemplar of individualistic political tradition. C. Ben Ross, governor during much of the New Deal period, symbolized Idaho's political resistance to the liberal Democrats who administered the programs that, as indicated in Chapter Twenty-two, were clearly advantageous for Idaho. Ross was Idaho's first native-born governor, the first to serve three terms (1931–37), a strong executive, a colorful campaigner, and an unforgettable personality.

"Cowboy Ben" grew up on a ranch near Parma, where the Snake and Boise rivers converge in Canyon County. Raised a Republican, he switched to the Populist-dominated Democratic Party in 1896, when he was twenty-one. His entry into politics was quick and successful. He was elected Canyon County Commissioner in 1915 and served six years. He was a founding father of the Idaho Farm Bureau Federation. In 1921 he moved to Pocatello, where he invested in irrigated farmland and urban real estate. Two years later he was elected mayor of Pocatello, and he served in that position for six years. Ross first ran for governor in 1928 but failed because of the presidential candidacy of Democrat Al Smith, whose "wet" and New York City image did not appeal to Idaho's rural voters. In a second try in 1930 Ross won the general election with a handy plurality over his GOP opponent, even though the legislature continued strongly Republican, as did the congressional delegation. He was successful in instituting the direct primary, an old-age pension law, an income tax to relieve property taxpayers, and a kilowatt tax on electricity generated in the state. He was reelected in the New Deal landslide of 1932 that put Franklin Roosevelt in the president's chair. His fellow Democrats won control of the legislature, both congressional seats, and a U.S. Senate seat for liberal Boise mayor James P. Pope.

During the turbulent early Thirties, Ross exercised strong yet restrained leadership. These were years of enforced austerity budgets, delinquent taxes, and confrontations with eastern liberals not always appreciative of Idaho's rural values. Ross put through a two-year moratorium on delinquent property taxes and a sixty-day freeze on mortgage foreclosures. Although he was pleased with such federal relief programs as the CCC, AAA, HOLC, and Social Security, the red tape, delays, and demands for state matching funds angered him. He won reelection easily in 1934. Juggling demands from federal programs for matching moneys with a need to relieve property taxpayers, Ross advocated a sales tax. When the legislature adjourned in March 1935 without passing the 2 percent tax he recommended, the FERA refused to fund further relief until the matching monies were advanced. Ross closed the state's relief offices, convened a special session of the legislature, and this time got a sales tax as law. The voters later punished him for extracting the "penny for Benny."

Ross had thought it was his destiny to unseat the most powerful of Idaho's politicians, Senator William E. Borah. In 1936, certain of a Democratic landslide, Ross expected his election as senator might be a part of it. He miscalculated his race. Roosevelt was reelected by the largest margin any presidential candidate had ever received, but Borah buried Ross by a margin of more than 54,000 votes. Ross's sales tax went down to defeat as well on a referendum vote. In 1938 Ross ran again for the governorship against the incumbent Democrat Barzilla W. Clark, winning the primary but losing by a small margin to Republican C. A. Bottolfsen. He returned to his Canyon County ranch, where he died at age sixty-nine in 1946.[10]

Ross's place as governor was taken by Barzilla W. Clark of Idaho Falls. Born in Indiana, Clark moved with his family to Eagle Rock in 1884, when he was only four. His father served as first mayor of the town after it had been renamed Idaho Falls. The younger Clark became a member of the Idaho Falls City Council in 1908, mayor in 1913, and, after a brief interlude when he ran for governor, was reelected mayor of Idaho Falls and served in that position until his nomination for governor in 1936.

Clark, a licensed engineer, was involved in many successful reservoir and water-development projects in Idaho. His term as governor, however, was riddled with failures. He had to find funds to replace the sales-tax revenues that the voters had rejected in the 1936 referendum. The legislature was unfriendly to him, since he was not a follower of Ross. Clark had little success with any of the measures he favored, and he vetoed several bills. In the 1938 Democratic primary he lost to ex-Governor Ross by just over 2,198 votes.[11]

Republican C. A. Bottolfsen, elected in 1938 and 1942, was

the only Idaho governor until recently to serve split terms. "Bott," as he was usually called, was born in Wisconsin and educated in North Dakota and at the age of nineteen moved to Arco, Idaho, to take over the *Arco Advertiser*. Elected to represent Butte County in the legislature in 1920, 1922, 1928, and 1930, he was chosen Speaker of the House during the 1931 session. By 1938 there was enough disillusionment with the national Democratic Party that Bottolfsen surprisingly won the election with a promise not to scuttle the relief program of the New Deal but to "house-clean" the Capitol. He also slashed the budget of the University of Idaho and other state educational institutions to avoid increasing taxes.

When Bottolfsen ran again in 1940, his opponent was Chase Clark, brother of Barzilla. The trend now favored Democrats, and Clark was elected by a narrow margin. Chase Clark, three years younger than Barzilla, was only one when his parents moved to Idaho. After a year of college study at Terre Haute, Indiana, he attended the University of Michigan Law School but did not graduate. Returning to Idaho, he settled at Mackay, passed his bar examination, practiced law, and developed mining, livestock, and banking interests. He served in the Judge Advocate General's Office of the army and as a lieutenant in a machine gun company during World War I. In 1930 he moved his law practice and family to Idaho Falls. He served two terms in the legislature, succeeded his brother as mayor of Idaho Falls, went to the Idaho State Senate, and was elected governor in 1940. At the conclusion of his term, the United States now at war, Clark and Bottolfsen faced each other again. "Bott" regained the office by fewer than 500 votes. Clark was appointed to the bench of the United States District Court in Idaho and served until his death in 1966. In 1947 his daughter Bethine married Frank Church, a young Boise attorney and later U.S. Senator.

In the 1942 election that returned Bottolfsen to office, voters approved an initiative calling for $40 per month for all Idaho citizens sixty-five and older. This Senior Citizens Grant Act created a potential financial crisis, since the governor and legislature had been elected on pledges of economy and no new taxes. Bottolfsen proposed a 5 percent sales tax to fund the Senior Grants, but the legislature promptly rejected the sales tax and then repealed the senior citizens' pensions by overwhelming majorities. Should the governor veto the legislation? In a dramatic appearance before a joint session of the legislature he announced that he approved the legislative action and that the pension plan had "joined all other patriotic endeavors of Idaho and gone to war."[12]

When his term of office was up in 1944, "Bott" decided to run for the U.S. Senate but was defeated by Glen Taylor. He retired to Arco, ran for the governorship again in 1946, but was defeated by Dr. C. A. Robins. He served two additional terms in the legislature, 1959 to 1963, and died at his Arco home in 1964.

The career of picaresque Glen Taylor demonstrated once again the unpredictability and independence of the Idaho voting public. Born in Portland, Oregon, Taylor was one of eight children of a retired Texas ranger and itinerant minister. Soon after his birth the family moved to Kooskia, south of Kamiah on the Clearwater River. Taylor quit school at twelve, worked as a sheepherder and sheet-metal apprentice, and joined some of his brothers in a repertory troupe that traveled the West. He met a young Montana actress, Dora Pike; they married, set up a vaudeville company known as Glendora Players, and continued barnstorming. Taylor played every kind of role from romantic lead to comedian. The "talkies," as sound movies were called, and the depression almost put them out of business, but they persevered and revived in 1937, only to be struck down by the "menace" of radio. Taylor, who had never played any musical instrument except the mouth organ, learned to play the trombone, banjo, and guitar; Dora mastered the piano and saxophone. With his brother Paul and Paul's wife, they played one-night stands in country towns in Montana and Idaho.

Once when playing in Driggs, Idaho, Taylor attended a rally at which "Cowboy Ben" Ross was speaker. A master campaigner, Ross could move his audience to laugh and cry and vote for him. Experienced from his own long years on the road, Taylor decided that he could entertain even better than Ross, so he ran for Congress. His troupe, mounted on trucks, moved from place to place and put on a show, playing and singing to attract a crowd, after which he would make a speech attacking politicians and pleading for the common man. Taylor had been moved by the large number of persons who, not having any income, wanted to pay to attend his shows by trading bushels of wheat or potatoes, pullets, or eggs. He accepted the "donations" and used to joke about the one who turned in a turkey and wanted a chicken in exchange. Taylor "read up" on economics to find some explanation for the poverty in the midst of plenty. He was beaten, but the people liked him.

When an election was held in 1942 to replace Senator Borah, who had died in 1940, Taylor decided to run. Many dignified political old-timers were embarrassed. A Boise newspaper editorialized: "Feature Idaho [if you will] telling the nation that the best it can do for a man to fill the great Borah's shoes is a sweet singer, wholly uneducated and wholly unfitted."[13] With little support from people with resources, Taylor bought a dapple-gray Arabian horse named Ranger, saddled up, and rode from house to house asking for votes—thus saving on rationed gas and rubber. Surprisingly, he won the Democratic primary, defeating the state's Democratic machine, but he lost by a close margin in the general election to Republican John Thomas, who had been senator from 1928 to 1933 and was then appointed to replace Borah.

Taylor applied for a defense plant job in Idaho but was turned down because of the unfavorable publicity from his campaigns. He finally got a position in San Francisco as a painter's assistant and later as a sheet-metal worker and spent his earnings keeping up his contacts in Idaho. When the 1944 campaign began, he returned to Pocatello, filed again for the Senate, won the primary by 216 votes against incumbent Senator D. Worth Clark, and easily defeated Clarence Bottolfsen in the runoff. A crazy six-year dream had come true.

As a senator, Taylor voted on domestic programs that were in the New Deal tradition—increased social security benefits, fair employment for black Americans (of whom there were less than 500 in Idaho), national health insurance, mammoth federal housing construction, pro-labor legislation, and numerous reclamation projects. Disagreeing with Harry Truman over international issues, he thought Truman's policy of trying to contain the supposed Communist conspiracy destroyed the effectiveness of the United Nations and made the Cold War inevitable. He believed the United States was losing friends, particularly among Third World countries in Africa, Asia, and Latin America, and that the Russians wanted peace. He feared the development of a military-industrial complex. In 1948 he bolted the Democratic Party and ran for vice president on Henry Wallace's Progressive ticket.

Although Taylor is best known for his international stance, so different from that of Borah and D. Worth Clark, he also was solicitous to help Idaho. He worked to secure the atomic energy plant near Arco; the Palisades and Lucky Peak dams; and the reactivation of Mountain Home Air Force Base. He wheedled federal money for flood control, conservation, reclamation, irrigation, schools, roads, and hospitals in Idaho. An entertainer, Taylor was also a very serious man with a fertile mind, good sense, and a dry wit. He was unaffected and interested in helping the common man. Although he sang and played the guitar on the Capitol steps, he was not a clown, hillbilly, or buffoon.[14] Nor was he a demagogue. Idaho voters appreciated his pertinacity, candor, and sincerity. He served six years but was defeated for renomination in 1950 when 5,000 Republicans crossed party lines in the primary to vote for D. Worth Clark, who was defeated in the general election by Republican Herman Welker.[15]

Bottolfsen's successor as governor in 1944 was Charles C. Gossett of Nampa. One of only two farmers to occupy the governor's office, Gossett had a host of elective experience—the only Idahoan to serve as state legislator, lieutenant governor, governor, and United States Senator. Born in Ohio, Gossett migrated at the age of eighteen to Cunningham, Washington, where he worked as a farmhand for three years. In 1910 he homesteaded in Nyssa, Oregon, and in 1922 bought an eighty-acre farm south of Nampa. Like other farmers, he complained about low prices, high freight rates, water fees, and taxes. Thinking the legislature could do something about it, he campaigned as Democratic nominee for representative from Canyon County and was elected in 1932. At odds with another Canyon County politician, Governor Ben Ross, Gossett voted against Ross's proposal to enact a sales tax to provide matching funds for the Federal Emergency Relief Administration in 1935. His opposition to the tax enhanced his reputation, and he was elected lieutenant governor in 1936. In 1942 he ran for the U.S. Senate but was defeated in the primary by Glen Taylor, who, as noted, lost in the November election. Gossett campaigned for governor in 1944 and was victorious. The ticket revealed Idaho's independent spirit because liberal Democrat Glen Taylor was elected to the Senate while conservative Gossett became governor.

Gossett did not serve long. When Senator John Thomas, Republican from Gooding who had been elected to take Borah's place in the Senate, died in November 1945, Gossett resigned as governor; he had served less than a year. Lieutenant Governor Arnold Williams of Rexburg now became Idaho's first

Mormon governor; he appointed Gossett to the Senate seat. Gossett had barely taken his place in the Senate when he had to stand for election. In 1946 Glen Taylor campaigned for George Donart, another Democrat, to replace Gossett, and Donart received the nomination but lost in the general election. Taking the seat was Republican Henry Dworshak.

Dworshak, a conservative newspaperman from Burley, was first elected to Congress in 1938, the year Glen Taylor first tried for office. Born in Duluth, Minnesota, Dworshak learned the printing trade and served as a printer there and in 1924, at the age of thirty, moved to Idaho to publish the *Burley Bulletin*. After his election Dworshak served the two remaining years of the senatorial term, but in the 1948 election was defeated by Bert H. Miller, a Utah-born Democrat from Boise who had been Idaho attorney general and Supreme Court justice. When Senator Miller died the next year, Dworshak was appointed to fill out his term, which, because of the death, expired in 1950. In the 1950 elections Dworshak retained his Senate seat, but he faced a tight race with Glen Taylor in 1954. It was a contest in which Herman Welker, Idaho's senior senator, employed the tactics of Senator Joseph McCarthy of Wisconsin, whom he admired, and opened a campaign of fear and innuendo, alleging quite falsely that Taylor was a Communist fellow-traveler and part of an alleged Communist conspiracy. (Taylor left himself open to these charges by the 1948 campaign and various pro-Russian statements.) The campaign of defamation, in which Dworshak played no part, succeeded, and Dworshak was handily elected. When the term was up, Dworshak was reelected in 1954 and again in 1960. He died in office in July 1962.

Welker, a rightist from Payette who had practiced law in Hollywood, was a friend of actor Wallace Beery and a bird-hunting companion of Bing Crosby. Crosby, who had a vacation home north of Coeur d'Alene, campaigned for Welker in Boise under the slogan "A pheasant in every pot."[16] Welker was elected in

1950 to replace Democrat D. Worth Clark, but he lost to Frank Church in 1956.

Frank Church was born in Boise in 1924. As a boy he read Borah's speeches, learned all he could about him, and decided he wanted to be a U.S. Senator. He became a high school debater, won a national contest in public speaking, became a lawyer, married Bethine, the daughter of Chase Clark, and got into politics. He was elected to the United States Senate in 1956, reelected in 1962, 1968, and 1974. As a member of the Foreign Relations Committee, he was opposed to the Vietnam War. He also took an interest in conservation and the environment and led the push to pass the Wilderness Act, about which more later.

Meanwhile at the state level Democrat Arnold Williams, who took Governor Gossett's place in November 1945, had the responsibility of calling the legislature to a special session in February 1946 to deal with post-World War II problems. Although both houses of the legislature had Republican majorities, they enacted most of Williams's recommendations, which increased appropriations to most government agencies; expanded public assistance to the aged, blind, and dependent children; enlarged control over the state's charitable institutions; and established a teachers' retirement program. Williams failed in his bid to retain the governorship in the 1946 elections, losing to Dr. C. A. Robins in an election that saw Republicans winning a U.S. Senate seat, both congressional posts, a full Republican slate of state offices, and large Republican majorities in both houses of the state legislature. Williams later closed out his political career by serving as Idaho's secretary of state from 1959 to 1966.

Robins, who was born in Iowa and raised in Colorado, taught high school for six years in Missouri, Montana, Colorado, and Mississippi and then entered medical school at the University of Chicago. He practiced medicine until he joined the Army during World War I. After the Armistice he went to St. Maries,

Idaho, where he established a successful practice and operated a twenty-five-bed hospital. He served in the state senate for three sessions beginning in 1939 and then in 1946 was chosen as the Republican nominee for governor to run against Arnold Williams. That election tested the validity of two axioms of Idaho politics: "You can't elect a north Idaho man governor," and "you can't elect a Mormon governor." When north Idahoan Robins won over Williams, he had proved that at least the first was not true.

Robins was the first Idaho governor to serve after adoption of a constitutional amendment that provided for four-year terms. As it was originally worded, governors could not serve consecutive terms, but this stipulation was changed in 1961 and Idaho has since had two governors (Smylie and Andrus) who served at least two consecutive four-year terms.

An important series of measures proposed by Governor Robins and approved by the legislature resulted from recommendations of the Peabody Report on Education.[17] Idaho's 1,118 school districts were consolidated to realize both educational improvement and economy. All high schools with fewer than 100 students were closed. Teachers' salaries, among the lowest in the nation, were raised. The Southern Branch of the University of Idaho at Pocatello was made a four-year, degree-granting institution separate from the University of Idaho at Moscow. The legislature also appropriated money for the purchase of a residence for the chief executive, and Robins became the first occupant of the home that remained the governor's mansion for most of four decades.

In typical independent Idaho fashion, in the next election after Robins was elected, that of 1948, a Democratic rebound gave that party control of the Senate and a large minority (34 to 25) in the House. Nevertheless, in a show of unusual harmony, nearly all of Governor Robins's proposals were adopted.

The victor in the 1950 governor's election was Republican

Leonard "Len" Jordan. Born at Mount Pleasant, Utah, Jordan moved with his family to Enterprise, Oregon, when he was an infant. In 1917 he enrolled at Utah State Agricultural College, where he played football and participated in the Special Army Training Corps. Commissioned a second lieutenant, he served with a machine gunnery unit in World War I. Upon discharge he went to the University of Oregon, where he earned his football letter and was elected to Phi Beta Kappa honorary. After graduate work in economics he settled in Portland, Oregon, to work as an accountant and office manager of the Portland Gas and Coke Company. He began ranching in Wallowa County in 1926 and in 1930 disposed of his interests to become foreman of the Tully Creek Ranch of Dobbin and Huffman on the Snake River, running about 6,000 sheep. In the fall of 1932 he and a partner ventured into ranching at Kirkwood Bar, south of Hells Canyon, where he had 17,000 acres of land and about 3,000 sheep, and in 1935 he bought his partner's interest. In 1941 he moved to Grangeville, Idaho, where he operated a farm, had a car dealership, and sold insurance. Active in civic affairs, Jordan was elected to the state legislature, where he served one term. When he was nominated as Republican candidate for governor in 1950, he won the office and served one four-year term.[18]

Len Jordan was the only person in the last seventy years to be elected to the governorship and then to the U.S. Senate. (The last had been Frank Gooding.) Seven other governors during that period tried and failed to win a Senate seat. Jordan's opponent in his successful 1956 Senate campaign was Gracie Pfost. Another political independent from Nampa, Pfost was Idaho's first Congresswoman—elected in 1952 by defeating her very conservative opponent, Dr. John T. Wood of St. Maries, by the slender margin of 591 votes. An able Congresswoman, Pfost was reelected in 1954. When one group proposed a high dam in Hells Canyon, Pfost gave her support to preserving the beauty of the canyon and earned the nickname "Hell's Belle." She made the mistake of running for the Senate in 1956 and was beaten by popular former governor Jordan.

Senator Jordan is best remembered for his lobbying in connection with Hells Canyon. Having spent years on his remote sheep ranch below the canyon, Jordan figured prominently in the discussions as to whether one large federal dam should be built, as Glen Taylor recommended; three small ones constructed by Idaho Power Company, as Jordan and other conservatives advocated; or none at all. The conservatives won—Brownlee began producing power in 1958, Oxbow in 1961, and Hells Canyon in 1967. Upon Jordan's insistence, however, there was an extended debate to examine all the issues. Jordan's wife, Grace, also a college graduate, wrote an interesting family narrative entitled *Home Below Hells Canyon*, published in 1954.

Jordan's successor as governor was Robert E. Smylie, Republican of Boise, who had been attorney general during Jordan's term. Smylie was born in Iowa, did undergraduate work at the College of Idaho in Caldwell, and went on to obtain his law degree from George Washington University in 1942. Initially practicing in Washington, D.C. during the war, he returned to Idaho and served as attorney general from 1947 to 1954. Smylie served three consecutive four-year terms as governor—one of the few governors in American history to do so. He was fortunate to have bipartisan support in the legislature for at least part of his program of governmental reform. He created the Department of Commerce and Development to attract industry to Idaho and to promote the state. He reorganized the Idaho State Historical Society in 1956 and with the generous assistance of J. R. Simplot placed the society under professional supervision. Its quarterly, *Idaho Yesterdays*, first appeared in the spring of 1957. Other actions will be apparent in subsequent chapters.

Smylie's most lasting contribution to the state was the establishment of a state park system. Although the state had created

Heyburn State Park near St. Maries in 1908 and Lava Hot Springs State Park in 1913, and had acquired the Packer John cabin (where Idaho's first Democratic convention was held in 1863) near McCall, the Spalding Mission property, some beautifully timbered lands on Payette Lake, and Register Rock, the state had lagged behind Oregon and Washington in the creation of state parks. Persuaded that a state park system would save the scenic beauty of the state and capture tourist trade, Smylie, after his election in 1954, urged the legislature to appropriate funds for the creation of a professional Parks Department and reorganization of the management of the state's natural resources.

Smylie, who wrote his own speeches, typed many of his own letters, and was a man of action rather than a politician who enjoyed status, employed John W. Emmert as the first director of state parks and initiated a system that by 1990 comprised twenty-four state parks. Round Lake and Mary Minerva McCroskey state parks were created in 1955, Lucky Park and Ponderosa in 1956 and 1957, and Priest Lake State Park in 1959. The land was acquired in 1961 by which Harriman State Park was later created, and Farragut and Henry's Lake state parks were opened in 1965. Smylie's fight for parks was one of many indicators of the rising national concern for conservation and recreation in the 1950s and 1960s.[19]

Clearly, Idaho has had some forceful, brilliant, and colorful political leaders. George L. Shoup, the first territorial governor and first state governor, established an operable state government. Fred Dubois, a champion of statehood and an anti-Mormon crusader, gave the state its first visibility in the national capital. William J. McConnell, author of one of the state's earliest histories, served as United States Senator and as Idaho's third governor (for two terms). Frank H. Gooding was elected governor twice and a U.S. Senator. Weldon B. Heyburn, also a senator from 1903 until his death in 1912, represented Idaho's mining, forestry, and grazing interests. Governor James H. Hawley was a noted attorney, historian, and legal advisor. Burton L. French, a congressman for twenty-six years, and Addison T. Smith, a congressman for eighteen years, were both honorable and intelligent representatives of their constituents. Senator William E. Borah, son-in-law of Governor McConnell, served for thirty-three years and had national, even international significance. William Jardine of Cherry Creek became secretary of agriculture under Calvin Coolidge, was Herbert Hoover's ambassador to Egypt, and served as president of Wichita State University until his retirement in 1949. C. Ben Ross, C. A. Robins, Gracie Pfost, Glen Taylor, and Frank Church were all leaders with stature. Ezra Taft Benson, a Republican from Whitney, who had been Idaho's agricultural economist in Boise and later national director of the agricultural cooperatives headquartered in Washington, D.C., became secretary of agriculture under President Dwight Eisenhower and served from 1953 to 1961.[20]

During the war years, state government had seemed to be overshadowed by the national war effort. When wartime inconveniences were lifted in 1946, Idaho exhibited an anomalous political tendency. Many elections were decided by small majorities. Because Idaho's voters were inveterate ticket-scratchers, Idaho government tended to be bipartisan. Democratic governors often worked with Republican legislatures, and in one instance a Republican governor had a split legislature. Idaho frequently elected one representative from one party and the other from the opposing party. In 1962 the state returned Frank Church, a liberal Democrat, and Len Jordan, a conservative Republican, to the United States Senate in the same election. Idaho politics has never suffered from dullness. Idaho voters show a political irascibility that is both admirable and exciting; many things are more important to them than party labels.[21]

Although sectionalism was once a dominant factor in state politics, issues common to all sections have developed in this century: questions of public finance, funding education, labor legislation, and environmental concerns. Local provincialism declined, especially during World War II when Idahoans became more closely allied with the developing national culture. Idahoans read the same magazines and syndicated press columns, listened to the identical radio and (later) television programs, attended similar concerts and plays, and read the same best-selling books as other Americans. San Francisco, Seattle, Salt Lake City, and Denver were almost as close for many Idahoans as Boise. The result was not a decline in interest concerning state problems, but a new level of national and international awareness.[22]

Nevertheless, Idaho's tradition of political independence and unpredictability remained. Randy Stapilus's recent book on *Paradox Politics: People and Power in Idaho* is aptly titled.

## CHAPTER TWENTY-FIVE: SOURCES

Idaho's political activity, especially in the period from 1930 to 1959, is treated especially well in Beal and Wells, *History of Idaho*, 2:262–68, 275–83; and F. Ross Peterson, *Idaho: A Bicentennial History*, 159–81. Other general sources are Neal R. Peirce, *The Mountain States of America* (New York: W. W. Norton & Co., 1972), 120–53; Robert H. Blank, *Regional Diversity of Political Values: Idaho Political Culture* (Washington, D.C.: University Press of America, 1978); Robert H. Blank, *Individualism in Idaho: The Territorial Foundations* (Pullman: Washington State University Press, 1988); Randy Stapilus, *Paradox Politics: People and Power in Idaho* (Boise: Ridenbaugh Press, 1988) and *Idaho Political Almanac* (Boise: Ridenbaugh Press, 1990); Robert C. Sims and Hope Benedict, eds., *Idaho's Governors: Historical Essays on Their Administrations*, 2d ed. (Boise: Boise State University, 1992); Gunther, *Inside U.S.A.*, 107–17; Chamberlain, "Idaho: State of Sectional Schisms,"

150–88; and Boyd A. Martin, "Idaho: The Sectional State," in Frank H. Jonas ed., *Western Politics* (Salt Lake City: University of Utah Press, 1961), 161–79.

A general study of the immediate postwar period is Ray Broadhead, "The History of Idaho Since World War II: 1945–1950" (M.A. thesis, University of Idaho, 1950).

The many sources on Senator Borah include Marian C. McKenna, *Borah* (Ann Arbor: University of Michigan Press, 1961); Robert James Maddox, *William E. Borah and American Foreign Policy* (Baton Rouge: Louisiana State University Press, 1969); John Chalmers Vinson, *William E. Borah and the Outlawry of War* (Athens: University of Georgia Press, 1957); Ashby, *The Spearless Leader*; Claudius O. Johnson, *Borah of Idaho* (New York: Longmans, Green, & Co., 1936: reprinted with a new introduction by the author, Seattle: University of Washington Press, 1967); Claudius O. Johnson, "William E. Borah: The People's Choice," *Pacific Northwest Quarterly* 44 (January 1953):15–22; William E. Leuchtenburg, "William Edgar Borah," *Dictionary of American Biography*, Supplement 2 (New York: Charles Scribner's Sons, 1958), 49–53; Richard L. Neuberger, "Battle of the Idaho Titans," *New York Times Magazine*, August 9, 1936, Sec. 7, 9, 20; Richard Neuberger, "Hells Canyon, The Biggest of All," originally in *Harper's* (April 1939) and "The Lion of Idaho," originally in *Coast* (November 1939), reprinted in Steve Neal, ed., *They Never Go Back to Pocatello: The Selected Essays of Richard Neuberger* (Portland: Oregon Historical Society Press, 1988), 15–29 and 70–78; Claudius Johnson, "Borah's Bequest to Democracy," *Idaho Yesterdays* 1 (Winter 1957–58):11–20; [Merle W. Wells], "The Lion of Idaho," *Idaho Yesterdays* 1 (Fall 1957):3–5; Orde S. Pickney, "Lion Triumphant," *Idaho Yesterdays* 3 (Summer 1959): 12–15, 18–24; and John Milton Cooper, Jr., "William E. Borah, Political Thespian," *Pacific Northwest Quarterly* 56 (October 1965): 145–58, an article followed by helpful comments and criticisms by Claudius O. Johnson and Merle Wells.

Other political figures are treated in Malone, *C. Ben Ross and the New Deal in Idaho*; Michael P. Malone, "C. Ben Ross: Idaho's Cowboy Governor," *Idaho Yesterdays* 10 (Winter 1966–67):2–9; F. Ross

Peterson, *Prophet Without Honor: Glen H. Taylor and the Fight for American Liberalism* (Lexington: University Press of Kentucky, 1974); F. Ross Peterson, "Glen H. Taylor: Idaho's Liberal Maverick," in Etulain and Marley, eds., *The Idaho Heritage*, 157–61; Robert C. Sims, "James P. Pope, Senator from Idaho," *Idaho Yesterdays* 15 (Fall 1971):9–15; and F. Forrester Church, *Father and Son: A Personal Biography of Senator Frank Church of Idaho by His Son* (Boston: Faber and Faber, 1985).

132. 133.

134. 135.

132. William E. Borah, United States senator from 1907 to 1940, was a brilliant orator who was often referred to as "The Lion of Idaho." ISHS 64–105.26.

133. C. Ben Ross, of Parma, served as governor during the early depression years, 1930–36. ISHS D–858.

134. Glen Taylor was elected United States senator in 1944 for a six-year term. A guitar-playing entertainer, he was also national candidate for vice president in 1948. ISHS 3645.

135. Henry C. Dworshak, a Burley newspaperman, represented Idaho as U.S. congressman, 1939–46, and as U.S. senator, 1947–62. ISHS 75–2.80.

136.

137.

138.

136. Frank Forrester Church III of Boise served as United States senator from 1957 to 1981. In 1984, shortly before his untimely death from cancer, the Frank Church River of No Return Wilderness was named for him. ISHS 66–49.

137. Len B. Jordan, of Grangeville, governor, 1951–55, was also United States senator, 1962–73. ISHS 66–36.57.

138. Robert E. Smylie, governor of Idaho, 1955–67, usually typed his own speeches—as he later did weekly columns for the *Idaho Statesman*. ISHS 77–163.46.

## CHAPTER TWENTY-SIX

# Expansion and Growth After World War II

IDAHO'S ambivalent attitude toward the federal government was demonstrated several times after World War II. On the one hand, the state appreciated federal expenditures for the National Reactor Testing Station at Arco; federal highways; the Bureau of Reclamation's Palisades and Anderson Ranch dams; the U.S. Army Corps of Engineers' Lucky Peak and Dworshak dams; and other dam, reclamation, and power projects. On the other hand Idahoans wanted to leave private enterprise free to develop the state's resources in an untrammeled, if responsible, manner. This viewpoint was particularly true in lumbering, mining, farming, food processing, hydroelectricity, transportation, television, and tourism, each of which developed spectacularly in the years from 1946 to 1960.

LUMBER. The lumber companies of the Weyerhaeusers and their coinvestors suffered from the post-World War I recession, as did other Idaho concerns, and their earnings were disappointing. Burdensome state and local taxes, heavy transportation charges, high percentage of woods other than marketable white pine, low percentage of clear timber, exposure to fire and insect pests, and costly logging charges all contributed to unprofitability, in addition to the faltering market.

Weyerhaeuser's Clearwater Timber Company held 200,000 acres of the finest western white pine in existence; but the company had done little to develop it, confining efforts primarily to the purchase of standing timber. In November 1924 the stockholders chose a new management team that inaugurated a bold program of development. Under the direction of J. P. (Phil) Weyerhaeuser and C. L. Billings, land was acquired in Lewiston in what had been the county fairgrounds and a large sawmill began operation in August 1927. A large dam was constructed across the Clearwater, a hydroelectric plant was installed, and logs were funneled to the mill by both river and rail. The plant also included a planing mill, a large remanufacturing plant, and a box factory to utilize trimmed remnants and spoiled lumber. The Union Pacific and Northern Pacific railroads were induced to complete a forty-one-mile line from Orofino to Headquarters, and a machine shop was erected to repair locomotives. Clearwater managers reported that 200 million board feet of lumber were sawed the first year.

The company also experimented in making wood-fuel briquettes from the mass of sawdust, splinters, and chips formerly discarded into the burner. The result was Presto-Logs, ideal for city fireplaces, dining cars on trains, and other places where concentrated, almost smokeless fuel was needed. By World War II the company had made thirty-five Presto Log machines that were installed on a rental basis at other western firms.

But depression struck the lumber industry as early as 1927. During the following Great Depression, domestic building averaged only 15 percent of 1925 construction. Large companies staggered, small businesses collapsed. The Bonners Ferry operation was one of the first to fall in 1926, the Edward Rutledge Timber Company failed to recover from two terrible fires, and Potlatch Lumber Company drifted along without any profits. Phil Weyerhaeuser and Billings concluded that Rutledge, Potlatch, and Clearwater should be merged. The new corporation, established April 29, 1931, was Potlatch Forests, Inc. (P.F.I. for short). The retail yards of the old Potlatch Lumber Company were transferred to Potlatch Yards, Inc. From this time forward there were two large Weyerhaeuser-associated companies in Idaho, P.F.I. in the north and Boise Payette in the south. Humbird Lumber Company stopped logging in 1931, ran its planing mills until 1934, and liquidated.

During the depressed thirties these and other western lumber companies did a quarter to a third of their normal business and registered consistent losses. Under expert leadership, however, they were able to survive and work out a conservation program that paid off over the long run.

During World War II P.F.I. earned profits, set aside a contingency reserve fund, launched selective cutting of timber, established tree farms, provided wood products for the war effort, and planned a plant at Lewiston to peel large white pine logs into rolls of veneer. In 1948 the initial output of veneer began. Men and women could now dream of living rooms, bedrooms, playrooms, and libraries paneled in knotty white pine veneer from the forests of northern Idaho. This undertaking proved to be expensive, and the veneer operation was later converted into a more profitable, fully equipped plywood plant.

In 1949 P.F.I. began construction of a pulp plant at Lewiston, along with three converting plants to produce paper milk cartons and other containers. The 150-ton pulp and 130-ton paper mill began producing at the end of 1950, and their rated capacity was later expanded many times. Beginning in 1952 the company added a paper mill in California, sawmills in Idaho and Washington, and enough timberland to raise P.F.I.

holdings to 425,000 acres in the Far West. In 1960 P.F.I. had plants in twelve states and was catering to markets throughout the nation.[1]

The Boise Payette Lumber Company was long considered an orphan, an expendable bantling. Its operations depended largely on ponderosa, a stately pine that did not do well in the market because of prejudice against its yellow wood. The company ran deficits throughout most of the 1920s, and its losses multiplied during the depression of the thirties. Many of the retail yards closed down; a bank at Burlington, Iowa, where Boise Payette had $100,000 on deposit, failed; the First National Bank of Boise closed; the Emmett mill was temporarily shut down. The Barber mill was closed and dismantled in 1934, the Intermountain Railway liquidated in 1935. The conviction grew that Boise Payette should harvest the profitable stands within reach and then cease operations. The company carefully inspected all of its holdings and mapped out the remaining timber for selective logging. During World War II the company skimmed the cream from its holdings. By the end of 1946 the company had 484 million feet of "leave" timber and 292 million feet marked "cut." Everything pointed to early liquidation.

In 1947, however, the company took an unexpected step and expanded, paying $5 million for the Merrill Company (which operated a wholesale lumber business and millwork factory in Salt Lake City) and the Tri-State, Sugarhouse, and Badger lumber companies, which ran thirty-nine retail yards in Idaho, Utah, and Wyoming. Except for the initial boost in retail marketing, however, the company still looked to an early termination of activities until 1949–50, when Norton Clapp and John Aram, youthful but experienced enterprisers, took charge. Nonpracticing physician Clapp had a connection with Norton lumber interests in the Midwest. Tall, stocky Aram, born on a cattle ranch "back in the hills" of the Salmon River country, studied business administration at the University of Idaho, went to work for Potlatch Forests, Inc., and was then appointed manager at Boise Payette.

Boise Payette's timber supply would not support the company long, little private timber could be bought, and state forests in the area were negligible. The United States Forest Service, however, could sell timber from its southern Idaho forests. Aram was successful in persuading it to sell timber to feed Boise Payette mills and to make mutually profitable trades of woodland, while the company held on to large acreages of cutover forests waiting for the new growth to mature (ponderosa pine mature more slowly than other pines). Grazing revenues were sufficient to render such lands self-supporting. By superior management, Aram made Boise Payette's mills efficient, bought timber from all available sources, and started a sustained-yield operation on a broad scale. He laid down a long-range program of selective cutting and tree farming.

In the spring of 1950 Boise Payette lands were officially certified as a Western Pine Tree Farm. Sound logging practices were enforced. High priority was given to working with the broad community. When a terrible fire broke out in the hills of the Payette National Forest, Aram halted all logging, closed the mill at Emmett and a small one at Council, and sent 350 men to help fight the fire. That fall another conflagration raged near Council and once again Boise Payette men battled the flames. This response built good will with government agencies and smaller companies. Through lobbying, sufficient federal money was obtained to enable the Forest Service to build roads up many canyons to increase access. The company also improved its marketing and manufacturing and purchased and virtually rebuilt a sawmill in Cascade. Moreover, Boise Payette was a leader in fighting the pine butterfly and spruce budworm that were killing ponderosa pine throughout southwestern Idaho.

By achieving friendly relations with national and state authorities, gaining the right to purchase a fair share of mature public timber, buying more timberland when possible, and developing a sustained-yield program on its own domain, Boise Payette solidified as a permanent operation. Employment approached 2,500, property valuations increased, and the company paid more local taxes. Small mills were delighted when the company purchased their rough lumber to be finished at the Emmett plant. When John Aram left Idaho for a post with the Weyerhaeuser Timber Company in 1956, he could take pride in having directed Boise Payette on a distinctive, successful path of development.[2]

**MINING.** Mining did not dominate Idaho's economy in the twentieth century as it had in the territorial period, but improved transportation and more efficient technology provided wealth far beyond the gold production of the early years. Although government orders suspended gold mining during World War II, Idaho led the nation in the production of tungsten and antimony, two metals vital to the war effort.

New plants played an important role. The blowing-in of the new Bunker Hill lead smelter in 1916 and the construction of an electrolytic zinc plant in 1928 by Bunker Hill and Hecla companies were followed in 1954 by a sulfuric-acid plant and in 1960 a phosphoric-acid plant. Low metal prices during the depression of the early 1930s forced a decreased output. Mines cut production and prices. In 1932 the average silver price was only 28 cents an ounce, lead was 3.2 cents per pound, and zinc was 3.25 cents per pound. For five years smaller producers were shut down or operated on a greatly curtailed basis. Larger mines, except for increasing silver output at the Sunshine, operated only half-time or less.

World War II brought its own frustrations. Lead and zinc production were desperately needed for the war effort, but experienced underground workers were scarce, and federal controls over prices and wages made it impossible to siphon workers away from the aircraft and shipping industries. Nevertheless, zinc production averaged about 80,000 tons a year, a record high. During the Korean War of the 1950s federal controls were not imposed, and Idaho operators surpassed previous top prices for lead and zinc. The annual gross value of metallic products in the Coeur d'Alene district reached $65 million in 1951.

The Coeur d'Alene district remained one of the great metal producers in American history, ranking with the Sierra Nevada in California in producing gold; the Mesabi in Minnesota, in iron; Keweenaw in Michigan, in copper; Bisbee in Arizona, in copper; Butte in Montana, in copper, silver, and zinc; and Bingham in Utah, in copper, lead, silver, and gold.[3]

The greatest success story in metals was the Sunshine Mining Company. In 1884 Dennis and True Blake discovered a silver-bearing lode on Big Creek, near Kellogg. With primitive tools the Blakes worked the Yankee Boy claim until they were bought out by the Sunshine Mining Company, incorporated in 1919. In 1931 a bonanza of high-grade ore was found, and Sunshine vaulted into the group of high silver producers. In 1937, when the claim yielded more than twelve million ounces of silver, Sunshine became the largest producer of silver in the world.[4]

The other metal mining success story is the Hecla Mining Company. "Hekla," Icelandic for the verb "to crochet," aptly describes the network of tunnels, shafts, and crosscuts honeycombing the Coeur d'Alene district. The Hecla and Katie May claims at Burke, located in 1884, became the foundation of the Hecla Mining Company, incorporated in 1891. In 1898 the company extended the tunnel and discovered the main ore body. By the 1920s, with the Hecla ore body decreasing, the company expanded its property holdings in Idaho and other states and Canadian provinces. Although a disastrous fire destroyed the plant and the town in 1923, a new mill was built. In 1931 Hecla purchased control of the Polaris Mining Company and worked on the Polaris Mine in Osburn, just west of Burke.

Those reserves were exhausted in 1943, but further explorations revealed a high-grade ore body with years of mining potential. Hecla and Polaris merged in 1958. Hecla purchased other properties and by 1959 Hecla and Bunker Hill formed the Star-Morning Unit Area. The Morning Mine, which Hecla obtained by lease from ASARCO and which shares a vein with the Hecla Star Mine, is the largest lead-zinc vein in the world.[5]

Aside from developments in the Coeur d'Alene district, and the production of cobalt and other rare new minerals, the most important development during and after World War II was in phosphate mining and manufacture. We noted in Chapter Twenty-three the founding of the industry by Jack Simplot in 1944, when he built a large phosphate factory near Pocatello. Southeastern Idaho has one of the nation's largest deposits of phosphate rock. Simplot added to its phosphate production in 1960 when he purchased the Conda Mine near Soda Springs from the Anaconda Company. The minerals and chemicals division of J. R. Simplot Company built the Pocatello plant into one of the largest fertilizer processors in the United States. The division ultimately moved into retail fertilizers, industrial minerals, agricultural chemicals, industrial chemicals, and feed phosphates.

Associated with Simplot in mining phosphate was Westvaco Chemical Company, acquired in 1948 by Food Machinery Corporation (later called Food Machinery and Chemical Corporation). In 1961 the name was shortened to FMC Corporation. Under the new direction, FMC jointly operated with Simplot the Gay Mine (named for Simplot's daughter), an open-pit mine about thirty-five miles northeast of Pocatello on the Fort Hall Indian Reservation. The company brought its first electric furnace on-line in its Pocatello plant and produced about 8,000 tons of elemental phosphorous. Another furnace was started in 1950 and two more in 1952. By 1968 some 125,000 tons of elemental phosphorous were being produced annually from about 2 million tons of phosphate shale, coke, and silica. Five days a week, from sunrise to sunset, April to October, ore was hauled from the Gay Mine to Pocatello in two hundred Union Pacific Railroad gondola cars, each gondola holding 100 tons of ore. A mountain of ore was stockpiled that would keep the plant in uninterrupted operation from November through March, when ore could not be moved because of weather conditions. FMC was committed to protecting the environment: when the ore was depleted in one area of the Gay Mine, the pit was back-filled, topsoil was brought in, and the land contoured, restored, and revegetated for the grazing of domestic and wild animals.[6]

Production by FMC's more than 600 employees totaled more than 100 million pounds annually, about 20 percent of the national total. The furnaces required about 90,000 kilowatts of electric power, about 27 percent of the entire output of Idaho Power Company in 1957. At FMC's plants in Kansas and California the material is converted to chemical products used in making alloys, safety matches, medicines, emulsifiers, detergents, soaps, foods, plastics, dyes, and gasoline additives.

Other companies soon joined in the industry. Monsanto Chemical Company erected a two-furnace plant at Soda Springs in 1952; Central Farmers' Fertilizer Company began operations in Georgetown Canyon in 1957; and Anaconda Copper and San Francisco Chemical developed mines at Conda. Other minerals and materials of value mined during the post World War II period include barite, near Hailey; fluorspar from Bayhorse, Wallace, and Meyers Cove; monazite from Cascade; thorium from Salmon; corundum from New Meadows; asbestos from Kamiah; garnet from Fernwood; sulphur from Swan Lake; rock salt from Soda Springs; and pumice from Idaho Falls.[7]

AGRICULTURE. Just as the scarcity of farm labor during the war had forced farmers to mechanize—to use tractors and powered harvesters—the thousands of sons and daughters returning to their farm homes at the end of the war ushered in an expansion of irrigated and dry-farm acreage. Assisting this process were the erection of new dams and the increased use of underground water. Anderson Ranch Dam, near Boise, which had been started before the war but was suspended "for the duration," was finally completed in 1952 at a cost of more than $26 million. A 450-foot structure that was then the highest earth-fill dam in the world, the half-mile-thick dam had long been needed to supply supplemental water to Boise Valley farms and stabilize farming in times of drought. The dam also contained power-generating facilities. Another $20 million flood-control dam, Lucky Peak, situated ten miles above Boise, was erected in 1950–52. This dam provided a large recreational reservoir for boating and water sports.

The Palisades Dam, a few miles west of the Idaho-Wyoming border, was authorized in 1941, suspended during the war, reauthorized in 1950, and completed in 1959 at a cost of $76 million. The additional water provided by the large reservoir permitted new land projects near American Falls and Rupert. The largest earth dam ever constructed by the Bureau of Reclamation, Palisades provides much of the hydroelectric power needed for the pumping and sprinkling projects described below. Additional dams were the Dworshak on the North Fork of the Clearwater near Orofino, initiated in 1959, and the Teton on the Teton River. Two other dams, C. J. Strike and Brownlee, both in southern Idaho, were built without federal funds by the Idaho Power Company. Dworshak Dam, the highest straight-axis concrete gravity dam in the western world, is the largest ever constructed by the U.S. Army Corps of Engineers. An integral unit in the comprehensive development of the water resources of the Columbia-Snake River drainage area, the dam regulates floodwaters of the North Fork of the Clearwater and adds important electrical generation to the Pacific Northwest power complex. The three generators are capable of producing enough power to light a city the size of Boise. The dam, constructed over a period of seven years, is more than 700 feet tall and cost an estimated $327 million. The reservoir extends fifty-three miles behind the dam.

The most revolutionary development was the use of underground waters that probably have their original source in the Snake. The leading role in this development was played by Julion Clawson, who operated out of Rupert during the years immediately following World War II. A great-grandson of Brigham Young, "Duke" Clawson served in the Navy during World War I, operated a building and loan company, and invested in a sheep ranch at Nounan in Bear Lake Valley. In 1946 he purchased a large tract of sagebrush land in Minidoka and Lincoln counties, north of Rupert. Intending to begin a dry-farming operation, he soon discovered nine culinary wells on the property, abandoned thirty years earlier by German immigrants who had come from eastern Washington and the Dakotas to homestead the land. Clawson studied geological reports indicating that there were enormous lakes of water under the vast lava plain of the Snake. "They thought I was after oil when I brought drilling equipment here from Oklahoma," he told friends. "They thought I was crazy. They were even more convinced of it when they learned I was drilling for water."[8] By the summer of 1947 Clawson found abundant water in the three deep twenty-inch wells. He arranged with Idaho Power for electricity from Minidoka Dam to supply the needs of large, specially designed pumps to water more than 3,800 acres of wheat, potatoes, and beans in 1948. His irrigation layout was engineered so as to prevent erosion and undue loss of water through evaporation.

The first year of his deep-well irrigation was successful. The Portneuf silt loam of the area, with the addition of proper fertilizer and water, seemed ideal for the production of potatoes and sugar beets. And seventy days of uninterrupted pumping brought no drop in the water table. Local farmers were quick to catch on, and it was not long before some 30,000 acres of private land in the vicinity were under pump-based irrigation. The Bureau of Reclamation also drilled test wells on adjacent land that had long ago been set aside for irrigation but had never been provided the promised water. The bureau confirmed Clawson's contention that the entire area had an ample supply of underground water. During the 1950s more than 60,000 acres of land in the area, administered by the Bureau of Reclamation, were opened for homesteading.

This effective beginning of pump-based irrigation in the Snake River Valley, which spread as far down the river as Nyssa, Oregon, constitutes one of the most significant postwar changes in Idaho agriculture. Hundreds of thousands of acres of good farmland were opened up in the following years. Although pump-based irrigation existed elsewhere, particularly in the Imperial Valley in California, Clawson's success did much to bolster Idaho's agriculture. He had concentrated on deep wells, but the Snake River itself also became an important source of water as enterprisers pumped its water to plateaus high above the river. Clawson's willingness to think big and his fearlessness in going heavily into debt to take advantage of the best available technology in pumps and sprinkling systems established his leadership in setting a pattern of change that many smaller farmers in the Snake River country soon followed.

A visitor to Magic Valley and Boise Valley, in particular, will now see enormous investment in land leveling; underground irrigation pipe systems; slip-form concrete head ditches; aluminum, canvas, rubber, and plastic pipe systems; sprinklers, valves, and automatic controls; check dams; holding reservoirs; and siphons, gates, gauges, and meters. Working in a land where water is as precious as gold, Idaho farmers have learned to save water and to be efficient in its use and management. With relatively cheap hydroelectric power, farmers have also expanded the value of electricity beyond lights, water pumps, and refrigerators to a myriad of uses: electrically warmed water for livestock, milking machines, feed-processing systems, heating livestock shelters and crop storage buildings, and extension of daylight in poultry buildings.

The supply of seeds from the low countries of Europe was cut off the world market during World War II. This shift increased the demand for seeds grown in the United States, and Idaho growers capitalized on the opportunity to grow and commercially market these crops. Idaho became the nation's largest producer of small seeds: alfalfa, onion, carrot, bean, seed corn, clover, and wheatgrass. Seed companies with an established national market contracted with Idaho farmers, whose land was level, uncontaminated by weeds, and assured of late-summer water, to grow these products. By 1950 Idahoans had planted 150,000 acres of seed beans, the most popular of which was the pinto bean, jointly developed by the University of Idaho Agricultural Experiment Station and the U.S. Department of Agriculture; another 150,000 acres of seed peas; 3,000 acres of onion seed; 85,000 acres of clover and grass seed; and 2,000 acres of carrot seed.

FOOD PROCESSING. Because of Idaho's imposing position in the growing of crops, the state also came to rank high in food processing: potato processing, canning, freezing, meat and dairy product industries, and commercial trout hatcheries. After World War II Jack Simplot organized the Food Processing Division of J. R. Simplot and aggressively went into the market. Simplot's impact was significant. He built a large plant at Heyburn where potatoes were not only dehydrated but prepared and frozen as french fries, mashed potatoes, and potato chips. Dehydrator production reached about 8 million pounds of potatoes and onions annually, and canning and quick-freezing operations were added in 1946–47. Some 1,000 employees produced the equivalent of 600 carloads of food products annually. Potato processing plants were also located at Caldwell and Aberdeen, and a meat-packing plant was built at Nampa. Among the twenty products from the Caldwell plant were "minute" potatoes, frozen french fries, frozen potato patties, frozen diced potatoes, onion flakes, onion powder, canned corn, fruit and vegetables, frozen corn, fresh fish fillets, strawberries, and microwaveable cheeseburgers and pasta-vegetable blends. Frozen-food packing at Caldwell had reached 1 million cases by 1952.

In another move Simplot purchased in 1946 the Shelley Processing Company facilities at Burley, which became one of the nation's largest buyers of potatoes. The company also had a daily production of 24,000 pounds of dried pea powder for soups. The same year Simplot joined C. J. Marshall of Jerome in manufacturing potato glucose. Their plant began to make potato starch in 1947, producing five million pounds annually.

By 1960 the Simplot Western Idaho Produce Company, with headquarters at Caldwell, operated ten warehouses in Idaho and Oregon, shipped 25 percent of all potatoes in western Idaho and eastern Oregon, and employed 1,500 people per season. Simplot also had several thousand acres of irrigated farms in the Snake River Valley, a large sheep enterprise, a cattle-feeding operation, and a box factory.

NATIONAL REACTOR TESTING STATION. Perhaps the most significant new industrial development in Idaho after the war was the establishment of the United States National Reactor Testing Station (NRTS) near Arco in 1949. (The name was changed to Idaho National Engineering Laboratory—INEL—in 1974.) The gunnery range the Navy used in World War II and a location to the southwest of the naval area that the U.S. Army Air Corps utilized as an aerial gunnery range, also in the 1940s, were chosen for the site. The station included all the former military area plus a large adjacent plot withdrawn from the public domain. It was 687 square miles (now 890 square miles) in area—larger than the state of Rhode Island. The former Navy administration shop, warehouse, and housing area became the Central Facilities Area of the NRTS site, its boundaries including a part of the Big Lost River Irrigation Project authorized under the Carey Act of 1894 but never completed.

The NRTS site, administered at the time by the Idaho Operations Office of the Atomic Energy Commission, was chosen in May 1949. Employment during the construction years peaked at more than 3,000 in 1951. Operation began with a few hundred employees and reached 2,000 in 1951; 5,000 by 1960; and about 13,000 in 1990. About one-half of the employees have been native Idahoans. The site was bounded by a Golden Triangle of Arco, Idaho Falls, and Pocatello. Each of these towns, plus Blackfoot, hoped to host the headquarters for the project, and all in the region eventually profited. Idaho Falls, 29 miles east of Arco, was chosen because it combined proximity, state of development, capacity for rapid growth, and general suitability. By 1956 the government had spent approximately $110 million on plants and equipment. Annual cost of operation at the time was around $65 million. There was enormous growth in the neighboring communities. For example, during the years 1949 to 1959 the population of Blackfoot doubled. Of the thousands who worked at the facility, riding the bus back and forth, about 70 percent have lived in Idaho Falls; 15 percent, Blackfoot; and 7 percent each in Pocatello and Jefferson County (Rigby and Roberts).

Several private corporations have been integrated into the NRTS program under a contractual agreement. They include Aerojet General, EG&G, North American Aviation, Phillips Petroleum, and Westinghouse Electric corporations.

In 1951 the NRTS was the site of one of the most significant accomplishments of the century—the first use of nuclear fission to produce electricity. This event took place at Experimental Breeder Reactor No. 1 (EBR-I) on December 20 of that year.

EBR-1 also produced the first usable electrical energy in 1951 when four bulbs, strung unceremoniously from a steam turbine generator to an adjacent hand railing, were lighted. It was a world first—an electrical moment from several points of view. A year and a half later, in June 1953, the Experimental Breeder Reactor demonstrated another milestone: the principle of "breeding"—that a reactor can actually "breed" more fuel than it consumes. This achievement was important because the uranium used for reactor fuel was in short supply. The large bodies of uranium ore found in the 1950s had not yet been discovered. Don Ofte, manager of the Idaho operations of the AEC, emphasized the importance of the EBR-1 this way: "If you say that the atomic age was born under the football stands in the University of Chicago when Enrico Fermi and the other pioneers built that first reactor and sustained that first chain reaction, then the nuclear industry had its adolescence in Idaho, because this is where it came into its maturity."[9]

Other firsts of EBR-1 included the first use of plutonium as a test reactor fuel and proving that the consequence of a core meltdown was not necessarily catastrophic. EBR-l remained in operation for ten years—until September 30, 1961, when Experimental Breeder Reactor II started up.

The second reactor at NRTS, the Materials Testing Reactor (MTR), became operational March 31, 1952. Materials proposed for use in new reactors still under design were tested to determine which would function best in the presence of intense radiation. The MTR produced the world's most intense neutron flux, enabling the reactor to run tests in a relatively short time, and made possible the production of radioisotopes of higher specific activity than in other reactors. Much radiocobalt used in cancer therapy and food irradiation was likewise produced in the MTR. Every reactor designed in the United States has been influenced by knowledge gained from the MTR, which was retired in 1970.

Boiling Water Reactors Experiments (BORAX-I), constructed in 1953, was the first in a series of five NRTS reactors designed to pioneer intensive work on boiling-water reactors, where steam generation was allowed to take place in the reactor pressure vessel at the core itself. BORAX-I was tested in July 1954 to determine its inherent safety under extreme conditions. Experiments at the BORAX-II reactor in the winter of 1954–55 demonstrated the feasibility of the boiling-water reactor concept. The power level of this reactor was six megawatts. BORAX-III started operating in June 1954 with a 2,000-kilowatt turbine generator. On July 17, 1955, it produced sufficient power to light the city of Arco for a period of two hours—a world first.

Special Power Excursion Reactor Test (SPERT) was conducted at the site in 1955, and other SPERT reactors operated in succeeding years; research concentrated on the major safety concern at the time, "runaway power." The SPERT program demonstrated that "runaway" accidents are less likely to happen than once thought, that the course of such an incident can be predicted, and that reactors have a strong tendency to shut themselves down if excessive fission occurs.

In August 1955 the Atomic Energy Commission decided to undertake the construction and operation of an Engineering Test Reactor (ETR) to provide irradiation facilities for the development of reactor components for military and civilian power reactors. When the ETR achieved nuclear start-up in 1957, it was the largest and most advanced materials test reactor in the world with a power level of 175 megawatts. It continued to operate until 1982. The work done in the MTR and BORAX experiments in 1953 and 1954, the SPERT experimental work in the later 1950s, and the expanded activities of the ETR contributed to basic knowledge of reactor materials and reactor behavior under abnormal conditions. Resulting improvements in the design of reactors helped ensure the safe and reliable operation of nuclear power plants across the United States and in the free world.

Other work in the 1950s included development of several reactor prototypes for the U.S. Air Force, Army, and Navy. The nuclear Navy at the NRTS was inaugurated on March 31, 1953, with the initial power run of the Submarine Thermal Reactor, a land-based prototype of the nuclear engine for American's first atomic-powered submarine, the U.S.S. *Nautilus*. The nuclear-powered submarine could run thousands of miles without having to put in at port for fuel, and because nuclear fuel is only a small bundle, a little larger than the size of a softball and weighing twenty pounds, the ship could carry more cargo. Unlike regular engines, a nuclear engine does not need oxygen, so an atomic submarine could operate under water much longer and much faster than regular submarines. In 1954 a sixty-six-day test run from small uranium rods that would fit into a two-pound coffee can generated as much power as 1.6 million gallons of diesel oil would have provided.

Powered by STR Mark II, the U.S.S. *Nautilus* traveled in excess of 25,000 miles, most of the time submerged. The submarine also cruised under water from New London, Connecticut, to San Juan, Puerto Rico, a distance of more than 1,300 miles taking 84 hours at an average speed of about 16 knots. At all times, the reactor performed satisfactorily. This first atomic or nuclear submarine ran for more than 96,000 miles on its second small load of fuel. The Naval Reactors Facility is one of the oldest sections on the NRTS; thousands of naval officers and enlisted personnel have received training in Idaho's desert in this sophisticated system. Other ships besides submarines now use atomic power: the U.S.S. *Enterprise* is a huge aircraft carrier free to roam much farther than older carriers because it runs on atomic power.

The nuclear airplane, however, was a failure. Work began on the first prototype power plant for a nuclear airplane in 1951. The commission of the Aircraft Nuclear Propulsion (ANP) project was to develop a nuclear-reactor aircraft engine capable of powering an airplane for extremely long periods—one that could stay in the air for a week. The program involved building and testing three heat-transfer reactor experiments that proved the feasibility of operating an aircraft turbojet engine with nuclear heat. But after ten years and $1 billion spent on development, the ANP project was canceled, mostly because of the parallel development of the intercontinental ballistic missile. Looking at the two giant stainless steel reactor vessels still parked in the desert, encumbered by a labyrinth of pipes, instruments, and support beams weighing 150 and 170 tons—necessary to shield anyone flying in it—one cannot visualize them hanging on an aircraft that could actually take off.

Work in the Army Reactor Experimental Area on the site in 1957 was aimed at developing a family of small reactors that could meet a number of military requirements, including being compact, lightweight, and mobile. Both the ANP project and the Army's mobile reactor experiments provided technology that is still in use, specifically in the planning and design of the Modular High Temperature Gas Cooled Reactor (New Production Reactor) project.

Finally, two other plants established by the NRTS in the early 1950s tidied up operations at the station. The first was the Radioactive Waste Management Complex (RWMC) established in 1952 in the southwest corner of the site as a thirteen-acre disposal area for radioactive waste generated at NRTS. Advanced and innovative radioactive-waste management programs were designed. During the early years the waste was buried, but in recent years contaminated wastes have been stored above ground in fifty-five-gallon steel drums, fiberglass-covered wooden boxes, and steel bins. A recent objective is to send all such waste to a Waste Isolation Pilot Plant near Carlsbad, New Mexico. There continue to be controversies over waste seeping into the Snake River Aquifer and the importation of waste into Idaho.

The second new plant was the Idaho Chemical Processing

Plant, established in 1953 to recover the usable uranium in spent nuclear fuel from government reactors. This unique recycling enterprise proved successful and continues.

Other industries and enterprises greatly expanded after World War II. Morrison-Knudsen at the end of the war was engaged in construction enterprises in sixty different countries. Total revenue from such contracts was $100 million in 1948 and by 1970 exceeded $1 billion. The surplus naval gun-relining facility in Pocatello was converted to a Bucyrus-Erie plant that turned out huge dragline excavators, cranes, and similar construction devices. Mobile homes and recreational vehicles were among the products added to Idaho's manufacturing potential. A mobile-home plant was established in Boise in 1954, and soon there were similar facilities in Nampa, Caldwell, and Weiser with a production of more than $25 million per year. Recreational vehicles, mostly camping units, added to the housing-fabrication industry. Sugar factories were enlarged, meat-processing plants were expanded, and egg and poultry production became a specialty in Franklin and Meridian. In 1948 Mountain Home Air Force Base reopened as a training facility and air transport base where Strategic Air Command bombers were stationed after 1953.

In the 1950 U.S. Census, Idaho's labor force was approximately 206,000, of whom about 55,000 were in agriculture, 868 in forest (excluding lumber manufacturing, in which there were 8,500) and fisheries, 5,000 in mining, 15,500 in construction (a sign of growth), 19,000 in manufacturing, and the remainder —far more than those mentioned—in transportation, communications, trade, services, and public services. Concurrently, Idaho ranked lowest among the Mountain States in per capita income, a reflection of large families and the vast proportion of workers in low-paying jobs. Wartime experience, however, demonstrated the loyal work ethic of most Idahoans, and the state became a target for a number of new businesses. Idaho was anxious to build its manufacturing sector and invested heavily in the necessary development of infrastructure—highways, schools, airports, trucking lines, hospitals, power, telephones, and television.

Despite the thousands who left the state during the war to work on the Coast, the state's population continued to expand. From 1940 to 1960 Idaho's population rose by 142,318, a gain of 27 percent compared with a national increase of 30 percent. Urban growth was more than sufficient to make up for the rural loss. Even with the trend away from the farm, Idaho's growers produced more than they did before. In 1960, though Idaho was still a rural state, about half its people lived in urban communities.

## CHAPTER TWENTY-SIX: SOURCES

General histories of the West and Pacific Northwest that cover the postwar period include: Johansen and Gates, *Empire of the Columbia*, 513–87; Pomeroy, *The Pacific Slope*, 293–332; Peirce, *The Mountain States of America*, 120–53; Schwantes, *The Pacific Northwest*, 341–67, 384; William G. Robbins, et al., *Regionalism and the Pacific Northwest*; Nash and Etulain, eds., *The Twentieth-Century West*; Morris E. Garnsey, *America's New Frontier: The Mountain West* (New York: Alfred A. Knopf, 1950); Malone and Etulain, *The American West*, 120–69; Nash, *The American West in the Twentieth Century*; Nash, *The American West Transformed*, 201–16.

Idaho histories that treat the postwar period include: Beal and Wells, *History of Idaho*, 2:275–314; Barber and Martin, *Idaho in the Pacific Northwest*, 264–325; Peterson, *Idaho: A Bicentennial History*, 182–92; Wells and Hart, *Idaho: Gem of the Mountains*; Wells, *Boise: An Illustrated History*; Jensen, *Discovering Idaho: A History*, 234–50.

Articles and books that deal with specific topics include: William E. Davis, "Portrait of an Industrialist [Jack Simplot]," *Idaho Yesterdays* 11 (Summer 1967):2–7; W. Darrell Gertsch, "Water Use, Energy, and Economic Development in the Snake River Basin," *Idaho*

*Yesterdays* 23 (Summer 1979):58–72; Thomas R. Cox, "Weldon Heyburn, Lake Chatcolet, and the Evolving Concept of Public Parks," *Idaho Yesterdays* 24 (Summer 1980):2–15; David H. Stratton, "Hells Canyon: The Missing Link in Pacific Northwest Regionalism," *Idaho Yesterdays* 28 (Fall 1984):3–9; Broadhead, "The History of Idaho Since World War II: 1945–1950"; Richard L. Neuberger, "Idaho's Fantastic Millionaire," *Saturday Evening Post* (June 19, 1948), 20–21+; Herbert Solow, "The Big Builder from Boise," *Fortune* (December 1956), 144–46, 196–204; David O. Woodbury, *Builders for Battle* [Morrison-Knudsen and the Pacific Bases] (New York: E. P. Dutton Co., 1946); Stapilus, *Paradox Politics: People and Power in Idaho*; *Idaho Yesterdays* 30 (Spring-Summer 1986), special issue on irrigation in Idaho—articles by ten persons on the impact of water and its use on Idaho life; Ralph Hidy, "Lumbermen in Idaho: A Study in Adaptation to Change and Environment," *Idaho Yesterdays* 6 (Winter 1962):2–17; Hidy et al., *Timber and Men*, 512–50; *INEL News*, May 1989; "INEL'S 40th Anniversary Celebration," *Idaho State Journal* (Pocatello), May 15, 1989; *Idaho National Engineering Laboratory* (Idaho Falls: INEL, 1989); "Submarines in the Desert?" in *The Prospector*, Idaho State Historical Society, no date.

139.

140.

139. This Ore-Ida potato-processing plant near Burley was one of several built in Idaho after World War II. ISHS 80–87.41.

140. The Experimental Breeder Reactor No. 1 was the first to use nuclear fission to produce electricity. IDAHO NATIONAL ENGINEERING LABORATORY.

141. 

141. The first nuclear-powered submarine, the U.S.S. *Nautilus*, whose engine was perfected at the National Reactor Testing Station near Arco, ran thousands of miles without having to put in to port for fuel. IDAHO NATIONAL ENGINEERING LABORATORY.

CHAPTER TWENTY-SEVEN

# The Public Lands Paradox: Idaho's Wilderness

IN the 1960s Idahoans developed a strong concern for their rivers, wildlife, trees, and mountains. Not that there was always agreement or consistency in what they wanted done; many questions about the environment are inevitably complex, often controversial. Exquisite, even dramatic, scenery was plentiful, but access roads and overlooks were limited. Should roads be built into a pristine wilderness? Should facilities be built so that people could enjoy the gorgeous panoramas? Campgrounds? Picnic tables? Outdoor toilets? Shelters in case of rain or snow? Cabins? Mineral deposits are known to exist in appealing mountain settings. Should miners be allowed to work them? A forest is the only habitat of a rare bird. Should lumbermen be allowed to cut down the trees? A secluded glen is a traditional grazing area for elk. Should cattle be allowed to graze there? A spectacular rushing river carries water down to the Snake and on to the ocean. Should farmers be allowed to dam the water and use it for irrigating their crops? There is an inadequate supply of electrical energy to power pumps. Should a power company be allowed to construct a plant and dam a creek to produce needed inexpensive hydroelectric energy?

The problems are so complex that complete agreement is unlikely. Preserving the serenity of the primitive is in conflict with mineral development, forest extraction, range appropriation, farming operations, and power production. It is also in conflict with the construction of accommodations for tourists, and tourism is a leading industry in Idaho. There is surprising agreement among Idaho's visitors that the state has the finest and most extensive wildernesses in the nation with the exception of Alaska, of course. Should they be preserved, or made more available, or exploited for the wealth they contain? Like other Americans facing similar questions, Idahoans are of different minds on the answer.

As early as 1872 Congress had established Yellowstone National Park, reserving more than 2.2 million acres from the public domain to ensure unique protection from commercial exploitation. A small strip on the western side of the park (31,500 acres) reaches into Idaho. In 1891 Congress passed the General Public Lands Reform Law, which authorized the president to create forest reserves from the public domain; their administration was initially placed with the General Land Office (predecessor to the Bureau of Land Management). In 1905 the Forest Service was established to administer and manage the forest reserves, which were renamed national forests in 1907. Idaho came to have more than 21 million acres of national-forest land. Boundaries of national forests have been rearranged and names changed over the years. At present, Idaho's twelve national forests are the Bitterroot, Boise, Caribou, Challis, Clearwater, Kootenai, Nez Perce, Panhandle, Payette, Salmon, Sawtooth, and Targhee. Under the direction of the Forest Service, the goal is multiple use of Idaho's forest resources, with sustained yields of wood, water, forage, wildlife, and recreation.

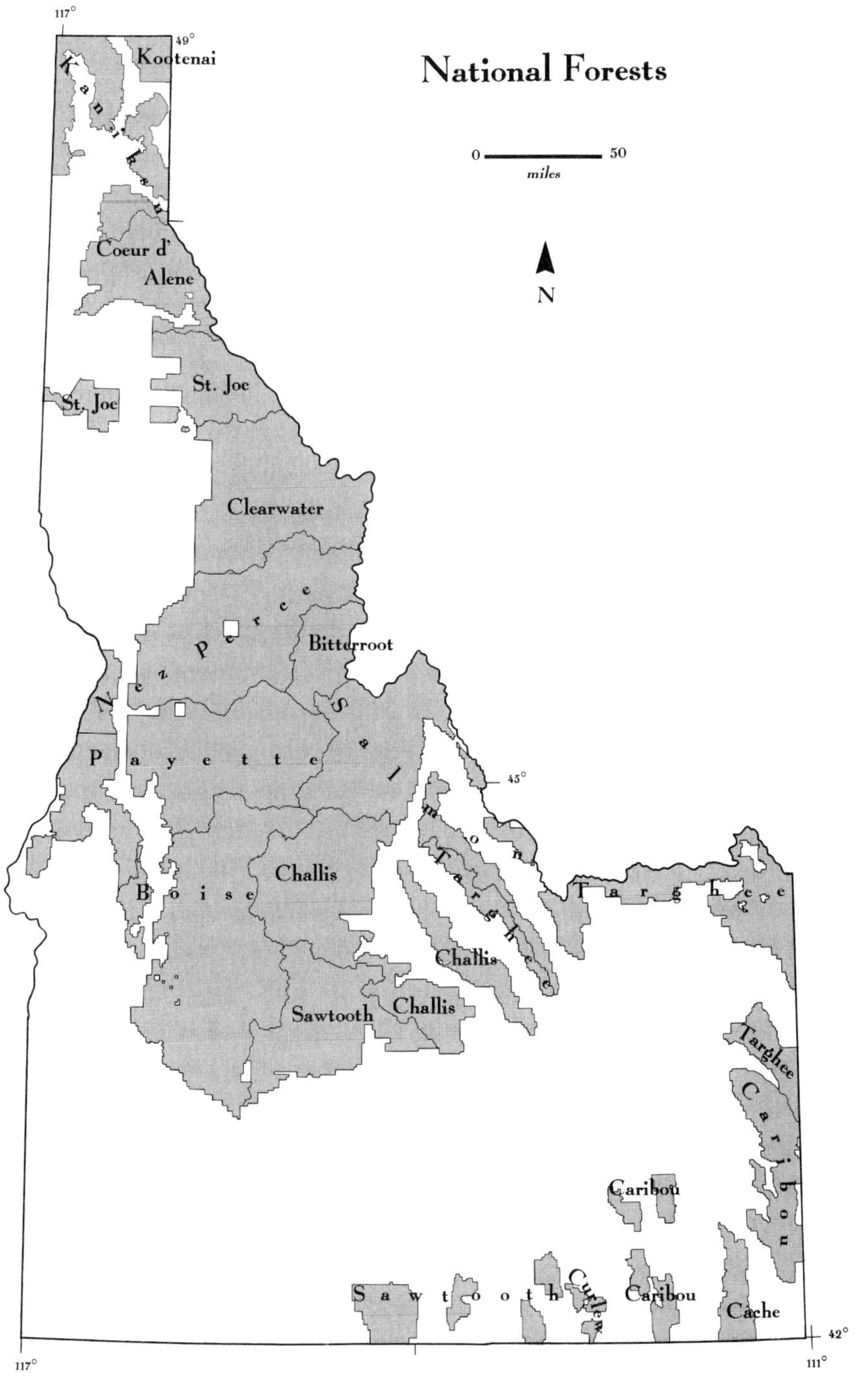
National Forests
0
50
miles
N
117°
49°
45°
42°
111°
Kootenai
Kaniksu
Coeur d'
Alene
St. Joe
St. Joe
Clearwater
Nez Perce
Bitterroot
Salmon
Payette
Boise
Challis
Targhee
Targhee
Challis
Sawtooth
Challis
Targhee
Caribou
Caribou
Sawtooth
Curlew
Caribou
Cache

Much of Idaho's national-forest land was added to the system by President Theodore Roosevelt, as interested in preserving the West as in developing it. As one of his biographers writes:

> For him, the preservation of the wilderness and the maintenance of the sport of wildlife hunting engendered qualities of manliness and self-reliance. It was always his hope to bring the individualism that he had found in the West back East, for it was in the West and in the history of western settlement that he felt were preserved the most truly American values and strengths of character.[1]

Roosevelt also supported the passage of the Antiquities Act of 1906 to preserve and protect prehistoric, historic, and scientifically significant sites on public lands and to create national monuments. Craters of the Moon National Monument, set aside by President Calvin Coolidge in 1924, is not a granite column placed prominently to commemorate an event but rather a desolate, eighty-three-square-mile area northwest of Arco that contains several dozen separate lava flows—some of them as recent as 1,600 years ago—as well as interesting patterns of lava resulting from relatively recent violent volcanic action.

A second historic site was recognized in 1965 as sentiment for environmental preservation was mounting. In an innovative partnership of federal and state agencies and private parties, the Nez Perce National Historical Park protects twenty-four notable areas in north central Idaho that retrace the history of the Nez Perce Indians, the Lewis and Clark Expedition, and other events in early Idaho history.

In 1962, with the help of Idaho's liberal Democratic senator Frank Church, Congress passed the National Recreation Area Act to help preserve and expand outdoor recreation opportunities throughout the nation. Idaho soon had two. The first was the Sawtooth National Recreation Area, established in 1972 to preserve rural, recreational, and scenic values in response to a proposed open-pit molybdenum mine at the base of Castle Peak in the White Cloud Mountains. The second, established in 1976, straddles a sixty-seven-mile stretch of Snake River on the west central Idaho border and is called Hells Canyon National Recreation Area.

Senator Church's leadership in wilderness legislation was surprising to some. In 1957 he had advocated the building of a 700-foot dam in Hells Canyon to generate power for mining the phosphate fields of southeastern Idaho. "I believe we have a trust," he said, "not only to ourselves but to our children, to develop the full potential of our God-given resources."[2] Five years later he had shifted from favoring development to being an outspoken environmentalist. This switch was certain to cause problems for him in his reelection campaign in 1962. Shortly before the election, former governor Chase Clark, his father-in-law, earnestly inquired:

> Tell me, Frank, how do you expect to win? All the organizations that count are against you: the cattlemen, the woolgrowers, the mining association, the forest products industry, the newspapers [all but one newspaper supported his opponent, Jack Hawley], the chambers of commerce . . . and for what? For wilderness! You don't just have rocks on your mind; you've got rocks in your head![3]

But Church was re-elected, by 25,000 votes.

In 1964 Church coauthored, sponsored, and was floor leader for the National Wilderness Act, which set aside undeveloped federal land so that some selected spots of the earth and its community of life would be unaffected by humanity—areas where persons might visit but could not remain. Such regions might contain ecological, geological, biological, scenic, or historical features and values. As part of the bill, more than 1 million Idaho (and some Montana) acres were designated as the Selway-Bitterroot Wilderness Area. This area included the first section seen by white men during the Lewis and Clark Expedition. In 1972, 217,000 acres of the Sawtooth National Forest were designated as the Sawtooth Wilderness Area. The district includes over 200 alpine lakes and many rugged peaks. Hells Canyon, overlooking the deepest gorge in North America and including the legendary Seven Devils Mountains, was designated a wilderness area in 1976; about four-fifths of it is in Oregon. Two years later the Gospel Hump Wilderness Area in the Nez Perce National Forest was created. The area is bordered on the south by the Salmon River. The name comes from Gospel Peak, where W. N. Knox preached an impromptu sermon to surveyors, prospectors, miners, and freighters in 1899, and for the local description—the peak looks like a buffalo hump.

In 1980 the famous River of No Return area, consisting of about 2.4 million acres, was designated a wilderness, the largest in the lower forty-eight states. This area, known for its jagged canyons and towering mountains, contains the Middle Fork of the Salmon. Senator Church later told how his wife, Bethine, had maintained her composure during the angry exchanges that took place in the hearings on this bill:

> During the public hearing in Salmon a cowboy flaunted his contempt by riding his horse through the front entrance of the hall, down the center aisle, out the side door. The wide-eyed editor of the local paper turned to Bethine and blurted out, "Well, what did you think of that?" "Why," she replied, "I thought that was a right handsome horse."[4]

In 1984, shortly before his untimely death from cancer, the wilderness area's name was changed to honor the senator's role in the designation of the area, making its official title Frank Church/River of No Return Wilderness.

The next step in preserving significant natural and historic sites, also suppored by Church, was the passage in 1966 of the National Historic Preservation Act—designed to protect prehistoric and historic properties of regional and local importance. Many Idaho properties, including homes, businesses, and historic structures, have now been nominated by the Idaho State Historical Society and certified by the Park Service as National Register sites.

In 1968, again with Senator Church's sponsorship, Congress passed the Wild and Scenic Rivers Act for the preservation of America's most spectacular free-flowing rivers. Nine rivers in Idaho have been thus designated because of their remarkable scenic, recreational, geologic, fish and wildlife, historic, cultural, or other significance in their natural free-flowing condition. The rivers are the Middle Fork of the Salmon, Main Salmon, Lochsa, Selway, Middle Fork of the Clearwater, St. Joe, Snake (sixty-seven miles from Hells Canyon Dam downstream to the northern border of the Wallowa-Whitman National Forest), Rapid, and West Fork of the Rapid. Senator George McGovern of South Dakota gave Church much of the credit for the bill's passage. Church was "an extraordinarily able floor manager. He did it by shaming people into standing for the future of this country—despite all the special interest claims."[5]

In 1971 Congress established the Snake River Birds of Prey Area to protect valuable raptor nesting areas in Idaho, and the 1973 Endangered Species Act more generally offered protection of plants and animals facing extinction, as well as their habitats.

The National Environmental Policy Act made protection of the environment a national priority by requiring all federal agencies to assess the impacts of their actions on the surroundings and to mitigate adverse effects. Following this legislation, in 1976 Congress passed the Federal Land Policy and Management Act, which directed federal agencies to retain public lands under federal sponsorship and to provide for the multiple use and sustained-yield management of public lands and resources through land-use planning.

Equally interested in conservation, ecology, and tourism from the state's standpoint, Governor Robert E. Smylie proposed in 1955 that Idaho move quickly to reserve the few remaining areas that would be splendid parks. A state park system was finally established in 1965, and since that time twenty-one state parks have been established; they are administered by the Idaho Department of Parks and Recreation, headquartered in Boise.

Idaho's first state park had been established fifty years before. In 1908 Senator Weldon Heyburn became interested in preserving the beautiful setting around Chatcolet Lake in north Idaho, and lobbied for its designation as a national park. When that effort failed, the land was conveyed to the state and became Heyburn State Park, the first state park in the Pacific Northwest. The 7,800-acre park remains one of Idaho's finest. In addition to Heyburn, there are five state parks in northernmost north Idaho: Priest Lake, Round Lake, Farragut, Old Mission, and Mowry. Farther south, but still in north Idaho, are Mary Minerva McCroskey, Dworshak, Hells Gate, and Winchester Lake. In central Idaho are Packer John, Ponderosa, and Centennial parks. State parks in southwestern Idaho include Eagle Island, Veterans Memorial, Lucky Peak, Bruneau Dunes, Three Island Crossing, and Malad Gorge. South-central Idaho has two: Silent City of Rocks (usually, simply City of Rocks) and Massacre Rocks. In the southeast lies Bear Lake State Park and in eastern Idaho Henry's Lake and Harriman. Harriman, eighteen miles north of Ashton and one of the largest of the state parks (4,300 acres), is named for W. Averell Harriman, formerly president of Union Pacific Railroad, governor of New York, ambassador to the Soviet Union, and founder of Sun Valley, who, with his brother E. Roland, presented the park—the family's famous "Railroad Ranch"—to Idaho in 1977. Geologists believe that the ranch, near the Montana line, occupies an extinct volcano. Along with the park the state also administers the 11,000-acre Harriman Wildlife Refuge, where hundreds of trumpeter swans winter and which is also a home for pelicans,

Canada geese, mountain bluebirds, moose, bald eagle, osprey, beaver, muskrats, otter, and sandhill cranes. The park offers gorgeous scenery, fantastic fly-fishing, and peaceful isolated tranquility.

Finally, there are seven National Natural Landmarks in Idaho, the earliest established in 1968 and the latest in 1980. The Great Rift Natural Landmark, consisting of 102,000 acres in the Bureau of Land Management wilderness in Blaine, Butte, Minidoka, and Power counties, marks the longest rift system in the United States and the deepest in the world. Big Southern Butte, in Butte County, rises 2,500 feet above the Snake River Plain and was an easily recognized geographic landmark for early travelers on Goodale's Cutoff from the Oregon Trail. Hell's Half Acre, in Bingham County, contains lava flows determined to be only 4,100 years old. City of Rocks in Cassia County, known to emigrants on the California Trail, features striking rock formations from a granite mountain. Hagerman Fossil Beds, in Twin Falls County, is one of the major fossil deposits in North America and is a National Monument. More than a dozen ancient horse fossils were uncovered here by the Smithsonian Institution in the 1930s. Menan Buttes, 1,200 acres in Madison and Jefferson counties, served as a navigation and rendezvous point for early explorers and travelers and is composed of rare volcanic tuff. Crater Rings, in Elmore County, features craters formed 1.4 million years ago when lava cones collapsed after loss of gas pressure, forming 200-foot depressions.

Policies ardently recommended, positions firmly held, and attitudes strongly expressed, with inevitable compromise, played a role in funding and establishing these forests, parks, monuments, and preserves, and in the administrative policies that govern them. As elsewhere, Idaho has seen vicious disputes between production-oriented enterprisers and nature-conscious environmentalists. The results have pointed, once again, to the inconsistency of Idaho's voters. Senator Church's sponsorship and support of the Wilderness Act, for example, gained him the animosity of many interests; many voters were upset with him. Church told Neal Peirce that in his 1962 election campaign, in spite of strident organized opposition against him, he learned that "Idaho people care a great deal about the outdoors. . . . Long dominant interests in Idaho politics can no longer . . . preserve their rights to the public domain as against the public interest."[6] The people, Church said, seemed to agree with Justice William O. Douglas's decision in the Hells Canyon case that "a river is more than an amenity; it is a treasure."[7]

Some of these emotional arguments surfaced in the late 1960s when the American Smelting and Refining Company (ASARCO) proposed a 740-acre open-pit mine to extract molybdenum from the magnificent White Cloud Range. Among other things, they required a huge tailing pond. Governor Smylie, who had served three four-year terms, had been defeated in the 1966 primary by fellow Republican Don Samuelson and was not now in a position to defend the conservationists. Born in Illinois, graduate of Knox College in Galesburg, Illinois, Samuelson served two years in the Navy at Camp Farragut and later established a business at Sandpoint, from which he was elected state senator for three terms. A fiscal and social conservative, Samuelson sided with ASARCO. The request became a volatile issue in the 1970 election. The Democratic candidate for governor, Cecil D. Andrus, who had lost to Samuelson in 1966, took advantage of the general negative reaction to the ASARCO proposal and defeated Samuelson. After his election, Andrus worked with Frank Church and others to create the Sawtooth National Recreation Area, which effectively defeated the ASARCO proposal.

The problem of environmental impact is indeed complicated. Forest operations provide hundreds of jobs, but they may destroy the habitat of birds or animals in danger of extinction. Mining companies employ thousands, but the discharge from the smelters severely impacts the surrounding communities.

The level of lead in the Coeur d'Alene River delta in the 1980s was perhaps the highest recorded in the United States. The smelter-polluted air above the plants had the highest levels of sulphur dioxide gas in the nation, and smelter effluents denuded the surrounding hillsides. The Environmental Protection Agency placed the Silver Valley on a list of hazardous sites to be cleaned up by the Superfund program.[8]

Not all the problems are related to pollution in the air and water. As long as farming is a major focus in Idaho, soil erosion will be a dominant concern. The fertile Palouse country, thanks to research in plant breeding and cultivation techniques conducted by the University of Idaho and Washington State University agricultural experiment stations, produces more wheat than its counterparts in any equivalent area in the nation. Annual yields of seventy and eighty bushels of winter white wheat per acre are common, and the region is also a leader in the production of dry peas, lentils, and barley. Yet the Palouse and Nez Perce prairies of Washington, Idaho, and Oregon are among the ten most erodible regions in the United States, with average annual erosion and sedimentation rates on cultivated cropland of 11.5 tons per acre; in the heart of the Palouse, average annual rates are 20 tons per acre. The equivalent of 360 tons of soil has been lost from every cropland acre since 1939; all of the original topsoil has been lost from 10 percent of the land. Three million tons of sediment are carried out of the basin in runoff water each year. Partly because of this erosion and sedimentation, the U.S. Army Corps of Engineers has had to abandon plans for 89 percent of its water-based recreation sites along the Snake River. "Palouse farmers," wrote Frederick Steiner, "have not killed the golden goose but are plucking it to death."[9]

Soil erosion affects agricultural productivity, contaminates waterways, and worsens air pollution. No dramatic solution seems possible, but the U.S. Soil Conservation Service has instituted a program that will reduce erosion to "tolerable" levels by the year 2010 and will permit a high level of crop productivity to be sustained economically and indefinitely.

Wherever there is work or activity, it would seem, there is pollution and environmental destruction. Federal agencies are studying the problems and recommending measures to curtail the trends. Idaho's largest corporations are also aware of the concerns and are taking measures to reduce their impact.

The single worst environmental disaster in Idaho's history—in human terms, even worse than the 1910 forest fire—was the Teton Flood of 1976. Until then scarcely anyone had questioned the design and engineering reputation of the Bureau of Reclamation; none of its major public works had ever failed. The Bureau was very proud of its contribution to western production potential. But on June 5, 1976, the Teton Dam on the Teton River in eastern Idaho collapsed.

There seemed to be a sound justification for building the dam. Within the Teton Basin Project area 114,000 acres were under irrigation, but the farmland was subject to water shortages in late summer months and spring runoffs caused frequent flooding. For example, in 1961 southeastern Idaho experienced a serious drought that was followed in February 1962 by the largest flood on record. Following congressional hearings in 1962 (all of Idaho's congressional representatives favored the project), construction of the dam was authorized in 1964. Environmental impacts were criticized by various groups, including the Environmental Protection Agency, the Bureau of Sports Fisheries, the Idaho Fish and Game Department, and—after its establishment in 1974—the Idaho Conservation League. The project's economic feasibility was also questioned by eastern economists, who have commonly contended that every western dam is a boondoggle. But construction commenced in 1972, with up to 500 men working three shifts around the clock (though winter crews were reduced to about seventy-five men). The 10-million-cubic-yard, 305-foot-high earth dam, 1,600 feet wide at the base, was essentially completed by the end of 1975, when the reservoir began filling.

The seventeen-mile-long lake was nearly full when the earthen embankment gave way on June 5. Eighty billion gallons of water burst through the collapsing barrier and raged across the Idaho countryside with incredible fury. Traveling at about fifteen miles an hour, the water hit Wilford first; six persons were drowned and 150 homes were destroyed. It then passed through Sugar City, Rexburg, Salem, Roberts, Hibbard, Shelley, Firth, and Blackfoot, and finally, three days after the break, entered the backwaters of the American Falls Reservoir. The torrent stripped crops and topsoil from fields, destroyed roads, uprooted trees, and swept away houses and farm buildings. Altogether, eleven people died directly or from related causes, 25,000 persons were driven from their homes, 18,000 head of livestock were lost, and thirty-two miles of railroad were washed out. Property damages totaled some $600 million.

The flood triggered a massive relief effort by religious, private, and governmental organizations. The Mormon Church, to which 90 percent of the affected people belonged, shipped in tens of thousands of pounds of food and an estimated 50,000 volunteers in June, July, and August to assist in the rebuilding. Ricks College, located on higher ground than the city of Rexburg, opened its doors and facilities to those in need and became a haven with food and shelter for the thousands of homeless. Volunteers working around the clock with the college food services personnel provided 2,000 meals on the evening of June 5 and some 9,850 the next day, and continued as needed until August 18. A total of 390,000 had been served, all without charge. A special example of brotherly love was shown by small groups of Mennonites who came from California, Canada, Minnesota, and Oklahoma to stay for a week and help in the food service and rebuilding efforts. As many as 1,000 Latter-day Saints from southern Idaho, northern Utah, western Wyoming, and southern Montana came in chartered buses on weekdays and 4,000 on Saturdays, and worked all day in assigned areas before returning home at night. In three months this volunteer relief service amounted to more than one million hours of donated labor valued at $10 million.

Business organizations, too, went the second mile to help in the communities' recovery. Bakeries, bottlers, dairies, grocery concerns, restaurants, and local retailers still able to operate donated needed food. Other firms and individuals supplied trucks, tractors, and front-end loaders as well as materials where they could. The Idaho Power Company sent a caravan of crews and equipment from other locations to help the Rexburg Division restore electrical service in a minimum of time to all the disaster area.

In the wake of the tragedy, two panels of experts were established to determine the causes of the failure. Their respective reports were issued in December 1976 and April 1977. The dam's failure was a complex phenomenon but, in the final analysis, it was concluded that Reclamation designers were at fault. Extraordinary geological conditions, especially highly permeable, cracked volcanic rocks at the damsite, were not effectively countered in the dam's design and construction process. Major recommendations to minimize the recurrence of failures included establishing an independent review board for dam design and construction, greater documentation of design decisions, closer project supervision and oversight by design personnel, and more intensive construction and post-construction monitoring of structures. The dam has not been rebuilt. Appropriately, Idaho native R. Keith Higginson became commissioner of reclamation in mid-1977; he had served as director of Idaho's Department of Water Resources from 1965 to 1977 (and returned to that position again in 1991). Higginson took initiatives to strengthen the agency's organizational structure and commitment to dam safety, environmental protection, economic efficiency, fair distribution of project benefits, and water conservation.[10]

Idahoans are quite aware of the severe restrictions that environmental controls have placed on parts of society. The family farmer is restricted in his use of cheap pesticides and fertilizers. Working families have lost their jobs because of restraints on small businesses. EPA rulings are sometimes regarded as unnecessary federal interventions in private business. Grace Jordan, whose husband (Senator Len) voted against the Wild Rivers Act when it was first proposed in 1966, commented: "The Wild River enthusiast was rarely the little taxpayer who couldn't afford expensive gear for outdoor sports; and the river selected for Wild status was rarely in the proponent's own state. No one was demanding that the reeking Potomac be returned to its pristine wild condition."[11] Outside interventions by activist groups (Sierra Clubs, Earth Lovers) have delayed or prohibited the growth of some operations generally regarded as beneficial.

In certain quarters pro-development studies are objects of derision and scorn. Observers think they see a hesitancy, a hanging back, an unsureness among Idaho enterprisers. It would be regrettable if the reformist and sometimes angry tone of the environmentalists were to halt the risk-taking, the technological innovation, and the "full speed ahead" approach that has built much of the new industry in Idaho.

## CHAPTER TWENTY-SEVEN: SOURCES

Particularly good among the Northwest histories is "An Environment at Risk," in Schwantes, *The Pacific Northwest*, 368–81. Recent histories of the West with discussions of the environment include John Opie, "Environmental History of the West," in Nash and Etulain, *The Twentieth-Century West*, 209–32; William L. Lang, "Using and Abusing Abundance: The Western Resource Economy and the Environment," in Michael P. Malone, ed., *Historians and the*

*American West* (Lincoln: University of Nebraska Press, 1983), 170–99; Malone and Etulain, *The American West*, 219–94; Nash, *The American West Transformed*, 201–16; Donald Worster, *Rivers of Empire: Water, Aridity, and the Growth of the American West* (New York: Pantheon Books, 1985); Nash, *The American West in the Twentieth Century*, 288–95; Neil Morgan, *Westward Tilt: The American West Today* (New York: Random House, 1963), 259–65; Peter Wiley and Robert Gottlieb, *Empires in the Sun: The Rise of the New American West* (New York: G. P. Putnam's Sons, 1982), 54–74; and Marshall Sprague and the Editors of Time-Life Books, *The Mountain States* (New York: Time-Life Books, 1967), 159–64. A recent book is Marc Reisner, *Cadillac Desert: The American West and Its Disappearing Water* (New York: Viking Penguin, 1986), 393–425; this author sees Western water development not as a triumph, but as a catastrophe.

Idaho histories helpful for this chapter include: Beal and Wells, *History of Idaho*, 2:377–392; Peterson, *Idaho: A Bicentennial History*, 168–69, 179–92; Stapilus, *Paradox Politics*, passim; Jensen, *Discovering Idaho*, 248–60; Loftus, *Idaho State Parks Guidebook*; Conley, *Idaho for the Curious*, passim; Wells and Hart, *Idaho: Gem of the Mountains*, 137–52. Of special help has been *Idaho Blue Book*, 1983–86 edition, published by Secretary of State Pete Cenarrusa for the State of Idaho.

Other sources include James Muhn and Hanson R. Stuart, *Opportunity and Challenge: The Story of BLM* (Washington, D.C.: U.S. Department of the Interior, Bureau of Land Management, 1988); Fred Rabe and David C. Flaherty, *The River of Green and Gold* (Moscow: Idaho Research Foundation, 1974), an environmental history of the Coeur d'Alene River; George Wuerthner, *Idaho Mountain Ranges*, Idaho Geographic Series Number One (Helena, Montana: American Geographic Publishing Co., 1986); United States Department of Agriculture, *Your Land: The National Forests in Idaho* (Hailey, Idaho: Peak Media, Inc., 1989); Elmo Richardson, *Dams, Parks, and Politics: Resource Development and Preservation in the Truman-Eisenhower Era* (Lexington: University Press of Kentucky, 1973); Grace E. Jordan, *The Unintentional Senator* (Boise: Syms-York Company, 1972); Church, *Father and Son*; Frederick R. Steiner, *Soil*

*Conservation in the United States: Policy and Planning* (Baltimore: Johns Hopkins University Press, 1990); David Cushman Coyle, *Conservation: An American Story of Conflict and Accomplishment* (New Brunswick, New Jersey: Rutgers University Press, 1957); Michael G. Robinson, *Water for the West: The Bureau of Reclamation, 1902–1977* (Chicago: Public Works Historical Society, 1979); Cox, *The Park Builders*; and Tim Palmer, *The Snake River: Window to the West* (Washington D.C. and Covelo, California: Island Press, 1991).

# CHAPTER TWENTY-EIGHT

# The Challenge of Education

IDAHO'S development is the result of abundant natural resources, entrepreneurial energy, the adoption of improved technology, and the infusion of capital from the Midwest, New England, Europe, and the West Coast. Another major factor is the education of its people. Idaho's pioneers, as with most westering peoples, early established schools along with churches, theaters, glee clubs, and other cultural institutions. Idaho has always ranked high in number of years of schooling completed and in the rate of literacy of its population. Idaho has always had many dedicated teachers.

Two Idahoans in education have received particular national attention in recent years. When NASA planned to send a teacher on an outer-space mission in 1986, two of the ten final candidates for consideration came from Idaho: David Marquart of Boise and Barbara Morgan of McCall. Morgan was one of two final choices for the honor. A California native and graduate of Stanford, she moved to Idaho in 1975, teaches at the McCall-

Donnelly Elementary School, and plays flute with the McCall Chamber Orchestra. She has represented Idaho with distinction, serving on several national committees and receiving wide acclaim as a lecturer, but she most enjoys her third-grade students in McCall.

Further indication of Idaho's status in education is that Dr. Terrel H. Bell, native of Lava Hot Springs, served as Secretary of Education for one president (1981–85) and as commissioner of education for two others. One of nine children raised by his widowed mother, Bell attended Albion Normal School because it was less costly than a university, then taught science and coached athletics for a year in Eden. He was principal in Rockland for seven years while he studied each summer to earn a master's degree in education from the University of Idaho. He later served as state superintendent of schools in Wyoming and Utah. Under his leadership as Secretary of Education the National Commission on Excellence in Education issued 12 million copies of the report *A Nation at Risk*, warning that American education, critical to the nation's future, was faltering and in many cases failing. In 1988 Bell published *The Thirteenth Man: A Reagan Cabinet Memoir*.

Having had an early start, Idaho's school system continued to grow with the population. By 1910, 722 school districts had an attendance of more than 35,000 students. Teachers' salaries averaged about $48 per month. A state board was established to supervise the schools (and take on duties of the university's board of regents) in 1912, and by 1920 it oversaw 1,771 school districts with 115,192 students. Idaho's schools were financed almost entirely by local property taxes. As mentioned in Chapter Seventeen, in 1887–88 the Latter-day Saints had established academies (high schools) in Paris (Fielding), Preston (Oneida), Oakley (Cassia), and Rexburg (Ricks). These remained in operation until the early 1920s, when, excellent public schools being available, the church turned the buildings over to local school districts and replaced these church schools with "seminaries." Adjacent to local high schools, the seminaries offer classes in religion (Old and New Testament, Christian history, Book of Mormon, and Mormon history) to supplement "secular" high school instruction. At the college level in the 1920s the LDS Church established "Institutes of Religion" adjacent to state college campuses to further religious study. Ricks Academy was renamed Ricks College in 1923 and, as we shall see, remains in operation.

Over the years, denominations other than the LDS Church also established parochial schools. By 1976 the Roman Catholics operated twelve elementary schools and one high school (Bishop Kelly in Boise); they had earlier operated St. Teresa's Academy, also in Boise. The Seventh-Day Adventist Church administered ten elementary schools and one high school (Gem State Academy near Caldwell). The Friends Church managed one combined elementary and high school at Greenleaf in Canyon County. Other Christian schools were operated in several locations.

The University of Idaho at Moscow was created in 1889. In 1893 normal schools were established in Lewiston and Albion and in 1901 the legislature founded a technical school, the Academy of Idaho, at Pocatello, about which more later. A state school for the deaf and blind was opened at Gooding in 1910. In 1904 the Idaho Industrial Training School was built at St. Anthony. The name was changed to State Youth Training Center in 1963, and to the Youth Services Center in 1974. Today this is the only state-operated institution in Idaho responsible for the care and rehabilitation of delinquent youth.

As we shall see, the Academy of Idaho in Pocatello became the Idaho Technical Institute, then the Southern Branch of the University of Idaho. After considerable study, discussion, and agitation, the legislature increased its stature in 1947, establishing Idaho State College with authority to grant bachelors' degrees as a liberal-arts institution. In 1955 the institution was authorized to grant the master of arts degree in education.

Although the college at Pocatello was given increased recognition and financial support, the normal colleges were not. In 1949 the legislature closed the colleges in Lewiston and Albion. Largely in response to much resistance to and resentment of the closing, in 1955 the legislature reactivated the Northern Idaho College of Education in Lewiston as the Lewis-Clark Normal School. It was charged with power to provide a two-year college course for elementary teachers under the general direction of the University of Idaho. The Lewiston school became a separate four-year college in 1963. A bill to reactivate the Southern Idaho College of Education at Albion was defeated, and in 1957 the state granted a long-term lease on the property to the Church of Christ. Magic Valley Christian College opened there in 1958, but it was discontinued after three years. Although other groups have attempted to put them to use, the buildings are now vacant.

In 1939 the legislature permitted the organization of junior college districts. Such districts were effectuated in Boise and Coeur d'Alene, and junior colleges already operating in these cities became tax-supported institutions. Boise Junior College had been founded in 1932 by the Episcopal Church; the Coeur d'Alene College had been founded in 1933 as a private institution. The three church colleges serving the people of Idaho have been the Northwest Nazarene College in Nampa; the College of Idaho (Presbyterian), now Albertson College of Idaho, in Caldwell; and Ricks College (LDS) in Rexburg.

Mention was made in Chapter Twenty-five of the reorganization of schools that began in 1947. Within five years the number of districts was reduced from 1,118 to 268 as a means of equalizing educational opportunity, achieving greater uniformity of school tax rates, and providing more effective use of state funds for the support of public schools. The greater centralization of administration has been accompanied by increased state appropriations for the schools.

In 1953 Governor Len Jordan entered into a regional compact with the governors of nine western states and Alaska under which certain high-cost professional programs might be operated on a reciprocal basis with no out-of-state fees. Idaho's students were admitted to medical, dental, and veterinary schools in other states, and students from those states were encouraged to register at the schools of pharmacy in Pocatello and forestry at Moscow.

Another policy change was in the training of Native Americans. Indian youth were schooled on the Coeur d'Alene, Nez Perce, Shoshoni-Bannock (Fort Hall), and Shoshoni-Paiute (Duck Valley) reservations until 1935, when they were integrated into nearby public schools.

A significant step in Idaho's educational achievement was the enactment in 1965 of a 3 percent sales tax, duly ratified by the citizenry in a 1966 referendum, which gave the state the wherewithal to equalize educational opportunity, support higher salaries for teachers, and maintain higher standards of instruction. In 1975 the legislature authorized state support for kindergartens.

Particularly significant to Idaho, to the West, and to the nation are the contributions of Idaho's major institutions of higher learning.

UNIVERSITY OF IDAHO. In one hundred years the University of Idaho has granted more than 60,000 degrees. It was at Moscow that most teachers in the state received their certificates, most of Idaho's lawyers graduated from law school, and many of the nation's finest agricultural, mining, and engineering scientists were given their first training. The university's principal problem has been its location so far north that enrollment has been limited.

From the very beginning the university has insisted on high academic standards. As early as 1905 Idaho required four years of high school for entrance, the first college in the Pacific Northwest to do so. That same year the Carnegie Foundation surveyed the academic standings of the nation's colleges and universities and rated the U of I high above most of its western contemporaries—indeed, among the select colleges of the nation. By then the university had grown to include colleges in letters and science, agriculture, law, forestry, and mines; and master's degrees were available in four areas of study. The student newspaper (*The Argonaut*) had begun printing, the Pacific Northwest's first summer school had been started, and the agricultural experiment station had published significant bulletins about the growing of peas and potatoes to contribute to a developing business of agriculture.

In 1917 the College of Agriculture, in cooperation with federal, state and county governments, began a cooperative extension service to dispense research knowledge statewide. "Field men" were employed to go directly into the homes, orchards, fields, and stables wherever farms were located to demonstrate the best methods to follow in various agricultural efforts. Eventually, a county farm agent system was developed in each of Idaho's forty-four counties. Branch stations were established in Caldwell, Parma, Kimberly, Aberdeen, Sandpoint, and Tetonia. Agriculture-related research in growing potatoes, sugar beets, and wheat and raising sheep improved yields and profits for farmers and stockmen throughout the nation. Home economists have met with women's clubs, teachers, and youth groups to provide instruction in cooking, sewing, and home management, and have developed departments in many home-related industries.

During World War I the School of Mines conducted a statewide geological survey of minerals that proved helpful to the war effort. Recognizing the value of this activity, the state in 1919 established the Idaho Bureau of Mines and Geology (now the Idaho Geological Survey) at the university. The bureau and the university over the years have jointly done research for Idaho's mining industry.

The School of Forestry, like Mines, conducted experiments from its first days on campus to help both farmers and foresters. In 1911 the Potlatch Lumber Company engaged the school to run experiments on its cutover lands to determine the best methods of removing stumps. The school published a bulletin entitled "Methods of Clearing Logged-Off Land" that was widely distributed in the region. In the mid-1920s the school cooperated with state and federal agencies in controlling white-pine blister rust and in studying wood lots and windbreaks. In 1927 the university named its first extension forester and began some of the country's earliest experiments on the potential uses of forestry by-products. The next year it established the Idaho Forest Experiment Station, precursor to the Forest, Wildlife and Range Experiment Station organized in 1939. In the latter year the university appointed its first extension conservationist.

The Schools of Business Administration and Education were established in the 1920s, as was the Graduate School, and the university was fully accredited by the Association of American Universities in 1928. Not until 1959 were doctoral programs initiated; both the Doctor of Philosophy (Ph.D.) and Doctor of Education (Ed.D.) degree are offered.

During the depression of the 1930s U of I faculty absorbed substantial cuts in salaries, worked with reduced office services, taught heavier loads, and gave students extra attention. The university was besieged by the sons and daughters of southern Idaho farmers who were unable to pay for campus housing. The U of I led the nation in establishing the first university cooperative, enabling students to get by on less than $300 a year. (The writer, who lived in one of these, kept a careful record of his spendings and survived on $285 for a ten-month period. Of this amount he earned $150 by working for college departments on a National Youth Administration program, received $75 in scholarship funds from the Union Pacific Railroad, and secured the remainder doing odd jobs for professors and townspeople.) More than 300 students attended each year as members of one of the cooperatives—the Idaho Club, Campus Club, Lindley Hall, Ridenbaugh Hall, and LDS Institute—doing their own meal preparation and serving, dishwashing, room cleaning, and clothes washing to keep down expenses. Director (and instigator) of the cooperatives was George S. Tanner, director of the LDS Institute of Religion adjacent to campus.

During World War II the university instituted a Naval Radio Training School, operated an Army Specialized Training Program, and installed an Air Force ROTC unit, making it one of the few colleges in the nation to have ROTC in all branches of the Armed Forces. A 1945 report by the George Peabody College Survey Commission ranked the University of Idaho among the upper 10 percent in the nation in academic standing and rated the faculty "of high scholarly competence."

In the 1940s the William E. Borah Outlawry of War Foundation began the sponsorship of annual symposia at which nationally and internationally renowed scholars and statesmen discuss problems of social importance. The symposia have attracted worldwide attention.

In 1949 the university introduced extension classes in five Idaho cities and organized adult education programs at Boise Junior College, Idaho Falls, and Mountain Home Air Force Base. Five years later, overseas programs got under way when faculty initiated teaching and research programs in two Ecuadorean universities, and in 1981 faculty participated in a water-management research project in Pakistan.

Other parts of the university also operate outreach programs. In 1949 the university started a service of renting films and audio-visual materials to schools and organizations. With the completion of the school's television center in 1955, it increased production of informational films. The university also established in the 1950s the Bureau of Business and Economic Research and the Bureau of Public Affairs Research. Both render valuable assistance to county and municipal governments as well as the state. The university provides advisory services to the Nez Perce Indian tribe in connection with school and adult programs. The Theatre Arts Department presents annual tours to Idaho high schools. Other departments sponsor conferences and institutes for high school students. The College of Forestry, Wildlife and Range Sciences sponsors study at its sixty-five-acre Wilderness Research Center in the heart of the Frank Church/River of No Return Wilderness area and in McCall. Off-campus resident instruction centers are located in Coeur d'Alene, Boise, Twin Falls, and Idaho Falls.[1] Statewide responsibilities include agriculture, architecture, engineering, law, mining, metallurgy, and forest, wildlife, and range sciences. In 1990 the university enrolled 8,500 full-time-equivalent students and was led by President Elisabeth Zinser—the first woman to head a four-year institution of higher education in Idaho.

IDAHO STATE UNIVERSITY. As with most of the colleges and universities in Idaho, ISU began as a high school. When the Fort Hall Indian Reservation was established in 1869, its boundaries extended from Red Rock south of Downey to the Blackfoot River, an area of 1.5 million acres. In 1889 482,000 acres were trimmed from the southern section because few Indians resided there. In 1898 an agreement was reached with the Shoshoni and Bannock, duly signed by President William McKinley in 1900, by which 418,000 acres were opened to white settlement. A land rush resulted on June 17, 1902, when thousands of men rode racehorses, buggies, wagons, and trains to stake claims for farming land and mines, after which they hastened to the land office in Blackfoot to file on the property.

Anticipating the creation of a city larger than the existing railroad terminal environs, State Senator Theodore Turner pushed a bill through the legislature establishing the Academy of Idaho at Pocatello to provide a two-year college preparatory and vocational school for eastern Idaho. The school opened in 1902 with forty students and four faculty members.

In 1915 the Academy was renamed Idaho Technical Institute and authorized to provide two years of college study along with preparation of students in technical and vocational fields. In 1927 the institution became the University of Idaho, Southern Branch, with greater emphasis given to traditional college curricula in the arts and sciences. The program remained two-year except for pharmacy, which was three years and later expanded to four. In 1930 the College of Pharmacy was established; by 1990 it was still the only college of pharmacy in Idaho.

The college's contribution during World War II was comparable to that of many of the largest universities in the nation. Civil Pilot Training under the jurisdiction of the Civil Aeronautics Authority was inaugurated in 1940; thirty classes offered training in auto and aviation mechanics, electricity, machine shop, air depots, welding, printing, foundry, sheet metal, and ordnance—all of this to train for specific military services or war-defense industries. Officials of the Kaiser Swan Island Yard at Portland, Oregon, were so pleased with the Pocatello-trained welders that they commissioned the successive training of twenty-four groups of men from 1943 to 1945. The college organized Idaho's first unit of American Women's Voluntary Service Corps. The 100 women who joined were trained in nutrition and communal feeding, motor-corps service, map reading, Morse Code, and first aid. A comparable number of men joined the Idaho Southern Enlisted Reserve Corps. In 1942 a Navy V-5 flight training program was started and continued through 1944, with from fifty to eighty-five persons assigned each ninety-day period for flight training.

In 1943 the college was one of 150 schools in the nation

chosen by the Bureau of Naval Personnel as an officer training school in the Navy V-12 program. One student described the program as follows:

> Every day has the same pattern to it; reveille, morning muster, breakfast, classes, mail call, muster and lunch, classes again, muster again, study hours, then in for a bit of sack time. But there is more than enough to break up that routine. In Graveley Hall there are watches to stand, "personal appearances" before the officers, and always visits to the Training Aids Library and Ship's Store.[2]

Classes were held year-round, and the college had an average of 825 cadets over a five-semester period. They fielded a creditable football team, the Battling Bengals basketball team won eleven of fifteen games, and there were baseball, boxing, and volleyball teams; plays; concert, marching, and dance bands; a Navy chorus; and two newspapers, the *Idaho Bengal* and the *Dittybag*. All told 2,200 Southern Branch men and 96 women served in the United States Armed Forces, of whom 61 died under the colors.[3]

Partly because of this exemplary war record, Idaho State College was created in 1947 from the Southern Branch as an autonomous, four-year degree-granting institution. Divisions included the College of Liberal Arts, College of Pharmacy, and School of Trade and Technical Education. The Division of Graduate Studies was organized in 1955, the College of Education in 1958, and the Division of Medical Arts in 1961. The final step in the institution's rank came in 1963 when the legislature changed its name to Idaho State University. At the same time the College of Business was created. Since 1975 the Medical Arts Division has been reclassified as the College of Health-Related Professions and the School of Engineering has been created. Because of its proximity to the Idaho National Engineering Laboratory, ISU offers a program leading to the Doctor of Philosophy degree in nuclear science and engineering.

In 1990 ISU had more than 7,000 full-time equivalent students. ISU is home of the Minidome (recently renamed Holt Athletic Arena), the first indoor stadium ever built on a college campus. In 1977 ISU also completed the Eli M. Oboler Library, at the time the largest educational building in Idaho. The university maintains continuing education centers in Idaho Falls, Twin Falls, and Sun Valley. The university also has close association with the Idaho Museum of Natural History, located on campus. One of the few institutions in the nation with a Dinomania Exhibit, the museum has attracted hundreds of thousands of visitors and houses one of the largest collections of the mammoth extinct Bison Latifrons.

BOISE STATE UNIVERSITY. Founded in 1932 by the Episcopal Church and private agencies as a community college called Boise Junior College, BSU became a district-supported school in 1939, a state college in 1969, and a university in 1974. It originally occupied St. Margaret's Hall, an Episcopal girls' school since 1892; the growing institution was relocated on the original site of the Boise Municipal Airport in 1940. Students and faculty enlisted in the military during World War II and enrollment dropped to about 200 in 1942, but a pilot-training program on campus kept the school from closing. By 1956 the student body exceeded 1,000. As enrollment continued to climb and new academic programs were added, three large new buildings were constructed: a grand Pavilion, 1982; the Morrison Center for the Performing Arts, 1984; and the Simplot/Micron Center for Technology, 1985. The college offers masters of arts and science degrees in several fields and masters in business administration, public administration, fine arts, and music. BSU has an extensive evening instruction program; does research to support the needs of business, government, and industry; operates a sizable academic program at the Mountain Home Air Force Base; and offers cultural opportunities to the public through its drama and music departments, popular concerts, art exhibits, lecture series, and special workshops.

Because Boise State is centered in the governmental, medical, and business heart of Idaho, students and the university interact with the school districts, health care institutions, government agencies, and corporations headquartered in Idaho's largest city. The Boise State University School of Nursing, for example, graduates from 80 to 100 students per year; trains students in medical, surgical, pediatric, and psychiatric nursing; and gives experience in nursing procedures at hospitals in Boise, Caldwell, Nampa, and rural hospitals. The university registered 9,500 full-time equivalent students in 1990.

LEWIS-CLARK STATE COLLEGE. In 1893, when the state legislature established a normal school at Lewiston, Idaho's rural grade-school teachers were required to complete only eight grades and pass a county examination. Classes were held that year on the second floor of the old Grostein and Binnard Building at Second and Main. The room was separated by canvas curtains into four classrooms to accommodate the forty-three students and three instructors. When the ten-acre "city park" became the campus and the administration building was completed in 1896, 137 students enrolled. In the years that followed, most of the students were women who took a two-year course preparatory to teaching in a one-room country school. By 1934 it was one of the nation's few remaining two-year normal schools. Lewis-Clark was authorized to issue four-year degrees in education in 1947 and was renamed the North Idaho College of Education. Closed in 1951 because of the failure of the legislature to appropriate funds, the school was reopened in 1955 as the Lewis-Clark Normal School. Once again a two-year school, under the supervision of the University of Idaho, the school "graduated" to four-year and independent status in 1963. The name, however, remained the same. In addition to a liberal arts course, the school also offered a nursing program and vocational-technical education classes. In 1971 the school was renamed Lewis-Clark State College. In 1990 the school's 2,600 students could select from four-year courses in business, criminal justice, education, and nursing, as well as in the arts and sciences.

COLLEGE OF SOUTHERN IDAHO. Although the Peabody Survey of 1946 had recommended the establishment of a junior college at Twin Falls, and although local citizens had privately employed professionals from Stanford University and elsewhere to help with the planning process, not until 1963 did passage by the legislature of the Junior College Act make possible the creation of a junior college district. In a subsequent election the citizens of Twin Falls and Jerome counties approved the creation of such a district. With funds obtained from the counties, the state, and the federal government, the college opened in September 1965 with 640 students. Its campus was located on 230 acres on the north side of Twin Falls near the Snake River Canyon. The college almost immediately was granted accreditation by the Northwest Association of Schools and Colleges for its standard junior college program with a strong vocational-technical curriculum. Within five years CSI had 1,500 full-time students and an equal number of part-time enrollees. In 1990 the college had 1,900 full-time equivalent students. The college has ranked very high in athletics, often earning the national championship for two-year colleges in basketball and ranking at the top in baseball, track, and rodeo. The college has a fine arts center; an expo center; academic facility, health-physical education, student union, multi-use, vocational-technical, administration, and farm management buildings; a gymnasium; and the Herrett Museum, LDS Institute, and Catholic priory adjacent to the campus. CSI graduates approximately 500 students each year.

NORTH IDAHO COLLEGE. At the bottom of the Great Depression in 1933 a group of citizens of Coeur d'Alene, for whom it was prohibitively expensive to send their children to the state university at Moscow ninety miles away, organized to found a junior college. The city council permitted them to use without charge the third floor of the city hall for classroom space and the city library on the second floor. Four full-time teachers with master's degrees were employed, several part-time instructors came from the community's local business school, a first-year president was chosen, and the school opened in the fall of 1933 under the name Coeur d'Alene Junior College. It had sixty-seven students. The school operated for the next six years with similar small enrollments. The University of Idaho agreed to give students credit for their course work; Orrin Lee, a graduate of Ricks College and the University of Idaho, was employed as "permanent" president; and the founding committee worked for approval of a legislative bill authorizing the formation of a junior college district that would provide tax dollars. The measure passed in 1937 but was vetoed by Governor Barzilla Clark. The legislature tried again in 1939 after the election of Governor C. A. Bottolfsen, who signed the measure, permitting tax support not only for Coeur d'Alene but also for Boise Junior College.

The junior college opened its doors as a tax-supported institution in the fall of 1939 under the name North Idaho Junior College, a name the college retained until 1971 when it became North Idaho College. Nestled among tall pines on a forty-acre site (originally, Fort Sherman) that includes beachfront on Lake Coeur d'Alene, the two-year college confers associate-degree certificates in thirty-eight transferable academic majors and several vocational programs. In 1990 the college had 2,000 full-time equivalent students.

RICKS COLLEGE. With an enrollment of 7,700 in 1990, Ricks College—a two-year, private institution—has become one of the largest institutions of higher learning in Idaho. Beginning as the Bannock Stake Academy, an LDS high school, the institution changed its name in 1903 to Ricks Academy in honor of Thomas E. Ricks and shifted to a college curriculum in 1915. It was named Ricks College in 1923. During the depression of the 1930s the LDS Church offered to give the college to the state of Idaho, but the donation was refused. With a large number of returning veterans enrolling at the end of the war, and the legislature decreeing that all teachers to be certified must have completed four years of college, the college added a third year of courses in 1948 and a fourth in 1949. New buildings were constructed, and new Ph.D.s were employed as instructors. Then in 1956, in a move designed to strengthen Brigham Young University in Utah, the upper-division courses were discontinued and Ricks students were encouraged to complete their classwork at BYU. Brigham Young University has now reached its 30,000 enrollment limit, however, and Ricks College looks forward to a restoration of its four-year, degree-granting status.

In 1957 the LDS Board of Education stunned the campus community with an announcement that it was considering moving the college to Idaho Falls. After several meetings and the presentation of arguments pro and con, the LDS First Presidency assured a visiting Rexburg delegation that the college would remain in Rexburg. Just the next year, however, the decision seems to have been reversed: land for the new location was purchased in Idaho Falls. Rexburg decided to fight the decision. A Committee of One Thousand published a booklet attacking the "underhanded" effort to move the college and rebutting the arguments used to support the removal. David O. McKay, the eighty-five-year-old LDS Church President, was inundated with letters, telegrams, and telephone calls. There was despair and bitterness in Rexburg but hopes rose with the repeated delays in implementing the removal. Finally, in April 1961, LDS headquarters announced that three new buildings would be constructed immediately on the Rexburg campus. By 1975 the church had spent $17 million on new structures. LDS authorities had heard from the "boondocks," were touched by the dedication, determination, and fervor of the One Thousand, and from that time gave full support to Ricks College at Rexburg. The episode is now dismissed with the comment that no one in Salt Lake (or Provo) could figure out how to get the buildings through the Rigby overpass.[4]

ALBERTSON COLLEGE OF IDAHO. The College of Idaho (renamed The Albertson College of Idaho in 1991) was originally opened by the Wood River Presbytery and residents of Caldwell in 1891 as an academy or high school. (College students were not yet available.) The leading advocate was William Judson Boone, local Presbyterian pastor and president of the college until his death in 1936. Among the initial faculty were John T. Morrison and Frank Steunenberg; both later became Idaho governors. (Former governor Robert Smylie would later serve as acting president.) College classes were first offered in 1906 and the first degree was granted in 1911. Secondary-level classes were discontinued in 1919. From then on, the college was a four-year, nonsectarian liberal-arts school. By 1990 the school, with 560 students, was granting bachelor degrees in thirty subjects and master's degrees in education and counseling.

Perhaps the most famous academic personality connected with the college (and with the University of Idaho) was Lawrence Henry Gipson. Born in Greeley, Colorado, in 1880, Gipson moved in 1893 with his parents to Caldwell, where his father published *Commonwealth of Idaho* and *Gem State Rural*, grew fruits and horticultural products, and managed the business of the Caldwell Real Estate and Water Company. Young Gipson learned the printer's trade and worked in the printing shop of the *Caldwell Tribune* and his father's *Gem State Rural* until he was sixteen, when he matriculated at the college. He remained two years and in 1899 transferred to the University of Idaho, where there were 106 students in the collegiate department and 120 in the preparatory school. Gipson took the classical course required for the A.B. degree, which meant Greek, Latin, English literature, history, mathematics, and political economy.

Gipson received his A.B. in 1903, was recognized as the class poet, and remained another year at the university to teach history and economics in the Preparatory Department. In 1904, he was designated Idaho's first Rhodes Scholar. Indeed, he was a member of the first delegation of Rhodes Scholars to attend Oxford University, one of forty-two to sail for England from the United States. After studying English history at Oxford, Gipson earned a doctorate at Yale and went on to become one of America's premier historians. He returned to the College of Idaho as an instructor and in 1907 accepted a post at the University of Idaho as a professor of history. In 1910 he was, like so many Idaho scholars, drawn to the East, to Lehigh University in Bethlehem, Pennsylvania, where he spent the rest of his life working on a fifteen-volume history of *The British Empire Before the American Revolution*—the last volume of which was published in 1971, just before his death at the age of ninety-one. His magnum opus was called by one American historian "the greatest single work by an American historian of our time. . . . A work of synthesis on a scale that few historians could have the temerity to attempt or the longevity to complete."[5] The work won the Pulitzer Prize. He was given an honorary Doctor of Humane Letters from the University of Idaho in 1953 and an honorary D. Litt. from the College of Idaho in 1969.

NORTHWEST NAZARENE COLLEGE. Founded at Nampa in 1913 as an elementary school, Northwest Nazarene began to offer high school and college courses in 1915. The school was accredited as a junior college in 1931 and fully accredited as a four-year school in 1937. The goal of the college is "to develop a Christian perspective on life and to encourage Christian commitment within the philosophy and framework of genuine scholarship." Although those of the Nazarene faith dominate the student population, almost every major Christian denomination is represented and students are not required to be church members. The college has six academic divisions: fine arts, language and literature, mathematics and natural science, philosophy and religion, professional studies, and social science. It has a well-earned reputation in debate. Enrollment in NNC in 1990 was 1,350 students.

BOISE BIBLE COLLEGE. Organized by Boise First Church of Christ in 1945 to train preachers, missionaries, and teachers, Boise Bible College offers bachelors of science and arts degrees. The nondenominational school had eighty students in 1990.

MUSEUMS. Other centers of learning in the state include the following museums:

Idaho State Historical Museum, Boise, with richly detailed interiors and exhibits telling Idaho's story in a clear and interesting manner;

Idaho Museum of Natural History, in Pocatello, depicting natural history of Idaho and the West, with animated dinosaurs;

Herrett Museum, in Twin Falls, featuring Idaho anthropology;

Latah County Historical Society, Moscow, with exhibits and a frequently used research library;

Boise Art Museum, offering twenty exhibitions annually, encompassing a wide range of historical and contemporary home and educational programs, lectures, films, art classes, and docent-guided tours.

In addition, many counties and communities have museums

that feature local and regional history, pioneer relics, wildlife specimens, fossils, works of art, artifacts, books and newspapers, native American and ethnic memorabilia, railroad cars, mining equipment, photographs, and farm machinery.

Outside observers have pointed out the financial cost to a population of 1 million people as they attempt to maintain three first-rate universities, Lewis-Clark, two junior colleges, and several private colleges. The investment this involves inevitably dilutes to some extent the excellence of the universities. But the political reality of the burden of higher education can be explained by the state's geography. Centers of population that are distant from a college or university want one of their own, and they want it to be a good one. Idahoans face a challenge as they continue to support, via taxes and donations, the impressive educational system they have devised to fill the needs of Idaho's citizens.

## CHAPTER TWENTY-EIGHT: SOURCES

Histories of Idaho that were helpful in the preparation of this chapter were Beal and Wells, *History of Idaho*, 2:316–26; Fisher, ed., *The Idaho Encyclopedia*; *Idaho Blue Book*, 1983–1986 ed.; *Idaho Almanac*, 1977 ed. (Boise: Office of the Governor and Idaho Division of Tourism and Industrial Development, 1977); Harold A. Farley, "An Unpublished History of Idaho Education" (1974), manuscript at the Idaho State Historical Society, Boise; Hawley, *History of Idaho*, 1:333–61; Wells and Hart, *Idaho: Gem of the Mountains*, particularly 176–244; and Wells, *Boise: An Illustrated History*.

Histories of particular educational institutions include: Kermit L. Staggers, "Coeur d'Alene Junior College, 1933–1939," *Idaho Yesterdays* 22 (Summer 1978):18–26; Gibbs, *Beacon for Mountain and Plain*; Keith C. Petersen, *This Crested Hill: An Illustrated History of the University of Idaho* (Moscow: University of Idaho Press, 1987); Merrill Beal, *History of Idaho State College* (Pocatello: Idaho State College, 1952); Norman E. Ricks, *A Brief History of Ricks College*

(Rexburg: Ricks College, 1970); Crowder, *Rexburg, Idaho*, on Ricks College; Bess Steunenberg, "Early Days in Caldwell," *Idaho Yesterdays* 10 (Winter 1966–67):12–17; Leslie V. Brock, "Lawrence Henry Gipson: Historian: the Early Idaho Years," *Idaho Yesterdays* 22 (Summer 1978):2–9, 27–31.

142.

143.

142. Ethel Cutler's pupils at Central School, Preston, 1910, gathered in front of the Oneida Stake Academy for a photograph. LDS CHURCH ARCHIVES PH 224.

143. The University of Idaho, founded in 1890, attracted students in a variety of disciplines including these 1898 female students in the Home Economics Laboratory, Ridenbaugh Hall. ISHS 65–169.1.

144.

145.

144. The Idaho State University campus in 1901. IDAHO STATE UNIVERSITY.

145. The Idaho State University campus in 1991. IDAHO STATE UNIVERSITY.

CHAPTER TWENTY-NINE

# Idaho's Amazing Entrepreneurs

AUDACIOUS men and women who risk their energy and sometimes their own capital to introduce new products, organize new businesses, and launch new processes are called entrepreneurs. They are noteworthy because, in pursuing their own motives and interests, they also provide jobs and income, open up markets, and introduce improved ways of doing things. Except for certain examples of collective endeavor—roads, canals, dams, airports, railroads, and public buildings—Idaho's growth and development have been the result of individual decisions to exploit natural resources, initiate new businesses, build new plants, and produce goods and services that people are willing to purchase. The flexibility and freedom of American institutions have offered opportunities for Idahoans—idealists, inventors, innovators, organizers, financiers, or just ambitious young people—to serve themselves, their families, and the citizens of the state, nation, and world.

There was an unprecedented blossoming of Idaho entrepreneurship in the late 1950s, 1960s, and 1970s. A few men (the "giants" seem to have been men, but women also achieved significant entrepreneurial gains) amazed the editors of *The Wall Street Journal*, *Fortune*, *Forbes*, *Business Week*, *Dun's Review*, and other prominent national business newspapers and magazines. Robert Smylie, who was governor during most of these years (1955–66), attributed Idaho's unexpected rise to business prominence to three factors: the increased ability of Idaho banks to put together major loans, the establishment of the Idaho Department of Commerce and Development in 1957, and the newfound confidence of Idaho capitalists in promoting development in the decades after World War II.[1]

This period from 1955 to 1980 was a critical turning point in the state's economic life—a climacteric, a decisive period in the development of Idaho's commerce and industry. The principals, each of whom has maintained a healthy relationship with the growing community, have built personal economic empires. The free-wheeling Idaho society has fostered the ultimate expression of such personalities and goals.

## BOISE CASCADE

Late in 1956, officials of Boise Payette Lumber Company replaced John Aram as president with thirty-six-year-old Robert V. Hansberger, manager of a small pulp mill at Albany, Oregon. A farm-born engineering graduate of the University of Minnesota with a subsequent MBA from Harvard, Hansberger had worked as an assistant to the executive vice president, divisional chief engineer, sales executive, and budget director for Container Corporation of America in Chicago until 1954, when he went west to manage the lumber and paper firm that later became Western Kraft.

At the time Hansberger became president of Boise Payette the lumber industry, the paper industry, and the company were burdened with overcapacity, declining prices, and intense competition. In fact, Boise Payette, as mentioned in Chapter Twenty-six, was cutting its timber in preparation for liquidation. An optimist and an aggressive leader, Hansberger, who looked a little like movie star Yul Bryner, persuaded the stockholders to go into debt to build a pulp and paper mill that could make use of the waste wood chips and sawdust. Boise Payette did not have the capital assets to build the mill, nor enough waste wood to feed it. Undaunted, Hansberger pored over maps, devised a method to obtain control of large stretches of timberlands in southwestern Idaho and south-central Washington, and proposed a merger with two other lumber companies holding substantial acreages that faced the same problems as Boise Payette. One of the companies, Valsetz Lumber Company, declined the offer; the other, Cascade Lumber Company of Yakima, Washington, agreed. Boise Cascade Corporation was the result. Two years later Valsetz also joined.

Boise Cascade borrowed $7 million to build a small pulp and paper mill and a corrugated-box plant on the Columbia River at Wallula, Washington, close to the apple, pea, and potato growers who were ready carton customers. Hansberger next acquired a chain of forty-one lumberyards in Washington and northern Idaho. He also constructed a plant at Burley to make corrugated shipping containers for the nation's frozen potato products industry. Acquisitions proceeded rapidly, and within ten years Boise Cascade, an almost totally integrated forest-products business—that is, owning everything from trees to trucks that hauled the finished products—was one of the nation's fastest-growing companies. In 1965 the company was selling more than $400 million worth of products and earning $17 million, compared with $35 million in sales and $2 million in profits in 1955. By 1965 the company had 60 manufacturing plants and 104 retail and wholesale distribution centers in the United States, in addition to interests in mills and plants in six other countries. To keep the enterprise moving forward, Hansberger was in the air much of the time. The company had two planes and four pilots, and Hansberger kept them busy. As a *Business Week* writer who followed him around for a week in 1963 reported: "It is not unusual for him to do business in San Francisco one day, fly all night to New York, and have his secretary and staff working simultaneously with him so that he can lay down in New York in the morning the results of the previous day's business in San Francisco."[2]

Bob Hansberger guided Boise Cascade until 1972. By that time the company had expanded thirtyfold and its annual sales reached more than $1.6 billion. Hansberger had hired dozens of ambitious MBA graduates from Harvard and Stanford, he had given them considerable leeway in what was called "free-form" management, and he had demonstrated a financial wizardry that eastern brokers had not expected from an Idahoan. In its expansion, however, the revitalized company had ventured into land development and home-building in California, an investment that turned into a disaster. The company was forced to write off more than $300 million in assets in 1971–72 and Hansberger resigned. Having fallen in love with Idaho, Hansberger remained in Boise to oversee interests combined under Futura Industries Corporation that included two metal-fabricating firms, several dude ranches, and part ownership of a golf-equipment manufacturing operation.

Boise Cascade chose as its new leader John B. Fery, its forty-four-year-old executive vice-president. Within two years Fery had the company back in the black, insisting that Boise Cascade concentrate on its basic line of business—timber operations—"businesses we know something about." Grandson of the Austrian-born pioneer artist John Fery, who is mentioned in Chapter Thirty, and the son of a forester, Fery grew up in western Washington, graduated from the University of Washington and Stanford, and then went to work for Boise Cascade under Hansberger. Overcoming its financial setbacks of the early

1970s, Boise Cascade, under Fery's leadership, emerged as one of the nation's premier forest-products companies. Its operations in the 1980s included an annual 3-million-ton paper industry, a large carton and corrugated-container division, an office-products division, and a lumber products and residential-construction section that accounted for sales of $4 billion in 1990. Plants and outlets in thirty-five states, as well as in Canada and Europe, included sixteen sawmills, fourteen plywood producers, fourteen paper mills, and twenty-two container factories. The company employed 27,000 workers. Boise Cascade owned 3 million acres of timberland and worked several million additional leased or contracted acres.

Boise Cascade's and Potlatch Forest, Inc.'s, prospects were greatly enhanced when University of Idaho scientists, in cooperation with the Forest Service, Bureau of Land Management, and these major companies, bred taller yellow pine seedlings with a higher survival rate and white pine seedlings capable of resisting blister rust and other diseases. Genetic research introduced straighter trees that provided superior lumber. Proven tree-seed farming methods developed improved varieties for restocking burned or cutover lands. Congress facilitated the implementation of some of these changes with the adoption of national forest management legislation in 1976.[3]

John Fery, who is committed not only to Boise Cascade but to Idaho's quality of life, has been a strong supporter of the Boise Future Foundation at Boise State University and the Idaho Community Foundation, a recently organized funding vehicle for Idaho's social, educational, and cultural needs. An avid outdoorsman, Fery describes Idaho as "a land of high altitudes and low multitudes."[4]

## J. R. SIMPLOT COMPANY

As noted in Chapter Twenty-four, John Richard (J. R.) Simplot got an early start in business. As a young teenager he sorted potatoes for a local firm of potato buyers, fed cull potatoes to a drove of pigs he bought, purchased seed potatoes and rented land to grow the crop, and with a partner bought an electrically driven potato sorter in Ashton. The two later flipped a coin to see which one would keep it. Simplot won the toss. Physically strong, vigorous, quick to move and decisive in manner, he was as much at home on a horse as in an executive suite. The fiery competitor soon became the biggest rancher and feedlot operator along the Snake River Plain. By the end of World War II, as described earlier, he had become the nation's largest supplier of dehydrated potatoes and operated a million-dollar fertilizer plant at Pocatello.

In 1957, the same year Hansberger founded Boise Cascade, Simplot met Ray Kroc of McDonald's Fast Foods Restaurants. Simplot assured Kroc that he could make frozen french fries as tasty as fresh ones. The two struck a deal and Simplot has supplied about 80 percent of the fries served by McDonald's in the years since.

Wall Street could not believe that an empire as large as the one "Jack built" could have been based on potatoes. By the end of the 1960s Simplot's private conglomerate included six potato plants (the three largest at Burley, Heyburn, and Caldwell); two immense fertilizer plants; and many mining operations, ranches, and other enterprises in thirty-six states, Canada, and Europe and Asia. He processed more "spuds"—2.5 million pounds, enough to fill sixty freight cars, daily—than anyone else in the world. He also grew more wool and potatoes, ran more cattle (270,000) and sheep, owned more land (160,000 acres), and employed more people (6,600) than any other person in Idaho. With sales of $200 million per month, his personal wealth was estimated by *Fortune* at $200 million. He has never found it necessary to "go public." He has made the decisions, and he has enjoyed doing so. Simplot is a singer, as anyone who listens to him skiing down a slope or riding up a mountain at the break of day can testify. He also hunts, fishes, golfs, swims, and sails. He has an infectious sense of humor, and a booming voice; he does not smoke and seldom takes a drink. He serves on the board of several private and public corporations.

In 1978 Simplot expanded from fries to "chips." As the computer industry was getting started he made a major investment in Micron Technology Inc., a manufacturer of memory chips. Still resisting the sale of his $1.8 billion-a-year Idaho agribusiness, Simplot, who in 1990 was eighty-two, and whom *Fortune* regards as the richest man in Idaho, says simply, "I'm just an old farmer who's been a little lucky. . . . The smartest thing I did was hang on—not sell out—just keep building things bigger and bigger."[5]

Because of Esther Simplot's interest in the arts (she had pursued an opera career in New York before her marriage to Simplot in 1972), the Simplots have suported the Boise Opera, the Boise Art Museum, and the American Festival Ballet. Esther Simplot has spearheaded efforts to establish a permanent home or institute for the performing arts in Boise—a place where dance, opera, and music groups can share administrative costs and practice facilities.

## ORE-IDA FOODS, INC.

In 1934 brothers Nephi and Golden Grigg of Nampa developed land on the Vale (Oregon) Irrigation Project and grew sweet corn that they sold door-to-door. At the end of World War II they joined with Ross E. Butler, a native of Manard (near Fairfield) and graduate of the University of Idaho, to form Grigg Bros. Produce; they bought transport trucks and hauled the produce to California. Contracting with Oregon and Idaho farmers to grow their products, they shipped freshly packed corn to Portland, Salt Lake City, and Butte. By 1948 the Grigg Brothers Produce Company was shipping corn to Washington, D.C., New

York City, and Los Angeles. In 1949 the Griggs leased a bankrupt quick-freeze plant in Ontario, Oregon, to freeze corn on the cob; two years later they purchased the plant and formed Oregon Frozen Foods Company. To extend their processing season they added potatoes to the frozen line; spuds were the major money crop in eastern Oregon as well as in southwestern Idaho. As their methods of processing and marketing became more sophisticated, the Griggs's business flourished. With 100 employees they formed Ore-Ida Potato Products, Inc., in 1952. They also organized the Oregon Feeding Company to use the waste from the plant as livestock feed.

Starting with raw potatoes, the company took the produce from processing to quick freezing, to zero storage, and finally to national markets—the beginning of frozen french-fried potato production. Ore-Ida started researching original and new products. In addition to regular-cut and crinkle-cut french fries and shredded and southern-style hash browns, in 1953 they developed "Tater Tots," potato puffs that are small round bite-size shredded potatoes which can be baked in an oven to a golden brown, fried, or deep-fried, with natural, bacon, or onion flavoring. They became enormously popular with restaurants and the general public.

In 1961, when Ore-Ida was producing one-fourth of the nation's 350 million pounds of finished potato products, and the 1,300 employees were receiving $3 million in pay, the company went public under the name Ore-Ida Foods, Inc. That year a $2-million plant was added in Burley; a second Burley facility opened in 1964. In 1962 the product line was expanded by processing and marketing french-fried onion rings and fresh-frozen chopped Idaho-grown onions. Ore-Ida was named as the official supplier of instant flake and quick-frozen potatoes to the Century 21 exposition at the 1962 Seattle World's Fair. Sales continued to increase, to $31 million in 1964, with a net income of $1.3 million. The company now looked to expansion into the Midwest and East.

In an attempt to revive the Michigan potato industry, Ore-Ida contracted for potato acreage around Greenville, Michigan, and transferred several Idaho and Washington farmers and their families there to grow russet Burbank potatoes. A grower-exchange program was initiated in which selected Idaho and Michigan farmers were transported in the company plane from one state to the other to observe farming techniques and solve special problems. The company began construction on a processing plant at Greenville on land donated by the city. Michigan-grown potatoes started through the factory in August 1965.

Later in 1965 the Griggs and other investors exchanged their interests in the growing company for stock in the Pittsburgh-based H. J. Heinz Company, "The King of Ketchup." The company would now operate as a wholly owned Heinz subsidiary under the name Ore-Idaho Foods, Inc. The former management would remain for at least two years. In a revolutionary expansion move, the new Ore-Ida established a national retail brand for its frozen potato products. Emphasis was placed on commercial sales to restaurants and institutions rather than the consuming public. The brand became synonymous with retail frozen potatoes, and by 1970 annual income had surpassed $175 million. Heinz believed in decentralized management and left most of the direction to loyal Ore-Ida officials.

In 1968 Boise became the company's new home, locating the headquarters close to the producing area and to the necessary transportation facilities. In 1979, when the company built its own distinctive headquarters in the Parkcenter office development along the Boise River, Ore-Ida had become the nation's largest diversified frozen-food company with more than 350 separate items from frozen pizzas to cookies to vegetables. Potato products accounted for three-fourths of the selections. By 1990 the company employed more than 4,000. The company began sponsorship in 1984 of Ore-Ida's Women's Challenge, a world-class cycling competition solely for women.[6]

## ALBERTSON'S

Joseph A. Albertson, who came with his parents from Oklahoma to Caldwell at age three, worked as a young man on a ranch, cleared land of sagebrush six feet high, and milked cows (six each night and morning). In 1927 at the age of twenty-one he was hired by Safeway, where he remained twelve years, managing stores in Boise, western Kansas, Emmett, Meridian, and Ogden, Utah. In 1939 Albertson joined L. S. Skaggs with a combined investment of $25,000 and they established their own self-service store. Albertson used his own $5,000 in savings and borrowed $7,500 from his aunt to fulfill his half of the bargain. When the first store opened in Boise, Albertson—the store operator—worked eighteen hours a day. To compete with the six Safeway stores in the Boise area, he offered his customers extras: the first in-store bakery, the first magazine rack, automatic doughnut and popcorn machines, and ice cream made by Albertson right on the store premises. He sold the largest ice cream cones in the area, survived a five-month price war, and ended up with a healthy profit. Within a year Albertson-Skaggs opened a second store at Nampa and a third in Boise. The nucleus of a supermarket chain was established.

The Albertson-Skaggs partnership was dissolved in 1945 and Albertson's was incorporated. By 1959, when the corporation went public, Albertson's had fifty-one stores, mostly in the Far West. The corporation had divisions for chickens and turkeys, a brooder farm and an egg farm. In 1970 Albertson's formed a partnership with Skaggs Drug Stores—which originated in the 1915 American Falls venture described in Chapter Twenty-two —to operate combination food-drug units. The football-field-sized stores, stocked with 30,000 items, were immensely successful. Shoppers not only bought food but also kept pushing their carts up and down other aisles, picking off cosmetics, perfumes, pharmacy products, camera supplies, electrical equipment—goods with higher profit margins. Ironically, this blending of food and drugs in one store was so successful that after seven years the two firms divided their fifty-eight jumbo-size stores in what they called an "amicable separation." Albertson's thereafter maintained twenty-nine of these formerly joint stores in the West and Southeast.

Albertson's continued to build and add stores and in 1974 reached its first $1 billion in sales. By the end of 1978 the figure surpassed $2 billion, and in 1983 sales exceeded $4 billion. By 1985 the firm employed 35,000 people and operated 434 retail outlets in 17 states. These included 81 superstores, 90 combination food-drug units, and 263 conventional supermarkets and other stores. By 1990 Albertson's was the sixth largest supermarket company in the nation and the nineteenth largest merchandising firm. The company operated 540 stores in seventeen western and southern states, employed 55,000 people, and grossed $7 billion.

Joe Albertson's success may be attributed to four factors. He worked hard; he believed in hiring high-quality executives and letting them run the company; he admonished all to give tender, loving care to customers; and he tried to run a big store that had low prices, convenience, and wide selection, and at the same time a specialty store in terms of quality, personal service, and specialized attention.

Albertson, who died in 1993, and his wife, Kathryn, whom he married in 1929, have made generous gifts to many Idaho philanthropic causes.

The other large merchandising firm, Safeway Stores, Inc., goes back to Marion Barton Skaggs and his grocery store in American Falls in 1915. In 1926 he merged his 428 stores with Sam Seelig's California-based business to form Safeway. By 1931 there were 3,500 retail outlets. The firm moved overseas in the 1960s with store operations in Great Britain, Germany, and Australia. By the 1970s Safeway was the world's largest food retailer.

## MORRISON-KNUDSEN

Harry W. Morrison, perhaps the most world famous of all of Idaho's entrepreneurs, was a dynamo and a superb organizer who contracted for many substantial projects—in Idaho and elsewhere. But contractors, unlike the industrial and mercantile executives described above, do not turn out the same product or service twice. No two buildings, bridges, roads, or dams are alike. The contractor sets up a factory to make one product in one place at one time, then dismantles it completely when he has finished. His bidding is risky and the inevitable gains and losses have to be spread over a number of jobs.

Major projects may go on for several years. Even before the first shovelful of earth is turned, the contractor has to establish a firm price for the job—with only a glimmer of what may happen to wages and the costs of material. One serious mistake in judging costs can finish his company.[7]

A contractor, of whom Harry Morrison was surely one of the top two or three in the nation, has to be a construction stiff, finance man, designer, politician, and human-relations expert. He has to know more engineering than his engineers, more about costs than his accountants, be his own chief salesman, know the details on progress at dozens of different projects, travel 200,000 miles a year, and survive on a few hours of sleep each night. "He had to be able to deal, equally well, with bankers, working stiffs, clients, project engineers, his competition, and officials of foreign governments. If he slips up anywhere along the line, he doesn't stay big."[8]

Morrison enjoyed his work; he claimed it was his hobby, but he also devoured mystery novels, organized barbershop quartets, and sang and played the guitar dressed in a white suit at company picnics in Municipal Park in Boise. With his own private plane, Morrison was "on the go" 80 percent of the time. His wife of forty-three years, Ann Daly, who was constantly at his side and traveled the globe to visit the far-flung projects of the company, was born and raised in Idaho and published a book of her travels, *Those Were the Days* (1951), which *Time* described as "a letter from home to 5,000 children spread around the world." In Ann Morrison Park in Boise is a bronze plaque with the inscription: "She knew the shrines, the people, the cities of faraway lands . . . yet dearest of all was this, her home, the place she knew as Boise the Beautiful." After her death in 1957, Harry married Velma Shannon; she was largely responsible for the opening of the Morrison Center for the Performing Arts in Boise in 1984.

Morris H. Knudsen, who was the first president of the firm, relinquished the presidency to Morrison in 1939; Morrison retained the position until 1960, when he became chairman of the board, and he served in that capacity until 1968.

Having started at the bottom, Morrison, the younger of the two men, knew his business from the ground up; he was willing to take risks on bidding for contracts; he worked for the firm; he was not insulated by a heavy organization; and he was never far from the flying dirt. Morrison got along well with labor because he was loyal to the company's employees, just as he expected them to be loyal to their boss. He was socially mobile; that is, he easily made the shift from the excavation site to the embassy reception.[9]

During the 1960s and 1970s, Morrison-Knudsen continued to expand in its traditional work—the large-scale, complex construction jobs. In 1964, for example, M-K's restless, far-flung organization was building something—a factory, a missile base, a pipeline, an airport, a power plant, tunnels, a bridge, a dam—at 317 locations in the United States and thirty-two other countries.[10] In 1964 the company recorded about $320 million in gross revenue.

Morrison-Knudsen also became involved in shipbuilding, contract coal mining, commercial real estate development, coating steel pipe for offshore oil and natural-gas lines, aircraft maintenance and repair, locomotive rebuilding, fabrication of steel, and power-generating units. A subsidiary built a 125-acre industrial park and office complex that eventually housed Ore-Ida, Albertson's, and other Boise businesses.

With many projects worldwide, M-K decided in 1969 to centralize most of its international management operations in a massive headquarters complex in Boise. With approximately 30,000 employees in 1990, about half international and half domestic, the M-K operation grossed $2 billion per year—more than double the revenues of Idaho's state government. Morrison died in 1971, aged eighty-five. *Time* magazine called him "the man who has done more than anyone else to change the face of the earth."[11]

Subsequent presidents of Morrison-Knudsen have included John Bonny, Bertram L. Perkins, William H. McMurren, William J. Deasy, and William M. Agee. Agee, who was president in Idaho's Centennial year, grew up in Boise near J. R. Simplot and took his first corporate plane ride on a DC-3 with Harry Morrison; Morrison-Knudsen had an interest in Agee's father's steel fabrication business. A graduate of the University of Idaho with an MBA from Harvard, Agee was initially employed in the accounting department at Albertson's, then worked for Robert Hansberger in the expanding days of Boise Cascade. He was thus under the influence of several of Idaho's extraordinary entrepreneurs. Agee, who became chief executive officer of Bendix Corporation when he was only thirty-eight, is expanding M-K's interests into light-rail transportation, waste disposal, and the design and construction of the Super Collider.

In June 1991 the Texas High Speed Rail Authority picked Texas TGV, a consortium led by Morrison-Knudsen, to build the 200-mph train line connecting the state's largest cities—and to build the $6-billion project without public money. During the same month M-K was chosen to lead a $1-billion joint venture to design, build, and operate a toll road that would be the main route between metropolitan Denver and the new Denver International Airport, which was scheduled to open in 1993.

## SUN VALLEY

In 1936 W. Averell Harriman developed Sun Valley as an attraction for national and international luminaries—European and Asian royalty; stars of screen, opera, and ballet; nationally famed authors and sportspersons. The resort featured the first "chair-type lifts" in the world, and a summer season was opened in 1938 that offered swimming, horseback riding, fishing, hunting, archery, tennis, and a nine-hole golf course. A stewardship of Union Pacific Railroad, the resort was noted for its high quality accommodations, food, entertainment, and sports, but it was not a money-maker. The corporation is said to have lost a half-million dollars each year—a fine tax write-off but still no delight to the board of directors.

In 1964 Union Pacific asked the Janss Corporation to assess the condition of the Sun Valley complex and present plans for a major restoration. Janss estimated that a total facelift would cost $6 million, a price Union Pacific was unwilling to pay to revive a property that had never yielded a profit. Bill Janss, who thought the potential was good, made the railroad an undisclosed offer; Union Pacific accepted.

Janss, a champion skier, took over sole ownership in 1968 and changed the tone of the resort from a gathering place of the rich and famous to an appealing area where the average family would want to spend their vacation. Condominiums were built near the lodge (the first condominiums in Idaho), a new mall was built to make the resort more self-sufficient, new runs were built, and new lifts installed. In 1977 Janss sold the Sun Valley Corporation to Earl Holding, native of Salt Lake City and president of Little America Hotels and Resorts and an executive of Sinclair Oil Corporation. Holding and his wife, Carol Orme Holding, who worked with him on the project, suspended the building policy; there would be no more condominiums or private residences constructed within the complex. Thousands of trees and shrubs were planted along ponds and housing areas, restaurants were renovated, the lodge was completely reroofed, and the remodeled lodge dining room was furnished with crystal chandeliers from Venice and silk wall coverings and draperies from England. All the rooms were remodeled and refurnished, marble bathrooms emplaced, and electric heat and television cables installed in each room. The ski lifts, which include three high-speed quad lifts, in 1990 could transport 22,000 people each hour. Excellent ski instructors are available, horse trainers direct dressage exercises, swimmers enjoy the outdoor heated pools (with water maintained at 100 degrees for winter comfort), hikers scale the mountains, and skaters skim over the ice at the rink. There are dazzling ice shows, sleigh rides are popular, and shoppers fill the mall. There are several elegant restaurants on Mt. Baldy.

Sun Valley Resort has the world's largest automated snowmaking system, all computerized, which covers 435 acres—over half the groomed area on Mt. Baldy. The sophisticated system has built-in temperature and humidity control and three cooling towers that cool 2,800 gallons of water per minute to thirty-two degrees or less. Water from the Warm Springs side of the mountain and a private well on the river side is processed by the $8-million machine to create consistently good snow conditions from a dense base to a very light powder. The system is reliable and gives the resort confidence in making reservations for guests to ski.[12]

## TRUS-JOIST CORPORATION AND COEUR D'ALENE RESORT

Arthur Troutner, an architect and self-taught engineer who had built a number of futuristic edifices in the Boise and Sun

Valley areas, invented an open-web, lightweight truss or joist that combined wood with webbing of hollow steel tubing. In 1960 he joined with Harold Thomas, a forester who owned a business selling lumber and glue-laminated beams, to form the Trus-Joist Corporation. The firm built headquarters in Boise in 1964. Further inventions by Troutner have resulted in a joist series and a lumber manufactured with veneer running in parallel grain permanently bonded under heat and pressure in a continuous process. The high-grade laminated structural product is marketed directly to builders of roofs, floors, and windows. The firm's special lumber is used in the electric-utility industry for transmission towers, cross arms, and transformer racks; concrete forming; highway signposts; furniture frames; bleacher seats; and spars for crop-dusting airplanes. By 1990 TJ International, as the company was renamed, had 1,500 employees at its thirteen plants in the United States and others in Canada and Asia.[13] Its president since 1979 is Walter C. Minnick, a native of Walla Walla, Washington, who had earlier served as an assistant to the President of the United States. Minnick has also been active in the Bogus Basin Recreation Association, The Wilderness Society, Boise Future Foundation, Idaho Conservation League, and the Nature Conservancy.

The enterprise and ambitious building plans of a father-and-son team, Burl and Duane Hagadone, remade central Coeur d'Alene. In the early 1930s Burl Hagadone, a native of Kootenai County whose family moved to Coeur d'Alene when he was a young boy, became publisher of the *Coeur d'Alene Press*. He also was co-owner and president of publishing companies in The Dalles, Oregon; Flagstaff, Arizona; and Santa Maria, California; and joined with Scripps League Newspapers in the operation of radio stations at Spokane, Coeur d'Alene, and Pocatello. In addition, he owned part of Inland Empire Stores in Kellogg and Wallace and Newport, Washington. As editor and investor he pioneered the development of irrigation in north Idaho and the introduction of natural gas as a source of energy. His son Duane—at times a controversial figure—inherited the *Coeur d'Alene Press* and other holdings; collected additional properties in the area, including a large apartment complex; and built the Coeur d'Alene Resort—a world-class hotel, restaurant, and convention center with a floating golf course out on the lake. The $60-million Coeur d'Alene Resort blends big-city lifestyle with an Idaho setting rich in natural beauty and outdoor attractions. Hagadone also is part owner of other accommodations in northern Idaho and has provided assistance to the Kutenai tribe in constructing and operating a prize-winning inn in Bonners Ferry. The Coeur d'Alene Resort and nearby Silver Mountain ski area are to northern Idaho what Sun Valley is to southern Idaho.

## IDAHO POWER COMPANY

Political scientists have often noted that one of the most powerful political forces in the Gem State is the Idaho Power Company. The company captured the national spotlight in the 1960s during the Hells Canyon public/private power conflict. The story of Idaho Power is centered on Sidney Zollicoffer Mitchell, who grew up on a plantation in Dadeville, Alabama. When he was seventeen, Mitchell was appointed to the U.S. Naval Academy in Annapolis; he graduated in 1883 and spent two years at sea during which time he installed an incandescent lighting system on the U.S.S. *Trenton*. In 1885, he resigned his commission to work for Thomas A. Edison, who had just opened his Pearl Street electric generating plant in New York City. After intensive training in electric-current generation technique and management in the infant electric-power industry, Mitchell moved to Seattle as sales agent of the Edison Electric Light Company for the Pacific Northwest. Since the Northwest had no electric plants that could use Edison's equipment, Mitchell, who was only twenty-three, proceeded to organize electric companies and help them install the generators, transformers, motors, and control apparatus he was marketing. He established the Northwest Electric Supply and Construction Company, which, in the next two years, organized electric lighting companies in Washington, Oregon, Idaho, and British Columbia.

Mitchell built two early plants in Idaho, at Hailey and on the Ridenbaugh Canal in Boise, both in 1887.[14] In 1892 the Edison companies merged with Thomson-Houston Company to form the General Electric Company, which Mitchell joined. In 1905, with General Electric's backing, Mitchell set up a holding company, the Electric Bond & Share Company, and served as its president until his retirement in 1933. In return for a fee, Electric Bond & Share, which became the largest holding company in the industry, provided financial, managerial, accounting, and technical assistance to operating companies that served small towns and cities. Drawing on his experience in the Pacific Northwest, Mitchell consolidated a number of small, contiguous operating companies, enabling them to achieve economies through common management to take advantage of large, centrally located turbine generators that could handle diverse "load" conditions.

An example of the service of Electric Bond & Share was the organization in 1915 of Idaho Power Company. In common with the proliferation of electric facilities elsewhere in the nation, plants were built with money from promoters in Chicago, Pittsburgh, New York, and New England to serve many new communities along the Snake River Plain. Companies were established, they were acquired by other companies, and they provided power for the operation of irrigation pumps, concentrating mills, interurban railways, and businesses and homes in the growing towns and cities. Between ruthless competition and the heavy costs in acquiring new technology, most of the companies ended up in receivership. The 7,000 investors in the bankrupt companies could pocket their losses or work out a combination that would furnish hope of recompense.

Dismayed that the whole economy of southern Idaho was in danger, based as it was on irrigation, Calvin Cobb, editor of the Boise *Idaho Statesman*, appealed to Mitchell (whom he had known since 1887) to work out a reorganization. Ten unrelated generating units stretched from American Falls to Rupert, Burley, Twin Falls, Buhl, Castleford, and on to Mountain Home, Boise, Nampa, Caldwell, Payette, and Weiser and ultimately connected with the coastal service in Portland. The earnings of these companies that served 31,000 business and residential customers were miniscule—far less than the interest charges on their bonds. Seven of the companies, with outstanding securities having a face value of $49 million, were in receivership in the U.S. District Court in Boise; the other three, seriously wounded, were expected to follow.

Mitchell recommended a complete integration of all thc companies and elimination of destructive competition, duplicated facilities, and personnel. The new company would take title to the property of all the companies free and clear of existing liens so financing could be raised. Mitchell insisted that the original directors of Idaho Power be chosen by vote of the customers and that the president be elected by residents of the communities served. In this way the common Idaho fear of being dominated by Wall Street—something of a "folk enemy"—would be avoided. The first president of Idaho Power was Frank F. Johnson, a vice president of Boise City National Bank, who ran Idaho Power until his death twenty-five years later.

Johnson, who was reared in Colorado as the son of a surveyor and mining engineer, moved to Idaho in 1887 when he was twenty-five and served as assistant cashier of the Bank of Murray. He later established the Bank of North Idaho at Murray; moved to Wallace, where he founded the First National Bank of Wallace; and removed to Boise in 1910 to serve as cashier and vice president of Boise City National Bank. He helped organize the First National Bank of Twin Falls and the Farmers State Bank of Nez Perce. Under the expert counsel of Sidney Mitchell, Johnson's focus was to reconcile the various business, financial, and regional interests involved in the operation of Idaho Power. Once the stockholders and bondholders had been induced to participate, Idaho Power Company took title to all the properties of the predecessor companies on July 31, 1916. The principal role of Electric Bond & Share was that of an investment engineer and banker. The reorganization was a success. Since then the company has furnished unlimited power to the residents of Idaho at low rates.

After World War II Idaho Power built six dams along the Snake River and in 1955, led by Tom Roach, was awarded federal licenses to create dams at Brownlee, Oxbow, and Hells Canyon. The company also cooperated in providing power to water the arid land of the Snake River Plain by pumping from the Snake River as well as from underground sources. By the mid-1980s nearly 2 million acres were under irrigation pumping. Idaho Power's cheap hydro power has helped develop one of the nation's largest irrigation empires and promoted the development of industrial products from agricultural crops. The utility has established parks and recreation areas at dam sites and built nesting places on its high-voltage lines for birds of prey. It funds fish hatcheries that protect and increase the runs of salmon and steelhead from the Pacific Ocean to their spawning grounds in the central Idaho mountains.

Idaho is also served by Utah Power and Light, which has four plants in Idaho; Washington Water Power Company, with customers in northern Idaho; Pacific Power and Light, with customers in the Sandpoint area; Citizens Utilities Company, serving Wallace; and several municipal and cooperative systems, including those of Idaho Falls, Weiser, Soda Springs, Bonners Ferry, and the towns of Burley, Declo, Heyburn, Rupert, and Albion.

## LESS DRAMATIC, SMALLER ENTERPRISES

In 1900 George L. Crookham II married Grace Steunenberg, a sister of Governor Frank Steunenberg, and in 1911 founded a seed business in Caldwell. Popcorn was first featured; sweet corn seed and onion seed were soon added. By 1931 the firm ranked first in the nation in the production of hybrid sweet corn seed, all produced in Treasure Valley.

In 1929 George Crookham III assumed ownership of the company and developed additional hybrids. He also served as Caldwell mayor, as a state legislator, and as chairman of the Idaho Water Resource Board. By 1990 the Crookham Company was shipping 6 million pounds a year to seed companies in the United States and to many countries in Europe and Asia. Crookham allocates about $1 million a year to research, constantly improving hybrid products. In addition to sweet corn, the company is also first in the nation in the production of hybrid popcorn seed, hybrid onion seed, hybrid carrot seed, and lettuce seed. New corn hybrids represent a major breakthrough, being sweeter than other varieties and having a shelf life of fifteen days.[15]

Idaho's other large seed business, Rogers Brothers Seed Company, now Rogers NK Seed Company, originated in New York in 1876 and built the nation's best-equipped seed plant at Idaho Falls in 1911. Other large seed plants were subsequently constructed in Twin Falls and Nampa. Southern Idaho is an excellent area for seed production because the dry climate produces disease-free seed of exceptional quality. In 1990, the Company expanded its focus beyond large seed when it merged with the Vegetable Seed Division of Northrup King, a sister company. Now, in addition to peas, beans, corn, and dry beans, Rogers NK is a leading supplier of seed for thirteen small seeded crops including broccoli, brussels sprouts, cabbage, cantaloupe, carrots, cauliflower, cucumbers, peppers, radish, spinach, squash, tomatoes, and watermelon. The company has developed numerous new varieties that meet users' requirements for cultivation, handling or processing, and consumption.[16]

Mining has always played an important role in the Idaho economy. By incorporating some remarkable new approaches to metal production developed by private and government researchers, most of Idaho's mining districts have remained in operation. Some, of course, have shut down, like the large, now outdated Bunker Hill smelter at Kellogg that closed in 1981. Kellogg residents have diversified and expanded their options by developing a magnificent ski resort. After one hundred years, with workings extending far below sea level, Idaho mines have produced about $5 billion worth of ore.

Many of the nearly 3,000 miners in Idaho in 1990 were involved in large open-pit ventures that process a high volume of low-grade ore by utilizing new equipment and chemical processing systems only recently available. With the assistance of sophisticated sampling procedures developed by the Bureau of Mines and Geology at the University of Idaho and the U.S. Geological Survey, and by innovations in technology, miners have operated open-pit systems at Delamar, Stibnite, Thunder Mountain, Volcano, and Clayton. Not far from Leesburg an open-pit operation promises to surpass all of Idaho's previous gold production, including that of Boise Basin.

Sunshine Mining Company descends from the discovery in 1884 of a silver-bearing lode on Big Creek, near Kellogg. The company's shafts and workings extend to a depth of 6,000 feet (3,300 feet below sea level), and Sunshine—which moved its headquarters from Kellogg to Boise in 1984—has produced 300 million ounces of silver, more than the combined total of all the mines in the famous Comstock Lode of Nevada. As a by-product of the ore the company produces antimony, used to harden lead and as a fireproofing agent for textiles. A recently constructed refinery has a daily capacity of 50,000 ounces of silver and 1,200 ounces of gold, in addition to 7,000 pounds of copper. Aware of environmental problems in both air and water, the company completed a thirty-five-acre impoundment pond in 1979 to control water pollution. Its refineries are equipped with a process that virtually eliminates emission of sulfur dioxide into the atmosphere.

The largest domestic producer of new silver, Hecla Corporation, has continued to expand and has moved its headquarters to Coeur d'Alene. The company's Lucky Friday shaft, reaching down 7,700 feet, is the deepest shaft in the world outside South Africa. The company has broadened its holdings to include ranches, the Escalante silver mine in Utah, and other properties.

One entrepreneur who began work for Hecla and subsequently took advantage of opportunities to create new enterprises in north Idaho was Harry F. Magnuson. Born in Wallace, son of a Scandinavian butcher and a mother of Italian ancestry who was born in Harrison (just north of Chatcolet on Lake Coeur d'Alene), Magnuson studied at Idaho State University and the University of Idaho and, as part of his active duty with the Navy during World War II, earned an MBA at the Harvard Business School. After three years of service as a naval supply officer in the Pacific, Magnuson returned to Wallace and opened an accounting office. When the mining industry went into a decline after the Korean War, Magnuson purchased Golconda Mining Company stock; when the company began to earn profits in the 1960s he acquired properties in Wallace—including the First National Bank of Wallace, which has since expanded to a dozen branches under the name First National Bank of North Idaho. (FNB was taken over by First Security in 1992.) As earnings increased, Magnuson engaged in land developments, including the University Inn of Moscow and shopping centers in Lewiston and Coeur d'Alene. When the Bunker Hill Company curtailed operations in Silver Valley in 1982, Magnuson and three other Idaho businessmen joined to purchase the Bunker Hill facilities and mines. Dedicated to the preservation of Wallace despite declining mining fortunes, Magnuson received the Idaho Distinguished Preservationist Award in 1989 and was chairman of the Idaho Centennial Commission.

Since 1970 Idaho has also developed a significant computer-products industry. American Microsystems of Santa Clara, California, established a plant in Pocatello in 1970. Hewlett-Packard, another California firm, followed, opening a larger plant in Boise in 1975; by 1990 it employed 3,000 there. The company produces magnetic disc drives, mass storage systems, and laser printers in Boise. Micron Technology, Inc., another notable Boise corporation, started in 1978. A Zilog plant was established in Nampa in 1979. All together, by 1990 Idaho had eight such plants, each with more than one hundred employees. J. R. Simplot, whose spirit of innovation helped finance the start-up of a micro memory chip firm, contributed $5 million to establish the Simplot/Micron Center for Technology at Boise State University in 1988.

New technology, influenced as it has been by scientific research and industrial innovation, has likewise contributed to Idaho's transportation, communications, and banking. Airports in Boise and Pocatello, constructed originally for military purposes, were enlarged and improved to serve many other cities. Such sophisticated facilities have enabled corporate administrators like those of Boise Cascade and Morrison-Knudsen to remain in Idaho and yet manage sprawling operations in many other states and nations. Improved highways have aided not only the building industries but also the tourist trade.

Idaho's first telephone exchange was opened in Hailey in September 1883, a second in Boise that December. By 1890 the state's exchanges consisted of about 500 subscribers each of whom paid $150 per year for service. Nationwide telephone service was routed through Salt Lake City in 1915. Rocky Mountain Bell, which bought up most of the smaller exchanges in 1898, became part of Mountain States Telephone and Telegraph (later known as Mountain Bell) in 1911. Long-distance lines were strung across southern Idaho in 1928 and 1929. Mountain Bell converted to dial telephones in 1952 and in 1965 instituted direct dialing of long-distance calls from Idaho to any place in the United States. The first electronic switching system in Boise was installed in 1970 and was updated with a digital system in 1982. In 1985 Mountain Bell put into operation in Idaho a light-guide cable system based on fiber optics that included a 270-mile long-distance link between Boise and Pocatello. Instead of electricity this system uses laser-generated light in tiny glass fibers to carry telephone conversations, video, and data. Strung in a cable one-half inch in diameter, the fibers, as thin as human hair, carry as many messages as seven copper cables each the size of a man's forearm. At one time Mountain Bell also used the light guide to carry local calls.[17]

The first telephone operator in Hailey in 1883 was twelve-year-old Nathan Kingsbury, an apprentice for the *Wood River Times*. Kingsbury, who later became vice-president of American Telephone and Telegraph Company (AT&T), was author of the 1913 Kingsbury Commitment with the U.S. Justice Department that crafted the interconnected telephone network that linked the United States until federal courts forced the breakup of the giant corporation in January 1984. In 1987, Mountain Bell, of which southern Idaho was still a part, became U.S. West, headquartered in Denver. At the time Mountain Bell had 260,000 Idaho customers, with about 500,000 telephones in service, all south of the Salmon River. Those north of the river were covered by General Telephone Company (twenty-eight communities, including Moscow); Pacific Northwest Bell (eight communities, including Lewiston); and smaller independent telephone companies. Some southern Idaho communities also had independent companies. Rupert and Paul, for example, are served by Project Mutual Telephone Company, organized after construction of the Minidoka Dam drew settlers to the region.

The operations of Idaho First National Bank, First Security Corporation, First Interstate Bank, and various local banks were revolutionized by computer equipment that utilized transcontinental automatic tellers in accessing deposits. First National, chartered to assist miners and mining-town businesses in 1867, grew out of B. M. DuRell's and C. W. Moore's 1864 Boise and Silver City banking services. After its brief suspension in 1932, First National resumed business, changed its name to Idaho First National, and established a statewide branch-banking system. It became the principal affiliate of Moore Financial Group, a holding company formed in 1981 and recognized as one of the top 100 banks in the nation with $3 billion in assets. In 1976 ground was broken for the nineteen-story Idaho First Plaza, tallest structure in Idaho, the Moore Group's headquarters. By 1990 seventy-four branches of the bank, now West One, were located around the state, with others in Utah, Oregon, and eastern Washington.

First Security Corporation, whose charter traces back to the Anderson Brothers Bank of Idaho Falls, founded in 1866, was organized as America's first multiple-bank holding company in 1928. Principal owners were Marriner and George Eccles—sons of David Eccles, who had earned a large income supplying lumber to Wood River mines and the Utah and Northern and Oregon Short Line railroads in the 1880s and by manufacturing lumber in Oregon from 1888 until his death in 1912. In the years that followed, Marriner and several associates acquired seventeen banks in Utah, Idaho, and Wyoming and organized First Security Corporation to manage them. By 1990 First Security Corporation had eighty branches in Idaho, extending from Bonners Ferry near the Canadian border to Preston on the Utah-Idaho boundary. The IBM system installed in its central operations system in 1983 is said to be one of the most advanced in the world. With $7 billion in assets, First Security is also among the largest banks in the nation.

The Bank of Idaho originated in 1957 with the merger of Continental State Bank of Boise, First National Bank of Caldwell, and the Bank of Eastern Idaho in Idaho Falls. In 1964 Western Bancorp constructed the thirteen-story Bank of Idaho headquarters building in Boise. The next year the bank joined Western Bancorporation, founded the previous year. With a national charter obtained in 1973, the firm became known as First Interstate Bank of Idaho in 1981. First Interstate Bancorp now operates in thirteen western states and has thirty-four international offices. The eighth largest banking organization in the United States, First Interstate was the first in Idaho to install fully automated day and night tellers, then known as "Ida." Using the newest technology, the bank constructed a million-dollar data-processing facility; in 1978 the bank established a communication network that connected all branch terminals and offices. The system allows tellers to check customer accounts in any First Interstate Bank.

The largest state-chartered bank in Idaho during the 1980s was the Idaho Bank & Trust Company, with assets approximating $500 million. Its story is one of systematic expansion. This bank opened in 1934 (after the passage of the branch-banking law of 1933) with the merger of four banks: State Bank of Blackfoot, founded in 1904; Bear Lake Bank of Paris, organized in 1905; Burley National Bank, opened in 1919; and the Power County Bank of American Falls, dating back to 1924. The Paris branch was closed in 1934, as was the bank in American Falls; the assets were moved to Pocatello, the new headquarters of the bank, which at the time of organization had assets of $1.5 million. By 1949 deposits exceeded $18 million. There were dramatic increases in facilities and deposits in the 1950s. Branches were opened in Paul, Chubbuck, Westwood Village in Pocatello, American Falls, Boise, Caldwell, Lewiston, and Nampa. In 1973 Idaho Bank & Trust acquired the Bank of Central Idaho, with branches in Grangeville, Kooskia, and Riggins.

In 1975 other branches were opened in Boise, Burley, and Pocatello, and in 1977 the bank acquired the First Bank of Troy with branches in Moscow and Plummer. Headquarters were moved to Boise in 1982, at which time the bank had twenty-five branches in Idaho and a computer center in Pocatello.

On October 16, 1988, Idaho Bank & Trust became a part of Key Bank Corporation, a multi-billion-dollar, multiregional bank holding company serving customers and businesses in smaller cities and towns along the country's northern tier. Headquartered in Albany, New York, Key Bank has 600 full-service branches in the northeast and northwest. In 1991 Key Bank of Idaho became Idaho's fourth largest bank as it took over the Treasure Valley Bank locations in Cascade, McCall, New Meadows, Midvale, Weiser, Fruitland, Emmett, and Boise. Key Bank then had thirty-nine branches in Idaho, with assets in excess of $825 million.

## MICROENTERPRISES

Although giants like Morrison-Knudsen, Boise-Cascade, J. R. Simplot, and Albertson's and their executives may get most of the national attention, one must not overlook the role of hundreds of microenterprises in providing modest primary and secondary incomes for Idaho's citizens. Lumped together, these "Lone Rangers" in economic development furnish the state with a sizable share of its total income. They include persons with small sewing jobs, furniture makers, toy-makers, pushcart peddlers, small factory owners—free enterprises in their most basic and spontaneous form. They are a business counterpart to subsistence farming, an alternative to welfare dependency. Some are sole sources of income; others consist of people earning second incomes out of their homes by selling dresses, caring for children, styling hair, writing for a newspaper, teaching a prekindergarten class, repairing electronic equipment, or painting portraits. These small undertakings, important to the individuals served, also deserve mention in Idaho's history.

## CONCLUSION

As Idaho approached its centennial year, the state was becoming less and less a producer of raw materials to be exported for processing elsewhere. Instead, the state's people were demonstrating different kinds of skills that are of value to the nation. Tourism is a fast-growing industry; manufacturing is also prospering. Light industries have increased momentum; the state's economy has become more diversified and more stable. As always, the state has benefited from infusions of eastern and coastal capital, and from helpful federal programs. Clearly, thanks to its amazing private entrepreneurs, Idaho is making more of her own way.

## CHAPTER TWENTY-NINE: SOURCES

*General.* Susan M. Stacy, ed., *Conversations* (Boise: Idaho Educational Public Broadcasting Foundation, 1990); Carlos A. Schwantes, *In Mountain Shadows: A History of Idaho* (Lincoln: University of Nebraska Press, 1991); *Here We Have Idaho: People Make the Difference* (Boise: Idaho Centennial Foundation, 1990); Wells and Hart, *Idaho: Gem of the Mountains*, particularly 176–244; and Wells, *Boise: An Illustrated History*. I am grateful for the opportunity to read "Industrial Development," an unpublished essay by Merle Wells. A splendid general introduction is Jonathan Hughes, *The Vital Few: The Entrepreneur and American Economic Progress*, expanded ed. (New York: Oxford University Press, 1986), which gives insightful portraits of men and women whose individual enterprise helped to carry the American economy forward from colonial times to the present. The book also has a helpful bibliography.

Sources on specific persons and businesses are given below.

On Hansberger, Fery, and Boise Cascade: "An Idaho Woodsman Makes the Chips Fly," *Business Week*, October 12, 1963, 144–48;

"Action in Idaho," *Time* 82 (December 20, 1963):78–79; Thomas G. Alexander, "It's Grow or Die at Boise Cascade," *Fortune* 72 (December 1965):180–83, 214–19; "Building a Case for Youth," *Business Week*, February 24, 1968, 148–53; John McDonald, "Bob Hansberger Shows How To Grow Without Becoming a Conglomerate," *Fortune* 80 (October 1969):134–38, 198–202; "Bob Hansberger Rides Again," *Dun's Review* 104 (September 1974):12–27; "John Fery Puts His Own Stamp on Boise," *Business Week*, June 1, 1974, 72–74.

On J. R. Simplot: *Declo—My Town and My People* (Burley: Declo History Commission, 1974), esp. 635–42; William E. Davis, "Portrait of an Industrialist," *Idaho Yesterdays* 11 (Summer 1967):2–7; "John Richard Simplot," in Beal and Wells, *History of Idaho*, 3:2–4; Charles J. V. Murphy, "Jack Simplot and His Private Conglomerate," *Fortune* 78 (August 1968):122–26, 166–72; "The Great Potato Bust," *Time* 107 (June 7, 1976):70; B. Saporito, "Cashing in on Food and Drink," *Fortune* 116 (October 12, 1987):152–53; E. F. Cone, "Shootout at the OKC Corral," *Forbes* 140 (December 14, 1987): 86–88; G. Eisler, "Potato Power," *Forbes*, 142 (July 11, 1988):137; D. Glick, "The Magic of 'Mr. Spud,'" *Newsweek* 114 (November 27, 1989):63; "J. R. Simplot: Still Hustling, After All These Years," *Business Week*, September 3, 1990, 60–65.

On Ore-Ida: Robert C. Alberts, "The Good Provider," *American Heritage* 23 (February 1972):26–47; Lisa Borsuk, "A Dream Became World's Largest Frozen Food Processor," Ontario (Oregon) *Daily Argus Observer*, ca. 1983, undated photocopy supplied by Ore-Ida; *The Ore-Ida Story*, ca. 1982, copy supplied by Ore-Ida; *Ore-Ida Foods, Inc.: 30 Years of Growing*, a company publication, 1981; *The Tater Tot: A Success Story*, 1989, copy supplied by F. Nephi Grigg; Kerry Hannon, "The King of Ketchup," *Forbes*, 141 (March 21, 1988):58–62; and Gregory L. Miles, "Heinz Ain't Broke, But It's Doing a Lot of Fixing," *Business Week*, December 11, 1989, 84–86.

On Albertson: "Home-Baked Bread, Anyone? TV Sets? Blue Jeans?" *Forbes* 119 (May 15, 1977):144–48; Barry Stavro, "In the Bag," *Forbes* 132 (December 5, 1983):118; Marc Beauchamp, "Food for Thought," *Forbes* 143 (April 17, 1989):73; Norm Alster, "One Man's Poison," *Forbes* 144 (October 16, 1989):38–39.

On Morrison-Knudsen: "Harry Winford Morrison," Beal and

Wells, *History of Idaho*, 3:49–50; *The eM-Kayan* 46 (March 1987), 75th Anniversary Issue; "Dams for Afghans," *Business Week*, February 11, 1950, 65–66; "The Master Builder," *Time* 55 (May 29, 1950):80–81; *Diary of Ann Morrison: Those Were the Days* (Boise: eM-Kayan Press, 1951); "The Earth Mover," *Time* 63 (May 3, 1954):86–93; "Carrying the Ball for West," *Business Week*, January 1, 1955, 54–55; Herbert Solow, "The Big Builder from Boise," *Fortune* 54 (December 1956):144–46, 196–204; "Builders of Anything, Anywhere," *Business Week*, December 5, 1964, 58–61; "Too Many Sandboxes?" *Forbes* 117 (March 15, 1976):79; "Morrison-Knudsen's Foray into Coal Mining," *Business Week*, June 20, 1977, 52–56; Glen Barrett, "Reclamation's New Deal for Heavy Construction: M-K in the Great Depression," *Idaho Yesterdays* 22 (Fall 1978):21–27; C. Knowlton, "Bill Agee Gets a Second Chance," *Fortune* 119 (March 27, 1989):94–96.

On Idaho Power: Wells and Hart, *Idaho: Gem of the Mountains*, 179; Idaho Power Company, *1990 Annual Report* (Boise, 1990), 6–27; "Sidney Zollicoffer Mitchell," in Rockwell, *The Saga of American Falls Dam*, 184–96; Sidney Alexander Mitchell, *S. Z. Mitchell and the Electrical Industry* (New York: Farrar, Straus & Cudahy, 1960), esp. 91–102; John Alden Bliss, "Mitchell, Sidney Zollicoffer," in *Dictionary of American Biography*, Supplement 3, 526–28. Susan Stacy, *Legacy of Light: A History of Idaho Power Company* (Boise: Idaho Power Company, 1991), was published after this history was completed.

On other enterprises, pamphlets and brochures have been furnished by the companies involved. One recent book is John Fahey, *Hecla: A Century of Western Mining* (Seattle: University of Washington Press, 1990).

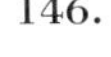

146.

147.

148.

146. Harry W. Morrison of Morrison-Knudsen Company, 1950, was a prominent Idaho businessman. *Time* carried a similar photo on the cover of its May 3, 1954, issue, which referred to Morrison as an "ambassador with bulldozers." ISHS 76–28.31C.

147. Robert V. Hansberger, president of Boise Cascade, played a significant role in the development of the modern timber industry. ISHS 72–190.16.

148. Jack Simplot (ca. 1940), founder of J. R. Simplot Company, made frozen potatoes for all of America. ISHS 77–2.45.

149.

150.

149. Joseph A. Albertson (ca. 1970), founder of Albertson's Inc., founded the grocery chain that has spread throughout the nation. ISHS 75–127.1.

150. W. Averell Harriman, founder, and Steven Hannagan, the original publicist who gave Sun Valley its name, observe lodge construction in 1936. ISHS 80–37.102.

## CHAPTER THIRTY

# Art and Literature

### THE ARTISTIC TRADITION

WHEN John C. Frémont conducted his expeditions to the Far West he took along Charles Preuss, a cartographer trained in Europe. Preuss not only prepared valuable maps of the vast domain beyond the Missouri but also executed sketches, including a view of American Falls in 1843. In the same tradition, George Gibbs and William Henry Tappan accompanied the U.S. Army's Regiment of Mounted Riflemen (the Cross Expedition) as they traveled on the Oregon Trail to Fort Vancouver in 1849. Tappan provided the earliest interior and exterior views of Fort Hall and Fort Boise, while Gibbs made the first extant drawing of Shoshone Falls. An artist who illustrated northern Idaho with graphite portraits and wonderful and sensitive scenes of Coeur d'Alene Indian life in the 1840s was Nicolas Point, native of France, the Jesuit missionary who opened Sacred Heart Mission in 1842.

The next three artists who captured on canvas scenes of early Idaho were among America's most talented. John Mix Stanley, an itinerant artist since 1835, was selected to accompany Isaac Stevens on his government-sponsored railroad survey to the Pacific in 1853–54. Although a graphic realist, Stanley also produced idealized interpretations, such as his scene *On the Snake River*, hoping Congress could be persuaded that the Northwest was a worthwhile destination. Another member of the Stevens railroad survey was Gustavus Sohon, native of East Prussia, who came to the United States in 1842 when he was seventeen. After he enlisted in the U.S. Army and served with Stevens's party, Sohon was assigned to Lieutenant John Mullan's party commissioned to develop a viable railroad route through northern Idaho. Sohon explored the difficult terrain of the Coeur d'Alene Mountains in 1853–54 and left watercolor and pencil drawings of the Mullan Road, of Indian life, and of the Coeur d'Alene Mission, as well as maps and other illustrations.

Another contemporary, George Catlin, was the first artist of any importance to pictorially document the culture of the American Indian. An accomplished watercolorist, Catlin visited Idaho's mountain country in 1855. He declared the Salmon River Valley "one of the most verdant and beautiful valleys in the world." His painting of a Crow village set against the rugged Salmon River range is one of his most captivating.[1]

Among artists who recorded the early mining rushes to Idaho was Charles Ostner, a native of Austria who arrived in 1862. He painted portraits, mining scenes, and landscapes with animals. He also left in Boise an equestrian statue of George Washington that he carved in 1869. An oil of Main Street in Boise that was painted in 1864 by Arm Hincelin is in the collections of the Idaho State Historical Society. A house, sign, and ornamental painter who worked in Boise, Hincelin depicted the wide expanse of the street, with men driving ox-teams, horses, and covered wagons; men conversing while leaning against a guard rail;

and such merchant signs as "City Brewery," "Oregon Tailor," "Tin Shop," "Chop House," and "Livery and Feed Stable." A historical record of life in the Boise Basin was provided by Margaretta Favorite Brown, a native of Pennsylvania who moved with her husband, Jonas W. Brown, to Idaho City in 1864 and Boise in 1882. She painted miners and merchants, landscapes, and scenes from daily life as well as moralistic murals for the walls of The Good Templar's Hall in Boise.

After the transcontinental railroad was completed in 1869, leading eastern pictorial magazines sent artist-reporters to the West to cover the "frontier territories." *Frank Leslie's Illustrated Newspaper* and *Harper's Weekly* carried lithographs that depicted the triumphs and struggles of Western settlers. Perhaps the most famous artist who visited in Idaho during this period was William Henry Jackson, who not only made photographic reports for *Harper's Weekly* but also produced vibrant paintings of landmarks such as Fort Hall. Thomas Moran, an English native who had been with Jackson on the Hayden survey of the upper Yellowstone in 1871, painted Shoshone Falls and the Tetons—works that are among the treasures left by this dean of American landscape artists.

In the same tradition was Mary Hallock Foote, a novelist and illustrator who married a mining engineer and spent the years 1885 to 1893 in Idaho, where she wrote and sketched not only for her novels and stories but also for *Century Magazine*. Her illustrations vividly capture the Idaho landscape and the nature of frontier life. Well before her marriage and move to Idaho Mary Hallock provided illustrations for Albert D. Richardson's *Beyond the Mississippi* (1867), referred to in Chapter Eleven.

Other painters of Idaho scenes at the turn of the century included James Everett Stuart (grandson of Gilbert Stuart, who painted America's most famous image of George Washington); Henry L. A. Culmer, a Utah artist who left a memorable scene of Shoshone Falls; Ella Knox Parrish, one of Idaho's few native pioneer artists; Mrs. M. J. Bradley, whose painting *Gem, Idaho and Gem Mill* is a thoughtfully delineated look at a bustling Idaho mining town in the 1890s; Abby Rhoda Williams Hill, who painted canvases of Idaho scenes for the Northern Pacific Railway Company; and John Fery. Born in Austria in 1859, Fery conducted tours and hunting trips in the Far West for European nobility and was employed as an artist in 1910 by the Great Northern Railroad to produce promotional paintings. He painted more than three hundred monumental paintings of western scenes displayed in railroad stations, hotels, and banks along the Great Northern line. They include magnificent paintings of Lake Pend Oreille and other Idaho panoramas.

Although Idaho has fostered no real art communities like those in many states, artists have always lived and worked here. Exhibitions were held in Boise as early as the 1870s and displays were mounted at territorial and state fairs. Amateur and professional Idaho artists exhibited their work in the Lewis and Clark Exposition in Portland (1905), Alaska-Yukon-Pacific Exposition in Seattle (1909), Panama-Pacific International Exposition in San Francisco (1915), Century of Progress at Chicago (1935), and New York World's Fair (1939). On October 17, 1898, the *Idaho Statesman* reported that in the art competition at the Intermountain Fair most of the prizes were won by Joseph Patrick McMeekin. Born in Dublin, Ireland, McMeekin had migrated with his family to the United States in 1872. Between 1890 and 1910 he lived with his sister's family on a homestead on Millet Island in the Snake River near Hagerman, and left paintings of farmers clearing sagebrush, spring plowing, livestock huddled against winter winds, and images along the Snake River—including paintings of Shoshone Falls and Twin Falls that were exhibited at the World's Columbian Exposition in Chicago in 1893.[2]

Two of McMeekin's peers were Idella Rogers Chester and her daughter Ruperta Chester. A native of Quebec, Idella came to the United States after a divorce and in 1895 married Horace

Chester, a miner in Atlanta, Idaho. She painted not only numerous landscapes of the Atlanta area but also homes, businesses, and local persons. On one occasion she painted a canvas of a semi-nude woman and sold it to a wealthy miner. When she discovered it was hung in the town saloon she marched down to the bar and demanded it back. On another occasion she interrupted a gathering of imbibing locals, who offered her a drink. She took the jug over her shoulder and walked back to her house with the jug turned upside down, liquor dripping all the way. Nobody challenged her. Her daughter Ruperta, also a painter, left realistic paintings of stamp mills, miners' cabins, and features of the mining town.[3]

One contemporary of the Chesters, George Schroeder, settled in Heyburn and Burley in 1906 and rendered views of the Sawtooth Range and other Idaho landscapes; the paintings adorned the Governor's Special Train that toured the eastern states in the early 1910s to advertise the wonders of Idaho. Other painters of this period were Cecelia May Southworth Beach, of Burley, who painted wildflowers and landscapes; Selma Calhoun Barker, of Bellevue, who painted cowboys and other western subjects; Marie Irvin, the first interior decorator in Boise; and Sara Annette Bowman, an art instructor at the University of Idaho.

During the 1920s and 1930s several ambitious local artists attended the Art Institute of Chicago and the Art Students League in New York, expanding beyond the frontier focus. The Federal Art Program of the Works Projects Administration assisted local artists during the depression. Under the direction of Professor Theodore J. Prichard of the University of Idaho, seventeen artists were employed. Murals were commissioned for Idaho post offices and other public buildings, the Boise Gallery of Art (now the Boise Art Museum) became a permanent exhibit space hosting regional and national shows, and the traditional Idaho regionalist paintings were complemented with works by artists influenced by Monet, Van Gogh, and Cezanne.

Among those who participated in the WPA artists' program

were Cecil Smith, reared on a ranch at Carey, who attended the Chicago Art Institute, worked as a cowboy, drew hundreds of sketches of cowboy life including freighting and muleskinning, exhibited widely, and received recognition in the United States and Europe; Ethel Lucile Fowler, native of Nebraska, who exhibited with the Boise Art Association in its early days and who, during her thirty years in Idaho, painted portraits, local scenery, flowers, and still life; and Alfred Dunn, raised in Twin Falls and graduate of the University of Idaho, who was a professor of art at Moscow from 1941 to 1974. Dunn's watercolors depict life in Idaho's small towns and the variety of the state's natural terrain. Dunn also designed artwork for University of Idaho publications.

Another participant in the WPA program was Archie Boyd Teater. Born in Boise, Teater spent much of his youth in the Hagerman Valley. Under the WPA program he painted mining and lumber camps in Boise Basin and occasionally panned for gold along the Snake River. A prolific painter of landscapes, portraits, and still lifes, Teater worked in a studio designed by Frank Lloyd Wright, one of two Wright structures in Idaho, jutting over the cliff rim of Snake River Canyon above Hagerman.

Still another participant in the Federal Arts Program was Fletcher Martin, resident of Emmett, who competed in the "48 States Competition," a contest to design a mural for a post office in each state. Martin's winning design for the Kellogg post office depicted two husky miners carrying an injured worker on a stretcher from a mineshaft. The mining community thought this equating of work and catastrophe was intolerable, so Martin was forced to replace it with a more palatable scene: the discovery by Noah Kellogg and his burro of the Bunker Hill and Sullivan claim.[4]

A contemporary of these artists was Minerva Kohlhepp Teichert. Raised on an isolated farm in the Fort Hall Bottoms near American Falls, she moved with her husband across the border to Cokeville, Wyoming, in 1927 when their home was inundated by the American Falls Reservoir. In addition to rearing five children and serving as a ranch wife, Teichert wrote *Drowned Memories* (1926) and *Romance of Old Fort Hall* (1952) and painted numerous murals—purchased for LDS Church buildings and for schools—that feature pioneers with oxen and Indians on the open range. Her narrative-like murals are full of movement and force.

Other painters of the "modern" period include Helen Hoff Aupperle, of Idaho Falls, who taught high school art classes and widely exhibited her paintings, which usually featured Indian festivals, dances, ceremonies, and personalities; and James Castle, who was born deaf in Garden Valley, Idaho, and was never able to read, write, or use sign language. He communicated visually. His drawings impart an ominous and quiet drama to everyday objects and scenes and show a sophisticated approach to space and tone. He exhibited in many western states in addition to Idaho.

Stalwarts in Idaho's art community in recent decades have been art instructors at the state's colleges and universities: Mary Kirkwood, Arnold Westerlund, and George Roberts, at the University of Idaho; Thomas Raymond Nielson, Idaho State University; Oliver Parson, Ricks College; Conan Mathews, Boise Junior College; and Max Peter, the College of Idaho now The Albertson College of Idaho.

In its centennial year, among Idaho's ten outstanding artists were Fred Ochi in Idaho Falls; Malcolm Renfrew, in Moscow; Don "Bemco" Bennett and Will Caldwell, in Ketchum; Richard Brough, formerly of Salmon Hot Springs; John Dawson, who designed the 1990 Idaho Centennial postage stamp; and John Killmaster, at Boise State University, who does acrylics and painted metal. John Takehara is an acclaimed ceramicist at Boise State University, Ed and Nancy Kienholz are recognized environmental sculptors living in Hope, and Rod Kagan is an innovative metal sculptor in Ketchum.

The most widely known sculptor with Idaho origins was

Gutzon Borglum, born in Ovid, Bear Lake County, in 1867. Robust, flamboyant, celebrator of America and the West, Borglum created one of the monumental patriotic shrines of the United States on Mount Rushmore, South Dakota. He was the son of Jens Møller Haugaard and Christiane Michelsen Borglum, natives of Hjørring, Denmark, who converted to Mormonism and moved to the Bear Lake Valley in 1865. They built a log cabin at Ovid, about five miles north of Paris, where Gutzon was born. (Some Bear Lake oldtimers later identified the place as St. Charles.) When the boy was about two years old the family moved to Ogden, Utah, where his father could take advantage of employment in building the transcontinental railroad. Later, after the completion of the railroad, the Borglums took the train to Omaha, remained there for a year or two, and then moved to St. Louis, where Jens Borglum went to the Homeopathic Medical College. After graduation in 1874 he returned to practice medicine in Omaha and Fremont, Nebraska. Some of the Borglum relatives remained in southern Idaho, however. Jens's sister Maren, who married Hans Christian Sorensen Høgsted (later anglicized to Hegsted), a friend of the family in Denmark, migrated to the upper Snake River Valley in 1880. Their son, Victor Hegsted, led in the settlement of Rexburg and served as a legislator. Their grandson, D. Mark Hegsted, a University of Idaho graduate and professor of biochemistry at Harvard, became an international nutrition expert and consultant.

Meanwhile, Gutzon Borglum studied art in California and in Europe and became an internationally renowned sculptor. At Rushmore, his most famous project, he carved out of a granite mountain the massive busts of George Washington, Abraham Lincoln, Thomas Jefferson, and Theodore Roosevelt, symbolic of the nation's most remarkable human endeavors. The monument was dedicated by President Calvin Coolidge on August 10, 1927. Visitors experience a feeling of reverence and awe—a reminder of American patriotism that will weather the millennia.

Increasing attention has been given in recent years to folk arts and material culture, aspects of aesthetics in which Idaho has a rich and expressive tradition. Art is not limited to drawing, painting, and sculpture; good taste and design can also create beauty in the simple, homely things of life. County fairs, museums, private homes, and folk art exhibitions feature objects that demonstrate the yearning for beauty. Hand-tooled leather saddles, exquisitely patterned quilts, hand-wrought gates and fences, Norwegian embroidery, Nez Perce baskets and beadwork, richly decorated cradleboards, braided horsehair bridles, well-shaped duck decoys, tablecloths, parfleches, rag rugs, miniature hay derricks, whittled caricatures, elegant bedsteads and lounges—all of these reflect artistic skill. Whether for the home, for work, for recreation, for ceremony and celebration, or for personal whimsy, the objects have been shaped with an eye for the aesthetic. The products of Idaho blacksmiths, tinsmiths, potters, furniture makers, housewives, needleworkers, quilt-makers, carvers, and gravestone engravers often represent the articulation of an intelligent, if not academically acquired, design skill. As in all countries and states, folk art is part of Idaho's artistic tradition.

## THE LITERARY TRADITION

For thousands of years Idaho's literary output consisted of the folktales and legends of her aboriginal inhabitants. This was an exclusively oral literature, delivered by an elderly man or woman as both instruction and entertainment. The tales, often called myths, were, of course, different for each band or tribe; they passed on the values and beliefs of the group and gave moral instruction to its members. Such stories explained the creation of the world and its beings, the significance of rituals and customs, and the religious meaning of birth, death, and other natural occurrences. The myths also were the means of teaching children proper behavior, the habits of animals, the location of food resources, how to use tools and implements, and the geography of the region. The stories helped to induce pride in their people and invoked supernatural powers in behalf of their survival. Myths displayed the negative, comical, and delightful aspects of earthly existence.[5]

A principal character in many Idaho stories was Coyote, the transformer-trickster who changed himself, animals, and natural objects into their present form. As one writer suggested:

> Coyote and his kin [raven, rabbit, blue jay] represent the sheerly spontaneous in life, the pure creative spark that is our birthright as human beings and that defies fixed roles or behavior. He not only represents some primordial creativity from our earlier days, but he reminds us that such celebration of life goes on today, and he calls us to join him in the frenzy. In an ordered world of objects and labels, he represents the potency of nothingness, of chaos, of freedom—a nothingness that makes something of itself. There is great power in such a being, and it has always been duly recognized and honored by Indian people.[6]

Much as Mickey Mouse and Donald Duck, Kermit the Frog and Big Bird talk to children in our day, animal characters instructed Indian children in why things are the way they are, and what one must strive to do in life. They did so in a religious setting. The titles of these spiritual and artistic stories, grouped according to Indian nation, illustrate some of their subject matter.[7]

Kutenai: "Coyote and Buffalo," "Origin of the Seasons," "Wolf," "Skunk," "Frog and Antelope."

Pend Oreille (Kalispel): "Coyote, Wren, and Grouse," "Coyote and Mountain Sheep," "Coyote and His Teeth," "Coyote and the Snake-Monster," "Coyote and the Shellfish Women."

Coeur d'Alene: "Chief Child of the Root," "Origin of Indian Tribes," "Story of Lynx," "Catbird," "Thunder."

Nez Perce: "Mosquito and Coyote," "The Glutton," "How Bear Led a Boy Astray," "Coyote and His Guests."

Shoshoni: "The Sun," "The Weasel Brothers," "The Sheep Woman," "The Bear's Son."

Northern Paiute: "The Creation of the Indian," "The Theft of Pine-Nuts," "The Stars," "Some Adventures of Coyote."

As presented, these stories were imaginative, inventive, and flexibly oriented to the intended audience. There was an aesthetic effect along with the religious and educational in this literature. Collections of the tales, even in cold print, are marvelously instructive of how Indian cultures worked.[8]

Early explorers who left literary accounts of their travels through what we now call Idaho include, of course, Meriwether Lewis and William Clark, mentioned in Chapter Four; Washington Irving's *Captain Bonneville*, described in Chapter Five; and Narcissa Whitman, from whose diary quotations were taken in Chapter Six. Many other Overland Trail diaries also capture a sense of Idaho's terrain. Later, several distinguished literary figures—Richard F. Burton, Robert Lewis Stevenson, Oscar Wilde, Rudyard Kipling—traveled in the American West, but none left memoirs of Idaho. A few travelers did make comments as they journeyed through the territory. The following is typical: "High and barren for the greater part, suited, as a rule, for nothing more than cattle-runs, conducted on a large scale, too vast for anyone but a great capitalist to occupy."[9] The following are representative samples of those who left published accounts of their Idaho sojourn.

Charles Nelson Teeter, born in 1832 in Genoa, Cayuga County, New York, the eldest son in a family of seven, went with his family to Wisconsin when he was ten. He helped his father on a farm, served as a raftsman on the river, taught school, and in 1862, age thirty, headed for the Colorado mines. Learning in the spring of 1863 that a mining camp had been opened in the Boise Basin, Teeter immediately left with others, arriving in "Bannack or Idaho City" in June 1863. His experiences during the next two years were later described in a journal, published by the Idaho State Historical Society under the title *Four Years of My Life.*[10] Teeter's experiences with Indians, drunken miners, wild animals, and wilderness preachers are simply and honestly recorded. A similar first-person account of Boise Basin in 1863 is by C. Aubrey Angelo, a correspondent for the *Daily Alta California*, a leading San Francisco newspaper, who joined the rush to Idaho and left his journalistic impressions. One of several "literary" newspaper reports, his impressions were published in *Idaho Yesterdays* during the centennial of Idaho Territory.[11]

In 1865 Speaker of the House Schuyler Colfax, editor Samuel Bowles of the Springfield (Massachusetts) *Republican*, and reporter Albert Richardson of the *New York Tribune* made a trip across the continent that involved journeying in Idaho. Bowles waxed ecstatic about Shoshone Falls, ranking it as the world's greatest "in majesty of movement and grandeur of surrounding features."[12] Richardson's description of Idaho was not uncharacteristic.

> We were now in Idaho, barest and most desolate of all our Territories, with vast rolling wastes of lava, sand and sage-brush. But its lack in agriculture is more than counterbalanced by its richness in minerals. Here, as in Dante's Inferno, "not green but brown the foliage." Yet this nutritive bunch-grass, requiring no rain, keeps the stage-horses fat, and often subsists great herds driven hither to escape the drouths of California. Here is the world's pasturage. Hundreds of valleys await the tinkling sheep-bells; cattle shall browse upon a thousand hills. . . . Governor Caleb Lyon, in one of his messages, characterizes Idaho as a "land of Italian summers and Syrian winters." The summers may outshine Araby the Blest; but I think he should have said Siberian winters.[13]

In 1866 two influential British writers and opinion makers, William Hepworth Dixon and Sir Charles Wentworth Dilke, made their way into Idaho. Dixon, editor of the distinguished London literary magazine *The Athenaeum*, had written biographies of Francis Bacon and William Penn, social commentaries on prison life and poverty among the working classes; he spent the summer of 1866 in America with Dilke, the twenty-three-year-old son of the proprietor of *The Athenaeum.* Dixon wanted the English readers of his two-volume *New America* to realize what it meant to be in a region with a ratio of four males to one female. "At the wayside inn," Dixon wrote, "when you call for the chambermaid, either Sam puts in his woolly head, or Chi Hi pops in his shaven crown. Hardly any help can be hired in these wastes; Molly runs away with a miner, Biddy gets married to a merchant."[14]

A New England visitor was John Codman, a retired clipper-ship captain who decided in 1874 to maintain a vacation home at Soda Springs, where he spent his summers for the next two decades.[15] Codman, who had traveled all over the world, was particularly impressed with Idaho stage-drivers:

> Our driver was an energetic fellow. He whipped, clubbed, swore, and yelled steadily at the "cussed" team. His swearing was something stupendous and perfectly exhaustive of Heaven, Earth, and Hell, and of all their inhabitants. No words could do it justice. But the climax was reached when it began to snow thickly, and some of us were staying along ahead of the wagon through a deep gorge in the hills [Codman was on the way to Caribou Mountain]. All at once, within ten rods of us, a grizzly set up a tremendous growl that drowned out the swearing of our driver. We just dropped on all fours and crawled back to the wagon, into which we tumbled rather quickly. We . . . drove along until we came to the place where he [the bear] was. When he heard the wagon coming he trotted out within two or three rods ahead of us. Then our driver set up a yell and commenced to swear in a style that exceeded all his previous efforts, and actually scared the grizzly so that it fairly made him turn tail and put for the woods.[16]

More important to Idaho history-lovers are two books by missionary bishops, both Episcopalians: Daniel S. Tuttle served in Idaho from 1867 to 1886, Ethelbert Talbot from 1887 to 1898. Tuttle, a native of Connecticut, was elected at age twenty-nine to serve as bishop in Montana, with jurisdiction in Idaho and Utah. During his first two months in Idaho he held services in Boise, Silver City, and Idaho City and organized a parish school in Boise. Beginning in 1870, he spent each summer in Idaho. In his *Idaho of Yesterday* Thomas Donaldson recalled his first meeting with Bishop Tuttle, who was busily at work on the cellar of a new wing for the chapel in Boise:

> The digger was a man of six feet in height and with whiskers of the style the English call "Picadilly Weepers." A tam-o'-shanter hat lolled on his head. With shovel in hand, he leaped from the hole and smiled at me. . . . "Glad to meet you, Mr. Donaldson," smiled the bishop. It was a hearty handshake he gave me, and then he chatted briskly for fifteen minutes. I said good-by, and Bishop Tuttle jumped into the hole and commenced digging again. I formed my opinion of him right then and there and never had reason to change it. I reasoned that if a bishop of a silk-stocking church could, and was willing, to handle a shovel in a public place he would certainly be able to touch the hearts of his people; sincerity and common sense made him outrank any churchman in the territory. . . . Bishop Tuttle was the best and most convincing pulpit preacher I have ever heard. . . . He fairly lifted me into space above earth by his eloquence and affectionate reception of the applicants.[17]

Tuttle, who had physical as well as mental strength, preached in log cabins and saloons and ate alkali dust in the deserts as he traveled by stage and horseback and afoot to fifty locations in Idaho. He left Idaho in 1886 to become Bishop of Missouri. From 1903 to 1923 he was presiding bishop of the Protestant Episcopal Church in the United States.[18]

Bishop Talbot, who replaced Bishop Tuttle in Idaho and also had charge of Episcopalians in Wyoming, wrote *My People of the Plains*, in which he discussed Chief Washakie, an Idaho mining camp, the Coeur d'Alene country, and the people "in my flock." His descriptions of religion and life in Idaho mining camps are vivid and informative.[19]

Some of the most vivid personal experience accounts are by women. Among these are Annie Pike Greenwood, Nelle Davis, Inez Puckett McEwen, and Grace Jordan.

Annie Pike Greenwood's *We Sagebrush Folks* is an account of the settlement and development of the Minidoka reclamation project. The book covers the 1910s, 1920s, and early 1930s. Annie Pike was born in Provo, Utah, in 1879, the daughter of Dr. Walter Pike, first superintendent of Utah's state mental hospital, and a Mormon mother who had given up her Mormonism when she married non-Mormon Pike. A graduate of Brigham Young Academy (later Brigham Young University), also a student at the Universities of Utah and Michigan, she worked for the *Salt Lake Tribune* and a Los Angeles newspaper before marrying Charles O. Greenwood in 1905. They soon moved to Idaho, near Acequia in Minidoka County, where they remained as farmers until the 1930s, when they lost their farm, and separated. Annie Greenwood then lived in Ogden, Utah, and finally in Sacramento, California, where she died in 1956. For some years she taught the one-room school in Acequia.

*We Sagebrush Folks* gives an authentic account of the daily life of farm families in southern Idaho. The book discusses schools, birth, death, recreation, outdoors, sex (surprising in this kind of book, written as early as 1934), the impact of World War I, politics, religion, and economics. Sympathetic with their neighbors' struggles, the Greenwoods were caught up in the farmers' cause. He was twice elected to the Idaho legislature; she wrote honest articles for national and local magazines about the farmers' vicissitudes. Exciting and interesting, her book was nevertheless a plea on behalf of the women and children on farms. Though often discouraged, she loved Idaho and its people and described them accurately and with spirit.[20]

*Stump Ranch Pioneer*, by Nelle Portrey Davis, is the true story of dustbowl refugees who carved out a home for themselves as stump ranch farmers in the Idaho panhandle. Born in Sidney, Nebraska, the fourth of eight children, Nelle Portrey began writing while still a teenager. Her family moved to Kiowa County, Colorado, in 1920. In 1936 she and her husband, Norman Davis, lost their 160-acre sheep ranch near Eads, Colorado, and moved with $160 in their pockets to "Welcome Ranch" in Boundary County, Idaho. Their experience is a testament to the American ability to overcome hardship through hard work and persistence. Nelle's writings for national and local magazines contributed substantially to the family's income. In 1947 the family moved to Eastport, northeast of Bonners Ferry, and established a second Welcome Ranch—a guest ranch on the Moyie River. *Stump Ranch Pioneer* celebrates the traditional American virtues of industry and inventiveness. It is a charming and informative story of neighborliness, resourcefulness, and tenacity.[21]

Inez Puckett McEwen was born in Iowa; came to Idaho as a child; spent years in California studying at the University of Southern California and Scripps and Pomona colleges; and taught in a southern California high school. In 1943 she settled down on a ranch at Cedar Draw, near Wendell, Idaho. Her book, *So This Is Ranching*, is a humorous account of southern Idaho ranch life in the 1940s.[22]

Another woman's experience on an Idaho ranch is recounted in *Home Below Hell's Canyon*, by Grace Edgington Jordan. During the depression days of the early 1930s Len and Grace Jordan and their three small children moved to a sheep ranch on the Idaho side of the Snake River gorge just below Hells Canyon. Short of cash but long on ingenuity, the Jordans raised and stored their food, made their own soap, and educated their children. This is an intensely human account of their experiences before they were thrust into the national spotlight with Len Jordan's election as governor and later as United States Senator. *Home Below Hell's Canyon* tells much about sheep ranching in the 1930s and 1940s.

Born in Wasco, Oregon, Grace Jordan earned a bachelor's degree in English from the University of Oregon and taught at the Universities of Oregon, Washington, and California before she moved to Idaho in 1933. She was not disturbed by the isolation she would expect at Kirkwood Bar, the name she gave to the ranch. The family lived at Kirkwood for seven years. After moving from there, she wrote a novel, *Canyon Boy* (1960) about the area. Still later, she wrote a book about her husband's service as senator entitled *The Unintentional Senator* and a book about the Brown family of McCall entitled *The King's Pines of Idaho.*[23]

We come now to Idaho's writers of fiction. We shall have room to mention only a few—those who became important figures in the history of American literature.

The first was Mary Hallock Foote, a proper Victorian lady who became wife, mother, novelist, and artist in the Far West, with a residence in Idaho from 1884 to 1895. Although she wrote many books and numerous articles, the most interesting to Idahoans is *The Chosen Valley*, first published as a serial in the *Century Magazine* and in 1892 as a book. She wrote much about Idaho miners, dam-builders, irrigators, and farmers. Her husband, Arthur D. Foote, a first cousin of Henry Ward Beecher and Harriet Beecher Stowe, was a mining engineer who, after reaching Idaho, became interested in supplying water to thirsty deserts. Her other Idaho novels included *Coeur d'Alene* (1894), *The Desert and the Sown* (1902), *A Picked Company* (1912), and *Edith Bonham* (1917). She also published many short stories, some of which are in *Exile* (1894), *The Cup of Trembling* (1895), and, for children, *The Little Fig-Tree Stories* (1899).

Born in 1847 on a farm near the Hudson River town of Milton, near Poughkeepsie, New York, Mary Hallock was reared in a Quaker home. After her graduation from the Poughkeepsie Female Collegiate Seminary, she went to the School of Design for Women at the Cooper Union in New York City. By the 1870s she was doing professional work as an illustrator. When her best friend married Richard Watson Gilder, one of the most influential literary figures of the oncoming generation, she came to have undreamed-of opportunities. Gilder became acting editor of *Scribner's Monthly* and founding editor of its successor, *Century Magazine*, one of the top literary magazines in the nation.

In 1876, when Foote came west to a California quicksilver mine as a bride, Gilder encouraged her to write about her new environment and to furnish illustrations. She became a leading national writer and illustrator of scenes that were "authentically western." When the Footes moved to Leadville, Colorado, in 1879, she began books and stories that featured an attractive, well-educated young eastern mining engineer as hero, a young eastern-type woman as heroine, and coarse western men or depraved easterners as villains.[24]

The Footes established their home on the outskirts of Boise in 1884; it was, Mary Foote wrote, "a very proper, decent little town [about 2,000 people] quite unlike the wild [mining] camps where my married morals have been cultivated . . . a little oasis in the desert."[25] Her reminiscences are a fairly pungent account of pioneer Idaho life.

Arthur Foote had made the decision to build an irrigation system in the canyon and valley of the Boise River. He and others organized the Idaho Mining and Irrigation Company to deliver water for irrigation and also for the Snake River gold placers. It was not a good time to launch a major enterprise, however—the country experienced a depression in 1884—and Foote eventually lost his investment. The two then went to Grass Valley, California. She died in 1938.

In 1972 Wallace Stegner, making use of the Mary Hallock

Foote-Helena Gilder correspondence, won the Pulitzer Prize for his novel *Angle of Repose*, a fictional account of the life of Mary Hallock Foote. The book has high value as a novel, but it is not a factual account of Foote and her career, in Idaho or elsewhere. Her reminiscences, published as *A Victorian Gentlewoman in the Far West*, are a delightful story in their own right.

In 1885 Mary Foote was, for a period, in Hailey; she may have met the parents of Ezra Pound, who was born there that year. The Pounds moved two years later to Pennsylvania, where he grew up. But this world-famous poet, literary critic, and translator, about whom more has been written than about any other Idaho-born writer, is almost always introduced by the words "Idaho-born," which suggests that a paragraph about him is in order.

After graduating from the University of Pennsylvania, Pound taught at Wabash College for a while but was asked to resign for being "a Latin Quarter type" and went to Europe in 1908. There, in Italy, he published his first volume of poems, *A Lume Spento*. He went on to London, where he became prominent in literary circles and published three other volumes of verse. He and others founded the Imagist school of poets, who advocated the use of free rhythms and concrete images, and he championed the work of avant-garde writers like James Joyce and T. S. Eliot. His later poetry demonstrated his knowledge of medieval literature and troubadour ballads. He did translations of Chinese and Japanese poetry that show great skill and tenderness. In 1920 he left England for Paris, where he formed part of the group of American expatriates who included Gertrude Stein and Ernest Hemingway. He had enormous influence on Hemingway, who later also had a connection with Idaho. Pound remained in Paris until 1924, when he went to Italy for most of the rest of his life. He established poetic journals and published anthologies. Often regarded as his major work is the "Cantos," which, in addition to poetic distinction, incorporated details and quotations from ancient, Renaissance, and modern history of the Western world and of the Orient. Pound also became preoccupied with economics, embraced free credit theories, and was convinced that modern credit capitalism was a failure. He gave at least partial support to the programs of Benito Mussolini in Italy. Having broadcast over Italian radio during the Second World War, he was charged with treason in 1946 but found unsound of mind and confined to a mental hospital until 1961, when he returned to Italy. He died in 1972 at the age of eighty-seven.[26]

A very different kind of writer, but also with a prodigious output, was Frank Robertson, a writer of Westerns.[27] Robertson was born near Moscow in 1890. His parents were converted to Mormonism when he was a boy, and in 1901 they moved to Chesterfield, in southern Idaho, a village of about three hundred people. After the rich topsoil of the Palouse, young Frank was not impressed by Chesterfield, a dryfarm region. He herded sheep, did freighting, and became a migratory worker at age fourteen. He married a local girl, farmed in Chesterfield, and began to submit stories and articles to Western magazines. He wrote about 100 Westerns and hundreds of stories in the years that followed, with titles like *Foreman of Forty Bar*, *Boss of Tumbling H*, *Clawhammer Ranch*, *The Boss of the Flying M*, *Wildhorse Henderson*, *Riders of the Sunset Trail*, and *The Fight for River Range*. Many of his novels were translated into German, Czech, Hungarian, Swedish, and Dutch. He also wrote juvenile books, *On the Trail of Chief Joseph* (1927) and *Sagebrush Sorrel* (1954), both of which won prizes. His autobiography, *A Ram in the Thicket*, is a gem. Nebraska writer Mari Sandoz wrote of it:

> It's been a long time since I read a book with the authentic smell and feel of this one. It has the freshness, the wry humor, the off-hand understatement in even the most appalling situations, that are the essence of our High Coun-

> try. The book has so much that is peculiar to the life of this man and his time and place, and very much, too, that is universal. I think it will be good reading fifty years from now.[28]

Another writer born in Moscow, and former student at the University of Idaho, was Carol Ryrie Brink. She published several novels of distinction, including an Idaho trilogy: *The Buffalo Coat* (1944), *Strangers in the Forest* (1959), and *Snow in the River* (1964). She attained greatest fame, however, for her juvenile and junior books, of which *All Over Town*, *Two Are Better Than One*, and *Louly* have Idaho settings. One of them, *Caddie Woodlawn* (1935), received the Newbery Medal as the "most distinguished contribution to American literature for children" in its year of publication. Other books were selections of the Junior Literary Guild and Children's Book Club. The University of Idaho awarded her an honorary Doctor of Literature degree in 1965.

A contemporary of Carol Brink who was also a student at the University of Idaho was Talbot Jennings. Born in Shoshone in 1894, raised in Caldwell and Nampa, he left his classes at the University of Idaho to fight in World War I. After the war he returned to Moscow, completed a degree in English, went on to earn an M.A. at Harvard, and returned to the University of Idaho to teach. After two years he went to the Yale Drama School, where Eugene O'Neill and John Mason Brown had also studied, then taught at Miami University in Oxford, Ohio. After writing for the professional theatre in New York, in 1934 he went to Hollywood to write screenplays. He remained there for the next thirty years, creating scripts for such well-known films as *Mutiny on the Bounty*, *Northwest Passage*, *Across the Wide Missouri*, *The Sons of Katie Elder*, *Romeo and Juliet*, *Anna and the King of Siam*, and *The Good Earth*. He won an Academy award for his script *So Ends Our Night*. Jennings also received an honorary doctorate from the University of Idaho, in 1970.

In more recent years a member of the Coeur d'Alene Nation, Janet Campbell Hale, has written several highly acclaimed young-adult novels. Born on the Coeur d'Alene Reservation in northern Idaho, she grew up mainly on the Yakima Reservation in Washington. She worked as a waitress; picked cherries, apricots, and peaches; stripped hops; painted; wrote poetry; read serious books; and then went to the University of California at Berkeley, where she received the B.A. She later received the M.A. from the University of California at Davis. Her books include *The Owl's Song* (1974), a novel about fourteen-year-old Billy White Hawk, who leaves his Idaho reservation in search of a better life in California only to find hatred and hostility there that he finds increasingly difficult to cope with; *Custer Lives in Humboldt County and Other Poems* (1978); and *The Jailing of Cecelia Capture: A Novel* (1985) that is the story of the struggles of a young Indian woman in a large city. Her poems and short stories have been widely anthologized and published in various journals and magazines.

A second native American writer born in Idaho was Mourning Dove (Hum-ishu-ma), the literary name of Christine Quintasket, born in a canoe near Bonners Ferry in 1888. Although she and her husband were migrant laborers, she took along an old manual typewriter and managed to write in the evenings. Her book *Cogewea, the Half Blood* (1927) is now recognized as the first novel by a Native American woman. Her book *Coyote Stories* (1933) contains the traditional tales of her tribe, the Okanogan. She died in 1936 at the age of forty-eight.[29]

Dwight William Jensen, a recent author of juvenile and adult literature and the author of an Idaho history, wrote *There Will Be a Road* (1978) about two young men who spend the winter in the Idaho mountains cutting trees for posts, living in a dugout, and ultimately fighting for their lives in a blizzard.

In the view of many, Idaho's greatest home-grown literary figure was Vardis Fisher. Fisher was born in Annis, Idaho, and grew up on an isolated homestead in the so-called Antelope country of southeastern Idaho. He graduated from Rigby High School the same year that Philo Farnsworth, as a student in chemistry there, invented television (see Chapter Twenty-one). Fisher went on to the University of Utah and University of Chicago and after completing a Ph.D. taught at the University of Utah, where one of his students was Wallace Stegner. Fisher left Utah to teach at New York University, where he formed a lifelong friendship with southern novelist Thomas Wolfe. In 1931 he returned to Idaho to live in Boise and the Hagerman Valley the rest of his life.

A product of a Mormon household far removed from a Mormon wardhouse, Fisher began to write such powerful novels about the Mormon countryside as *Toilers of the Hills* (1928), *Dark Bridwell* (1931), and *In Tragic Life* (1932). The last was the first in the Vridar Hunter autobiographical tetralogy that went on to include *Passions Spin the Plot* (1934), *We Are Betrayed* (1935), and *No Villain Need Be* (1936). In 1935 Fisher became director of the Idaho Writers' Project and Historical Records Project of the New Deal's Works Progress Administration and published *Idaho: A Guide in Word and Picture* (1937), the model for other state guides; *The Idaho Encyclopedia* (1938); and *Idaho Lore* (1939). He also wrote a light-hearted Idaho novel, *April: A Fable of Love* (1937).

In 1939 Fisher published *Children of God*, a historical novel about Mormonism that won the $10,000 Harper Prize. Other western novels that followed were *City of Illusion* (1941), about the Comstock Lode, and *The Mothers: An American Saga of Courage* (1943). Fisher began a twelve-volume series that he called the *Testament of Man*, which traced the development of the human race from prehistoric times to the twentieth century, and then returned to western-based novels: *Pemmican* (1956), about the Hudson's Bay Company; and *Tale of Valor* (1958), about the Lewis and Clark Expedition. His last novel, *Mountain Man: A Novel of Male and Female in the Early American West* (1965), was later filmed under the title *Jeremiah Johnson* and has been widely distributed and viewed. With his wife, Opal Laurel Holmes, he also wrote *Gold Rushes and Mining Camps of the Early American West* (1968).[30]

Fisher was an "honest" writer and rebelled against the hardships and repressive effects of the frontier. He wrote:

> If there is any general theme running through my novels, it must be this, that the human race has been betrayed by an assumption of compensatory virtues which are beyond fulfillment, and in self-defense has fled into countless evasions that have become so indelibly fixed in patterns that it is difficult to get out of them or understand what they have been doing to us.[31]

Because he was critical of Idaho frontier life and the Puritan rigidity of his family and church standards, he was regarded by many Idahoans as a controversial writer. He had a vivid style and clearly drawn characters and showed prodigious scholarship and understanding of civilization in the *Testament of Man* series. As he grew older, Fisher was able to look at Mormon and frontier values with greater appreciation. The last volume in his *Testament of Man* series, *Orphans in Gethsemane*, is a restructuring and rewriting of the Tetralogy—with a mellower look at his childhood and young manhood.

Fisher also produced *Sonnets to an Imaginary Madonna* (1927), considered by some as the finest book of verse by an Idahoan. His "power of imagery, command of language, technical knowledge of form, and general power to stir the imagination" demonstrated remarkable creative powers.[32] Fisher died in 1968.

Idaho has been home to one other literary figure of international importance: Ernest Hemingway.[33] Hemingway was born four years after Fisher, in Oak Park, Illinois. The son of a small-town doctor, he reported for the *Kansas City Star* until World War I. Because of an eye defect he was not inducted, but he volunteered as an ambulance driver in France and in the Italian infantry, where he was wounded just before his nineteenth birthday. While working in Paris as a correspondent for the *Toronto Star* after war's end, he joined the expatriate circle that included Gertrude Stein and Ezra Pound. He began to write short stories and novels that attracted attention. His first major work, *The Sun Also Rises* (1926), made him a spokesman for the "lost generation" of American expatriates. There followed *A Farewell to Arms* (1929) and several volumes of short stories. He wrote *Death in the Afternoon* (1932) about bullfighting, and *Green Hills of Africa* (1935) about big-game hunting. He served as a correspondent on the Loyalist side during the Spanish Civil War, and from this experience came a great novel, *For Whom the Bell Tolls* (1940). The last two chapters of this novel were written in Sun Valley, during which time he gained an appreciation for Idaho. In particular, he liked the pheasant hunting.

A foreign correspondent during World War II, Hemingway settled in Cuba, where he wrote the celebrated short novel *The Old Man and the Sea* (1952), a parable of man against nature, for which he was awarded the Nobel Prize in Literature in 1954. When Fidel Castro assumed control in Cuba in 1959, Hemingway moved to Idaho, where he lived until his self-inflicted death in 1961.

Hemingway's writings, composed in a simple, terse style, glorified virility, bravery, stoicism, and other primal qualities.[34] Idaho's eminent literary historian, Richard Etulain, suggests that some of Hemingway's popularity was his fascinatingly active life. "He went everywhere, did everything, and, above all, experienced all things."[35]

L. J. Davis, a Boise native living in Arizona, has written fine novels about Idaho. Marilynne Robinson, who grew up in Coeur d'Alene, published *Housekeeping* (1980), a novel set in Sandpoint, her birthplace, which won both the Hemingway and Rosenthal prizes. Several other novelists and poets of the present are doing creditable work.

Idaho has had two Pulitzer Prize winners for historical writing. The first was Lawrence Henry Gipson, mentioned in Chapter Twenty-seven, who won the prize in 1962. The second, Laurel Thatcher Ulrich, won the prize in 1991 for her book *A Midwife's Tale: The Life of Martha Ballard Based on her Diary, 1785–1812*. She had previously won the Bancroft and John H. Dunning awards, and the Joan Kelly Memorial Prize in Woman's History—all top prizes in the field of American history. Her book was praised for its imaginative use of the "minutiae regularly recorded in Martha Ballard's diary to construct an intricate mosaic of life on the . . . frontier." Ulrich's interpretation of data "discloses the operation of a female economy, reveals the importance of the midwife in the life of a rural community, and provides insight into gender roles and relationships."[36]

Ulrich had previously written the well-reviewed *Good Wives: Image and Reality in the Lives of Women in Northern New England* and many professional articles. She was born in St. Anthony but grew up in Sugar City, where her father, John Kenneth Thatcher, who had a master's degree from the University of Idaho, was principal and later superintendent of schools. He was a state senator from Madison County for eight years and a member of the State Board of Education and the board of the Idaho Falls Vocational-Technical School. Ulrich graduated from Sugar-Salem High School and the University of Utah and later completed her doctorate at the University of New Hampshire. Her grandfather was John B. Thatcher, who gave Thatcher, Idaho, its name; her ancestors were also among the early settlers in Teton City and Idaho Falls.

Inez Callaway Robb was a prizewinning reportorial writer who grew up in Caldwell, worked for the *Idaho Statesman*, joined the staff of the New York *Daily News*, and was a roving reporter for the International News Service from 1938 to 1953. One of the first woman war correspondents during World War II, she went on to become a nationally syndicated writer and her column appeared regularly in 160 newspapers for another decade. She wrote a widely acclaimed book, *Don't Just Stand There* (1962), a collection of her best columns that give a picture of her childhood in Caldwell and Boise, her beginnings as a newspaperwoman, and her happy married life. She reveals her enchantment with the scenic wonders of America and her firm stand on equal rights for men. The book is lively, provocative, and witty.

Another Idaho writer, Rosalie Sorrels, who grew up in Boise, lives in a cabin alongside Grimes Creek in Boise County. She has written and performed songs of her own composition, her haunting voice breathing life into the Idaho experience. Her Idaho songbook is entitled *Way Out in Idaho*. Mother of five, Sorrels has made sixteen records.

Finally, Idaho has produced writers of history—custodians and recorders of the territory's and state's conscience, experience, and wisdom. They have included the elders who transmitted the oral history of native peoples to their children and grandchildren; early residents who left diaries, letters, reminiscences, and personal histories of the events in which they participated; and more recent observers of the Idaho scene who felt an obligation to "write up" events in which they had a personal interest. They sometimes spoke several languages (especially Indian tongues), were often successful businessmen, and were active in the territory's and state's political life. They rode on Idaho's mountain trails, fished in its streams, felt the wind in their faces, and played poker with frontier roughnecks. By recognizing their responsibility to tell the territory's and state's story as they had witnessed its unfolding, they helped unite Idahoans by reminding them of their common origins and experiences.

Idaho's historians have included John Hailey, whose *History of Idaho* (1910) was commissioned by the state legislature and contains detailed and authentic coverage of each legislative session; William J. McConnell, whose *Early History of Idaho* (1913), also published by authority of the state legislature, is especially rich in discussing the lawlessness in the Boise Basin in the 1860s and 1870s; and Hiram T. French, author of a three-volume *History of Idaho* (1914) that, in addition to two volumes of biographies, provides excellent treatment of the history of the various cities and counties and agricultural development.

The first major history of the state written by a professionally trained historian was *History of the State of Idaho* (1918) by Cornelius J. Brosnan, long-time professor of history at the University of Idaho. An informative four-volume *History of Idaho* was published in 1920 by James H. Hawley, prominent lawyer, mayor of Boise, and governor (1911–15). Byron Defenbach published a three-volume work, *Idaho: The Place and Its People* (1933), that concentrates on the territorial period.

The most definitive history of the state, the one used by all historians and researchers in the thirty years after its publication, is the three-volume *History of Idaho* (1959) by Merrill D. Beal and Merle W. Wells. Beal taught at Ricks College and Idaho State University and wrote *A History of Southeastern Idaho* (1942), *"I Will Fight No More Forever": Chief Joseph and the Nez Perce War* (1936), and many articles. Merle Wells was director of the Idaho State Historical Society from 1969 to 1975 and state historian from 1959 until his retirement in 1989, and has published a half-dozen books and hundreds of articles on elements of Idaho history. Their *History of Idaho* covers almost every aspect of life—economics, politics, education, fine arts, religion, and sports. The body of their work and the contribution it has made to Idaho have earned both authors honorary degrees from the University of Idaho.

The national bicentennial occasioned a series of state histories under the sponsorship of the American Association for State and Local History. Idaho's history was written by F. Ross Peterson, a native of Montpelier and professor of history at Utah State University. Peterson's charming *Idaho: A Bicentennial History* (1976) pays special attention to the impact of the state's physical environment.

Idaho's centennial in 1990 promoted the writing of an additional volume, Carlos Schwantes' *In Mountain Shadows*, published in 1991 by the University of Nebraska Press. The book is amply illustrated and written in spritely style by this professor of history at the University of Idaho. Colorful personalities and raging controversies accent this fine Idaho history.

There are also excellent books for young people, especially those taking junior high school classes in Idaho history. Those still widely used in 1990 included Dwight William Jensen, *Discovering Idaho: A History* (1977) and Virgil M. Young, *Story of Idaho* (Centennial [3d] edition, 1990).

All of these historians have assiduously tried to get the facts right and at the same time tell a coherent story. They are fully conscious of the diversity and multidimensional nature of human experience and of the relativity of values, cultures, and traditions.[37]

Clearly, Idaho is not New England. Its settlement has been too recent, its energies too largely devoted to survival, to support a "flowering" such as Van Wyck Brooks chronicled for Massachusetts and her neighbors. Nevertheless, for a sparsely inhabited western state, Idaho has performed well in the literary arena. Its writers, especially when we include both those born in the state and those who later moved there, are far from insignificant. And prospects for the future are bright.

## CHAPTER THIRTY: SOURCES

The section on Idaho's art history is based primarily on Sandy Harthorn and Kathleen Bettis, *One Hundred Years of Idaho Art, 1850–1950* (Boise: Boise Art Museum, 1990). I have also made use of entries in Lamar, ed., *Reader's Encyclopedia of the American West*; Robert Taft, *Artists and Illustrators of the Old West, 1850–1900* (New York: Charles Scribner's Sons, 1953); Paul Rossi and David C. Hunt, *The Art of the Old West* (New York: Alfred A. Knopf, 1971); Larry Curry, *The American West: Painters from Catlin to Russell* (New York: Viking Press, 1972); William H. and William N. Goetzmann, *Looking at the Land of Promise: Pioneer Images of the Pacific Northwest* (Pullman: Washington State University Press, 1988); William H. and William N. Goetzmann, *The West of the Imagination* (New York: W. W. Norton & Co., 1986); Phil Kovinick, *The Woman Artist in the American West, 1860–1960* (Fullerton, Calif.: Muckenthaler Cultural Center, 1976); and William H. Gerdts, *Art Across America: Two Centuries of Regional Painting*, 3 vols. (New York: Abbeville Press, 1990), esp 3:98–101.

The Borglum paragraphs are based on Richard L. Jensen, "The Mormon Years of the Borglum Family," *Task Papers in LDS History*, No. 26 (Salt Lake City: Historical Department of the LDS Church, 1978); Lincoln Borglum, *My Father's Mountain* (Rapid City, S.D.: Fenwinn Press, 1965); Robert J. Casey and Mary Borglum, *Give the Man Room: The Story of Gutzon Borglum* (Indianapolis: Bobbs-Merrill Co., 1952); Willadene Price, *Gutzon Borglum: Artist and Patriot* (Chicago: Rand McNally Company, 1961); and Walker Rumble, "Gutzon Borglum: Mount Rushmore and the Agrarian Tradition," *Pacific Northwest Quarterly* 59 (July 1968):121–27.

The paragraph on folk art has used Steve Siporin, ed., *Folk Art of Idaho* (Boise: Idaho Commission on the Arts, 1984). See also Henry Glassie, "Artifacts: Folk, Popular, Imaginary, and Real," in *Icons of Popular Culture*, ed. Marshall Fishwick and Ray B. Browne (Bowling Green, Ohio: Bowling Green University Popular Press, 1970); John A. Kouwenhoven, *The Arts in Modern American Civilization* (New York: W. W. Norton & Co., 1948, 1967); Kenneth L. Ames, *Beyond Necessity: Art in the Folk Tradition* (New York: W. W. Norton & Co., 1977); and Louie W. Attebery, ed., *Idaho Folklore: Homesteads to Headstones* (Salt Lake City: University of Utah Press, 1985).

Sources on Indian myths and legends include Walker, *Myths of Idaho Indians*; "Visioning: Oral Literature of Idaho's Indian People" in James H. Maguire, ed., *The Literature of Idaho: An Anthology* (Boise: Boise State University, 1986), 3–37; "World View," in Walker, *Indians of Idaho*, 158–65; Richard Erdoes and Alfonso Ortiz, eds., *American Indian Myths and Legends* (New York: Pantheon Books, 1984); William R. Palmer, *Pahute Indian Legends* (Salt Lake City: Deseret Book Company, 1946); Joseph Bruchac, Gerald Vizenor, and Arlene B. Hirschfelder, "Indian Literature and the Oral Tradition" in *Halcyon: A Journal of the Humanities*, published by the Nevada Humanities Committee in 1990, 35–61; Ake Hultkrantz, "Mythology and Religious Concepts," and Sven Liljeblad, "Oral Tradition: Content and Style of Verbal Arts," in D'Azevedo, ed., *Handbook of North American Indians: Great Basin*, 630–59; and Sven Liljeblad, "The Oral Traditions of the Shoshoni and Bannock Indians of Idaho," *Rendezvous: Idaho State University Journal of Arts and Letters* 6 (Spring 1971):1–11.

Travelers' accounts, narratives of personal experience, and sources on creative works of fiction and their authors are listed in the appropriate footnotes.

Splendid compilations on Idaho literature are Maguire, ed., *The Literature of Idaho: An Anthology*; and Ronald E. McFarland and William Studebaker, eds., *Idaho's Poetry* (Moscow: University of Idaho Press, 1988). Also helpful are J. Golden Taylor, *The Literature of the American West* (Boston: Houghton Mifflin Co., 1970); J. Golden Taylor, et al., *A Literary History of the American West* (Fort Worth: Texas Christian University Press, 1986); and Dexter Fisher, ed., *The Third Woman: Minority Women Writers of the United States* (Boston: Houghton Mifflin Co., 1980), esp. 39–43, 54–57, 106–8.

151. 

 152.

155. Vardis Fisher, of pioneer Idaho parentage, became Idaho's most noted writer of fiction. ISHS 77–90.1.

156. Merle W. Wells (ca. 1982) is recognized as long-time Idaho State Historian and State Historic Preservation Officer. ISHS 82–2.42.

# CHAPTER THIRTY-ONE

# Idaho's Ethnic Heritage

FOR thousands of years Idaho was the homeland of aboriginal peoples who hunted in its mountains and labyrinthine valleys, fished along its mountain creeks and rivers, and dug for roots on its arid plains. Then, starting about 1860, Idaho was invaded by diverse peoples from California, the Pacific Northwest, Utah, the Southern Confederacy and border states, and New England and the Old Northwest. These new citizens represented a variety of cultures: Protestants from the backcountry of Appalachia and the Southern Highlands, New York-New England descendants of English Puritans, Virginia descendants of Cavaliers and their farm laborers, Hispanics from the Southwest, frontiersmen from the Midwest and Great Plains, and Mormon farmers and craftsmen from Utah, many of whom were themselves new converts from Scandinavia, Wales, and England.

This pluralism, this lack of a common culture, resulted in a general tolerance for different faiths and values, a respect for individual differences, a belief in private enterprise, and a diversified democratic society. Inevitably, differences existed—among whites, Chinese, early Americans, and African-Americans—among nationalities with their differing languages, religions, customs, and social institutions. The state's history might well have been expected to be one of friction and strife.

But all of these differences were overshadowed by the common experience of new and old residents with the environment, whether along the Clearwater, Boise, Owyhee, Snake, Bear, or Salmon. The isolation, the struggle with nature, and the unpredictable opportunities fostered a resourcefulness, self-reliance, and spirit of working together. Nature was spectacularly beautiful, but the state's difficult terrain, its aridity, meant a constant struggle for survival. There were pockets of incredible wealth in rich underground deposits, but the expense of extraction was prohibitive, the market was 2,000 miles away, and there was always the danger of skullduggery or attack by hostiles in the wilds. Cooperation was not a luxury; it was absolutely necessary.

The territory continued to attract new residents from many countries and states. Although the vast majority were from the American Midwest and Plains states, significant numbers came from Europe, Asia, Mexico, and Canada. Idaho is proud to boast that different cultures have prospered together without being overwhelmed. Those groups of greatest significance in the state's history will be reviewed briefly in this chapter.

NATIVE AMERICANS. The first people to live in Idaho were, of course, the Native Americans.[1] In 1990 there were approximately 12,000 Native Americans living in Idaho, about the number present when Lewis and Clark passed through the region in 1805–6. During the decades that followed that first white contact, these native peoples retained their distinctive cultures, languages, and traditions. Despite the efforts of the dominant white society to assimilate them, the Native Americans still cherish a respectful attitude toward the land and try to maintain some of their traditions.

The Indian response to white occupation shifted with the changing face of white policy. The first phase began in 1867 when Congress created a Peace Commission that dropped the treaty as a negotiating instrument with the various tribes and substituted agreements that required the approval of both houses of Congress. Such an agreement, designed to force the Indians onto reservations, was approved at Fort Laramie in 1868. The Quaker or Peace Policy that sought to "conquer by kindness" followed. Indians were taught white practices, elementary education was provided for children, and annuities were proposed to help the Indians become self-supporting. Unfortunately, Congress allowed the agreements to languish without ratification or appropriations, and some hard-liners continued to demand extermination. In 1869 Congress appropriated money and created the Board of Indian Commissioners, consisting of prominent Quakers, Episcopalians, and others, to oversee the disbursement of Indian funds. Methodists supervised the Fort Hall Agency, Presbyterians the Nez Perce Agency, and Roman Catholics the Colville Agency that included part of northern Idaho. Unfortunately, religious influences on Indian administration did not measure up to expectations, and the reservation system proved ineffective. As the years passed the entrenched bureaucracy of the Indian Service demonstrated both incompetency and dishonesty, Indian rations fell below subsistence levels, and reservation land was mined and farmed and grazed by whites with the right connections. Church representatives continued to push for crop agriculture, private property, education, and Christianity over traditional Indian religion and land uses.

In 1887 Congress passed the Dawes Severalty Act, in which Indians were each given a standard 160-acre allotment of land and the rest of their property was made available for use by whites. Of the approximately 138 million acres in Indian hands at the time, about two-thirds, including most of the best land, had passed into white possession by 1934. Whites continued to believe that communal ownership of property had deprived the Indians of the self-interest that was essential to "civilized" advancement. Programs continued to provide Christian education—mission schools, reservation schools, and off-reservation boarding schools—to instruct boys in farming and trades and girls in skills that would make them good housekeepers and farmers' wives. One praiseworthy step was the employment of Indian policemen and judges. Another came on June 2, 1924, when Congress gave full citizenship to all Indians.

Nevertheless the "civilization program" had hamstrung one way of life without replacing it with one more satisfactory. With the onset of the Great Depression the time was ripe for a new approach. In June 1934 Congress passed the Wheeler-Howard (Indian Reorganization) Act, which enabled tribes to purchase additional land, made loans available for tribal business ventures, gave Indians preference in employment, and permitted tribes to draft constitutions that would establish self-government. Under the leadership of Commissioner John Collier, Indian cultures enjoyed a new respect as Native Americans were given a larger voice in their own affairs. Infant mortality dropped, food production increased, and the Native land base expanded. A program was launched to relocate reservation Indians to urban centers, but it never achieved much success. There were many problems—infant mortality, disease, and alcoholism. County and state governments were asked to assume a larger role in providing Indian health care and education.

In 1946 Congress created the Indian Claims Commission to settle tribal claims against the government. In the many suits filed by Indians and their lawyers, some sizable judgments were rendered in their behalf. Nevertheless, the Indians suffered the dubious distinction of being the most depressed American minority.

The strategy of government Indian policy in the last three decades has been to encourage self-determination. Substantial sums were committed to develop an improved system for Indian social, economic, and political growth; many federal programs were turned over to Indian control. Native Americans were appointed to policy-making positions in the Bureau of Indian Affairs. Efforts also were made to attract tourists and light industry to reservations.[2]

Within this general framework, Idaho's natives have tried to make the best of their diminished property. The Nez Perce, who once shared about 14 million acres between the Clearwater and Salmon and from the Bitterroot Divide on the east to the mouth of the Snake River on the west, were limited in 1863 to an 800,000-acre reservation, later reduced through allotment to about 200,000 acres. Similarly, the Coeur d'Alene were restricted in 1885 from 4 million acres between the Clearwater and Pend Oreille rivers of Idaho and reaching into Montana and Washington to 345,000 acres around the town of Plummer. By 1990 Indians retained ownership of only about 58,000 acres. Various bands of Shoshoni, who once ranged all over south and central Idaho, down into the Great Basin and north to Canada, were placed on the 1.8 million-acre Fort Hall Reservation, now only 500,000 acres, which consisted of more than half the total reservation land in Idaho. Among those gathered together at Fort Hall were the Bear Lake Shoshoni, the Lemhi Shoshoni, the Sheepeaters or Mountain Shoshoni, and the Northern Paiute Bannock. The Boise, Bruneau, and Weiser Shoshoni—all Northern Shoshoni—were sent in 1869 from Boise Valley to Fort Hall, and the Mountain Shoshoni group of Weiser "Sheepeater" Indians followed shortly before 1900. The Western Shoshoni, who lived primarily in Nevada, reside on the 300,000-acre Duck Valley Reservation in southern Idaho and northern Nevada with some Northern Paiute from central Oregon. A Northern Shoshoni band from Bruneau Valley is also located at Duck Valley. (The Kutenai and Kalispel did not sign a treaty for a reservation within Idaho and have petitioned for recognition and land, as have the Delaware, who came into Idaho during the trapper era and have lived as a people in Payette Valley for more than 100 years, but more self-consciously since 1922.) In the case of each nation or tribe, the reduced acreage granted to the Indians made traditional food sources unavailable or insufficient.[3]

More recently, the Nez Perce have won important legal claims—payment for the loss of traditional Indian fisheries at Celilo Falls due to the construction of The Dalles Dam on the Columbia River and for losses from royalties for gold found on Indian land. Still working through the courts are suits for the protection of their salmon runs and fishing rights on the Clearwater, Snake, and Salmon rivers and their tributaries. The tribal council has pushed to create employment to support the 3,000 members by developing timber and limestone resources. They have sought to keep alive the Nez Perce language, to change the approach to Native American history in Idaho public schools, and to introduce Nez Perce history, culture, and language into the instruction their own tribal members receive. They have also enriched their cultural days and powwows with dances, songs, and feasts that honor the traditions of their people.

There are only about eighty members of the Idaho Kutenai tribes, most living in the Bonners Ferry area. In recent years, this small group has built thirty homes, a community building, a school, and the elegant forty-eight-room Kootenai River Inn. They have improved their educational system, held regular culture days and pow-wows, and helped the teachers of non-Indian children to prepare sessions on Indian history and culture.

The 900 Coeur d'Alenes on the reservation readily adapted to a farming and ranching lifestyle and embraced the Catholic faith. Obtaining an award from the Indian Claims Commission for land the tribe had owned, they used the money to buy additional property. Some $500,000 of this fund was invested in a six-thousand-acre farming venture that proved successful. The largest Indian-owned farm in the nation, the property grows winter wheat, lentils, spring wheat, and spring barley. Its earnings support construction, logging, hog-raising, and a gasoline station. The Coeur d'Alene hold an annual Indian Fair, with handicrafts, arts and agricultural displays, horse-racing, and other sports. Each July they celebrate Wha-Laa Days with a powwow. The tribe has kept oral histories of tribal elders and prepared slide shows to commemorate their Coeur d'Alene heritage. A Native American who is a former chairman of the Coeur d'Alene Tribe, David J. Matheson, currently (1991) serves as deputy Commissioner of Indian Affairs in Washington, D.C. Matheson, born on the Coeur d'Alene Reservation in Plummer, attended the University of Washington. He has responsibility for the day-to-day operations of the Bureau of Indian Affairs and is expected to stimulate much-needed economic development on tribal lands in the United States.

The 3,500-enrolled members of the Shoshoni-Bannock nation, sometimes called the "Sho-Ban," have developed economic activities that employ its members and bolster the tribe's economy. The tribal-owned Shoshone Bannock Trading Post Complex includes a grocery store, gas station, restaurant, and arts, crafts, and clothing store. A museum displays Indian baskets, pottery, clothing, and photographs. The tribe also derives income from the Gay Mine, a phosphate mine leased to the J. R. Simplot Company, and also owns and operates a 1,500-acre farm on which they raise potatoes, grain, and hay. Its 300-head buffalo herd supplies the buffalo burgers sold at the tribe's Oregon Trail Restaurant. With its profits the tribe has completed a $12 million housing improvement and development project. Its young people are encouraged to continue education beyond high school and bring back their advanced training to the reservation to help strengthen and broaden the tribe's many enterprises. The Shoshone-Bannock Indian Festival and All Indian Rodeo, held each August, features a parade, art show, food booths, recreational gambling, softball tournament, Indian games, dance competition, drum and singing contests, and a Miss Shoshone-Bannock contest.

The 2,000 Western Shoshoni and Northern Paiute on the isolated Duck Valley Reservation depend heavily on the Owyhee River diversion dam and canals to carry water to their farming tracts. Wildhorse Reservoir was completed in 1937, and the tribe for many years has been farming 11,000 acres of land. The Duck Valley people have retained some of their traditional crafts and customs including willow baskets, cradleboards, and rag rugs.

FRENCH CANADIANS. The first ethnic group to follow Indians in settling present-day Idaho were French Canadians.[4] Several, including the husband of Sacajawea, were in the Lewis and Clark Corps of Discovery. Others were fur traders with the North West Company and Hudson's Bay Company who remained in the area when the two companies consolidated. Among these were Michel Bourdon, who came with David Thompson in 1808, and François Payette, who traveled with John Jacob Astor's company and later was postmaster at Hudson's Bay Company's post at Fort Boise. French Canadians also found representation as Catholic priests. Andre Zapherin, for example, was assigned to Boise Basin and Alex J. Archambault to Idaho City and other mining and farming camps in the region. The impact of French Canadians is clear from many Idaho names: Coeur d'Alene, Pend Oreille, Nez Perce, and Payette River. Godin Valley in Custer County was named for French Canadian (actually an Iroquois) Thyery (Henry) Godin, who explored the country with Donald Mackenzie in 1820 and named the river and mountains after himself. The river was later renamed Lost River. Pattee Creek in Lemhi County recognized Joseph B. Pattee, who came into the area as an employee of the

American Fur Company and later settled on land at the mouth of the stream.

Many French Canadians joined the rush to Boise Basin with the mining boom of the 1860s. One of these was Joseph Perrault, from Montreal, who went to California, Walla Walla, Lewiston, and finally to Boise, where he became assistant editor and part owner of the *Statesman*. Lafayette Cartee built the first sawmill and quartz mill at Rocky Bar, moved with his family to Boise in 1866, and was appointed the first surveyor general of Idaho Territory.

French Canadians homesteaded land throughout the region. Frenchman's Island in Minidoka County was named for two French Canadians who filed a claim on the island. One of them ran a ferry across the Snake called "Frenchman's Ferry." A group of Quebec and Montreal natives moved to the Deer Flat area south of Nampa in 1903 and established a barber shop, bakery, carpenter shop, and farms. At the 1980 reunion of descendants of the original French Canadian settlers held at Saint Paul's Church and Lakeview Park in Nampa, the crowd numbered more than 300.

The north Idaho community of Colburn, nine miles north of Sandpoint, was named in Anglicized form for John Courberon, a French Canadian who worked for the Great Northern Railroad. From St. John the Baptist, Quebec, five of the thirteen children of the Poirier family moved into north Idaho and made it their home. A cove, falls, creek, and dam bear the name of Albeni Poirier. Beginning in 1883, he and a brother ran a cattle ranch in Spirit Valley. Later, the brothers built a road from Rathdrum to Albeni Falls, and the site became the headquarters for navigation of Priest River. Albeni Poirier built a small hotel, boarding house, and saloon just below the dam located there. The Poirier family now operates a museum that traces the history of the Blanchard community and the family farm.

In 1910, Idaho counties included 202 French Canadians in

Kootenai, 115 in Shoshone, and 140 in Bonner. Other populations were in the lumbering counties of Latah, Nez Perce, Boundary, and Benewah.

BRITISH ISLANDERS. The British had, of course, been in the Oregon country with the fur trade. They had explored the land, named geographic features, directed international attention to the region, operated trading posts at Fort Hall and Fort Boise, and indirectly paved the way for subsequent American settlement.[5] Most of the large percentage of British migrants to Idaho, mirroring mainstream American society, assimilated easily. They did not retain ethnic enclaves, were not subjected to the job discrimination that others experienced, and were sometimes referred to as "invisible immigrants." The three exceptions were the Cornish, Welsh, and Irish. The Cornish came in comparatively large numbers to work in the mines and concentrated in Silver Valley and the Owyhees. The Welsh came directly from their homeland or indirectly through Utah to settle in Malad Valley and Bear Lake Valley in the 1860s and 1870s. The Irish worked in Idaho mining camps, some as prospectors, others as shoemakers, grocers, saloonkeepers, butchers, and livery operators.

The discovery of gold in Idaho during the 1860s coincided with a depression in the mines in Cornwall, and hence many of the miners were attracted to Idaho. They were often referred to as "Cousin Jack," a complimentary nickname that suggested they had a cousin back home ideal for a vacant mining job.[6] Most of them, however, stayed in the United States and sent for their families.

Because of their experience and their strong sense of family and social stability, the influence of the Cornish in mining camps was often out of proportion to their numbers. Many of them were Methodist, and they filled in as lay preachers when formally trained ministers were not available. (One of the ministers was John Andrewartha, who served in Rocky Bar and Atlanta.) They refused to work on Sunday, formed church choirs and brass bands, and sponsored such recreational activities as wrestling matches. They also favored their own foods—meat and vegetables wrapped in pie crust, called "pasties." Some of the men rose to political prominence, such as legislators Richard Tregaskis and Luke Williams.

The Welsh who were not Mormons were dominant in mining areas in north Idaho. Wardner, the first mining town in the Bunker Hill region, was made up mostly of Welsh miners who had worked the Cornwall tin mines. They later moved to Kellogg. Most were single men, lived in boarding houses, and were sometimes the butt of jokes by other miners because of their difficulties with the English language. A group of Welsh and Cornish miners from Butte worked in the mines at Gibbonsville in Lemhi County during the peak mining years of 1880 to 1906. A few Welsh also settled in American Falls, one of whose children was blue-eyed, red-haired David Davis, elected governor of Idaho in 1919.

The Irish sometimes favored settling together because of the strong anti-Catholic sentiment among Americans. In his statistical study of Idaho mining camps in 1870 and 1880, Elliott West discovered that one in four miners and one in four of the skilled persons in mining towns were Irish. Most were males; in Boise County, for example, Irish men outnumbered women 285 to 37.[7]

Half the miners in the Wood River area in the 1880s were also Irish, and they likewise comprised a substantial proportion of the military in territorial Idaho. These Irish also contributed individually. Robert Dempsey, a glassblower in Ireland before he came to Idaho, mined, worked as an Indian interpreter, and established a trading post near Blackfoot on the Snake River. He founded the town of Dempsey, which later became Lava Hot Springs. Another early resident was an Irishman named Murphy who built a toll gate and charged a fee for using his private road near the present town of McCammon.

Irish women also were enterprising. Anna, Margaret, and

Mary O'Gara, sisters from County Cork, operated a rooming house and restaurants catering to timber workers in St. Maries. Witty, amiable, and "respectable," the O'Garas did not hesitate to do a little bootlegging on the side. As Ruby El Hult reported, once when officers raided their place, Margaret "poured her whiskey into a clean and sterile chamber pot and placed it under the bed. The officers found it but did not recognize its contents as whiskey." During another raid Margaret "brought her small whiskey keg into the kitchen and spread her voluminous skirts around it. There she stood adamant while officers searched the quarters."[8]

As part of labor-union activity, which they sometimes dominated, the Irish were highly visible in activities on St. Patrick's Day. Fenian Clubs, Irish Clubs, the O'Conner School of Dancers, and other such organizations allowed immigrants from the Emerald Isle to continue to celebrate their own culture and history.

CHINESE. The next national group to come to Idaho in force were the Chinese.[9] As we saw in Chapter Eleven, many Chinese fortune seekers followed the gold boom to Idaho in the 1860s. By 1870 there were 4,274 in Idaho, more than one-fourth of all the people in the territory. That year, approximately 60 percent of all Idaho miners were Chinese. They were also packers, cooks, domestics, merchants, doctors, launderers, and gardeners. Of the 445 Chinese men and 8 Chinese women living in Pierce in 1870 the average age was approximately thirty-two years; one to eleven people lived together in households. The group consisted of 411 miners, 14 gamblers, 3 hotel cooks, 3 blacksmiths, 3 gardeners, 2 laundrymen, and 1 each as clerk, trader, hotel keeper, merchant, hotel waiter, barber, doctor, and Chinese agent. One was a brothel-keeper, and eight women were listed as prostitutes.

Substantial numbers of Chinese worked in all Idaho mining

districts, not only in the 1860s but also in the 1870s and 1880s. Many "celestials" grew fruits and vegetables for mining camps, hauling them in two large hemp baskets equally balanced on either side of a heavy, wooden shoulder yoke, or in a wooden vegetable cart. Several communities boasted Chinese gardens. The community known today as Garden City was so named in honor of the Chinese who lived and worked there. In Lewiston, Boise, St. Maries, and elsewhere Idahoans were eating Chinese food well before the East or Midwest acquired a taste for it. C. K. Ah-Fong of Boise was a well-known herb doctor, duly licensed by the territory.

Some 4,000 Chinese worked on the construction of the Northern Pacific Railway; others worked on the Oregon Short Line, Great Northern, and Chicago, Milwaukee, and St. Paul and their branches. They also helped build the railroad and bridge at American Falls and worked in the railroad shops at Eagle Rock and Pocatello.

The number of Chinese in Idaho declined after 1870. There were 3,379 in Idaho in 1880; 2,500 in 1890; and 1,500 in 1900. Part of the reason for this decline was the anti-Chinese sentiment of the 1880s mentioned briefly in Chapter Eleven. In 1890 the Idaho legislature barred Chinese or "Mongolians" from holding mining lands. In 1897 the legislature restricted them from any mining activity. They suffered from several savage attacks; dozens were killed in prejudicial violence. Their religions, customs, clothes, burials, manners, queues of hair, insistence that their bones be transported back to China—all were ridiculed. The Chinese population declined everywhere except Boise, which was known as Cowrie City, the central Chinese community. Boise's Chinatown was first located on Idaho Street between 6th and 8th streets. About 1900 city authorities demanded that it be moved to 7th and Front streets, where it remained for the next seventy years.

After World War II the American attitude toward Chinese

changed. As allies in the war they were viewed positively. Those born in the United States saw themselves as American citizens and worked to bring family members from "the old country." The Chinese Exclusion Act of 1882 was repealed in 1943, making naturalization possible. Nevertheless, Idaho's Chinese population remains small. In 1980 only 625 people in the state claimed Chinese ancestry. They still have the traditional Chinese New Year, which is celebrated throughout the day and night with firecrackers, roast-pig dinners, Chinese and American candies, and special Chinese whistles. Paper dragons are popular in city and national parades, and Chinese paper lanterns adorn local festivities.

**THE MORMONS.** An extended essay on the Mormons in *The Harvard Encyclopedia of American Ethnic Groups* written by Dean May, a historian formerly of Middleton, Idaho, suggests that the Mormons have always regarded themselves as a people in the same sense that Jews, blacks, Hispanics, and Basques are considered a distinct people. The history of prejudice toward the Mormons in Idaho clearly fits into the perspective of ethnic relations.

The case for understanding Mormons as an ethno-religious people rather than simply as another religious group rests on many considerations. Mormons have (or at least used to have) a distinctive vocabulary, shared history, unique theological beliefs, definite in-group boundaries (prohibitions on the use of alcohol, tobacco, tea, and coffee), emphasis on in-group marriage, and a strong sense of peoplehood, which includes the "brother" and "sister" terminology. Mormons' bloc settlement, their modified self-sufficient economy, their gradual identification with Idaho, and their rural-urban transition all parallel the experience of many other ethnic groups in Idaho. Their agricultural skills, English-language background, and knowledge of western culture made their transition easier than that of many others, but the broad process of adjustment and accommodation was similar to other ethnic groups. Like others described in this chapter, the Mormons were gradually accepted into the larger society because of their economic contribution, their growing political power, and their own accommodation to the underlying values of the dominant society.[10]

Mormons who settled in Idaho were, in approximately equal numbers, British, Scandinavians, and Americans. A substantial number of the British were Welsh, who settled in the Malad Valley, Bear Lake Valley, and Iona.[11] Many of the Welsh spoke Cymric, were clannish, and expressed their fierce nationality in their music, poetry, and the perpetuation of their language and national customs. They celebrated Saint David's Day (first two days of March); held "eisteddfods" for the development of their literary, theatrical, and musical abilities; and organized Cambrian societies. Census figures of Malad Valley showed 400 Welsh in 1890. The people were zealous Mormon converts, and one reason is that their religion helped them preserve their language and customs. Mormon scriptures were published in Cymric, and Mormon communities vied for Welsh settlers because this would assure, or so they believed, good singers for the choir. The person who gave the Mormon Tabernacle Choir national status was Evan Stephens, a Welshman whose family settled in St. John, just north of Malad. That singing tradition continued; the Welsh chorus from Malad was invited to sing at the two inaugurations of Governor John V. Evans, of Welsh Mormon heritage, in Boise.

Another large group of Mormon settlers in Idaho were Scandinavians.[12] Some came directly from Sweden, Norway, and Denmark; others went to Utah in the 1850s and 1860s, worked on the Utah and Northern Railway, and then relocated in the upper Snake River area. Scandinavians represented about one-third of all the Mormons who settled in Idaho in the last third of the nineteenth century. Scandinavians from Utah's Brigham

City and Hyrum established St. Charles and Ovid in Bear Lake Valley in 1864, Mink Creek in 1871, Weston in 1875, and Driggs in the 1890s. In 1890 almost 1,000 Mormon Danes were located in Oneida, Bingham, and Bear Lake counties. They were farmers, stockmen, craftsmen, or worked for ranchers, the railroad, and the U & I Sugar Company. They were good builders of homes, business establishments, flour mills, bakeries, and power plants.

Many of the Scandinavians brought with them a folk tradition of celebrating May Day Eve with bonfires, merrymaking, group singing, and speech-making, followed the next day by a colorful Maypole dance and feast. The children might pick spring flowers and fill May baskets and place them on the steps of friends' and neighbors' homes. In some communities attention was paid to Midsummer Day, "Midsommarfest" (June 24), a celebration of the summer solstice—the beginning of summer in the Northern Hemisphere—that dates back to pre-Christian times. It was a time for visiting friends and relatives, enjoying traditional foods, wearing traditional costumes, singing folk songs, and performing folk dances. There were picnics, parades, and pageants. In some communities this holiday was postponed and celebrated in connection with Mormon Pioneer Day on July 24; in others, Midsummer and May Day Eve were celebrated together. In still others the celebrations were scheduled on June 14, the day the Mormon mission opened in Scandinavia in 1850. Scandinavians enjoyed dances, music festivals, and theatrical performances throughout the year and had a salutary influence on the communities in which they settled.

The minutes of meetings of Mormon men and women in these ethnic villages where Danish, Norwegian, or Swedish was still the predominant languages are fascinating reading, weaving, as some of them did, a mixture of English and Danish, Norwegian, or Swedish. Many residents left life histories similarly charming. Many poems included plays on words. It has been written:

"Then Danish speech falls on the ear, The sweetest sound a soul can hear."[13]

A third important group of Mormons were the Swiss, who settled villages in the Bear Lake Valley (including Bern and Geneva) in the 1860s and 1870s. Farmers and stockmen, they accumulated large cattle herds, made Swiss cheese and butter, held Swiss Days, and continued to maintain their traditions and customs.[14] Most of Idaho's Swiss settlers were Mormons. There were 249 Swiss natives in Bear Lake County in 1890, 362 in 1900. There were also 219 Swiss in Fremont County in 1910.

Bern was founded by John Kunz in 1873 when he was called by Brigham Young to raise cattle and make cheese for the local settlers and for export to Salt Lake City. Geneva was founded by Henry Touvscher in 1879. Both towns enjoyed Swiss yodeling, sauerkraut parties, and competition in handcrafted articles.

SCANDINAVIANS. Like the Mormon Scandinavians, their fellow nationals of other faiths also adapted well to the Idaho settlement process.[15] In 1900 Scandinavians constituted approximately one-fourth of the total foreign-born in Idaho. They included not only Danes, Norwegians, and Swedes but Finns as well. Finnish immigrants came in smaller numbers than the other three but were nevertheless an important segment.

Most non-Mormon Scandinavians had migrated first to Minnesota, Wisconsin, and Michigan, where they worked in the forests, before moving on to north Idaho to become loggers. Some worked in north Idaho mines during World War I, settling in Coeur d'Alene, Wallace, Potlatch, Moscow, Bonners Ferry, Sandpoint, and Troy. Maintaining cultural ties for many years, they sponsored group excursions, held midsummer festivals, and organized ethnic clubs. Norwegians celebrated Norwegian Independence Day (May 17); Swedes celebrated Walpurgis Night or Spring Festival (April 30) with singing, folk dancing, bonfires, and Swedish-style refreshments. Some communities included both of the two denominational Lutheran churches.

New Sweden, west of Idaho Falls, was a result of the formation of the Great Western Land Company, which constructed the Great Western and Porter irrigation canals in 1895. The settlers built a Lutheran church and large barns even before they finished their houses. By 1919 about 12,000 acres had been cleared and a system of dams and reservoirs established, and settlers filled up the area. The New Sweden Pioneer Association was formed to "keep alive the old memories of pioneer days" and to operate the New Sweden School.[16] Residents celebrated occasionally with potluck picnics, Swedish accordion music, square dances, horse-drawn wagon rides for children, a midsummer pole raising, and folk music.

Other communities of non-Mormon Swedes were in Firth, Minidoka County, and Nampa. Swedish children in Minidoka sometimes complained that other children laughed at their Swedish dialect, clothing, and food; their parents laughed right back at the Missouri dialect, Ozark dress, and cornpone and "chittlins" of their southern neighbors. Among the traditional foods of the Minidoka Swedes were clabbered milk; "valling," a dish made from potato starch with nuts and raisins; fruit compotes; "sill" or salt herring; head cheese; "kalvost" or milk pudding; and "skorpor," a rusk (sweet raised bread dried and cooked again in the oven). The large Swedish community around Nampa had gone first to Illinois and then moved to Canyon County. They also had an active Scandinavian Society.

Most Finnish immigrants came to Idaho between 1890 and 1920, the majority of them settling in Silver Valley in north Idaho and in Long Valley in central Idaho; most of those in north Idaho were miners from Minnesota and Wisconsin. Politically active, the north Idaho Finns constructed six workers' halls within a forty-mile radius of each other but built no church. In Enaville, their chief center, they held workers' meetings and performed monthly amateur plays sometimes infiltrated with socialist doctrine. Many of them sympathized with the Industrial Workers of the World. There were dances at the halls, weddings, basket socials, and dramas. They organized athletic teams and held track meets in which only Finns participated. Once, when loggers were moving logs down the North Fork of the Coeur d'Alene River, a group of Finnish women came to loudly protest their use of dynamite—it scared the setting hens off their nests and killed the embryos in the eggs.[17]

The Long Valley Finns, primarily at Elo in a high mountain valley, were farmers and loggers. More conservative and religious, they worshipped in the Suomi Synod of the Lutheran Church. Because Finnish is not a Germanic-based language, as is English, the Finns had difficulty learning English.

A well-known Finnish cultural artifact was the sauna, which contained two rooms, a dressing room, and a steam room with a wood-burning stove. Several apple-sized rocks were heated on the top of the stove with a water barrel nearby. Tiered benches were built around the wall, and the hardiest bathers sat on the highest bench where the temperature was hottest. The men often hit themselves with branches to stimulate their circulation. After sufficient steaming, they raced out and dove into a nearby lake or river to cool off. Saunas were heated Saturday nights. When the men had finished and the temperature had cooled somewhat, women used the sauna.

Another Finnish custom was celebrating "Juhannus," or St. John's Day, on June 24 (the equivalent of the midsummer festival), commemorating the return of summer. An all-day picnic included music, footraces, speeches, and food and drink. The community band played, a church choir sang, and the children recited verses.

The Finns in both north and central Idaho, adults and children, knew or soon learned how to ski. They fashioned their skis from red pine and old leather harness straps.

WESTERN EUROPEANS. The Germanic peoples who came to Idaho were from Holland, Prussia, various states of southern and western Germany, diverse sections of the Austrian Empire, Switzerland, and the Volga and Black Sea areas of Russia where Germans had moved generations earlier yet retained their identity.[18] There are problems in categorizing these people because "Germans," of whom 5,221 were listed in the 1910 census, might have been listed separately in the census under Russians, Prussians, Austrians, or Dutch (often confused with Deutsch). Many of Idaho's foreign-born Germans came from the Midwest rather than directly from Europe; the peak year of German immigration to the United States was 1882. Many of them fled their homeland to avoid lifetime military conscription.

Germanic people began coming to Idaho Territory in the 1860s as miners, investors, assayers, brewers, and bakers. In the 1880s other Germans joined the rush to Coeur d'Alene and nearby districts. Still others arrived when Indian reservation land was opened for settlement around the turn of the century. Groups of Germans worked in mines and on farms in Bonners Ferry around 1900; others maintained a German Methodist Church at Rathdrum. Post Falls, in Kootenai County, was named in honor of Frederick Post of Herburn, Germany, who moved to north Idaho in 1871. Frank Bruegeman, who lived in the Cottonwood area of Camas Prairie, wrote to a German-language newspaper in the Midwest and recruited a group of Germans from Illinois, who settled the town of Keuterville and built a Catholic church there. Others who settled around Cottonwood also built a Catholic church and parochial school. Another company of Germans formed the neighboring town of Greencreek, named after Greencreek, Illinois, from which they came. With so many German Catholics in the vicinity, they persuaded the Benedictine order to establish a convent, the Priory of St. Gertrude. Farther north, German Lutherans settled around Leland and Kendrick, and in their communities in Juliaetta and Cameron they built two churches.

A small community of Germans from a drought-stricken area of Kansas settled Council Valley; others went to Minidoka County; still others to St. Maries and Moscow. There were Mormon Germans around Blackfoot, Rexburg, Iona, Soda Springs, the Bear Lake Valley, and Teton County. Russian Germans settled as groups in the Aberdeen (Mennonites), Dubois, and Tabor areas in eastern Idaho. Another group of German Russians was in American Falls, where Lutheran and German Congregational churches were built.

Germans were also early settlers of Boise, where there were 1,000 in 1900 and 6,000 in 1910—approximately 10 percent of the population. The young men organized a Turnverein, a club dedicated to physical fitness and patriotism. They sponsored picnics, gymnastic exhibitions, singing, and dancing. In 1904 the German-American architect Charles Hummel built a Turnverein Hall in Boise with a stage, a 400-seat auditorium with a 200-seat balcony, and an exercise area in the basement. The hall was sold in 1916 when Germans and their organizations became objects of suspicion during World War I.

The Germans made important contributions to Idaho music. Nearly every small town had a brass band. Towns with a substantial number of Germans celebrated Oktoberfest, the Feast of St. Nicholas, and May Day. During the 1930s an elite group of Germans and Austrians came to Idaho to teach skiing at Sun Valley Resort. As a result, German and Austrian folk-music festivals, decorations, food, and chalet architecture became prominent in the area.

In addition to Germans and Austrians, there were three unique Dutch communities in Idaho. One, founded in 1908, was on the Camas Prairie in Idaho County where the Dutch established Christian Reformed and Dutch Reformed churches in Grangeville. Some of these settlers moved to the Salmon Tract in south Idaho and founded the town of Appledorn, later changed to Amsterdam. They built a Dutch Reformed Church and parsonage. Although many later left for other settlements, enough Holland Americans remained to maintain its ethnic character. A third Dutch settlement is much more recent. It began in the 1970s when a group of Dutch dairymen left California and relocated in the Jerome-Gooding area where they continued their dairy product operations. Their Dutch Reformed church serves about 100 families around Jerome, Buhl, and Twin Falls.

Belgian, Luxembourg, and French immigrants have established no ethnic communities. A non-Mormon Swiss group settled Island Park in Fremont County in the 1880s. Although the company that attracted them, the Arangee Land and Cattle Company, went broke in 1898, many of the Swiss remained as homesteaders and ranchers. After World War I a group of about 120 Czechs moved to Castleford, in Twin Falls County, where they maintained cultural traditions through lodges and community celebrations. Senators William E. Borah and Henry Dworshak, although not of this community, were of Czech origin.

SOUTHERN EUROPEANS. Italians came to Idaho, mostly during the years 1890 to 1920, to mine, farm, ranch, construct railroads, and start businesses.[19] In 1910, 2,627 Italians in Idaho lived in enclaves in Kellogg and Wallace, Bonners Ferry, Naples, Lava Hot Springs, Roston in Minidoka County, and Mullan and east of Priest River. The largest concentration was in Pocatello, where as many as 400 families were supported by railroad jobs. Almost half of these left after workers lost a nationwide railroad strike in 1922.

With 1,860 Greeks working on railroad construction, about 40 percent of the total railroad work force in Idaho in 1910 consisted of Italian and Greek immigrants. Many of the Greeks, who lived where rail-line activity was busiest, also left the state in 1922 as the result of the strike. Most of the Greeks and Italians lived in the railroad center of Pocatello, although there were pockets in Boise, St. Maries, Potlatch, Sandpoint, Orofino, Wallace, and Rupert. In addition to railroads, they worked in sawmills and mines and opened small businesses such as shoe repair shops, restaurants, and saloons. The Roman Catholic and Greek Orthodox churches played a central role in fostering an ethnic consciousness among the state's Italian and Greek citizens.

There were also Portuguese, mostly from the Azores, and some Syrians and Lebanese, particularly in Gooding County. The Basques, who are from northern Spain and southern France, are discussed below.

JEWS. Like the Mormons, the Jews are not, collectively, one ethnic group—they make up peoples from many nationalities and cultures. But in relation to the Gentile majority in the countries where they have lived, Jews have been treated as a distinct people. That ethnicity results from a combination of their religion, their European cultures, and their experiences in the United States.[20]

A few Jews, mostly single young men who were born in Germany (which included parts of Poland, Austria, and Hungary), spent a few years in the East and then ventured to Idaho in the 1860s and 1870s. Coming as peddlers, small traders, and wage earners, they quickly learned English, opened stores, and rose rapidly out of poverty. Others got their start in business as sutlers for the U.S. Army.

Larger numbers, mostly from Central and Eastern Europe, entered the territory and state between 1881 and 1919. They spoke Yiddish, shared a common European culture, and practiced a more conservative form of Judaism than did their German predecessors. As they settled in the Boise and Pocatello areas, their large numbers made possible a group ethnic identity.

Most of the Jews from Eastern Europe remained orthodox, obeyed dietary laws and laws of ritual and ceremony in their religious and personal lives, and held religious services in

Hebrew. Members of the Reform sects came to the United States from Western Europe and brought a more liberal form of Judaism. Services were conducted in English, and they more easily acculturated to American society. As East Europeans made adaptations and adjustments to American life, in religion as in other aspects of life, they established Conservative congregations that were similar to the Reformed; both Conservative and Reformed represented an Americanization of Judaism. Whatever the form of their religion, Idaho's Jews celebrated such festivals as the Feast of the Booths, Hanukkah or the Festival of Lights, Passover, and such High Holy Days as Yom Kippur and Rosh Hashannah.

Among the early Jewish residents of Idaho was Robert Grostein, born in what later became Poland, who came to America at age four, went to California when he was nineteen, and in 1862 joined the rush of miners to Idaho and opened a store in Lewiston. For thirty-three years Grostein and his partner and brother-in-law Abraham Binnard, who joined him in 1865, ran a profitable business. Grostein built several public buildings and "one of the finest residences" in the city, owned 3,500 acres of farmland, and operated a branch store in Warrens that he supplied by using his 200 pack mules. Louis Grostein, possibly a nephew of Robert, operated stores in Elk City, Warrens, and Lewiston.

Joseph Alexander left Adelsheim, Germany, at age sixteen, worked in New York until he learned English, and in the 1860s moved to the Idaho gold fields and opened retail businesses in Lewiston, Genesee, and Grangeville. His partner was Aaron Freidenrich, who was born in Bavaria and went to Lewiston in 1868. He later opened a general store in Florence, then Warrens, and then moved to Grangeville.

David and Nathan Falk, brothers, were born in Eggenhausen, Bavaria. They came to the United States while still teenagers. In 1866 Nathan moved to Boise and worked as a bookkeeper for his brother, who had gone to Boise in 1864. In 1868 the two opened their own general store and five years later expanded to include a third brother, Sigmund.

Alexander Rossi was born in Zybrechken on the Rhine, came to the United States at age eighteen, worked in New York three years, joined the California gold rush in 1849, later went to Oregon City, and then in 1861 moved on to Lewiston. He went the next year to Idaho City, where he engaged in the lumber busi ness and operated an assay office. In 1865 he relocated in Boise and built that city's first sawmill with his partner Albert H. Robie, from Lewiston. Rossi headed the construction of the Ridenbaugh Canal, was the first assayer in charge of the Boise City Assay Office, and did survey work in Idaho and Oregon.

Later comers included Simon Friedman, a German native, who moved to the Wood River gold and silver district in 1881, opened a general store, and invested in mining property. Another was Nate Block, who was born in Omelno, Russia, came to the United States when he was twenty-two, and moved in 1909 to Pocatello, where he operated a clothing store.

Perhaps the most prominent immigrant was Moses Alexander, who came to Boise in 1891 and was later elected governor. We have described him briefly in Chapter Twenty. His election as governor in 1914 was astonishing to the Jews since there were not more than 250 voting Jews in the state. But a survey of Boise newspapers reveals that Jewish merchants were regarded as "pillars of the community," and their comings and goings were reported as regularly as those of other prominent citizens.

In 1895, at Alexander's suggestion, Boise Jews incorporated under the name Congregation Beth Israel. A temple was dedicated in 1896, with David Falk presiding over the services. It is the oldest synagogue in continuous use west of the Mississippi. In 1899 the first B'nai B'rith Lodge in Idaho was established. By 1912 there were enough orthodox Jews in Boise to organize Congregation Ahavath Israel, which built a synagogue in 1949. In 1990 the Reform and Orthodox groups were combined.

Pocatello, a younger community than Boise, established a

Reform congregation about the time of World War I, a B'nai B'rith Lodge in 1923, and its first synagogue in 1947. In 1961 Temple Emanuel was built. Eli M. Oboler described Pocatello Judaism as "Conformoxaho," meaning part Conservative, part Reform, part Orthodox, "and a lot Idaho."[21]

JAPANESE. The first generation of Japanese immigrants made Idaho their home in the 1880s.[22] During the course of their lives in Idaho they lifted themselves, through back-breaking work, from the migrant laborers who followed the railroad and agricultural circuit to become successful merchants, tenant farmers, and other business people.

Most of the early Japanese migrants came from Hawaii, where they had contracted to work on sugar plantations. Many came with wives and families, and others sent for brides as soon as they could settle down. Most of the immigrants paid for their passage and had more money in their pockets than the average European immigrant. Japanese society thus took on an air of permanence unlike that of many other immigrants, even though the Issei, those born in Japan, could not own land or become American citizens.

The Japanese were not always welcomed. The *Idaho Daily Statesman* carried articles in 1892 supporting Mountain Home, Nampa, and Caldwell residents who had ordered "Japs" to keep out of the state.[23] Japanese immigration was, in fact, barred from the United States from 1924 to 1942. However, Japanese immigration had lasted for more than forty years (1882–1924), during which time the Issei could establish themselves, summon their families, teach their children Japanese traditions, and at the same time encourage their acculturation. Issei could not buy land, but they could and did lease it until 1923, when Idaho passed an act prohibiting Japanese from securing property. (The act remained on the books in Idaho until 1955.) Bonneville County had from 200 to 250 Japanese throughout 1900, 1910,

1920, and 1930. By 1980 there were 2,066 persons claiming Japanese ancestry in Idaho.

When the Oregon Short Line began construction in 1882, recruiters were sent to California and Hawaii. Within two years 1,000 Japanese men were working on the line, and by 1892 there were about 3,500. Japanese labor camps sprang up along the line through south Idaho, with shop headquarters in Nampa and Pocatello. In 1900 Japanese railroad crews worked in Ada County, Rexburg, and St. Anthony. By 1900 about 3,500 men were building branch lines in south Idaho, such as those from Murphy to Nampa and Emmett and from Weiser to New Meadows. In north Idaho a high proportion of the work force on the three transcontinental railroads was Japanese. Their earnings were low—from $1.10 to $1.50 per day—and they were lodged in broken-down boxcars fitted with wooden bunks that accommodated from six to twelve men.

Many of the railroad workers took leaves of absence to work for Utah-Idaho Sugar Company and other firms in the sugar beet fields. In 1907 all the 4,000 acres of sugar beets in Idaho Falls, Sugar City, Blackfoot, and Moore were worked exclusively by Japanese. Thinning beets by stooping with a short-handled hoe, and topping by reaching down for each harvested beet and cutting off the top, were hard work—"the kind of work to break not only backs but spirits too."[24] But then, as Buddhists and Shintoists, the Japanese had learned to accept whatever happens, to show gratitude for what they had, and to know that everything would come out right. They were not afraid of hard manual labor. By 1910 about 1,000 Japanese in south Idaho were employed in thinning and topping sugar beets, building railroads, constructing irrigation ditches, working as domestic labor, and employed in such private businesses as supply stores, boarding houses, restaurants, barber shops, pool rooms, and tailor shops.

Because the Japanese had achieved, by the 1920s, a near balance of sexes, they were more easily able to retain their language and customs within the privacy of their homes, where the Butsudan shrine (representation of Buddha) commemorating ancestors had its niche. Traditional foods were served, and traditional marriages and funerals were held. The Japanese also had social gatherings, dinners, and annual picnics. They honored their elders and took care of each other. Although the men learned English, the women, more protected, had less opportunity to learn the language. The husband spoke Japanese with his wife in the home, thus helping the family retain its language. Many adopted the dominant religion of the region and affiliated with Christian denominations.

Japanese children (Nisei), being born here, had access to the vote, the right to own land, and the civil protections denied their parents. They formed the Japanese American Citizen League (JACL) to assist in the process of Americanization and to insure their civil rights. By the 1920s the Nisei outnumbered the Issei. Parents were caught between the desire to preserve traditional ways and the hope that their children would find success in America.

After the attack on Pearl Harbor that brought America into World War II, as described in Chapter Twenty-three, 110,000 Japanese from the West Coast were forcibly taken to war relocation camps in Idaho, Utah, Wyoming, and other places in the interior. These relocatees did not affect the permanent settlers in Idaho, who were, nevertheless, often subjected to prejudice, abuse, and hatred.

After the war, many of the internees remained in Idaho to make their home, especially in the Nampa, Caldwell, and Weiser areas. Work and educational opportunities gradually expanded, anti-Japanese legislation was repealed, and the people were allowed to live as they wished. In 1952 legislation made alien Japanese eligible for citizenship; Japanese immigration resumed. In 1955 Japanese Americans successfully obtained repeal of the Alien Land Law and in 1962 Idaho voters passed a constitutional amendment that deleted the section disqualifying Japanese from full citizenship rights.

BASQUES. The people who call themselves "Euskaldunak" or "speakers and lovers of the Basque language" are perhaps the most well-known of all of Idaho's European ethnics.[25] The Idaho Basques came from the Pyrenees in north-central Spain, mostly from farms and villages within a twenty-mile radius of the Basque capital of Guernica. Beginning about 1895 and continuing for another fifty years, they worked as sheepherders, ranch hands, and sheep shearers. Their life was lonely and isolated, something to which the gregarious and community-oriented Basques were not accustomed. They often took part of their wages in ewes that they ran alongside those of their employer. Once their own flocks were substantial, they broke away, seeking their own range by leasing from private landowners or moving onto unclaimed rangeland. Thus Basque-owned sheep outfits spread throughout southwestern Idaho. Most made certain their children received an education to obtain different work. Not many second-generation Basques are sheepherders.

Most Basques coming to Idaho were single, expecting to earn and save money and return home. But many remained, sent for families, and established ethnic centers in several Idaho communities. Boise was the center of Basque settlement in southwestern Idaho, and the southeastern section of the city's downtown came to be dotted with boarding houses and pelota courts. A Basque priest served the people's needs beginning in 1911, and the parish established the Church of the Good Shepherd in 1918. The enclave started to decline in 1920 as more Basques became "Americanized" and settled in other parts of the city. They abandoned their separate church and reaffiliated with other Catholics. Nevertheless, Boise still remains an important center for Basque life and culture and, drawing from smaller Basque communities in Mountain Home, Nampa, Hagerman,

Twin Falls, Shoshone, and Hailey, boasts the largest concentration of Basques outside Europe.

Basques have contributed color and variety to Idaho life in the continued existence of Basque hotels and boardinghouses that feature delectable ethnic cuisine and informal, family-style atmospheres. The Basque boardinghouse was an important home away from home for Basque herders, and the women cooks and helpers treated all the men as sons or brothers. Towns like Shoshone had half a dozen such boardinghouses in the 1930s and 1940s. At Basque festivals, held annually in Boise, Mountain Home, and Shoshone, hundreds of spectators are treated to Basque cooking, athletic events (stone-lifting and woodchopping), and folk dancing. A Basque Museum and Cultural Center in Boise preserves artifacts, books, music, and other elements of Basque history to acquaint Idahoans and other visitors with their heritage. The Oinkari Basque Dancers have performed throughout Idaho and in festivals and tours throughout the nation.

HISPANICS. Idaho's largest ethnic group has its roots in Mexico and the American Southwest.[26] Many Hispanics and "mestizos"—people of mixed Spanish and Indian heritage—worked their way up from New Mexico prior to Idaho's gold rush of the 1860s. Once gold mining ensued, Hispanics arrived in Idaho Territory to work as miners and packers. Mexican miners worked placers in the hills near Idaho City; others found rich quartz deposits in the Salmon River mountains. Ramon Meras and Anthony Yane operated pack strings out of Lewiston; "Spanish George" ran a pack outfit out of Grangeville for twenty years; another group was based in the Loon Creek Mining District. Jesus Urquides had a large pack-string in the Boise district and built thirty cabins to house packers. He once moved nine tons of steel cable several miles in length up a mountain range to a mine in the Boise Basin. In Boise the enclave between Main Street and the Boise River was known as "Spanish Town"; some of its buildings were still standing as late as 1972.

In the 1870s Mexican vaqueros—cowboys—were hired to work ranches in Owyhee County and elsewhere, where some acquired land and stock of their own. Joseph Amera raised hundreds of cattle near White Bird, and Guadalupe Valez had a large herd in south-central Idaho.

Hispanics were employed by the hundreds to lay railway track in Idaho in the 1880s and 1890s, and many found secure employment in railroad towns like Nampa and Pocatello. Others worked in north Idaho in the Bunker Hill mine and smelters. In this century the development of large-scale agriculture in south Idaho and its subsequent need for cheap labor encouraged Mexicans to come in large numbers. Hand labor was required to pick fruit, thin and top sugar beets, weed and harvest beans, and pick potatoes. Many of these farm workers later became permanent residents, and by 1920 Idaho had 1,125 residents of Mexican birth.

World War II generated a new demand for agricultural workers. Growers induced Congress to create the "bracero" program that allowed farmers to use Mexican nationals to harvest crops. Employers were required to pay transportation costs, cover living expenses, and provide proper treatment. The Forest Service also hired Mexicans to plant seedlings and fight fires; crews of Mexicans were paid to fight blister rust.

The construction and expansion of food-processing plants in Idaho in the 1950s and 1960s increased industry demand for laborers to work in fields and in the new factories. In 1950 only 326 persons of Mexican birth were counted as permanent residents; many had gone to California during World War II. By 1960, 2,241 were calling Idaho home. Although job opportunities expanded, difficult problems emerged. The migratory farm work, the language barrier, and little financial and counseling assistance combined to give Hispanics the highest school dropout rate in Idaho; as late as the 1980s less than 40 percent graduated from high school.

In 1990 there were about 65,000 Hispanics in Idaho, about two-thirds of whom were citizens. A developing industry, the production of hops—a labor-intensive crop—employs many Hispanics. In 1986 Anhaeuser-Busch established a camp for about 150 Mexicans working in the hops fields north of Bonners Ferry.

Concern has increased for the operation of "decent" and "sanitary" labor centers. The Twin Falls office of the Idaho Migrant Council has taken over the maintenance and operation of the labor center a mile south of Twin Falls that has housed migrants for decades. The dilapidated housing has been transformed into a model labor camp equipped with new insulation, wiring, bathrooms, kitchen cabinets, and doors and windows.

With more Mexicans establishing permanent residence in the state, the Idaho Association of Mexican Americans was formed in 1976 to perpetuate Hispanic customs among their children. There are now dozens of Mexican restaurants, local tortilla factories, and bilingual teachers, nurses, and store clerks in most southern Idaho towns. Spanish-language radio stations and churches flourish, and Mexican bands play for dances, weddings, and fiestas. Mexican Americans give strong emphasis to familial bonds, and extended families have gathered in many places, with parents, siblings, cousins, uncles, aunts, and grandparents. The importance of an extended family is reflected in the care with which Mexican Americans choose godparents for their children—someone to look after them in case of death of the biological parents.

Religion has played an important role in Mexican American communities. Although the vast majority are Roman Catholics, there are many who are Mormons, and some have joined the Assembly of God and other charismatic groups. In the Burley-Rupert area, for example, there were in 1990 eight Spanish-language churches. A large tinted picture of the appearance of the Virgin Mary to Juan Diego had a prominent place at the front of the Burley Little Flower church, and small statues of the Virgin graced the front or back yards of many Hispanic homes. A statue of the Virgin was in the center of the lawn in front of the Guadalupe Center in Twin Falls.

Recognizing that Mexican Americans are a permanent part of their communities, Anglos have learned to enjoy many local Hispanic customs: the celebration of quincineras (the rite of passage for young women); Our Lady of Guadalupe and Las Posadas holidays that begin the Hispanic Christmas; fiestas and celebrations honoring patron saints; Cinco de Mayo, celebrating the Mexican defeat of the French army in 1862; Mexican Independence Day, September 16; and such musical groups as "Los Pequeños Ballerinas" and "Ballet Folklorico de Pocatello."

BLACKS. Although their numbers have never comprised as much as 1 percent of Idaho's population, African-Americans have made important contributions to the state's history.[27] York, the personal servant of Captain William Clark, served with the government-sponsored expedition of Lewis and Clark. A few black explorers and trappers ventured into the area in the years that followed; and blacks mined in Idaho in the 1860s, even though whites in Boise County passed a law in 1863 to exclude blacks and Chinese from prospecting, and the territorial legislature considered a bill to prohibit black migration to Idaho.

Silver City reportedly had the largest concentration of black miners in the territory in the l860s, and there were pockets of blacks in Boise County, near Wallace in northern Idaho, and at the mining camp of Custer in Lemhi County. The territorial census of 1870 reported sixty "free colored" people in Idaho. Of the twenty who lived in Boise, some were barbers, others cooks. With the growth of stockraising, black cowboys were also attracted to Idaho in the 1870s.

A few black converts to Mormonism came to the Salt Lake Valley in the late 1840s and later went to Idaho. Green Flake, for example, who drove Brigham Young's wagon to the Salt Lake Valley in 1847, later moved to Gray's Lake, near Idaho Falls, where he homesteaded and raised his family. Ned Leggroan, a former slave from Mississippi, also homesteaded in Bonneville County in the 1880s. Gobo Fango, orphaned in Africa, was smuggled into the United States by an LDS family in Layton, Utah. He herded sheep for the family north of Oakley Basin and was fatally shot there by a white cattleman in 1886.

Members of the Twenty-Fifth Infantry Regiment from Missoula, an all-black unit, were ordered to the Coeur d'Alene mining region in 1892 to crush the labor unrest. Seven years later, the Twenty-Fourth Infantry, another company of black soldiers, returned to the region to arrest striking miners. The Twenty-Fifth also fought devasting forest fire blazes near Avery and Wallace in 1910. One reporter wrote: "Black fire fighters made the mountains echo with their songs."[28]

The 1910 census indicates that most of the 651 black residents in Idaho were waiters, servants, barbers, farm and railroad laborers, and, in the case of employed women, domestic or personal servants. A few were farmers or miners. About half lived in Pocatello and Boise, where they worked for Union Pacific Railroad Company. Ten years later there were 920 blacks in Idaho. In Boise in the 1920s they worked in clubs and hotels and in homes as handymen and domestics. They ran barbershops, roominghouses, a pool hall, a grocery. The Owyhee Hotel in the 1920s had fourteen black waiters. The largest concentration of blacks in the 1920s, however, was in Pocatello, where the men worked as laborers in the railroad yards, on section gangs, and as porters. Black railroad workers for the Union Pacific in Pocatello refused to join the 1922 strike led by white employees because they were not allowed to be members of the union.

As elsewhere, some prejudice and discrimination existed. The leading theater in Pocatello required blacks to sit on the left side of the theater; others reserved balconies for blacks and Indians. Yet blacks did have employment, lodges, clubs, and friends. They often sponsored educational events for blacks and whites. Social life usually centered around the church. Boise had an African Methodist Episcopal church and the Bethel Baptist Church, Pocatello the Bethel and Corinth Baptist churches.

During the Great Depression of the 1930s, many blacks left Idaho. There were only 595 blacks in Idaho in 1940, four-fifths of whom lived in cities. Programs of the New Deal provided road-building and construction jobs and several all-black Civilian Conservation Corps camps. One of these was at Arrowrock Dam near Boise; two others were in Coeur d'Alene National Forest.

Idaho's African American population was 1,050 in 1950, some of them soldiers or former soldiers. Until the 1950s blacks were excluded from the YMCA and from working or dining in some restaurants. But in the years since World War II there have been black teachers in schools, black athletes at all the state's colleges and universities; and Les Purce became one of the first black mayors in the West when he was elected mayor of Pocatello in 1975. Purce, formerly a faculty member at Idaho State University and now president of Evergreen State College in Washington, served as chairman of the Idaho Democratic Party. Business, military, educational, and professional opportunities are now available to blacks in Idaho. There were 2,711 blacks in Idaho in 1980.

SOUTHEAST ASIANS AND FILIPINOS. The most recent ethnic group to come to Idaho were the Vietnamese, Cambodians, Laotians, and some Filipinos.[29] Approximately 1,800 Southeast Asian immigrants were resettled in Idaho between 1975 and 1988. Living primarily in Boise and Twin Falls, they have found employment in fish hatcheries, food-processing plants, electronics factories, and service occupations and on farms. The women have made curtains and upholstery. Like other immigrants, they wish to assimilate but do not want to lose their culture. For instance, the Lao Association of Twin Falls sponsors cultural events as well as mutual assistance. There are traditional weddings, funerals, and New Year celebrations.

Some Filipinos came to Idaho in the early decades of the century as farm workers. By 1960 there were about 200 Filipinos in Idaho, most of them in rural areas. Since then, most of the immigrants have been professional people—nurses, engineers, business people. Half of the Filipinos in Idaho in 1990 lived in Boise or surrounding towns.

Idaho has been culturally rich from the time the first immigrants arrived. The state's history demonstrates that, despite occasions of intolerance and bigotry, the different cultures could prosper together without being submerged or crushed. The most compelling proof occurred as Idaho concluded its centennial celebrations in 1990 with the re-election of Pete Cenarrusa, a Catholic Basque, as secretary of state, and the election of Larry EchoHawk, an Indian Mormon, as the state's attorney general. Both their stories are satisfying to Idahoans.

Cenarrusa was born in Carey, the son of Basque immigrants, and graduated from Bellevue High School, then from the University of Idaho, where he was a member of the university's first national intercollegiate championship boxing team. After teaching at secondary schools in Cambridge, Carey, and Glenns Ferry, he became a Marine pilot during World War II, retiring with the rank of major, and then a farmer and sheep rancher in Carey. He was elected to the Idaho House of Representatives, where he served nine consecutive terms including three as Speaker of the House. In 1967 he was appointed Secretary of State to fill the unexpired term of Edson Deal, who had died, and was elected in succeeding terms so that, by 1990, when he was reelected, he had served as a continuously elected state official for forty years—longer than any person in Idaho history.

Larry EchoHawk was born in Cody, Wyoming, one of six children of members of the Pawnee Tribe. He was educated in New Mexico and then attended Brigham Young University, where he played football and was named to the Academic All-Conference team. Like Cenarrusa, he served in the U.S. Marine Corps, then went on to earn a Juris Doctor degree from the University of Utah Law School and taught law at BYU, the University of Utah, and Idaho State University. He was named chief general counsel of the Shoshoni-Bannock tribe in 1977 and held that position for eight years. He was elected to the Idaho House of Representatives, served two terms, and then became Bannock County prosecutor. He was elected attorney general in 1990, the first Native American in U.S. history to hold statewide office.

Cenarrusa, seventy-three in 1990, represented an older generation, and EchoHawk, only forty-two at the time of his election, a younger. Early in 1991 *USA Weekend* featured EchoHawk on its cover as one of America's twenty most promising people in politics.

## CHAPTER THIRTY-ONE: SOURCES

The principal source for this chapter is the three-volume work by Laurie Mercier and Carole Simon-Smolinski, *Idaho's Ethnic Heritage: Historical Overviews* (Boise: Idaho Ethnic Heritage Project, 1990). I have even borrowed the title for this chapter from that valuable work. I hope the authors will regard my freely borrowing from their summary chapter as a complimentary acknowledgment of their valuable compilation. The particular sources on each section of this chapter are listed in the notes below. The third volume of their work is an extensive bibliography.

Also indispensable is Stephan Thernstrom, ed., *Harvard Encyclopedia of American Ethnic Groups* (Cambridge: Harvard University Press, 1980).

153. 

 154.

153. Larry EchoHawk, elected Idaho's attorney general in 1990, occupied the highest political office ever held by a Native American. ATTORNEY GENERAL'S OFFICE, BOISE.

154. Pete Cenarrusa, a Basque from Gooding, served as Idaho's secretary of state beginning in 1971. ISHS 72–43.4.

## CHAPTER THIRTY-TWO

# Search for Community

LIKE Americans elsewhere, Idahoans have struggled to maintain a sense of community. Crime, drugs, geographical rootlessness, and changing generational standards have militated against identifying oneself with a larger group. Yet centripetal forces have also been at work, strengthening the unity and sense of belonging. As the state changed from its predominantly rural status of 1890, the small-town-and-country relationship diminished but did not disappear. The spirit of fellowship and loyalty has continued to be expressed with undisguised enthusiasm. Idahoans do not like crowds but, independent as they are, they have developed enduring allegiances to their localities.

As it had been in the nineteenth century, life in Idaho in the first third of the twentieth century continued to be dominated by the horse. On farms horses pulled plows, planters, cultivators, mowers, and harvesters. People rode to the general store, to church, and to visit relatives in nearby towns in horse-drawn buggies, wagons, and stagecoaches. Children rode horses to school, to swimming holes, and to deliver milk. One heard sleighbells in the winter and the sound of passing teams in the summer. One sat on the porch on Sunday afternoon and watched the high-stepping elegantly caparisoned team of the local judge or bishop pull a democrat—a high, lightweight wagon with two seats—down the road to Main Street. The clop-clop of horses' hoofs was as much a part of Idaho village life as listening to the gossip in the local barbershop. The few automobiles were often mired in country roads, and RFD mail carriers frequently had to ford streams and ditches. By and large, each town or village furnished its own society and amusements.

A strong sense of community, a willingness to work together, was evidenced by road-building projects, church construction, the digging of irrigation canals, maintenance of public buildings, town picnics, Fourth of July parades, and occasional projects to render humanitarian assistance to people around the world—for example, earthquake victims in China and Turkey. Churches were the centers of social life, and bankers, physicians, and bartenders knew their clients by name.[1]

Community spirit was also evident in the many festivals developed in the years after statehood—celebrations that continue to this day. They include Soda Springs's two rodeos: the Henry Stampede and Stockmen's Reunion, the latter the fourth oldest rodeo in the Northwest; Old Settlers Day in Fairfield, celebrated August 15, a rodeo with horseracing and cowboy events; the Lewiston Air Fair, Dogwood Festival, Hydroplane Races, and Roundup; the Snake River Stampede in Nampa; International Folk Dance Festival at Rexburg; National Old Time Fiddlers Contest in Weiser; and the County Fair and Rodeo and Western Days at Twin Falls. Spencer hosts a Stockmen's Rodeo, Nez Perce sponsors the Lewis County Rodeo, and the War Bonnet Round-Up is held every year at Idaho Falls. There are winter carnivals in Sandpoint, McCall, and Grangeville; Lumberjack

Days at Orofino; Mardi Gras and Beaux Arts Ball in Moscow; Massacre Rocks Rendezvous in American Falls; and Salmon River Days in Salmon. Burley sponsors the Speedboat Regatta; Sandpoint the International Draft Horse Show and Sale and an August music festival; Buhl the Sagebrush Days and Harvestfest festivals. The Shoshone-Bannock Indian Festival is held at Fort Hall; the Rendezvous-Pioneer Days Celebration in Lava Hot Springs; Arts in the Park and Old Time Fiddlers' Jamboree in Shoshone; and Boise River Festival in Boise. Septemberfest is in Kellogg, and Oktoberfest and Jazzfest in Coeur d'Alene. The famous American Dog Derby was held annually at Ashton from 1917 to 1951, attracting hundreds of mushers and a huge crowd of spectators.

In addition to fairs in most counties, Idaho had two "state fairs" that attracted large numbers of exhibitors and visitors: the Western Idaho State Fair in Boise in August, and the Eastern Idaho State Fair in September in Blackfoot.

Other twentieth-century festivals that have garnered attention throughout the state and the region are Pioneer Day (July 24) in Mormon communities, the Flower Show in Idaho Falls, the Cherry Festival in Emmett, Music Week in Boise (the first in the nation), Spud Day in Shelley, and the Spring Poetry Festival in Pocatello.

That the symbiotic small town-and-country arrangement that characterized territorial Idaho continued into the first three decades of the twentieth century is verified by census data. In 1890, the year statehood was achieved, Idaho had no "cities"—defined by the Census Bureau as places with more than 2,500 inhabitants. People lived in small mining towns, logging camps, railroad towns, trading centers, Mormon villages, or—in most cases—on scattered farms and ranches. Even by the middle 1920s Idaho had only two cities with more than 10,000 residents—Boise with about 21,000 and Pocatello with about 15,000. As late as 1930 only twenty Idaho communities qualified as urban centers. In that year, a little over one-fourth of Idaho's people (29 percent) lived in cities, with the remaining 71 percent in or near towns and rural villages.

The town-and-country arrangement that dominated Idaho lifestyles provided healthy values, democratic patterns of behavior, and a sound educational system. One of America's most penetrating social theorists, Thorstein Veblen, described the country town as "one of the great American institutions; perhaps the greatest, in the sense that it had and continues to have a greater part than any other in shaping public sentiment and giving character to American culture."[2]

The automobile, electricity, radio, and motion pictures wrought a revolution in the 1920s and 1930s. The adjustment, wrote Idaho historian Peter Buhler, meant electrically lighted main streets; the conversion of livery stables into garages; the gradual replacement of village blacksmiths, wheelwrights, and saddlemakers by machinists, mechanics, and upholsterers; the prevalence of interurban electric streetcars; the substitution of fire trucks for horsedrawn hand pumpers; the paving of main streets to accommodate the "Model T"; the family gathered around the radio to hear "Amos and Andy," "The Shadow Knows," and "One Man's Family"; and weekly visits to town movie theaters to view Al Jolson, Charlie Chaplin, and Mary Pickford.[3]

Not all towns were transformed, of course. Mining towns at higher elevations and remote logging settlements continued to be served by mule trains that brought supplies, equipment, and food; stagecoaches still transported passengers and mail to a few outposts; and winter mail continued to be delivered in mountain hamlets by men on skis accompanied by dogsleds.

A unique town in many respects was Potlatch.[4] Founded in 1905 at a bend in the Palouse River in northern Latah County, about twelve miles north of Moscow, Potlatch was owned by Potlatch Lumber Company. Part of the Weyerhaeuser syndicate,

Potlatch was one of the West's largest lumber company towns. The company built not only the houses, but also the schools, the churches (one, later two, Protestant and one Catholic), hospital, hotel, bank, jail, opera house, library, gymnasium, and company store. Over and under the precisely laid streets were trees, water and sewer pipes, street lights, and electric power lines providing residents with the essentials of modern living. Although the term "company town" stirs memories of overpriced goods and credit policies keeping employees in debt, this stereotype was not true of Potlatch, where low prices prevented anyone "from owing their souls" to the company store. Potlatch historian Keith Petersen concluded that most town residents were proud of their community store; it generally served them well.

The town kept time with the rhythm of the mill, waking with the morning march of workingmen to the plant; taking noon lunch when the sawmill (largest in the world) paused at midday; and preparing for evening activities at the night whistle. The residents slept in company houses, sent their children to company schools, walked on company sidewalks, kept company yards, and shopped in the company "Merc." Yet there was diversity in the community.[5] Once a company attorney, William E. Borah, on more than one occasion, launched his campaigns at Potlatch during his thirty-four years in the Senate.

Since Potlatch had served its purpose of attracting and keeping a contented work force, the company made the decision to sell the town in 1951. Virtually everything—churches, schools, town hall—was sold or donated by 1954. The town declined to 880 people in a self-governing community, and by 1980 all the homes, businesses, buildings, and lots were privately owned. In 1983 the company announced permanent closure of the mill.[6]

The urbanizing process that was already under way elsewhere in the nation is evident in the decennial census for Idaho, beginning especially in 1930. Here are the urban (people in places with 2,500 or more inhabitants) and rural populations of Idaho for the years 1930 to 1990:

| | URBAN | | RURAL | |
|---|---|---|---|---|
| *Year* | *Number of people* | *Percent of total* | *Number of people* | *Percent of total* |
| 1930 | 129,507 | 29.1 | 315,525 | 70.9 |
| 1940 | 176,708 | 33.7 | 348,165 | 66.3 |
| 1950 | 234,138 | 39.8 | 354,499 | 60.2 |
| 1960 | 276,258 | 41.4 | 390,933 | 58.6 |
| 1970 | 385,434 | 54.1 | 327,133 | 45.9 |
| 1980 | 509,805 | 54.0 | 434,233 | 46.0 |
| 1990 | 563,779 | 56.0 | 442,970 | 44.0 |

Source: U.S. Department of Commerce, Bureau of the Census. "Urban" means places with 2,500 or more inhabitants; all the rest are "rural." Beginning in 1970 the urban definition includes unincorporated places of 2,500 or more; this was not done for earlier decades.

Not until the 1960s did the number of Idahoans living in urban areas begin to exceed the number living in towns and villages and on farms and ranches. Even in 1990 Idaho retained many characteristics of a rural society, with only one city over 100,000 and only six over 25,000. Nevertheless, more than half of Idaho's residents in that year lived in what the Census Bureau called urban places—cities over 2,500, of which there were forty-two in 1990. Another thirty communities had 1,000 to 2,500 residents, and 108 had populations from 100 to 1,000. Of the 127 with population under 1,000, 89 lost residents between 1980 and 1990.

The urbanizing trend has occurred in all sections of the state, north as well as south, east as well as west. Urbanization has brought freeways, traffic jams, thousands of shoppers in suburban malls, the construction of central office buildings, urban renewal, sports facilities, convention centers, and larger airports.

Annexation drives have sometimes accompanied the physical construction.

The progress in urban growth is dramatically illustrated in Boise:

| *Census Year* | *Population* |
|---|---|
| 1900 | 5,957 |
| 1910 | 17,358 |
| 1920 | 21,393 |
| 1930 | 21,544 |
| 1940 | 26,130 |
| 1950 | 34,393 |
| 1960 | 34,481 |
| 1970 | 74,990 |
| 1980 | 102,249 |
| 1990 | 125,738 |

While the state population rose 6.6 percent from 1980 to 1990, Boise's increased 23 percent.

In 1962 Boise reached U.S. Census Bureau status as a Standard Metropolitan Statistical Area. That growth brought frustrating efforts at civic planning and urban development. Transportation improvements included airport modernization and interstate highway construction. A veterans home, new schools, hospitals, parks, housing, sewage lines, and disposal facilities were built. A greenbelt development connected all of Boise's river-area parks. The LDS Church built a temple in Boise to meet the religious demands of more than 200,000 Latter-day Saints in the region. Forest Service lands were made available for a major expansion of Bogus Basin ski runs and facilities; popular as a regional winter resort, the nonprofit, community-managed area expanded to make available additional ski lifts, a ski lodge, and night skiing.

In addition to permanent migration to the Boise Metropolitan Area and other large cities, intermittent or short-term flows of population from the rural to the urban setting were set in motion. The same westerners who adamantly refuse to *live* in major cities make 150- or 200-mile shopping trips from Grangeville to Boise, from Mackay to Idaho Falls, from Stanley to Twin Falls, or from Bonners Ferry to Coeur d'Alene. In a reciprocal relationship, weekend recreation zones have been located beyond the range of daily commuting but clearly serve the populous areas. There are metropolitan connections to cities as superficially isolated as Sandpoint.[7]

Urban growth led to the expansion of suburban areas. Indeed, most of the urban increase has been registered in the suburban or fringe districts, not in the central city. The complex of suburbs around Boise, for example, most of them older towns at heart, has grown at a staggering rate and sprawled steadily into the once rural landscape. Although a majority of Idahoans are city-dwellers, they are in style suburbanites, fashioning the good life in split-level ranch homes with broad lawns and attractive patios. Along the fringes (and sometimes near the heart) of cities, large planned communities of condominiums, small single-family homes, and garden-apartment developments with their own shopping centers have mushroomed.

As urbanization and suburbanization have proceeded, Idaho's architectural styles have come to reflect both the old and the new.[8] Next to ostentatious new shopping centers are historic structures of another era. Images have become progressively more eclectic. Of particular note at the turn of the century was the construction in Boise in 1900 of the Idanha Hotel, a grand French chateau designed by Boise architect W. S. Campbell. The turreted, six-story hotel was joined in its Romance motif by the city hall and the Columbia Theater, both created by John Paulsen of Helena, Montana, who had an office in Boise from 1891 to 1893. Similar picturesque structures were the Seavers Building in Pocatello, the Hotel Moscow in Moscow, and the Northern Pacific Depot in Wallace. Other popular buildings were the Hotel Boise, an Art Deco design with vertical piers and decorative concrete panels that opened in December of 1930 in a gesture of faith by Boise's business community; the Bannock Hotel in Pocatello, completed in 1919, which according to the plans of Frank Paradice would have three towers, though only one was constructed; and the Union Pacific depot in Nampa, built in 1924–25, with a single round arch window as its main focus.

Boise City National Bank, built in 1890–92, referred to more recently as the Simplot Building, is a four-story structure styled in Richardsonian Romanesque by Boise architect James King. Trained in West Virginia, King came to Idaho to establish his architectural practice in 1888. He incorporated Boise sandstone in the building, taking advantage of its location to create a round corner similar to Marshall Field's department store in Chicago. In the next two decades other buildings in cities' business sections followed this example. Steel framing also was introduced to commercial construction during this period. Tested in Chicago in the 1880s, the new skeleton structure was a precursor to the simpler styles popular in the early twentieth century.

The Lewiston Normal School and the Boise Natatorium—a fanciful Moorish structure with towers, side wings, and keyhole arches—were both examples of important public projects. Another public commission was the Bear Lake County Courthouse in Paris, designed by Salt Lake City architect Truman O. Angell, Jr. These public facilities usually focused on space for foot traffic, a large reception or entertainment area, a central hallway, and perhaps a tower. The more compact rooms were for offices and instruction.

Residential areas were likewise eye-catching. Normal Hill in Lewiston (around the Lewiston Normal School) and the area surrounding the Academy of Idaho in Pocatello were indicative of distinctive architectural elements applied to residences.

Exclusive neighborhoods included a parade of picturesque homes with crested towers, brick French Chateaux design, Romanesque arches, Palladian windows, Queen Anne shingles, and fanciful wood ornamentation.

While urban communities were expanding, the rural landscape was adapting as well. Traditional log construction, which had dominated in the early years of settlement, was replaced with frame farmhouses in which the interior floor plan was expanded with parlors, halls, and wings. These structures, too, benefited from advances in transportation, architectural publishing, and the trends in towns nearby.

In railroad towns, the commercial area expanded with mercantiles, office buildings, banks, hotels, stables, lodge halls, a city hall, sometimes a fire station, and the railroad depot. Depots were not always imposing. Through the 1890s railroads introduced cast-iron storefronts—cornices, window heads, and facades of galvanized sheet iron pressed to mimic carved stonework and enhance architectural designs. There are good examples in Hagerman, Bellevue, Oakley, Franklin, and Ketchum.

The Forest Service used standard plans and styles to create a distinctive image for its service facilities. The "Use Book" published in 1906 suggested: "Whenever possible cabins should be built of logs with shingle or shake roofs." Manuals also carried suggestions for administrative buildings, ranger housing, barns, blacksmith shops, fire lookouts and barracks, and called for attention to the local materials. One plan book advised: "If the timber on the site is predominantly conifer, a log building is the type; if broad leaf, a frame building is the proper one. If there is neither conifer nor broad leaf plainly in view from the site, a frame building is the type."[9]

Ranger stations were built in the Caribou, Challis, and Salmon national forests in the 1930s, and Sun Valley Resort was opened by W. Averell Harriman as the "St. Moritz of America." Recreational facilities near Yellowstone National Park, Island Park, and Targhee National Forest began to develop seriously in the 1940s. Private ranch resorts and dude ranches also became popular. Cottages, guesthouses, and barns were built in traditional log construction with green and white detail. Many summer homes began to dot the hillsides. Owners of such homes and resorts had been applying for permits to use public land since 1902. Private facilities from the Big Springs Complex to Yellowstone National Park employed mostly rustic designs with a touch of the bungalow, Colonial Revival, and Tudoresque motifs that became synonymous with recreation. Lakeshore property on Payette and other lakes flourished. Resorts were also established at Priest Lake in the Idaho panhandle.

The State Board of Education in the early 1900s published one-, two-, and three-room school plans that could be adopted by local boards and used in the system quickly and easily. A study of Boise schools by Suzanne Lichtenstein indicates that the school environment was initially designed with a primary emphasis on natural light and safety. Art and music rooms were a low priority, but student desks were arranged in each room to focus light over the left shoulder. To satisfy fire regulations, doors opened outward and stairs were at least five feet wide. As designs matured, the school plans shifted as well.[10] Spori Hall at Ricks College in Rexburg utilizes an early Beaux Arts design. The Lewiston Normal School, Albion Normal School, the Academy of Idaho at Pocatello, the state university at Moscow, and the College of Idaho at Caldwell all appeared in this burgeoning building period from 1890 to 1905. Boise Junior College and the dairy science building at the University of Idaho, built in the 1940s, reflected a neo-Gothic design.

Churches and hospitals also showed signs of change, and many echoed or duplicated styles used by similar groups elsewhere. The Mormon ward building in Boise's Fort Street neighborhood resembled a Georgian-period Colonial church. The LDS temple in Idaho Falls, started in 1940, served all Northwest Mormons and fostered an expanded sense of community. Delayed by World War II, the $750,000 building with its gleaming white cast stone and center spire was finally dedicated September 23, 1945. Neo-Gothic designs were created by Tourtellotte and Hummel for twenty Catholic churches, parish schools, and rectories, including St. Theresa's in Orofino (1937), St. Mary's in Boise (1937), St. Mary's in Moscow (1930), and St. Anthony's in Pocatello (1941). An excellent example of a Gothic structure is Holy Rosary Catholic Church in Idaho Falls (1947).

In 1889 the first Catholic bishop of Boise, the Right Reverend Alphonsus J. Glorieux, invited the Sisters of the Holy Cross in Notre Dame, Indiana, to establish Saint Teresa's Academy in Boise. With the encouragement of the Idaho State Medical Association, which was formed in 1893, the Sisters also founded Saint Alphonsus Hospital in 1894. The hospital, located at Fifth and State streets, had twenty-four beds. St. Alphonsus installed Idaho's first X-ray machine in 1900. By 1936 the hospital was treating more than 3,000 patients annually. As the medical needs of the region expanded, Saint Alphonsus in 1972 moved to a $14 million, six-story facility. By 1990 the hospital—then known as the Saint Alphonsus Regional Medical Center—had 269 beds and specialized in emergency care, neurology, kidney dialysis, mental health, orthopedics, ophthalmology, plastic surgery, and outpatient surgery. Like many other modern hospitals, it now has a complex of medical office buildings adjacent. The hospital operated a School of Nursing until 1969, when the program was transferred to Boise State University. It operates a Family Maternity Center, Geriatric Assessment Center, Health Promotion Institute, and Family Practice Residency.[11]

St. Luke's Hospital was opened in Boise in 1902 when Episcopal Bishop James B. Funsten converted a small cottage into a hospital with six beds. The hospital was expanded three times in the next five years, and in 1928 a four-story building was constructed at First and Bannock streets with 135 patient beds. St. Luke's Regional Medical Center, as it was known in 1990, had a bed capacity of 300 and served about 20,000 patients annually. It too has medical offices and outpatient facilities clustered around it. St. Luke's has concentrated on obstetrics, neonatal intensive care, pediatrics, and cardiac care, including open-heart surgery. Regionalization of cancer treatment came with the addition of the Mountain States Tumor Institute, established in 1969, which offers radiation therapy, chemotherapy, and surgery. In 1903 St. Luke's established a School of Nursing whose program was transferred to Boise State University in 1957.[12]

Hospitals that emerged soon after St. Alphonsus and St. Luke's were the Central Miners' Union Hospital at Wallace, the Wardner Hospital (which later moved to Kellogg), and the St. Anthony Mercy Hospital. Other hospitals were built in Ashton, Arco, Blackfoot, Rexburg, Pocatello, Montpelier, Jerome, Sandpoint, Moscow, Lewiston, Weiser, Caldwell, Nampa, Gooding, Salmon, and Hailey.

In the 1920s an imposing hospital was built by the Latter-day Saints on the east bank of the Snake River at Idaho Falls. This five-story structure with 135 rooms served the entire upper Snake River region. In 1952 the Magic Valley Memorial Hospital in Twin Falls ushered in a new era for medical care in that region. Other hospitals were constantly updating.

The Blackfoot mental-care facility, now called the State Hospital South, opened in 1881. During its first year sixty-six patients were received, fourteen were discharged, and five died. By 1900 the facility averaged 167 patients and by the 1950s about 713. In 1990, with different patterns of care for the mentally ill, the figure was less than 300. Another such facility, the State Hospital North, was opened in Orofino in 1901 and averaged about eighty patients. The state supports several regional mental health centers around the state that serve many outpatients.

Idaho has had a medical practice act since 1898; district medical societies operate in eight locations in the state. By

1990 1,450 physicians were practicing in Idaho, the fewest per capita of any state in the nation—probably because of the isolation of many rural practices, the low Medicare reimbursement, and the absence of a medical school in Idaho. Prospective physicians in Idaho can compete for reserved places in area medical schools under various consortium plans.[13]

Architectural Modernism, growing out of an international culture and devoid of the ornamentation of previous periods, has had a profound impact on Idaho building styles, particularly since World War II. School systems, interstate freeways, commercial zones, and sprawling residential suburbs all have been marked by this movement.

International Modern designs include the boldly styled Federal Building in Boise, built in 1967; its concrete and other construction materials have no stated relationship with the Boise hills or environs. The cylindrical auditorium at the University of Idaho was an advance in campus design. The engineering of the roof of Kibbie Stadium at the University of Idaho, which spans 400 feet with trusses adapted from Arthur Troutner's lightweight steel-and-wood Trus-Joist system, earned its designers the Outstanding Civil Engineering Achievement from the American Society of Civil Engineers. During their years of expansion the College of Southern Idaho in Twin Falls, the Albertson College of Idaho in Caldwell, Northwest Nazarene College in Nampa, and Ricks College in Rexburg have all experienced significant campus construction with a modern flair. A number of large administration buildings and classrooms have dominated the university campuses, dwarfing some of the quadrangle structures that had been sufficient for half a century and had added to the campus landscape. Some campuses simply tore down the old to make way for the new.

Many Idahoans saw little value in the gaudy, excessive architectural styles of the past. Although temporarily out of favor, not all old buildings fell to the wrecking ball. A national effort at historic preservation reached Idaho in the 1970s following the passage of the 1966 National Historic Preservation Act. The restoration program under Merle W. Wells, Idaho's historic preservation officer for two decades, had a major effect on preserving and restoring historic buildings.

Many observers have become concerned that urbanization and suburbanization have been accompanied by (but not necessarily as a cause of) changes in gender roles and family life. In 1990 more than half the married women in Idaho were employed outside the home. Children were often in need of the supervision provided by public and private day-care and pre-school centers. Families were less patriarchal. Communities witnessed sharp increases in crime and juvenile delinquency, higher divorce rates, drug addiction, and greater cosmopolitan diversity. (No cause-and-effect relationship is implied.) Idahoans, along with other Americans, seem to have a "cultural schizophrenia" or "bifurcation outlook" in regard to the role of women.[14] On the one hand, little opposition was manifested to the larger number of women working outside the home; on the other hand, women were expected to hold to the traditional roles of wife and mother. Caught between such earlier images of womanhood and the pressures of the workplace, women suffered mounting stresses evidenced in soaring rates of family breakup and addictions to tranquilizers and alcohol. The birth rate dropped as fathers and mothers tried to devote more time and energy to each child in the perilous journey from childhood to young adulthood. Help in childrearing and acculturation came from such organizations as public schools, Boy Scouts, Girl Scouts, Campfire Girls, YMCA, YWCA, 4-H, FFA, and churches. These institutions helped parents in maintaining standards of morality and patterns of correct behavior.

Strangely enough, religious activity increased. Many denominations recorded substantial gains. This may have been due in part to the social advantages of membership, but those attracted to the different religions say that their faith helps them to resist moral breakdown and adds meaning to their lives. There is no reason to doubt their sincerity.

Voluntary community activity, particularly by women, has also increased. Idaho women have, as we have noted in these pages, exercised leadership in many areas—religion, politics, education, music, art, literature, agriculture, business, the professions, and the family. From the time of early Indian settlement to the present, they have contributed individual and collective effort to worthy causes. As pioneers, immigrants, shopkeepers, farm housewives, and suburban mothers, they have helped to make Idaho a better place in which to live. Women of various hues and ethnicities, from aboriginal shamanesses of ancient times to the dual-role career woman and mother of 1990, have played memorable roles—sometimes created by them, sometimes forced upon them by society—in the significant social and political events of Idaho's history.

Although in many parts of the United States the sense of community tended to decline as society became more expansive and mobile, the problems of transportation and communication in territorial Idaho were such that modern developments actually strengthened the unity and sense of belonging of Idaho's residents. In contrast to earlier generations, there was no longer a strong yearning for separatism in northern Idaho, and Mormon settlers in the upper Snake River Valley felt a far stronger kinship with their native state. A witness of such commitment was evidenced when Idahoans all over the state participated enthusiastically in the centennial celebrations of 1990.

## CHAPTER THIRTY-TWO: SOURCES

Many of the sources listed for Chapter Seventeen were also useful in connection with this chapter. Particularly valuable were: Stacy Ericson, ed., *The Idaho Small Town Experience: 1900–1925* (Boise:

Idaho State Historical Society, 1981); Frederick Lewis Allen, *The Big Change: America Transforms Itself 1900–1950* (New York: Harper and Brothers, 1952); "Social Patterns in the Modern West" in Malone and Etulain, *The American West*, 120–69; and Walter Nugent, "The People of the West since 1890," and Carl Abbott, "The Metropolitan Region," in Nash and Etulain, eds., *The Twentieth-Century West: Historical Interpretations*, 35–70, 71–98.

Other helpful sources include Leonard J. Arrington, "Recalling a Twin Falls Childhood," *Idaho Yesterdays* 15 (Winter 1982):31–40; Wells, *Boise: An Illustrated History*, esp. 119–89. See also James B. Gardner and George Rollie Adams, eds., *Ordinary People and Everyday Life: Perspectives on the New Social History* (Nashville, Tenn.: American Association for State and Local History, 1983); Carl Degler, *At Odds: Women and the Family in America from the Revolution to the Present* (New York: Oxford University Press, 1980); Sara M. Evans, *Born for Liberty: A History of Women in America* (New York: Free Press, 1989); Betty Penson-Ward, *Idaho Women in History* (Boise: Legendary Publishing Company, 1991); and David J. Russo, *Families and Communities: A New View of American History* (Nashville: American Association for State and Local History, 1974).

155.

156.

155. A common meeting place for men in the early years of the twentieth century was the village pool hall. At Matt's Place in Grangeville in 1916, Matt Geary is behind the bar; the man with the cue is Mort Martin. DONATED BY VERNA MCGRANE, UIL 5–117–3C.

156. The fire department, like this one in Twin Falls, was usually made up of community volunteers. BISBEE PHOTO, ISHS 73–221.407/A.

157.

158.

157. Twin Falls residents celebrated their May Festival in 1910 with typical style. BISBEE PHOTO, ISHS 73–221.761/B.

158. *The Mikado,* produced in Twin Falls in 1912, drew on the theatrical talents of the residents for the cast. BISBEE PHOTO, ISHS 73–221.521.

159.

160.

159. The streets of Preston in 1910 were similar to those in agricultural villages around the country. USHS.

160. For most of this century, as in this 1940 photo, Pocatello was Idaho's second largest city. USHS.

161.

162.

161. Oinkari Basque Dancers in 1965 illustrate the diversity of settlers who continued to maintain their cultural heritage. UIL 6–78–2D.

162. The Nez Perce Rodeo, 1971, bespeaks the acculturation of north Idaho Native Americans. UIL 5–101–3A.

163. 

164. 

163. In the foreground in this 1965 view of Idaho Falls is the Snake River and falls; in the left foreground is the LDS Temple; right foreground is the Idaho Falls Hospital. ISHS 78–2.108.

164. Now a seaport, Lewiston provides services for many people, including this splendid St. Joseph's Hospital, shown in 1969. WILSON, LEWISTON, PHOTOGRAPHER, UIL 5–7–3N.

165.

165. The June 5, 1976, collapse of the Teton Dam damaged millions of dollars' worth of property in the southeastern Idaho communities downstream. ISHS 82–114.3/A.

# CHAPTER THIRTY-THREE

# Politics, Economics, and the Centennial

## POLITICAL PARADOXES

FROM just after World War II until January 1971—a total of twenty-four years—Idaho's governors were Republicans. The vagaries of Idaho politics are clearly evident in that Idaho elected Democratic governors for the next twenty-four. Some of the explanation for this paradox can be traced to Verda Barnes, a brilliant Idaho political analyst who never held office. She came from an active Democratic family in Fremont County. As a young mother she received a letter from Jim Farley, the Democratic National Chairman, asking her to get involved in Idaho politics. She accepted the challenge and spent the next thirty years shaping political thought and action in the Gem State. She became national vice chairman of the Young Democrats and then joined the staff of Glen Taylor in 1944 and moved to Washington. In 1957 Barnes went to work for Senator Frank Church as his in-house analyst. She kept him out of trouble at home and in front of the voters on all the right issues. She retired in the early seventies and died in May 1980—before Church's defeat that year. Above all, wrote Randy Stapilus, Barnes had "the political equivalent of a musician's perfect pitch: with a dozen phone calls she knew precisely what was happening in Idaho and how to deal with it."[1]

In 1970 Barnes persuaded Senator Church that his future was tied to a strong gubernatorial candidate. The two of them urged the nomination of Cecil D. Andrus, a "liberal" Democrat who was in the forefront of promoting environmental issues. Andrus, a friend of Church, and only forty years of age (Church was forty-six), was born in Hood River, Oregon, attended Oregon State University one year, and joined the U.S. Navy, where he served as a crew member of a patrol bomber in Korea. In 1955 he and his wife, Carol Mae May, went to northern Idaho, where he worked as a lumberjack and helped operate a sawmill at Orofino. He later sold insurance in Lewiston. "Cece" entered politics in 1960, when at age twenty-nine he was elected to the Idaho State Senate from Clearwater County. He became the Democratic gubernatorial candidate late in the 1966 campaign when the party's original nominee, Charles Herndon of Salmon, was killed in a plane crash. Andrus returned to the senate in 1968. Thanks to the effective work of Barnes and others two years later, Andrus received the Democratic nomination over conservative Max Hanson and went on to win the election over incumbent Republican governor Don Samuelson. Andrus was reelected in 1974 with a margin of 71 percent of the vote, the largest winning margin in Idaho history except for Frank Stuenenberg's in 1896.

After the 1976 election of Jimmy Carter as president, Andrus resigned as governor to accept appointment as Secretary of the Interior in Carter's cabinet. Andrus was automatically replaced as governor by Democratic lieutenant governor John V. Evans, a native of Malad, who was subsequently elected governor in his own right in 1978 and reelected in 1982. Evans had attended Idaho State University and Stanford and served as an Army infantryman in World War II; he was a rancher and Malad banker and businessman. He had been active in Idaho politics for many years, serving as a state senator, 1953–57; senate majority leader, 1957–59; mayor of Malad, 1960–66; and senate minority leader, 1969–74.

After Andrus returned to Idaho in 1981, he established a natural-resources consulting firm and then, at the end of Evans' second full term in November 1986, was again elected governor. He was reelected in 1990.

Andrus and Evans were consistent advocates of an adequately funded educational system, took steps to build a stronger economy, and sought to strike a wise balance between the positions of "conservationists" and "developers." Both men championed local land-use planning laws and protection of wild and scenic rivers. Andrus served as chairman of the Western Governors' Association and the National Governors' Association.

Meanwhile, conservative Republicans strengthened their numbers in the legislature. Clashes were common between farm interests anxious to expand irrigation along the Snake River Plain and customers of Idaho Power Company preferring to assign water to hydroelectric generators. Contentious negotiation and litigation continued for several years.

In 1972, James A. McClure, a Republican, took Len Jordan's place in the United States Senate. A native of Payette, McClure served in the Navy during World War II, earned his law degree at the University of Idaho, and practiced law with his father in Payette. He and Andrus were both elected to the Idaho Senate in 1960. McClure served three terms in the state legislature and then in 1966 was elected congressman, a position he also held for three terms before successfully running for the Senate. Reelected in 1978 and 1984, he retired in 1991 to serve as a consultant in Boise and Washington, D.C. He served as chairman of the Senate Energy and Natural Resources Committee from 1981 to 1987 and was also a member of the Appropriations and Rules committees.

Having served eighteen years in the Senate, including a term as chairman of a powerful committee (only the third Idahoan to serve as a committee chairman), McClure left his imprint on every major piece of energy, public-lands, and natural-resources legislation in those years. He was instrumental in creating the Hells Canyon National Recreation Area, arranging the Snake River water-rights settlement, and securing approval for the $6.6 million ski gondola for Kellogg, $8 million to pave the remote Forest Service road along the South Fork of the Salmon, and $1 million for the Fall River Electric Cooperative's hydro project at Island Park.

Idaho's other senator in 1990 was Republican Steve Symms, a native of Nampa who attended the University of Idaho, served in the U.S. Marine Corps, managed a family fruit ranch, and in 1972 was elected to Congress, where he served four terms before his election to the U.S. Senate in 1980. He was reelected in 1986 and retired in 1993.

Idaho's First District congressman in 1990 was Larry E. Craig, Republican, of Council, a graduate of the University of Idaho who was elected to the state senate in 1974 and served three terms. Craig was elected to the U.S. House of Representatives in 1980, reelected in 1982, 1984, 1986, and 1988, and then was elected to McClure's Senate seat in 1990. When Craig moved to the Senate in January 1991, his place as representative was taken by Democrat Larry LaRocco, a Boise stockbroker. The representative from the Second District was Democrat Richard Stallings, a professor of history at Ricks College, who was elected in 1984 and reelected in 1986, 1988, and 1990, and who ran unsuccessfully for Symms's Senate seat in 1992.

Each of these men tends to demonstrate Idaho's tradition of choosing individualistic leaders who act independently from party-line political patterns.

## IDAHO'S CENTENNIAL-YEAR ECONOMY

The livelihood of the people of Idaho, like that of many other Rocky Mountain citizens, is based primarily on the production and processing of agricultural commodities, nonfuel minerals, and timber, and on such other sources of income as tourism and the federal government. Since Idaho's transportation system was designed to assist in the exploitation of its natural resources rather than to unify the northern with the southwestern and southeastern regions, the regions are not well tied together. Although Idaho is about the size of the United Kingdom of Great Britain, and Northern Ireland, it has less than one-fiftieth of Britain's population and so provides only a minimal market for its own products; it must rely on out-of-state markets for its well-being. No section of the state is an important market for the output of any other region. Moreover, persons with the largest disposable incomes tend to buy the luxury items they can afford in Spokane, Seattle, Portland, San Francisco, and Salt Lake City rather than at home.[2] Nevertheless, approximately 500,000 persons find employment in Idaho, of whom about 140,000 are in agriculture; 35,000 in mining, construction, transportation, and communications; 60,000 in manufacturing, including lumber and wood products; 80,000 in government; and the remaining 185,000 in trade, finance, and services.

AGRICULTURE. Idaho's largest industry is agriculture, and much of the state's activity is geared to agricultural production and related service industries. Most communities in the Snake River Plain, for example, are heavily dependent on agriculture. And the state's agriculture is as diverse as the state's geography; Idahoans receive revenues from many different crops and livestock products.

Idaho is a major producer nationally in eight crops including potatoes, with a production of about 100 million hundred-pound sacks annually—about 30 percent of total U.S. volume. The state also ranks first in barley production, with about 52 million bushels, almost one-fifth of the nation's total. Idaho ranks third among the states in the production of sugar beets (4 million tons annually), hops (4 million pounds), mint (1 million pounds), and onions (4 million hundredweight). The state ranks fourth in the supply of fresh plums and prunes (6,500 tons) and fifth in dry edible beans (2.3 million hundredweight). It is among the top ten states also in sweet cherries (2,300 tons), sweet corn for processing (170,000 tons), alfalfa hay (3.5 million tons), wheat (76 million bushels), and apples (135 million pounds).

Idaho also is recognized for many livestock products. The state ranks number one in trout (36 million pounds—85 percent of the national harvest). The state ranks fifth in American cheese (almost 100 million pounds); eleventh in honey (6 million pounds), sheep and lambs (300,000 head), and wool (1 million pounds); and thirteenth in milk production (2.7 billion pounds).

Cattle, potatoes, milk, wheat, barley, sugar beets, and hay, in that order, account for about 85 percent of all agricultural income. The total agricultural income from all sources exceeds $2 billion in 1990.

The vast majority of Idaho's 24,000 farms are small—operated by families who farm part-time and have off-farm sources of income. About 40 percent of all Idaho farmer heads of households have nonfarm occupations. Idaho relies more heavily than many states on non-family labor, partly because of the large number of farms along the Snake River that require much labor to move irrigation pipes. Nevertheless, 85 percent of all farms are individually or family owned; only 5 percent are corporate farms.

Geographical diversity is significant. Wheat is the major crop in the amply watered hills of north Idaho. The Palouse hills also lead the nation in the production of peas and lentils. Grass seed is grown on the Rathdrum Prairie in Kootenai County and the western part of Benewah County; high-quality wild rice is raised along the St. Joe and Coeur d'Alene rivers. Lewiston is a major trading center for the livestock industry of the Inland Empire.

Southwestern Idaho is a major cattle- and milk-producing area and is also an important supplier of sugar beets, potatoes, and seed crops. The region is significant in fruit growing—sweet cherries, apples, peaches, plums, apricots, and grapes—and also has a thriving wine industry.

South-central Idaho encompasses highly productive irrigated farms and also excellent upland grazing regions. Sheep and wool production are prominent in Blaine, Gooding, and Minidoka counties, whereas in Twin Falls, Cassia, Jerome, Gooding, and Minidoka counties thousands of irrigated farms grow grain, beans, corn, and sugar beets. Idaho's famous potatoes are cultivated mostly in southeastern Idaho, where the summer days are sunny and the nights cool. Beef cattle, hogs, sheep, hay, and wheat are also abundant in the region; much of the wheat is produced by dry farming.

Because of the importance of agriculture, enterprisers in the state develop specialized machinery; chemical fertilizers and weed-killers; implements for planting, cultivating, and harvesting; and irrigation systems. Surface mines in Bingham and Caribou counties yield phosphate from which fertilizer is manufactured in plants near Pocatello and Soda Springs. Idaho maintains a large food-processing industry as well, with about twenty-five potato, sugar beet, and frozen-vegetable plants in the state that employ 16,000 people.

MINING. Since the discovery of gold along the Clearwater in 1860, Idaho has been a leading national producer of metallic minerals. The role of the state's miners was particularly crucial during World War II. Idaho's mineral production, which varies from $200 to $500 million annually, depends on prices, foreign production, the value of the dollar, and technological developments. The industry is highly competitive.

Idaho is the leading U.S. producer of newly mined silver, accounting for almost half of national production, and the state is the second largest producer of rock phosphate. Idaho molybdenum accounts for 25 percent of the nation's output. The state ranks fifth in the production of lead, zinc, and gold and is the leading producer of antimony, pumice, and industrial garnets. It has significant reserves of cobalt, tungsten, mercury, uranium, copper, clays, and zeolites.

There is mining in every Idaho region. The most productive areas are Silver Valley, in Shoshone County, which has produced almost $5 billion in metals since 1884; the phosphate region in southeast Idaho, where six major mines produce about $100 million annually; and the central Idaho mountains in Custer County that produce molybdenum, silver, and other minerals. About 5,000 persons work in the eighty-three active mining and processing operations in the state.

TIMBER. In 1990 Idaho had ninety-one operating sawmills that furnish a variety of wood products, including five plywood mills, a wafer-board plant, and a particle-board plant. The state also has seventy or eighty other producers of wood products. Idaho's single pulp and paper mill, in Lewiston, is owned by Potlatch Corporation. Containers made from pulp and paper products are manufactured at plants in Nampa, Twin Falls, and Burley. Employment in the industry is approximately 13,000, and the industry is highly competitive because of automation. The largest companies are Boise Cascade, Potlatch, and Louisiana-Pacific. Although the state's forest industry is concentrated in the northern counties, the Boise area is also significant as the headquarters of Boise Cascade, TJ International, Idaho Timber Corporation, and Canfor U.S.A. Corporation.

MANUFACTURING. In addition to forest products and food processing, Idaho machinery businesses manufacture pump and irrigation equipment and farm implements, logging and sawmilling equipment and tools, and mining machinery. Idaho also has attracted high-technology firms that have grown rapidly in recent years. Hewlett-Packard's plant in Boise employs 3,500 workers, making printers and disk drives. Micron Technology in Boise employs 3,100 workers. Other firms include Advanced Input Devices in Coeur d'Alene (280 workers), Gould Electronics in Pocatello (900 workers), and Zilog in Nampa (425 workers). Electrical and non-electrical machinery and instrument manufacturers employ almost 10,000 workers in Idaho. About 3,500 persons are employed in chemical manufacturing plants, including those owned by J. R. Simplot Company, FMC Corporation, and Monsanto.

Printing and publishing is another important sector with 4,500 employees. Firms attracting national business include Caxton Printers in Caldwell, Pacific Press in Nampa, Commtek, Inc., in Boise, and Stylart Manufacturing in Rexburg.

One significant business development of the 1980s was the increase in companies trading on the global market. By 1990 Idaho businesses sold more than $1.3 billion abroad, creating jobs for some 40,000 Idahoans. A related source of income is the earnings of hundreds of Idahoans who work overseas for such firms as Morrison-Knudsen and who remit much of their earnings to their families in Idaho.

FEDERAL AND OTHER GOVERNMENTS. Employing about 12,000 people in Idaho, the federal government spends about 30 percent more in the state than it collects there in taxes. One reason is that the government owns and manages about two-thirds of the state's land. Another large expenditure provides support for several large enterprises, including Gowen Field, a major National Guard training facility; Mountain Home Air Force Base, with approximately 4,000 military and 500 civilian employees; the Idaho National Engineering Laboratory, with about 13,000 employees, both government and private; the Boise Interagency Fire Center, the national hub of the joint U.S. Forest Service, Bureau of Land Management, and National Park

Service fire-control system; and the Forest Service and BLM, with employees in many small communities in the state.

The other public sector, the state and local governments, employs far more people than the federal government but is not a net source of outside income. Funding support of these entities and their activities comes from within Idaho; as much money is collected in the state as is paid out. Employing about 56,000 compared with only 12,000 by the federal government, state and local governments serve those engaged in agriculture, mining, forestry and fisheries, manufacturing, the service trades, and tourism. Their focus, defined by the citizens collectively, includes maintaining streets, parks, and libraries; keeping the peace; operating water systems; putting out fires; and teaching the young.

TRAVEL AND TOURISM. In recent years travel and tourism have become a significant contributor to the state's economy. Lodging, entertainment, restaurant and beverage establishments, sports facilities, transportation services, and consumer retail businesses have expanded and earn a substantial proportion of the state's total income. This expansion is evident in such locations as Sun Valley and Ketchum, Coeur d'Alene, Sandpoint, Riggins, and McCall. Expenditures for travel and tourism were estimated to be $1.5 billion in Idaho's centennial year, and employment approached 30,000 workers.

Tourism and travel are promoted by visitor and convention centers in Boise, Coeur d'Alene, and Pocatello; by such destination resorts as those at Sun Valley, Coeur d'Alene, Lava Hot Springs, Island Park, Cascade/McCall, and Sandpoint and Priest Lake; by the group-tour industry; and by the wide selection of outdoor recreation resources. Camping, boating, fishing—taking advantage of world-renowned trout streams—backpacking, and hunting attract thousands. Professional river-runners operate in twenty-two of Idaho's rivers. Special events that bring large numbers of visitors to the state include the Women's Bicycle Challenge, Burley Boat Regatta, Teton Hot Air Balloon Rally, Weiser National Old Time Fiddlers' Festival, Boise Shakespeare Festival, McCall Winter Carnival, and Lewiston Dogwood Festival.

TRENDS IN POPULATION. Idaho was one of the fastest growing states in the nation in the 1970s. During the 1960s the state experienced net out-migration as young people left the state for better job opportunities, but a flood of people returned in the 1970s to take advantage of new openings, particularly in machinery and transportation-equipment manufacturing. Coupled with a high birth rate, this in-migration caused a 23 percent increase in population—from 712,641 in 1970 to 944,127 in 1980. This boom period was followed, beginning by 1979, by a severe recession that eliminated 8 percent of the state's employment base. Several large manufacturing plants shut down or curtailed production. Once again, Idaho experienced net out-migration. The downturn ended in 1983, and employment levels resumed their climb to 1979 levels. The state, once more, began to enjoy a net in-migration—a large proportion of it from California.

Idaho's population in 1990 was 1,006,749, an increase of 62,622 over 1980. The ten largest cities in 1990 were:

| | |
|---|---|
| Boise | 125,738 |
| Pocatello | 46,080 |
| Idaho Falls | 43,929 |
| Nampa | 28,365 |
| Lewiston | 28,082 |
| Twin Falls | 27,591 |
| Coeur d'Alene | 24,563 |
| Moscow | 18,519 |
| Caldwell | 18,400 |
| Rexburg | 14,302 |

Forty-eight cities had more than 2,000 population and seventy-two more than 1,000 residents. Federal defense expenditures were a factor in growth of some of the cities, the rise of a leisure society was important in others, and in still others growth came from bursts of innovation and entrepreneurship.

One result of the 1970s and 1980s was the loss of population in rural areas. Although the state retained its essential rural character in 1990, some rural areas lacked adequate medical and dental care, children had to travel many miles to attend quality central schools, and rural underemployment continued to prevail.

## POTENTIAL FOR THE FUTURE

Except for government spending, Idaho's future is largely dependent on the competitiveness of its farms and industries. Persons who have studied thc state's economy are confident that Idaho is indeed in a strong, aggressive position. Of course, the state has abundant natural resources, an enormous advantage, but that is not enough. Japan, Switzerland, and Korea, for example, have fewer resources than Idaho, and yet they generate high and increasing income for their millions of people.

Most important in the modern world economy is the share of national and world markets that Idaho's businesses can command. On the assumption that what is good for its largest businesses is likely good for the state as well, economic consultants admonish the state and its elected representatives to create the proper environment in which Idaho businesses can grow and prosper. Regulations must not be too burdensome nor intrusive, taxes must not be too high, and the state must be aggressive in selling itself to other states and foreign countries. At the same time, the state must ensure that its businesses face enough "internal" competition to sharpen their fighting edge for "outside" rivalry.

Conservative politicians seek to remove constraints, alleviate tax burdens, encourage private investment, and cut public spending. Liberals look more favorably on subsidizing and protecting firms with potential for growth. Business and economic consultants insist that competitiveness can only be achieved and maintained by continuous innovations in product and process. Problems arise when firms stop innovating, seeking instead to live off past accomplishments.[3]

There is no single "magic bullet" for rendering a state's businesses more competitive. With its comparative advantage in producing certain food products, chemicals, minerals, and wood products, Idaho is gaining an advantage in high technology. Companies in the state have been able to take advantage of advances in technologies of communication and transportation worldwide (via satellite, fax, fiber-optic cable, cargo ship, and container) as they go global—financing, designing, producing, and marketing their wares all over the world. The level of living of the states' citizens is coming to depend more on how the world economy values their labors than on the value of the corporate assets they own. Human capital—the skills, insights, and intellectual capacities of the state's work force—is replacing financial and physical capital as the key determinant of the region's wealth.

Idaho's status in the national and world economy ultimately turns on the quality of its work force, as well as the dexterity of its firms' managers. Its highly skilled workers—many of them cosmopolitan professionals in Boise and elsewhere linked to worldwide enterprises from desks and computer terminals in glass and steel high-rises—will reap the benefits of a rapidly growing world market for their designs, plans, inventions, and insights. In support, the state must ensure its citizens a good education, adequate training, health care, and the means of linking their skills to the wider economy through efficient systems of transportation and communications.[4]

## THE CENTENNIAL CELEBRATION

During its centennial of statehood in 1990 Idaho and Idahoans, in a "celebration of one million," had a birthday to remember. Some 1,600 official centennial events were programmed in every corner of Idaho—events that celebrated the state's heritage and its unique place among the fifty states. The Idaho Centennial Commission, chaired by Harry Magnuson of Wallace, sponsored 175 local and statewide projects. The commission was funded by a budget of about $6 million, some $3.5 million of which was raised through sales of Centennial license plates. The second-largest source of funds was the sale of Centennial products, including state flags and the Centennial logo used by commercial firms that marketed baseball caps, T-shirts, sweatshirts, belt buckles, ornaments, pens, and other memorabilia. Private corporations also donated money, and the state legislature appropriated $100,000. Approximately another $12 million was raised by community fund-raisers for local projects.

Newcomers from California and elsewhere and fourth-generation Idahoans joined in celebrating the hundred years of progress that brought the state from covered wagons to jet planes; from 160-acre homesteads scratched out of sagebrush to miles and miles of potato, wheat, and sugarbeet fields irrigated with a complicated series of dams and ditches; from dusty stage stops to cities with gleaming towers and shopping malls; from the telegraph to the microchip.[5]

Festivities reached a high point on July 3, 1990, the hundredth birthday. Events included the conclusion of the Centennial Float through Hells Canyon; the Moscow premier of a centennial musical called "The River Song," about the Lewis and Clark Expedition; a celebration in Franklin, the first pioneer settlement; a week-long, seventy-mile trek across the desert from Rupert to Arco by wagon-weary travelers seeking to imitate the Oregon Trail emigrants; and a seventeen-leg steam train excursion that left Montpelier and zigzagged through southern Idaho to Boise, where the main celebration was planned. Events in the state capital the day before included dedication of the county shields display along streets approaching the capitol, featuring designs from all forty-four counties; and an All-Idaho Homecoming Celebration that included street entertainment, a strolling supper, music, dances, and a Celebrate Idaho laser light show staged in The Grove. All the city's bells tolled at midnight to mark the end of the first century of statehood. With 20,000 revelers in the streets, this was the closest Boise ever came to Mardi Gras. Towns all over the state were decorated and draped in red, white, and blue.

On Statehood Day a day-long picnic at Boise's Julia Davis Park featured a birthday cake that fed 3,000, and a potato jamboree on the Capitol grounds was sponsored by state employees who washed, baked, transported, and served about 6,000 Idaho potatoes. A "potato" wearing black tights and Birkenstock sandals danced across the grounds, hugging children and extolling the virtues of the state's famous export. On the backside of his burlap sack were the words "Idaho No. 1."

At the Boise Convention Center 700 people attended a luncheon that marked the debut of the Centennial book *Here We Have Idaho: People Make a Difference.* Special guests were the 100 Idahoans the book profiled—from politicians to scientists to musicians. Among those honored was Walter Sparks of the University of Idaho's Research and Extension Center in Aberdeen, who developed storage techniques that allowed potatoes to be kept in storage for twelve months, cutting processors' costs to the minimum and thus keeping potatoes on the plate year-round. Other living Idahoans spotlighted in the book were Gretchen Fraser, Olympic gold medalist in skiing, woman pilot, and equestrian; Gene Harris, jazz pianist; Cort Conley, writer, publisher, and river runner; and Mary Brooks, who served eight years as director of the U.S. Mint.

Featured on the luncheon program was storyteller and folk-singer Rosalie Sorrels of Robie Creek, who sang "Coming Home," a ballad of her own composition about returning to Idaho. At the luncheon Sorrels explained that her presentation represented the people from whom she collected songs and stories while traveling the state for an Idaho songbook.[6]

During the elaborate Statehood Day ceremony at the capitol, for which about 20,000 persons packed the steps and Capitol Park, an invocation was offered by Father Thomas Connolly of DeSmet; Richard Shoup, former Montana congressman and great-grandson of Idaho's first governor, George L. Shoup, read portions of a letter from his ancestor written shortly after Idaho became a state; and Robert Sims, dean of Boise State University's School of Social Science and Public Affairs, recounted the enactment of the Idaho Statehood bill in Washington, D.C. Governor Andrus, his voice hoarse after two weeks of giving addresses throughout the state, told the crowd: "There are many wonderful things about this celebration, but the very best thing is that, more than any event in our history, this one has brought Idahoans together as a people." Centennial Commission chairman Harry Magnuson added:

> Idaho's challenging geographical barriers have often been cited as one of the unfortunate drawbacks of living in Idaho. Yet we love this state, not in spite of its geography but because of it. The diversity of mountains and rivers, wilderness and deserts, and most of all, Idaho's peoples, are attributes of the state that are a continual source of strength. We're enriched by a renewing sense of discovery. Idaho is raw, untamed and unconquered, and the landscape instills a sense of humility in us. The spirit of the Centennial has regenerated us. It has bridged party lines, spanned the interests of all ages, transcended geographical barriers, taught our hearts, and instilled good will.[7]

As the thousands broke out in singing the state song, "Here We Have Idaho"—as if they had been rehearsed—some of the happy faces in the audience had tears on their cheeks.

The crowd was treated to a flyover by four Idaho National Guard F-4 Phantom Jets and a 43-cannon salute by the Guard's 148th Artillery. At the end of the hour-long ceremony, persons queued up to be served some of Idaho's birthday cake by Idaho's chief grocer, Joe Albertson.

The evening ended in an extravaganza of dancing and dazzling fireworks at Boise State University's Bronco Stadium that illuminated the night sky with spectacular bursts of color for thirty minutes. The dancing highlighted aspects of Idaho's culture: Native American dancing, Basque dancing, a Chinese dragon dance, square dancing, Irish jigs, tap dancing, ballroom dancing, and an old-fashioned two-step.

A moving part of the evening program, representative of Idaho's varied citizenry over the previous hundred years, was the naturalization ceremony for twenty-six persons who had been Poles, English, Filipinos, Vietnamese, Mexicans, and citizens of ten other countries.

The spectacular fireworks crackled to musical accompaniment, ranging from Neil Diamond singing "America" to a rousing rendition of "Stars and Stripes Forever." The memorable finale came when all 20,000 in the audience, furnished as they entered the stadium with candles and matches, lit their candles and joined in singing once again "Here We Have Idaho."

The next day, July the Fourth, an estimated 50,000 people lined the two-and-one-half-mile parade route to see the 63 floats and 214 entries, constituting the most colorful and magnificent parade in Idaho's history.

## THE HISTORIAN'S VIEW

The Centennial celebration demonstrated that Idaho's future is unquestionably influenced by its past. There were visual and aural reminders of the important role that Native Americans played in assisting the early explorers, missionaries, and travelers; the influence of northern, southern, midwestern, and coastal Americans in establishing basic institutions and securing territorial status; the influx of large numbers of Mormons who swelled the population enough to permit statehood; and the labor of Chinese, Japanese, Mexicans, Scandinavians, Germans, and others in building railroads and irrigation dams and reservoirs, cutting timber, and developing mines that launched the territory and state on the material progress that it continues to enjoy.

The celebration also awakened memories of the refractoriness of Idaho's voters. In 1953 they voted for anti-gambling candidates, the legislature outlawed slot machines, and the Supreme Court declared the acts unconstitutional. A generation later, in 1989, they voted for a state lottery. For decades the people relied on the property tax to provide strong local schools, and then in 1978 they voted for the One Percent Tax limit that threatened to suffocate many local school districts. They voted against right-to-work legislation in 1958 and 1982 and turned around to affirm it in 1986. Anti-liquor initiatives were defeated in 1942 and 1946. When the legislature voted in 1987 to raise the drinking age from 19 to 21, the bill was vetoed by the acting governor. When the "real" governor returned, a follow-up bill was approved and the governor signed it. In 1972 the legislature ratified the so-called Equal Rights Amendment; in 1977 a later legislature rescinded its ratification. At times Idahoans are quite predictable, at other times nothing short of cantankerous.

A major concern of Idahoans during the centennial year was safeguarding the state's beauty. With a booming economy and forecasts of growth twice the national average, Idaho has been "discovered." The pressing question is whether the people can preserve its vast landscapes, cascading water, and clear skies and still make a living. It will be hard to satisfy both the traditional view that rapid development is good and the environmental concerns of those who call for preservation and nonconsumptive use of natural resources. Everyone seems to agree that the wilderness issues need to be resolved so Idaho's rural communities can plan for a stable economic future. But no consensus exists on what should be done. Should people be camping in forests rather than clear-cutting them? Floating their rivers rather than damming them? Conflict seems inevitable.[8]

The governor, legislators, state administrators, and the voters wrestle with problems like how best to protect the sockeye and chinook salmon that come upstream to spawn and the juveniles that head back to the ocean; whether to allow a large-scale residential development in a hitherto secluded wilderness area; whether to allow wolves into central Idaho grazing areas; whether to increase taxes in order to spend more money for higher education; how much to invest in advertising the state in national magazines; and what kind of an abortion law to adopt. Opinions on these and other pressing issues sway back and forth.

Certain institutions are so solidly established that they will always be with us; they give security that the future will not be entirely unlike the past. A central convention is the institution of property. Modern taxation, eminent domain law, zoning, land-use restrictions, and other regulations have reduced the scope of our private property rights, but our society continues to be motivated by the desire to acquire property, to engage in enterprises that will enable us to have more comfortable homes, more dependable automobiles, tastier and more nutritious foods, and more stylish clothes. With the blessing of abundant natural resources, much of it still unexploited, we have assurance that growth is still likely, that there will be economic improvement. The questions are how much and whether environmental concerns will also be protected. Whatever the problems, Idahoans continue to live peacefully and productively in a stable society.

## CHAPTER THIRTY-THREE: SOURCES

A profile of Idaho in 1990, including government, education, economy, demographics, and recreation, is found in *Idaho Blue Book 1989–1990* (Boise: Office of the Secretary of State, 1990). The economic section, pp. 255–80, is extremely well written and informative, and I have borrowed heavily from it. Other information is provided by publications of the Idaho Department of Commerce, including especially *Idaho Facts* (Boise: Division of Economic Development, 1990). *Idaho's Economy* has been published quarterly by the College of Business at Boise State University since 1984 and contains industry reviews and state and national statistics with helpful interpretations of developments and trends. Also helpful are Harry H. Caldwell, ed., *Idaho Economic Atlas* (Moscow: Idaho Bureau of Mines and Geology, 1970); and Michael J. DiNoto and Joy Passanante Williams, "Idaho's Economy: A Look Under the Hood," in *Idaho: The University* 2 (March 1985):10–18.

The political picture is described in Randy Stapilus, *The Idaho Political Almanac* (Boise: Ridenbaugh Press, 1990), and Stapilus, *Paradox Politics: People and Power in Idaho.*

Environmental concerns are discussed in "Conservation of Natural Resources" and "Our Scenic and Recreational Resources," in Beal and Wells, *History of Idaho*, 2:361–92; Peterson, *Idaho: A Bicentennial History*, 182–92; William Ashworth, *Hells Canyon* (New York: Hawthorn Books, 1977); Rabe and Flaherty, *The River of Green and Gold*; Jack G. Peterson, "Vision for the Future: Water in the Twenty-first Century," *Idaho Yesterdays* 30 (Spring-Summer 1986):71–76; and Ed Marston, ed., *Reopening the Western Frontier* (Washington, D.C., and Covelo, California: Island Press, 1989).

A companion book to Idaho Public Television's "Proceeding on Through a Beautiful Country: A History of Idaho" is Stacy, ed., *Conversations.* Including portions of interviews with 220 persons, the book looks at how Idahoans got where they were at the time of the Centennial, and what their outlook was for the future.

Articles in the state's newspapers have been helpful, as have publications of the Idaho Centennial Commission and broadcasts of the state's television stations. Other specific sources are indicated in the footnotes.

In preparing this chapter I have been stimulated by reading Hughes, *American Economic History*, esp. 577–85. Jonathan Hughes, raised in Twin Falls, was until his untimely death in 1992 a distinguished professor at Northwestern University.

166.

167.

166. Cecil D. Andrus, governor of Idaho, 1971–77 and 1987–95, was Idaho's first four-term governor as well as United States Secretary of the Interior, 1978–82. ISHS 76–209.1.

167. The Coeur d'Alene Lake region, known for timber, marine, and mineral resources, is also a popular recreation area. UIL 6–41–2.

CHAPTER THIRTY-FOUR

# Idaho: Today and Tomorrow

JUDGING by public opinion polls, visitors to Idaho, like the people, are impressed with what its citizens have accomplished, and believe the quality of life in the Gem State is attractive. But they are overawed by the scenery. They use words like "spectacular," "awe-inspiring," "breathtaking," and "magnificent." Part of the attraction of nature in Idaho is the difference in regions. Each part of the state is distinct in its geography as well as in its history, economics, and politics. A reflective trip around the state in 1990 not only gives one an understanding of the state in its centennial year and of its future potential, but also suggests the positive characteristics that illustrate how national, regional, and local issues can be addressed and resolved in a harmonious manner.

Idaho's eastern and northeastern border is well preserved and remains pristine. The Continental Divide constitutes 312 miles of Idaho's border. One of the great tragedies of the 1863 Congressional surgery that created Idaho is that the Teton Range is in Wyoming: the magnificent Yellowstone National Park and the border of the Teton Range, small parts of which are in Idaho, can be seen from Idaho but are hard to enter from the western side. These mountain vistas viewed from the Teton Valley, carrying a tributary of the Snake, have not changed much since trappers camped on their numerous streams. The Grand Targhee ski resort on the west side of the Teton Range boasts fine powder snow and enough distance from population centers to avoid crowded lift-lines. Skiing, hunting, fishing, backpacking, and camping are all part of the sport of Idaho.

Another trapper's tributary of the Snake in eastern Idaho is Henry's Fork, a fishing stream of rare productivity with waters cascading over two Mesa Falls, the upper one 114 feet high, flowing toward the Upper Snake River Valley. This stream originates at Big Springs, spawning ground for the kokanee salmon, and eventually feeds the spectacular Island Park reservoir, a way-station for numerous migrating ducks and geese and a popular summer retreat for many Idahoans.

The northeastern border leaves the backbone of the Rockies near U.S. Highway 93 at Lost Trail Pass and turns westward along the Bitterroot Mountains. This vast Idaho interior is a major collector for hundreds of brooks, creeks, and rivers that ultimately find their way to the Snake River. The imposing Salmon River and its drainage in central Idaho make up the largest block of federally legislated preservation land in the forty-eight contiguous states. This 25,000-square-mile region, larger than entire states and even countries, includes national primitive areas, recreation areas, national forests, and wilderness preserves. In numerous mountain ranges six peaks extend over 12,000 feet high and another fifty reach 10,000 feet. The mountain peaks, river canyons, and alpine valleys remain virtually unspoiled as places where the sights, sounds, and smells are timeless.

This part of Idaho has already experienced transitions from

the frenetic activity of early mining areas to reverence for its natural splendor. The great mountain ranges—the Sawtooth, Salmon, White Cloud, Boulder, Big Horn Crags, and Lost River—demonstrate what geologists call batholith. These large granite upthrusts, exposed by glaciers and erosion, form majestic peaks that once contained vast mineral wealth. Well over $100 million worth of gold and silver was extracted from this area prior to 1900. From the Wood River mines on the east to Idaho City on the west, the region felt the prospector's imprint just as it had the trapper's and the Native American's before. But mining industries are now largely gone and nature has regained control.

Another great resource in Idaho's central mountains is the wildlife and game. Although Idaho abounds with deer and elk, rare species that risk extinction exist in the protected areas. Numbered among these are the mountain lion or cougar, whose predatory nature makes it an enemy to livestock owners; the lordly bighorn sheep, distinctively identified by circular horns; and the pronged mountain goat, whose shaggy coat gives protection from winter's icy blasts against mountain ridges. Moose and bear also roam the mountains. River wildlife still find a home in Idaho. Otter frequent the streams near the Middle Fork of the Salmon. Lightning quick, the otter can catch the fastest fish that swims but is usually spotted chuting into the water on slides nature built along the stream's banks. The lakes and streams abound with native trout that attract anglers from all over the nation.

The Salmon River country hosts one of nature's more spectacular dramas—or miracles. All five of the Pacific salmon species still attempt the arduous task of swimming back to their spawning ground in central Idaho. Not all make it; but after traveling nearly 1,000 miles, climbing eight ladders over dams, jumping up natural falls and various human hazards, the successful ones find the very stream where they were born. There they rest, spawn, and die. This sensational migration contains something both mysterious and victorious. The Frank Church "River of No Return Wilderness Area" preserves the Salmon and its most famous tributary, the Middle Fork. The salmon are not alone in navigating the dramatic waters. For rafters, the rivers provide some of the sport's most exciting, thrilling, and frightening white rapids. Regulated by licensing procedures, the raft operators introduce unbelieving enthusiasts to the vast wilderness river canyons.

Central Idaho will always be a center of environmental controversy. Timber harvests are regulated and reforestation is constant. However, the real conflict of the future may be balancing the needs for energy and water and the growing desire for wilderness, conservation, and preservation. While the Snake River is totally controlled from Jackson Lake to Hagerman, the wild and scenic Salmon runs free—as does the Snake for over 100 miles through Hells Canyon, the continent's deepest gorge at nearly 8,000 feet.

North of the Salmon River to the North Fork of the Clearwater is another stretch of Idaho wilderness that was the traditional home of the Nez Perce. Like other Native Americans, the Nez Perce lived in harmony with nature and viewed the animals, trees, grass, and fish as friends. The north Idaho forests of spruce, red cedar, white pine, and larch comprise 30 percent of the state's 54 million acres, making Idaho one of the nation's top timber states.

Northern Idahoans have lived with forest fires and logging for so long that they have become adept at managing their resource. This remote region of Idaho commands awe, and it is still fairly unknown. The Lolo Trail stretches from the Montana border westward along the ridges above the Lochsa River until it joins the Clearwater. Two of the great historic events in Idaho history are tied to this trail: Lewis and Clark used it in 1805 and again in 1806, and the great Chief Joseph and his band of Nez Perce fugitives fled across this trail toward Canada. There is a mystical stillness about the trail that is able almost to freeze time.

To the north and west of the Clearwater away from the rushing streams and tree-covered slopes is one of Idaho's richest farming areas, the Palouse. This thick blanket of loam that surrounds Moscow and Lewiston provides fertile ground for abundant crops of grains and vegetables. These agriculturally rich rolling hills produce soft white wheat, peas, alfalfa, and other crops in amazing quantities. The Palouse country is a small agricultural interlude in the midst of timber, lakes, rivers, and wildlife. It also serves as a window to the northern panhandle, which is perhaps the most isolated of Idaho's regions.

Idaho's panhandle is rich in beauty and resources. The rivers and lakes are tied to the northern Columbia system, not the Snake. Its rounded tree-covered mountains surround three of the most beautiful lakes on the continent: Pend Oreille, Coeur d'Alene, and Priest. The surface of these three covers more than 150,000 acres. The elevation is so much lower than most of the rest of Idaho that the region's rainfall is greater and the overall climate is significantly milder. Still, there is considerable snow for winter-sports facilities.

The abundance of lakes and rivers in the panhandle also belies the comment that Idaho suffers from aridity. French Canadian missionaries and trappers, as well as the influence of Native Americans, are reflected in the place names—names that are a testament to the diversity of the region. Several of the northern lakes and streams have been reclaimed in recent years from near ecological death. Although the large lakes have always boasted great kamloops or mackinaw trout, the reality of mining and sewage pollution proved nearly fatal. The seriousness of the problem demanded a massive clean-up and control effort that succeeded.

Silver ore is still mined in the Kellogg-Wallace area, but its heyday is long past. Rich mining and labor history and lore still attract the scholar to the region, but the $2-billion lode is nearly played out. This gradual diminution of mining has been replaced by tourism and winter recreation in the area as Kellogg tries to take advantage of its proximity to Interstate 90. The expanding network of roads has made available many previously inaccessible areas.

Northern Idaho—rural and remote—remains a fish and game paradise, though not as rugged as the various national recreation and wilderness areas to the south. There are caribou and moose as well as grizzly bear; trappers seek marten, beaver, and mink. Dog-sledding contests in the winter hearken back to earlier days. In fact, the far north is a constant reminder of the need for ecological balance and care between man and nature.

The fastest route between the two extreme corners of Idaho takes a traveler through Montana for about 350 miles on Interstates 90 and 15. It is more than 700 miles from Bonners Ferry to Montpelier. However, the Bear River drainage shares with the north a legacy of environmental and ecological concern.

The Bear River does not connect to the Snake River system. When the river's waters turn south toward salty death in the Great Salt Lake, it is only a few miles from the Portneuf, a Snake River tributary. Nearly all of the rest of Idaho drains into the Pacific, but the Bear irrigates high mountain valleys in Wyoming, Idaho, and Utah. Like Pend Oreille, Coeur d'Alene, and Priest lakes in the north, Bear Lake, the crown jewel of the Bear River basin, is a natural lake of magnetic appeal. Like its sister waters it continues to be a battleground among environmentalists, developers, and managers. The region's phosphate-rich mountain ranges create problems similar to those of the silver and lead mines of the panhandle. The ore, taken from open-pit mines and processed in smoke- and slag-producing smelters to be used in many ways, provides needed jobs for an economically depressed region. Mine operators must adhere to legislation that requires certain degrees of restoration and reforestation, yet enforcement may not always be meticulous.

County Seats
0 50
miles
N
117°
49°
45°
42°
111°
117°
BOUNDARY
Bonner's Ferry
Sandpoint
BONNER
KOOTENAI
Coeur d' Alene
Wallace
SHOSHONE
St. Maries
BENEWAH
LATAH
Moscow
CLEARWATER
Orofino
NEZ PERCE
Lewiston
Nez Perce
LEWIS
Grangeville
IDAHO
Salmon
LEMHI
ADAMS
Council
VALLEY
WASHINGTON
Cascade
Challis
Weiser
CUSTER
Payette
PAYETTE
GEM
Emmett
BOISE
Idaho City
CANYON
Caldwell
Boise
ADA
ELMORE
CAMAS
Fairfield
Hailey
BLAINE
BUTTE
Arco
CLARK
Dubois
FREMONT
St. Anthony
JEFFERSON
Rexburg
MADISON
Rigby
TETON
Driggs
Idaho Falls
BONNEVILLE
BINGHAM
Blackfoot
Murphy
Mountain Home
GOODING
Gooding
LINCOLN
Shoshone
JEROME
Jerome
MINIDOKA
Rupert
American Falls
POWER
Pocatello
BANNOCK
CARIBOU
Soda Springs
BEAR LAKE
Paris
OWYHEE
Twin Falls
TWIN FALLS
Burley
CASSIA
Malad City
ONEIDA
FRANKLIN
Preston

Another similarity between Idaho's northern and southeastern extremities is their traditional ties of transportation, communication, economy, and culture to a population center outside the state. The northerners have looked to Spokane and the southerners to Salt Lake City as much as to Boise or each other. This too, is changing. Idaho is more unified now than at any time in its history. In part because of technology and transportation, the media have brought Idaho to all of the people. Citizens watch Idaho television stations and read Idaho newspapers. Boise is the capital of the entire state and is more dominant than Spokane and Salt Lake City. To be sure, these contiguous centers still impact the state, but not as they did even two decades ago. Not only have the media brought Idaho together, but the state's transportation system is more refined and accessible. Private, corporate, and governmental enterprises, as we saw in Chapter Twenty-nine, have also focused the state's regions on each other.

When one moves west across southern Idaho, as the Overlanders did in the 1840s and '50s, the traveler passes through a land of infinite variety. There are awesome canyons, waterfalls higher than Niagara, ice caves not far from natural hot springs, underground aquifers bursting from sheer canyon walls, and the huge granite columns of the Silent City of Rocks. Above all, however, one is struck by the sweetness of green and productive valleys, more fertile and ripe than the Promised Land. There are fields of waving grain; endless rows of sugar beets, corn, beans, and potatoes; cheerful cherry orchards and heavy-bearing apple, peach, and prune trees; long gardens of carrots and tomatoes; and hundreds of acres of vineyards. Miles of sprinklers bring water to green alfalfa and clover. The traveler is entranced; he is in a land of unimaginable riches. Chicken farms, dairies, and cattle feedlots dot the landscape, as do wineries, canneries, milk condenseries, and fish hatcheries. In the southwestern corner are rugged, high mountain deserts and North America's tallest sand dunes. Peregrine falcons, golden eagles, and screeching owls are seen and heard. North of Boise, "City of Trees," one encounters lush forests, serene mountain lakes, and remains of prehistoric villages. The tensions of Idaho's conflicting responsibilities are clearly evident: to provide water and electricity for hard-working farmers and the industries that use their animals and produce; and, at the same time, to preserve the state's endowment of natural wonderwork for the enjoyment of kayakers, waterskiers, fishermen, and hikers—who may come from far places or head for the out-of-doors after work.

Diverse as are the regions, the larger communities and cities of Idaho, most of them within fifty miles of the Snake River, create a unifying factor. Idaho Falls depends on agricultural as well as federal energy spending; Pocatello on industrial and manufacturing growth; Twin Falls on agricultural prices; Lewiston on timber products; and Boise on all of the above as well as state government. If the cities create a unity that drives the state toward cooperation rather than competition, the character of the ethnically diverse people in the state also holds the state together. In their struggle to survive and coexist in a tough and harsh environment, multiple tribes of Native Americans displayed a strength and knowledge that served as a schoolground for successive waves of trappers, pioneers, explorers, miners, and self-sufficient farmers and ranchers. Assisted by ingenious private, state, and federal efforts, the settlers provided water to a thirsty volcanic soil deemed unproductive and uninhabitable. Idaho's rich and dramatic human saga is replete with success stories based on diligence, perseverance, determination, and cooperation. This willingness to individually and communally conquer a harsh and unrelenting environment is a part of Idaho's legacy. Idaho continues to be a place of discovery, conquest, and achievement. If Idaho follows its traditions, there will always be leaders with character and heart like Borah, Thomas, Ross, Smylie, Church, McClure, and Andrus to guarantee Idaho's place as sanctuary and as innovator.

More important, Idaho will remain a state where young

people can still dream dreams, reach out to nature and each other, and see visions of a more perfect society. In fact, it is a place where one's soul can simultaneously receive inspiration and refreshment from the landscape. If our eyes and ears remain keen to the vistas and solitude, the natural beauty can remain permanent. As with other states, Idaho offers opportunity to use and not abuse, to reclaim and restore, the great gifts that nature bestows upon all its creatures. Romance continues to reside in her name—Idaho.

# APPENDIX A

## Governors of the Territory of Idaho, 1863–1890

| *Governor* | *Appointed* |
|---|---|
| William H. Wallace | March 10, 1863 |
| Caleb Lyon | February 26, 1864 |
| David M. Ballard | April 10, 1866 |
| Samuel Bard | March 30, 1870 |
| Gilman Marston | June 7, 1870 |
| Alexander H. Connor | January 12, 1871 |
| Thomas M. Bowen | April 19, 1871 |
| Thomas W. Bennett | October 24, 1871 |
| David P. Thompson | December 16, 1875 |
| Mason Brayman | July 24, 1876 |
| John P. Hoyt | August 7, 1878 |
| John B. Neil | July 12, 1880 |
| John N. Irwin | March 2, 1883 |
| William M. Bunn | March 26, 1884 |
| Edward A. Stevenson | September 29, 1885 |
| George L. Shoup | April 1, 1889 |

Source: *Idaho Blue Book, 1989–1990*, 49.

# APPENDIX B

## Territorial Delegates to U.S. Congress, 1863–1889

| *Name/Party* | *Term of Office* | *Remarks* |
|---|---|---|
| William H. Wallace | 3/3/1864 to 3/3/1865 | elected 1863 |
| Edward D. Holbrook | 3/4/1865 to 3/3/1869 | elected 1864; reelected 1866 |
| Jacob K. Shafer | 3/4/1869 to 3/3/1871 | elected 1868 |
| Samuel A. Merritt | 3/4/1871 to 3/3/1873 | elected 1870 |
| John Hailey | 3/4/1873 to 3/3/1875 | elected 1872 |
| Thomas W. Bennett | 3/4/1875 to 6/24/1876 | elected 1874, election challenged, unseated |
| Stephen S. Fenn | 6/24/1876 to 3/3/1879 | seated by Congress; elected 1876 |
| George Ainslie | 3/4/1879 to 3/3/1883 | elected 1878; reelected 1880 |
| Theodore F. Singiser | 3/4/1883 to 3/3/1885 | elected 1882 |
| John Hailey | 3/4/1885 to 3/3/1887 | elected 1884 |
| Fred T. Dubois | 3/4/1887 to 3/3/1889 | elected 1886 |

Source: *Idaho Blue Book, 1989–1990,* 38

APPENDIX C

# Elected Governors of the State of Idaho, 1890–1990

Note: *Party Designations:* (R) *Republican;* (D) *Democrat;* (P) *Populist*

| *Name/Party* | *Term of Office* | *Remarks* |
|---|---|---|
| George L. Shoup (R) | 1890 to 12/1890 | elected 1890; resigned to become U.S. Senator |
| Norman B. Willey (R) | 12/1890 to 1/1893 | succeeded to office |
| William J. McConnell (R) | 1/1893 to 1/4/1897 | elected 1892; reelected 1894 |
| Frank Steunenberg (P-D) | 1/4/1897 to 1/7/1901 | elected 1896; relected 1898 |
| Frank W. Hunt (D) | 1/7/1901 to 1/5/1903 | elected 1900 |
| John T. Morrison (R) | 1/5/1903 to 1/2/1905 | elected 1902 |
| Frank R. Gooding (R) | 1/3/1905 to 1/4/1909 | elected 1904; reelected 1906 |
| James H. Brady (R) | 1/4/1909 to 1/2/1911 | elected 1908 |
| John M. Haines (R) | 1/6/1913 to 1/4/1915 | elected 1912 |

| | | |
|---|---|---|
| Moses Alexander (D) | 1/4/1915 to 1/6/1919 | elected 1914; reelected 1916 |
| D. W. Davis (R) | 1/6/1919 to 1/1/1923 | elected 1918; reelected 1920 |
| Charles C. Moore (R) | 1/3/1923 to 1/3/1927 | elected 1922; reelected 1924 |
| H. C. Baldridge (R) | 1/3/1927 to 1/5/1931 | elected 1926; reelected 1928 |
| C. Ben Ross (D) | 1/5/1931 to 1/4/1937 | elected 1930; reelected 1932, 1934 |
| Barzilla W. Clark (D) | 1/4/1937 to 1/2/1939 | elected 1936 |
| C. A. Bottolfsen (R) | 1/1/1939 to 1/6/1940 | elected 1938 |
| Chase A. Clark (D) | 1/6/1941 to 1/4/1943 | elected 1940 |
| C. A. Bottolfsen (R) | 1/4/1943 to 1/1/1945 | elected 1942 |
| Chas. C. Gossett (D) | 1/1/1945 to 11/17/1945 | elected 1944; resigned 11/17/1945 |
| Arnold Williams (D) | 11/17/1945 to 1/6/1947 | succeeded to office |
| Dr. C. A. Robins (R) | 1/6/1947 to 1/1/1951 | elected 1946 |
| Len B. Jordan (R) | 1/1/1951 to 1/3/1955 | elected 1950 |
| Robert E. Smylie (R) | 1/3/1955 to 1/2/1967 | elected 1954; reelected 1958, 1962 |
| Don Samuelson (R) | 1/2/1967 to 1/4/1971 | elected 1966 |
| Cecil D. Andrus (D) | 1/4/1971 to 1/24/1977 | elected 1970; reelected 1974; resigned 1/24/1977 |
| John V. Evans (D) | 1/24/1977 to 1/5/1987 | succeeded to office; elected 1978; reelected 1982 |
| Cecil D. Andrus (D) | 1/5/1987 | elected 1986; reelected 1990 |

Source: *Idaho Blue Book, 1989–1990*, 49.

# APPENDIX D

## United States Senators

Note: *Party Designations:* (R) *Republican;* (D) *Democrat;* (S.R.) *Silver Republican;* (P) *Populist*

| *Name/Party* | *Term of Office* | *Remarks* |
|---|---|---|
| | FIRST POSITION | |
| George L. Shoup (R) | 12/18/1890 to 3/3/1901 | elected by legislature 1890; reelected 1894 |
| Fred T. Dubois (D) | 3/4/1901 to 3/3/1907 | elected by legislature 1900 |
| William E. Borah (R) | 3/4/1907 to 1/19/1940 | elected by legislature 1907; reelected 1912; elected by voters 1918; reelected 1924, 1930, 1936; died in office |
| John Thomas (R) | 1/27/1940 to 11/10/1945 | appointed to fill vacancy; elected 1940; reelected 1942; died in office |

| | | |
|---|---|---|
| Charles C. Gossett (D) | 11/17/1945 to 11/5/1946 | appointed to fill vacancy |
| Henry C. Dworshak (R) | 11/6/1946 to 1/2/1949 | elected 1946 |
| Bert H. Miller (D) | 1/3/1949 to 10/8/1949 | elected 1948; died in office |
| Henry C. Dworshak (R) | 10/14/1949 to 7/23/1962 | appointed to fill vacancy; elected 1950; reelected 1954, 1960, died in office |
| Len B. Jordan (R) | 8/6/1962 to 1/2/1973 | appointed to fill vacancy; elected 1962; reelected 1966 |
| James A. McClure (R) | 1/3/1973 to 1/2/1991 | elected 1972; reelected 1978, 1984 |
| Larry Craig (R) | 1/3/1991 to | elected 1990 |

## SECOND POSITION

| | | |
|---|---|---|
| William J. McConnell (R) | 12/18/1890 to 3/3/1891 | elected by legislature 1890 |
| Fred T. Dubois (R) | 3/4/1891 to 3/3/1897 | elected by legislature 1891 |
| Henry Heitfeld (P) | 3/4/1897 to 3/3/1903 | elected by legislature 1897 |
| Weldon B. Heyburn (R) | 3/4/1903 to 10/17/1912 | elected by legislature 1903; reelected 1909; died in office |
| Kirkland I. Perky (D) | 11/18/1912 to 2/5/1913 | appointed to fill vacancy |
| James H. Brady (R) | 2/6/1913 to 1/12/1918 | elected by legislature 1912; elected by voters 1914; died in office |
| John F. Nugent (D) | 1/22/1918 to 1/14/1921 | appointed to fill vacancy; elected 1918; resigned |

| | | |
|---|---|---|
| Frank R. Gooding (R) | 1/15/1921 to 6/24/1928 | appointed to fill vacancy; elected 1920; reelected 1926; died in office |
| John Thomas (R) | 6/30/1928 to 3/3/1933 | appointed to fill vacancy; elected 1928 |
| James P. Pope (D) | 3/4/1933 to 1/2/1939 | elected 1932 |
| D. Worth Clark (D) | 1/3/1939 to 1/2/1945 | elected 1938 |
| Glen H. Taylor (D) | 1/3/1945 to 1/2/1951 | elected 1944 |
| Herman Welker (R) | 1/3/1951 to 1/2/1957 | elected 1950 |
| Frank Church (D) | 1/3/1957 to 1/2/1981 | elected 1956; reelected 1962, 1968, 1974 |
| Steven D. Symms (R) | 1/3/1981 to 1/2/1993 | elected 1980; reelected 1986 |
| Dirk Kempthorne (R) | 1/2/1993 | elected 1992 |

Source: *Idaho Blue Book, 1989–1990*, 38.

# APPENDIX E

## United States Representatives

Note: *Party Designations:* (R) *Republican;* (D) *Democrat;* (S.R.) *Silver Republican;* (P) *Populist*

| *Name/Party* | *Term of Office* | *Remarks* |
|---|---|---|
| **AT-LARGE DISTRICT** | | |
| Willis Sweet (R) | 1890 to 1895 | elected 1890; reelected 1892 |
| Edgar Wilson (R) | 3/4/1895 to 3/3/1897 | elected 1894 |
| James Gunn (D-P) | 3/4/1896 to 3/3/1899 | elected 1896 |
| Edgar Wilson (D-SR) | 3/4/1899 to 3/3/1901 | elected 1898 |
| Thomas L. Glenn (D-P-SR) | 3/4/1901 to 3/3/1903 | elected 1900 |
| Burton L. French (R) | 3/4/1903 to 3/3/1909 | elected 1902; reelected 1904, 1906 |

| | | |
|---|---|---|
| Thomas L. Hamer (R) | 3/4/1909 to 3/3/1911 | elected 1908 |
| Burton L. French (R) | 3/4/1911 to 3/3/1913 | elected 1910 |

TWO AT-LARGE SEATS

| | | |
|---|---|---|
| Addison T. Smith (R) | 1/3/1913 to 1/2/1919 | elected 1912; reelected 1914, 1916 |
| Burton L. French (R) | 1/3/1913 to 1/2/1915 | elected 1912 |
| Robert M. McCracken (R) | 1/3/1915 to 1/2/1917 | elected 1914 |
| Burton L. French (R) | 1/3/1917 to 1/2/1919 | elected 1916 |

FIRST CONGRESSIONAL DISTRICT

| | | |
|---|---|---|
| Burton L. French (R) | 3/4/1919 to 3/3/1933 | elected 1918; reelected 1920, 1922, 1924, 1926, 1928, 1930 |
| Compton I. White (D) | 3/4/1933 to 1/2/1947 | elected 1932; re-elected 1934, 1936, 1938, 1940, 1942, 1944 |
| Abe McGregor Goff (R) | 1/3/1947 to 1/2/1949 | elected 1946 |
| Compton I. White (D) | 1/3/1949 to 1/2/1951 | elected 1948 |
| John T. Wood (R) | 1/3/1951 to 1/2/1953 | elected 1950 |
| Gracie Pfost (D) | 1/3/1953 to 1/2/1963 | elected 1952; reelected 1954, 1956, 1958, 1960 |
| Compton I. White, Jr. (D) | 1/3/1963 to 1/2/1967 | elected 1962; reelected 1964 |

| | | |
|---|---|---|
| James A. McClure (R) | 1/3/1967 to 1/2/1973 | elected 1966; reelected 1968, 1970 |
| Steven D. Symms (R) | 1/3/1973 to 1/2/1981 | elected 1972; reelected 1974, 1976, 1978 |
| Larry Craig (R) | 1/3/1981 to 1/3/1991 | elected 1980; reelected 1982, 1984, 1986, 1988 |
| Larry LaRocco (D) | 1/3/1991 to | elected 1990; reelected 1992 |

## SECOND CONGRESSIONAL DISTRICT

| | | |
|---|---|---|
| Addison T. Smith (R) | 3/4/1919 to 3/3/1933 | elected 1918; reelected 1920, 1922, 1924, 1926, 1928, 1930 |
| Thomas C. Coffin (D) | 3/4/1933 to 6/8/1934 | elected 1932; died in office |
| D. Worth Clark (D) | 3/4/1935 to 3/3/1939 | elected 1934; reelected 1936 |
| Henry C. Dworshak (R) | 1/3/1939 to 1/2/1947 | elected 1938; reelected 1940, 1942, 1944 |
| John Sanborn (R) | 1/3/1947 to 1/2/1951 | elected 1946; reelected 1948 |
| Hamer Budge (R) | 1/3/1951 to 1/2/1961 | elected 1950; reelected 1952, 1954, 1956, 1958 |
| Ralph R. Harding (D) | 1/3/1961 to 1/2/1965 | elected 1960; reelected 1962 |
| George V. Hansen (R) | 1/3/1965 to 1/2/1969 | elected 1964; reelected 1966 |
| Orval Hansen (R) | 1/3/1969 to 1/2/1975 | elected 1968; reelected 1970, 1972 |

| | | |
|---|---|---|
| George V. Hansen (R) | 1/3/1975 to 1/2/1985 | elected 1974; reelected 1976, 1978, 1980, 1982 |
| Richard Stallings (D) | 1/3/1985 to 1/2/1993 | elected 1984; reelected 1986, 1988, 1990 |
| Mike Crapo (R) | 1/2/1993 | elected 1992 |

Source: *Idaho Blue Book, 1989–1990*, 39–40

APPENDIX F

# Idaho Population Growth, 1870–1990

| *Year* | *Population* | *Increase: Number* | *Percent* | *Estimated Net Migration* |
|---|---|---|---|---|
| 1870 | 14,999 | — | — | — |
| 1880 | 32,610 | 17,411 | 117 | 1,700 |
| 1890 | 88,548 | 55,938 | 172 | 34,200 |
| 1900 | 161,772 | 73,224 | 83 | 39,800 |
| 1910 | 325,594 | 163,822 | 101 | 104,100 |
| 1920 | 431,866 | 106,272 | 33 | 37,300 |
| 1930 | 445,032 | 13,166 | 3 | -50,600 |
| 1940 | 524,873 | 79,841 | 18 | -20,500 |
| 1950 | 588,637 | 63,764 | 12 | -29,600 |
| 1960 | 667,191 | 78,554 | 13 | -39,300 |
| 1970 | 713,015 | 45,824 | 7 | -42,000 |
| 1980 | 944,127 | 231,112 | 32 | 130,000 |
| 1990 | 1,006,749 | 62,622 | 7 | 35,000 |

Source: *U.S. Department of Commerce, Bureau of Census*

# APPENDIX G

## Data on Idaho Counties

| *County* | *Year Established in Idaho* | *County Seat* | *Population in 1990* |
|---|---|---|---|
| Ada | 1864 | Boise | 205,775 |
| Adams | 1911 | Council | 3,254 |
| Bannock | 1893 | Pocatello | 66,026 |
| Bear Lake | 1875 | Paris | 6,084 |
| Benewah | 1915 | St. Maries | 7,937 |
| Bingham | 1885 | Blackfoot | 37,583 |
| Blaine | 1895 | Hailey | 13,552 |
| Boise | 1864 | Idaho City | 3,509 |
| Bonner | 1913 | Sandpoint | 26,622 |
| Bonneville | 1911 | Idaho Falls | 72,207 |
| Boundary | 1915 | Bonners Ferry | 8,332 |
| Butte | 1917 | Arco | 2,918 |
| Camas | 1917 | Fairfield | 727 |
| Canyon | 1891 | Caldwell | 90,076 |
| Caribou | 1919 | Soda Springs | 6,963 |
| Cassia | 1879 | Burley | 19,532 |

| | | | |
|---|---|---|---|
| Clark | 1919 | Dubois | 762 |
| Clearwater | 1911 | Orofino | 8,505 |
| Custer | 1881 | Challis | 4,133 |
| Elmore | 1889 | Mountain Home | 21,205 |
| Franklin | 1913 | Preston | 9,232 |
| Fremont | 1893 | St. Anthony | 10,937 |
| Gem | 1915 | Emmett | 11,844 |
| Gooding | 1913 | Gooding | 11,633 |
| Idaho | 1864 | Grangeville | 13,783 |
| Jefferson | 1913 | Rigby | 16,543 |
| Jerome | 1919 | Jerome | 15,138 |
| Kootenai | 1881 | Coeur d'Alene | 69,795 |
| Latah | 1888 | Moscow | 30,617 |
| Lemhi | 1869 | Salmon | 6,899 |
| Lewis | 1911 | Nez Perce | 3,516 |
| Lincoln | 1895 | Shoshone | 3,308 |
| Madison | 1913 | Rexburg | 23,674 |
| Minidoka | 1913 | Rupert | 19,361 |
| Nez Perce | 1864 | Lewiston | 33,754 |
| Oneida | 1864 | Malad | 3,492 |
| Owyhee | 1863 | Murphy | 8,392 |
| Payette | 1917 | Payette | 16,434 |
| Power | 1913 | American Falls | 7,086 |
| Shoshone | 1864 | Wallace | 13,931 |
| Teton | 1915 | Driggs | 3,439 |
| Twin Falls | 1907 | Twin Falls | 53,580 |
| Valley | 1917 | Cascade | 6,109 |
| Washington | 1879 | Weiser | 8,550 |

# NOTES

## CHAPTER 21

1. Betty B. Derig, *Weiser, The Way It Was* (Weiser: Rambler Press, 1987), 143–49.

2. Quoted in Bob Waite, "The Ethnic Experience in Idaho," *Snake River Echoes* 11 (1982):77.

3. Crowder, in *Idaho's Governors*, 98.

4. Brosnan, *History of the State of Idaho*, 361–65.

5. Ibid., 365–66.

6. Hawley, *History of Idaho*, 1:581.

7. Crowder, in *Idaho's Governors*, 100–101.

8. Ruckman, "Knit, Knit, and Then Knit," 30; *Pocatello Tribune*, January 5, 1919.

9. Ruckman, "Knit, Knit, and Then Knit," 29, based on report in the *Pocatello Tribune*, November 3, 1917.

10. Lovin, "World War Vigilantes," 6.

11. Hawley, *History of Idaho*, 1:582.

12. Lovin, "World War Vigilantes," 2–3.

13. Ibid., 6.

14. Crowder, in *Idaho's Governors*, 101.

15. See Arrington, "The Influenza Epidemic," 19–29.

## CHAPTER 22

1. Edison K. Putman, "Travail at the Turn of the Century," 16.

2. Mowry, *The Urban Nation*, 34.

3. Chalmers, *Hooded Americanism*, 219.

4. Wells and Hart, *Idaho: Gem of the Mountains*, 125.

5. Mowry, *The Urban Nation*, 5.

6. *Rexburg Journal*, April 21, 1922.

7. T. C. Stanford to William E. Borah, May 26, 1922. The papers of Thomas C. Stanford are in the possession of Gwynn (Glen) Barrett, Boise State University.

8. Shideler, *Farm Crisis*, 196–97, 324; *New York Times*, January 28, 1922, 2; *Idaho Daily Statesman*, October 1, 1922.

9. Gilbert C. Fite, *George N. Peek and the Fight for Farm Parity* (Norman: University of Oklahoma Press, 1954), 4.

10. *Yearbook of Agriculture*, 1919, 523, 660, 669; 1922, 595, 671, 687, 823, 871; Leonard Arrington, *Beet Sugar in the West* (Seattle: University of Washington Press, 1966), 94.

11. Clara E. Aldrich, *The History of Banking in Idaho* (Boise, 1940), 56–58.

12. *Idaho Daily Statesman*, September 7, 1920, July 1, 1921.

## CHAPTER 23

1. Theodore Morgan, *Introduction to Economics* (New York: Prentice-Hall, 1950), 509–13.

2. The statistics and interpretations are based upon Arrington, "Idaho and the Great Depression."

3. The following account is based on Arrington and Barrett, "Stopping a Run on a Bank."

4. Malone, *C. Ben Ross and the New Deal in Idaho*, 39.

5. The report may be found among the papers of the Ross Administration, Box 27, folder entitled "Drouth Relief, 1932–1935," Idaho State Archives, Boise.

6. The statistical information in the description of programs below has been compiled from Office of Government Reports, Statistical Section, Report No. 10, Idaho, Volume II (Washington, D.C., 1940). A photocopy of this 54–page mimeographed report is in the Utah State University Library, Logan, Utah.

7. Austin, "The CCC in Idaho," 14–15.

8. The information in this section comes from Dean H. Lundblad, "The Indian Division of the Civilian Conservation Corps" (Plan B master's thesis, Report No. 2, Utah State University, 1968); Final Report of the Director, 1933 to 1942, in Records of the CCC, Record Group 35, National Archives; and Office of Government Reports, Statistical Section, 1940, "Federal Loans and Expenditures 1933–39," Vol. II, Idaho, mimeographed copy in Utah State University Library, Logan, Utah.

9. The overwhelming majority of Idaho farmers favored these programs. In a nationwide wheat referendum in May 1935, Idaho producers voted 88 percent in favor of an AAA program. In October 1935, when corn-hog producers were asked if they favored a program for 1936, Idaho votes were 3,319 for and 425 against, a favorable majority of 89 percent.

10. Fisher, *Idaho: A Guide in Word and Picture.*

11. See Barrett, "Reclamation's New Deal for Heavy Construction," 21–27.

12. Keith C. Petersen, "Frank Bruce Robinson and Psychiana," *Idaho Yesterdays* 23 (Fall 1979):9–15, 26–29. See also Petersen's *Psychiana, The Psychological Religion* (Moscow: Latah County Historical Society, 1991).

## CHAPTER 24

1. Bill Loftus, *Idaho State Parks Guidebook* (Lewiston: Tribune Publishing Company, 1989), 17–22.

2. Clark, "Idaho Made the Desert Blossom," 651.

3. Beal and Wells, *History of Idaho*, 2:270.

4. Brosnan, *History of Idaho*, 373D–73E.

5. Ibid., 373G–73I.

6. Clark, "Idaho Made the Desert Bloom," 641.

7. Ourada, "Reluctant Servants," 9.

8. Busco and Alder, "German and Italian Prisoners of War in Utah and Idaho," 72.

9. Hausler, "History of the Japanese-American Relocation Center," 23.

10. Ibid., 39.

## CHAPTER 25

1. See, for example, Beal and Wells, *History of Idaho*, 1:440–54.

2. Blank, *Individualism in Idaho*; Stapilus, *Paradox Politics*.

3. Blank, *Individualism in Idaho*, 2–7.

4. Duane A. Smith, *Rocky Mountain Mining Camps: The Urban Frontier* (Bloomington: Indiana University Press, 1967), 244.

5. Gunther, *Inside U.S.A.*, 115.

6. Ibid., 115–17.

7. Peterson, *Idaho: A Bicentennial History*, 158.

8. Claudius Johnson, "Borah's Bequest to Democracy," *Idaho Yesterdays* 1 (Winter 1957–58):12.

9. I have borrowed heavily from the succinct biography of Borah by Merle Wells in Lamar, ed., *The Reader's Encyclopedia of the American West*, 114–15.

10. See Malone's first-rate biography, *C. Ben Ross and the New Deal in Idaho*; also Malone's brief biography in Sims, ed., *Idaho Governors*, 130–37.

11. See Willard Barnes's biography of Clark in Sims, ed., *Idaho's Governors*, 138–44.

12. Robert C. Sims, "C. A. Bottolfsen," in Sims, ed., *Idaho's Governors*, 149.

13. *Idaho Pioneer* (Boise), October 18, 1940, as quoted in Peterson, *Prophet Without Honor*, 16.

14. Gunther, *Inside U.S.A.*, 108.

15. An excellent biography is Ross Peterson, *Prophet Without Honor*. Short biographies are in Peterson, "Glen H. Taylor: Idaho's Liberal Maverick," in *The Idaho Heritage*, 157–61; John Gunther, *Inside U.S.A.*, 107–13; and Stapilus, *Paradox Politics*, 81–85, 90–92.

16. Stapilus, *Paradox Politics*, 101.

17. The excellent commissioned study of Idaho's schools, *Public Education in Idaho*, was the Report of the Idaho Education Survey Commission, George Peabody College for Teachers, Nashville, Tennessee, 1946. Copy in the library at University of Idaho, Moscow, and in many local libraries.

18. Beal and Wells, *History of Idaho*, 3:37–38.

19. See especially "Robert E. Smylie and Idaho's State Parks," in Thomas R. Cox, *The Park Builders: A History of State Parks in the Pacific Northwest* (Seattle: University of Washington Press, 1988), 104–20; and *Idaho Recreation Review* 2 (Spring 1990), commemorating the twenty-fifth anniversary of the Idaho Department of Parks and Recreation.

20. This is based in part on Martin, "Idaho: The Sectional State," 172–73.

21. Compare Merle W. Wells, "The Context of Gubernatorial Politics in Idaho," in Sims, ed., *Idaho's Governors*, 1–11.

22. Martin, "The Sectional State," 174–79.

## CHAPTER 26

1. Hidy, et al., *Timber and Men*, 512–33.

2. Ibid., 534–50.

3. Henry L. Day, "Mining Highlights of the Coeur d'Alene District," *Idaho Yesterdays* 7 (Winter 1963–64):8–9.

4. "Sunshine Mining Company," in Wells and Hart, *Idaho: Gem of the Mountains*, 194.

5. "Hecla Mining Company," in ibid., 222.

6. "FMC Corporation," in ibid., 220–21.

7. Beal and Wells, *History of Idaho*, 2:310.

8. *Salt Lake Tribune*, October 3, 1948. Further information on the life and agricultural efforts of Julion Clawson is in clippings from the *Minidoka County News* (Rupert), *Salt Lake Tribune*, and other newspapers collected by Clawson's secretary, Anona Kunz Clawson, LDS Church Archives, Salt Lake City; and oral history interviews with Irwin Clawson, Yale Holland, and Rodney Hansen by Richard L. Jensen, James Moyle Oral History Program, LDS Church Archives.

9. Statement of Don Ofte, Idaho Operations Manager, in *Idaho State Journal*, May 15, 1989, 11–12.

### CHAPTER 27

1. G. Edward White, "Roosevelt, Theodore," in Lamar, ed., *The Reader's Encyclopedia of the American West*, 1046. See also G. Edward White, *The Eastern Establishment and the Western Experience* (New Haven, Conn.: Yale University Press, 1968).

2. Church, *Father and Son*, 72.

3. Ibid., 56.

4. Ibid., 73.

5. Ibid., 72.

6. Peirce, *Mountain States of America*, 149. See also Peterson, *Idaho: A Bicentennial History*, 179.

7. Neal Peirce, *Mountain States of America*, (N.Y.: Norton, 1972) 147.

8. Schwantes, *The Pacific Northwest*, 373–74.

9. Steiner, *Soil Conservation in the United States*, 94; see also, 60, 91, 106.

10. An excellent summary is given in Robinson, *Water for the West*, 106–8. The best treatment is F. Ross Peterson, *The Teton Dam Disaster: Tragedy or Triumph?* 66th Faculty Honors Lecture (Logan: Utah State University Faculty Association, 1982). See also Louis J. Clements, *Teton Flood Revisited* (Rexburg: Eastern Idaho Publishing Co, 1991).

11. Jordan, *The Unintentional Senator*, 152.

### CHAPTER 28

1. See Petersen, *This Crested Hill*, 213–32.

2. Quoted in Beal, *History of Idaho State College*, 127.

3. Ibid., 131.

4. Crowder, *Rexburg, Idaho*, 245–48. See also Ernest L. Wilkinson and Leonard J. Arrington, eds., "The Ricks College Controversy," in *Brigham Young University: The First One Hundred Years*, 4 vols. (Provo: Brigham Young University Press, 1976), 3:156–75.

5. Petersen, *This Crested Hill*, 30.

## CHAPTER 29

1. Robert Smylie in *Conversations*, 169–72.

2. "An Idaho Woodsman Makes the Chips Fly," *Business Week*, October 12, 1963, 148.

3. Wells and Hart, *Idaho: Gem of the Mountains*, 180–83.

4. *Here We Have Idaho*, 72.

5. Ibid., 70.

6. The best write-up on the company's history is an undated article by Lisa Borsuk, "A Dream Became Largest Frozen Food Processor," *Daily Argus Observer* (Ontario, Oregon), probably written in 1983. Copy furnished by Ore-Ida.

7. "Off-Beat Men for Off-Beat Jobs," *Business Week*, July 20, 1957, 167–68.

8. Ibid., 172.

9. Ibid., 167.

10. "Builders of Anything, Anywhere," *Business Week*, December 5, 1944, 58.

11. "The Earth Mover," *Time* 63 (May 3, 1954):86.

12. Wells and Hart, *Idaho: Gem of the Mountains*, 232–35; *Here We Have Idaho*, 49.

13. Wells and Hart, *Idaho: Gem of the Mountains*, 129; Wells, *Boise: An Illustrated History*, 198.

14. Mitchell's recollections are that the plant at Hailey was finished first, but his son's biography of his father says the one in Boise was completed on July 4, 1887, and the one at Hailey was finished by Christmas Eve of the same year: Mitchell, *S. Z. Mitchell and the Electrical Industry*, 48–49.

15. Wells and Hart, *Idaho: Gem of the Mountains*, 213.

16. Ibid., 231.

17. Ibid., 206–7.

## CHAPTER 30

1. George Catlin, *Episodes from Life Among the Indians and Last Rambles Amongst the Indians of the Rocky Mountains and Andes* (Norman: University of Oklahoma Press, 1959), 147.

2. *One Hundred Years of Idaho Art*, 68–69.

3. Ibid., 72–73.

4. Ibid., 101.

5. Walker, *Myths of Idaho Indians*, 7–8; Walker, *Indians of Idaho*, 158.

6. Introduction to "Coyote Laughs and Cries," in *American Indian Myths and Legends*, 335–36.

7. These and other stories comprise the text of Walker, *Myths of Idaho Indians*.

8. Bruchac, "Storytelling and Native American Writing," *Halcyon*, 40; Jon P. Dayley in *The Literature of Idaho*, 15.

9. William Hepworth Dixon, *White Conquest*, 2 vols. (London, 1876), 2:364. This was a report of Dixon's second trip, one made in 1875.

10. Charles Nelson Teeter, *Four Years of My Life or My Adventures in the Far West (May 14, 1862–December 13, 1865)* Thirteenth Biennial Report of the Board of Trustees of the State Historical Society of Idaho (Boise, 1932), 26–128.

11. "Impressions of the Boise Basin in 1863," *Idaho Yesterdays* 7 (Spring 1963):4–13. See also Angelo, *Idaho: A Descriptive Tour and Review of Its Resources and Route* (San Francisco, 1865; reissued, Fairfield, Washington: Ye Galleon Press, 1969).

12. Bowles, *Our New West: Records of Travel Between the Mississippi River and the Pacific Ocean* (Hartford, Conn., 1869), 488.

13. Richardson, *Beyond the Mississippi*, 494–95, 507.

14. William Hepworth Dixon, *New America*, 2 vols. (London, 1867), 2:21.

15. John Codman, *The Mormon Country* (New York, 1874); and Codman, *The Round Trip: By Way of Panama through . . . Idaho* (New York, 1879).

16. Codman, *The Mormon Country*, 32–33. A similar account is Wilmot Woodruff Van Dusen, *Blazing the Way, or Pioneer Experiences in Washington, Idaho, and Oregon* (Cincinnati: Jennings and Graham; New York: Eaton and Mains, 1905).

17. Donaldson, *Idaho of Yesterday*, 61–62.

18. See Betty Derig, "Pioneer Portraits: Bishop Tuttle," *Idaho Yesterdays* 12 (Winter 1968–69):13–22; and Daniel S. Tuttle, *Reminis-*

*cences of a Missionary Bishop* (1906; reissued, Logan: Utah State University Press, 1991).

19. For example, Ethelbert Talbot, *My People of the Plains* (New York: Harper & Bros., 1906), 96–97.

20. I have especially profited from reading the "Foreword" to the new edition of *We Sagebrush Folks* by JoAnn Ruckman.

21. The introduction by Susan Hendricks Swetnam is very helpful.

22. McEwen, *So This is Ranching* (Lincoln; University of Nebraska Press, 1948).

23. Jordan, *Home Below Hell's Canyon* (Lincoln: University of Nebraska Press, 1954, 1962).

24. For example, Foote's novel, *The Led-Horse Claim: A Romance of a Mining Camp* (1883). I am using Rodman Paul's splendid introduction to *A Victorian Gentlewoman in the Far West: The Reminiscences of Mary Hallock Foote* (San Marino, California: The Huntington Library, 1972); and James H. Maguire, *Mary Hallock Foote* (Boise: Boise State University, 1972).

25. Paul, ed., *A Victorian Gentlewoman*, 25.

26. See the biography by Noel Stock, 1970; and Eric Homberger, ed., *Ezra Pound: The Critical Heritage* (1973).

27. The following is based on Robertson's autobiography, *A Ram in the Thicket: The Story of a Roaming Homesteading Family on the Mormon Frontier* (New York: Hastings House, 1950, 1959).

28. From the dust jacket of *A Ram in the Thicket.*

29. Jay Miller, ed., *Mourning Dove: A Salishan Autobiography* (Lincoln: University of Nebraska Press, 1990).

30. In addition to the write-up in *The Literature of Idaho*, 237–38, I have examined Joseph M. Flora, *Vardis Fisher* (New York: Twayne Publishers, 1965), and Wayne Chatterton, *Vardis Fisher: The Frontier and Regional Works* (Boise: Boise State College, 1972); Tim Woodward, *Tiger on the Road* (Caldwell: Caxton Printers, Ltd., 1989); Beal and Wells, *History of Idaho*, 2:330–33; and Leonard J. Arrington and Jon Haupt, "The Mormon Heritage of Vardis Fisher," *Brigham Young University Studies* 18 (Fall 1977):27–47.

31. Quoted in Beal and Wells, *The History of Idaho*, 2:331.

32. Comment taken from Beal and Wells, *History of Idaho*, 2:331.

33. The essay "In Papa's Shadow," in Tim Woodward's *Tiger on the Road*, 190–205, has been very helpful. Also Carlos Baker, *Ernest Hemingway: A Life Story* (New York: Charles Scribner's Sons, 1959); Hemingway, *How It Was*; Arnold, *High on the Wild with Hemingway*; and "Father L. M. Dougherty Talks About Ernest Hemingway," in *Rendezvous: Idaho State University Journal of Arts and Letters* 5 (Winter 1970):7–17. An excellent review of the Hemingway literature is Richard Etulain, "Ernest Hemingway and His Interpreters of the 1960's," in *Rendezvous*, 53–70.

34. See Robert Andrews, *The Concise Columbia Dictionary of Quotations* (New York: Columbia University Press, 1987), 176.

35. Etulain, "Ernest Hemingway and His Interpreters," 53.

36. *Perspectives* (American Historical Association newsletter), May/June 1991, 1.

37. See Leonard J. Arrington, "Celebrating Idaho's Historians," *Idaho Yesterdays* 34 (Winter 1991):2–9.

## CHAPTER 31

1. Carole Simon-Smolinski, "Idaho's Native Americans," in *Idaho's Ethnic Heritage*, 2:1–51; Walker, *Indians of Idaho*; Liljeblad, *The Idaho Indians in Transition, 1805–1960*; Patricia K. Ourada, ed., *Indian Peoples of Idaho* (Boise: Boise State University Press, 1975); Haines, *Indians of the Great Basin and Plateau*; and Alvin M. Josephy, Jr., *The Indian Heritage of America* (New York: Alfred A. Knopf, 1968).

2. See William T. Hagan, "United States Indian Policy," in Lamar, ed., *Reader's Encyclopedia of the American West*, 565–69; and William T. Hagan, *American Indians* (Chicago: University of Chicago Press, 1961).

3. Carole Simon-Smolinski, "Idaho's Native Americans," in *Idaho's Ethnic Heritage*, 2:1–12.

4. See especially "Canadian and French Canadian Americans," in *Idaho's Ethnic Heritage*, 2:1–18.

5. See Bobbi Rahder, "Idaho's British Isles Americans," in *Idaho's Ethnic Heritage*, 1:8.

6. A. C. Todd, "Cousin Jack in Idaho," *Idaho Yesterdays* 8 (Winter 1964–65):5.

7. West, "Five Idaho Mining Towns," 112.

8. Ruby El Hult, *Steamboats in the Timber* (Caldwell: Caxton Printers, 1953), 94–95.

9. Carole Simon-Smolinski, "Idaho's Chinese Americans," in *Idaho's Ethnic Heritage*, 1:7–43; Alfreda Elsensohn, *Idaho Chinese Lore* (Cottonwood: Idaho Corporation of Benedictine Sisters, 1970).

10. See Dean L. May, "Mormons," in Thernstrom, ed., *Harvard Encyclopedia of American Ethnic Groups*, 720–31; also articles by Armand L. Mauss and Keith Parry in Brigham Y. Card, et al., eds., *The Mormon Presence in Canada* (Edmonton: University of Alberta Press, 1990), 329–65.

11. On Welsh Mormons see Bobbi Rahder, "Idaho's British Isles Americans," in *Idaho's Ethnic Heritage*, 1:32–49; Glade F. Howell, "Early History of Malad Valley" (Master's thesis, Brigham Young University, 1960); Philip A. M. Taylor, *Expectations Westward: The Mormons and the Emigration of British Converts in the 19th Century* (Ithaca, N.Y.: Cornell University Press, 1966); and Herbert Glee, ed., *Malad Stake Centennial History Book, 1888–1988* (Malad: Malad LDS Stake, 1990).

12. Mary E. Reed, "Idaho's Northern European Americans," in *Idaho's Ethnic Heritage*, 2:31–44; Cleo J. Johnson, "The Scandinavian Organization," *Snake River Echoes* 11 (1982); William Mulder, *Homeward to Zion: The Mormon Migration from Scandinavia* (Minneapolis: University of Minnesota Press, 1957).

13. Mulder, *Homeward to Zion*, 272.

14. See Carole Simon-Smolinski, "Idaho's Western European Americans," in *Idaho's Ethnic Heritage*, 2:36–45; Zina Kunz Hatch Fuit Cox, *The Hills of Bern* (Montpelier, ca. 1980).

15. See Mary Reed, "Idaho's Northern European Americans," in *Idaho's Ethnic Heritage*, 2:1–64.

16. Hal Cannon, "New Sweden Pioneer Day," in Attebery, *Idaho Folklife: Homesteads to Headstones*, 68–79.

17. Bert Russell, *North Fork of the Coeur d'Alene River* (Harrison, Idaho: Lacon Publishers, 1984), 66–67.

18. Carole Simon-Smolinski, "Idaho's Western European Americans," in *Idaho's Ethnic Heritage*, 2:1–89.

19. Laurie Mercier, "Idaho's Southern Europeans," *Idaho's Ethnic Heritage*, 2:1–53; Andrew F. Rolle, *The Immigrant Upraised: Italian Adventurers and Colonists in an Expanding America* (Norman: University of Oklahoma Press, 1968); and Leonard Dinnerstein, Roger Nichols, and David Reimers, *Natives and Strangers: Ethnic Groups and the Building of America* (New York: Oxford University Press, 1979).

20. Carole Simon-Smolinski, "Idaho's Jewish Americans," in *Idaho's Ethnic Heritage* 1:1–35, an excellent essay. See also Juanita Brooks, *The History of the Jews in Utah and Idaho* (Salt Lake City: Western Epics, 1973).

21. Eli M. Oboler, "Being Jewish in Pocatello, Idaho," *SH'MA*, April 4, 1980.

22. Carole Simon-Smolinski, "Idaho's Japanese Americans," in *Idaho's Ethnic Heritage*, 1:44–89; Robert Sims, "The Japanese American Experience in Idaho," *Idaho Yesterdays* 22 (Spring 1978):2–10.

23. Issues of July 9, 26, 28, 1892.

24. Simon-Smolinski, "Idaho's Japanese Americans," 1:63.

25. See Laurie Mercier, "Idaho's Southern Europeans," in *Idaho's Ethnic Heritage*, 2:17–34; Pat Bieter, "Reluctant Shepherds: The Basques in Idaho," *Idaho Yesterdays* 1 (Summer 1957):10–15; Richard W. Etulain, "Basque Beginnings in the Pacific Northwest" *Idaho Yesterdays* 18 (Spring 1974):26–32; William A. Douglass and Jon Bilbao, *Amerikanuak: Basques in the New World* (Reno: University of Nevada Press, 1975).

26. Laurie Mercier, "Idaho's Latin Americans," in *Idaho's Ethnic Heritage*, 2:1–47; Gamboa, *Mexican Labor and World War II*.

27. Laurie Mercier, "Idaho's African Americans," in *Idaho's Ethnic Heritage* 1:1–49; Mamie O. Oliver, *Idaho Ebony: The Afro-American Presence in Idaho State History* (Boise: privately published, 1990); Quintard Taylor, Jr., "History of Blacks in the Pacific Northwest, 1788–1970" (Ph.D. dissertation, University of Minnesota, 1978).

28. Marvin Fletcher, "Army Fire Fighters," *Idaho Yesterdays* 16 (Summer 1972):12–15; *Idaho Press*, August 18, September 1–8, 1910, as quoted in Mercier, "Idaho's African Americans."

29. Laurie Mercier, "Idaho's Southeast Asian and Filipino Americans," in *Idaho's Ethnic Heritage*, 1:90–108.

## CHAPTER 32

1. Peter Buhler, in Ericson, ed., *The Idaho Small Town Experience*, 4–5.

2. "The Country Town," *The Portable Veblen*, Max Lerner, ed. (New York: Viking Press, 1961), 407, as quoted in Robert Sims, in Ericson, ed., *Idaho Small Town Experience*, 7.

3. Ibid., 2.

4. These paragraphs are based on Petersen, *Company Town: Potlatch, Idaho, and the Potlatch Lumber Company*, 98, 135.

5. Ibid., 141.

6. Ibid., 139, 206.

7. Abbott, in Nash and Etulain, *Twentieth Century West*, 89–90.

8. As with Chapter Seventeen, this section borrows heavily from Attebery, *Building Idaho*.

9. Attebery, *Building Idaho*, 125.

10. Ibid., 121, 133 n12.

11. "St. Alphonsus Regional Medical Center," in Wells and Hart, *Idaho: Gem of the Mountains*, 188–89.

12. Ibid., 184–85.

13. See also "Blue Cross of Idaho Health Service," in Wells, *Boise: An Illustrated History*, 157.

14. The phrases are from Malone and Etulain, *The American West*, 162.

## CHAPTER 33

1. Stapilus, *Paradox Politics*, 206.

2. Gregory A. Raymond, "Idaho: A Third-World Country?" *Idaho's Economy* 7 (Spring 1990):16.

3. Michael E. Porter, *The Competitive Advantage of Nations* (New York and London: The Macmillan Co., 1990); Michael L. Dertouzos, Robert M. Solow, and Richard K. Lester, *Made in America: Regaining the Productive Edge* (Cambridge, Mass.: MIT Press, 1990).

4. See also Robert B. Reich, "But Now We're Global," *London Times Supplement*, August 31–September 6, 1990, 925–26.

5. "Pioneer Spirit Guides Idaho into Next 100 Years," editorial in *Idaho Statesman*, July 3, 1990.

6. Nancy Reid, "The Start of the Party," *Idaho Statesman*, July 3, 1990.

7. *Idaho Statesman*, July 4, 1990.

8. Compare Dan Popkey, "Idaho's Future: Learning to Balance Growth and Environment," *Idaho Statesman*, July 3, 1990.

# BIBLIOGRAPHY

IDAHO HISTORIANS are fortunate in having available several repositories of historical documents. The Idaho State Archives and Historical Society library in Boise has not only the official documents of the state's history—the papers of the governors, state officers, state agencies, Capitol Building Commission, and other materials—but a large collection of other material that is a historian's joy—books, newspapers, presidential papers, diaries, letters, maps, photographs, and miscellania. The University of Idaho Library in Moscow has a full collection of books, newspapers, diaries, theses, maps, photographs, and other materials. Likewise, the Idaho State University Library in Pocatello has a similar, if smaller, collection. The Boise and Twin Falls public libraries are remarkably complete, as is the Latah County Historical Society in Moscow. Many other public libraries throughout the state are particularly helpful on local history. The best introduction to these is Terry Abraham and Richard C. Davis, "Directory of Manuscript and Archival Repositories in Idaho," *Idaho Yesterdays* 34 (Fall 1990):21–33.

All of these libraries have the standard bibliographical aids and many rolls of microfilm copies of materials preserved elsewhere. Many libraries outside the state are helpful, including the National Archives, Washington, D.C.; Bancroft Library, Berkeley, California; Henry E. Huntington Library, San Marino, California; Utah State University Library, Logan, Utah; University of Utah Library, Salt Lake City, Utah; Oregon Historical Society Library, Portland; and University of Washington Library, Seattle.

The most useful bibliographical aids are: Judith Austin and Gary Bettis, "A Preliminary Checklist of Guides to Sources in Idaho History," *Idaho Yesterdays* 21 (Fall 1977):19–26; Richard W. Etulain and Merwin Swanson, *Idaho History: A Bibliography* (Pocatello: Idaho State University Press, 1974, 1979); Milo G. Nelson and Charles A. Webbert, eds., *Idaho Local History: A Bibliography with a Checklist of Library Holdings* (Moscow: University Press of Idaho, 1976); Melville R. Spence, *Bibliography and Union List of Idaho Newspapers, 1862–1955* (Moscow: University of Idaho, 1956); *Monthly Checklist of Idaho Government Publications*, 1990 Annual Cumulation (Boise: Idaho State Library, 1990); John E. Rees, *Idaho: Chronology, Nomenclature, Bibliography* (Chicago: W. B. Conkey Co., 1918; reprinted, Seattle: Shorey Book Store, 1970); and Merle W. Wells, *Idaho: A Students' Guide to Localized History* (New York: Teachers College Press, 1965).

Of special help are several state documents: *Idaho Digest and Blue Book* (Caldwell: Caxton Printers, 1935; Boise: Secretary of State, 1963; biennial updating since 1970); and *Idaho Almanac* (Boise: Department of Tourism and Industrial Development, 1963, 1977); *Idaho's Highway History, 1863–1975* (Boise: Idaho Department of Transportation, 1985).

Professional journals with significant Idaho material are:

*Idaho Yesterdays*, quarterly, 1957-present date;

*Rendezvous: Idaho State University Journal of Arts and Letters*, annually 1966-date;

*Idaho's Economy*, quarterly, 1984-present date;

*Montana: The Magazine of Western History*, quarterly, 1951-present date;

*Oregon Historical Quarterly*, quarterly, 1900-present date;

*Pacific Northwest Quarterly*, quarterly, 1906-present date (originally the *Washington Historical Quarterly*);

*Pacific Historical Review*, quarterly, 1931-present date;

*Western Historical Quarterly*, quarterly, 1970-present date;

*Nevada Historical Society Quarterly*, quarterly, 1957-present date;

*Forest and Conservation History* (originally *Journal of Forest History*), quarterly, 1956-present date.

Semi-professional magazines published in recent years in Idaho include: *Scenic Idaho*, 1946–64, 1976-present date;

*Incredible Idaho*, 1969-present date;

*Snake River Echoes*, 1974-present date;

*Idaho Heritage*, 1975-present date; and

*Oh! Idaho*, 1989-1992.

## GENERAL HISTORIES OF THE AMERICAN WEST

A particularly useful volume because of its comprehensive coverage is Howard R. Lamar, ed., *The Reader's Encyclopedia of the American West* (New York: Thomas Y. Crowell Co., 1977). Most of the entries relating to Idaho were written by Idaho's senior historian, Merle Wells. Other general histories, usually organized by chronological periods or topics that contain information on aspects of Idaho history, include:

Ray Allen Billington, *Westward Expansion: A History of the American Frontier*, 2d ed. (New York: The Macmillan Co., 1960).

——, *The Far Western Frontier, 1830–1860* (New York: Harper & Bros., 1956).

Dan Elbert Clark, *The West in American History* (New York: Thomas Y. Crowell Co., 1937).

Thomas D. Clark, *Frontier America: The Story of the Westward Movement*, 2d ed. (New York: Charles Scribner's Sons, 1969).

LeRoy R. Hafen and Carl Coke Rister, *Western America: The Exploration, Settlement, and Development of the Region Beyond the Mississippi*, 2d ed. (Englewood Cliffs, N.J.: Prentice-Hall, 1950).

William H. Goetzmann, *Exploration and Empire: The Explorer and the Scientist in the Winning of the American West* (New York: Alfred A. Knopf, 1966).

John A. Hawgood, *America's Western Frontiers: The Exploration and Settlement of the Trans-Mississippi West* (New York: Alfred A. Knopf, 1967).

Robert V. Hine, *The American West: An Interpretive History* (Boston: Little, Brown and Co., 1973).

Gerald D. Nash, *The American West in the Twentieth Century: A Short History of an Urban Oasis* (Englewood Cliffs, N.J.: Prentice-Hall, 1973).

David Lavender, *The Rockies* (New York: Harper & Row, 1968).

Patricia Nelson Limerick, *The Legacy of Conquest: The Unbroken Past of the American West* (New York: W. W. Norton & Co., 1987).

Michael P. Malone, ed., *Historians and the American West* (Lincoln: University of Nebraska Press, 1983).

—— and Richard W. Etulain, *The American West: A Twentieth-Century History* (Lincoln: University of Nebraska Press, 1989).

Gerald D. Nash and Richard W. Etulain, eds., *The Twentieth-Century West: Historical Interpretations* (Albuquerque: University of New Mexico Press, 1989).

Rodman W. Paul, *The Far West and the Great Plains in Transition, 1859–1900* (New York: Harper & Row, 1988).

## GENERAL HISTORIES OF THE PACIFIC NORTHWEST
(Listed chronologically)

Hubert Howe Bancroft, *History of the Northwest Coast*, 2 vols. 1543–1800 and 1800–1846 (San Francisco: A. L. Bancroft & Co., 1884).

George W. Fuller, *A History of the Pacific Northwest* (New York: Alfred A. Knopf, 1931).

Sidney Warren, *Farthest Frontier: The Pacific Northwest* (New York: The Macmillan Co., 1949).

Oscar O. Winther, *The Old Oregon Country: A History of Frontier*

*Trade, Transportation, and Travel* (Lincoln: University of Nebraska Press, 1950, 1969).

———, *The Great Northwest: A History*, 2d ed. (New York: Alfred A. Knopf, 1955).

Earl Pomeroy, *The Pacific Slope: A History of California, Oregon, Washington, Idaho, Utah, and Nevada* (New York: Alfred A. Knopf, 1965).

Dorothy O. Johansen and Charles M. Gates, *Empire of the Columbia: A History of the Pacific Northwest*, 2d ed. (New York: Harper & Row, 1967).

D. W. Meinig, *The Great Columbia Plain: A Historical Geography, 1805–1910* (Seattle: University of Washington Press, 1968).

William G. Robbins, Robert J. Frank, and Richard E. Ross, eds., *Regionalism and the Pacific Northwest* (Corvallis: Oregon State University Press, 1983).

G. Thomas Edwards and Carlos A. Schwantes, *Experiences in a Promised Land: Essays in Pacific Northwest History* (Seattle: University of Washington Press, 1986).

David H. Stratton and George A. Frykman, *The Changing Pacific Northwest: Interpreting Its Past* (Pullman: Washington State University Press, 1988).

Carlos A. Schwantes, *The Pacific Northwest: An Interpretive History* (Lincoln: University of Nebraska Press, 1989).

A book about the Pacific Northwest, its environment and cultural heritage, written for students in the secondary schools is Dale A. Lambert, *The Pacific Northwest: Past, Present, and Future* (Wenatchee, Washington: Directed Media, 1979).

## GENERAL HISTORIES OF IDAHO

The major histories of Idaho are discussed, with statements about their authors, in Leonard J. Arrington, "Celebrating Idaho's Historians," *Idaho Yesterdays* 34 (Winter 1991):2–9. The following, listed chronologically, have been particularly helpful in writing this history:

Hubert Howe Bancroft, *History of Washington, Idaho, and Montana, 1845–1889* (San Francisco: The History Company, 1890).

John Hailey, *The History of Idaho* (Boise: Syms-York Company, 1910).

W. J. McConnell, *Early History of Idaho* (Caldwell: Caxton Printers, 1913).

Hiram T. French, *History of Idaho*, 3 vols. (Chicago: Lewis Publishing Company, 1914). The narrative is in the first volume, biographies in the second and third.

Cornelius J. Brosnan, *History of the State of Idaho*, rev. ed. (New York: Charles Scribner's Sons, 1918, 1948).

James H. Hawley, *History of Idaho: The Gem of the Mountains*, 4 vols. (Chicago: S. J. Clarke Publishing Company, 1920). The narrative history is in the first volume, the other volumes contain biographies.

Byron Defenbach, *Idaho: The Place and Its People*, 3 vols. (Chicago: American Historical Society, 1933). Narrative in the first volume, biographies in the second and third.

Vardis Fisher, *Idaho: A Guide in Word and Picture* (Caldwell: Caxton Printers, 1937).

Vardis Fisher, ed., *The Idaho Encyclopedia* (Caldwell: Caxton Printers, 1938).

Thomas Donaldson, *Idaho of Yesterday* (Caldwell: Caxton Printers, 1941).

Merrill D. Beal and Merle W. Wells, *History of Idaho*, 3 vols. (New York: Lewis Historical Publishing Company, 1959). Narrative in the first two volumes, biographies in the third.

Robert O. Beatty, *Idaho* (Caldwell: Caxton Printers, 1974).

Richard W. Etulain and Bert W. Marley, eds., *The Idaho Heritage: A Collection of Historical Essays* (Pocatello: Idaho State University Press, 1974).

Don Moser, *The Snake River Country* (New York: Time-Life Books, 1974).

F. Ross Peterson, *Idaho: A Bicentennial History* (New York: W. W. Norton & Co., 1976).

Cort Conley, *Idaho for the Curious: A Guide* (Cambridge, Idaho: Backeddy Books, 1982).

Merle Wells and Arthur A. Hart, *Idaho: Gem of the Mountains* (Northridge, California: Windsor Publications, 1985).

Carlos O. Schwantes, *In Mountain Shadows: A History of Idaho* (Lincoln: University of Nebraska Press, 1991). This most recent history is an exciting and informative introduction to Idaho history. With many well-chosen maps and photographs, the book is filled with historical insight and human interest.

## TEXTS ON IDAHO HISTORY AND GEOGRAPHY USED IN THE PUBLIC SCHOOLS

(Listed chronologically)

Cornelius J. Brosnan, *History of the State of Idaho*, rev. ed. (New York: Charles Scribner's Sons, 1918, 1948).

Henry Leonidas Talkington, *Heroes and Heroic Deeds of the Pacific Northwest*, 2 vols. (Caldwell: Caxton Printers, 1929). Volume I, entitled "The Pioneers," is for the elementary grades. Volume II, "Empire Builders," is for "advanced grades."

Claire Boyle Bracken, *A Child's Idaho* (Boise: Syms-York, 1941). Written for children of the elementary grades.

Francis Haines, *The Story of Idaho* (Boise: Syms-York, 1942).

Thelma M. Rea, *Living in Idaho* (Caldwell: Caxton Printers, 1947?).

Floyd R. Barber and Dan W. Martin, *Idaho in the Pacific Northwest* (Caldwell: Caxton Printers, 1956).

Jennie Brown Rawlins, *Exploring Idaho's Past* (Salt Lake City: Deseret Book Co., 1963). Concerned with Idaho's history up to statehood.

Dwight Williams Jensen, *Discovering Idaho: A History* (Caldwell: Caxton Printers, 1977).

Helen M. Newell, *Idaho's Place in the Sun* (Boise: Syms-York, 1977).

David A. Bice and Ellen Sue Blakey, *Horizons of Idaho* and *A Panorama of Idaho* (Marceline, Mo.: Walsworth Publishing Co., 1988); the latter is organized by topic instead of chronologically.

Ronald K. Fisher, *Beyond the Rockies: A Narrative History of Idaho*, 2nd ed. (Coeur d'Alene, Idaho: Alpha Omega, 1989). Treats the history up to 1890, when Idaho became a state.

Virgil M. Young, *The Story of Idaho*, Centennial edition (Moscow: University of Idaho Press, 1990).

# INDEX

## ABOUT THE AUTHOR

LEONARD J. ARRINGTON was born on a farm in Twin Falls County, Idaho, about two miles south of Shoshone Falls, and attended public school in Twin Falls. At Twin Falls High School he majored in agriculture, was national first vice president of the Future Farmers of America, earned the American Farmer degree with a project that featured Rhode Island Red chickens, and was a member of the state-champion debate team.

Arrington did his undergraduate work at the University of Idaho, where he majored in economics, was a member of the student government, and continued as a debater. He graduated with high honors in 1939 and was elected to Phi Beta Kappa. He later earned the Ph.D. in economics from the University of North Carolina.

As a professor of economics at Utah State University, he maintained enormous interest in Idaho history. An active member of the Idaho State Historical Society, he has written several articles for its journal, *Idaho Yesterdays*, and has often spoken to groups on aspects of Idaho history. In addition to prizewinning biographies of David Eccles, Charles C. Rich, Brigham Young, and others, he has written more than a dozen books on western American history.

Arrington owns an irrigated farm east of Twin Falls. He received an honorary Doctor of Humanities degree from the University of Idaho in 1977 and is an honorary alumnus of that institution. He has served as president of the Western History Association, Agricultural History Society, and Pacific Coast Branch of the American Historical Association. He is a fellow of the Society of American Historians.